Visual Studio 6:
The Complete Reference

Visual Studio 6: The Complete Reference

John Paul Mueller

Osborne/**McGraw-Hill**

Berkeley   New York   St. Louis   San Francisco
Auckland   Bogotá   Hamburg   London   Madrid
Mexico City   Milan   Montreal   New Delhi   Panama City
Paris   São Paulo   Singapore   Sydney
Tokyo   Toronto

Osborne/**McGraw-Hill**
2600 Tenth Street
Berkeley, California 94710
U.S.A.

For information on translations or book distributors outside the U.S.A., or to arrange bulk purchase discounts for sales promotions, premiums, or fund-raisers, please contact Osborne/**McGraw-Hill** at the above address.

Visual Studio 6: The Complete Reference

1234567890 AGM AGM 90198765432109

ISBN 0-07-882583-0

Publisher	**Copy Editor**
Brandon A. Nordin	Dennis Weaver
Editor in Chief	**Proofreader**
Scott Rogers	Stefany Otis
Acquisitions Editor	**Indexer**
Wendy Rinaldi	Irv Hershman
Project Editor	**Computer Designer**
Ron Hull	Jani Beckwith
	Ann Sellers
Editorial Assistant	
Monika Faltiss	**Illustrator**
	Brian Wells
Technical Editor	Beth Young
Russ Mullen	

This book is dedicated to the latest addition to our family, Bubba.

Contents at a Glance

Contents

Part I
The Interface

Part II

Working with Others

Part III

Desktop Applications

Part V

Server Applications

About the Author

John Mueller is a freelance author and technical editor. He has writing in his blood, having produced 40 books and almost 200 articles to date. The topics range from networking to artificial intelligence and from database management to heads down programming. Some of his current books include a Visual C++ programmer's guide and a Windows NT Web server handbook. His technical editing skills have helped over 22 authors refine the content of their manuscripts, some of which are certification-related. In addition to book projects, John has provided technical editing services to both *Data Based Advisor* and *Coast Compute* magazines. A recognized authority on computer industry certifications, he has also contributed certification-related articles to magazines like *Certified Professional Magazine.*

When John isn't working at the computer, you can find him in his workshop. He's an avid woodworker and candle maker. On any given afternoon you can find him working at a lathe or putting the finishing touches on a bookcase. One of his newest craft projects is glycerin soap making, which comes in pretty handy for gift baskets. You can reach John on the Internet at JMueller@mwt.net. John is also setting up a new Web site at http://www.mwt.net/~jmueller/. Feel free to take a look and make suggestions on how he can improve it.

Acknowledgments

Thanks to my wife, Rebecca, for working with me to get this book completed. I really don't know what I would have done without her help in researching and compiling some of the information that appears in this book. She also did a fine job of proofreading my rough draft and page proofing the final result.

Russ Mullen deserves thanks for his technical edit of this book. He greatly added to the accuracy and depth of the material you see here. In addition, his Visual Basic insights greatly added to the quality of the Visual Basic material in this book.

Matt Wagner, my agent, deserves credit for helping me get the contract in the first place and taking care of all the details that most authors don't really think about.

The technical support staff at Microsoft deserve credit for answering the questions that helped fill in the blanks and made the Visual Studio learning experience go faster. Likewise, I'd like to thank the people on the various Internet newsgroups I visited who helped provide insights into Visual Studio programming techniques.

Finally, I would like to thank Wendy Rinaldi, Ron Hull, Dennis Weaver and the rest of the production staff at Osborne for their assistance in bringing this book to print. I especially appreciate Wendy's patience when things didn't go exceptionally well.

Introduction

Visual Studio is the product to get if you want to see everything that Microsoft has to offer in the way of programming language product support. Of course, your first question may be why you even need more that one programming language. That's one of the first topics we talk about in this book. You'll learn how each of these products can help you develop applications faster and with less code. Using the right programming language for the job means that you spend less time in your office and more time having fun at the beach (or wherever you like to have fun).

Team programming is another concept that Microsoft is trying to promote. If you're working in an enterprise environment, you may need to manage an entire team of programmers rather than just one or two people like developers in days gone by. The enterprise environment provides a lot of opportunities to use more than one language by dividing the project at hand into smaller components that can be handled by individual team members. This can cause headaches because it takes more effort to make a project flow smoothly. This book will help you get more out of the individual team members and still have a project flow smoothly by providing scenarios that show how you can make the examples work in practice. In other words, you'll get some real world management techniques in addition to coding theory and practice.

Anyone who has used Microsoft Visual Studio over the years will attest to the enormous amount of change that has occurred in this product. Microsoft has gone to great lengths to make the latest version of Visual Studio easier to use and more feature-complete than previous versions. However, for the Visual Studio programmer, writing programs is still more art than science. Just about the time that Microsoft creates a new wizard to take the mystery out of one area of programming (like the updated ATL wizard in the version of Visual C++ included with Visual Studio 6.0), some new technology comes along to put the mystery right back in (like OLE-DB and ADO support).

Change is also the reason that you need yet another Visual Studio book. Microsoft is constantly adding new features to Visual Studio. While this book won't tell you much about basic usage for any of the programming languages or programming from a theoretical perspective, it will tell you how to use the new features that Microsoft has added in. For example, you'll find a lot of updated database and Internet-related features in recent releases of this product.

Database programming is getting more and more advanced as Microsoft and other companies try to answer the age old question of how to make data accessible and still keep it secure. ADO is one of the latest technologies to make it into Visual Studio. In addition, you'll find lots of new ways to use existing technologies like ODBC in environments like Visual InterDev when creating Web pages to view your database.

The Internet has played a more predominant role with every release of Visual Studio, and version 6.0 isn't any different. It's the quest for speed that's driving use of Visual Studio in certain Internet components. Downloading a large application from the Internet isn't practical; users want small, fast applications. Sound familiar? We'll be spending a lot of time looking at how you can use Visual Studio to best advantage within today's Internet-driven programming environment.

This version of Visual Studio also includes support for adding a browser right into your application. You can use this browser support for a variety of purposes, including placing help files on your Web server so that people can access them wherever they may be. Just think about the advantages of adding a help desk view into your application. The reduction in support calls alone makes such an addition worth the effort. This same browser support can provide a method for employees on the road to upload information to the company and to download things like the most recent sales statistics and brochures.

The choice of programming language defines the kinds of things a programmer can do within an application and how fast he or she can do them. Visual Studio is known for its outstanding flexibility: You can literally do anything with it without contorting your code into a mass of spaghetti. Visual Studio provides products such as Visual C++, which is known for creating very fast applications when used correctly. Visual Basic is king when it comes to prototyping and creating complex applications quickly. You'll find that Visual InterDev is indispensable when it comes to creating the Web pages that will allow users on the road interact with those that remain behind at the office. Finally, Visual J++ provides more than just a way to dress up your Web pages, you can now use it to create COM technology objects like ActiveX controls.

What's in This Book

This book is divided into five parts that are designed to help you use Visual Studio in just about any environment that you can image. The first part concentrates on the Visual Studio interface. You'll find information that will help you get started. We'll talk about the typical development workstation and server setup that you'll need in order to use Visual Studio effectively. You'll also take a quick tour of the various IDE elements in each of the Visual Studio language products. Next, this part will help you create your first application—a simple prototype of the applications to come. Finally, we'll talk about all of the support tools that Visual Studio provides to make your programming efforts easier.

The second part of the book talks about the principle difference between working alone and working in the enterprise environment—working with other people. We'll look at the tools you can use to reduce friction between users as they rush to get their part of an application put together. Obviously, one of the biggest parts of working with others is using Visual SourceSafe to ensure one programmer doesn't overwrite another's work (or worse yet, open the same file for editing at the same time). There is a wealth of enterprise-specific tools provided with Visual Studio as well, and this part of the book will talk about the ones that you'll use most often.

In the third part of the book you'll find a series of desktop applications, including the first multilanguage example in the book. This is also the first place you'll run into the Scenario section that will help you understand team-programming needs for the example at hand. Along with a simple text editor, you'll find applications that deal with database management and working with the Internet in this section of the book. The DHTML example is especially exciting because it allows you to combine traditional and new Internet programming techniques into one desktop application.

If the Internet is where you're headed today, then you'll want to definitely take a look at the fourth part of the book. We'll begin by looking at some existing technology in a new way by combining ActiveX with a standard Web page. You'll also learn about some of the pizzazz features of Visual InterDev like themes and layouts. More importantly, this part will introduce you to the concepts of remote data access—something that more companies will need to know about as more people find they need to access data over the Internet. This section will talk about user collaboration through an exciting technology known as ActiveDocument. An ActiveDocument application can make it possible for two users to collaborate on a single document, even if they're in different countries, without incurring any additional cost for travel. Finally, we'll talk about the bane of most network administrators, the help desk application. Supporting an entire network of hardware, software, and users can be a challenge for even the best support team. A help desk application can take some of the load off of the support staff by enabling users to help themselves.

The final part of the book talks about the server. We'll begin by looking at a basic Java application. In this case, we'll use the new Windows Foundation Classes (WFC) technology found in Visual J++ and how you can use it in the enterprise. This section will also look at ISAPI in the form of both ISAPI Extensions and ISAPI Filters. We'll look at how you can use ISAPI to create custom Web pages and as a debugging tool for your current Web applications. This part will also provide an overview of ISAPI as a whole—what you can expect from it and what limitations you need to be aware of.

What You'll Need

Most of the applications in this book rely on the features found in Visual Studio 6.0. In fact, if you want maximum use of all the book has to offer, you'll need the Enterprise Edition of this product. Make sure you also have the latest patches and service packs installed for whatever version of Windows you're using. I used the OSR2 version of Windows 95, the initial release version of Windows 98, and Windows NT 4 with Service Pack 3 installed while testing the examples for this book.

If you plan to work with the Internet Information Server (IIS) examples in the book, make sure you install Windows NT Server 4 and update it with Service Pack 3. You'll also need a copy of IIS 4.0 on your server. Some of the example code may not work at all with older versions of IIS. All of the IIS examples assume you're using a full-fledged copy of IIS with all features installed, not one of the alternatives that you could potentially use for a Web server.

You'll also need to install SQL Server version 6.5. The examples in this book were tested using the Developer's Edition of SQL Server 6.5 that comes with the Enterprise Edition of the Visual Studio package. There's no guarantee that any of the examples will work with earlier versions of SQL Server or SQL Server version 7.0, though they were tested with a beta version of SQL Server 7.0.

Note   *Many of the concepts you'll learn in this book won't appear in your online documentation. Some of it is so new that it only appears on selected Web sites. You'll find either a Tip or a Note alerting you to the location of such information throughout the book. In addition, Microsoft made some material available only through selected channels, such as MSDN subscription. Other pieces of information are simply undocumented, and you won't find them anywhere except within a newsgroup when someone finds the feature accidentally.*

You'll also need a computer running Windows 95/98 or Windows NT 4.0 to use as a workstation. Both your Web server and workstation will require enough RAM and other resources to fully support the tools you'll need throughout this book. In most cases, that means you'll need a minimum of a 200 MHz Pentium MMX computer with 64MB of RAM and at least 5GB of hard disk space. Even though you could potentially get by with less, you'll find that a lower-end computer will quickly bog down as you try to write code and test it. I did try running Visual Studio on a 166 MHz Pentium with 32MB of RAM and the performance was terrible.

Conventions Used in This Book

In this section, we'll cover usage conventions. We'll discuss programming conventions a little later when we look at Hungarian Notation and how to use it. This book uses the following conventions:

[<Filename>]	When you see square brackets around a value, switch, or command, it means that this is an optional component. You don't have to include it as part of the command line or dialog field unless you want the additional functionality that the value, switch, or command provides.
<Filename>	A variable name between angle brackets is a value that you need to replace with something else. The variable name you'll see usually provides a clue as to what kind of information you need to supply. In this case, you'll need to provide a filename. Never type the angle brackets when you type the value.
ALL CAPS	There are three places you'll see ALL CAPS: commands, filenames, and case-sensitive registry entries. Normally, you'll type a command at the DOS prompt, within a PIF file field, or within the Run dialog field. If you see all caps somewhere else, it's safe to assume that the item is a case-sensitive registry entry or some other value like a filename.
File | Open	Menus and the selections on them appear with a vertical bar. "File | Open" means "Access the File menu and choose Open."
italic	There are three places you see italic text: new words, multi-value entries, and undefined values. You'll always see a value in italic whenever the actual value of something is unknown. The book also uses italic where more than one value might be correct. For example, you might see FILE*xxxx*0 in text. This means that the value could be anywhere between FILE0000 and FILE9999.

monospace   It's important to differentiate the text that you'll use in
                                    a macro or type at the command line from the text that
                                    explains it. This book uses monospace type to make
                                    this differentiation. Every time you see monospace text,
                                    you'll know that the information you see will appear in
                                    a macro, within a system file like CONFIG.SYS or
                                    AUTOEXEC.BAT, or as something you'll type at the
                                    command line. You'll even see the switches used with
                                    Windows commands in this text. There is another time
                                    you'll see monospace text. Every code listing uses the
                                    monospace font to make the text easier to read. Using
                                    monospaced text also makes it easier to add things like
                                    indentation to the coding example.

Icons

This book contains many icons that help you identify certain types of information. The
following paragraphs describe the purpose of each icon.

Note
*Notes tell you about interesting facts that don't necessarily affect your ability to use the
other information in the book. I use notes to give you bits of information that I've picked
up while using Visual Studio, Windows NT, or Windows 95.*

Tip
*Everyone likes tips, because they tell you new ways of doing things that you might not
have thought about before. Tips also provide an alternative way of doing something that
you might like better than the first approach I provided.*

Caution
*This means watch out! Cautions almost always tell you about some kind of system or
data damage that'll occur if you perform a certain action (or fail to perform others).
Make sure you understand a caution thoroughly before you follow any instructions that
come after it.*

Web Link
*The Internet contains a wealth of information, but finding it can be difficult, to say the
least. Web Links help you find new sources of information on the Internet that you can
use to improve your programming or learn new techniques. You'll also find newsgroup
Web Links that tell where you can find other people to talk with about Visual Studio.
Finally, Web Links will help you find utility programs that'll make programming faster
and easier than before.*

Making sure your code will run in a variety of situations and on a variety of platforms is always a good idea. Whenever you see this icon, you'll learn about an issue that could affect your ability to move code or executable from one machine to another. Make sure you pay special attention to these icons if the ability to use your program on more than one machine type or in more than one operating system environment is important.

An Overview of Hungarian Notation

Secret codes—the stuff of spy movies and a variety of other human endeavors. When you first see Hungarian Notation, you may view it as just another secret code. It contains all the elements of a secret code including an arcane series of letters that you have to decode and an almost indecipherable result when you do. However, it won't take long for you to realize that it's other programmers' code that's secret, not the Hungarian Notation used in this book.

Hungarian Notation can save you a lot of time and effort. Anyone who has spent enough time programming realizes the value of good documentation when you try to understand what you did in a previous coding session or to interpret someone else's code. That's part of what Hungarian Notation will do for you—document your code.

An understanding of Hungarian Notation will also help you gain more insight from the examples in this book and from the Microsoft (and other vendor) manuals in general. Just about every Windows programming language vendor uses some form of Hungarian Notation in their manuals. In addition, these same concepts are equally applicable to other languages like Visual FoxPro, Delphi, and Visual BASIC. The codes remain similar across a variety of programming languages, even when the language itself doesn't.

So what precisely is Hungarian Notation? It's a way of telling other people what you intend to do with a variable. Knowing what a variable is supposed to do can often help explain the code itself. For example, if I tell you that a particular variable contains a handle to a window, then you know a lot more about it than the fact that it is simply a variable. You can interpret the code surrounding that variable with the understanding that it's supposed to do something with a window.

The first stage of development for this variable-naming system was started by Charles Simonyi of Microsoft Corporation. He called his system Hungarian Notation, so that's the name we'll use here. There are many places where you can obtain a copy of his work, including BBSs and some of the Microsoft programming Web sites on the Internet. (Many online services like CompuServe also carry copies of Hungarian Notation in its various incarnations.) Simonyi's work was further enhanced by other developers. For example, Xbase programmers use their own special version of Hungarian Notation. It takes into account the different types of variables that Xbase provides. An enhanced Xbase version of Hungarian Notation was published by Robert A. Difalco of Fresh Technologies. You can find his work on a few DBMS-specific BBSs as well as the Computer Associates Clipper forum on CompuServe.

The basis for the ideas presented in this section is found in one of the two previously mentioned documents in one form or another. The purpose in publishing them here is to make you aware of the exact nature of the conventions I employ and how you can best use them in your own code. There are four reasons why you should use these naming conventions in your programs.

- **Mnemonic Value**   This allows you to remember the name of a variable more easily, an important consideration for team projects.

- **Suggestive Value**   You may not be the only one modifying your code. If you're working on a team project, others in the team will most likely at least look at the code you have written. Using these conventions will help others understand what you mean when using a specific convention.

- **Consistency**   A programmer's work is often viewed not only in terms of efficiency or functionality but also for ease of readability by other programmers. Using these conventions will help you maintain uniform code from one project to another. Other programmers will be able to anticipate the value or function of a section of code simply by the conventions you use.

- **Speed of Decision**   In the business world, the speed at which you can create and modify code will often determine how successful a particular venture will be. Using consistent code will reduce the time you spend trying to decide what someone meant when creating a variable or function. This reduction in decision time will increase the amount of time you have available for productive work.

Now that I've told you why you should use Hungarian Notation, let's look at how I implement it in this book. I use the rules in the following section when naming variables. You'll also see me use them when naming database fields or other value-related constructs. Some functions and procedures will use them as well, but only if Hungarian Notation will make the meaning of the function or procedure clearer.

Rule 1: Prefixing a Variable

Always prefix a variable with one or more lowercase letters indicating its type. In most cases, this is the first letter of the variable type, so it's easy to remember what letter to use. The following examples show the most common prefixes for Visual BASIC,

Delphi, and C. (There are literally hundreds of combinations used in Windows that don't appear here.) You'll also see a few database-specific identifiers provided here:

a	Array
c	Character
d	Date
dbl	Double
dc	Device Context
dw	Double Word
f	Flag, Boolean, or Logical
h	Handle
i	Integer
inst	Instance
l	Long
li	Long Integer
lp	Long Pointer
msg	Message
n	Numeric
o	Object
pal	Palette
psz	Pointer to a Zero Terminated String
ptr	Pointer (or P when used with other variables like psz)
r	Real
rc	Rectangle
rgb	Red, Green, Blue (color variable)
rsrc	Resource
sgl	Single

si	Short Integer
sz	Zero Terminated String
u	Unsigned
ui	Unsigned Integer or Byte
w	Word
wnd	Window

Rule 2: Identifying State Variables

Some variables represent the state of an object like a database, a field, or a control. They might even store the state of another variable. Telling other programmers that a variable monitors the current state of an object can help them see its significance within the program. You can identify state variables using one of the following three-character qualifiers:

New	A New state
Sav	A Saved state
Tem	A Temporary state

Rule 3: Using a Standard Qualifier

A standard qualifier can help someone see the purpose of a variable almost instantly. This isn't the type of information that the variable contains, but how it reacts with other variables. For example, using the Clr qualifier tells the viewer that this variable is used in some way with color. You can even combine the qualifiers to amplify their effect and describe how the variable is used. For example, cClrCrs is a character variable that determines the color of the cursor on the display. Using one to three of these qualifiers is usually sufficient to describe the purpose of a variable. The following standard qualifiers are examples of the more common types:

Ar	Array
Attr	Attribute
B	Bottom

Clr	Color
Col	Column
Crs	Cursor
Dbf	Database File
F	First
File	File
Fld	Field
L	Last/Left
Msg	Message
Name	Name
Ntx	Index File
R	Right
Rec	Record Number
Ret	Return Value
Scr	Screen
Str	String
T	Top
X	Row
Y	Column

Rule 4: Adding Descriptive Text

Once you clearly define the variable's contents and purpose, you can refine the definition with some descriptive text. For example, you might have a long pointer to a string containing an employee's name that looks like this: lpszEmpName. The first two letters tell you that this is a long pointer. The second two letters tell you that this is a zero (or null) terminated string. The rest of the letters tell you that this is an employee name. (Notice that I used the standard qualifier, Name, for this example.) Seeing a variable name like this in a piece of code tells you what to expect from it at a glance.

Rule 5: Creating More Than One Variable

There are times when you won't be able to satisfy every need in a particular module using a single variable. In those cases, you might want to create more than one of that variable type and simply number them. You could also designate its function using some type of number indicator like those shown here:

1, 2, 3	State pointer references as in cSavClr1, cSavClr2, etc.
Max	Strict upper limit as in nFldMax, maximum number of fields
Min	Strict lower limit as in nRecMin, minimum number of records
Ord	An ordinal number of some type

Part I

The Interface

Chapter 1

Getting Started

Today's computing environment is getting more and more complex. All you need to do is look at the wealth of new hardware that's becoming commonplace on newer machines to see where the complexity begins. In addition, the advent of Internet computing has increased complexity as well, by adding new capabilities through unreliable connections. In general, people expect more out of their machines today than they did just a few months ago because they're able to do more.

All of this new complexity in the computing environment has made the programmer's job harder, just at the time when programming tools are finally making programming less of an arcane art and more of a science. While devices like digital video disks (DVDs) aren't all that difficult to program, imagine what you'd need to write a program for one of the new Windows 98 devices that support broadcast television. Since the ability to view broadcast television is now part of the Windows 98 operating system, you can bet that some customers will want to use that new capability in some way to improve business productivity.

Note   *Some special device support relies on specific hardware. For example, as of this writing, only the ATI All-In-Wonder display adapter fully supported broadcast television under Windows 98. What this means to you, as a programmer, is additional checks to make sure that a specific device is actually supported by the operating system before you use it. You can be sure that this situation will change as vendors release the required drivers once Windows 98 is released.*

Complexity occurs in areas where the user isn't likely to look. A new programming application programming interface (API) may solve some old problems or provide you with new operating system features, but it's just as likely to result in some hand programming when a favorite programming tool doesn't include automatic support for the API. As we all know, more hand coding results in longer development times and increased occurrences of programming errors. New networking technologies like COM+ will likely make for interesting programming situations. In days past, you could rely on the connection between your test computer and a database manager. That's no longer true. When you deal with the Internet, you also have to take the possibility of a bad connection into account. Because COM+ is an enabling technology for the Internet, you can count on finding programmers who are frustrated trying to find bugs that appear and disappear at the whim of a connection.

With Visual Studio, Microsoft has attempted to create a tool that an enterprise programming team can use to take some of the complexity out of today's programming environment. Not only does this suite of tools include multiple languages so that you can use the programming language that best fits the job at hand, but it contains a wealth of useful team coding tools as well.

This chapter provides an overview of what Visual Studio is and how it can help your programming team create the perfect application. Will we cover every feature in the package? Probably not, since I could probably write an entire book that looked at all the features that this product contains. What we will cover are the features that you need to know about most, especially the new features for this version of Visual Studio. You'll also get a better idea of what Visual Studio can do—for you individually, for your programming team, and for your company. It's important to know that everyone will benefit from this latest weapon in Microsoft's arsenal of complexity fighting tools.

What Is Visual Studio?

You've probably seen Visual Studio, or at least parts of it, in the past. First and foremost, Visual Studio is a packaging concept. Rather than asking the programmer to find the right tools and buy them as separate products, Microsoft has bundled all their most popular programming products in one package. You can look at Visual Studio in two ways: as a collection of programming languages and as a collection of development tools. There are too many tools to cover in just one paragraph, so we'll cover them as the chapter progresses and throughout the rest of the book (make sure you look at Chapter 5 "Understanding the Other Visual Studio Tools" for tool details). Here's a list of the programming language products in the package:

- Visual Basic
- Visual C++
- Visual InterDev
- Visual J++
- Visual FoxPro

Note

This book covers the first four programming language products in the preceding list, but it does not cover Visual FoxPro. Instead, we'll concentrate on using SQL Server when needed for database applications. Even though Visual FoxPro has a well-deserved following in the database community, SQL Server provides much more in the way of enterprise-related features and lends itself better to the needs of the enterprise developer.

There's more to Visual Studio than packaging. Microsoft is striving to create an enterprise product that'll allow a team of programmers to create robust applications in the minimum amount of time. With that in mind, Microsoft has done a few things to make it easier to use the individual programming languages within Visual Studio. For example, they're working on a common integrated development environment (IDE). While you won't see this feature completely in this release of Visual Studio, Microsoft has partially met that goal. The first two subsections that follow will talk about the common elements that you should look for in Visual Studio and those that Microsoft still has to work on.

The third subsection will talk about the special features of Visual C++. Microsoft chose to retain the appearance that Visual C++ has had in the past. Part of the reason that they retained the old Developer Studio IDE is that Visual C++ provides lower-level programming features that the other Visual Studio products don't provide. Trying to make Visual C++ look precisely like these other products proved difficult. However, the differences between Visual C++ and the other products go deeper than the IDE; this section will examine some of those differences.

The last subsection talks about the differences between the Enterprise Edition of Visual Studio and the Professional Edition. We'll use the Enterprise Edition throughout the book, but it's important to know about the differences between the two products, just in case you have the Professional Edition. There are some features that the Enterprise Edition includes that you'll need for some examples in the book. The fourth subsection will help you know when an example will use features that require the Enterprise Edition.

Common Features

Part of the learning curve for using a new programming language product is learning the integrated development environment (IDE) that it uses. The IDE determines what the menus will look like and what windows a programming language product will have. Modern programming products provide so much in the way of features that a programmer could end up spending quite a bit of time learning to use them efficiently. (Of course, most of us will eschew the manuals to figure out how things work by trial and error, which certainly doesn't help the situation much.)

In the past, if you wanted to learn how to use both Visual InterDev and Visual Basic, you had to learn two completely different IDEs. One of the methods that Microsoft plans to use to reduce the Visual Studio product learning curve is to provide a common (or as common as possible) IDE for all of the products in the Visual Studio suite. Figure 1-1 shows the IDEs for Visual Basic, Visual J++, and Visual InterDev. (The figure only shows two windows since Visual J++ and Visual InterDev use precisely the same IDE.) As you can see, there are a lot of common features in the interfaces for all three products. For example, all three products have common menu entries, as well as an assortment of common windows (like the Properties window that displays the properties of the currently selected object).

 Visual C++ will continue to use the IDE that programmers have been familiar with for quite some time now. Microsoft plans to upgrade the Visual C++ IDE during a future update.

 Make sure you read the discussion about the Visual Studio IDE used by Visual Basic, Visual InterDev, and Visual J++ in Chapter 2. It discusses the various interface elements you'll use to create applications and how to modify the IDE to meet your personal needs. You'll also learn more about differences between the Visual Basic and Visual InterDev/J++ IDEs.

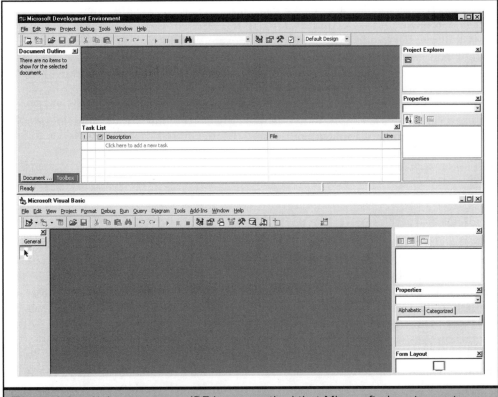

Figure 1-1.   Using a common IDE is one method that Microsoft plans to use to reduce the learning curve for the Visual Studio language products

Anyone using the Enterprise Edition of Visual Studio will notice another common theme throughout the entire package—database access. Microsoft has spent a lot of time figuring out what an enterprise-level application requires in the way of database access. You'll find new features like OLE-DB, which is a low-level method of accessing remote data, and visual database tools, which make it easier to create a connection to the database in the first place. The whole purpose of all these new database features is to make both remote and local database access less of a black art and more of a science.

Note   *One of the more important changes in this version of Visual Studio is the level of database support provided.*

As with every current Microsoft product, you'll find that the Internet is playing a much bigger role in Visual Studio features. The new features range from ADO (ActiveX

Data Object), which can help you create applications that don't care where data resides, to new data-aware ActiveX controls. Microsoft is also working to make Internet accessibility easier to add to applications. For example, Visual Basic provides an entirely new set of Web classes.

Visual is another word that you'll come to associate with the latest edition of Visual Studio. There are a lot of new wizards that will make designing an application or component easier. In addition, many of these tools provide a visual interface that you can use to draw various application relationships. The emphasis is on more automation and less hand coding of applications.

Note   *Microsoft has worked hard to put more emphasis on the visual aspects of Visual Studio.*

Differences Between Products

Now that we've seen how the various Visual Studio products incorporate similar features to make them easier to use, let's look at some of the differences between them. There are some obvious differences, and we won't discuss them here. For example, the language used for each product will be different, as are some of the intended purposes for that product. We'll still look at these obvious differences as the book progresses, but in a more practical way as part of creating enterprise-level team projects that show the various projects working together as a cohesive whole.

The most obvious differences from a product user perspective are in the IDE. For example, Visual Basic provides a Form Layout window that allows you to place the various dialog boxes in your application on-screen. Visual InterDev and Visual J++ don't really require this kind of functionality since you're not really working with a set of dialog boxes that you can position on a screen.

But there are some differences in the IDE that you can't write off as quickly. For example, the toolbox used by Visual Basic is much simpler than the hierarchical toolbox provided with Visual InterDev. You'll find that the hierarchical view allows you to retain more controls within reach and still not clutter your display with unnecessary icons.

Toolbars are another area where the Visual InterDev IDE has a distinct advantage. You'll find a wealth of new toolbars at your disposal. For example, there is a new Analyzer toolbar that makes it easy to more accurately determine when events occur in your application. You can even record these events and then play them back to better see how your application functions—sort of like instant replay.

In sum, even though the IDEs of these three products look very much the same, there are subtle differences that you need to be aware of. While none of these differences will make it difficult for you to create an application, you need to keep the various advantages offered by one product over another in mind when determining which product to use for a particular task. Any assistance you can get from the programming environment can make your programming session more enjoyable and allow you to create the application faster.

The Visual C++ Difference

As mentioned earlier, the most noticeable difference between Visual C++ and the rest of Visual Studio is the IDE. Figure 1-2 shows a typical Visual C++ setup. As you can see, it looks nothing like the rest of Visual Studio. Microsoft plans to correct this oversight in a future version of Visual Studio, but for now, you'll still need to learn unique IDE for Visual C++ before you can use it.

The main reason for the difference between the Visual C++ IDE and that provided by Visual Basic is the kind of programming you can perform with Visual C++. This

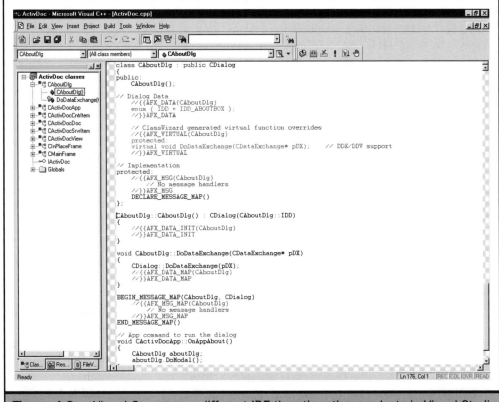

Figure 1-2.   Visual C++ uses a different IDE than the other products in Visual Studio

particular product is designed to create low-level applications. For example, it makes a superior platform for creating light ActiveX controls. Even though you can create ActiveX controls with Visual Basic, you'll find that it's more difficult to gain the level of control over them that you can with Visual C++. In addition, the Visual Basic version of an ActiveX control will always be larger than its Visual C++ counterpart, given equal levels of programmer ability when creating them.

> **Tip**   *Make sure you read about the Visual C++ IDE in Chapter 3 if you're unfamiliar with this product. The whole intent of that chapter is to help you get the most out of the Visual C++ IDE without spending a lot of time searching through the help files for information. We'll not only discuss the interface features, but you'll learn how to do things like customize the IDE for your personal needs.*

Another way in which Visual C++ differs from the rest of the Visual Studio product line is in the level of automation provided by the various utilities it provides. Unlike the other Visual Studio products, Visual C++ is designed to work with a broad range of application and operating system element types. As a result, many of the utilities provided with Visual C++ are designed to provide an in-depth look at precisely what Windows is doing. However, this depth of information comes at a price—automation. You'll find that many of the automatic features you take for granted in other language products like Visual Basic just don't appear with Visual C++.

Objects also play a very different role in Visual C++ than they do in the other Visual Studio products. When you work with Visual Basic, the very first thing you do is design the user interface. After that, you add code to make those interface elements do something. Visual C++ programmers may not begin with the user interface; they may choose to work on another part of the application first, such as designing the classes that'll eventually do all the work within the application. What all this boils down to is a very basic difference in the way that you'll interact with Visual C++. Even when Microsoft does come up with a new IDE for Visual C++, it's still certain that you'll work on a Visual C++ application in a different manner than you will its Visual Basic counterpart.

The Enterprise Version Difference

There are a lot of good reasons to buy the Enterprise Edition of Visual Studio if you're going to work on team projects. Even if you aren't working on team projects, getting some features like Visual Source Safe is well worth the price of entry. The point is that if you're planning on working on a major project (whether alone or as part of a group), you need the tools that the Enterprise Edition provides.

Table 1-1 provides a complete overview of the features you'll get with the Enterprise Edition of Visual Studio versus the Professional Edition. I've provided separate columns for the various tools just in case you plan to buy one or more of the tools separately. Obviously, you'll get all of the features listed in the table if you get the Enterprise Edition of Visual Studio.

It's important to note that Table 1-1 doesn't list all the new features you'll find in Visual Studio, nor do all of the Enterprise features found in one Visual Studio programming language product necessarily appear in the others. In addition, the Professional Edition of some language products does partially implement some Enterprise Edition features. You'll see an asterisk (*) next to the check mark when the Professional Edition partially implements an Enterprise Edition feature. If you don't

Feature	Visual InterDev	Visual J++	Visual Basic	Visual C++
Application Performance Explorer	√	√	√	
ASA400 and VSAM database access through OLE-DB			√	√
Client/server application development			√	√*
Component Object Model Transaction Integrator (COMTI) for CICS and IMS (mainframe proxy services)			√	√
Data Binding Software Development Kit (SDK)			√	
Data Environment Designer			√	
Data Object Wizard			√	
Extended Stored Procedure Wizard			√	√
Internet Information Server (IIS) 4.0	√	√	√	√
Microsoft Transaction Server	√	√	√	√
New Database Wizard	√	√	√	√
Posting Acceptor	√	√	√	
Proxy Server				√
Remote automation components (Remote Data control)			√	√
Remote Data Object (RDO) User Connection Designer			√	
SNA Server			√	√

Table 1-1. Visual Studio Feature Comparison by Edition

Feature	Visual InterDev	Visual J++	Visual Basic	Visual C++
SQL editing, debugging, and stored procedures debugging	√	√	√	√
SQL Server 6.5 Developer Edition and Service Pack 3	√	√	√	√
System Management Server (SMS)				√
Table Designer	√	√	√	√
Trigger Editor	√	√	√	√
TSQL debugging	√	√	√	√
User Connection Editor			√	
View Designer	√	√	√	√
Visual database tools such as Database Designer and Query Designer	√	√	√	√*
Visual Component Manager	√	√	√	√
Visual Modeler			√	√
Visual SourceSafe Version Control	√	√	√	√
Visual Studio Analyzer	√	√		
Visual Studio Enterprise Edition (VSEE) Solutions Book or Solution Deployment Reference	√	√	√	√
Webclasses			√	

Table 1-1. Visual Studio Feature Comparison by Edition (continued)

see a check mark in a column, the product either doesn't provide that feature or the feature is common to both the Professional Edition and Enterprise Edition.

Installing the Client Components

Every workstation you plan to use for development purposes will require some or all of the client components. Of course, exactly which components you install depends a great deal on what you plan to do at that workstation. Supervisors will likely require a full installation of Visual Studio so that they can help other workers get the most out of the product. On the other hand, someone who builds Web pages all day can probably get by with a Visual InterDev and Visual J++ installation. However, you can't ever assume anything about a particular installation since even Web pages use ActiveX controls, which may require a Web page developer to also have either Visual Basic or Visual C++ installed on their machine.

 You'll need a minimum of a 200 MHz Pentium MMX computer with a 3GB hard drive and 64MB of RAM to use Visual Studio efficiently. See the Introduction for further details on system requirements.

This section isn't designed to tell you everything there is to know about Visual Studio from an installation perspective. The main focus of this section is to show you what kind of installation you'll need to get the most out of this book. In addition, the setup used for this book will help you get the most out of the common Visual Studio products. Obviously, this section will also provide you with pointers that you can use for any installation, especially considering that we are going to perform a custom installation. With these criteria in mind, let's get the client part of Visual Studio installed on our development workstation.

Note *The examples in this book are based on the Enterprise Edition of Visual Studio. Readers using the Professional Edition may find that some examples do not work for them as written. In addition, the Professional Edition lacks some features included with the Enterprise Edition. Nevertheless, Professional Edition users will still be able to follow the examples and get some ideas of what can be done with Visual Studio.*

1. Start the Visual Studio Setup program. In most cases, all you'll need to do is place the CD in your drive since the Visual Studio CD includes an AUTORUN.INF file. However, you can also start Setup manually from Explorer. You'll see an Installation Wizard dialog box like the one shown here:

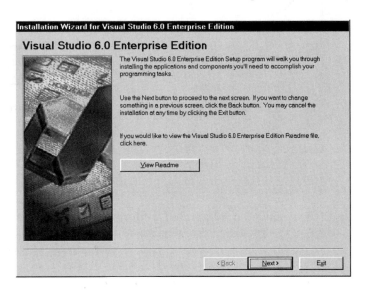

Caution   *The installation program may appear to stop running for extended periods. Unless your machine has definitely stopped responding, wait for the program to resume the installation. Such delays typically last about 20 minutes, but they may take up to an hour. In addition, you may get error messages if something unexpected happens during the installation. For example, the program may report an error if you remove the CD from the drive after a reboot. Check for simple problems even if error messages appear to be unwarranted.*

2. Click Next. You'll see a standard Microsoft license agreement. Make sure you read the agreement so that you know what licensing terms Visual Studio provides.

3. Select the "I accept the agreement" option, then click Next. The Installation Wizard will ask for your product ID, user name, and company name. The product ID should appear on the CD jewel case that came with Visual Studio.

4. Enter the requested information, then click Next. You'll see a Setup Options dialog box like the one shown here. This is where you'll decide what type of installation to perform. We'll be using the Custom installation for this book since it offers the greatest flexibility. Using the other two options means that you'll give up some flexibility for installation speed; the Installation Wizard will make certain assumptions for you. Note that even Microsoft assumes that you'll want to perform a Custom installation since it's the default option.

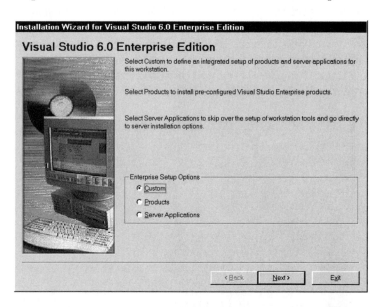

5. Click Next. The Installation Wizard will perform a few tasks in the background and then display the initial Setup dialog box as follows.

6. Click Continue. Setup will display a dialog box showing your full product ID. Make sure you record this number for future reference.

7. Click OK. Setup will look for existing copies of the product. This procedure assumes that this is the first time you've installed Visual Studio and that there are no previous copies on the development workstation. Once Setup completes its search, you'll see the Custom dialog box shown here:

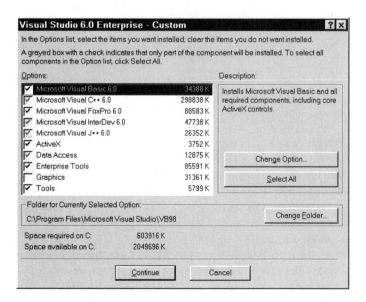

8. Choose the custom installation options that you need for the development workstation. This book will use four language products: Visual Basic, Visual C++, Visual InterDev, and Visual J++. We'll also use the additional ActiveX controls, the SQL Server data access options, all of the enterprise tools, and all of the general tools.

9. Click Continue. Setup will spend some time installing all the required files for you. Once it completes this task, you'll see a Setup Environment Variables dialog box. All this dialog box tells you is that you can use a batch file to set up a command prompt environment so that you can build applications manually from the command prompt if desired. We won't use that feature in the book, but it does come in handy when you have complex applications to create.

10. Click OK to clear the Setup Environment Variables dialog box. Setup will perform some additional background tasks and then display a Restart Windows dialog box like the one shown here:

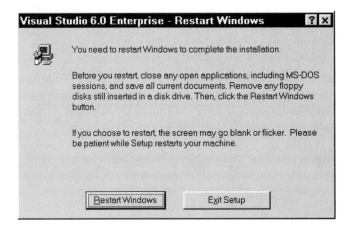

11. Restart Windows. The core development workstation installation is complete.

Once you restart Windows, Setup will allow you to install several additional Visual Studio features. The first feature is Microsoft Development Network (MSDN). You'll want to install this feature to gain access to help on your machine. Once you get past the MSDN installation, you'll have an opportunity to install other client tools such as InstallShield and FrontPage. We won't use any of these optional tools in the book, though you'll want to install them on your development machine in some cases. For example, if you plan to create a setup program for your C++ application, then you'll need to install InstallShield. You'll also get a chance to install any server components you need on your development machine. We'll cover server installation in the next section, because the book assumes you'll be using two machines: one for development and another as a test server. At the very end of the installation process, you'll see a Congratulations dialog box.

Installing the Server Components

In most cases, you'll want to create a separate server and development workstation, even if you're working alone on a project. (Team projects would require a separate server for file storage anyway, so there isn't much additional work involved in creating a test server setup.) While some developers do use one machine for both client and server, such a setup doesn't result in the most accurate test setup possible. For example, there are timing issues that you can't take into account when you use the local machine as your server. In addition, you can't test security at all. How do you know that someone using the application you create will be able to use it at all unless you test their ability to access all of the required files over a network connection? There are other considerations as well, like reliability. Using a two-machine setup for development purposes allows you to create a more realistic environment in which to test your application as a whole.

Note *You'll need a minimum of a 200 MHz Pentium computer with a 5GB hard drive and 64MB of RAM to use Visual Stuidio efficiently. (A faster processor is highly recommended if you want to see any kind of performance at all.) See the Introduction for further details on system requirements.*

The following procedure won't help you create the test server required for every kind of application development. You'll need to design a test server to meet your specific needs, which is something I can only guess about in this book. What this procedure will do is help you set up a test server that'll allow you to work with the examples in this book with the fewest potential conflicts.

Note *The examples in this book are based on the Enterprise Edition of Visual Studio. Readers using the Professional Edition may find that some examples do not work for them as written. In addition, the Professional Edition lacks some features included with the Enterprise Edition. Nevertheless, Professional Edition users will still be able to follow the examples and get some ideas of what can be done with Visual Studio.*

1. Start the Visual Studio Setup program. In most cases, all you'll need to do is place the CD in your drive since the Visual Studio CD includes an AUTORUN.INF file. However, you can also start Setup manually from Explorer. You'll see an Installation Wizard dialog box.

2. Click Next. You'll see a standard Microsoft license agreement. Make sure you read the agreement so that you know what licensing terms Visual Studio provides.

3. Select the "I accept the agreement" option, then click Next. The Installation Wizard will ask for your product ID, user name, and company name. The product ID should appear on the CD jewel case that came with Visual Studio.

4. Enter the requested information, then click Next. You'll see a Setup Options dialog box like the one shown here. This is where you'll decide what type of installation to perform. We'll be using the Server Applications option for this installation because we don't need the workstation products installed on the server.

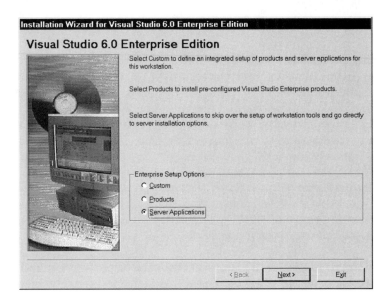

> **Caution** *The installation program may appear to stop running for extended periods. Unless your machine has definitely stopped responding, wait for the program to resume the installation. Such delays typically last about 20 minutes, but they may take up to an hour. In addition, you may get error messages if something unexpected happens during the installation. For example, the program may report an error if you remove the CD from the drive after a reboot. Check for simple problems even if error messages appear to be unwarranted.*

5. Click Next. The Installation Wizard will ask where you want to install the common server application files. In most cases, you'll choose the default directory. (Obviously, you'll choose a different drive if the current drive doesn't provide the required space.)

6. Click Next. You'll see a Server Setups dialog box like the one shown here. This is where you choose from the various server components. You must choose the standard Server Component Setup option as a minimum.

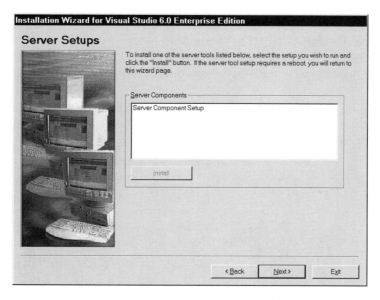

7. Choose a server setup option from the list, then click Install. (The Installation Wizard may ask you to insert the second CD at this point.) You'll see a BackOffice Server Setup dialog box like the one shown here. At this point, you have two choices: a Complete setup will reduce installation time and ensure you have everything you need, while a Custom setup will reduce the amount of disk space required for the installation. For the purposes of this book, we'll perform a Custom installation.

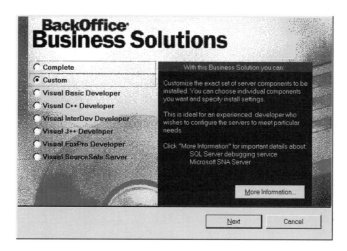

8. Click Custom, then Next. You'll see a Disk Space Requirements dialog box. This dialog box will allow you to determine which components you can install in the space available on your machine.

9. Click Next. You'll see a BackOffice Programs and Their Components dialog box like the one shown here. The illustration shows which of the programs I installed for my test sever. (The Windows NT 4 Options Pack isn't shown, but you'll need to install it if you haven't done so already.)

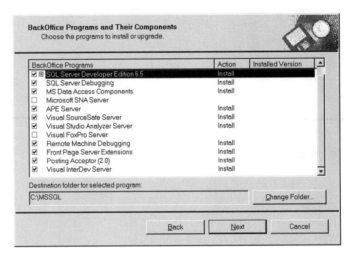

10. Click Next. BackOffice Server Setup will ask where you want to save your data. In most cases, you'll choose the default directory supplied.

11. Click Next. At this point, BackOffice Server Setup will ask you to provide an account name for each of the programs that require a login. The only program in this category for the test setup in this book is SQL Server.

12. Click Assign Account, choose an Account Name, Domain, and Password. Confirm the password that you typed, then click OK. You should see an assignment for the SQL Server entry, as shown here:

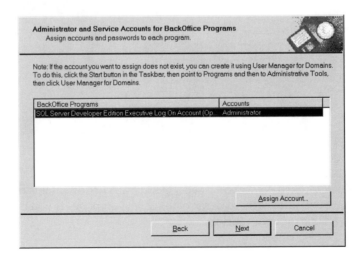

13. Click Next. You'll see a list of SQL Server database settings.

14. Accept the default settings by clicking Next. BackOffice Server Setup will provide a summary of the settings you chose.

15. Click Next to accept the settings and begin the installation. You'll see a BackOffice Component Installation dialog box. This dialog box will keep you informed about the progress of the installation. Eventually, you'll see a Completing the BackOffice Setup Wizard dialog box.

16. Click Finish to complete the installation process. BackOffice Server Setup will ask you to restart your machine. When your machine restarts, you'll see a Windows NT Setup dialog box and a list of items that will get set up on your machine. After a few minutes, this dialog box will disappear and your machine will continue to start normally. (Once the server restarts, you may need to reinsert the first Visual Studio CD.) At this point, you'll see the Installation Wizard Server Setups dialog box seen in Step 6.

17. Click Next. You'll see a Congratulations dialog box.

18. Click Finish.

At this point, your server should be set up and ready to go. Make sure you follow any required setups as the book progresses. Some of the server components aren't fully configured when you first install them.

Creating a Test Setup

So far, we've looked at how to install the client and server components on your machines (development workstation and server). The procedure shows the test setup that I'm using while writing this book. My goals are to show you how to create a broad range of application types and to demonstrate how to use the various programming languages in Visual Studio together.

Hopefully, you can see how my goals have affected the test setup that I'm using. You need to consider what your goals are when creating a test setup as well. In fact, it generally pays to create a list of goals as part of the initial setup process. Make sure that you're installing everything you need, but not more than you need. Not installing enough components will make completing the task at hand nearly impossible, but few people consider that having too many features installed can cause problems like memory shortages and unexplainable errors due to interactions between various suite components.

So, how do you know what to install for the perfect test setup? The following list provides some ideas that you can use to create your own test setup. However, you'll definitely want to modify this list to take any special needs you might have into account as well.

■ **Languages** You'll want to define which languages the project will require, then install the required level of support for those languages. There are two areas where you won't want to skimp on support. First, always provide as many of the help files as you can. Speeding access to help is one way to reduce programmer research time. Second, if this is a relatively new programmer, you'll probably want to install most or all of the example code as well, since examples can be a big help when learning to do something new.

■ **Application type** Database applications require much more support than any other kind of application on your machine. You not only need to test local connections, but remote connections as well. Ensure your server setup includes all of the components required to completely test your application. Make sure you provide a full SQL Server installation if that's your database product of choice.

■ **Internet capability** Any application that requires Internet or intranet connectivity requires a two-machine setup. There isn't any way to fully test an Internet application of any kind using just one machine and a local Web server like Personal Web Server.

■ **Hardware capacity** Some programmers will try to cut expenses by using an older machine, or one with fewer capabilities, for testing purposes. In most cases, this is a self-defeating way to set up a test server. Make sure your test server has adequate hardware capacity for the type of testing you intend to perform. On the other hand, you don't have to spend thousands of dollars for fancy features like RAID support that you'll never use. The main requirements are that the server have a large enough hard disk, plenty of memory, and a high-speed processor.

■ **Operating system support** If you can guarantee that your users will only have one operating system installed on their machines, then you can get by with testing for a single operating system. On the other hand, if your company has a setup like most companies do, you'll need to create a dual boot partition on your development machine: one for Windows 95/98 and the other for Windows NT. Make sure you test any application you write under all of the operating systems you expect to support. Of course, you'll also want to cover the bases with hardware support as well. While it's probably not possible to test every configuration of the machines in your company, you can test for configurations that have caused problems in the past.

Chapter 2

Working with the Visual Studio Interface

Visual Basic, Visual J++, and Visual InterDev all use what's commonly referred to by Microsoft as the Visual Studio interface (or IDE). The IDEs for all three products include essentially the same features, which makes moving from product to product easier than it was in the past. You can program with Visual Basic today and then use the same interface tomorrow to work with Visual InterDev. Only the language itself changes—not the way that you work with that language. (There are some obvious language-specific features of the IDE, and you won't find those in languages that don't require them.)

This chapter will acquaint you with the Visual Studio interface. I'll use Visual Basic for most of the discussion since it contains the greatest number of IDE features. However, the same techniques will work for the IDEs used by the other two language products. We'll cover four main IDE topics:

- Working with the interface.
- Differences between the IDEs used by the three languages.
- Working with standard windows like the Project Explorer.
- Working with the debug windows.

Note *Make sure you check out Chapter 3 to learn about the Visual C++ IDE if you intend to use that product. Visual C++ uses a unique IDE that was designed specifically for it. This chapter only covers the Visual Studio interface that Microsoft plans to make the standard IDE for all Visual Studio language products some time in the future.*

There are three additional topics in this chapter that'll allow you to get the most from the IDE. The first topic that we'll cover is how to define a view. You'll use views to make it easier to see just what you need to see to work with your application. The next topic is customizing toolbars. Most of the Visual Studio toolbars are well designed, but you may want to add a button or two to perform a special task without using a menu. For example, you may want to add the Build button to the standard toolbar. Finally, we'll look at using the Analyzer to make your code run better. Getting the fastest possible result from your coding efforts will make users more willing to learn how to use the final application. We'll explore various ways that you can use the Analyzer to optimize your code.

Getting Around Visual Studio

The Visual Studio IDE has been refined over the years to make it easy to use and understand. However, before you can really learn to use the IDE, you have to know what the various components of that IDE are. Figure 2-1 shows a typical Visual Basic IDE. There are small differences between the Visual Basic IDE and the one used by both Visual J++ and Visual InterDev. Figure 2-2 shows a typical example of the second IDE. The callouts in both figures will help you identify the various components that I describe in the following list.

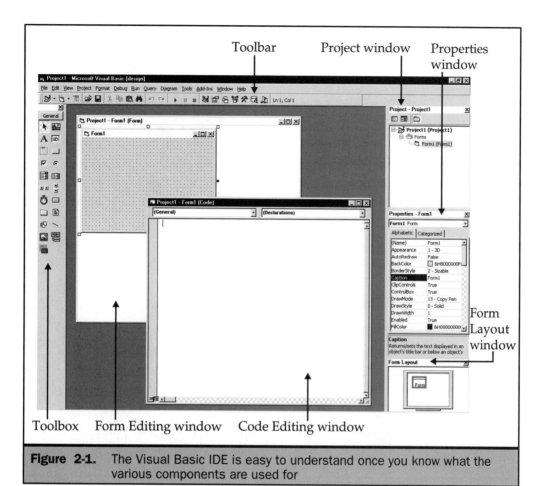

Figure 2-1.   The Visual Basic IDE is easy to understand once you know what the
various components are used for

- **Toolbars**   Toolbars contain one or more buttons that allow you to access an
  IDE feature without navigating the menu system. One of the more common
  toolbar buttons allows you to open a file with a single click rather than use the
  File | Open command. We'll see later in the chapter that Visual Studio allows
  you a great deal of freedom in designing your own special purpose toolbars.

- **Project window/Project Explorer window**   This window contains a
  hierarchical display of the major components in your project. The components
  are identified by the kind of file that holds them. For example, the HTM file
  uses a different icon than a JAVA file does.

- **Properties window**   Whenever you select an object on-screen, its properties
  will appear in this window. Changing the object properties allows you to define
  the appearance and functionality of the object. In many cases, you need to
  define specific object properties before the object becomes operational. For
  example, a database object requires a source file reference before you can use it
  to access the data within the database.

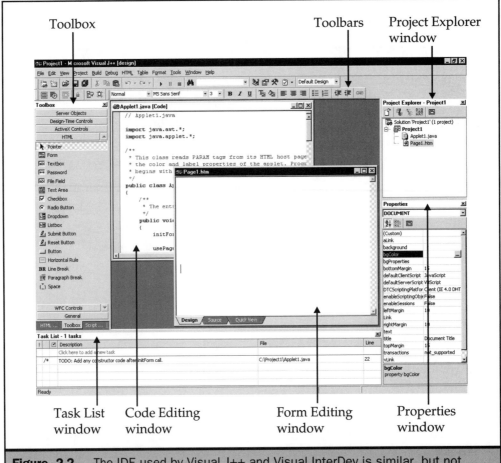

Toolbox   Toolbars   Project Explorer window

Task List window   Code Editing window   Form Editing window   Properties window

Figure 2-2. The IDE used by Visual J++ and Visual InterDev is similar, but not precisely the same as the one used by Visual Basic

- **Form Layout window (Visual Basic only)** Use this window to define the initial starting location of a form on-screen. Creating an easy to use form layout is just as important as the placement of controls on the form itself. Obviously, the user can still move forms about on-screen once they are displayed. This window only shows the starting position of the form.

- **Task List window (Visual InterDev/Visual J++ only)** This is one of several ancillary windows you can display when using Visual InterDev or Visual J++. It allows you to quickly find any pending tasks for your project. For example, you may need to add code to a wizard-generated stub before your application will do anything when the user interacts with a control. Double-clicking on one of the tasks will take you to that line within the source code file.

- **Code Editing window**   As suggested by the window name, this is where you'll edit the code required to make your application work. Obviously, the language of the code you'll see is determined by the language product you're using.

- **Form Editing window**   The Form Editing window allows you to design the user interface portion of an application. In essence, it presents a blank canvas on which you place a variety of controls. The user will interact with these controls in the process of using your application. In most cases, the number of controls you have at your disposal is limited only to the capability of the language product to display them and their availability on the design machine. The controls always appear in the toolbox once you register them with the IDE for use (some controls are registered by default).

- **Toolbox**   This window contains an iconic display of the controls you can use to create forms for your application. Note the big difference between the Visual Basic toolbox shown in Figure 2-1 and the one for Visual J++/Visual InterDev shown in Figure 2-2. Visual Basic displays all of the controls registered for use with the current project at one time, while the other two products provide hierarchical views that allow you to see the controls by category.

Like most products designed for Windows these days, Visual Studio is easy to customize to your personal tastes. There are several good reasons for customizing Visual Studio. For example, if you're working on a smaller monitor, you can undock and minimize one or more windows or toolbars to free space for writing code. Rearranging the order in which the windows and toolbars appear might increase your coding speed, because you can see everything you need to write the code at a glance.

Note   *Customizing Visual Studio can allow you to increase programmer productivity in a variety of ways, including making the display easier to see.*

Obviously, there are other reasons for rearranging or undocking toolbars and windows. For example, you may want to compare the code in one Code window with the code in a second Code window. Undocking the windows and placing them side by side allows you to perform the comparison with ease.

Sometimes you'll want to view only the Code window. For example, you may want to see the big picture when diagnosing an error. Using the Full Page View option allows you to see just the Code window—it will consume the entire display area.

The following sections help you understand how you can customize the Visual Studio IDE to make it easier and faster to use. While the default setup will work just fine for most people, you'll find that there are little things you can do to make the IDE meet your personal needs better.

Working with Windows and Toolbars

Visual Studio doesn't place many limits on you when it comes to working with windows and toolbars. You move them around on-screen, close and open them as needed, resize them, and even modify them to a certain extent. Most windows and all toolbars start out in what's known as the docked position. In other words, they appear to be part of the main IDE frame. Undocking a window or toolbar allows you to see it as a separate entity from the main IDE frame, which can be quite useful when short on display area.

To undock a window, all you need to do is click the title bar and then drag the window to wherever you want it outside of the IDE frame. As you move the window around, you'll see phantom boxes appear like the one shown in Figure 2-3. In this case, I'm moving the Project window to a new location. Note that the box will change size and shape if you move it near a dockable portion of the frame. The size and shape of

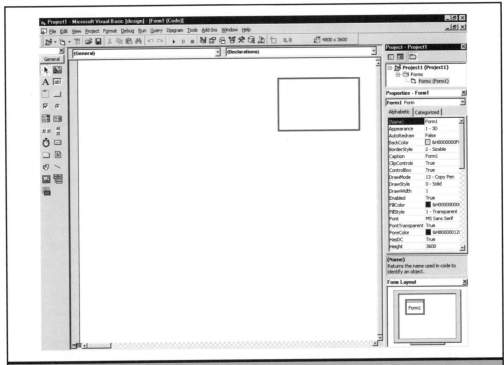

Figure 2-3.   You'll see a phantom box showing the final size and shape of the toolbar or window once you drop it on-screen

the phantom window indicates its final appearance when you drop it and also serves as an indicator of whether the window will be docked or free-floating.

Windows also include their own context menu. Right-click on the title bar for a window and you'll see a context menu like the one shown here:

Note that there are only two entries on the context menu: Dockable and Hide. The Dockable option is normally selected by default. Unchecking this option would mean that you couldn't dock the window on the Visual Studio IDE frame, the window would always be free-floating. The Hide option allows you to hide the window from view. You can get the same effect by clicking the Close icon (box with a square in it) on the title bar.

Most of the windows that you'll use in Visual Studio only have two options when it comes to display: Show and Hide. However, you can minimize, maximize, and resize the Code Editing window and Form Editing window. These options allow you to clear space as needed on-screen during the editing session.

Like windows, toolbars display a phantom box when you move them around. To move a toolbar, all you need to do is click the double vertical lines on the left side of the toolbar, then drag the toolbar where you need it. Unlike windows, toolbars don't include a title bar when docked. They do, however, include a title bar when free-floating as shown here:

Toolbars also include a context menu like the one shown here:

There's a very distinct difference between this context menu and the one provided by a window. In this case, you get to see a list of standard toolbars. Checking one of the toolbar names displays the toolbar and unchecking it hides the toolbar. There's also a Customize option on the context menu that we'll discuss in the "Customizing Toolbars" section of the chapter.

Using the Full Screen View

What happens if you've cleared as much space on your display as possible and you still can't see as much of the code as you'd like? That's where the Full Screen View feature comes into play. This feature will clear the entire display, except for the menu, and use the space to display your Code Editing window or Form Editing window. You'll also see a single toolbar, the Full Screen toolbar shown here:

 As of this writing, Visual Basic doesn't include the Full Screen View feature. Since this is such a useful feature, it's very likely that Microsoft will have added it to Visual Basic by the time you read this section.

As you can see, the Full Screen toolbar includes a single button, the one used to restore the IDE display to its normal state. However, you can customize this toolbar to include anything you want. Since this is the only toolbar displayed in Full Screen view, you'll want to add any tools needed to complete the task you're performing. For example, you'll want to include the Save button if you plan to save your work while in Full Screen view.

 The Full Screen View button appears on the Full Screen toolbar, which you can access from the toolbar context menu. Simply right-click on any toolbar, then select Full Screen from the context menu to display the Full Screen toolbar.

Using the Standard Windows

You'll use the standard windows that Visual Studio provides during the entire design and coding process for your application. The following sections provide an overview of the standard windows that you'll use on a regular basis. While these descriptions won't necessarily tell you everything there is to know about the window in question, you'll have a good idea of what the window is for and how to use it once you get done reading the section.

The following sections provide an overview of the common windows in all Visual Studio products. (See the "Using the Debug Windows" section of this chapter for a description of the various debugging windows.) Individual products may not include one or more of the windows listed in this section. Check the View menu of your application to determine if a particular window is available.

Project/Project Explorer

The Project and Project Explorer windows serve the same purpose; they provide an overview of your project. You'll use one of these windows to see how a particular file fits into the project as a whole. The Project/Project Explorer window also provides the means to interact with the files. For example, you can use this window to open the file in a specific way (either in the Form Edit window or Code Edit window). Here's a typical example of a Project window:

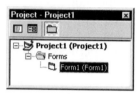

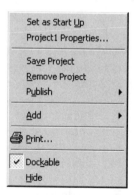

Note *You use the Project or Project Explorer window to get an overview of your project, then interact with the objects it contains.*

Note that each kind of object within the Project/Project Explorer window uses a different type of icon and that you can organize them in a variety of ways. For example, in Visual Basic, you can either display the objects within folders (to organize them by type) or by themselves (to organize them in alphabetical order). Visual J++ includes a Package View and a Directory View option.

Right-clicking any of the objects, even those not associated with a specific file (like the Project icon), displays a context menu containing a list of things you can do with that object. In most cases, all you need to do to interact with any major application object, then, is to find its entry in the Project/Project Explorer window. Here's an example of a context menu associated with a Project object:

Most of the entries on this menu are specific to the project. For example, the Project Properties option will display a dialog box that allows you to configure the settings for the project as a whole. The Add option is interesting because it displays a submenu that allows you to add new objects, such as forms, to the project. Finally, you'll see one or more menu options that are common to all objects. For example, the Publish option falls into this category. It allows you to publish the object (and any objects under it within the project hierarchy).

Properties

The Properties window is the one window that you'll always keep open for every project. You need it to define the characteristics of the various objects in your project. For example, you'll use it to change the caption on any command buttons you add to a form. Since even the form is an object, you'll use the Properties window to change background color and the border type.

There are two ways to view the properties for an object. You can either list them alphabetically or by category. The alphabetical listing comes in handy when you know the name of the property that you want to change and want to find it quickly. The category listing comes in handy when you want to find a particular property when you don't know its name. You can also use the category option when you need to change a group of properties. For example, you may need to change the width and height of a form.

The text box at the bottom of the Properties window will tell you about the selected property. In most cases, this is a simple text description of how the property affects the object.

Toolbox

Anyone who builds something needs a toolbox. A toolbox contains all the widgets you use in the actual construction of a project. The tools you have in your toolbox partially decide the kind of project you can build.

You can add tabs to the Visual Basic toolbox to make it look more like the one provided with the other Visual Studio products. Just right-click on the toolbox and choose Add Tab from the context menu. Visual Basic will ask you for a name for the new tab. Removing a tab is easy, too. Just right-click on the tab and choose Delete Tab from the context menu. Both Visual InterDev and Visual J++ provide this feature as well.

Visual Studio provides you with a toolbox filled with basic tools. For example, you can't build much of an application without at least one command button, so the command button is a standard part of the toolbox. However, you may find your assortment of tools somewhat limited when building specific kinds of projects, especially those that are complex. Visual Studio provides you with a whole assortment of tools that you can't see. All you need to do to use these other tools is take them out of the tool bin and add them to your toolbox. Let's take a quick look at the process for doing that.

1. Right-click the toolbox. You'll see a context menu like the one shown here. (Note that the context menu provided with Visual InterDev and Visual J++ is somewhat different, but the functionality is the same.)

2. Choose the Components… option if you're using Visual Basic, or the Customize Toolbox… option when using either Visual InterDev or Visual J++. You'll see a Components dialog box similar to the one shown here. (Visual InterDev and Visual J++ display a Customize Toolbox dialog box that looks slightly different than the one shown here but has similar functionality.) Notice the list of controls you can add to your project. Checked controls have already been added to your project, and the unchecked controls can be added.

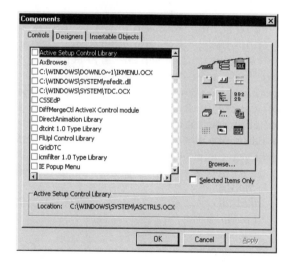

3. Find the control you need and check it. Make sure you see a check in the check box or the control won't be added to your project.

4. Click OK. You'll see the new control added to your toolbox.

Removing a control from the toolbox that you no longer need is just as easy. Just open the Components or Customize Toolbox dialog box and uncheck the item. Visual Studio will remove it from the toolbox. As an alternative to opening a dialog box, you can always choose the Delete Item option from the toolbox context menu. (The Delete Item option isn't available in the Visual Basic IDE.)

Removing controls that you're not using from the toolbox will normally decrease IDE loading time. In addition, it could marginally improve overall performance since each control that you remove from the toolbox also frees memory that Windows can use for other purposes.

So, how do you organize your toolbox? One of the easiest ways to do it is to move controls around within the various tabs. Just drag the control to the new tab. When you drop it, the control icon will move from its original tab in the toolbox to the new location.

Visual InterDev and Visual J++ provide a special toolbox feature not found in Visual Basic—a Paste option on the toolbox context menu. The Paste option allows you to paste all kinds of things in the toolbox. For example, you might need to add the name of your company to every Web page you design. Rather than type this text every time you need it, you can type it once, copy it to the clipboard, then paste the text into your toolbox. Now, whenever you need to add your company name to a Web page, you can select it like any other control.

Form Layout

Only Visual Basic provides a Form Layout window. The purpose of this window is to help you position the various dialog boxes and other forms in your application on-screen. The way you present forms on-screen can affect how easy the application is to use. For example, forcing the user to reposition every dialog box in your application because they have a smaller screen than you do is distracting in the extreme. It's unlikely that a user will want to work with an application that makes every task a major evolution in screen reorganization.

Fortunately, Visual Basic provides some special features that make the Form Layout window even more convenient to use. You'll find these features on the context menu. Just right-click on a form that you want to position and you'll see a context menu like the one shown here:

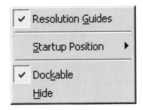

Using the options on the Startup Position is the easiest way to ensure the user will be able to see your form without repositioning it. Visual Basic provides three automatic settings, as described in the following list, that ensure your form will appear in a specific place on-screen:

■ **Center Owner** This option tells Windows to place the dialog box within the center of the owner window. You'd use this option for things like error message or configuration dialog boxes.

■ **Center Screen** Use this option to center a window or dialog box on the user's screen. It doesn't matter what the resolution of your screen is; Windows will use the center of the user's screen for placement purposes. In most cases, this option represents optimal placement for main windows and most dialog boxes.

■ **Windows Default** Windows provides a default placement option in the upper-right corner of the display based on a 640 × 480 resolution. Using this option means that everyone will be able to see your dialog box, no matter what kind of screen they have. Unfortunately, this isn't necessarily optimum placement for users with large displays. What usually happens is that the dialog box appears in the upper-right corner and the user ends up looking for it because their attention is focused on the center of the display.

So, what happens if none of these automatic placement options suit your needs? You can always manually place the form on-screen. Of course, then you take the chance that the user won't be able to see your form. If you want to make sure that every user of your application will be able to see a form, then you can always turn on the Resolution Guides feature found on the Form Layout Window Context menu. Here's an example of a Form Layout Window with Resolution Guides turned on:

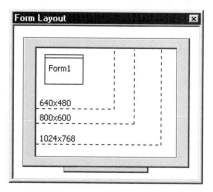

As you can see, the resolution guides make form placement a lot easier. All you need to do is choose the screen resolution that you want to accommodate with your application, then make sure the form fits within that area. This particular option allows you to perform custom form positioning that could make it possible for a user to use your application without ever moving the form around on-screen. For example, you could make it possible to see all of the forms in a cascaded view so the user could pick the one needed without moving the others around.

Task List

We previously looked at the Task List window as one of the optional windows that appear at the bottom of the Visual InterDev or Visual J++ IDE. The various wizards that work with these programming languages leave TODO notes. The Task List windows list all of these notes, making it easier for you to figure out where you need to add code to make your application functional. This is only one kind of Task List note that you'll run into. In fact, there's a whole range of Task List entry types, including comment, compile/build/deploy, user, shortcut and smart editor. Of these Task List entry types, you can add comment, shortcut and user tasks to the list.

Adding a user task is relatively easy. All you need to do is click on the *Click here to add a new task entry* button at the beginning of the list of tasks. Visual Studio will prompt you to type some text in the Description field. When you complete the task, there's a check box you can check. The next time you start the IDE, the task will be removed from the list. The unfortunate thing about user task entries is that they're global in nature. You won't find them associated with a particular file. This means that you'll want to reserve user task entries for tasks that affect your application on a global scale.

What if you wanted to be able to find a specific piece of code quickly and easily? That's where the shortcut task comes into play. All you need to do to add a shortcut task to the Task List window is right-click in the Code Editor window at the line of code where you want to create the shortcut, then choose Toggle Shortcut from the context menu. Whenever you want to find this line of code again, you can double-click on its task entry in the Task List window. The shortcut task entry includes the line of code where the task entry appears and the name of the source code file. The only description is the text contained on the line where you create the shortcut, which means you don't want to add shortcuts to blank lines. Choosing Toggle Shortcut from the Code Editing window a second time will remove the task from the Task List window. You can also check the check box associated with the shortcut task in the Task List window.

 Tip *You can delete most tasks by right-clicking the task entry in the Task List window, then choosing Delete Task from the context menu.*

Wizards aren't the only way to add comment entries to the Task List window. You can add them as well. All you need to do is start out a remark in your source code like the one shown here:

```
// TODO: This is my comment.
```

Make sure you add a descriptive comment after the TODO: part of the comment. The entire comment will appear as a task in the Task List window. Double-clicking the comment task will take you directly to the comment in your source code. This type of

Task List window entry is most appropriate for those times when you want to remind yourself to do something in a local procedure. The only way to remove a comment task is to remove the comment from your source code. This feature makes sense since you don't want to leave a lot of unneeded comments in your source code when you're finished with the application. As with the shortcut task, the comment task includes a description, the line of code where the task entry appears, and the name of the source code file.

HTML Outline/Class Outline/Document Outline

Depending on what kind of object you're trying to create, you could see a number of names in the Outline window. The three most common window types are HTML Outline (HTML documents), Class Outline (Java applets), and Document Outline (forms). No matter what name Visual Studio uses, the Outline window serves the same purpose with each kind of file—to map the relationships between components in an application file. In this respect, the Outline window serves as a means for zooming in on one file in your project. Just as you use the Project window to view the organization of the entire application, you use the Outline window to view the organization of a single file within that application. Here's a typical outline for an HTML page:

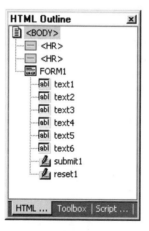

Outline is used in the literal sense of the word in this case. Just as a writer uses an outline to organize a book, you'll use the various Outline Windows to help organize your application files. One way in which the Outline Window helps is that you can click on any element and Visual studio will take you to that location on the form or within the source code. You can use this feature to quickly find a program element that you need to modify in some way or move to a different location.

Note   *The Outline window is designed to help you organize an application file, much like the Project window helps you organize the entire application.*

Unfortunately, the Outline window falls short of being a true organizational tool in the same sense that you use an outline for a word-processed document. You can't move program elements around within the Outline window, nor can you remove or add elements. The only thing that the Outline window will help you do is move from one place in your application to the next with relative ease.

Output

Every programming environment needs some way to display the status messages from the applications you create. The Output window serves this function with Visual Studio. Not only does the Output window allow you to view the status messages from most applications, but it also displays strings you use for debugging purposes.

The Output window contains two sections. The upper section is a list box where you select the output pane that you want to view. Visual Studio allows you to create as many output panes as you require for debugging purposes (within the limits of memory, of course). The panes can't be created dynamically at run time. The lower section of the Output window is where the output of the selected pane appears.

Using the Debug Windows

Debugging an application can be one of the more frustrating things that a programmer has to face during the development process. Visual Studio provides a wealth of debugging windows that allow you to troubleshoot your application without fighting the IDE as well. The following sections describe the various debug windows and tell you how you can use them to make debugging your application easier.

 The following sections provide an overview of the common windows in all Visual Studio products. Individual products may not include one or more of the windows listed in this section. Check the View menu of your application to determine if a particular window is available.

Immediate

The Immediate window is one of my favorites because it allows me to check out function calls and other programming constructs with a minimum of fuss. Not only does this window come in handy during design time, but when you're debugging the application as well. It allows you to play "what if" with your application. For example, if you type

```
MsgBox ("Hello")
```

in the Immediate window, then you'll see a dialog box like the one shown here:

This is exactly the same output that you would get if you were to use the MsgBox( )
function within an application. If you wanted to expand on the example, you could test
the effects of using various parameters. Once you're happy with the function call code,
you can cut it from the Immediate window and paste it directly into your application.

Autos

Visual Studio automatically displays the values of variables that are in scope for the
current line of code within the Autos window. (Being *in scope* means that the current
line of code can "see" and access the variable in question.) If you see a variable that
you'd like to track, you can drag the variable from the Autos window to the Watch
window. Likewise, if you want to manipulate the value of the variable in some way,
you can drag the variable to the Immediate window. Here's what the Autos window
looks like:

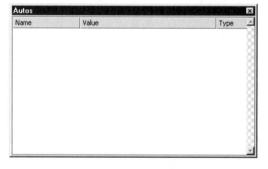

Note   *Most debug windows like the Autos window don't update their contents continuously.
A continuous update would slow application speed and could introduce problems in
tracking timing problems in applications. The Autos window, like most other debug
windows, only gets updated when you reach a breakpoint in the application or pause it
to work with one of the other debug windows.*

    As you can see, the Autos window allows you to track the name, value, and type of
every variable that's within scope. Of course, that could be quite a few variables,
depending on the size and complexity of your application. With this in mind, the
Autos window is better used as a way for finding out whether a variable is in scope
and using the variable within some other debug window. In most cases, you'll want to
place the variable within the Watch or Immediate window to track its value over the
long term.

Locals

The Locals window serves about the same function as the Autos window. However, the scope of the Locals window is limited to the variables declared in the local procedure. In other words, the Locals window won't show global variables, even if the current line of code could see the variable. Like the Autos window, the Locals window provides you with the name (or expression), value, and type of the variable. Here's an example of the Locals window:

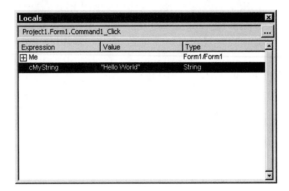

Watch

There are several debug windows designed to allow you to monitor all of the variables available at the current line of code. However, most programs are too complex for you to track every variable. In addition, you may only be interested in tracking the value of a loop variable, because the value of the other variables in the application are of minor or no importance.

The Watch window allows you to define specific variables to watch. Every time the application breaks for some reason, the Watch window gets updated. Unlike the other debug windows we've explored so far, the Watch window always tracks the variables that you ask it to track, even when they're not in scope (some language products use context). Here's an example of the Watch window:

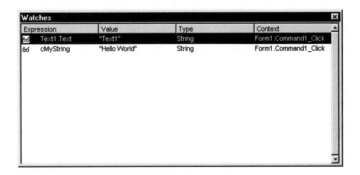

As you can see, the Watch window tracks more than just the name, value, and type of the variable that you want to track. It also includes information about the variable scope.

There are several ways to add a variable to the Watch window. You can drag it there from the Code Edit window, the Locals window, or the Intermediate window. Another way to add a watch is to right-click the variable, then choose Add Watch from the context menu. You'll see an Add Watch dialog box that allows you to define how Visual Studio watches the variable. In addition, this dialog box allows you to tell the debugger to stop the application should certain events, like a change in variable value, occur. The nice part about using this technique is that Visual Studio automatically inserts all of the correct variable information for you. Finally, you can right-click in the Watch window itself and choose Add Watch from the context menu. You'll see the same Add Watch dialog box as you would if you right-clicked on the variable, but this time you'll need to enter all of the field values manually.

Call Stack

Knowing how you got somewhere is pretty important when it comes to application programs. You may think that you reached a point in the application using one route when, in reality, you got there going some other path. That's what the Call Stack window is all about. It allows you to track how you got to the current position in your application. Here's what the Call Stack window looks like:

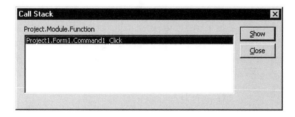

Notice that the Call Stack window uses standard dot notation to show precisely what module you're in and how you got there. Since modules in two different projects or forms could have the same name, the use of complete dot syntax as shown is very important. Obviously, it's equally important that you actually look at the complete line when using the Call Stack window.

Threads

The Threads window is used for multithreaded applications—those with more than one thread of execution. For example, if you had an application that printed in the background while running a spell check in the foreground, then it would have three threads of execution: one for the print routine, another for the spell checker, and yet another for the main application.

Each thread of execution in your application has to be tracked by the system. A thread is always owned by a single process, but each process can have more than one thread of execution. Windows assigns each thread a TID (thread identifier) and each process a PID (process identifier). The TID is the first entry that you'll see in the Threads window.

In addition to the TID, the Threads window displays the thread name and its current state of execution. There are three common states of execution that you'll see listed in the Threads window: running, suspended, and finished.

The last column in the Threads window tells you the thread's suspended count. The process or another thread could suspend the thread that you're looking at more than one time. Each time a process or thread tells the thread you're looking at to run, the suspended count gets decremented by 1. It's important to know the suspended count if you want to track problems with the way a process suspends the current thread of execution. A running thread always has a suspended count of 0.

The Threads window also allows you to access a thread. All you need to do is double-click on it to view its source code.

Finally, you can choose to look at another process using the drop-down list box in the Threads window. This feature allows you to look at other applications that are executing on your machine to see how they affect the application that you're troubleshooting.

Running Documents

The Running Documents window allows you to track which documents are loaded into the current application. For example, if you're currently testing an HTML document that uses frames, then you would see a hierarchy of documents starting with the main frame document and working it's way through the subordinate documents used to create the frame content.

Defining Views

A Visual Studio view is a combination of windows and toolbars that you can use to create your application. You access the views using the View | Define Window Layout command. Here's the Define Window Layout dialog box that you'll use to create, delete, and apply views to your Visual Studio setup:

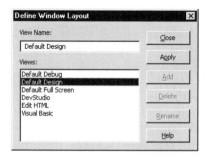

Applying an existing view is easy. All you need to do is highlight the name of the view that you want to use, then click the Apply button. Visual Studio takes care of the rest automatically. In fact, you can just go down the list of views and click Apply after highlighting each one to see what the view looks like. Using views like HTML Edit can greatly increase the area available for editing forms.

Visual Studio also allows you to delete old views (the only exception is the Default views, which you can't delete or rename). All you need to do is highlight the view you want to delete, then click the Delete button. Be careful about deleting views, though; there isn't any way to undo this action once you complete it and Visual Studio gives little notice that the view will be gone.

Renaming a view is easy. Highlight the view that you want to rename, type the new name in the View Name field, then click Rename. Visual Studio will give the view the name you typed in the View Name field.

Adding a view takes a little more work. The first thing you need to do is set up the IDE the way you want to see it. Once you get the IDE set up, use the View | Define Window Layout command to display the Define Window Layout dialog box. Type the name of the new view that you want to add, then click Add. Click Close to close the Define Window Layout dialog box and you're ready to go.

Customizing Toolbars

Creating an efficient set of toolbars is one way to get that programming project done in less time and with lower stress levels. You don't want to spend a lot of time during an intense programming session looking through the menu system for something you need. On the other hand, it's no fun working with a toolbar packed with icons that you'll never use. Both of these situations are somewhat common because most programmers have their individual ways of working.

Getting ready to customize your toolbar is easy. Right-click on any toolbar and select the Customize option from the context menu. You'll see the Customize dialog box shown in Figure 2-4.

Figure 2-4.   The Customize dialog box allows you to modify your toolbars as needed

There are three ways to customize a toolbar so that it meets your needs. (We'll explore all three methods in the paragraphs that follow.) First, you can create your own custom toolbars that contain just the buttons you need for specific tasks. The advantage of this method is that you don't have to spend any time at all changing Microsoft's default set of toolbars. In addition, someone using your machine will still have the standard set of toolbars you use. You won't have to spend time teaching them your way of doing things.

If you're the only one who will ever work at your machine, then there probably isn't any harm in making some modifications to the default Microsoft toolbars. I normally limit my activities to adding new buttons that I feel should be on the toolbar, but that Microsoft didn't include for whatever reason. Obviously, if you change the default toolbars too much, you may even find it difficult to explain how to accomplish certain tasks using your machine.

Finally, you can change the options found on the Options tab of the Customize dialog box. For example, you can use one option to change the size of the toolbar icons. Another option will allow you to control how the ScreenTips appear.

Adding and Deleting Toolbars

The Toolbars tab of the Customize dialog box shown in Figure 2-4 is where you add, delete, and rename toolbars. To add a new toolbar, all you need to do is click the New... button. You'll see the New Toolbar dialog box shown here:

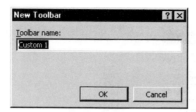

Visual Studio will suggest a name of Custom 1, but you can type any name you want in the Toolbar name field. Click OK to make the addition permanent. Visual Studio will automatically display a blank toolbar for you to work with. The "Working with Commands" section that follows will tell you how to add buttons to the toolbar and prepare it for use.

What if you decide that you no longer need a toolbar? All you need to do is highlight it, then click the Delete button. Visual Studio will display this Warning dialog box asking if you're sure you want to delete the toolbar. Just click OK to complete the process.

Renaming a toolbar is also relatively easy. All you need to do is highlight the toolbar that you want to rename, then click the Rename button. You'll see a Rename Toolbar dialog box similar to the Add Toolbar dialog box. Just type a new name in the Toolbar name field, then click OK to complete the change.

 Visual Studio won't allow you to rename or delete most of the default toolbars. If you don't see these two buttons highlighted when you select a toolbar from the list, then the toolbar is most likely a default toolbar provided with Visual Studio.

Working with Commands

A toolbar is nothing without its buttons. Some of the default toolbars are just fine; they're just lacking a couple of the buttons you use on a regular basis. Likewise, a new blank toolbar isn't much good until you populate it with some buttons. Adding or removing buttons is easy. All you need to do is open the Customize dialog box shown in Figure 2-4, then select the Commands tab. You'll see a menu list like the one shown in Figure 2-5.

The contents of the Categories column should look familiar since they're the names of the menus that Visual Studio provides. The Commands column contains the names of commands found in the menu selected in the Categories column. All you need to do

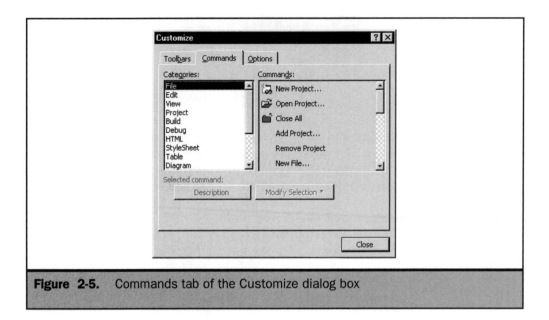

Figure 2-5. Commands tab of the Customize dialog box

to add a command to a toolbar is drag the command from the Commands column and drop it on the toolbar. Likewise, if you want to get rid of a command on a toolbar, just drag it off and drop it somewhere other than a toolbar. Visual Studio will remove the button from the toolbar.

Once you've placed a button on a blank toolbar, you'll notice that the Modify Selection button on the Commands tab of the Customize dialog box becomes active. If you click this button, you'll see a menu like the one shown here:

As you can see, this menu allows you to do a variety of things with the new button. For example, you can use it to change the icon used to represent the command. (Many of the commands don't come with a default icon, so you either get a text button or add your own icon to the command.) Notice the Reset option at the top of the menu. There have been a number of times when I was less than thrilled with the effects of a modification I made to a toolbar button. This option allows you to reverse any changes you make. In other words, you can modify the button to your heart's content and still have a presentable IDE when you get done. If you do add an icon, you'll want to choose either the Default or Text Only (in Menus) option on the context menu. Otherwise, you'll see both the text and the icon when looking at the toolbar button. (Text on a toolbar button can waste quite a bit of space that you could use for other purposes.)

A Look at the Toolbar Options

You can't really do much when it comes to displaying a toolbar. However, Microsoft has provided a few display options that can make life a little easier. You'll find them on the Options tab of the Customize dialog box (see Figure 2-6).

If you're anything like me, a 16-hour programming session sends your eyes into some kind of zone of darkness. It gets to the point where everything looks blurry. That's when the Large Icons option comes into play. Not only do the icons get bigger, but the ScreenTips text does as well. A set of large icons can be a real lifesaver during those midnight programming sessions.

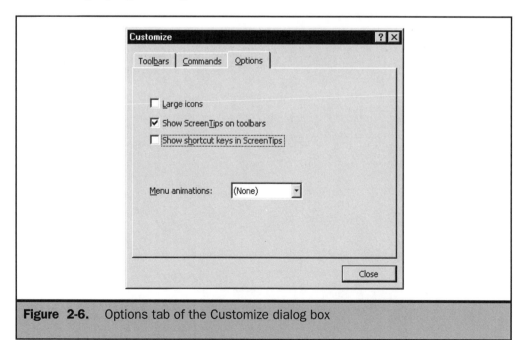

Figure 2-6. Options tab of the Customize dialog box

Microsoft keeps changing the name of what most people call balloon help. The new term for Visual Studio is ScreenTips. You'll still see the same thing as before—a little bit of text telling you about the purpose of a button when you place your mouse over the button for a few seconds. You can turn this feature off once you're familiar enough with the toolbars, but I normally keep it on. For those of you who like to keep your hands on the keyboard, you can add shortcut keys to your ScreenTips by selecting the Show shortcut keys in ScreenTips option.

The last option, Menu animations, doesn't affect the toolbar at all. It affects how your menu gets displayed when you click on it. For the most part, the animations are interesting but won't help you get your work done one iota faster.

Chapter 3

Working with Visual C++

O f all the Visual Studio products, Visual C++ is the only one that sports a unique interface. The reason is simple: Visual C++ is a lower-level programming tool than the rest of the products in the Visual Studio suite. While Microsoft does intend to eventually replace the Visual C++ IDE with something that looks more like the other Visual Studio products, that revision isn't going to happen for this release of Visual Studio.

The whole purpose of this chapter is to acquaint you with the Visual C++ IDE. We'll spend some time looking at the interface itself, which includes the three views, the standard windows, and the special windows you'll use for debugging purposes. Since this book uses as many of the Visual C++ automated programming technologies, like wizards, as possible, it really pays to know where things are.

Note   *You should know where things are located in Visual C++ so that you can make maximum use of automated programming features.*

The last section of the chapter will cover methods you can use to customize the Visual C++ programming environment. More than any other of the Visual Studio products, Visual C++ requires some level of customization to make the product fit your way of programming. I'll provide an overview of the various types of customization you can perform. You'll definitely want to spend some time looking at the customization features when you get done with this chapter in order to set Visual C++ up to be as efficient as possible.

Note   *As with the Visual Studio IDE presentation in Chapter 2, this chapter won't tell you anything about the programming constructs, runtime library routines, or any other part of the programming language provided with Visual C++. This book assumes that you have at least a rudimentary knowledge of Visual C++ programming techniques. We'll also see how various programming constructs are used in the example programs.*

Getting Around in Visual C++

This section of the chapter is going to provide an overview of the various Visual C++ IDE elements (you'll get detailed IDE information in the three sections that follow). It's easier to learn the Visual C++ IDE if you break it into manageable pieces. When you're editing a program with Visual C++, you can divide the display into three functional areas: toolbars, views, and the Editor window. Each area works independently of the others so that you can move around as needed. Figure 3-1 shows a typical editor display and the locations of these three areas.

Note   *We're going to talk about the various windows, views, and toolbars in this section. You'll find information about them in the sections that follow.*

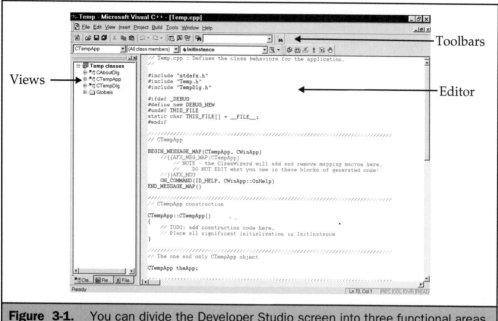

Figure 3-1.   You can divide the Developer Studio screen into three functional areas

There are three types of windows that you'll commonly run into: text-editing, resource, and graphics-editing. The window shown in Figure 3-1 is a typical text-editing window. Any time you need to modify your code or view a text file, you'll see this kind of window. Resource windows are where you'll define things such as shortcut keys or application information such as version numbers. A graphics window is used to modify things like icons and dialog boxes.

Note   *Visual C++ provides three window types: text-editing, resource, and graphics-editing.*

Visual C++ uses a variety of methods to make your coding experience easier. The first thing you'll notice in the text-editing window is that your code gets highlighted. For example, the default color for keywords is blue, while comments appear in green. Using color coding in this way helps you see the code for what it is.

Along the left edge of the text-editing window you'll see a bar. This is where Visual C++ places various symbols, and you may even see it colored to differentiate between data and control areas of your code. For example, when you set a breakpoint in your code, Visual C++ displays a stop sign here. If the breakpoint is enabled, the stop sign is red; otherwise, it's white.

You can also right-click in various areas of the text-editing window to display a context menu. The context menu contains options for the things you'll do on a regular basis—unlike other aspects of the Developer Studio interface; there isn't any straightforward way to modify it. Here's an example of the context menu you might see if you right-click in the text editor:

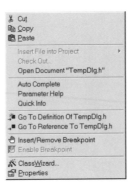

Notice that you can cut, copy, or paste text, just as in any editor. I've also highlighted an #include file entry, so the context menu gives you a chance to open it. If you hadn't already included this file in a project, the Insert File into Project option would give you a chance to do so. The Check Out option is used with team projects and allows you to take control of the file for a while so that you can edit it. The next three entries allow you to find out more about the current entry. For example, the Parameter Help option allows you to learn about the parameters associated with a function call, while Auto Complete helps you finish typing the function call. The next two entries are used for browsing your project. You can find where a particular entry is either referenced or defined. Since these entries rely on the BSC file created during a build of the project, you'll want to make sure you have a recent build available before using them. The next two entries, Insert/Remove Breakpoint and Enable Breakpoint, are for debugging your application. Finally, you can open the ClassWizard to work with the highlighted object some more (we'll do this a lot throughout the book) or view the properties for this document.

The second kind of window that you'll use is the Resource window. These text strings allow you to do things like assign shortcut keys to menu entries or add the name of your company to an application's header. Figure 3-2 shows a typical example of a Text Resource window. In this case, we're looking at the Text Resource window that allows you to add version information to your application. However, most of the other Text Resource windows follow the same tabular format as this one. The table consists of a string name (like "CompanyName" in the figure) and a string value (like "DataCon Services" in the figure). We'll see the other kinds of Resource windows as the book progresses. Remember that a text resource isn't code, it's a string that's used to make some part of the application easier to use or to provide identification of some sort.

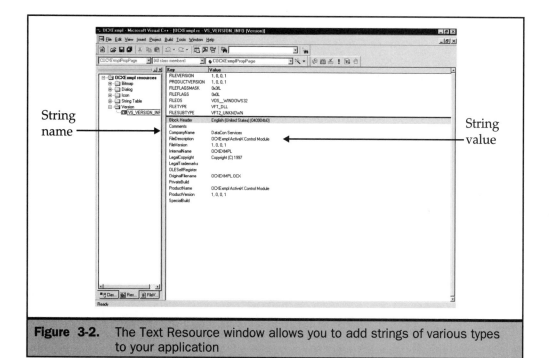

Figure 3-2. The Text Resource window allows you to add strings of various types to your application

Our final window example is one of the ones you'll see when editing graphics like dialog boxes and icons. Graphics are a form of resource and will be called resources throughout the book. Visual C++ always compiles graphics as part of the resource compilation process. Figure 3-3 shows a typical example, though the graphics-editing windows are far more varied than any other type that we've talked about so far. (Don't worry, we'll cover just about every kind of graphics-editing window somewhere in the book.)

In this case, we're looking at a dialog box. Notice that there are four controls, two of which are selected (you can see the sizing handles surrounding the two selected controls). You should also see a faint line around the edge of the dialog box (it's blue when using the default color settings). This line determines the outer limit for all the controls you want to place on the dialog box.

In the lower-left corner of the screen shot shown in Figure 3-3, you'll see the Controls toolbar. This contains an assortment of controls you can place on the dialog box. If you want to add a new control to the toolbox, use the Project | Add to Project | Components and Controls command. Right next to the toolbox you'll see a Dialog Box toolbar. It contains quite a few features that make it easier to line things up on the dialog box. For example, the Make Same Size button makes any number of controls you've selected the same size as the first control. There's also a Test push button that allows you to see how the dialog box will look when it's complete.

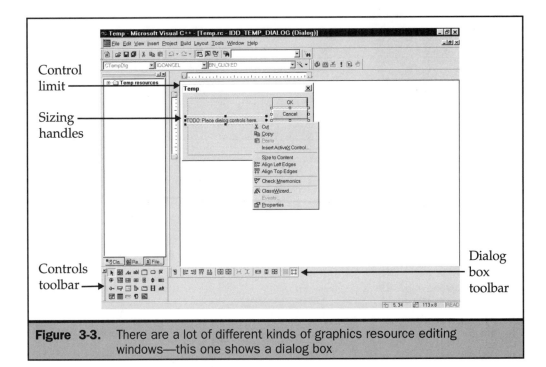

Figure 3-3.   There are a lot of different kinds of graphics resource editing
windows—this one shows a dialog box

Let's talk about the context menu shown in Figure 3-3. Since we've already talked
about the majority of these options, let's look at the three most important options. The
Insert ActiveX Control option allows you to add an ActiveX control to the dialog box
without actually adding it to the project. This allows you to see how the control will
work before you generate a lot of code for it. Remember to add the control to the
project later if you do decide to use it. The Check Mnemonics option tells Visual C++ to
look at all of the controls you've added and make sure that none of them have the same
name or violate any rules. It's an important check to make once you have the dialog
box all put together. Finally, the Events option displays a dialog box that tells you what
events the selected object supports. The same dialog box allows you to create a handler
for any of the events that you want to monitor.

Views

Views are a way to look into your application from the screen. As with views in the
real world, a view in Visual C++ is a panorama of the application you're designing; a
view is meant to provide an overview of the application, not the details. Selecting the
right view is the first way to find information in Visual C++. You need to know which
view to use if you want to see where a piece of code is located, whether a graphic

contains the right icon, or whether you've included a much-needed file. The following sections of the chapter will provide you with detailed information about the views provided by Visual C++.

Unlike the completely customizable windows in Visual Studio, the views in Visual C++ always appear together in one window. You can, however, undock the View window from the rest of the IDE, hide it, move it around the screen, and resize it as needed. Even though the IDE provided with Visual C++ isn't as flexible as the one provided with the rest of Visual Studio, you can still customize the display to meet personal needs.

ClassView

You'll probably spend most of your time with ClassView showing. This view provides a hierarchical listing of all the classes in your project. You can expand them to show what these classes contain. For example, your classes will contain member functions that you'll want to edit. Figure 3-4 shows a typical ClassView.

Notice that a special icon precedes each of the entries in the hierarchy. For example, each of the classes has a special class icon that looks like three boxes connected with

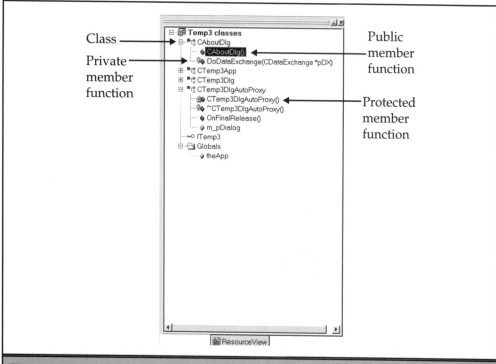

Figure 3-4. ClassView shows all of the classes in your project

lines. There are three kinds of member functions that ClassView will display. The first is the public member function, which uses a single purple box as an icon. The second is the private member function, which uses the same purple box but adds a key to the icon. The third is the protected member function, which has a purple box and lock icon. Likewise, there are three kinds of variables, all of which use turquoise icons. If you see a green box, you know that you're looking at a method for a COM object. There are a few other icon types, but these are the six you really have to know to create most projects.

You can hide ClassView (or any of the other views for that matter) by right-clicking in the ClassView window and then selecting Hide from the context menu. Use the View | Workspace command to display the ClassView window again.

ResourceView

ResourceView contains a hierarchical listing of all the resources in your project. Any graphic image, string value, toolbar, or other noncode element needed for the program to work could be considered a resource. Figure 3-5 shows a typical ResourceView window.

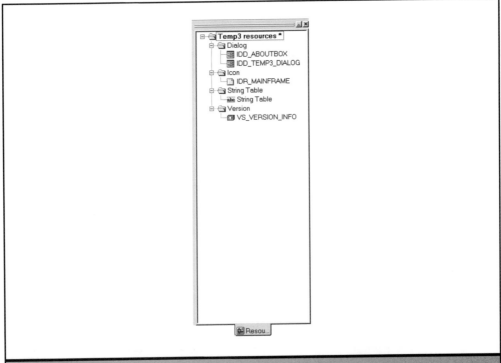

Figure 3-5. ResourceView provides a complete listing of all the resources required by your application

Each kind of resource you can create in Visual C++ has its own folder. If you don't use a particular resource, you won't see a folder for it. Within each folder, you'll find the resources for your project. For example, the Dialog folder would contain all of the dialog boxes in your project, including the About box. Every resource also uses its own kind of icon.

Right-click the topmost folder in ResourceView and you'll see a context menu that gives you access to the two resource-specific dialog boxes: Resource Includes and Resource Symbols. Right-click on a specific resource folder and you'll get a context menu that includes special options for adding new resources of that type.

FileView

FileView contains a complete list of all of the files in your project, whether they include code or not. Figure 3-6 shows a typical example of what you'll see in this window. Notice that it includes everything from source code files to the ReadMe.TXT file that Visual C++ generates automatically for you.

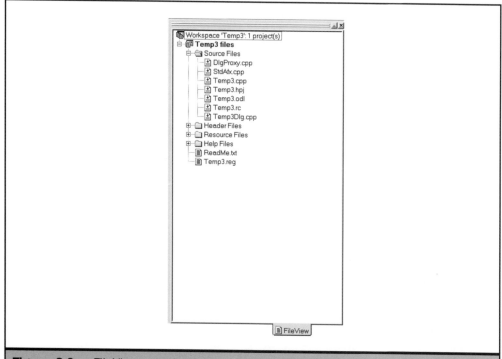

Figure 3-6.   FileView contains a complete list of all the files in your projects—even if they don't contain any code or resources

Each file type normally has its own folder. For example, all of the source code files appear in the Source Files folder. Not only can you move files from folder to folder, but you can create new folders to hold specific types of files based on their extension. I often create a Text File folder to hold all of my TXT extension files. All you need to do to create a new folder is right-click on the folder or project entry where you want to add the folder, and then select New Folder from the context menu. You'll see a New Folder dialog box like the one shown here. Just type the name of the folder and associated file extension, then click on OK to complete the process.

Using the Standard Windows

The IDE used by Visual C++ provides a number of standard windows. Each of these windows helps you to perform one type of programming related task like write code or create an icon. It's likely that you'll use every one of these windows when creating a typical application, though you'll definitely use some windows, like the Code window, much more than others. Even if you don't use a particular window very often, it's still important to know that the window is available so that you can use it if needed. For example, I usually use the Version window once during the programming process— when I first put the application together. However, I wouldn't want to release an application that didn't include my company name and the product version number as a minimum. The following sections will provide you with an overview of all the standard windows provided by Visual C++.

Code

The Code window (Figure 3-1) is the place where you'll spend most of your time when working with Visual C++. There isn't much in the way of special features in the Code window. It's a standard text editor that includes highlighting for keywords. You'll perform all code text editing in this window.

This version of Visual C++ provides some new features that you need to know about in the Code window. The following sections provide an overview of these new features and what you can expect them to do for you.

AutoCompletion

The AutoCompletion feature helps complete statements in your C++ header and source code files. What you'll see is a list box with possible completion lines. For example, consider the following code:

```
Cstring     oMyString;

    oMyString.
```

As soon as you type the period for oMyString, you'll see a list box containing the various methods and properties associated with a CString object. At this point, you could simply scroll down to the method or property you wanted to use and click on it. As an alternative, you could type the first few letters of the method or property that you wanted to use; the list will scroll to show you methods and properties of that name. Once you do select a method or property, Visual C++ will automatically type the name of the method or property you want to use. The result is that you'll spend a whole lot less time tracking down typos and more time coding.

 If you lose the AutoCompletion list box, right-click next to the place it originally appeared and choose Auto Complete from the context menu. The list box will reappear.

Delete Member Function

You now have the ability to remove a member function with a lot less work. All you need to do is place the cursor anywhere within the member function and choose Delete from the WizardBar Actions drop-down list box or Delete Function on the Message Maps tab of the ClassWizard dialog box. In either case, Visual C++ will remove the function declaration from the header file and comment out the function body from the source code. (You'll instantly see the commented source in the Code window.) The automatic commenting feature allows you to recover the function later if you decide you need it after all.

Doc Comments

What are Doc Comments? Let's say you're looking through the AutoComplete list and aren't sure about the limitations of the AnsiToOem( ) method of the CString object. If you highlight this item and then position your mouse over it, what you'll see is some balloon help telling you there is a 255-character maximum. This form of balloon help is another new Visual C++ feature called Doc Comments.

Not only do Doc Comments come as part of the Visual C++ package, but you can add them to your functions and variables as well. All you need to do is add a comment either before the function or variable declaration or on the same line as the declaration. You can use this feature to tell someone all about a function or variable that you've provided. Obviously, you don't want to make this comment too large. Microsoft places a 12-line limit on Doc Comments, which should be sufficient for most purposes.

Doc Comments aren't limited to the AutoCompletion list box. Try positioning your mouse over a variable or function. What you'll see is the same balloon help that Doc Comments provides within the AutoCompletion list box. As you can see, Doc Comments is a very fast way to provide continuous documentation for your application and makes it less likely that someone will have trouble using the code that you've designed.

Dynamic Parsing

The Code window is better linked with the ClassView window. The ClassView window is now automatically updated as you type new class, function, and variable information into your application. This allows you to see changes to your application as you make them rather than waiting until you save the source file. It also means that elements like the WizardBar and ClassWizard are always up to date.

| Note | *There are currently some problems with this feature that Microsoft promises to fix by product release (at least, as of this writing). For example, certain types of typos can cause Visual C++ to parse what you're trying to do incorrectly, and the IDE will freeze as a result. In all cases, restarting the IDE will clear the problem.* |

Empty Class Tracking

In the past, you might have spent more time in the Code window than you really wanted to just because Visual C++ didn't track classes without member functions. Finding what you needed in the source meant opening it in the Code window, then scrolling until you found the empty class declaration. The WizardBar now tracks all classes, even those without member functions. The Members combo box on the WizardBar will display "No Members - Create C/C++ Member Function" if you choose a class without members. The default WizardBar action is to add a new member function to empty classes.

Go to Dialog Editor

There are also new links between the Code window and the resource editor. For now, this option is only available when you're creating an application with a dialog box. Select the class containing the dialog box, then choose the Go To Dialog Editor option from the WizardBar Actions drop-down list box.

Dialog Boxes

Creating dialog boxes is a big part of creating many types of applications. The Dialog window (refer to Figure 3-3) provides you with all of the tools required to create standard dialog boxes. Dialog boxes begin with a blank form to which you add controls. Since the form is provided as part of the dialog box creation process, all you really need to worry about are the controls. Here's the standard Controls toolbar that acts as your palette for drawing on the form:

We'll see later in the book that you can add controls to your Controls toolbar—you're not limited to the choices shown in the standard setup. Of course, placing a control on the form is only part of the process. Getting the controls positioned correctly on the form could be a chore if you didn't have help. Fortunately, Visual C++ provides the Dialog toolbar shown here:

Most of the buttons here allow you to accurately place controls on the form. There is a special button that looks like a toggle switch, and it is called the Test button. The Test button allows you to check the final appearance of your dialog box. Notice the two buttons at the end of the toolbar. The first allows you to add grid lines that make it easier to place the controls correctly. The second displays guides that act as rulers, again to help you accurately place the controls.

Icon

Icons are part of every application in Windows. Even if you don't plan to use any icons within the application itself, you'll need an icon to display within Windows Explorer and as part of the Start menu. About dialog boxes normally include an icon as well. In fact, Visual C++ provides a default icon that gets used for the application and the About dialog box. Figure 3-7 shows what the Icon window looks like.

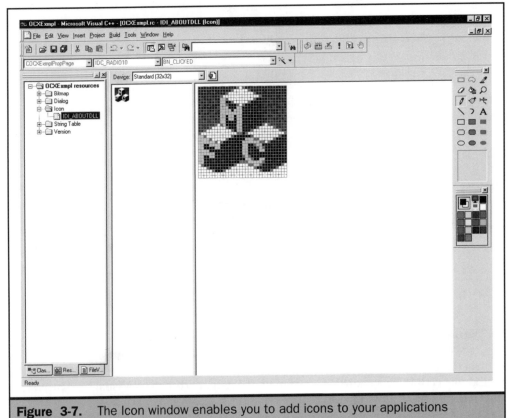

Figure 3-7.   The Icon window enables you to add icons to your applications

There are two specialty toolbars supplied with the Icon window by default. The first is the Graphics toolbar, shown here:

As you can see, the Graphics toolbar contains a variety of standard shapes. In fact, there isn't much to differentiate it from any other drawing program toolbar. You do get to choose from three variations of each shape: outline, filled, and the shape by itself. In addition, when using tools like the line drawing tool you get to choose the shape and size of the pen used to draw.

Black and white drawings are nice, but color is much nicer. With color you can add various effects to an icon and make it look like more than it first appears. In fact, I've seen some rather amazing icons that use color to effectively make the icon look bigger or more complex than it really is. The other specialty toolbar, Color, is shown here:

There are several points of interest when looking at the Color toolbar. The first is the box in the upper-left corner. It shows the current foreground and background colors. Left-click on a color in the palette area and the foreground color will change; right-click on the color and the background color will change. Unfortunately, you can't change the color palette—you have to use the one shown in the illustration. There are two special colors in the palette. They appear as little monitors in the illustration. The top color (looks green when you see it in the Color toolbar) allows you to make part of the icon invisible. In other words, the background will show through. That's how people make icons that take on a variety of nonstandard shapes. The bottom color of the two colors (looks red when you see it in the Color toolbar) allows you to add the Windows foreground color to the icon. Whatever the user has set the Windows foreground color to will appear in the icon if you select this color.

Menu

Except for dialog-box-based applications and things like ActiveX controls, most applications have at least one menu. You use it to allow the user to interact with the application's feature set. For example, the File menu normally contains an option to open an existing file or to create a new one. Figure 3-8 shows a typical Menu window.

Unlike many of the other windows that we've reviewed so far, there aren't any special toolbars associated with the Menu window. All you need to do to add a new

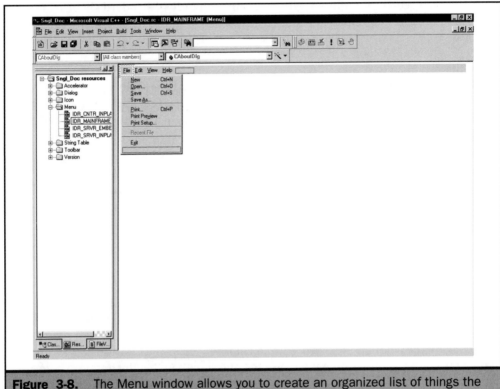

Figure 3-8.   The Menu window allows you to create an organized list of things the user can do with your application

menu entry is find a blank spot and type the new menu option. Once you start typing in the blank area, you'll see a Menu Item Properties dialog box like the one shown here:

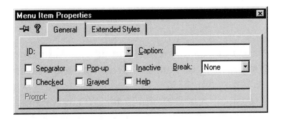

Deleting a menu entry is even easier than creating one. All you need to do is select the menu entry that you want to delete, then press the Delete button. Obviously, any submenus will disappear along with a main menu entry. Double-clicking a menu entry displays the Menu Item Properties dialog box. You can rename or redefine the menu entry using this dialog box.

We'll talk about what you need to do to create a new menu later in the book. All you need to know for now is that the Menu window allows you to create, define, rename, and delete menu entries.

String Table

Strings are used for a variety of purposes in any application. Many of those strings change as the application runs, so you have to define variables to hold them. However, there are some strings, like the application name, that don't change as the user runs the application. It would waste memory and make the application more complex than it needs to be if you defined variables to hold these constant strings. That's where the String Table window comes into play. It provides a place for you to define constant strings, ones that don't change while the application executes. Figure 3-9 shows what the String Table window looks like.

The string table consists of three entries: an ID, a value, and a caption. The ID is a human-readable string that you'll use to identify a string within an application. The value is a number attached to the string. This number helps Visual C++ identify the string;

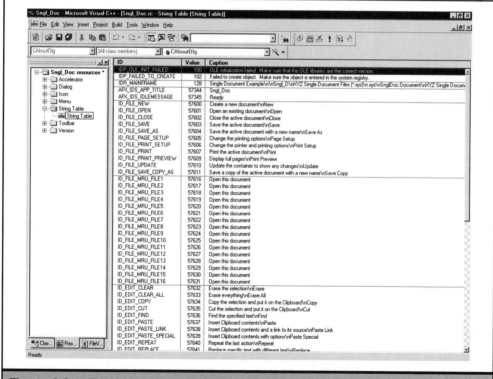

Figure 3-9.   The String Table window allows you to define constant strings for use throughout the program

you don't need to provide a specific number, but every string has to have a unique number to identify it to the compiler. The caption entry is the string itself. When you tell Visual C++ to display ID_MY_STRING, it will display the caption that you've provided.

Toolbar

The first thing you should know is that Visual C++ comes with a lot more toolbars than you'll see when you first start it up. Right-click anywhere in the toolbar area and you'll see a context menu like this one:

What you're seeing is a list of all the standard toolbars that Visual C++ provides. Any menu entries with a check mark next to them are currently displayed in the toolbar area. If you want to add a toolbar to the toolbar area, just click on its entry in the context menu. Likewise, to remove a toolbar, click on its entry again to remove the check mark.

Version

Adding version information to your application is important if for no other reason than making your support tasks easier. Figure 3-2 shows a typical example of a Version window. Since I've already described this window earlier in the chapter, I won't discuss it again here.

Output

The Output window is actually listed with the toolbars. It's a place where you and Visual C++ can display messages of various types while you're building or debugging an application. You can also use the Output window to display the results of searches.

In fact, there are separate tabs that show every purpose that you can use the Output window for. Here's what the Output window looks like:

Using the Debug Windows

There isn't any doubt about it, once you get enough of your application built to test, you'll need to use the various debugging windows to find errors in it. In fact, most applications go through several debug cycles during their development. During the latter part of the development cycle, you'll spend a lot more time than you ever wanted debugging your application. It's little wonder, then, that most programming language products are judged as much by the level of debugging features they provide as by other features such as language compliance and the kind of library capability they include.

Microsoft has worked hard to provide Visual C++ with a relatively capable debugger. It may not rival some of the hardware-assisted debuggers on the market, but you'll find that you can debug most applications. This version of Visual C++ provides a wealth of new debugger features that make it even easier to find bugs in your application. Table 1-1 contains a complete list of these new features and provides an overview of each one.

Feature	Description
Auto expansion of VARIANTs and GUIDs	The AUTOEXP.DAT (auto-expand) file contains new rules that allow you to display VARIANTs and GUIDs in more meaningful ways. (The AUTOEXP.DAT file appears in the Program Files\Microsoft Visual Studio\Common\MSDev98\Bin directory on your hard drive.) For example, a VARIANT will now appear as the data type that it actually contains; a string will actually look like a string. In addition, Visual C++ will display the VARIANT type along with its value. GUIDs won't necessarily display as a string of numbers; Visual C++ will attempt to find the GUID name in the registry and display the name instead.

Table 3-1. New Debugger Feature Overview

Feature	Description
Debugger formatting symbols	Visual C++ sports a whole list of new debugger symbols as shown in the following list.
	■ **, hr** Displays 32-bit result or error codes as common COM return values like S_OK or E_NOTIMPL. If it can't display a precise error value, then Visual C++ will attempt to turn the return value into a comment like "Not enough memory."
	■ **,mq** Allows you to display memory as four quadwords to compensate for 64-bit registers.
	■ **,st** Displays strings in Unicode or ANSI format, depending on the Unicode Strings setting in the AUTOEXP.DAT file.
	■ **,wc** Displays numeric values as decoded Windows class flags (WC_ constants).
	■ **,wm** Displays numeric values as decoded Windows message values (WM_ constants).
Disassembly output	You'll see a lot more information in the disassembled output, including symbolic information (when available).

Table 3-1. New Debugger Feature Overview (continued)

Feature	Description
Load COFF & Exports	You'll find this option on the Debug tab of the Options dialog box (accessed using the Tools | Options command). It allows you to load additional debugging information used by compilers other than Visual C++ (which uses CodeView format debug information). For example, Visual Basic provides Common Object File Format (COFF) debug information in the MSVBVM50.DBG file. The Exports option comes into play when no other debugging information (at least that Visual C++ can recognize) is available. Visual C++ will load the contents of the Exports table of each DLL and attempt to convert it into symbolic information for debugging purposes.
Registers	There are several new registers that will help you to find out more about your application. The Thread Information Blocks (TIBs) psuedo-register provides information about the current thread. The ERR psuedo-register displays the error code of the last error that occurred in your application. This register performs the same task as the GetLastError( ) function call. Adding the ,hr modifier to the ERR register tells it to display a 32-bit error code along with a comment like "Not enough memory." The 64-bit MMX register set now appears in both the Watch and Quick Watch windows. You'll see these registers displayed on all x86 machines, even if they don't suport pthe MMX instruction set.

Table 3-1.   New Debugger Feature Overview (continued)

Feature	Description
Undecorated symbols	What this means in simple terms is that you'll no longer see long lists of meaningless garbage characters with a function name hidden somewhere inside. In addition, all function names will include parameter information, when available.
V-Table and Function Pointer display	Function pointers and virtual table entries get displayed as text entries (symbolically), including parameters whenever possible instead of hex addresses.

Table 3-1.   New Debugger Feature Overview (continued)

Now that you have a better idea of what debugging is all about within Visual C++, let's look at the individual debugging windows. The following sections provide an overview of each debugging window and what it can do for you. (Make sure you look at the debug window descriptions in Chapter 2 as well. The following sections don't cover debug windows that work the same as their Visual Studio counterparts.)

Memory

The Memory window allows you to bypass all of the formatting that Visual C++ provides in the other debug windows and look at what's in memory directly. Sometimes it's handy to know whether you have a memory-overrun problem or if Visual C++ is correctly interpreting the contents of memory for you. All you need to do to use the Memory window is type the address you want to look at, then press ENTER. The address you want will be centered in the display area. You can usually get a general idea of what address to look at using one of the other debug windows like the Watch or Variables window. Here's what the Memory window looks like:

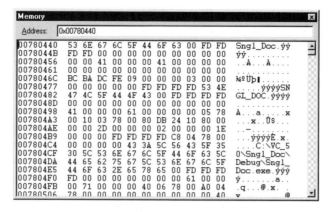

Variables

Visual C++ normally shows the Variables window as a default. This window shows a hierarchical view of all the variables currently in scope. One of the major differences between Visual C++ and the other Visual Studio products is the level at which you're working. Remember that Visual C++ is a low-level programming language and the Variables window reflects this orientation. You'll find that this window not only displays the variables in your application, but the objects as well. The object hierarchy can become quite difficult to navigate because you also have to consider the objects that the object in your application has inherited from. Here's an example of the Variables window. As you can see, the object hierarchy in this example (a simple About dialog box) is quite complex:

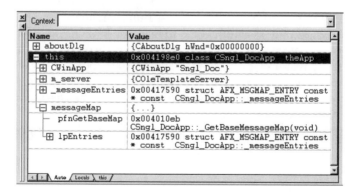

Registers

Those of us who have programmed extensively in assembler remember how important it was to keep track of what values were placed in the various processor registers. Part of the debugging process was to check those register values and make sure the right value got in the right place. Most modern programming languages don't require you to spend hours figuring out what value to place in which register. However, Visual C++ does allow you to manipulate the register values directly if you so desire, which means that you need some way to check what value the registers contain. That's where the Registers window comes into play. It displays the current content of the processor registers on the test machine. Here's what the Registers window looks like:

```
Registers                                                           ✕
EAX = 0065F820 EBX = 0065FC2A ECX = 00000064 EDX = 0065F820
ESI = 005301C0 EDI = 0065FB68 EIP = 00402683 ESP = 0065F7D4
EBP = 0065F890 EFL = 00000202 CS = 0137 DS = 013F ES = 013F
SS = 013F FS = 3357 GS = 0000 OV=0 UP=0 EI=1 PL=0 ZR=0 AC=0
PE=0 CY=0 ST0 = +0.00000000000000000e+0000
ST1 = +0.00000000000000000e+0000
ST2 = +0.00000000000000000e+0000
ST3 = +0.00000000000000000e+0000
ST4 = +0.00000000000000000e+0000
ST5 = +0.00000000000000000e+0000
ST6 = +5.12000000000000000e+0003
ST7 = +0.00000000000000000e+0000 CTRL = 027F STAT = 0100
TAGS = FFFF EIP = 1024A4D7 CS = 0137 DS = 013F
EDO = 10250140
```

Disassembly

You may not care how Visual C++ is putting your application together, but sometimes it does pay to take a look. Every programming language provides a human-readable format, but that's not the end of the story. Those human-readable statements have to be converted to tokens, usually assembly, then to machine language (also known as hexadecimal format) before you can use the resulting code on the computer.

The Disassembly window is designed to allow you to look at the C++ code statement that you're used to seeing, followed by all the assembly language statements required to implement the C++ code. Here's an example of the Disassembly window:

```
Disassembly                                                   _ □ ✕
  199:        aboutDlg.DoModal();
⬥ 00402683   lea          ecx,[ebp-70h]
  00402686   call         CDialog::DoModal (004038e6)
  200:   }
  0040268B   mov          dword ptr [ebp-4],0FFFFFFFFh
  00402692   lea          ecx,[ebp-70h]
  00402695   call         @ILT+325(CAboutDlg.:~CAboutDlg) (0040114a)
  0040269A   mov          ecx,dword ptr [ebp-0Ch]
  0040269D   mov          dword ptr fs:[0],ecx
  004026A4   pop          edi
  004026A5   pop          esi
  004026A6   pop          ebx
  004026A7   mov          esp,ebp
  004026A9   pop          ebp
  004026AA   ret
```

This illustration shows two lines of Visual C++ code: a call to aboutDlg.DoModal( ) and a curly brace (}). These two statements are displayed in bold type. The assembly language required to implement these two statements appears in lighter type.

Customizing Your Environment

Creating the right work environment is an important part of learning to use Visual C++. A good work environment makes programming less frustrating and can result in improved efficiency. Of course, what makes a good work environment for one person may be totally unusable for someone else. Since every programmer has an individual style of working, Microsoft provides a basic setup, then lets you customize your work environment as needed.

Most of the customization options we'll discuss in this section appear in the Customize dialog box shown in Figure 3-14. You access this dialog box using the Tools | Customize… command. We'll also work with some of the macro commands on the Tools menu in the next to last part of this section.

There isn't any way that this book can begin to suggest every potential customization you can make within the Visual C++ environment, but it can provide an overview of what's possible and provide some suggested ways to get the most from the product. The following sections break customization down by functional area. Once you've finished reading the section, try customizing your IDE to make it faster and easier to use.

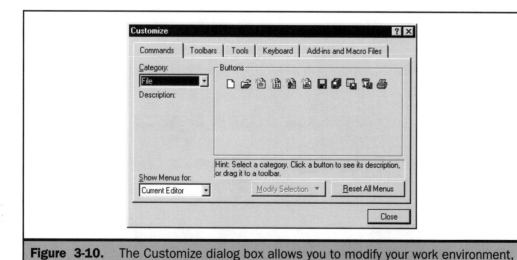

Figure 3-10.   The Customize dialog box allows you to modify your work environment, making it faster and easier to use

Commands

The Commands tab of the Customize dialog box shown in Figure 3-10 contains a series of icons (which represent commands) or text commands for every menu and toolbar. If you want to add a command to one of the existing toolbars, just grab one of the icons (or text commands) and drag it over to the toolbar. The command you've selected will appear on the toolbar, making it a lot faster to access. If you select a command that doesn't already have an icon associated with it, you'll see a Button Appearance dialog box that will allow you to select an icon for the command.

This same feature works with menus, too. All you need to do is lower the drop-down menu you want to change, grab the command you want to add from the Commands page, and then drag it over to the position where you want to see it on the menu. In this case, you'll always see the text version of the command rather than an icon.

Removing unneeded commands from a toolbar or menu is just as easy. Simply grab the command you no longer want and drag it over to the Customize dialog box. The command will disappear from the menu or toolbar; though it'll still be accessible anytime you want to add it back in.

You can also move toolbars around as needed to make space. Just click on what looks like a set of double bars at the left edge of the toolbar, then drag it where you want it. Likewise, if you don't like the current position of a menu, just grab it (with the Customize dialog box open) and move it where you want it.

Toolbars

You can customize toolbars in a number of ways. The Commands section of the chapter tells you one way to do it by adding or removing a command. However, there are other ways to customize a toolbar if you want to. For example, you can add a new toolbar or change the way the icons are displayed. To customize a toolbar using one of these other techniques, you'll need to open the Customize dialog box shown in Figure 3-10 using the Tools | Customize… command. Once there, click on the Toolbars tab and you'll see a dialog box like the one shown here:

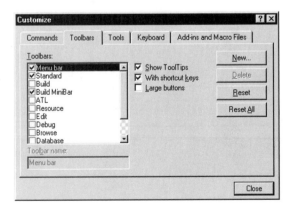

Let's begin with the Toolbars list. This list displays the default set of toolbars provided with Visual C++ along with any toolbars that you've defined. Checking one of the toolbars will make it appear so that you can use the commands that it contains. If you select a toolbar that you've created, you'll also be able to change the toolbar name by typing a new name in the Toolbar name field and clicking on another toolbar in the list.

Adding a toolbar is relatively easy. Click the New button and you'll see a New Toolbar dialog box like the one shown here:

Type the name of the new toolbar in the Toolbar name field, then click OK to complete the process. You'll see the new toolbar appear in the Toolbars list. Visual C++ will automatically display the blank toolbar for you as well. Just add commands and you're ready to go.

To remove a toolbar you no longer want, simply highlight the toolbar and then click Delete. Visual C++ will allow you to remove any toolbars that you've created. Standard toolbars can be modified, but not deleted.

Finally, notice that there are three check boxes on the Toolbars tab. The first, Show ToolTips, tells Visual C++ to display bubble help whenever you keep your mouse over a button for a few seconds. Normally, the help provided tells you the button's function and not much more. You can add shortcut keys to the bubble help by clicking the second option, With shortcut keys. The last option, Large buttons, increases the size of both the buttons and their associated icons on the toolbars. This feature comes in handy during those late-night programming sessions when your eyes are tired.

Tools

One of the nicer customization options provided by Visual C++ is the ability to launch other applications from within the IDE. Microsoft even includes a list of standard applications in the list for you. All of the applications you select will appear on the Tools menu. You could also add them to a toolbar if you wanted to.

Adding a new tool to the list is easy. Use the Tools | Customize... command to display the Customize dialog box shown in Figure 3-10. Select the Tools tab of that dialog box and you'll see a dialog box like the one shown here:

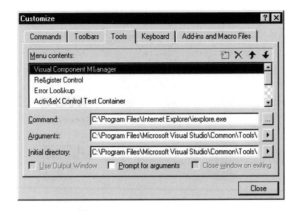

The list at the top contains all of the tools (applications) that you've added so far, along with any that Visual C++ added for you. Above and to the right of the Menu contents list are four buttons. The first adds a new tool to the list, while the second deletes tools from the list. The third and fourth buttons move items up and down on the list (and therefore change their position on the Tools menu).

Click the New button and you'll see a blank spot added to the Menu contents list. Type the name of the application you want to add. If you add an ampersand anywhere in the name, then Visual C++ will underline that letter in the menu and allow you to access the application using that letter. Once you type the application name, press ENTER. Now you need to provide three additional pieces of information as a minimum in the Command, Arguments, and Initial directory fields. These are the same entries you would provide for any Windows shortcut, so I won't spend time explaining them here.

There are also three option buttons for each application. The Use Output Window option tells Visual C++ to place the output from the application in the Output window that we talked about earlier in the chapter. This comes in handy for DOS applications that provide some type of text output. The Prompt for arguments option forces Visual C++ to display an arguments dialog box every time you start the application, which allows you to provide input to the application before it starts. Finally, the Close window on exiting option tells Visual C++ to automatically close the Application window when it finishes execution, another handy feature for DOS applications.

Keyboard

Many programmers make heavy use of the keyboard rather than the mouse. It's a lot easier to keep your hands on the keyboard rather than move them to switch between the keyboard and the mouse when executing commands. Unfortunately, not every Visual C++ menu command has a shortcut key, which means you have to use extra key presses to work with the menu. The extra key presses aren't a problem if you only use the command once in a while, but shortcut keys are definitely handy when you use a command with any regularity.

The Keyboard tab of the Customize dialog box allows you to change the shortcut key settings for Visual C++. All you need to do is open the Customize dialog box using the Tools | Customize... command to display the dialog box shown in Figure 3-10. Select the Keyboard tab and you'll see a dialog box like the one shown here:

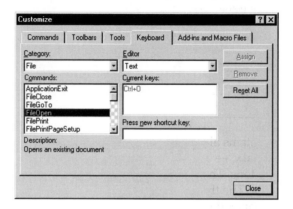

Assigning a new shortcut to a command is easy. First, select the command that you want to attach a shortcut to. Next, select the editor that you want to create a shortcut for in the Editor drop-down list box. Select the Press new shortcut key field, then type the key combination you want to use. If the key combination is already in use, Visual C++ will display a message saying so under the Press new shortcut key field. Click the Assign button to complete the process. You'll see the key combination added to the Current keys list.

Removing a shortcut when you no longer need it is just as easy. Select the command and editor that you want to remove the shortcut from. Find the shortcut key that you want to remove in the Current keys list. Click Remove to complete the process.

Chapter 4

Creating Basic Applications

Before we begin our tour of Visual Studio as a package, it's important to know how to use the package components individually. Every one of the language products in Visual Studio is a full-fledged application development environment in its own right. The whole purpose of this chapter is to show you how to create some basic applications using the individual language products.

None of the applications in this chapter will cause your friends to ooh and ah. What they will do is show you how to use the various programming aids like Application Wizards to create an application as quickly as possible. As the book progresses, we'll expand on the principles you learn here to build complex, multilanguage examples.

This chapter contains four major sections, one for each of the products that the book covers as a whole. You'll find one or two simple examples in each of the language areas that show some of the basics of using the product. The examples will also illustrate how the programming language product will be used throughout the book. While this chapter won't provide a primer on the programming language itself, it will help those of you with knowledge of other programming languages to at least gain a foothold in the four major languages supported by Visual Studio.

Visual Basic

Visual Basic can be used for a wide variety of application types. All you need to do is look at the New Project dialog box to see the vast array of programming tasks you can perform with this product. For the purposes of this book, though, we'll concentrate on the strengths Visual Basic possesses when it comes to creating applications. The form design tools and prototyping capability make writing applications with this product fast and efficient. Not only will you be able to create applications faster with Visual Basic than you can with other Visual Studio programming products, but the customer will be happier with the finished result since you can prototype the application with the customer present.

The following sections show two simple Visual Basic application types: Dialog based and single document. Both examples are designed to show some relatively simple design concepts and how to use the wizards provided with the product. We'll also explore some of the ways you can complete a simple application by adding buttons and other controls. (These examples aren't representative of the rest of the book; rather, they're specifically designed to teach product usage details.)

Visual Basic Dialog-Based Application

One of the simplest kinds of applications you can create is the dialog-based application. It normally contains a single form that you place controls on and that performs a limited task of some sort. Dialog-based applications are commonly used for utility programs because they're quick and easy to create, and a utility program normally doesn't require a complex interface. You'll also find dialog-based applications used for a wide variety of operating system tasks, and even for configuration and setup program applications.

The dialog-based application is a real plus for the programmer as well. For example, I use dialog-based applications to test new programming techniques or ActiveX controls that I create. In many cases, dialog-based applications also come in handy if I need to demonstrate to a client how something will work, or even help another programmer understand a programming principle. In other words, dialog-based applications are the workhorses of the programming community.

This example isn't going to do anything complicated. What you'll learn is how to create a dialog-based application, populate it with some standard controls, and then test it out to see if it works as intended. Even though the following procedure is designed to create this specific example, it will also help you design a dialog-based application of any type:

1. Start Visual Basic. You'll see a New Project dialog box like the one shown in Figure 4-1. This is where you'll start every time you start Visual Basic. The New Project dialog box will allow you to create a new project or select an existing project.

2. Choose the Standard EXE option, then click Open. Visual Basic will create the default EXE project, a dialog-based application, as shown in Figure 4-2.

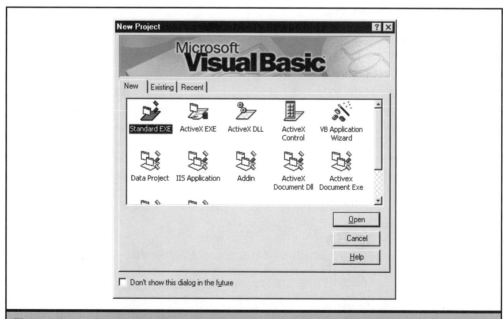

Figure 4-1. The New Project dialog box allows you to create a new project or open an existing one

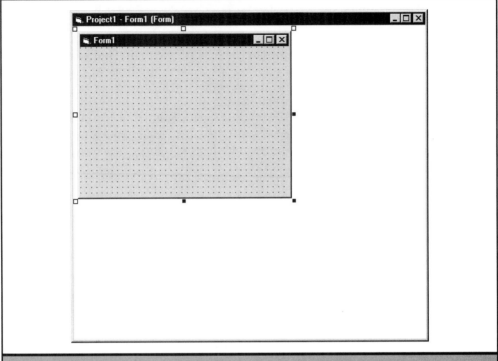

Figure 4-2.   You'll start with a blank form when creating a dialog-based application

> **Tip**   *If you're working on the same project every day, you can choose it from the Recent tab of the New Project dialog box. On the other hand, if you need to open a project that you worked on a long time ago but haven't opened recently, then use the Existing tab of the New Project dialog box. Finally, you can choose not to use the New Project dialog box at all by clicking the Don't show this dialog in the future option at the bottom of the New Project dialog box. This allows you to choose a project from the File menu. If you decide later that you'd like to see the New Project dialog box when starting Visual Basic, use the View | Options command to open the Options dialog box. Click on the Environment tab, then choose the Prompt for project option.*

That's all there is to the application creation process. Now that you've got a blank form, you can add controls to it, then some code, compile it, test it, and you're ready to go. The first thing you'll probably want to do, though, is provide some identification information for the application by changing entries in the Properties window. Here's a list of the changes I made for the example program. This represents the minimum changes you should consider making to any application; in most cases, you'd want to make more.

Property	Value
(Name)	MainForm
BorderStyle	1 - Fixed Single
Caption	My Test Dialog
StartUpPosition	2 - CenterScreen

Now that we've got the preliminaries out of the way, let's begin by adding some controls to the blank form. Obviously, you have to add whatever controls your application requires to get the job done. Since this application is going to perform a simple task, we'll work with three of the basic controls: a command button, an edit box, and a few labels. Here's what your dialog box should look like:

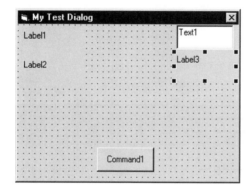

One of the things that I normally do next is give the "active" controls (those I'll work with during program execution) easy to remember names. Select Text1, then the (Name) property in the Properties window. Type **DataEntry** in the blank next to the property name. Select Label3, then the (Name) property. Change this control name to **DataOutput**. Finally, select Command1 and change its name to **DataChange**. Now you have three easy to work with names for your controls.

Tip   *Many programmers use Hungarian Notation when naming their controls. This convention makes it easier to determine the exact type and purpose of every control you create. However, it's not absolutely necessary to use this convention with Visual Basic because it provides so many helps in determining the purpose of a control for you.*

Now that we have our active controls labeled, let's get the rest of the form configured. Table 4-1 provides a complete list of the changes you'll need to make. Any value that appears blank in the table should also be blank in the Properties window, which means you'll need to erase any existing text.

Control	Property	Value
Label1	Caption	Type any string:
	Width	2000
Label2	Caption	Here's what you typed:
	Width	2000
DataEntry	Text	
	Left	2250
	Width	2300
DataOutput	Caption	
	Left	2250
	Width	2300
	BorderStyle	1 - Fixed Single
DataChange	Caption	Change It

Table 4-1.   Simple Visual Basic Dialog-Based Application Control Settings

At this point, you'll want to save your application. I gave the sample application a name of SmplDlg, but you can use any name you want. It's time to add some code to the application. Double-click on the DataChange control and you'll see a Code Editing window. Type the code shown here:

```
Private Sub DataChange_Click( )
    DataOutput.Caption = DataEntry.Text
End Sub
```

As you can see, this is a very simple program. When the user clicks DataChange, the value contained in DataEntry gets copied to DataOutput. At this point, you can compile and run the application by clicking the Start button. Type some text, then click Change It. You'll see a dialog box similar to the one shown next. (Stop the program by clicking the End button in Visual Basic or by clicking the Close button on the dialog box.)

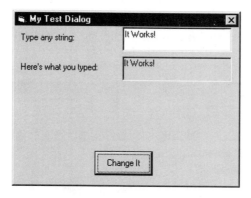

Visual Basic Single-Document Application

The single-document application is the basis for the multidocument application. A multidocument application is like Microsoft Word. You can open more than one document at once and more than one document type is normally supported. A single-document application is one like Notepad. You can only open one document at a time and it's not unusual for such an application to support only one document type.

It would appear at first that the multidocument application is superior to the single-document application because it contains more features. However, that's really just part of the picture for the programmer. There are situations where you only need to support one document at a time, and a single document application is perfect for those situations. Multidocument applications are more complex to create because you have to keep track of the number and type of documents open.

Obviously, some things are the same whether you select a single-document or multidocument application. For one thing, both have a requirement to display the document. It doesn't matter how many windows you have; the display process is essentially the same. Both kinds of applications have to provide a menu interface and both have to provide some type of help functionality (unless, as in this example, you're creating the application for test purposes).

Working with the VB Application Wizard

Our single-document application will demonstrate how to use the VB Application Wizard, work with menus, and create a very simple text editor. We'll pursue some of the other things that I mentioned in the previous paragraph as the book progresses. For example, you'll find the technique for adding help to your application in Chapter 9. The following procedure will help you get started with the sample application. You can also use this procedure, with minor modifications, to create other types of applications.

1. Start Visual Basic. You'll see the New Project dialog box, as shown in Figure 4-1.

2. Select the VB Application Wizard icon, then click Open. You'll see the Application Wizard-Introduction dialog box shown next. Notice that you can

use a profile to create your application. We'll go the longer route this time, but it's important to keep this feature in mind since it will reduce the amount of work required to create an application.

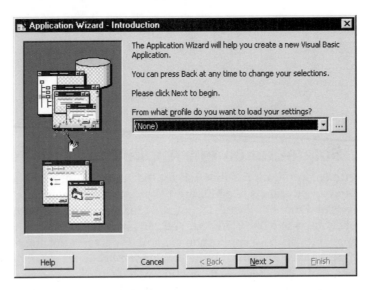

3. Click Next. You'll the Application Wizard - Interface Type dialog box shown here. This is where you choose the type of application to create: Multidocument, single-document, or dialog-based. Since we've already talked about the differences between application types, I won't discuss them again here.

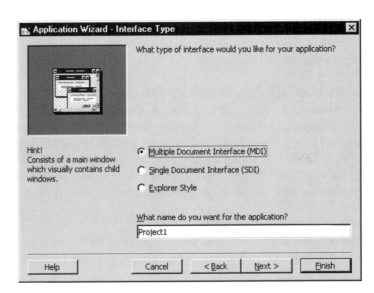

4. Select the Single Document Interface (SDI) option. You now have an option of typing the name of your application as you define it. I usually name the application at this point rather than waiting until later.

5. Type an application name in the "What name do you want for the application?" field (the example uses SmplSDoc), then click Next. You'll see the Application Wizard - Menus dialog box shown here. Visual Basic provides a wealth of standard menus that you can use to reduce the work required to get your application up and running. Read the "Using Standard Menus" sidebar for further details on using menus in your application.

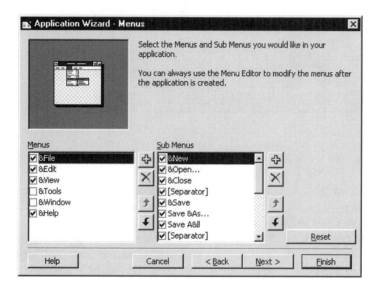

6. Select one or more standard menus from the Menus list. (See the "Using Standard Menus" section for details on adding custom menu entries.) The example application uses the File and Help menus, but you'd normally add the Edit menu as a minimum for a production application.

7. Verify the Sub Menu list contains the entries that you want for each standard menu selection. Make sure you add any required entries for custom menus (see the "Using Standard Menus" section for details). The example application includes the New, Open, Save, and Exit entries in the File menu. The Help menu only includes the About entry. Uncheck all of the other entries unless you intend to add code for them later.

8. Once you've made all the appropriate changes to your menu setup and double-checked them for accuracy, click Next. You'll see the Application Wizard - Customize Toolbar dialog box shown next. Notice that this toolbar provides the default set of buttons that you've seen with many applications in the past. Like menus, Microsoft wants to help you standardize your toolbars.

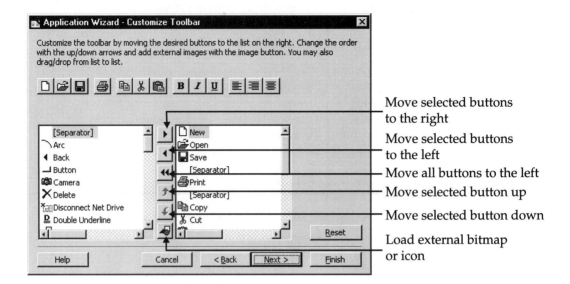

9. Configure your application's toolbar as needed to reflect the menu selections you made in Steps 6 and 7. The button list on the left tells you which buttons are available; the one on the right shows which buttons are selected for inclusion in the application. Use the arrow buttons to move a button from one side to the other. Move the button to the right if you want to include it or to the left if you want to exclude it. If you don't like the current position of a button, you can use the UP and DOWN arrows to move an entry in the right-hand list to the desired position. Finally, you can use the Load an External Bitmap or Icon button to add custom art to the application. The example application only provides three buttons on the toolbar: New, Open, and Save. Move all of the other buttons to the left-hand list.

10. Verify the toolbar contains all the icons you need to support the menu you created, then click Next. You'll see the Application Wizard - Resources dialog box shown next. This dialog box asks if you want to use an external file to hold the resources for your application. If you plan to distribute your application to more than one country, it's usually a good idea to select this option. All you need to do to prepare the application for use with another language is to change the resource file contents. Otherwise, you have to make the changes within the application, then recompile it for every language you plan to support. Since our sample application won't be used in more than one country, we don't need this support.

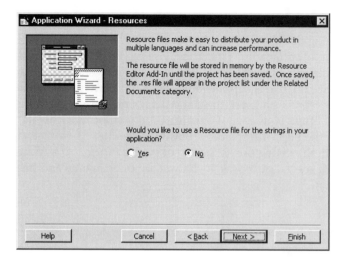

11. Choose No, then click Next. You'll see the Application Wizard - Internet Connectivity dialog box shown here. This dialog box allows you to add an Internet connection to your application. In addition, you can set that connection to start at any location on the Internet, including your company's home page. We won't be adding Internet connectivity to the sample application, but you can see how to use this feature in Chapter 10.

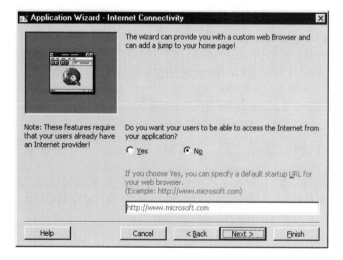

12. Choose No, then click Next. You'll see the Application Wizard - Standard Forms dialog box shown here. This dialog box allows you to add standard forms to your application. Of course, you can customize the form as needed. For example, even though most About dialog boxes look the same, you do expect to see the correct application name and perhaps a company name. The dialog box contains a list of the standard forms that programmers are likely to need most often. However, there are additional forms available. All you need to do is click the Form Templates... button to see them. One of the entries not included in the dialog box is the Tip of the Day form. You can use this form for a variety of special purposes, including announcements and help desk information.

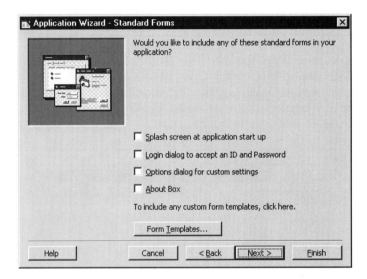

13. Choose any of the standard forms that your application requires. The sample application uses the About Box option. Click Next. You'll see the Application Wizard - Data Access Forms dialog box shown next. This is where you'd add database support for your application. We'll talk more about data access in Chapter 9.

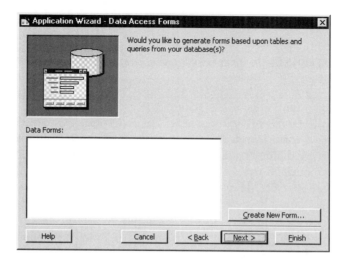

14. Click Next. You'll see the Application Wizard - Finished dialog box shown here.

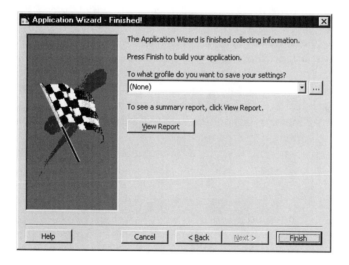

Tip   *Make sure you provide an entry for the "To what profile do you want to save your settings?" field if you plan to create this type of application with any regularity. Using profiles means that you spend less time answering Application Wizard questions and more time getting your application created.*

15. Click Finish to complete your application. You'll see an Application Created dialog box.

16. Click OK to close the Application Created dialog box.

Using Standard Menus

Microsoft wants to make Windows as a whole easy to use, which is why they promote the use of standard menus and dialog boxes in applications. Fortunately, using standard menus has a lot of appeal for the developer as well as the individual user. For one thing, using a standard menu saves you the time and effort of creating your own menu system for common tasks. In addition, using the standard menus will give your application the standard Windows look; your application will look and feel like other Windows applications that the user may have installed in the past.

The Application Wizard - Menus dialog box, shown in Step 5 earlier in this chapter, contains everything you'll need to add standard menu to your application during the initial design process. The menu entries that normally appear across the top of the application are in the Menus list. Submenus that appear when you click on one of these main menu entries, like the File menu, appear in the Sub Menus list. A check box next to each item in the two lists determines whether that item will appear in the application.

Fortunately, you can add custom main menu and submenu entries using the Application Wizard - Menus dialog box as well. Notice that there are four buttons to the side of each list. The first button adds a new menu entry, the second one deletes an existing menu entry, and the last two buttons move entries up or down, changing their position on the menu or submenu.

Adding a new menu entry (either main menu or submenu) is easy. Click the New button and you'll see the Add New Menu dialog box shown here:

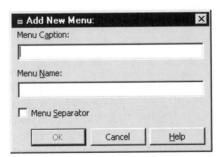

Notice that you need to provide information in two fields. The first field, Menu Caption, is what the user will see when they use your application. Type an ampersand (&) somewhere in the caption if you want the user to be able to use the keyboard to access your menu. Make sure you select a letter that's not already in use. The second field, Menu Name, is what you'll use to access the menu entry from within your application. Just adding a new menu doesn't make it functional; you'll need to add code to support the new menu entry as well.

Submenus provide an optional Separator check box in the Add New Menu dialog box. You don't need to provide either a Menu Caption or Menu Name field entry if you check this option since the menu entry will act as a separator (horizontal line) between menu entry groups.

So, what happens if you make a lot of changes to the menu setup, then decide that the changes were ill advised? Just use the Reset button. Any changes you made to the default menu setup will be reversed. Of course, you'll want to use this button with care since you can't put the changes back once they're gone.

Getting Ready to Edit

So, now that we have a program shell, complete with menus, toolbars, and an About Box, what do we need to do to make it functional? Well, the first thing we'll need to do is add some place for the user to view the document you want to display. Since this is a simple text editor, you can add a Text Box control to frmMain. We'll need to change the name of the control to ctrlTextEdit by changing the (Name) property (ctrl is short for control). Here's a list of the other property changes you need to make to ctrlTextEdit. (A blank value indicates a blank value for the property.)

Property	Value
Left	0
MultiLine	True
ScrollBars	2 - Vertical
Text	

There are several issues we need to take care of with the ctrlTextEdit control before we can actually use it as a text editor. For one thing, it doesn't fit the form as you would expect it to. Another problem is that the top of the editing area doesn't fall right below the toolbar (unless you were very lucky in placing the ctrlTextEdit control). Both problems have a simple solution. Double-click on the form to display the Code Edit window. Select Resize from the drop-down list box on the right side (this list box provides a list of functions associated with the form and is called the Procedure list box). Here's the code you'll need to add:

```
Private Sub Form_Resize( )
    'Make sure the text editing control fits on the form.
    ctrlTextEdit.Move 0, tbToolBar.Height, ScaleWidth, ScaleHeight
End Sub
```

Notice that you need to take the height of the toolbar into account when positioning ctrlTextEdit. If you don't take the toolbar into account, the Edit box control will be too high and you won't be able to see the first few lines of text. Likewise, if you move the toolbar to another location, then you need to reposition the Edit box to take up the slack space at the top of the form.

Opening a File

Now that we have a way to show the user the contents of a file, it's time to provide a method for opening one. If you try to open a file right now, you'll see the standard File Open dialog box, but nothing will happen. That's because the VB Application Wizard couldn't assume that you wanted to open text files. What we need to do is find a way to process the file once the user has selected one to open.

Open the Code Editing windows. Select mnuFileOpen from the Object list (list box on the left side of the window) and Click in the Procedure list. You'll see the mnuFileOpen_Click( ) subprocedure. We'll need to add the code shown in Listing 4-1 to this subprocedure (I'll explain how it works after you look at the code).

Listing 4-1

```
Private Sub mnuFileOpen_Click( )
    Dim sFile As String
    Dim sContent, sFullText As String

    With dlgCommonDialog
        .DialogTitle = "Open"
        .CancelError = False

        'Added the Text File entry in addition to All Files
        .Filter = "All Files (*.*)|*.*|Text Files (*.txt)|*.txt"

        .ShowOpen
        If Len(.FileName) = 0 Then
            Exit Sub
        End If
        sFile = .FileName
    End With
```

```
'Process the selected file.
Open sFile For Input As #1

'Read the contents of the file into a string.
Do While Not EOF(1)
    Input #1, sContent
    sFullText = sFullText + sContent + Chr(13) + Chr(10)
Loop

'Display the contents on screen.
ctrlTextEdit.Text = sFullText

'Close the file.
Close #1

End Sub
```

Some of this code was provided as part of the original subprocedure. The first thing you'll need to do is add two strings: One to hold the current line of text read from the file, the second to hold the entire contents of the file.

The VB Application Wizard created most of the dialog box code for us. However, since this is going to be a text editor, it's important that we be able to look for text files. Notice that the dlgCommonDialog.Filter property has two filters assigned to it: All Files and Text Files. When you open the File Open dialog box, you'll be able to choose between the two.

By the end of the common dialog box display sequence, we have a filename to use. That's all we need to open the file using the Open( ) function. Once the file is open, we can use a Do While loop to read it into a string one line at a time. Note that we have to add an end of line character to the string during each pass. Otherwise, you end up with one long string displayed for the entire file. The order of the two-character end of line is important as well since this order of characters is the only one that the text box control accepts as end of line.

The very last thing we do in the subprocedure is to close the file. Never forget to perform this important step. Otherwise, you'll end up with an open file that's locked for other users. Here's what our application looks like to this point:

Creating a New Document

New documents can be either easy or difficult to create, depending on the document type and what kinds of error trapping you provide for them. For example, most applications detect when the user has made a change to the document. They ask if the user wants to save the document before creating a new document or closing the application. Our sample application isn't going to get that fancy. All we'll do is create a blank document. (Unfortunately, this means that the user will need to remember to save before creating a new document.)

For some strange reason, adding this functionality to a Visual Basic application is a two-step process, versus the one-step process we followed in the previous section. The first step is to associate the New button with the File | New command. Access the New button procedure by selecting tbToolBar in the Object list and ButtonClick( ) in the Procedure list. Listing 4-2 shows the code required to line the New button to the File | New command procedure. (The new lines of code are in bold type.)

Listing 4-2

```
Private Sub tbToolBar_ButtonClick(ByVal Button As ComctlLib.Button)
    On Error Resume Next
    Select Case Button.Key
        Case "New"
            'Call the File | New command code.
            mnuFileNew_Click
        Case "Open"
            mnuFileOpen_Click
        Case "Save"
            mnuFileSave_Click
    End Select
End Sub
```

The advantage to associating a button with its related menu command is that you only have to write the code required to make both operational one time. In addition, any changes you make to one will automatically get reflected in the other. Finally, using one set of code instead of two reduces overall application size by a small amount.

Now that we can perform the same task with either the File | New command or the New button, let's make the command functional. Select mnuFileNew in the Object list and Click in the Procedure list. Listing 4-3 shows the code you'll need to add to make both the menu option and the button functional.

ting 4-3

```
Private Sub mnuFileNew_Click( )
    'Clear the current document.
    ctrlTextEdit.Text = ""
End Sub
```

Saving a Document

A text editor isn't much use if you can't save the changes you make to any files you open. That's where the File | Save command and the Save button come into play. We'll add a simple file-save routine to our application. As before, there are little or no safeguards built into this procedure. The sole intent of this section is to make you familiar with the basic steps for writing the file-saving code. We'll look at various kinds of error-trapping routines later in the book.

The first thing we need to do is move the sFile variable created for us by the VB Application Wizard from the mnuFileOpen subprocedure to the (General) (Declarations) area of the program—select (General) in the Object list and (Declarations) in the Procedure list. Doing so will change the variable's scope from local (the mnuFileOpen subprocedure) to global (the entire application). You use can use cut and paste to perform this part of the process. The reason we need to make the sFile variable global is so the File | Save command knows which file to save the changed information to.

The second step is to create a File | Save subprocedure. Select mnuFileSave in the Object window and click in the Procedure window. Listing 4-4 shows the code you'll need to save text to the file.

ting 4-4

```
Private Sub mnuFileSave_Click( )
    Dim sFullText As String

    'Open the file for output.
    Open sFile For Output As #1

    'Output the data
```

```
        sFullText = ctrlTextEdit.Text
        Write #1, sFullText

        'Close the file.
        Close #1

        'Tell the user that the file is saved.
        MsgBox "The file is saved."
End Sub
```

As you can see, the process of saving our data is relatively simple. The first thing we need to do is create a variable to hold the data. The next step is to open the file for output. Notice that we're using the same global variable that we used for the File | Open subprocedure. Unlike the input procedure, outputting the data doesn't require a loop. Finally, we close the file and display a success message for the user.

Visual C++

You'll find that Visual C++ provides much better contact with the operating system and your hardware than any other product provided with Visual Studio. The low-level programming features make Visual C++ perfect for creating ActiveX controls, utility programs, and other low-level applications like DLLs.

Obviously, Visual C++ isn't limited to working with low-level applications. You can literally use it for any kind of application you want to create. However, Visual Basic is much easier to use for certain kinds of applications because it does more of the work for you. In other words, while you can use Visual C++ for any application type, you'll definitely pay a price in development time for certain types of applications.

The following sections show you two of the kinds of applications we'll create with Visual C++ throughout the book. These two kinds of applications represent the low-level programs that you'd expect to create with this product (though not necessarily as functional as you'd like to see them). The first example is a simple ActiveX control. Since ActiveX controls are used with every other programming language in the book, it's very important to know how to create them using Visual C++. The second example is a simple utility. In this case, we'll test the ActiveX control that we created in the first section of the chapter. (You'll find that you always need to test your ActiveX controls in several environments before pronouncing them totally safe and usable.)

Simple ActiveX Control

I can't think of a single application on my machine that doesn't rely on a push button or two. In fact, the push button is one of the very few Windows controls that you could say every application has. Even an application that displays information in a simple dialog box usually relies on an OK push button to close the dialog box once you're done with it. Suffice it to say, then, that the push button (or command button as some programming environments refer to it) is the one control on your machine that has to work well. It's also the control that absolutely has to provide all of the features you need and the one that programmers change the most.

Note *The push button is the one control that every application uses and is the best place to start looking at the potential for custom controls.*

With this much emphasis on the utility of one control by programmers, it didn't take me too long to figure out which control to show you how to create in this section of the chapter. I also wanted to add a new feature that you may not find very often in a push button, something that everyone will need eventually. That's why I chose an On/Off button as the basis for the control in this chapter—just about everyone needs to turn something on or off during the course of programming an application. It's nice having that feature built right into the control you're using. I also added a few other bells and whistles to the default push button that you get with Visual C++. Even though my push button may not contain all of the fancy features of commercially available controls, it will get you started creating your own custom controls.

Using the MFC ActiveX Control Wizard

It's time to take a look at a simple coding example. This chapter uses Microsoft Visual C++ version 6.0 (though you can also use versions 4.2 and above), as mentioned earlier. Let's begin with a new C++ project. However, unlike other projects you may have created, you'll want to start with the MFC ActiveX Control Wizard to create your workspace. To do that, use the File | New... command to display the New dialog box. Select the Project Workspace option, and you'll see a dialog box like the one in Figure 4-3. Notice the MFC ActiveX Control Wizard entry in Figure 4-3. That's the one you'll need to start the project. The wizard provides you with an OCX framework that you can build on to create the final version of this example.

Note *I used the new Microsoft Developer Studio setup for this example. All the screen shots you see will reflect the Windows 95 orientation of that setup. If you choose to use the older interface, your screens won't match mine. There may be subtle differences even if you do use the Developer Studio interface due to the variety of configuration options this product provides.*

To get the project started, you'll have to type something in the Name field. This example uses OCXExmpl for a project name. You'll also need to click on the MFC ActiveX Control Wizard entry in the project list, and then on OK. Microsoft Visual C++ automatically selects the Win32 option for you. It also creates a project directory.

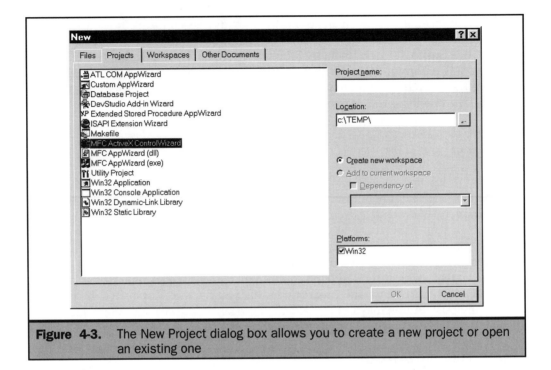

Figure 4-3.   The New Project dialog box allows you to create a new project or open an existing one

What you'll see next are two dialog boxes worth of MFC ActiveX Control Wizard screens. I accepted the defaults on both screens except for the subclass entry on the second page. You'll want to select the BUTTON class here if you want to create an example like this one. Otherwise, look through the list of available classes to determine what you want to use as a basis for your control. Notice that Visual C++ allows you to create your own basic class.

Once you click on the Finish button in the second wizard screen, you'll see a New Project Information dialog box like the one shown in Figure 4-4. You'll want to look through the list of features presented here just to make certain the project contains everything you need. After you verify that the project setup is correct, click on OK to get the project started. Visual C++ will churn your disk for a few moments, and then you'll see the project framework, as shown in Figure 4-4.

Modifying the Default About Box

Now that you have a framework put together, it's time to start filling it out. I usually start by tackling the easy stuff first—who doesn't? The first thing you'll want to do is modify the About box. Yes, Visual C++ creates one of those for you automatically—all

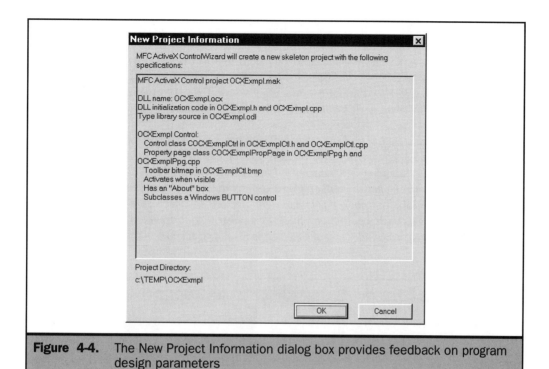

Figure 4-4. The New Project Information dialog box provides feedback on program design parameters

you need to do is customize it. Getting access to the About box is easy. Just use the View | Resource Symbols... command to display the Resource Symbols dialog box shown here:

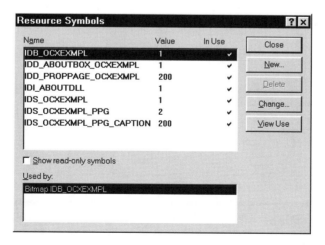

You'll want to select the IDD_ABOUTBOX_OCXEXMPL entry, and then click on the View Use push button to display it. Figure 4-5 shows one way to modify the About box for this example. You'll probably want to include additional copyright and company information in your About box. Notice the variety of tools that Microsoft provides for the dialog box. One of them is the Custom Control button. You can stick another OCX within the About box or any other dialog boxes you create.

Right-click on a control and then choose Properties from the context menu to make its Properties dialog box appear. You alter the text for a static text control by changing the Caption property on the General page of the Properties dialog box. Right-clicking on most objects in Visual C++ will display a context menu—most of which have a Properties option. The whole purpose of right-clicking on objects in Visual C++ is to see what you can do with a particular object. Remember that objects aren't limited to controls; they also include lines of code, the toolbar, and even the various windows.

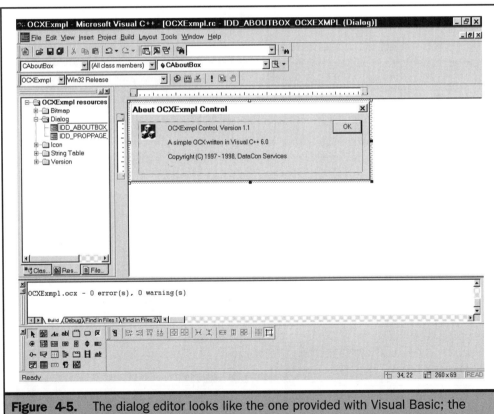

Figure 4-5. The dialog editor looks like the one provided with Visual Basic; the difference is that you'll have to access it separately from the main editor screen

The latest version of Visual C++ may require you to take an additional step that you didn't have to do in the past for the About box. You may need to create a class for the About box—previous versions of Visual C++ just assumed that you wanted to do so. Double-click on the About box and you'll see an Adding a Class dialog box like the one shown here. (If you don't see this dialog box, you'll know that there's already a class assigned to the About box and you don't need to go any further.)

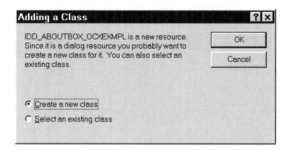

Make sure the Create a New Class option is selected and then click OK. Visual C++ will display a New Class dialog box like the one shown here:

We'll use CAboutBox as the class name. Just type it in the Name field. Everything else needed for this example is already added for you. Click OK to create the required class. You'll see a new entry in the MFC ClassWizard dialog box like the one shown in Figure 4-6. (You may need to select the Class Info tab before your screen will match the figure.)

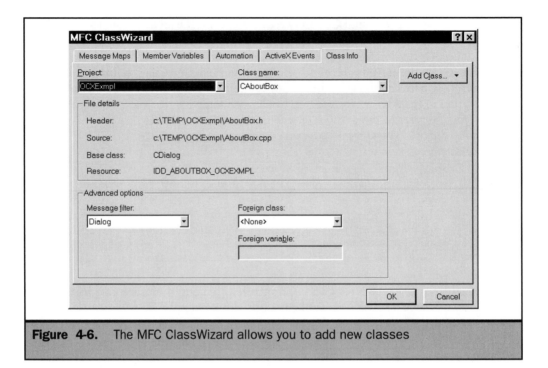

Figure 4-6. The MFC ClassWizard allows you to add new classes

This dialog box tells you about the new class. For example, the Header and Source entries tell you the location of the files associated with this class. You'll also see that IDD_ABOUTBOX_OCXEXMPL is the dialog box resource associated with this class. Go ahead and click OK to close the MFC ClassWizard dialog box.

Adding Properties and Events

Customizing the About box is fun, but let's get down to the business of creating an OCX. The first thing you'll want to do is make some of the button control properties and events visible to someone using the OCX. For example, it might be nice to be able to detect when the user clicked the button. You'll definitely want to be able to change default properties like the caption displayed on the button front. There aren't very many properties visible when you first create a button. To make these various elements visible, you'll need to use the ClassWizard. Use the View | ClassWizard... command to display the MFC ClassWizard dialog box. Choose the Automation page and then select OCXExmplCtrl in the Class Name field.

Visual C++ assumes very little about the control you want to create, not even which properties and methods you want to make visible.

We'll use two different kinds of properties in this example—Microsoft provides access to a lot more. The first type is a stock property. You'll find that things like the Caption property that we all take for granted aren't visible when you first create an OCX. A *stock property* (denoted by an S in Figure 4-7) is one that the parent class supports by default. The second type is a custom property (denoted by a C in Figure 4-7). A *custom property* is one that you've added to a particular class when you subclass it. One of them is the OnOff property that we'll use to create an On/Off switch. We'll look at the process for doing this in the "Adding Some Code" section of this chapter. Figure 4-7 shows a complete list of all the properties that we'll create in this example.

Note

Stock properties are part of the base class, while custom properties are created for the subclassed control.

S (Stock property) ——→

C (Custom —— property)

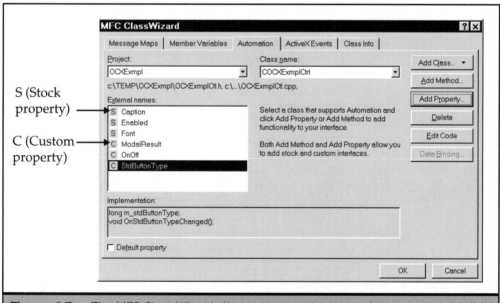

Figure 4-7. The MFC ClassWizard allows you to make properties and events visible to the OCX user

Creating a new property is fairly simple. All you need to do is click on the Add Property... push button to display the Add Property dialog box shown here:

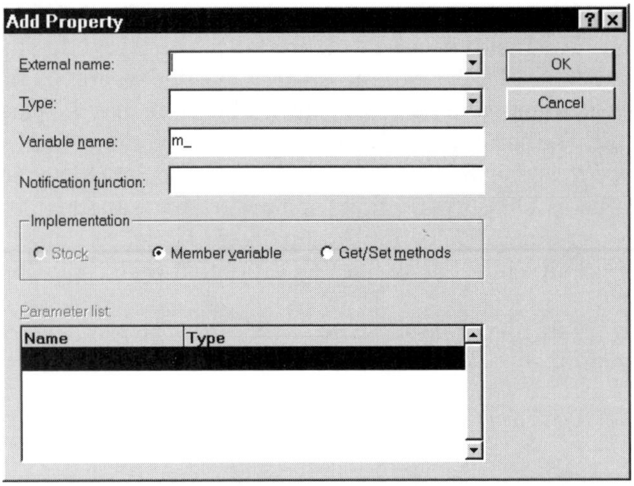

Add Property	? X

External name: [▼]   [OK]

Type: [▼]   [Cancel]

Variable name: [m_   ]

Notification function: [   ]

┌─ Implementation ─────────────────────
│ ○ Stock   ◉ Member variable   ○ Get/Set methods
└─────────────────────────────────────

Parameter list:

Name	Type

The Add Property dialog box has some important features that you might not see at first. The External Name combo box contains a complete list of the default properties for the base class that you selected when creating the OCX. In this case, you'll see things like the Caption property. To create a stock property, just select one of the items from this list and click on OK. Visual C++ will take care of the details for you in this case. Go ahead and create all of the stock properties for this example program now (refer to Figure 4-7).

We'll also need three custom properties: ModalResult, OnOff, and StdButtonType. To create these properties, type the names I've just mentioned into the External Name field. You'll need to select a data type in the Type field as well. In this case, the ModalResult and StdButtonType properties are the long type, while OnOff is a BOOL. (At this point, you may want to close and then reopen the MFC ClassWizard dialog box—there are some situations where your property selections won't get recorded otherwise.)

All of the events we'll use in this example are stock—they come as part of the button base class. All you need to do is click on the ActiveX Events page to display the dialog box shown in Figure 4-8. Adding a stock event is about the same as adding a stock property. Just click on the Add Event button to display the Add Event dialog box. Select a stock name from the External Name combo box, then click on OK to complete the process. Figure 4-8 shows all of the stock events you'll need for this example.

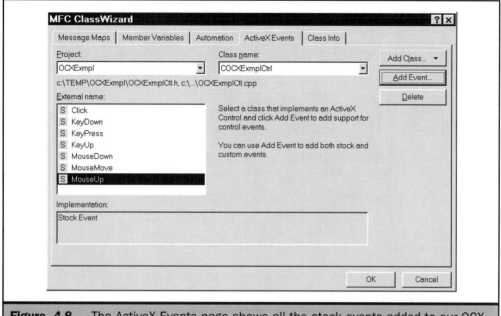

Figure 4-8. The ActiveX Events page shows all the stock events added to our OCX programming example

Defining the Property Page

Now it's time to add some functionality to the property page. You access it the same way that you did the About box, using the View | Resource Symbols... command. In this case, you'll select the IDD_PROPPAGE_OCXEXMPL entry in the Resource Symbols dialog box. The Property page is used for a wide variety of purposes—most of them configuration oriented.

There are two standard sizes of Property pages supported by Visual C++. The small size, which is the default for an OCX, is 250 × 62. This is going to be too small for our purposes, so we'll need to resize it to the large Property page size of 250 × 110. Make sure you use one size or the other when creating a control. Nothing bad will happen if you don't use a standard size, but users will get warning messages saying that you didn't use a standard-sized property page.

What we'll do now is add a method for defining standard button types to the page, as shown in Figure 4-9. These are radio buttons. You'll need ten of them. (Don't worry about how to configure them just now; I'll tell you how in the paragraphs that follow.)

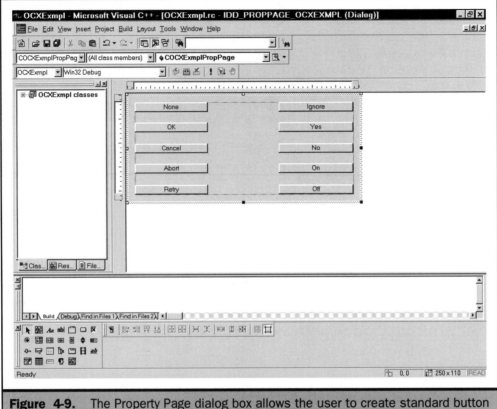

Figure 4-9. The Property Page dialog box allows the user to create standard button types in addition to the On/Off button

Each radio button should have a different ID so that you can detect which one the user clicks (see the ID field on the General page of the Radio Button Properties dialog box).

Now that you have ten standard radio buttons sitting on your Property page, it's time to do something with them. Right-click on a radio button and then choose Properties from the context menu to display the Radio Button Properties dialog box shown here:

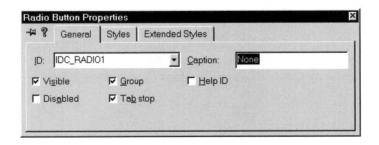

You'll need to make a few subtle changes to your radio buttons before they look like the ones in Figure 4-9. First, select the Styles page of the Radio Button Properties dialog box, and select the push-like check box for each button. You'll also need to place the radio buttons into a group so that the current selection gets deselected when you choose a new button. To do that, check the Group and the Tab stop check boxes on the first radio button in the group that uses the default ID of IDC_RADIO1. Check only the Tabstop check box for all of the other radio buttons, or you'll end up with ten groups of one button instead of one group of ten buttons. Visual C++ starts with the first button it sees that has the Group check box selected as the starting point for the group. The group continues with each radio button in tab order until Visual C++ sees the next one with the Group check box selected.

Tip *Most Microsoft products prefer that you use a Property page size of 250 × 62 or 250 × 110 dialog box units. However, you can use any size you need. When you try to access the Property page, the only thing you'll see is a message stating that you used a nonstandard size. Simply clear the message, and the Property page will appear as usual.*

We have to do one more thing with the radio buttons in this dialog box. To create an OLE connection between the radio buttons and the OCX control, you have to assign their output to an OLE property. CTRL-double-click on the first radio button (None) in the group to display the Add Member Variable dialog box shown here:

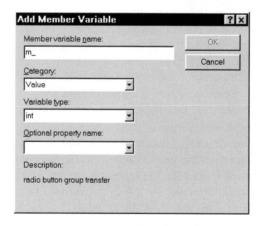

Tip *You can also access this dialog box by pressing CTRL-W to display the MFC ClassWizard dialog box, selecting the Member Variables page, and then clicking the Add Variable button.*

The entries you make here are crucial because Visual C++ doesn't check them for errors, and there isn't any way to select them from a list. In the Member Variable Name field, type **m_stdButtonType**. That's the internal name for one of the custom properties that we created earlier. Leave the Category and Variable Type fields alone. Type **StdButtonType** in the Optional Property Name field. This is the entry that links the property page to your OCX control. Remember that C++ is case sensitive; capitalization is important.

 The drop-down list box for the Optional Property Name field normally contains a complete list of the properties inherited from the base class of your control.

Adding Some Code

Up to this point, we haven't added a single line of code to our application. That's because we've been building a framework for the code. Now it's time to start adding code to the OCX. The first thing we want to do is add some code so our control can exchange data with the client it's being used with. For example, when you see a Properties dialog box for a control, you normally want to see the current values of those properties. Likewise, when you change a property value, you want to be sure that the actual control state will change. Listing 4-5 shows the code you'll need to add.

Listing 4-5

```
void COCXExmplCtrl::DoPropExchange(CPropExchange* pPX)
{

    // Default actions on the part of the Class Wizard.
    ExchangeVersion(pPX, MAKELONG(_wVerMinor, _wVerMajor));
    COleControl::DoPropExchange(pPX);

    // Make all of our properties persistent.
    PX_Bool(pPX, "OnOff", m_onOff, FALSE);
    PX_Long(pPX, "ModalResult", m_modalResult, mrNone);
    PX_Long(pPX, "StdButtonType", m_stdButtonType, 0);
```

Now, let's say that you don't like the default size of the button and you want it to display a specific caption when the user inserts it onto a Web page or other layout. You can change both properties in the OnReset( ) function. Listing 4-6 shows the code you'll need to change. Notice that we use the COleControl class functions to make the required changes. The SetText( ) function allows us to change the caption of the button. Every time the user inserts this control, the caption "Button" will appear. The SetControlSize( ) function allows you to set the control size of 75 × 25 pixels. Obviously, you can set these properties any way you wish, and you can even select one of the default buttons if you so choose.

isting 4-6

```
void COCXExmplCtrl::OnResetState( )
{
    COleControl::OnResetState( ); //Resets defaults found in DoPropExchange
    //Modify the Microsoft control to match custom size settings.
    COleControl::SetText("Button");
    COleControl::SetControlSize(75, 25);
}
```

Now that we have a method for exchanging information and we've set the control up the way we want it to look, it's time to implement the three custom properties that we created. That's right, every time you create a custom property, you'll need to define some code to make that property do something. Otherwise, it'll just sit there and do nothing at all. Listing 4-7 shows the code you'll need to add to implement the ModalResult, OnOff, and StdButtonType properties. I'll explain the inner workings of this code in the next section. For right now, all you need to know is that it implements the properties we created.

isting 4-7

```
void COCXExmplCtrl::OnModalResultChanged( )
{
    // We don't need to do anything here except set the modified flag.
    SetModifiedFlag( );
}

void COCXExmplCtrl::OnOnOffChanged( )
{
    //If the programmer set the OnOff property true, take appropriate action.
    if (m_onOff)
    {
        COleControl::SetText("On");        //Change the caption.
        m_SetOn = TRUE;                    //Set an internal caption flag.
        m_modalResult = mrOn;              //Set the modal result value.
    }
    else
    {
        COleControl::SetText("Button");    //Restore default caption.
        m_SetOn = FALSE;                   //Turn our caption flag off.
        m_modalResult = mrNone;            //Use the default modal result.
```

```
    )

    //Perform the default action.
    SetModifiedFlag( );
}

void COCXExmplCtrl::OnStdButtonTypeChanged( )
{
    // Change the modal result and button caption
    //to match the user selection.
    switch (m_stdButtonType)
    {
    case 0:
        m_modalResult = mrNone;
        COleControl::SetText("Button");
        break;
    case 1:
        m_modalResult = mrOK;
        COleControl::SetText("OK");
        break;
    case 2:
        m_modalResult = mrCancel;
        COleControl::SetText("Cancel");
        break;
    case 3:
        m_modalResult = mrAbort;
        COleControl::SetText("Abort");
        break;
    case 4:
        m_modalResult = mrRetry;
        COleControl::SetText("Retry");
        break;
    case 5:
        m_modalResult = mrIgnore;
        COleControl::SetText("Ignore");
        break;
    case 6:
        m_modalResult = mrYes;
        COleControl::SetText("Yes");
```

```
        break;
    case 7:
        m_modalResult = mrNo;
        COleControl::SetText("No");
        break;
    case 8:
        m_modalResult = mrOn;
        COleControl::SetText("On");
        break;
    case 9:
        m_modalResult = mrOff;
        COleControl::SetText("Off");
    }

    //Set the OnOff property to false since the user selected another type.
    m_onOff = FALSE;

    //Set the modified flag.
    SetModifiedFlag( );
}
```

We need to do one last bit of coding in the OCXEXMPLCtl.cpp file. What happens when a user clicks the button? If he or she is using one of the standard button types, the On/Off button will return a standard modal result value. However, the On/Off button also has a special behavior. If you set the OnOff property to TRUE, the button should switch between On and Off as the user clicks it. We need to add some special event code to handle this situation. Use the View | ClassWizard... command to display the MFC ClassWizard dialog box. Choose the Message Maps page, and then the COCXExmplCtrl entry in the Class Name field. Highlight the OnClick entry in the Messages list. Click Add Function to add a function skeleton to the class. Your MFC ClassWizard dialog box should look like the one shown in Figure 4-10.

Now it's time to add some code to the OnClick( ) function. Click the Edit Code button and Visual C++ will take you to the new function. Listing 4-8 shows the code you'll need to add.

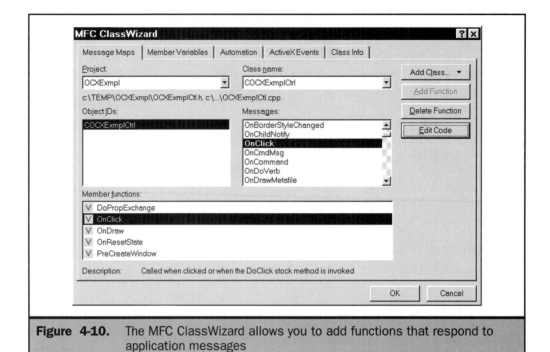

Figure 4-10.   The MFC ClassWizard allows you to add functions that respond to application messages

Listing 4-8

```
void COCXExmplCtrl::OnClick(USHORT iButton)
{
    // See if the OnOff flag is set.  If so, change the caption and
    // internal caption flag.
    // The effect you should see from this code is a toggling
    // of the caption text.
    if (m_onOff)
    {
        if (m_SetOn)
        {
            COleControl::SetText("Off");
            m_SetOn = FALSE;
            m_modalResult = mrOff;
        }
        else
        {
            COleControl::SetText("On");
            m_SetOn = TRUE;
```

```
            m_modalResult = mrOn;
        }
    }

    // Call the default OnClick processing.
    COleControl::OnClick(iButton);
}
```

Now that we've taken care of the function-coding part of the picture, we do need to add two support items to the OCXEXMPLCtl.h file. The first is an enumerated type. Its only purpose is to make the source code easier to read. Each entry corresponds to a standard button type. The second item is a special variable. If you'll notice in the code, I keep referring to an m_SetOn member variable, but this variable isn't part of the class right now. Listing 4-9 shows how you'll need to add the enumerated type and special variable to your header file—right between the Event maps and the Dispatch and event IDs entry:

sting 4-9
```
// Event maps
    //{{AFX_EVENT(COCXExmplCtrl)
    //}}AFX_EVENT
    DECLARE_EVENT_MAP( )

// Create a new enumerated type for the modal result.
    typedef enum
    {
        mrNone = -1L,
        mrOK = 1L,
        mrCancel = 2L,
        mrAbort = 3L,
        mrRetry = 4L,
        mrIgnore = 5L,
        mrYes = 6L,
        mrNo = 7L,
        mrOn = 8L,
        mrOff = 9L,
    }MODALTYPE;

// Special On/Off state variable.
    BOOL     m_SetOn;

// Dispatch and event IDs
```

```
public:
    enum {
    //{{AFX_DISP_ID(COCXExmplCtrl)
    dispidModalResult = 1L,
    dispidOnOff = 2L,
    dispidStdButtonType = 3L,
    //}}AFX_DISP_ID
    };
```

Breaking the Code into Pieces

Your initial reaction to all this code might be one of sheer terror, but it's actually pretty easy to figure out if you take it one function at a time. The fact is that you haven't written much more code than you would have for a standard application, since Visual C++ writes most of it for you as part of the ActiveX control definition process. The functions we did have to add are to address the special things that we want this control to do.

Let's start taking this code apart. The first function that you modified is DoPropExchange( ). This function only performs one service in this example—it allows you to make your custom properties persistent. Essentially, the PX_ series of function calls allow you to store the value of a particular property from one session to the next. There's one function call for each variable type that you define. Each one of them accepts four variables like this:

```
PX_Bool(pPX, "OnOff", m_onOff, FALSE);
```

The first variable is a pointer to a property exchange structure. Visual C++ defines this structure for you automatically—all you need to do is use it. The second parameter contains the external name of the property, the one that the user will see in the Property Inspector. (There are a variety of names for the Property Inspector—Visual C++ uses the Properties dialog box and Delphi uses the Object Inspector, for example.) The third parameter is the internal name for the property. That's the one you'll use throughout the program to define the property. Finally, we have to define a default value for the property (unless you want the user to see a blank field in the Property Inspector).

The next function you have to modify is OnResetState( ). This function provides some of the aesthetic details that users will see when they add the component to a form. In this case, we'll give the component a default caption and resize it to match a custom size that works well on Web pages, since this is the place we intend to use the control most often. You'll need to change this setting to meet the needs of the programming language you use most often if you design an ActiveX control for some other purpose. The important thing to remember is that the OnResetState( ) function allows you to perform any setup required to use your control.

The default component size used by Microsoft is about twice the size of the one provided by Borland products such as Delphi. Internet controls vary in size, but the 75 width × 25 height we use in the example works in most cases.

Two of the three modified functions in the message handlers section of the code require some kind of change. The ModalResultChanged( ) function doesn't require any modification, so I won't talk about it here. The property associated with the ModalResultChanged( ) function, ModalResult, gets changed by the other two functions. The OnOffChanged( ) function is the first one we'll look at. What we need to do is set an internal caption flag and the initial caption. If the programmer set the OnOff property to TRUE, we'll set the control up as an On/Off switch button by setting its caption to On. We also provide a different modal result value when the push button is used as an On/Off switch. Notice that the m_onOff internal property variable tracks the status of the flag. The m_SetOn internal property tracks the current condition of the On/Off switch (on or off). Since the button is initially On, we set the m_SetOn flag to TRUE.

Now it's time to look at the processing required for the Property page feature of this OCX. The OnStdButtonTypeChanged( ) function is nothing more than a simple case statement. It changes the button's Caption and ModalResult properties as needed to create various default button types. Notice that we also have to turn off the On/Off push-button processing if the user selects a default button type.

The OnClick( ) message-handling function is active during run time. There are two levels of action here. First, we need to determine whether the programmer defined this button as an On/Off switch. If so, we change the internal state variable (m_SetOn) and the button caption. The function switches the button state between On and Off as needed. Once we finish with the internal processing needed to make the button work, we call the default OnClick( ) processing routine. Failure to call this default routine will cause the OCX to skip any code specific to the programming environment that you attach to button events. For example, if you were to use this control in a Visual C++ application, any code attached to the exposed events in Visual C++ would be ignored.

Before you can use this component, you'll have to build it within Visual C++. Part of the build process automatically registers the OCX for you with Windows. I really liked this feature because it saved me some time when testing the OCX later. The only downside is that preregistration contaminates your working environment. You'll have to go to another machine to test this component from an Internet point of view as an ActiveX control.

Visual C++ Dialog-Based Application

Once you create a new ActiveX control of any kind, you have to perform some type of testing to make sure it works as anticipated. I'm going to use Visual C++ 6.0 throughout the following sections. You could use any programming environment that supports OCXs. For example, you might want to test the OnOff control with Visual Basic or Visual InterDev to see how it works with those languages. The important consideration is not the language you use for testing, but that you test the control fully with some programming language that includes full debugging support. You want to make sure that the control you've created actually works as anticipated in the safest possible environment designed to do so. Since many Internet tools are in the testing stage, you may find that a control that seems like it should work doesn't. Being able to eliminate the control itself by testing it in a known environment is one step toward troubleshooting the problem.

Using the MFC AppWizard

The first step in creating a dialog-based application to test our ActiveX control is to use the MFC AppWizard to design an application shell. The following procedure will help you create a dialog-based application for just that purpose. With a few modifications, you can use this procedure for creating just about any kind of dialog-based application that you might need.

1. Open Visual C++ (if you haven't done so already).

2. Use the File | New... command to open the New dialog box. In this case, you'll want to choose the MFC AppWizard (exe) selection in the Projects list box.

3. Type a name for your application in the Project Name field. The sample application uses the name Dialog, but you could easily use any name you like. Make sure you change the Location field if necessary. The Browse button next to the field makes things relatively easy.

4. Click on OK. You'll see an MFC AppWizard - Step 1 dialog box like the one shown here:

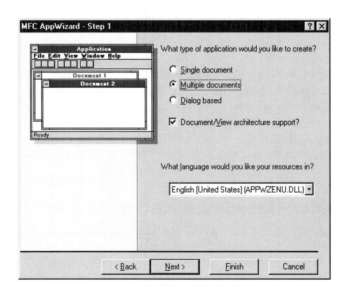

5. Choose the Dialog-Based option button, and then click on Next. You'll see an MFC AppWizard - Step 2 of 4 dialog box like the one shown here:

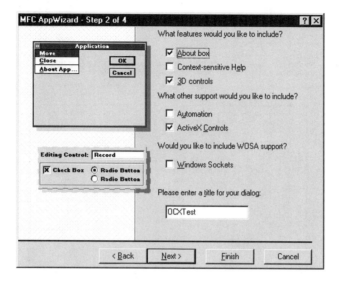

6. Type **Sample Dialog Application** in the Please enter a title for your dialog field. Notice that this dialog box will also allow you to add some features to your dialog-based application like context-sensitive help. The Automation check box allows you to add OLE automation to your application, which is essentially a form of scripting. You can also add Windows Sockets support to your application on this page, which allows it to communicate over TCP/IP networks.

7. Click Next, and then Next again. We don't need to change anything on these last two dialog boxes, but it's handy to know what's available should you need it later. The first page allows you to choose whether to add comments to your code or not. You also get to choose whether MFC is statically or dynamically linked to your application.

Tip

Statically linking MFC to your application has the benefit of reducing the number of files you have to distribute with your application. In fact, you'll only need to give someone the executable if you want to. It may also improve the chances that your application will run on every machine it's installed on since your application will always have access to the same version of MFC that you used to design it. The downside to static linking is that your application will be a lot bigger and waste a lot more memory when loaded. In addition, you'll need to relink your application any time you want to add a new feature to it, which can become quite a nuisance after a while.

8. Click Finish. Visual C++ will display a New Project Information dialog box like the one shown here. This is your last chance to make sure all of your program settings are correct. A poor choice in settings can actually make your project development time longer rather than shorter.

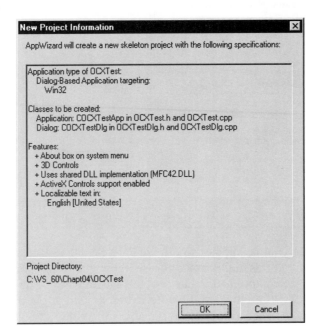

9. Click OK. The MFC AppWizard will generate a program shell for you.

Adding the On/Off ActiveX Control

Now we've got a basic program shell to work with and it's time to start putting our sample application together. The first thing we'll want to do, since this program uses the OnOff control that we created in the previous example, is to install the ActiveX controls we need. Use the Project | Add to Project | Components and Controls... command to display a Components and Controls Gallery dialog box like the one shown next:

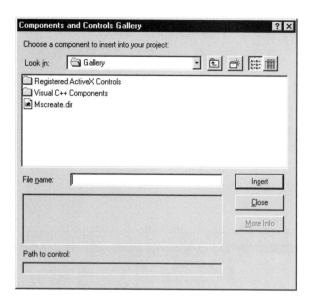

Note *Make sure you have the OCX controls that come with Visual C++ installed or you may not have a copy of the Microsoft Calendar control to work with.*

Double-click the Registered ActiveX Controls folder and you'll see a list of controls registered on your machine. Find the OCXExmpl entry. Visual C++ automatically registers ActiveX controls for you, so the control we created in the previous example should appear in the list of controls available to you. (Other programming environments may force you to register your ActiveX control separately.) Click on Insert. Visual C++ will display a dialog box asking if you really want to insert this control into your project. Click on OK. Visual C++ will have to add some wrapper classes to your application to accommodate the ActiveX control. It displays the names of those classes in a Confirm Classes dialog box like this one:

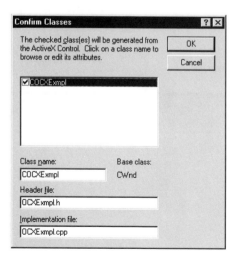

Designing the Application Dialog Box

Once you have a new project in place and some controls installed to use with it, you'll need to design your application dialog box. Figure 4-11 shows the dialog box for the test program I created to debug this example. It also shows the Properties dialog box with the Control page selected.

 Remember that you need to use the Project | Add to Project | Components and Controls... command to display the Components and Controls Gallery dialog box, which is used to add the OCXExmpl control to the current project.

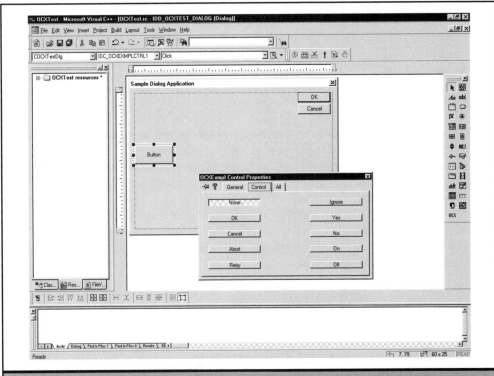

Figure 4-11. The Control page of the Properties dialog box shows the special features for this push button

Most programming environments also provide a way to view all of the properties associated with a control at one time. Here's the All page of the OCXExmpl Properties page; notice that the OnOff property is set to TRUE.

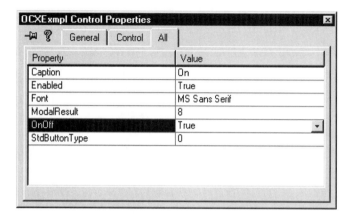

Adding Some Code

You'll probably want to add some test code to the program as well. That way, you can check the effects of various control events. For example, the On/Off switch button in our example provides a variety of modal result return values, depending on how you set the button properties. Setting the OnOff property to TRUE creates a special switch button. The ModalResult property switches between two values. However, you could just as easily select one of the standard button values from the Control page of the Properties dialog box.

The first thing you'll want to do is CTRL-double-click on the control. You'll see an Add Member Variable dialog box. Type **m_OnOffButton** in the Member Variable Name field. You'll also want to make sure that the Category field is set to Control and the Variable Type field is set to COCXExmpl. Now that we can access the control's properties from within the test application, right-click on the control and then choose Events from the context menu. You'll see a New Windows Message and Event Handlers dialog box like the one shown next:

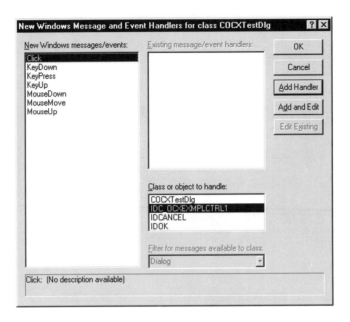

Notice that Visual C++ automatically selects the Click event and the IDC_OCXEXMPLCTRL1 object. All you need to do is click the Add and Edit button to add a new function to your program. Click OK when you see the Add Member Function dialog box to accept the default function name. At this point, you'll see the function skeleton for this button.

Listing 4-10 shows the C++ test code for this example. Notice the use of the GetModalResult( ) wrapper class function that Visual C++ automatically creates for the control. You'll find all of the declarations that Visual C++ makes for you in the OCXEXMPLE.h file. It's educational to look at this header file, since it shows how Visual C++ is interacting with your control. Looking at this file could help you find interface problems that you might not otherwise see (especially if you don't test every property of the control completely).

Note *You can create the OnClickOcxexmplctrl1( ) function in several ways. The easiest way to do it is using the MFC ClassWizard (which you can display using the View | ClassWizard... command). Highlight the IDC_OCXEXMPLCTRL1 entry in the Object IDs list box, and then the Click entry in the Messages list. Clicking the Add Function button at this point will add the function to your program.*

Listing 4-10

```cpp
void COCXTestDlg::OnClickOcxexmplctrl1( )
{
    //Get the current ModalResult value.
    long liModalResult;
    liModalResult = m_OnOffButton.GetModalResult( );

    //Determine which modal result was returned and display a message.
    switch (liModalResult)
    {
    case -1:
        MessageBox("None button pressed", "State of Control", MB_OK);
        break;
    case 1:
        MessageBox("OK button pressed", "State of Control", MB_OK);
        break;
    case 2:
        MessageBox("Cancel button pressed", "State of Control", MB_OK);
        break;
    case 3:
        MessageBox("Abort button pressed", "State of Control", MB_OK);
        break;
    case 4:
        MessageBox("Retry button pressed", "State of Control", MB_OK);
        break;
    case 5:
        MessageBox("Ignore button pressed", "State of Control", MB_OK);
        break;
    case 6:
        MessageBox("Yes button pressed", "State of Control", MB_OK);
        break;
    case 7:
        MessageBox("No button pressed", "State of Control", MB_OK);
        break;
    case 8:
        MessageBox("Button is On", "State of Control", MB_OK);
        break;
    case 9:
        MessageBox("Button is Off", "State of Control", MB_OK);
        break;
    }
}
```

Testing the Results

Now that you have a simple form with your control attached to it, try testing it. The example program will display a simple dialog box with the ActiveX control on it. Click the control and you'll see another dialog box telling you the state of the button, as shown in Figure 4-12. A click on either the OK or Cancel button (provided free of charge by Visual C++) will end the program. As previously stated, this is a simple test of basic control functionality. What we've done so far is check the Property page, the properties, and the results of using the control.

Visual J++

The Internet is a fact of life when it comes to computing today. Not only is the Internet being used for commercial and information-sharing purposes, but you'll find it in the corporate environment for more mundane purposes like keeping employees on the road in touch. In fact, the Internet (and the local corporate alternative of an intranet) is finding use in all kinds of applications, including computer support services. We'll get a better look at just how this works in Chapter 14, when I show you how to create a help desk application.

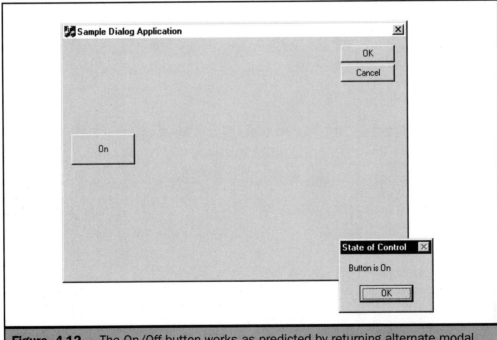

Figure 4-12. The On/Off button works as predicted by returning alternate modal result values

Visual J++ is a programming language designed specifically for the Internet, though you could easily use it for other purposes. It's Microsoft's version of Java, the product originally introduced by Sun Microsystems. One of the major differences between the Sun version of Java and the Microsoft version is that the Microsoft version provides some additional packages, some of which provide access to the Windows API.

We'll use Visual J++ for a wide variety of Internet-related tasks throughout the book, but in this section we're going to explore the kind of application that defines Visual J++ as a unique entity—the applet. An applet is a mini application that allows your Web page to work dynamically with the user in some way. This interaction could be something as small as a counter used to record the number of visitors or something more complex, like an aid in computing the total cost of the products ordered by the user from your company. Applets come in all shapes and sizes, and you can use them to replace ActiveX in many situations because Visual J++ allows better access than Java to the Windows environment.

Our example applet isn't going to do anything very spectacular. All it'll do is create an area that you can use to test various text manipulation features that Java provides. Since HTML doesn't normally allow you to change text dynamically, the use of this applet will at least improve on the Web page features you may have seen in the past.

Starting the Applet

The first order of business in creating the example is to create the applet skeleton. The following procedure will get you started. While the procedure is specifically tailored to this example, you can use it to create any kind of applet with a little modification.

1. Start Visual J++. You'll see a New Project dialog box like the one shown here:

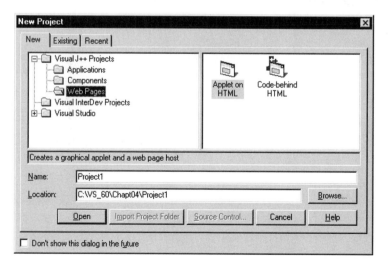

2. Open the Visual J++ Projects folder, then the Web Pages folder.

3. Highlight the Applet on HTML option.

4. Type a name for your project in the Name field (our example uses VJApplet), then click Open. Visual J++ will create a new project for you consisting of an HTML page for testing purposes and a JAVA file, which contains the applet.

Adding Code to the Applet

The applet that Visual J++ creates for you is functional, but not spectacular. What it does is display a form, which contains a label containing text displayed in a specific foreground and background color. The sample code doesn't allow you to control the label and form colors separately—they both appear in the same color. The applet can accept three parameters to begin with: label (the text you want displayed), background (the background color), and foreground (the foreground color). It might be nice to control the label colors separately from the rest of the box, so we'll add two more label color parameters (labelbackground and labelforeground) to answer that need. We'll also add the ability to change the color of the various applet elements dynamically while the applet is running on a Web page, which means that we'll need to perform some event tracking. Listing 4-11 shows the complete source for this applet. I'll explain how it works once you get a chance to look at the source.

| Note | *The example in this chapter doesn't rely on the Windows Foundation Classes (WFC) for a couple of reasons. First, it's important to know how to build an applet using standard Java code in case you want to use a third-party product to modify it later. Second, while you'll definitely gain a wide variety of features using WFC, you'll also lose platform independence. It's important to know how to design an applet that will work on any platform that supports a Java interpreter.* |

Listing 4-11

```
// Applet1.java

import java.awt.*;
import java.applet.*;

/** Add any required imports.
 */
import java.text.*;
import java.awt.event.*;
import com.ms.ui.*;

/**

 * This class reads PARAM tags from its HTML host page and sets
 * the color and label properties of the applet. Program execution
 * begins with the init( ) method.
```

```java
 */
public class Applet1 extends Applet
{
    /**
     * The entry point for the applet.
     */
    public void init( )
    {
        initForm( );

        usePageParams( );

        // TODO: Add any constructor code after initForm call.
    }

    private     final String labelParam = "label";
    private     final String backgroundParam = "background";
    private     final String foregroundParam = "foreground";

    // Add two label color parameters to our applet.
    private final String labelBackParam = "labelbackground";
    private final String labelForeParam = "labelforeground";

    /**
     * Reads parameters from the applet's HTML host and sets applet
     * properties.
     */
    private void usePageParams( )
    {
        final String defaultLabel = "Default label";
        final String defaultBackground = "C0C0C0";
        final String defaultForeground = "000000";
        final String defaultLabelBack = "FFFFFF";
        final String defaultLabelFore = "000000";
        String labelValue;
        String backgroundValue;
        String foregroundValue;
        String labelBackValue;
        String labelForeValue;
        String stateTextValue;

        /**
         * Read the <PARAM NAME="label" VALUE="some string">,
         * <PARAM NAME="background" VALUE="rrggbb">,
```

```
      * and <PARAM NAME="foreground" VALUE="rrggbb"> tags from
      * the applet's HTML host.
      */
     labelValue = getParameter(labelParam);
     backgroundValue = getParameter(backgroundParam);
     foregroundValue = getParameter(foregroundParam);
     labelBackValue = getParameter(labelBackParam);
     labelForeValue = getParameter(labelForeParam);

     if ((labelValue == null) || (backgroundValue == null) ||
         (foregroundValue == null))
     {
         /**
          * There was something wrong with the HTML host tags.
          * Generate default values.
          */
         labelValue = defaultLabel;
         backgroundValue = defaultBackground;
         foregroundValue = defaultForeground;
     }


     if ((labelBackValue == null) || (labelForeValue == null))
     {
         /**
          * Set the default values for the label colors.
          */
         labelBackValue = defaultLabelBack;
         labelForeValue = defaultLabelFore;
     }

 /**
  * Set the applet's string label, background color, and
  * foreground colors.
  */

     label1.setText(labelValue);
     label1.setBackground(stringToColor(labelBackValue));
     label1.setForeground(stringToColor(labelForeValue));

     labelForeColor.setBackground(stringToColor(labelBackValue));
     labelForeColor.setForeground(stringToColor(labelForeValue));

     labelBackColor.setBackground(stringToColor(labelBackValue));
     labelBackColor.setForeground(stringToColor(labelForeValue));
```

```
        foreColor.setBackground(stringToColor(labelBackValue));
        foreColor.setForeground(stringToColor(labelForeValue));

        backColor.setBackground(stringToColor(labelBackValue));
        backColor.setForeground(stringToColor(labelForeValue));

        this.setBackground(stringToColor(backgroundValue));
        this.setForeground(stringToColor(foregroundValue));

        // Display the current color values in the color text boxes.
        labelForeColor.setText(colorToString(label1.getForeground( )));
        labelBackColor.setText(colorToString(label1.getBackground( )));
        foreColor.setText(colorToString(this.getForeground( )));
        backColor.setText(colorToString(this.getBackground( )));

        // Enable our application to listen for events.
        labelForeColor.addTextListener(localTextListener);
        labelBackColor.addTextListener(localTextListener);
        foreColor.addTextListener(localTextListener);
        backColor.addTextListener(localTextListener);
    }


/**
 * Converts a string formatted as "rrggbb" to an awt.Color object
 */
private Color stringToColor(String paramValue)
{
    int red;
    int green;
    int blue;

    red = (Integer.decode("0x" + paramValue.substring(0,2))).intValue( );
    green = (Integer.decode("0x" + paramValue.substring(2,4))).intValue( );
    blue = (Integer.decode("0x" + paramValue.substring(4,6))).intValue( );

    return new Color(red,green,blue);
}


/**
 * Converts an awt.Color object to
 * a string formatted as "rrggbb".
 */
private String colorToString(Color colorValue)
```

```
{
    String sColorOut;

    if (colorValue.getRed( ) < 16)
    {
        sColorOut = "0" +
                    Integer.toString(colorValue.getRed( ),
                    16);
    }
    else
    {
        sColorOut = Integer.toString(colorValue.getRed( ),
                    16);
    }

    if (colorValue.getGreen( ) < 16)
    {
        sColorOut = sColorOut + "0" +
                    Integer.toString(colorValue.getGreen( ),
                    16);
    }
    else
    {
        sColorOut = sColorOut +
                    Integer.toString(colorValue.getGreen( ),
                    16);
    }

    if (colorValue.getBlue( ) < 16)
    {
        sColorOut = sColorOut + "0" +
                    Integer.toString(colorValue.getBlue( ),
                    16);
    }
    else
    {
        sColorOut = sColorOut +
                    Integer.toString(colorValue.getBlue( ),
                    16);
    }

    return sColorOut;
}
```

```
/**
 * External interface used by design tools to show properties of an applet.
 */
public String[][] getParameterInfo( )
{
    String[][] info =
    {
        { labelParam, "String", "Label string to be displayed" },
        { backgroundParam, "String", "Background color, format \"rrggbb\"" },
        { foregroundParam, "String", "Foreground color, format \"rrggbb\"" },
        { labelBackParam, "String", "Background label color, format \"rrggbb\"" },
        { labelForeParam, "String", "Foreground label color, format \"rrggbb\"" },
    };
    return info;
}


Label label1 = new Label( );

/**
 * Add some new labels to identify the other controls.
 */
Label label2 = new Label("Text Value:");
Label label3 = new Label("Label Foreground Color: ");
Label label4 = new Label("Label Background Color: ");
Label label5 = new Label("Display Foreground Color: ");
Label label6 = new Label("Display Background Color: ");

/**
 * Add some new controls that allow us to change the label
 * dynamically.
 */
TextField labelForeColor = new TextField( );
TextField labelBackColor = new TextField( );
TextField foreColor = new TextField( );
TextField backColor = new TextField( );


/**
 * Initializes values for the applet and its components
 */
void initForm( )
{
    // Set the colors.
    this.setBackground(Color.lightGray);
```

```
            this.setForeground(Color.black);

            // Initialize the label.
            label1.setText("label1");

            // Define the layout.
            setLayout(new GridLayout(5, 2, 0, 10));

            add(label2);
            add(label1);

            add(label3);
            add(labelForeColor);

            add(label4);
            add(labelBackColor);

            add(label5);
            add(foreColor);

            add(label6);
            add(backColor);
        }

/**
 * An instance of our special TextListener class.
 */
TextListener2 localTextListener = new TextListener2( );

/**
 * The TextListener2 class allows us to detect changes to the color
 * settings of the four labels and change them as appropriate. The
 * only criteria is that the user maintain 6 numbers in each label
 * for a change to take place.  Note that we do have to repaint the
 * background and foreground areas, but that any control changes
 * are reflected automatically.
 */

public class TextListener2 implements TextListener
{
    public void textValueChanged(TextEvent event)
    {
        if ((labelForeColor.getText( ).length( ) == 6) &&
            (labelBackColor.getText( ).length( ) == 6) &&
```

```
            (foreColor.getText( ).length( ) == 6) &&
            (backColor.getText( ).length( ) == 6))
    {

        // Set the colors to their new settings.
        setBackground(stringToColor(backColor.getText( )));
        setForeground(stringToColor(foreColor.getText( )));
        label1.setForeground(stringToColor(labelForeColor.getText( )));
        label1.setBackground(stringToColor(labelBackColor.getText( )));

        // The background color changes won't show up until
        // we repaint the affected areas.
        repaint( );
        label2.repaint( );
        label3.repaint( );
        label4.repaint( );
        label5.repaint( );
        label6.repaint( );
    }
  }
 }
}
```

At this point, you're probably saying that even this simple applet has too much code for comfort. However, most of the code is easy to understand once you break it apart a little. Some of the code is automatically produced for you by the wizard, but there are areas where we have to modify the default code. We won't cover any of the unchanged or standard code provided by the wizard in this section.

The init( ) method calls two other methods: initForm( ) and usePageParams( ). We'll be making most of our changes to these two methods first, then adding some new methods as needed to make the applet work properly. However, before we look at these areas, let's look at some applet-wide variable additions you'll need to make. If you look right under the init( ) method, you'll see that I've added two new parameters: one for the label background color and another for the label foreground color.

The other applet-wide variable additions appear between the getParameterInfo( ) and the initForm( ) method near the bottom of the listing. We need five new Labels to identify the controls displayed on the form, and four TextFields to allow the user to change the colors used on both the form and the text display label dynamically. We could have used a different technique for adding the identification labels using code like this in the initForm( ) method:

```
add(new Label("My component identification"));
```

There's only one problem using this second method—you'll find that it's impossible to perform a repaint of the display area later. Java provides more than a few ways to perform every task, but some of these methods won't work in specific situations. If you think you'll need to repaint the display area when working with an applet, every component on the form will need a name (otherwise, you can't access the component to repaint it).

Now that we have some parameter variables and new components to use, let's get the form displayed. That's where the initForm( ) method comes into play. The first two steps, setting the form color and initializing our text display label, are provided for you by the wizard. You will need to change the setLayout( ) method contents. Java provides several layouts that you can use to organize the components on your form. The BorderLayout( ) used by the wizard works fine for some situations, but not this one since there are too many components to display using the BorderLayout( ) method. The GridLayout( ) method provides a simple way to display the components without a lot of extra work. Obviously, you'll need to decide precisely how you want to lay your components out before deciding on which layout method to use.

Once we have a form and layout, it's time to add components. The rest of the initForm( ) method adds components to our grid layout (five rows by two columns). Notice that we haven't done anything with the components yet. All we've done is get the form ready for use. The next method we'll talk about, usePageParams( ), is where the components get configured for use and finally displayed.

The first thing we do in the usePageParams( ) method is define five constants containing default values for the parameters that the user will pass to the applet. The reason is simple: It's important that the applet be able to display an error message if the user doesn't provide everything needed. In addition, the two label color parameters aren't absolutely essential, so providing default values for them isn't a problem. We also need five variables to hold the final value of each parameter. These variables will allow us to manipulate the parameter values as needed to make the applet actually work. For example, we'll have to convert the color string to an actual color somewhere along the way, since a string containing color values won't do us much good. You'd also have to perform this kind of manipulation for other nonstring data types like numbers (we'll see how to perform these types of manipulation as the book progresses).

The next usePageParams( ) task is to retrieve the parameter values supplied by the user so that we can test to ensure they're actually usable. We'll use the getParameter( ) to get the parameters supplied to the applet.

Testing of the parameter values comes next. The getParameter( ) method returns null if the user hasn't supplied a particular value. All we need to do then is test the parameters to see if they're equal to null. The first if…then structure is supplied for you by the wizard. It checks to make sure that we have a label value, form foreground color, and form background color. If not, we assign default values to them. The second if…then structure does the same thing for the label foreground color and label background color values. The reason for using two structures (when one would theoretically do) is to make the applet a little more flexible. The user has a choice between mandatory and optional parameters. How you address this matter when you create an applet is determined entirely by parameter groupings (you wouldn't want a label foreground color without also supplying a background color) and need (there are situations where you can assign a default value without changing the applet's functionality).

We have everything needed to configure the components on the form, so the next section of the usePageParams( ) method assigns color values to each of our components. Note that only label1 requires a text value at this point, since we assigned values to the other labels during initialization. Notice the use of the stringToColor( ) method for converting our color string of six characters (two each of red, green, and blue) to an actual color.

Now that the form and components are set up, we can add some refinements. In this case, I display the current color values in the four TextFields that we set up earlier. Notice that I use a special colorToString( ) method to perform the task rather than display the parameter values that we retrieved earlier. The reason for this extra processing is that we want to get the actual display colors rather than the ones requested. The Java runtime engine may have had to perform some color translation due to limitations of the host machine, and it's important that the applet reflect these translation values.

The very last thing that we do in the usePageParams( ) method is set up four instances of the TextListener interface. For those of you who are familiar with the action( ) method, it won't work with Visual J++; you must use the newer Java-specific interface or WFC methods for handling component events like key presses or mouse clicks. In this case, we're looking for changes in the text displayed in the four TextField components, so we'll use the addTextListener( ) method to add a TextListener to the four components. The localTextListener variable referenced in the addTextListener( ) method is an instance of the TextListener2 class that I'll discuss next.

That takes us to the bottom of the listing, where you'll see a TextListener2 class that implements the TextListener interface. Notice that I nested this new class within the main Applet1 class. You have to do this to gain access to the Applet1 components.

The TextListener2 class is relatively easy to figure out. We add one method to it, textValueChanged( ). This is the same method provided by the TextListener interface. All we need to add to the textValueChanged( ) method is a way of determining when the user has typed in enough characters to change the display color. Once done, we use the same stringToColor( ) function as before to make the actual change. There's one difference here from the technique used in the usePageParams( ) method discussed earlier. Notice that we have to use the repaint( ) method to update the form and associated label components. The color change won't show up if you don't perform this extra step.

Modifying the HTML Test Page

The files automatically created for you by the Visual J++ Wizard include a test Web page. This Web page contains just about everything you need from the very beginning. You can change the page title if you want to make it a little more descriptive. However, the item that we're most interested in is our ability to change the applet's behavior using HTML tags. That's where the change we'll talk about in this section comes into play. Listing 4-12 shows the source code for the text HTML page.

Listing 4-12

```
<HTML>
<HEAD>
<META NAME="GENERATOR" Content="Microsoft Visual Studio 98">
<META HTTP-EQUIV="Content-Type" content="text/html">
<TITLE>Applet Test Page</TITLE>
</HEAD>
<BODY><!-- Insert HTML here -->
<APPLET code=Applet1.class
codeBase=file://C:\VS_60\Chapt04\VJApplet\height=200 name=Applet1 width=500>
  <PARAM NAME="foreground" VALUE="FFFFFF">
  <PARAM NAME="background" VALUE="008080">
  <PARAM NAME="label" VALUE="This string was passed from the HTML host.">

  <!-- Add the two new parameters -->
  <PARAM NAME="labelforeground" VALUE="0000FF">
  <PARAM NAME="labelbackground" VALUE="FFFFFF">
  </APPLET>


</BODY>
</HTML>
```

Most of the code shown here is automatically generated for you, so there isn't any need to discuss it. However, what you'll want to look at is the <APPLET> tag that appears halfway down the listing. Notice that the arrangement of this tag follows the tag used for displaying an ActiveX control rather closely. The first line tells the name of the applet we want to display. The codebase parameter tells where to find the applet. You'll need to change this value once you upload the applet and Web page to your Web site (otherwise, no one will be able to download and use the applet). There are also parameters that affect applet size and name.

The <PARAM> tags are where you'll make major changes to the way the applet reacts when the user opens the Web page. Three of the <PARAM> tags get supplied by the wizard when it creates the test page for you. You'll need to add two new <PARAM> tags to adjust the label color as shown in Listing 4-12. Remember that you can't supply just a foreground or background color, you must supply both or the applet will use the default color scheme. Obviously you can change this behavior if you so desire.

Testing the Result

We now have a completed applet and a Web page for testing it. Clicking the Start button on the Visual J++ standard toolbar will allow you to see the applet in its native

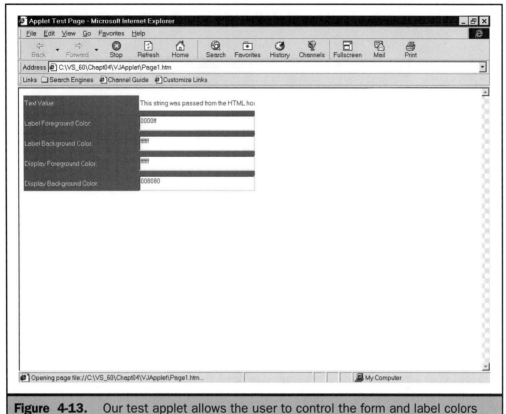

Figure 4-13. Our test applet allows the user to control the form and label colors dynamically, and the designer programmatically

environment, a Web browser (in this case, Internet Explorer 4). Figure 4-13 shows what our applet looks like in action.

As you can see, our applet starts using the label text and colors that the designer chose to use. However, you can modify the four TextField values to change the form background and foreground colors, along with those used by the label.

Visual InterDev

We're going to use Visual InterDev as the primary tool for creating Web pages in the book. For the most part, you'll find that using Visual InterDev is very much akin to using any form design tool. The difference, of course, is that you probably won't do a lot of coding using Visual InterDev unless you need to provide complex scripts for your Web page. Let's look at the process for creating a simple Web page. The following procedure will get you started:

1. Start Visual InterDev. You'll see a New Project dialog box like the one shown here:

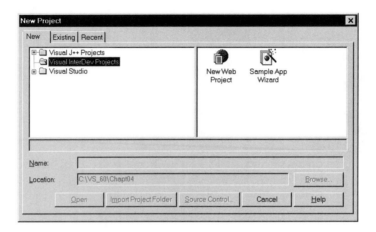

2. Open the Visual InterDev Projects folder.

3. Highlight the New Web Project option.

4. Type a name for your project in the Name field (our example uses SmplWeb), then click Open. Visual InterDev will display the Web Project Wizard - Step 1 of 4 dialog box shown here. There are three things you need to decide: What kind of Web server you'll use, whether you need secure access, and if you want to use Local or Master mode. Master mode will allow you better access to the project from a remote location. Unless you're working from a local network, you'll want to use the Master mode option. (We'll avoid security issues for this example, but cover them later in the book, in Chapter 12, when we talk about remote data access.)

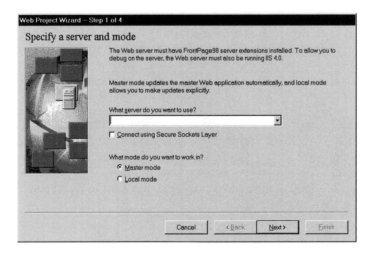

5. Type the name of your test server in the What server do you want to use? field.

6. Choose between the Master mode and Local mode options. Since we're working on test pages using a test Web server, I'm assuming in this procedure that you want to use Master mode.

Tip

Local mode allows you to work on a project locally, then update the files on the Web server manually. This is the mode that you'll want to use when working on projects on a production server since this option provides the least interruption in service to users who rely on the Web site. Master mode makes all of the changes automatically. You'll use it when working on a test server so that everyone working on the project will see your changes immediately. In addition, using Master mode means that you don't have to remember to make the changes manually, which means that you'll be less likely to lose important changes to your project.

7. Click Next. You'll see the Web Project Wizard - Step 2 of 4 dialog box shown here. This is where you'll decide on using an existing project or creating a new one. Since we're creating a new project, you can leave the settings as is.

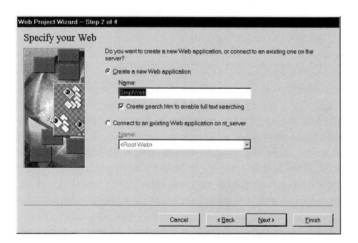

Note

The Create search.htm to enable full text searching option on the Web Project Wizard - Step 2 of 4 dialog box tells the wizard to automatically create a generic search page for your project. However, this option assumes certain setups on your server. For one thing, you need to install the Microsoft Index Server (or a suitable substitute). This option doesn't magically add indexing capabilities to a server that doesn't possess them. You also need to enable indexing for the Web site. If you're using Internet Information Server (IIS) 4, you'll find this option on the Home Directory tab of the Web Site Properties dialog box. You can access the Web Site Properties dialog box using the Microsoft Management Console (MMC).

8. Click Next. You'll see the Web Project Wizard - Step 3 of 4 dialog box shown here. This is where you'll choose a layout for your Web page. Using layouts helps keep your Web site organized and neat looking. If every page has a similar layout, then users will know where to find specific pieces of information. You'll find that using layouts also speeds the process of placing controls and adding new features. We'll use layouts later in the book to speed the process of creating test pages.

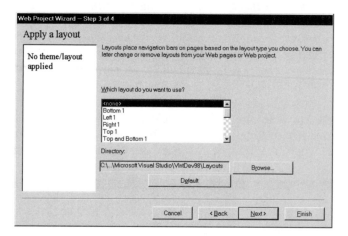

9. Click Next. You'll see the Web Project Wizard - Step 4 of 4 dialog box shown here. This is where you'll choose a theme for your Web page. Using themes gives your Web pages a consistent look. All of the Web pages will use similar art, contain the same types of features, use the same colors, and in general look about the same. This is a great option to use with large teams. Otherwise, you'll end up with the ransom note look that we all hate to deal with on other people's Web sites. We'll look at themes a little later in the book. For now, we'll keep the Web project simple by using a minimum of bells and whistles.

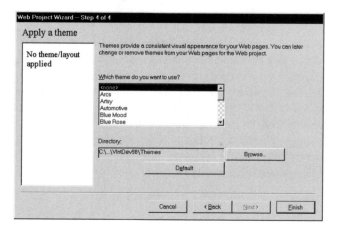

10. Click Finish to complete the project shell.

Normally, you'd start creating a start page for your project at this point, but we'll look at the process of designing pages later in the book. For right now, it's important that you know how to create a project. However, it would also be nice to test what we've done so far, and without a start page you can't do that. Look for the Search.htm entry in Project Explorer. You'll see it sitting near or at the bottom of items listed in Project Explorer. Right-click on Search.htm and you'll see a context menu like the one shown here:

Select the Set as Start Page option. You now have a start page with which to test your project. All you need to do now is click the Start button. What you'll see is a dialog box like the one shown in Figure 4-14. This is the default Search page that the Web Project Wizard creates for you. As you can see, it's plain but very serviceable. You'll soon learn that most users find this particular feature indispensable on a Web

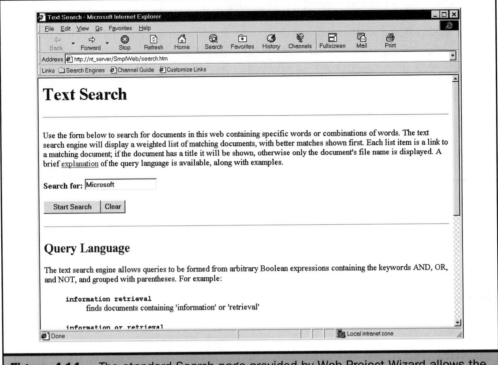

Figure 4-14.   The standard Search page provided by Web Project Wizard allows the user to find information on your Web site quickly

site since there isn't any other good way to find information. The benefit to you of providing a Search page is that you'll spend less time supporting the user and helping them to find the information they need.

Chapter 5

Understanding the Other Visual Studio Tools

Visual Studio provides you with a wealth of utility-level tools in addition to the main programming language offerings. The purpose of these tools varies, but for the most part they're designed to make writing and testing code easier. In other words, you need to know what tasks these tools perform to get the most out of Visual Studio as a whole. Look at these as the hand tools that any good craftsman would have in addition to the latest power tools provided by the main programming language packages. Just as it takes a combination of tools to build a house or create a meal with eye appeal, it takes a combination of programming tools to craft a really great application.

The following sections are going to provide you with an overview of the task performed by each Visual Studio utility program. These sections aren't meant as a full-fledged demonstration of every task the utility can perform. What you'll walk away with from this chapter is enough information to use these utilities as you build the various applications found in this book.

 Consider this list of tools as the default that every programmer starts out with. Any programmer will recognize these tools as the minimum required to get the job done. Just like any other craft, programmers have access to a variety of "luxury" tools. The professional tools that you use should augment the capabilities of the tools that we'll look at in this chapter.

ActiveX Control Test Container

Component technology has freed many programmers from the need to perform some types of repetitive tasks. For example, the addition of standard dialog box support, like the File Open dialog box, to Windows has reduced the need for everyone to create their own version of this very standard application feature. Command buttons, labels, and text controls have all had their share in reducing the programmer's workload as well. Consider what it would take to write a modern application using only the C code that programmers of the past had to use and you can see why component technology is so important.

Microsoft's latest term for component technology is ActiveX. Creating an ActiveX control allows you to encapsulate within a single object some of the functionality that you'll need for every program you create (or at least a good many of them). ActiveX controls appear everywhere, including Web pages and applications.

ActiveX Control Test Container will work with a variety of objects, not just ActiveX controls. For example, you'll find that many Visual J++ design time controls (DTCs) work just fine with this utility. In addition, most Java classes also work fine.

Because of the faith that many programmers place in the ActiveX controls they use, it's important to test controls fully. That's when the ActiveX Control Test Container comes into play. This utility allows you to test the features of your ActiveX control in a special environment designed to help you locate flaws quickly. In addition, the ActiveX Control Test Container utility allows you to test your control outside of the programming language IDE or test application, where errors could get introduced outside of the control itself. Here's what the ActiveX Control Test Container looks like with the ClockIt control that we'll create in Chapter 8 loaded:

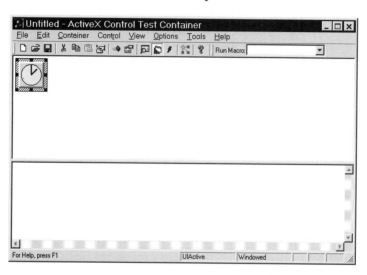

Note   *To load an ActiveX control in the test container, use the Edit | Insert New Control command. You can also insert an ActiveX control into the current test container from a stream or from storage using the appropriate Edit menu command.*

The following sections are going to explore a few of the more important tasks you can perform with ActiveX Control Test Container. You'll likely need to perform one or more of these tasks as the book progresses. For example, when using an ActiveX control in a multilanguage environment, you'll normally want to test it using this utility. As a minimum, you'll want to check to see that you can access the methods and properties that the control provides.

Checking Methods and Properties

There have been a number of situations when I thought I had defined a property or method properly only to have it fail to appear when needed in the final application. In some cases, the failure isn't anything in my code, but a difference in the way two languages support ActiveX controls. Unfortunately, unless you can isolate the control and test it in an independent test environment, you'll have trouble figuring out precisely what the problem is.

ActiveX Control Test Container allows you to check the availability of both methods and properties. In addition, you can change these features of your ActiveX control to see if they work as intended. Let's look at properties first. The normal method used to change the properties is through a property page (which is one of the reasons I normally include a property page for the most important value. Simply click on the Properties button (or use the Edit | Properties command) to display control's Properties dialog box. Here's a Properties dialog box for the OCXExmpl control that we created in Chapter 4:

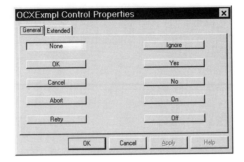

If you'll remember from that example, there was an OnOff property that we didn't put on the property page. This property allows you to turn the button into an On/Off button when set to TRUE. Even if your properties aren't listed in their entirety on property pages, you can still access them by looking through the list of methods supported by your control. You'll find that ActiveX Control Test Container creates a get and set method for every property your control supports. However, it's still easier to access properties through a property page for the most part.

Let's talk about methods for a moment. All you need to do to look at the methods your control supports is use the Control | Invoke Methods command (you can also click the Invoke Methods button on the toolbar). In addition to the get and set methods for various properties, you'll find all of the other methods that your control supports in the Invoke Methods dialog box shown here:

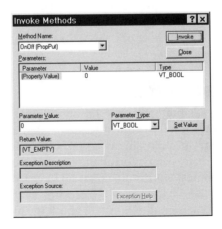

Notice that this is the set method (indicated by PropPut in the Method Name field) for the OnOff property. If you wanted to change this property, you could type a **-1** (for TRUE) in the Parameter Value field and click Invoke. ActiveX Control Test Container will send this value to the control and then the control will perform the required action.

Some methods will have more than one parameter. You can highlight the parameter in the Parameter list, change the value in the Parameter Value field, then click Set Value. This method will allow you to set multiple properties before you try to invoke the method. In some cases, you must set a group of properties prior to invoking the method to get the desired results.

Tracking Events

Events are the basis of a lot of ActiveX control activities. ActiveX Control Test Container has two windows. The upper window displays the controls you have loaded for testing, while the bottom window displays any output from the control. Output, in this case, occurs (at least in most cases) because some event has fired.

ActiveX Control Test Container provides two levels of event logging. The first level is at the container level. To set these logging options, use the Options | Logging... command to display the Logging Options dialog box shown here:

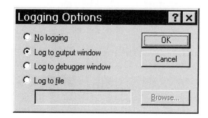

As you can see, the Logging Options dialog box allows you to choose where the logging output appears. As mentioned earlier, the default setting sends any log entries to the Output window. You can also choose to stop logging all events from all controls that you currently have loaded or to place the log entries in a file. The Log to debugger window option is supposed to send the log entries to the debug window of your favorite programming language product, but support for this feature is flaky at best.

The second level of logging is at the control level. Normally, ActiveX Control Test Container logs all control events, but that can lead to overload and make the detection of a specific event more difficult. It's important to select a specific set of events to monitor, in most cases, if you want to get optimal results. You must select the control that you want to work with before using the Control | Logging... command to display the Control Logging Options dialog box shown next:

There are three tabs on the Control Logging Options dialog box. The first contains a list of all of the events that your control can fire. For example, when a user clicks the control, it normally fires an event. The second tab contains a list of all the standard property changes, not necessarily all of the properties that the control provides. In the case of the On/Off switch, you'll find that only the Caption, Enabled, and Font property changes get tracked. These logging events only get fired if an actual change takes place, not if the client requests the current value or the ability to change the property. The third tab contains a list of property edit requests. In this case, you'll only find the Caption and Enabled properties listed since the Font property uses a special property page. This logging event gets fired whenever the client requests the ability to edit the property. In other words, a log entry will appear even if no actual change takes place. Here's what the Property Edit Requests tab looks like:

Notice that the Property Edit Requests tab allows you to do something that the other logging options don't. The Always, Prompt, and Never options allow you to tell ActiveX Control Test Container what to do with edit requests. In most cases, you'll want to allow the control to accept changes as normal. However, there are some situations when you may want the control to prompt you before it grants permission or to deny permission so that the property value remains constant during testing. Whatever option you choose, the edit request event will still get logged so that you can maintain a record of control activity.

You can load more than one ActiveX control at a time to see how two or more controls interact. This is especially important when working with data-related controls like those used to set the database and table source.

Testing Persistence

Persistence is the ability of an ActiveX control to retain its values from one session to the next. In most cases, you want your control to retain any property values that the user sets. Read-only properties, on the other hand, may change from session to session and therefore don't require persistence. It doesn't matter whether a property is persistent or not, you still have to ensure that it reacts as intended.

ActiveX Control Test Container provides three levels of persistence testing: property bag, stream, and storage. Generally, it's a good idea to test your control in all three environments to make sure that the persistence it provides actually works. Two of the testing methods—stream and storage—require you to save the control to disk, then read it back into the test container. The third method, property bag, provides instant feedback.

Let's look at the property bag method first. Set the control properties as needed for the test (verify that they are indeed set). Once you've set the properties, use the Control | Save to Property Bag command to display the Property Bag dialog box shown here:

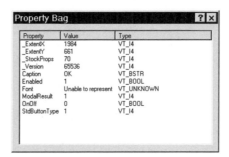

All you need to do now is make sure that the settings in the property bag match the settings you made on the control. If they don't, then your control has failed the most basic test of persistence.

The Property Bag dialog box provides you with the opportunity to check more than just the persistence of your control—it also allows you to see how a client views your properties. It's important to note inconsistencies in both the value and type of the properties that your control provides. Some subtle errors, like the size of an integer, are easy to spot this way.

The other two persistence tests rely on saving the control to disk, then reading it back in. If the control's persistence is working properly, then persistent properties should have the same value as when you set the control up in the first place. This six-step procedure will work for testing both storage and stream methods of persistence.

1. Set the control's properties.

2. Use the Control | Save to Stream or Control | Save to Storage command to display a Save As dialog box.

3. Type the filename you want to use for storing the control (properties set), then click Save.

4. Close ActiveX Control Test Container, then start it again.

5. Use the Edit | Insert Control from Stream or Edit | Insert Control from Storage command to display the control.

6. Check the control's properties to ensure they are the same (for persistent properties) as when you stored the control on disk. It's equally important to check nonpersistent controls for some default value when supplied, or a random value if not.

API Text Viewer

The API Text Viewer was originally designed for Visual Basic users. It's a simple tool that allows you to view the contents of the API declare files in an easy-to-read format. In addition, you can search the API for specific pieces of information. Finally, this utility allows you to cut and paste API defines and constants, which reduces the amount of work you need to do to use the Windows API. Here's what the API Text Viewer looks like:

Using API Text Viewer is easy. All you need to do is load a declare file like Win32api.TXT. As an alternative, you can load a database file containing the same information as the declare file would (API Text Viewer provides a utility for performing this task). Once you have a declare file loaded, choose the API Type that you want to view: Constants, Declares, or Types. To search for specific API information, just type a value in the blank provided.

Getting the information you find from API Text Viewer to Visual Basic is easy. Just highlight the entry you're interested in, like ClearCommBreak, then click Add. (Note that you can choose either a Public or Private declaration.) You'll see the declare appear in the Selected Items list like this:

```
Public Declare Function ClearCommBreak Lib "kernel32" Alias
"ClearCommBreak" (ByVal nCid As Long) As Long
```

The Copy button allows you to copy a single entry (you must highlight the entry first) or all of the entries in the Selected Items list will be copied to the clipboard. Use the Clear button to remove all entries from the Selected Items list. You can remove a single entry by clicking the Remove button.

AVI Editor

The AVI Editor is a very simple tool for working with AVI and other multimedia files. It comes in handy for purposes including cutting the size of a multimedia file (editing) and merging a sound file with a visual file. In addition, you can use it to perform a frame-by-frame examination of a file or to determine the quality of the presentation. Here's what AVI Editor looks like with an AVI file loaded (note that the AVI file includes a stereo audio track):

Tip	*The Cut and Paste option of this program provides a very convenient way of getting still images from a filmed multimedia presentation. All you need to do is choose the frame that you want to use for a presentation, highlight it, and copy it to the clipboard. You can use any standard graphics program to paste the image and then save it on disk for future use. The same feature allows you to create audio segments for future use or to insert new tracks into an existing presentation.*

The AVI Editor utility controls are simple. You'll find the usual Cut, Copy, and Paste commands on the Edit menu, along with a special Info command that allows you to view and set the properties of the sound or video source that you're working with. (In most cases, you'll use the properties displayed by the Set Stream Info dialog box displayed with the Edit | Info command for informational purposes only.) The Zoom menu allows you to change the size of the presentation, an especially useful feature when looking at video presentations. On the File menu, you'll find a Merge command that allows you to combine two multimedia files. You can use it to attach a sound source to a video. Finally, the Play menu contains options for starting and stopping playback of the multimedia file that you're currently viewing. (There isn't an option for slow playback or pausing, which can make editing the multimedia file more difficult—you'll find it harder to stop at a precise location in the file.)

Data Object Viewer

You're working with a data object that supports the IDataObject interface and want to know more about it. The Data Object Viewer is designed to do just that. It helps you determine how a data object will react when you perform certain standard operations on it, which in turn helps you build an application better suited to working with that kind of data object.

There are two ways to work with data objects when using the Data Object Viewer. You can either drag and drop the object onto the viewer (as in the case of dragging a file from an Explorer window to the Data Object Viewer window) or copy the data object to the clipboard and work with it using clipboard-specific methods. Each method of working with the data object has specific uses. In most cases, however, you'll get more information about the data object if you work with it using the clipboard, so that's what we'll explore in this section. (Since working with a drag-and-drop object is about the same as working with the clipboard, the information provided here applies equally to both manipulation methods.)

The first thing you'll need to do is get a copy of the object onto the clipboard. For the purposes of this discussion, I've copied the Word document that I'm working with right now to the clipboard. The results you get when working with Data Object Viewer depend a great deal on the kind of data that you're working with and the capabilities of the application that supports it.

If you're interested in working with the data object using the clipboard, then you need to know what clipboard formats it supports. Use the Clipboard | View Clipboard Data Object command to display a list of the formats supported by the object currently stored on the clipboard. Here's an example of what you might see for a Word document:

```
IDataObject Viewer - OLE Build 23.824                                  _ □ ×
 File   Clipboard   Data Object   Options   Help
Object Descriptor       ptd={NULL}   dwApsect={Content  }   lindex={-1}   tymed={hGlobal  }
Rich Text Format        ptd={NULL}   dwApsect={Content  }   lindex={-1}   tymed={hGlobal  }
CF_TEXT                 ptd={NULL}   dwApsect={Content  }   lindex={-1}   tymed={hGlobal  }
Unknown Clipformat      ptd={NULL}   dwApsect={Content  }   lindex={-1}   tymed={hGlobal  }
CF_METAFILEPICT         ptd={NULL}   dwApsect={Content  }   lindex={-1}   tymed={MFPict   }
Embed Source            ptd={NULL}   dwApsect={Content  }   lindex={-1}   tymed={IStorage }
Link Source             ptd={NULL}   dwApsect={Content  }   lindex={-1}   tymed={IStream  }
Link Source Descripto   ptd={NULL}   dwApsect={Content  }   lindex={-1}   tymed={hGlobal  }
ObjectLink              ptd={NULL}   dwApsect={Content  }   lindex={-1}   tymed={hGlobal  }
Hyperlink               ptd={NULL}   dwApsect={Content  }   lindex={-1}   tymed={hGlobal  }
```

It's no surprise that Word documents support both the CF_TEXT (standard text) and Rich Text Format clipboard formats. You can also display the Word document as a graphic or embed it in another object. The ptd column of this display tells you what target device this object is designed to work with (what it has been formatted for). Since you can work with Word documents with a wide range of devices, this value is set to NULL (as it will be for most of the data objects that you work with). The dwApsect value tells you what role this data serves. In this case we're looking at content. Other common role values include Thumbnail, Icon, and DocPrint. The index field isn't commonly used for anything, but you can see its purpose in the OLE2 Programmer's Reference. Finally, the tymed column tells you what type of media may be used to transfer the data. In most cases, you'll see a value of hGlobal, which means that you can transfer it using any acceptable method. Note that some clipboard formats do require special handling. For example, if you want to embed the Word document in our example, then you have to use IStorage to transfer the data.

Another bit of information you need to know about a data object is the object descriptor. You access this information using the Data Object | Show Object Descriptor command. Here's what the object descriptor looks like for our example Word document:

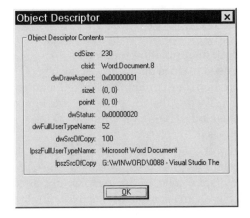

Notice that the Object Descriptor dialog box tells you all about the data object with regard to creating a link. The dialog box includes important information like the class ID (clsid field) and the data source.

Testing is another important feature of the Data Object Viewer. There are three essential application-specific tests that you can run: data format enumeration, data linking, and data embedding. When testing data linking using the Data Object | OleQueryLinkFromData command or data embedding using the Data Object | OleQueryCreateFromData command, all you get is a simple success or failure message.

DDE Spy

For those of you who thought that DDE was dead, OLE really has failed to kill it completely. Microsoft Exchange, for example, relies on DDE fairly heavily. On the other hand, you won't find that DDE is used very extensively at all when it comes to data manipulation because working with OLE is a better choice.

While it's unlikely that you'll make extensive use of DDE in your next application, you may find a situation when this older technology will work better than anything else in your programming arsenal. Unfortunately, DDE can be a little hard to debug, so you'll probably need to keep DDE Spy by your side whenever you use DDE in an application.

Let's take a look at a few of the features this utility provides. There are only a few choices to make when it comes to configuration. First, you need to decide where you want to send the output of the conversation items that you want to track or monitor. In most cases, you'll want to send the output to the screen since your only other alternatives are a file (which can be useful for large applications with a lot of discussions, but not for your run-of-the-mill application) or a debugger screen.

The second thing you need to decide is what you want to "spy" on. There are two menus for these items: Monitor and Track. Anything you track is going to be active. In other words, if you choose to track the current conversations, you'll see an active display of any servers and clients engaged in a conversation. Every item that you can track relies on a specially designed screen. For example, the Active Conversations window tells you about the service that's involved in the conversation, the name of the client, the name of the server, and the topic being discussed.

Monitoring DDE is more of a static process that involves tracking various message types. For example, you can track when a client sends or posts messages to the DDE server. The Message Filters and Callback Filters options on the Monitor menu allow you to select specific messages to monitor. Here's an example of what DDE Spy sees when you start Internet Explorer to view a JPG file on disk (all of the message-monitoring features are turned on in this case):

```
DDESpy                                                          _ □ ×
 Output  Monitor  Track  About...
Task:0x2b76 Time:27046251 hwndTo=0xf6c Message(Posted)=Ack:
             hwndFrom=0xdc0, lParam=0x3396000c
             App=0xc("#12")status=c()
             Topic=Item=0x3396("#13206")
Task:0x6076 Time:27046276 hwndTo=0xdc0 Message(Posted)=Terminate:
             hwndFrom=0xf6c, lParam=0x0

             dFrom=0xf6c, lParam=0x0
Task:0x6076 Time:27048062 Callback:
             Type=Disconnect, fmt=0x0("?"), hConv=0x1e0dc0, hsz1=0x0("")
             hsz2=0x0(""), hData=0x0, dwData1=0x0, dwData2=0x0
             return=0x0
Task:0x2b76 Time:27048088 hwndTo=0xf6c Message(Posted)=Terminate:
             hwndFrom=0xdc0, lParam=0x0

             dFrom=0xdc0, lParam=0x0
```

Dependency Walker (Depends)

Have you ever sent out an application and found out later that the person using it didn't have all the files needed to use it? Most of us have done that at one time or another and, in most cases, it wasn't our fault that a file or two was missing. It seems as if every file in Windows relies on every other file in some way—trying to untie this knot is something even Houdini would have had a problem doing.

Dependency Walker (or Depends as it's listed on the Microsoft Visual Studio 6.0 Tools menu) helps you prevent the problem of the missing file. It lists every file that an application, DLL, or other executable file depends on to execute. You can use the output of this application to create a list of required files for your application. Loading a file for examination is as easy as using the File | Open command to open the executable file that you want to examine. Here's an example of the output generated for the OCXExmple.OCX file that we created in Chapter 4:

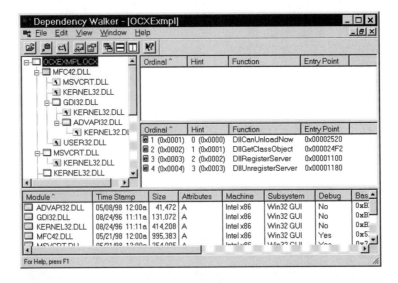

| Tip | It's interesting to note that Dependency Walker doesn't include any kind of print functionality. (Microsoft may add a print feature in a later release.) Fortunately, you can highlight a list of items you want to print, press CTRL-C to copy them to the clipboard, then use the Paste function in your favorite word processor to create a document you can print for future reference. |

As you can see, this application provides you with a lot of information about the dependencies of your file. In the upper-left corner is a hierarchical view of dependencies, starting with the executable file that you want to check. To the right of this hierarchical view are two lists. The upper list tells you which functions the parent executable imports from the current file. The lower list tells you which functions this executable exports for other executables to use. At the very bottom, you'll see an alphabetical list of all of the files along with pertinent information like the executable file's version number and whether you used a debug version of that file while creating and testing your application.

DocFile Viewer

When a user sees something like a Word document, what they see is the content they've created, not how the document is put together. In fact, Word makes the construction of a compound document pretty much invisible to the end user. That's why DocFile Viewer is such an important tool.

This relatively simple program allows you to take a compound document apart to see how various elements within it are put together. You can use this information for a variety of tasks, including the creation of your own compound document applications. Here's what a typical DocFile Viewer display looks like with a Word document loaded (there are two embedded files in this particular document):

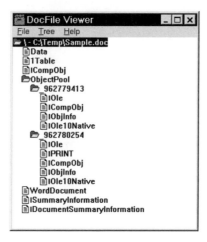

As you can see, the main display provides a hierarchical layout of the various compound document elements, including the two embedded files. Of course, you may still need additional information about the document. For example, you may need to know how the various elements look at the hexadecimal level so that you can reproduce them in your application. Double-click on any document elements (not folders) and you'll see a window like the one shown here:

```
Stream: ICompObj [0x0000006A bytes]                    _ □ x
0x00000000: 01 00 FE FF 03 0A 00 00  FF FF FF FF 06 09 02 00   ...............
0x00000010: 00 00 00 00 C0 00 00 00  00 00 00 46 18 00 00 00   ...........F....
0x00000020: 4D 69 63 72 6F 73 6F 66  74 20 57 6F 72 64 20 44   Microsof t Word D
0x00000030: 6F 63 75 6D 65 6E 74 00  0A 00 00 00 4D 53 57 6F   ocument. ....MSWo
0x00000040: 72 64 44 6F 63 00 10 00  00 00 57 6F 72 64 2E 44   rdDoc.... Word.D
0x00000050: 6F 63 75 6D 65 6E 74 2E  38 00 F4 39 B2 71 00 00   ocument. 8..9.q..
0x00000060: 00 00 00 00 00 00 00 00  00 00                     ............
```

Error Lookup

Sometimes the simplest utilities are the most useful. Have you ever spent time scratching your head trying to figure out what that weird error number was all about? Error Lookup will convert an error number to some text that will make things a little clearer. While the text isn't always as self-explanatory as it should be, at least you'll have some idea of where to look for additional information about the error your application is experiencing. Here's a sample of what the Error Lookup utility looks like in action:

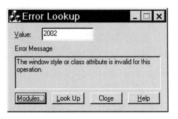

Tip   *You don't have to enter the error number for Error Lookup manually in most cases. All you need to do is drag and drop it from the Developer Studio or other OLE-enabled application window. Failing drag-and-drop capability, you can also highlight the error value, copy it to the clipboard by pressing CTRL-C, and then paste it in Error Lookup by pressing CTRL-V (paste).*

Note that Error Lookup assumes that you need the text associated with a system error number. You can load additional modules for error definition as well as using the Modules… button. Just type the module name and click Add when you see the Additional Modules for Error Lookup dialog box. If you decide that you no longer need the error message definitions contained in a specific module, click the Modules… button, highlight the module name in the list, and click Remove.

Heap Walk Utility

Memory is the one resource that every application has to have in order to run. It's no wonder then that Visual Studio includes a utility—Heap Walker—for viewing memory. This utility will help you find out a number of things about how the applications running on your machine are using memory. Here's one of the most common views that you'll find in Heap Walker; it shows the global heap:

```
HeapWalker- (Main Heap)                              _ □ ×
File  Walk  Sort  Object  Add!
ADDRESS   HANDLE    SIZE LOCK     FLG HEAP OWNER      TYPE
0000C7E0                 0                            Sentinel
0000C7E0  0117     46176 P1       F        KERNEL     Code 1
00017C40  1D5F      4512 P1       F   Y    AUDDRIVE   DGroup
00018DE0  1D1F      1824 P1       F        AUDMPU     Code 1
00019500  1CFF       512 P1       F   Y    AUDMPU     DGroup
00019700  1CDF       320 P1       F        MSACMMAP   Code 3
00019840  1C5F       288 P1       F        MMTASK     Private
00019960  016E        64                   KERNEL     Private
000199A0  36CE        32                   PWRCHUTE   Data
000199C0  012F      9600 P1       F        KERNEL     Code 4
0001BF40  1B1F       288 P1       F        Mprexe     Private
0001C060  2827      1024 P1       F        NETWARE    Private
0001C460  3087       576 P1       F        NETWARE    Private
0001C6A0  307F       576 P1       F        NETWARE    Private
0001C8E0  2F17       288 P1       F        NWPOPUP    Private
0001CA00  2DC7       288 P1       F        Mdm        Private
0001CB20  2CC7       288 P1       F        Rpcss      Private
0001CC40  2B07       288 P1       F        Explorer   Private
0001CD60  2D3F       288 P1       F        ESSDAEMN   Private
0001CE80  2957       288 P1       F        Systray    Private
0001CFA0  3947       288 P1       F        Loadwc     Private
0001D0C0  318F       288 P1       F        Winword    Private
0001D1E0  3867       288 P1       F        RUNDLL     Private
0001D300  2CDE        64                   GDI        Private Bitmap
0001D340  2D16        64                   GDI        Private Bitmap
```

Notice that every entry in the list includes the address of the memory, the memory handle, how much memory is allocated, the number and type of locks (blank if the memory isn't locked), any flags associated with the memory, whether there is a local heap, the owner of the memory, and the type of memory being viewed. However, all of this information doesn't do you much good unless you can associate it in some way. That's where the various Sort menu options come into play. You can use these options to reorder the data in a way that makes patterns obvious or allows you to perform some type of analysis. For example, you can sort by module if you want to see all of the memory usage for your application. The default sorting method is by address, which allows you to see where things are located in memory but doesn't necessarily tell you much about how the memory is used.

Tip

You can use the Object | LocalWalk command to display local heap information if a memory object has a local heap. Look at the Heap column of the global heap display to determine if a memory object has a local heap. A "Y" in the column indicates there is a local heap.

There are a number of memory views that you can select in Heap Walk. The most common is the global memory view that you can display using the Walk | Walk Heap command. Less common views include a least recently used memory and free memory spaces. You can also choose to display the global heap with or without garbage collection. Displaying the global heap with garbage collection removes old data that may confuse troubleshooting efforts. On the other hand, you may want to leave the old data in place so that you can see what objects have been discarded.

Heap Walk doesn't stop with an overview of memory allocation on your machine. You can get a detailed view of what that memory contains as well. Just double-click the memory object that you want to view and you'll see a detail view that looks like this:

```
Global Object - 0001DF40 49E7      288 P1      F      Ocxtest  Private  _ □ ✕
0000  CD 20 E7 4A 00 9A F0 FE 11 D6 B7 8C 7E 0C 52 23   Í çJ..ŏþ.Ö..~.R#
0010  79 FD 08 00 F0 0A A7 00 01 01 01 00 02 FF FF FF   yý..ŏ.§......ÿÿÿ
0020  FF FF FF FF FF FF FF FF FF FF FF FF 5F 49 28 02   ÿÿÿÿÿÿÿÿÿÿÿÿ_I(.
0030  55 0C 14 00 18 00 F4 1D FF FF FF FF 00 00 CE 01   U....ô.ÿÿÿÿ..Î.
0040  07 0A F7 3A 00 00 00 00 00 00 00 00 00 00 00 00   ..÷:............
0050  CD 21 CB 00 00 00 00 00 00 00 00 00 20 20 20 20   Í!Ë.........
0060  20 20 20 20 20 20 20 20 00 00 00 00 20 20 20 20       ....
0070  20 20 20 20 20 20 20 20 00 00 00 00 00 00 00 00       .....
0080  00 0D 43 4F 4E 20 4C 49 4E 45 53 3D 34 33 0D 00   ..CON LINES=43..
0090  00 00 00 00 00 00 00 00 00 00 00 00 00 00 00 00   ................
00A0  00 00 00 00 00 00 00 00 00 00 00 00 00 00 00 00   ................
00B0  00 00 00 00 00 00 00 00 00 00 00 00 00 00 00 00   ................
00C0  00 00 00 00 00 00 00 00 00 00 00 00 00 00 00 00   ................
00D0  00 00 00 00 00 00 00 00 00 00 00 00 00 00 00 00   ................
00E0  00 00 00 00 00 00 00 00 00 00 00 00 00 00 00 00   ................
00F0  00 00 00 00 00 00 00 00 00 00 00 00 00 00 00 00   ................
0100  5E 12 30 8C 01 80 00 00 00 00 00 06 53 59 53   ^.0.........SYS
0110  54 45 4D 00 00 03 57 45 50 0A 00 04 5F 5F 47 50   TEM...WEP..._GP
```

Help Workshop

All applications require some type of help file support, most rely on the HLP (help) file that has been with us since the days of Windows 3.*x*. In days gone by, creating a help file was a time-intensive task that involved writing massive quantities of text files. To make matters worse, you had to compile these files with a DOS command line utility that spewed out hardly recognizable error messages of dubious origin.

Help Workshop is one of the few utilities provided with Visual Studio that's not totally complete by itself. You still need a text editor that can produce rich text format (RTF) files. A word processor like Microsoft Word should work just fine—it's what I use.

There's a lot of work involved in creating a good help file. Help Workshop is one of the most complex utilities provided with Visual Studio. As a result, the sections that follow provide only a glimpse at what you'll need to do to create a help file for your application.

Note *If the Microsoft utilities don't fulfill all your help file-writing needs, then look at the Windows 95 Winhelp Tools and Utilities site at http://win95.daci.net/webwhelp.htm. There are a variety of products at this site designed to meet just about every need. For example, the Help Maker Plus utility is designed as a complete replacement for the Microsoft Help Compiler. Another good site to visit is the WinHelp WWW Index at http://www.hyperact.com/winhelp/FTP_and_file_Archives/index.html. While this site doesn't contain any helpful information, it does have a wealth of links that take you to Windows Help-specific sites. For example, you'll find a link to the RTF file specification and another for the SHED file format. You'll also find links for places that provide alternative help-file compilers and design utilities.*

Visual C++ Considerations

Visual C++ requires you to perform an extra step before you actually start to create your help script or make file. Fortunately, that extra step will save you some time later on, especially if you remember to do it before you start working on the RTF or make files. You need to use the MakeHM (make help map) utility located in your Visual C++ BIN directory to create a help map before you do anything else. (Some Visual Studio users will find the MakeHM utility in the Program Files\Microsoft Visual Studio\ Common\Tools directory if they've used the default directory locations during setup.) All you need to do is type the following at the command prompt to create the help map you'll need later on to link the help file to the application:

```
MAKEHM ID_,HID_,0x10000 RESOURCE.H MY.HM
```

What you'll get is a listing of the help IDs in your application like the one shown in Listing 5-1. These help identifiers will allow you to make the link between Visual C++ and your help file, as we'll see later. For right now, all you need to know is that you'll include that list of help IDs in your help file. You'll also use the help ID names in your help script.

isting 5-1
```
HID_CANCEL_EDIT_CNTR              0x18000
HID_CANCEL_EDIT_SRVR             0x18001
HID_UNDERLINE                    0x18006
HID_STRIKETHROUGH                0x18007
HID_BOLD                         0x18008
HID_ITALIC                       0x18009
HID_FONT_DIALOG                  0x1800A
HID_VIEW_FORMATTOOLBAR           0x1800B
HID_FORMAT_FONT2                 0x18010
HID_HELP_CONTENTS                0x18012
HID_HELP_WHATSTHIS               0x18013
```

Creating the Script Files

Help Workshop requires a minimum of two files: The help script and a make file. The make file is created as part of the process of defining the help file. That's the part of the picture that Help Workshop provides for you in addition to the compilation of the script into a help file.

You'll need a word processor to create the help script. I normally use Microsoft Word to create the help script, since it provides full RTF support and it's my word processor of choice when writing.

Note	*It doesn't matter which word processor you use—you could even use a programmer's editor if you'd like. The only requirement to use the Microsoft Help Compiler is that the script file be in RTF format. Fortunately, RTF is really an ASCII file containing special formatting commands. You'll want to be careful about using a text editor created strictly with the CRichEdit MFC class, since older versions of this class don't implement some of the RTF commands you'll really need to create a help file. The CRichEdit class provided with Visual C++ 5.0 and above still isn't as complete as a dedicated word processor, but it should work fine for creating help files.*

There are several steps to creating the help file script. The first thing you'll want to do is separate the various help file sections. You do this by adding a hard page break before each new section. The page break is symbolized as the \page statement in an RTF file. (I'll be including some of the more important RTF statements in my discussion so that you can troubleshoot any problems in your RTF file, if necessary.)

Adding one or more footnotes to each heading comes next. Footnotes are used for a variety of hyperlink functions. For example, the search words for your index will come from this source. You'll also use footnotes to define links between words in the glossary and the help file. Table 5-1 shows a partial list of footnotes. You'll find that these are the footnotes you use most often. You should also check the documentation for the Microsoft Help Compiler for additional ideas—there are times when those alternatives to the standard footnote come in handy. So what do you type in the footnote? You have to add one of several things, depending on the footnote types. For example, when using the # footnote, you add the name of a hyperlink. Make sure you read the text that follows each footnote in the table to learn about any requirements for using them. It's extremely important to create unique names for each of your footnotes. Descriptive names are also essential since you'll have to remember what those names mean later. One thing that you need to remember is that hyperlink names, like variables, don't contain spaces. Footnotes are symbolized by the <footnote type>{\footnote <text>} RTF file statement.

Footnote Type	Purpose
*	You'll eventually end up with a lot of RTF files on your machine and you may not want to include all of the topics they contain in every help file. For example, I have one help file that I include with a communication program that talks about online courtesy. It's very generic and most users find it helpful when trying to figure out the various acronyms they see online. It appears in an RTF file of general topics. While I wouldn't want to include that topic in a utility program, the general file does have topics I do want to include. This footnote defines a build tag. It works in concert with the help project (HPJ) file that I'll describe later. The help compiler looks at the list of help topics you want to include, then looks at the build tags in the RTF file to find them. You must include this footnote as the very first footnote for a topic. Build tags are case insensitive, but I still type mine in uppercase so that any future changes to the way that Microsoft handles help files won't break mine. A typical build tag in an RTF file looks like this: *{/footnote BUILD_TAG}.
#	This is a topic identifier footnote. Think of this as a label used by a GOTO statement. Whenever you "call" this topic identifier using a technique I'll describe in just a bit, Windows Help changes the focus to this particular footnote. This is the first half of a hyperlink within the help file. You can use hyperlinks for a variety of tasks, including menus and to create links to a glossary. Like build tags, topic identifiers are case insensitive, but I still type mine in uppercase so that any future changes to the way that Microsoft handles help files won't break mine. One example of this kind of footnote in an RTF file is: #{/footnote SOME_LINK}.
$	Use this footnote type to create a topic title. The topic title appears in the gray area above the help text in the Help window. You'll also see the topic title in the Topics Found and the History dialog boxes. This footnote accepts any kind of text. For example, you could use ${/footnote This is a title.} as a topic title.

Table 5-1. Standard Footnote Styles for the Microsoft Help Compiler

Footnote Type	Purpose
+	There may be times when you want to create a sequence of help topics to allow the user to move from one area of the help file to another with relative ease. For example, a lengthy procedure may be inconvenient to use if you make it fit in one window. One alternative to this is to break the procedure into window-sized elements and then allow the user to browse from one window to the next. Adding the browse-sequence identifier footnote to an RTF file does just that. It activates the two Browse buttons >> and << in the Help window. Windows will allow you to use any identifier for a browse sequence—it sorts the identifiers in alphabetical order to determine which sequence to display next—but I usually use a page-numbering sequence. For example, +{/footnote Page:1} would be the first page in a sequence. The only limitation to using sequences is that you can only have one per topic. You have to enable the Browse buttons by adding a BrowseButtons macro to the HPJ file. Windows Help looks for this macro as part of the help file initialization process. I'll show you how to add it in the "Creating the Make File" section of the chapter. The browse sequence identifier is one of the handier help file footnotes because you can use it to break up long sections of text without causing any confusion for the user. I also find it essential when I need to display a multipage graphic like a hierarchical chart. For example, one of the help files I created contained a complete hierarchical chart of all the Novell forums. Since the chart required more than one page, I used a browse sequence to make it easy for the user to move from one area to the next. You could also use this feature in a reference-type help file to move from one command to the next. The applications for this particular footnote are almost unlimited.

Table 5-1. Standard Footnote Styles for the Microsoft Help Compiler (continued)

Footnote Type	Purpose
K	The search capability of your help file depends on the keyword footnote. You define one or more descriptive words for each topic and subtopic in your help file. I always err on the side of too many rather than too few keywords. The keywords you define appear in the Index page of the Search dialog box if you're using the Windows 95/98 interface. A keyword can contain any sequence of characters, including spaces. Windows also preserves the case of your keywords—making it easier for you to come up with descriptive terms that the user can identify easily. One topic can also have more than one keyword—just separate them with semicolons.
	There's a flaw in the DOS version of the help compiler—HC31—that you need to compensate for when using this footnote. You'll need to add an extra space between the footnote and the next character in the RTF file or it won't appear in the help file. In addition, if your keyword begins with a K, you'll need to precede it with an extra space or a semicolon.
	One example of a keyword footnote might be: K{/footnote Control;Exit Pushbutton;Leaving the Program}. In this case, the user could find the same help topic using three different routes: Control, Exit Pushbutton, and Leaving the Program. You'll find it easier to build a comprehensive yet consistent help file if you maintain a sorted list of keywords as you build the RTF files. Make sure that you use the same keyword in every place a topic appears. For example, if you say "Control" in one place, don't use the plural form or a different term in another place. A user can adapt to a help file that's consistent—it's when the help file uses terms inconsistently that you start running into problems.

Table 5-1.   Standard Footnote Styles for the Microsoft Help Compiler (continued)

Footnote Type	Purpose
@	What would a program be without comments? You couldn't figure out what you did during the previous build the next time you needed to add a new feature. In addition, other help file programmers need comments to understand what you've done and why. As you can tell by looking at the examples in this book, I like to add a lot of comments. I've found that comments are an essential part of any programming effort. Help files can get quite complex. You could easily forget why you added a macro or did something in a particular way between editing sessions. The author-defined comment footnote solves this problem. It's like adding comments to your help file. The only difference is that you won't see the comment, in most cases, until you open the footnote for viewing (assuming, of course, that you're using a standard word processor to create the file). A typical author-defined comment footnote looks like this: @{/footnote This is a comment.}. Needless to say, since the help compiler ignores this footnote, you can include any kind of text within it.

Table 5-1. Standard Footnote Styles for the Microsoft Help Compiler (continued)

What you should do, at this point, is compile a list of the topic identifier (#) footnotes you've created. Armed with this list, you can go through the rest of the help file and create the appropriate hyperlinks. Just how do you go about doing this? When you look at a standard help file and see the green text that signifies a hyperlink, what you're looking at is a double underline (/uldb in an RTF file) or a strikethrough (/strike in an RTF file). So the first part of creating a hyperlink is to double underline or strikethrough the text that you want the user to see as green text. Right after the double underline, add the topic identifier of the hyperlink in hidden text (use the /v statement in an RTF file). This is the same identifier that you typed in the # footnote.

At this point, you'll probably need to decide a variety of things. For example, do you want to add graphics to your help file? A few graphics in the right places can go a long way toward making your help file truly user-friendly. Some people like to add sound or other multimedia. Unless you're proficient at using these mediums, I'd probably avoid them for the first few projects.

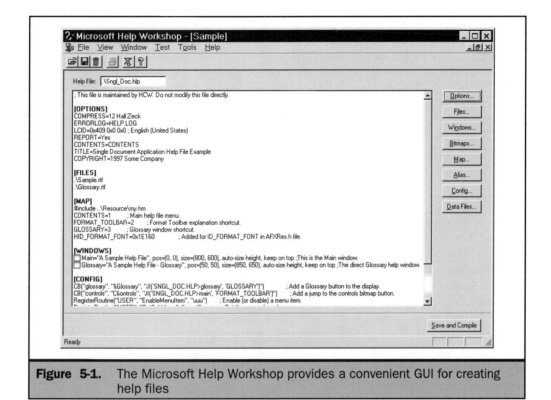

Figure 5-1.   The Microsoft Help Workshop provides a convenient GUI for creating help files

Creating the Make File

As previously stated, the Microsoft Help Workshop allows you to create help project files (another name for a help make file) and compile them from within Windows. Figure 5-1 shows a typical view of the Microsoft Help Workshop.

Using Microsoft Help Workshop is relatively easy. The first step is to create a new project. Simply use the File | New command to display the New dialog box shown here:

Select Help Project and click on OK to complete the action. As you can see from Figure 5-1, I've already created a new help project. It starts out as a blank page that you fill in with the characteristics of your help file.

Caution	*The files you'll create using the Microsoft Help Workshop aren't compatible with those created using the older DOS-based Windows Help utilities. You have to decide on a single application strategy. I think that the new Help Workshop makes life a lot easier for the developer, but only if you work with 32-bit operating environments. If you still need Windows 3.x compatibility, you have to use the DOS utility versions of the Help compiler.*

Defining a Project's Options

Once you have a new project to work with, it's time to start defining at least some of the project options. For example, you should at least have some idea of what you want to call your help file and what type of copyright information to add. I always use the contents topic as my main topic, so adding that entry at the beginning is a good idea as well. All you need to do is click the Options... button and you'll see the Options dialog box shown here:

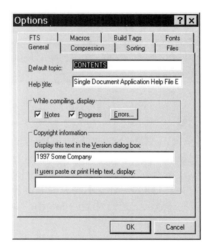

Notice that I've already defined some general options in this case. The most important field is Default topic, which tells Help Workshop which topic you want to display first. This is also the tab where you define copyright information and how much information the compiler displays as it creates the help file.

You'll find that the options on the Compression page are pretty self-explanatory. In most cases, you'll set compression to None while creating the help file to reduce compile time. Once you have a working help file, you'll set compression to Maximum to reduce the resulting help file size and to decrease loading time. There's also a custom compression option that you can use if you have special file compression requirements (you won't normally need this feature).

Tip   *At this point, some programmers may feel that they won't get much benefit out of using this tool, especially if they have a lot of predefined files sitting around on disk. It's important to remember that this dialog box provides a simple form for you to fill out—no longer do you need to remember what statements to use to accomplish a specific task.*

The Sorting page of the Options dialog box contains two areas. The first area determines the language of the help file. Language makes a difference in the way things are sorted, since everyone's alphabet is slightly different. The second area contains two options. The first allows you to ignore nonspacing characters. For example, the "^" that appears over ê would affect the sort order if you didn't select this option. The second option tells the help compiler to ignore any symbols in the help file when sorting. This comes in handy if you want to create a nonspecialized index for a data entry program or other general application. On the other hand, it would actually get in the way when creating an index for a reference help file. Consider the fact that many C functions begin with an underscore. Ignoring those underscores would make the function more difficult to find.

The next thing we'll need to look at is the Files page of the Options dialog box, shown here:

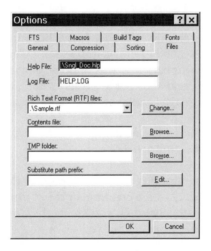

You can change the name of the help file by changing the contents of the Help File field. Normally, the help compiler uses the name of the project file as a basis for naming the help file. The Log File field contains the name of a log file. Fortunately (as we'll see later), this particular option isn't really required with the new help compiler. I still use a log file to keep track of the status of various help file projects, but it's an option now.

One of the most important fields on this page is the Rich Text Format (RTF) files list box. You'll find a list of the files for the current help project here. Clicking the Change button next to the field displays the Topic Files dialog box shown here:

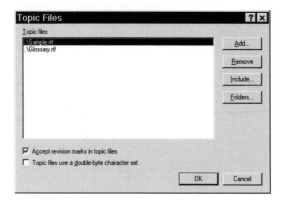

This is where you add and remove topic files from the list in the FILES section of the project file. Notice the two check boxes at the bottom of this dialog box. They're important because they control how the help compiler reacts to your RTF files. The first option allows the help compiler to automatically implement any changes you make to the RTF files during the next compile. If you leave this box unchecked, the help compiler will ignore any changes. The second option is important if you use a double-byte character set (DBCS) within your help file. This option changes the way the help compiler works with your file and allows it to preserve the special characters. (This feature is mainly used by languages with complex character sets, such as Chinese.)

Tip   *Another way to access the Topic Files dialog box is to click on the Files button on the Main window shown in Figure 5-1.*

There are a couple of other options on the Files page of the Options menu. One of them is the Contents file field. If you're creating a project from scratch, Help Workshop will fill this in for you automatically when you create the Contents page. This is useful when you already have a contents page that you want to use with the current project. The TMP Folder field only comes into play when your help file gets over 8MB in size. It allows you to specify something other than the current directory for the temporary files that Help Workshop creates when it compiles your help file. In most cases, you won't need to change this entry unless the current drive is short on disk space. The final field, Substitute path prefix, comes into play if you move the files used to create the help file, and don't want to change all the path information in the project file.

Windows 95/98 and newer Windows NT help files offer something that you won't find in those of its predecessors—full text search. That's the database created when you select the Find page of the Help Topics dialog box. It allows you to search an entire help file word by word. The FTS page of the Options dialog box contains an option to generate this file when you compile the help file. Since Windows 95/98/NT generates this file anyway, I normally leave this option blank. The GID file that the help compiler creates takes up a lot of room on the distribution disks and increases compile time by a considerable margin for large files.

You'll want to spend some time learning to use the Macros page shown here:

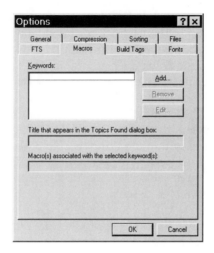

This is where you can define keyword macros to use on a file-wide basis. Not only that, but these macros also appear on the Index page of the Help Topics dialog box when the user tries to search for a particular topic.

Clicking the Add push button on this page displays a Keyword Macros dialog box containing three fields. The first field contains the name of the macro. The second field contains the macro itself. The third field contains a string that tells Help Workshop how to display the macro on the Index page. I use this particular entry when I have more than one help file but want to display a particular keyword file-wide. For example, I often place the glossary and list of acronyms in a separate file, and then use the JI macro to create a file-wide jump to them. The keyword macro is the method I use to do this. The user never even realizes that he or she has loaded another file—it's that transparent.

Note *Remember that the Macro page on the Options dialog box is for macros that affect the entire help file—not just one window.*

I previously talked about the * footnote with regard to build tags. The Build Tags page of the Options dialog box is where you make use of this feature. I covered this topic pretty thoroughly earlier, so I won't go into detail again here. The main idea is to provide Help Workbench with a list of build tags that you want to include in a help file. Even if an RTF file contains other topics, it won't include them in the help file if you don't include that topic's build tag. If you leave this page blank, Help Workbench assumes that you want to include all of the topics in all of the RTF files you've included as part of the final help file.

The Fonts page of the Options dialog box is your first chance to customize the look and feel of your help file. I normally don't use this page to control the appearance of the help file, preferring to rely on the formatting capabilities of my word processor instead. However, if you're creating an RTF file using a text editor, this particular feature can save you some time. The Character Set field allows you to select a particular character set for your help file—the default is ANSI. You can also choose from several different language types, such as Arabic. The Font in WinHelp Dialog Boxes field is where you define a default font type. Click on the Change push button and you'll see a Font dialog box with three fields. The first defines the font name, the second the font point size. The third field defines the character set you'll use with dialog boxes. The list box below the Font in WinHelp Dialog Boxes field allows you to change the general fonts used within the Windows Help file. It lets you substitute one font for another. The Add push button displays an Add/Edit Font Mapping dialog box that contains two groups of three fields. The three fields are precisely the same as the ones used in the Font dialog box that I just described. The only problem with using this particular page is that it doesn't work if your word processor overrides the settings— something that generally happens if you use a product like Word for Windows.

Defining Windows

Defining options is only the first phase of creating a project file. Once you have the options in place, you need to define some windows to display your data in. I always create one window called *Main*. It's the main window that my application will use.

Creating a window is fairly simple. All you need to do is click on the Windows push button in the Main window (refer to Figure 5-1) to display the Window Properties dialog box shown here:

The first page you'll need to look at is the General page, shown in the illustration. Click the Add push button on this page and you'll see an Add a New Window dialog box with two fields. The first field contains the name of the window. The second field contains the window type. There are three window types that Help Workbench can create: procedural, reference, and error message. There's very little difference between the procedural and reference windows. They're both auto-sizing and contain the three system buttons. The only difference between the two is their placement on screen— which you can override with the settings I'll show you next. The error message window differs from the other two in that it doesn't include the three system buttons. It looks somewhat like a dialog box.

The Title bar text field determines what Windows Help places on the title bar. This entry doesn't affect the appearance of the topic title area of the help window. The Comment field allows you to place a comment next to the entry in the project file— something that I always take advantage of. There are also three attribute check boxes. Help Workbench may disable one or more of these check boxes, depending on the situation. For example, you can't make the main help window auto-sizing. If you do make an ancillary window auto-sizing, you can't choose to maximize it when it opens. Most procedural windows default to staying on top. This is a handy feature if you want to keep help available to a user who is trying to work with an application.

> **Tip**
>
> *I normally turn the Auto-Size Height feature off to provide better control over the appearance of a window on screen. The options on the Position page that we'll look at next allow you full control over the appearance of your help window on screen.*

You'll almost always want to spend some time working with the Position page of the Window Properties dialog box shown next. The name of this page is a bit deceiving because it provides a little more functionality than you might initially expect. While it does control the actual starting position and size of the various help windows you create, this dialog box provides some easily used features that you'll really find handy.

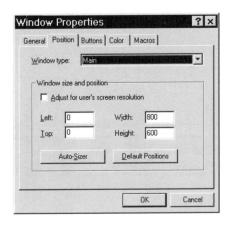

There are four fields on the Position page: Left, Top, Width, and Height. These control the size and position of your window. I normally position my first help window in the upper-left corner and use a size of either 640 × 480 or 800 × 600, depending on the capabilities of the target machine for my application. This may seem a bit small, but the user can always resize the window as needed. Trying to find a help window on an older display when the programmer positions it near one of the edges is frustrating to say the least. I really like the Adjust for User's Screen Resolution option on this page because it prevents the help window from becoming totally hidden when the user has a low-resolution display.

There's one very special feature on this page, and you may not notice it at first. Look at the Auto-Sizer push button. Clicking on this button displays the example window shown in Figure 5-2. If you change the window's position, the Left and Top field values also change. Resizing the window changes the value of the Width and Height fields. This graphic method of changing the window size will definitely reduce the number of times you have to recompile the help file to take care of aesthetic needs.

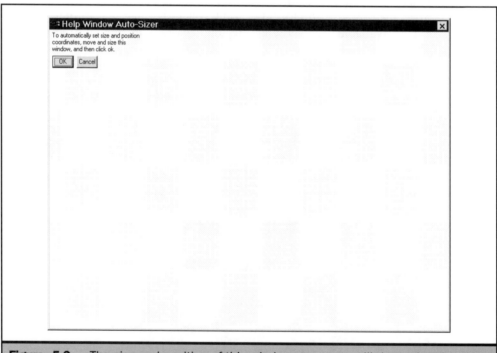

Figure 5-2. The size and position of this window on screen will determine the size and position of the help window

Windows 95/98/NT defines a lot of default buttons that you can add to your help file. There are situations when you may not want to add all of them. For example, the Browser buttons aren't all that important if you don't define a browse (+ footnote) in one of your RTF files. The Buttons page, shown here, allows you to define the buttons used with your help window:

All ancillary procedure and reference windows lack both the Contents and Index buttons. Main windows contain both of these buttons as a default, as well as the Print and Back buttons. On the other hand, a Main window won't allow you to select the Help Topics button. Unlike all the other window types, an error message window has no restrictions. You can include any of the default buttons that you like on it.

You can get around the Help Workbench-imposed limitations on buttons for the main help window by clicking the No Default Buttons check box. This check box only appears for the Main window, which means that you can't override the restrictions for ancillary procedure and reference windows.

The next page that you'll want to look at is the Color page. This contains two fields: Nonscrolling area color and Topic area color. Each has a Change button. All you need to do is click on the Change button to display a color palette. Selecting a different color from the palette changes the appearance of the help window.

The final page of the Window Properties dialog box is the Macros page, shown here:

The Main window type always uses the macros in the CONFIG section of the project file as a default. All of the macros you see in this section are self-executing— that's why the macros in the CONFIG section are added to the Main window. You want those macros to execute when the Main window opens. Adding a new macro to the Main window always adds it to the CONFIG section of the help project file. Adding macros to other windows changes the way those windows appear in comparison to the Main window. For example, if you add a browse to one of the ancillary windows, you might need to add a macro or two here to set up any conditions not taken care of by the default Browse button selection on the Buttons page. Each of these ancillary windows will have their own special CONFIG-<window name> section in the help project.

Another way to access the Macros dialog box for the Main window is to click on the Config button on the Main window, shown in Figure 5-1.

Mapping Help Topics

I've already expressed the importance of this particular part of creating a help project file. If you don't map the topic identifiers in your help file to a help context number, you can't attach context-sensitive help to the controls in your application.

Clicking on the Map push button displays a Map dialog box like the one shown here:

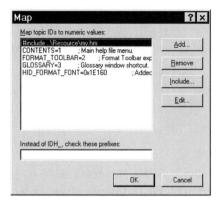

This is where you define the relationship between a topic identifier and a particular context number. Notice that I've already defined a few in this case. The topic identifier is set equal to a help context number. It's followed by a comment that describes the entry.

There are a lot of ways to keep the context numbers straight. I usually start at one and count up from there until I reach the last topic identifier for small help files. Large help files require something a bit more complex, though, or you'll find yourself reusing numbers. I normally use a three- or four-digit number in this case. The first two numbers are the position of the control or menu item described by the help context within the application. For example, the File menu is normally 01 and the Edit menu is 02. A description of the File | New command would receive a help context number of 0101, since the New option is usually the first one on the File menu. I assign a value of 0001 to the first nonapplication topic. For example, the glossary would fall into this category. The first two numbers for a control on the form of an application would be one greater than the last menu item. I use the tab order for the last two numbers since it's unlikely that a label or other nonactive component would ever appear in the help file.

It's easy to add a new map entry. Simply click on Add and you'll see the Add Map Entry dialog box shown here:

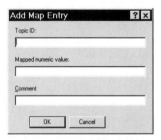

This dialog box contains three fields: The Topic ID, the Mapped numeric value (help context number), and a Comment. Fill out the three fields and click on OK to add a new map to the project.

As I previously mentioned, you'll normally want to include an HM file with your help file if you're using Visual C++ to reduce the amount of work you need to do when creating the help file mapping and to provide a quick and easy method for checking your work. Nothing is more frustrating than to release a help file that you thought was complete at the time of testing but turns out to be missing one or more crucial entries after you release it. All you need to do to include a file is click on the Include button. You'll see an Include File dialog box like the one shown here:

Notice that this dialog box provides a Browse button so that you can simply search for your include file on the hard drive. The Browse button opens a standard Open dialog box, just like the ones you've used with other applications.

Compiling Your Help File

Once you get a help project file put together, it's time to try to compile it. All you need to do is click on the Save and Compile button at the bottom of the Main window shown in Figure 5-1. The Help Workbench window will minimize while it compiles the help file. This allows you to work on something else—compiling a large help file can take a very long time. Once the compilation is complete, you'll see a dialog box similar to the one shown in Figure 5-3.

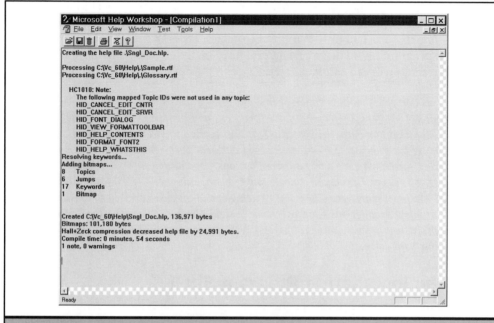

Figure 5-3.   This compilation screen shows the current status of the help file and any error messages

You should notice something almost immediately about this dialog box—it shows that there are errors in the help file (actually they're notes, but you'll still want to count them as errors in most cases). We didn't define help file entries for every entry in the HM file. What this means is that there are holes in the coverage provided by the help file that need to be filled. As you can see, using the HM file is a great help because it at least reduces the chance that you'll miss an important topic.

InstallShield for Microsoft Visual C++

Packaging your application is one of the more important aspects of the development process. The way you present the application package determines for the most part what kind of first impression the user will get from your application. InstallShield is a product that helps you create a package for your Visual C++ applications.

The first thing you need is a complete list of the files needed to run your application, which you can get using the Depends tool mentioned earlier in the chapter. Make sure your file list includes specific installation areas for each file. For example, you'll want to note which files you have to install in the SYSTEM folder. In addition, you should have tested your application and associated files on a clean machine—one that has had only Windows installed. It doesn't pay to start writing an installation program until you're certain you have included all of the files it requires and that the setup works as anticipated on a clean machine.

Note *This section relies on the version of InstallShield provided with Visual C++ 6.0. Earlier versions of Visual C++ may not have this version of InstallShield, which means you'll probably need to modify the procedures in this section to meet your needs. Even if you are using the same version of InstallShield outlined in the book, you may see slightly different screens or have a few different options, depending on the application you're trying to package. In short, it's not going to be too unusual to see a few variations from what I'm presenting here when you're using InstallShield. You'll need to install the InstallShield product—it's located in the IShield directory on your Visual Studio CD. The procedures in this section assume you've already installed the InstallShield product on your hard drive.*

Creating the Installation Program Shell

The following procedure is going to show you how to put a typical installation program together. I've targeted the corporate environment, so the procedure will have certain biases that developers will need to be aware of (I've discussed those biases as part of the procedural steps). This is for a small utility program written in Visual C++ (the actual application isn't important right now—I just want to show you the InstallShield Free Edition feature set). We won't do anything really fancy; the whole idea is to get the application ready to send to someone else. We'll cover a generic installation program in this section; you'll need to modify it to meet the needs of your particular application and installation environment.

Note *The Single-Document Application (SnglDoc) example program used for this installation program isn't shown in the book. The example code and compiled result are provided as part of the CD provided with the book. Just look in the Chapt05 folder.*

1. Start the InstallShield 6 Free Edition program. You'll see a window similar to the one shown in Figure 5-4. Notice that we don't have any project defined yet, but that there's a wizard entry in the Projects window. This window doesn't look precisely like the one in Visual C++, but as the procedure goes on you'll notice certain similarities that tend to ease the installation program creation process. Notice also the InstallShield link in the lower-right corner. Clicking it will open your browser and take you to the InstallShield online help site on the Internet.

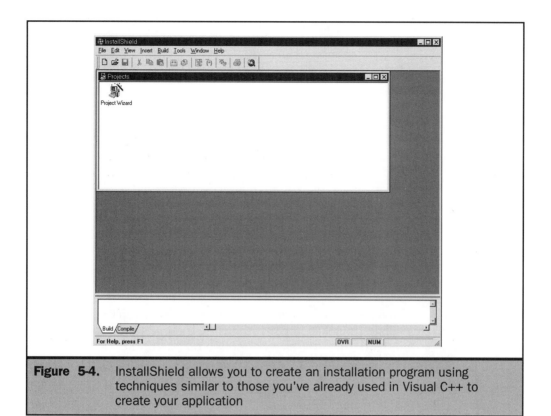

Figure 5-4. InstallShield allows you to create an installation program using techniques similar to those you've already used in Visual C++ to create your application

2. Double-click on the Project Wizard icon in the Projects window. You'll see a Project Wizard - Welcome dialog box similar to the one shown here:

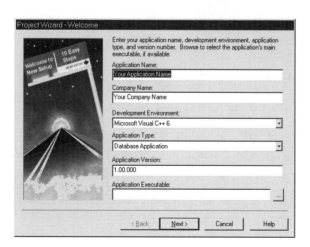

Tip *The Professional Edition of InstallShield offers advanced features on the Welcome (and other) page—make sure you read about the enhancements in the help file.*

3. Type the name of your application. The example program is **Single Document Application Example**.

4. Type your company name. The example program uses **A Sample Company**.

Note *The Free Edition of InstallShield only provides one Development Environment field entry—Microsoft Visual C++ 6.*

5. Choose one of the entries in the Application Type field. The example program uses **Software Development Application**—there isn't a standard utility program type, and the Software Development Application type does allow for utility programs.

6. Type the application version number in the Application Version field. Our example program uses **1.0**, but you can use any numbering scheme consistent with your company policies.

7. Click the ... button next to the Application Executable field. You'll see a standard Open dialog box that you can use to find the application you want to package on your hard drive. The sample application uses SNGL_DOC.EXE.

8. Click Next. You'll see a Project Wizard - Choose Dialogs dialog box like the one shown here:

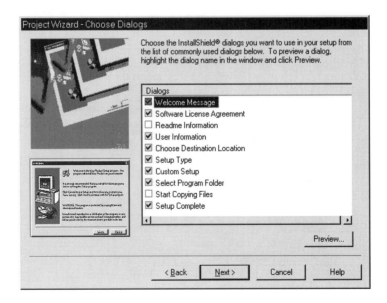

This is where you'll choose the series of dialog boxes that the user will see when installing your application. Since we're using the corporate model for our installation program, I unchecked the Software License Agreement, Setup Type, and Custom Setup dialog boxes. You'd choose some or all of these dialog boxes for other kinds of packaging environments. There are a few things you should notice about this particular dialog box. First, look in the lower-left corner as you move from one dialog box entry to the next. You'll see that the Project Wizard gives you a thumbnail view of the dialog box in question to make it easier to determine whether you actually want it. Highlighting a dialog box and then clicking the Preview button will display a dialog box that looks exactly like the one the user will see. Obviously, you'll be able to modify this dialog box later, but it helps to know what you're starting with.

9. Choose which dialog boxes you want to add to the installation program and then click Next. You'll see a Project Wizard - Choose Target Platforms dialog box like the one shown here. Since we want to be able to install our program on any of the supported programs, we won't have to make any changes. However, there may be situations when you'll want to be a little more selective. Reducing the number of supported platforms accomplishes two things. First, it reduces the size of the installation program you create—a real plus for shareware developers who are short on space to begin with. Second, it reduces the chance that someone will try to use your program under the wrong version of Windows—a real plus for any developer.

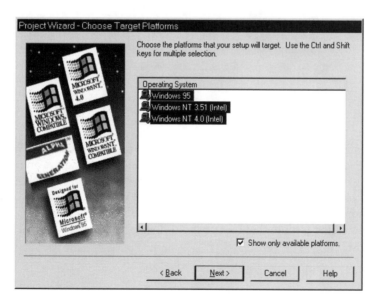

It's educational to uncheck the Show Only Available platforms check box to see all of the choices offered by the Professional Edition of InstallShield. The same thing holds true for language support and other dialog boxes where there is a Show Only Available... check box. The free edition of the product supplied with Visual C++ limits the number of choices you have available when creating an installation program—limitations that may not matter if you're distributing the application locally.

10. Select one or more platforms as needed (but at least one) and then click Next. You'll see a Project Wizard - Specify Languages dialog box like the one shown here. Since the Free Edition only supports one language, we don't have to make any changes here. Like other selections you've had to make so far, more is not necessarily better. Adding languages will increase the size of the installation program and could add user confusion as well—choose only the languages you need.

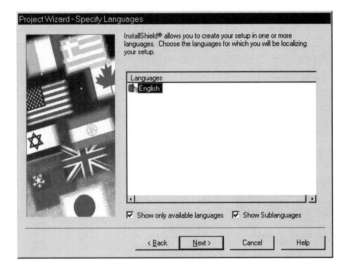

11. Highlight one or more languages (but at least one) and then click Next. You'll see a Project Wizard - Specify Setup Types dialog box like the one shown next. Since we're using the corporate packaging model, I've already chosen the Network setup type. Other packaging models will require you to make other selections, including the most common of all: Custom, Typical, and Compact. It's interesting to note that InstallShield does offer a wealth of other choices, though.

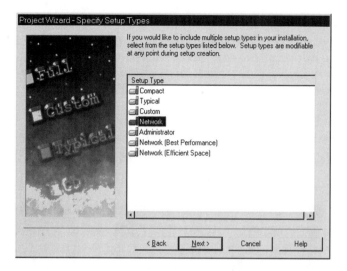

12. Choose one or more setup types and then click Next. You'll see a Project
    Wizard - Specify Components dialog box like the one shown here:

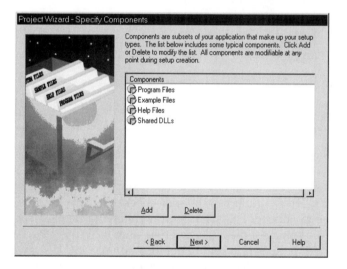

The Project Wizard doesn't assume anything about the components you want to
install. The example program uses Program Files, Shared DLLs, and Help Files.
You'll need to choose each of these options one at a time to define the files that
go under each component type. A component type is a definition of a major
program area. For example, the user may want to include all of the sample files
but none of the help files. A component type doesn't necessarily define which
files you'll need to perform the task, simply that the task is a separate entity that
the user could either choose to install, or perhaps that needs to be installed in a
different directory from the rest of the files.

> *You can add new component types as needed to your installation program. For example, you might need to add a Database File component if you've written a database application. All you have to do is click the Add button, and the Project Wizard will add the new entry for you. Type the name of the component and press ENTER to complete the addition process.*

13. Highlight Example Files and then click Delete. Project Wizard will remove this component type from our installation program.

14. Add or delete component types as needed and then click Next. You'll see a Project Wizard - Specify File Groups dialog box like the one shown here:

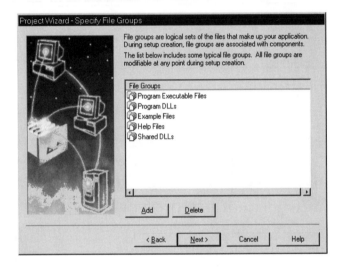

Our example program uses Program Executable Files, Help Files, and Shared DLLs. Normally, you'll create file groups so that all of the files needed for a specific task are copied at one time. File groups can cross component type boundaries. For example, say the spell checker and the grammar checker both rely on the same set of DLLs, but require different rule files. You could define a common file group for the DLLs and two other file groups for the rule files. If the user selected the spell checker but not the grammar checker, InstallShield would copy the spell checker file group and the common DLL file group but not the grammar checker file group.

15. Highlight Program DLLs and then click Delete. Highlight Example Files and then click Delete. We've just eliminated the two file groups that we won't need for the example program. Obviously, the selection of file groups will depend on

how your application is put together and where you need to copy the files. Remember that all the files in one file group will go to the same directory on the hard drive.

16. Add or delete file groups as needed, and then click on Next. You'll see a Project Wizard - Summary dialog box like the one shown here. At this point, you should check the list of options to make sure everything is correct before you ask the Project Wizard to build the installation program for you.

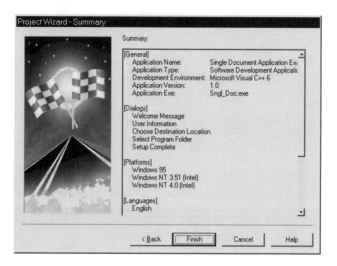

17. Click Finish. InstallShield will create the installation program using the parameters you've just specified. At this point, the InstallShield interface will change as shown in Figure 5-5. Notice that you can now see the C++ code required to create the installation program and that you can modify it just like you would any other project.

Note

Don't get the idea that InstallShield generates source files that are precisely like the ones used in a general project. There are some ancillary files that you haven't seen in the past, such as the setup rule (SETUP.RUL) file shown in Figure 5-5.

At this point, you should have a barely usable installation program shell. There's still quite a bit of configuration to do, though, and we'll look at all of it in the sections that follow. The important thing to realize is that you'll write very little code during this process—InstallShield will do most of the work for you as you define the various program elements.

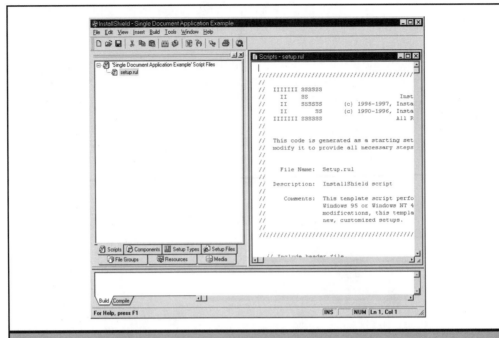

Figure 5-5. Once you've created a project, InstallShield will generate it for you, and then display the resulting source code

If you've still got questions about how to use InstallShield after reading this section, there are a couple of ways to find out more information. This is one of those times when it really pays to look in the product README file, because it contains links to a lot of places you need to know about on the Internet. For example, you'll find a link to the newsgroups site at http://support.installshield.com/newsgroups/default.asp. This site contains links to several InstallShield-specific newsgroups. Just clicking one of the links will create a new folder in your newsreader containing the newsgroup you wanted to look at. There's even a special newsgroup for the Free Edition at installshield.is5.free-edition. You'll also find links for newsgroups covering things like the IDE, scripting, and the use of multimedia. In short, these newsgroups provide you with the contacts you need with other developers interested in finding solutions to packaging their applications successfully.

Setting Up the Components

The first task we'll need to accomplish is setting up the various components. Remember that a component is a selection that appears during the installation. If you've ever used the custom install feature of an installation program, then you know what a component is. It's the series of check boxes that allow you to choose whether you want to install a particular program feature, such as the help files.

Configuring the components for your installation program is fairly easy. Click on the Components tab and you'll see a Components - Program Files dialog box like the one shown here:

The Components dialog box contains a complete list of all the values for the selected component. Remember that we have three components in this case: Program Files, Help Files, and Shared DLLs. It's important to set up all three before you go to the next section. Double-click on the Description property and you'll see a Properties dialog box like the one shown here:

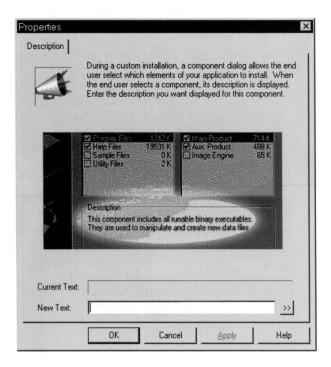

All of the other properties will show similar dialog boxes. Each Properties dialog box will describe what you're supposed to do with this particular property. It'll also allow you to type in a value for the property. In this case, type **All the files required to run the application.** and then click OK. The Description property will now contain the text you just typed.

You don't need to change all of the component properties—what you do need to change depends on the kind of application package you're creating. For example, in our corporate model installation, we don't ever allow the user to choose the components that get installed, so providing a component description is pointless. The user won't ever see it anyway. There are some properties that you should consider changing regardless of the packaging model you're using, and the following list looks at each one.

- **Status Text**   This is the text that the user will see while the installation program copies the files from the source to the destination. The Progress dialog box will say something like "Copying program files...", which works fine for default components. You may want to define something special for custom components.

- **Installation**   If you've ever been annoyed by the fact that some program came along and copied over the new DLLs you just installed with really old ones that don't work, then you'll know why this property is important. It tells

InstallShield whether you want to look at the time and date stamp on the component files first before you overwrite them. I always choose NEWERVERSION/NEWERDATE or SAMEORNEWERVERSION/ SAMEORNEWERDATE instead of the default ALWAYSOVERWRITE. In essence, these options tell InstallShield to only overwrite a file if the source has both a newer (or same) date and a newer (or same) version than the one on the user's hard drive.

■ **Destination** The standard destination for all of your application files is the target directory, the one the user chose for the program. However, there are some circumstances when using the target directory won't work like it should or could waste space on the user's machine. For example, most Visual C++ applications require the C run-time files and the MFC files. What if every application you installed added these files to a program directory instead of a centralized place? It wouldn't take very long to fill your hard drive with useless files. In most cases, you'll probably want to copy your Shared DLLs component files to the Windows SYSTEM folder. All you need to do is change this property. (When you open the Property dialog box, you'll see a map of the various locations you can use for copying the file; just choose the one you want.)

■ **Required Components** This is where you'll set up dependencies between components as shown here:

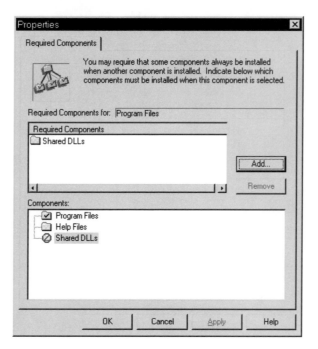

What I'm telling InstallShield, in this case, is that if the user installs the Program Files component, he or she must install the Shared DLLs component as well (which only makes sense since without the Shared DLLs, the program won't run).

Pay special attention to the FTP Location and HTTP Location properties if you plan to install your application from an Internet or intranet site. These properties will allow a user to start the installation from a Web site link and then copy the needed files from your Web server. You would normally choose the FTP Location property if the files were under the control of the FTP server.

There's one last item that you absolutely must take care of to configure the components. Look at the Included File Groups property. Right now we haven't assigned any to the Program Files (or any other) component. Double-click on this property and you'll see a Properties dialog box like the one shown here:

This Properties dialog box contains a complete list of the file groups assigned to a particular component. Remember that I previously talked about an example where you might want to make the spell checker and grammar checker optional components of your installation. They both use the same DLLs but require different rule files. I mentioned setting up three file groups: one with the spelling rule file, another with the grammar rule file, and a third with the common DLLs needed by both. This is the property where you set up that relationship. Click on the Add button and you'll see an Add File Group dialog box like the one shown here:

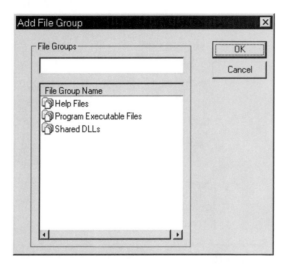

As you can see, the Add File Group dialog box contains the three file groups we defined using the Project Wizard. You'll need to make the following assignments between components and file groups before going on in the chapter. Table 5-2 shows the settings I used for the example program.

Component	Property	Value
Program Files	Description	All the files required to run the application
	Status Text	Copying Program Files
	Overwrite	SAMEORNEWERVERSION /SAMEORNEWERDATE
	Required Components	Shared DLLs
	Included File Groups	Program Executable Files
Help Files	Description	Files that show you how to use the program

Table 5-2. Component Settings for the Sngl_Doc Installation Program

Component	Property	Value
	Status Text	Copying Help Files...
	Overwrite	SAMEORNEWERDATE
	Included File Groups	Help Files
Shared DLLs	Description	Common files used by the program
	Status Text	Copying Shared DLLs...
	Overwrite	SAMEORNEWERVERSION /SAMEORNEWERDATE
	Destination	<WINSYSDIR>
	Included File Groups	Shared DLLs

Table 5-2. Component Settings for the Sngl_Doc Installation Program (continued)

Setting Up File Groups

Creating a set of components doesn't help the installation program very much. You've told the user what components can be copied to the hard drive, but you still haven't told the installation program what those files are. This is the step when you do that. We'll define a set of files for each of the file groups that we defined previously.

The first thing you'll need to do is click on the File Groups tab. What you'll see is a list of the file groups and the File Groups dialog box shown in Figure 5-6. Choosing which file group you want to configure is easy. Just click on its entry in the File Groups window on the left side of the display.

Click on the plus sign (+) next to the Help Files folder in the File Groups window. Click on the Links entry under the Help Files folder and you'll see the File Groups - Help Files\Links dialog box shown next.

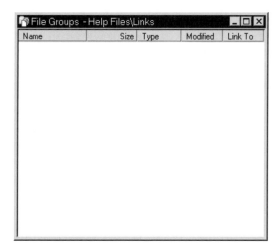

This is where you'll define a list of one or more files to include for this file group.

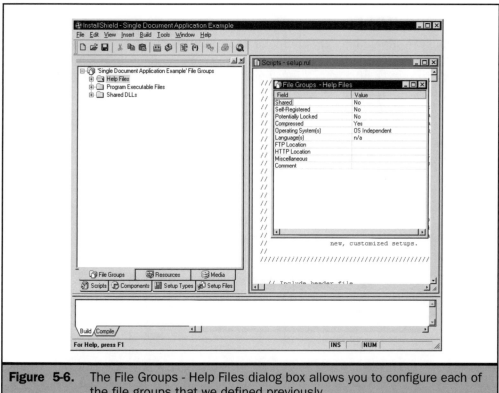

Figure 5-6. The File Groups - Help Files dialog box allows you to configure each of the file groups that we defined previously

Right-click on the File Groups - Help Files\Links dialog box and choose Insert Files from the context menu. You'll see a standard File Open type dialog box. Find the Sngl_Doc.HLP file that we created earlier in the chapter. Click OK to add this file to the Help Files file group. You'll need to add the Sngl_Doc.EXE file (supplied as part of the CD that comes with this book) to the Program Executable Files file group. The last file group, Shared DLLs, requires that you add the following list of files: MFC42.DLL and MSVCRT.DLL. You'll find these files in the Windows SYSTEM folder.

Note   *The Sngl_Doc.EXE file actually relies on quite a few more files than I have listed here, but the user's machine should include these other files. The other files include ADVAPI32.DLL, GDI32.DLL, KERNEL32.DLL, USER32.DLL, and VERSION.DLL. One of the best ways to determine which files your application relies on is to use the Depends utility discussed earlier in the chapter, then eliminate common files that the user will most likely have installed on their machine from the list. Always make sure you send a complete set of files with your application. In some cases, this may mean sending common files when your application depends on a specific version of a DLL rather than the DLL in general.*

Defining Resources

By this time, you should have the components and the file groups set up. What we need to do now is provide some identification information for the users. After all, they'll want to know a little something about the program they're installing. Click on the Resources tab and you'll see the Resources window shown in Figure 5-7. This same window contains two dialog boxes: Resources - String Table and Resources - String Table\English. The resources we want to change are in the Resources - String Table\English dialog box.

Most of the changes we'll make in the Resources - String Table\English dialog box won't affect the program at all. We're making them for identification purposes or to help the user in some way. Changing one of the resource values is much the same as changing a property in one of the other dialog boxes. All you need to do is double-click on the Identifier you want to change and InstallShield will display a dialog box that allows you to make the required change. Here's an example of the COMPANY_NAME identifier:

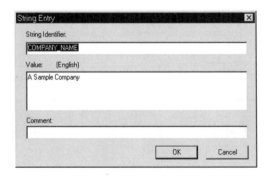

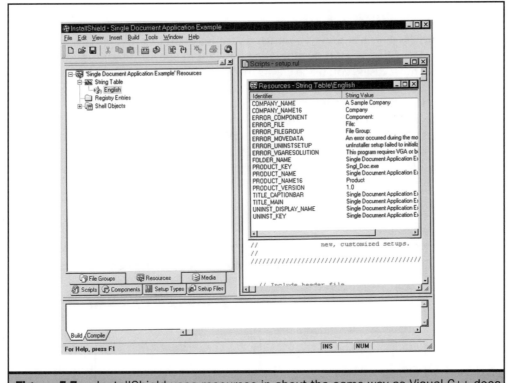

Figure 5-7.   InstallShield uses resources in about the same way as Visual C++ does

Table 5-3 shows the changes I made for the example program—obviously, many of the strings will be different for your installation program.

Identifier	Value
COMPANY_NAME	A Sample Company
PRODUCT_KEY	Sngl_Doc.EXE
PRODUCT_NAME	Single Document Application Example
UNINST_DISPLAY_NAME	Single Document Application Example
UNINST_KEY	Sngl_Doc.EXE

Table 5-3.   String Values for the Sngl_Doc Installation Program

Determining a Media Type

We've come to the very last thing you must do from a configuration perspective—simply tell InstallShield what type of media you want to use for distributing your application. In most cases, you'll use CD as the main distribution method, and may decide to use floppies as a secondary method if the application is small enough. If your only distribution method is going to be CD, you're done. Otherwise, choose the Media tab. You'll see a Media dialog box and window like the ones shown in Figure 5-8.

As you can see, the CD media is already in place (as shown by the CD folder in Figure 5-8). You'll need to use the Media Build Wizard to add another media to your installation program. The following procedure will take you through the steps required to add a floppy media type.

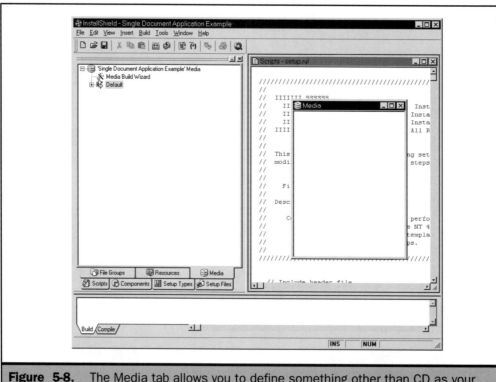

Figure 5-8. The Media tab allows you to define something other than CD as your distribution media

1. Click on this entry and you'll see the Media Build Wizard - Media Name dialog box shown here:

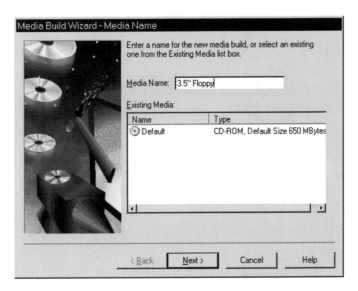

2. Type **3.5" Floppy** and then click Next. You'll see the Media Build Wizard - Disk Type dialog box shown here. Notice that InstallShield supports a wide variety of media types, including 2.88MB floppies:

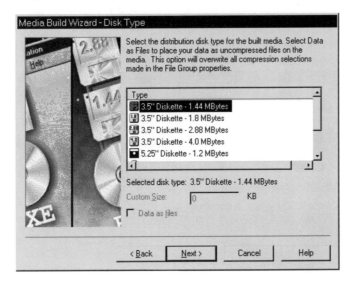

3. Highlight the 3.5" Diskette - 1.44 MBytes option and then click Next. You'll see the Media Build Wizard - Build Type dialog box shown here. A full build will compress all the files for your application, create the required CAB files, and create the full-fledged installation program. The Quick Build option is designed for testing purposes. It allows you to see if your installation program works as anticipated.

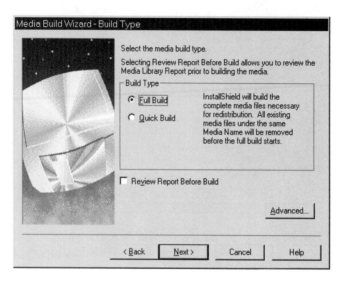

4. Choose the Full Build option and then click Next. You'll see the Media Build Wizard - Tag File dialog box shown here. All this dialog box does is allow you to enter your company name and associated application information.

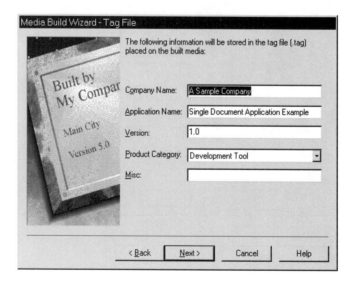

5. Type all the required information into the dialog box. The example program uses **A Sample Company** for the Company Name field, **Single Document Application Example** for the Application Name field, **Word Processor** for the Product Category field, and **Utility Style Text Editor** for the Misc. field.

6. Click Next. You'll see a Media Build Wizard - Platforms dialog box. All you need to do is make sure the three platform choices are highlighted—they should be by default.

7. Click Next. You'll see a Media Build Wizard - Summary dialog box like the one shown here. This is your last chance to verify the settings you've used.

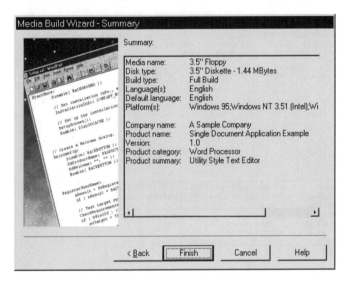

8. Verify your settings and then click Finish. InstallShield will create the new build that you requested.

The Free Edition of InstallShield may present an error message at this point, saying that it doesn't have enough memory to create the requested build. Ignore the problem and try setting up the build again. If you still can't get it to work, try using the default build setting. What you'll need to do is right-click on the Default folder and choose Media Build Wizard... from the context menu. Choose the Default option on the first screen of the Media Build Wizard dialog box and then click Next until you get to the final screen, where you got the error before. Click Finish and InstallShield will create the media for you.

At this point, you'll see a Building Media... dialog box. InstallShield is actually creating your installation program for you. When the process is complete, you'll see a completion message. Just click the Finish button and you're finished!

IROTView

The IROTView utility allows you to view OLE's running object table. So, what does this buy you? Well, if you're testing the OLE capabilities of your application, you can use this ability to see how well your application interfaces with other objects. For example, what happens if you open a compound document object? Does your application actually make the connection? Here's what the IROTView utility looks like with several objects loaded:

The upper window gives you a complete list of the currently running objects. Every time an application receives focus, this list gets updated. You can also perform a manual update using the Update! menu option.

The lower window gives you more information about the highlighted object. The following list tells you what each field contains.

A moniker *is a name for some kind of a resource. For example, C:\MyStuff\ MyDoc.Doc is a moniker for a document file that appears in the MyStuff folder on the C drive of your machine. Monikers can include all kinds of resource types. For example, http://www.microsoft.com is the moniker for Microsoft's Web site. You can even reference objects by their moniker by using the class ID (ClsId). For example, the moniker for Microsoft Word is {000209FF-0000-0000-C000-000000000046}.*

- **Name**   The display name of the moniker. For example, in the case of a file, you'd see the complete path for the file. Applications normally use their class ID.

- **Reduced**   The reduced name of the moniker. Normally, this is the same value as the Name field.

- **Inverse**   The anti-moniker for this object. You add this value to the end of the moniker to destroy it. This value is set to \.. in most cases.

- **Enumerated**   A list of the items in this moniker. If this isn't a composite moniker (as is the case in most situations), the field displays N/A.

- **Hash Value**   The 32-bit hash value associated with the moniker.

- **Running**   Displays TRUE to show that the application is running or FALSE to show that it's halted. The entry for the application will always disappear when the application is terminated, so FALSE always indicates a halted, but active, application.

- **Last Change**   This is the last time that the moniker's data was updated.

- **Type**   The type of moniker displayed. Standard values include Generic Composite Moniker, File Moniker, Anti-Moniker, Item Moniker, Pointer Moniker, and Not a System Moniker.

OLE View

Every OLE object you create, whether it's an application or an ActiveX control, relies on interfaces of some sort. Even language extensions like ActiveX Scripting rely on interfaces. An interface is a method for bundling functions in a way that is independent of programming language. Interfaces are one of the basics of OLE. In addition to the custom interfaces you'll create for your object, every object also supports standard interfaces like IUnknown.

Visual Studio provides a handy utility named OLE View (also known as OLE/COM Object Viewer), which you can use to see these interfaces in more detail. We'll use this utility several times in the book, so you may want to install it if you haven't done so already.

It's important to understand how OLE View can help you during the development process. Say you want to find out about the interfaces provided by a document object server (we talked about one previously in this chapter called Sngl_Doc.EXE—the source for this example is provided on the CD). Go ahead and open OLE View. You'll see a set of folders that encompass the various types of objects. Open the Document Objects folder and then open the XYZ Single Document folder (or another document objects folder if you don't have the Sngl_Doc.EXE program installed on your machine). You'll see a list of interfaces that MFC implemented for you as you built the application, as shown in Figure 5-9.

Figure 5-9. OLE View shows a hierarchical view of objects starting with the object type, then the name, then the interfaces the object supports

Notice that I've highlighted the IOleWindow interface in the left pane. If you look in the right pane, you'll see that this interface has five methods. In addition, you could find the class ID of the proxy stub for this interface. Further research would show that one of the methods for the IOleWindow interface is GetWindow( ), which is what a client would call to create a new application window. Since IOleWindow is a standard interface, you can be certain that it will always contain the GetWindow( ) function— this is just part of the interface's standard package.

This bit of research would tell you something about this application in addition to the fact that it supports the IOleWindow interface. The presence of an IOleWindow interface without the IActiveScriptSiteWindow interface means that your application supports OLE automation, not ActiveX Scripting. So, you'd have to write an application that interfaces with this one in such a way that it wouldn't rely on ActiveX Scripting. Let's extend this research further. If you look at every other application in this list, including Office 97 if you have it, you won't find a single application that supports ActiveX Scripting—yet. As you can see, with the proper knowledge of interfaces, you can use OLE View to perform all kinds of research on various objects without building a test application first.

Strange things can happen if you create an instance of an application or control in OLE View and then don't release it. For example, your machine might freeze unexpectedly. Every time you view the interfaces supported by an application or control, you have to create an instance to do it. You can tell if there is an instance of an object by looking at the application name. OLE View displays any open objects with bold type. To release the instance of the object you created, right-click on the object name (like XYZ Single Document) and then choose Release Instance from the context menu. Fortunately, OLE View is good about closing instances of objects before you leave, but you may need to do this during a viewing session if your machine begins to run out of memory. Remember that every instance you create also uses some memory.

Let's pursue the ActiveX Scripting line of research a bit further. The client-side support for ActiveX Scripting is available—at least in a preliminary form. Release the instance of the XYZ Single Document and then close the Document Object folder. Now open the ActiveX Scripting Engine folder. You'll see two entries, one for JavaScript and another for VBScript. Both of these entries are for Internet Explorer, but expect to see Netscape Navigator to implement them as well. Open the JScript Language (JavaScript) entry and you'll see a typical list of interfaces like the ones shown in Figure 5-10 (your list may vary slightly from the one shown).

Notice the highlighted entry, IActiveScript. This is the first of two client-side interfaces you need to implement client-side ActiveX Scripting. Right below it you'll see the IActiveScriptParse interface entry, which is the second client-side interface. Having both of these interfaces means that Internet Explorer currently supports

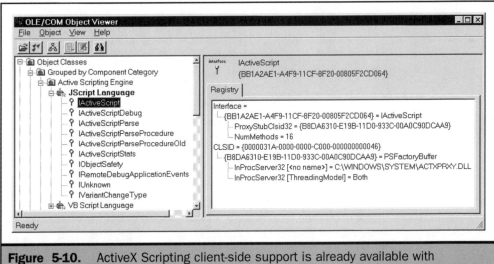

Figure 5-10. ActiveX Scripting client-side support is already available with Internet Explorer

ActiveX Scripting as a client, but you won't find any associated server entries in this section of OLE View either.

If you're absolutely and totally confused by all of this talk about interfaces, make sure you spend plenty of time reading through the various pieces of OLE documentation that Microsoft provides—most important of which is the OLE 2 SDK. You'll also want to invest in a magazine like Microsoft Systems Journal. *This particular magazine painstakingly explains most of the new interfaces that Microsoft designs in detail. Finally, make sure you check out Osborne's book on OLE technology,* OLE Wizardry *by William H. Murray III and Chris H. Pappas (ISBN 0-07-882102-9).*

Process Viewer

The Process Viewer utility allows you to see what processes are currently running on your machine, what threads they've spawned, and the priority of those threads. You can also use this utility to kill a process that isn't working as intended, using the Kill Process button. Here's what the Process Viewer utility looks like in action—notice that I've started a copy of the OCXTest application that we created in Chapter 4 for explanation purposes:

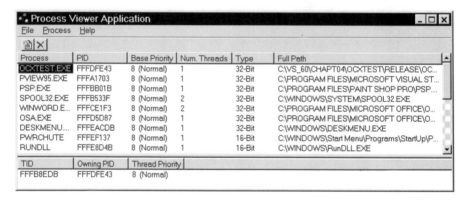

The Process Viewer automatically updates its display at a given interval (depending on current processor load). You can force an update of the display by pressing F5 *or by using the Process | Refresh command.*

The upper window contains a list of all of the processes currently running on the machine. It includes information about the process, such as the process ID number, the number of threads that it owns, the base priority of the process (used for multitasking), whether this is a 16-bit or 32-bit process, and the full path to the process.

Highlighting a process displays thread information for it in the lower window. In this case, we see the one thread owned by OCXTest.EXE. Thread information includes the thread ID, the ID of the process that owns the thread (useful when you have threads starting other threads), and the priority of the thread (normally the same or lower than the base priority for the process as a whole).

Spy++

Spy++ is a complex utility that can give you more information about your application than you might have thought possible. This section is going to give you a very brief overview of this utility. What I'll do is point out some of the more interesting features that will make working with the applications in this book easier. Make sure you take time to work with this utility further once you've learned the basics.

The first thing you'll see when you start Spy++ is a list of windows. A window can be any number of object types, but the most familiar is the application window. Here's an example of what you might see when you start Spy++ with the OCXTest sample application (see Chapter 4) running:

Notice that there are three windows that belong to the main application window—all three of which are controls on the dialog box. In this case, the OK, Cancel, and On/Off buttons are all considered windows. In fact, when you try to change the caption on one of these buttons, you'll find that you're working with the CWindow MFC class, which means that Spy++ is right on track displaying the information as it has.

Working with Window Properties

Windows are a central part of working with Spy++. They represent the method you'll normally use to begin deciphering how an application works and how well it runs. It makes sense, then, that you can access every aspect of an application, its child windows, processes, and threads through the Window Properties dialog box shown next:

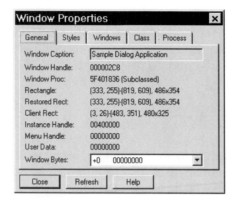

Accessing this dialog box is easy. All you need to do is right-click the window you want to view, then choose Properties from the context menu. You can also access this dialog box using the View | Properties command.

The General tab of the Window Properties dialog box tells you about the window as a whole. It includes the window's display name, the window handle, the virtual address of the window procedure, the size of the rectangle used to display the window (both present and restored sizes), and various other pieces of general application information.

The Styles tab contains a list of the window style constants used to create the window. For example, you'll commonly find WS_VISIBLE as one of the items in the list unless you're dealing with an invisible window. This same tab contains extended styles for the window, such as WS_EX_APPWINDOW. These constants should be very familiar to C/C++ programmers.

The Windows tab contains five entries. You can move between windows at the same level by clicking the links in the Next Window and Previous Window fields. The Parent Window field will contain a link if this is a child window or (None) if this is a main window. If the window contains child windows (like the controls for the OCXTest.EXE program), you'll see an entry in the First Child field. Clicking this link will take you down one level in the hierarchy so that you can examine any child windows that belong to the current window. Finally, the Owner Window field will contain a link if the current window is owned by another window—except for the Desktop, in which case the field displays a value of (None).

The Class tab tells you about the MFC (or other) class used to create the window. For example, the main window for the OCXTest.EXE program uses the Dialog class, while the controls are all listed as being part of the Button class. You'll also find class-specific information like the class style codes, number of data bytes used by this instance of the class, an instance handle for the window, number of bytes used by the window itself, and window details such as the name of any associated menus.

The Process tab provides a list of process IDs and thread IDs associated with the current window. Clicking the links associated with each field will display the Properties dialog box associated with the process or thread ID. We'll look at this Properties dialog box in more detail in the Viewing Processes and Threads section that follows.

Viewing Messages

Windows runs on messages. Every activity that the user engages in generates a message of some sort. It's important to monitor those messages and see how your application reacts. For example, if you expect a certain message to get generated when the user clicks a button, you can monitor the message stream to see if it really does get sent.

There are a number of ways to display the Messages window for a window that you're debugging. You could right-click on the window and choose Messages from the context menu. However, in this particular case, the best way to start the message-monitoring process is to use the Spy | Messages command. Using this command will display the Message Options dialog box shown here (you don't get this dialog box when you use the context menu method of displaying the Messages window):

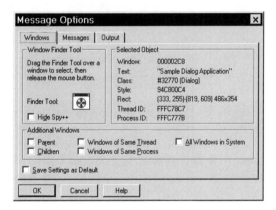

Notice the Selected Object frame on the right side of the dialog box. This frame provides you with some information about the object you've selected, which enables you to determine if this is the window you want to monitor. The Finder Tool on the left side of the dialog box is interesting as well. Drag this tool to any displayed window, then release the mouse button, and the information on the right side will change to match the data for that window. (The windows will get highlighted as you drag the mouse cursor over them so that you can see which one is being selected.) The Windows tab also allows you to choose additional windows. For example, you may want to monitor the child windows as well as the parent window for a specific kind of message.

There are 849 different messages that Spy++ can track for the average window. Needless to say, you could end up with a lot of useless tracking information if you don't trim this number down to a more reasonable number. That's why the Messages tab is so important. This tab allows you to choose which messages get tracked in the Messages window. You can choose messages singly or by group. A Select All button allows you to choose all of the messages, while a Clear All button allows you to clear the current selections. Make sure you tune these settings before you display the Messages window or your chances of getting the input you need are very small indeed.

It's also important to determine how you want information displayed in the Messages window. In most cases, the default options on the Output tab will work just fine. Spy++ assumes that you want to display only decoded information and only on-screen. However, there are options for displaying raw message information. You can also choose to send the output to a file as well as to the screen.

Once you have the options set for your Messages window, you can click OK and Spy++ will display it for you. Here's an example of what a Messages window would look like if you chose to monitor a subset of button and mouse events:

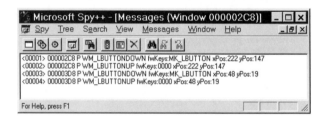

In this case, I clicked on the OCXTest application twice. The first time, I clicked on the main window, while the second time, I clicked on the On/Off button. Notice that the log entries contain the handle of the window where the action occurred, the action performed (mouse button up or down), and the position where the action occurred. Obviously, this is a simple test case, but it's also easy to see that monitoring messages can provide you with very important debugging clues for your application.

Viewing Processes and Threads

Every application you create will have at least one process and one thread. Consider a process as the overall application identifier, while a thread consists of a particular set of actions taking place within that process. In a multithreaded application, each thread of execution is performing a single task that affects the application (the process) as a whole.

Spy++ allows you to monitor both processes and threads. All you need to do is use the Spy | Processes or Spy | Threads command to display the appropriate window. Here's an example of the Processes window:

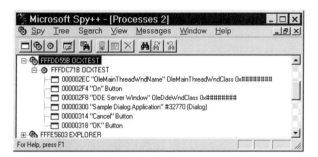

It's interesting to note that the Processes window also contains a list of any threads owned by the process in a hierarchical format. For this reason, you'll normally want to use the Processes window over the Thread window. You get more information in an easier-to-use format using the Processes window.

Notice also that there's a complete list of windows provided, even those that aren't visible. This listing differs from the one you saw for the Windows window, which lists only visible windows such as controls. Our application still contains three control windows, but it also includes an invisible OLE main thread, a DDE server, and a Dialog class window. Double-clicking any of these window entries will display a Window Properties dialog box like the one we talked about in the "Working with Window Properties" section of the chapter.

Stress Utility

Development machines tend to be state of the art, contain lots of memory, and provide plenty of speed. On the other hand, the workstation owned by the user may not have much in the way of memory, state-of-the-art hardware, or speed. Theoretically, everyone takes his or her application to a least common denominator workstation for testing. That way, a developer can ensure that the application written on a development machine looks and works just as nice on a user's workstation.

The Stress utility jumps in to provide a little reality to this scenario. How many developers have both a test workstation and all of the development machines they require at their disposal? Not many, is the likely answer. So, the Stress utility allows you to simulate that memory-constrained stress situation that an application you create will run into when going from your development machine to the user's workstation.

Note   *Obviously, not having to move the application from the development machine to a test workstation during the development process saves a lot of time. Just as obviously, you still need to test the application on a workstation once you complete it to ensure that it will run as intended.*

You can also use the Stress utility for other kinds of testing. For example, what happens when the user's machine runs out of GDI memory? Will your application degrade gracefully or crash indignantly? Stress can help you test resource-related problems that your application may run into. You can also use Stress to test error handling when a resource isn't available, and other kinds of problems that it would normally be difficult to test.

The first thing you'll see when you start the Stress utility is a display of the current resource values for the machine you're using it on. These values include the total amount of global memory, percentages of 16-bit user and GDI memory in use, available hard drive space, the number of available file handles, and the 32-bit memory available for user, GDI, and menu usage. Here's an example of the starting display:

Resource	Remaining	
Global	65036.00	KB
User	77	%
GDI	83	%
Disk Space	2047.69	MB
File Handles	119	
Wnd32	2014.51	KB
Menu32	1936.04	KB
GDI32	2022.29	KB

Stress — Settings Options Help

There are two ways to test your application using Stress. The first is to set fixed values for a specific resource using the Fixed Settings dialog box. You access this dialog box using the Settings | Fixed Settings command. The Fixed Settings dialog box contains a list of all the resources shown in the main window. Setting the value for a resource to -1 deallocates all Stress utility usage of that resource, while setting it to 0 completely allocates all of the available resource to simulate an out-of-resource condition. You can also set a field to a specific value so that Stress will allocate a specific amount of a resource. This is how you can test for workstation performance on your development machine.

The second form of testing is random resource allocation. Stress will allocate and deallocate resources in the background so that you can see how your application reacts to varying amounts of free resources. To start random resource allocation, you use the Settings | Executer command. What you'll see is an Executer Options dialog box. Like the Fixed Settings dialog box, this one contains entries for each of the resource categories displayed on the main window—only this time you'll see check boxes in place of fields that you can use to set specific values. You'll also need to set a stress level from 1 to 4 (with 4 being the most difficult for your application to endure), the seed used for determining the random allocations (using the same seed results in the same series of allocations being used), and the interval between allocations. Stress also allows you to use a message-based allocation strategy. Every time a specific kind of message appears in the message queue, Stress will make an allocation. This setting allows you to test for event-related problems in your application.

> *You can set the parameters for the various stress levels by clicking the Advanced button on the Executer Options dialog box. This will display a Stress Level Ranges dialog box where you can set the range of values that Stress will use for resource allocations during the application testing process.*

Tracer

Normally, your debugger will only trace events that happen within your application. In other words, events that happen outside of your application, such as accessing a database, are somewhat invisible. Tracer changes all that. It allows you to trace MFC calls in your debugger, in addition to those that happen within the application. When you open this utility, you'll see a list of trace options like the ones shown here:

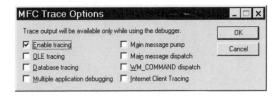

Notice that the Tracer utility allows you to turn tracing on or off using the Enable tracing option. The other options control exactly which external occurrences your debugger will trace. Some of the more useful options include database and OLE tracing. The Multiple application debugging option comes in handy when using Visual Studio in a multiple-language scenario, as we'll do in this book. There are even options for tracing the Windows message queue and events that occur on the Internet. The important thing to remember is that this utility works with MFC calls, not every call that can occur on the test machine.

WinDiff

WinDiff is a utility of comparisons. You can compare two files, two directories, or even two disk drives if you want. The point of this utility is that you can find out how two file storage objects differ in a matter of moments, rather than the hours it might take to perform a comparison by hand.

When comparing two files, WinDiff will also allow you to edit one file or a composite of both of them. You can also expand the comparison of the two files and perform a variety of other analyses on the two files.

Let's begin by looking at an example of two files that started out being the same—I then added a sentence to each file to make them different. (You can perform a similar experiment if you'd like—just create two files with the same content, then make a small change to each.) To perform a comparison, use the File | Compare Files command to load the files. WinDiff will ask you for two filenames. The outline display will tell you that the two files are different, which is important, but not all that useful. Now click the Expand button and you'll see the kind of analysis that can help you locate problems quickly. Here's the result of my file experiment:

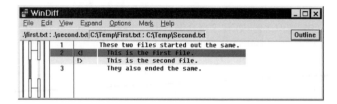

As you can see, the first and last sentences of the two files are exactly the same. The second sentence of both files is different. Now look on the left side of the display. There is an outline that you can use to get to file differences quickly. A difference in the first file is shown in one color, a difference in the second file is shown in a second color, and exact comparisons are shown in a third color.

Let's look at an example of a directory comparison. You perform a directory comparison using the File | Compare Directories command. WinDiff will ask you to provide a path for each directory. I filled two directories with test files and then compared them. The two directories contained some files that were exactly the same, a few that were modified versions of the ones found in the other directory, and a few files that appear only in one directory. Here's a typical example of what you might see:

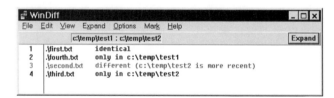

ZoomIn

If you've ever had to squint to see the details of an icon or read some small text, you'll appreciate the ZoomIn utility. This utility acts just like a magnifying glass. Here's a typical example of ZoomIn in action:

Tip	*You can copy the contents of the ZoomIn window to the clipboard for use in another application by pressing* CTRL-C *or by using the Edit	Copy command.*

Using this utility is easy. All you need to do is click within the display window, then drag the magnify box out and place it over whatever you want to magnify on-screen. The size of the magnify box is determined by the amount of zoom that you've selected and the size of the display window.

Adjusting the amount of zoom is easy. Just move the scroll bar on the right side of the ZoomIn window up and down. Moving the thumb up reduces the magnification, while moving it down increases magnification.

You can also set ZoomIn to automatically refresh the display. Just use the Options | Refresh Rate command to display the Refresh Rate dialog box. Check the Enable Refresh Time option to start automatic updates. You set the time between updates using the Interval (Tenths of Seconds) field.

Part II

Working with Others

The
Complete
Reference

Chapter 6

Using Visual SourceSafe

Most large projects today require some form of team development if you expect to get them done in the required time. In addition, the inclusion of multimedia and database management in a project requires the use of specialists. These specialists will work with other team members to create a cohesive project that one person may not be able to do due to a lack of skills. In short, team development is a very real part of the world that programmers deal with today.

Team development means allowing more than one person to work on a project. There are some problems that a manager will encounter as soon as there is more than one person working on a project, problems that Visual SourceSafe is designed to help you avoid. The following list talks about some of the ways that Visual SourceSafe can help in a general way to make life easier for the project manager (we'll talk about more specific ways as the chapter progresses).

■ **Limiting individual team member access** If a particular part of the project is outside of a person's expertise, then normally that person doesn't require access to that part of the project. Even if they do require access, they'll normally need to work with another team member while doing so. Visual SourceSafe makes it easier for the project manager to maintain control over project access. Limiting access can help the team members focus on their part of the project and reduce security problems that might occur if team members have access to the entire project.

■ **Controlling file access** The possibility of two people trying to access the same file at the same time is fairly high on a programming project. However, if both parties do access and then modify the file, there are going to be problems resolving the changes made to the file by each individual. Visual SourceSafe provides the means for team members to check a file out for editing. This practice prevents two problems. First, it prevents another team member from modifying the file, which means that all the edits that take place on the file remain intact. Second, team members who need access to the file will be able to find out who has it open. Nothing can cause more problems with a project than having a problem with organization. Team members need to know who is using what resource and when.

■ **Source control** Even individual programmers make code-editing mistakes that they wish they could recover from later. Visual SourceSafe makes it possible to retrieve a previous version of a source code file. In effect, this feature allows the team as a whole to undo mistakes or a manager to undo an incorrect assumption on module direction by a team member.

■ **Centralized storage** Visual SourceSafe helps the team as a whole to keep track of where code is stored. Even if different pieces of a project are stored in different areas of the network, what the team sees is a centralized storage methodology. Using centralized storage means that every team member can access the parts of the project when they need to access them without having to spend a lot of time looking.

- **File backup**   The ability to archive all or part of a project means that you can create small backups of your project as the coding process continues. It's important to have some means for creating backups in a comprehensive, easy-to-restore manner, which is one of the features Visual SourceSafe provides for you.

- **Archival**   Creating an archive of a finished project is always important. You never know when you'll be called upon to make some change to the existing code. Visual SourceSafe makes it easy to archive an entire project and then restore it later in such a way that it appears the code was always present on the server.

- **Local file updates**   A programmer or program tester can obtain the latest version of one or more files as the project develops without affecting the current build. The file update gets stored on the user's local hard drive, not the central copy used for source control. This means that your testers can always use the latest code without interfering with anyone else's efforts (especially those of the people coding the application).

As you can see, Visual SourceSafe is an important tool for both team and individual developers, though the team benefits are much greater. The following sections will help you understand more about Visual SourceSafe and how you can use it to make your team development efforts safer, more efficient, and easier.

We'll begin by looking at Visual SourceSafe administration. I won't cover every concern for security in this section, nor will we look at every security feature that Visual SourceSafe has to offer. What you'll get is an overview of how to administer Visual SourceSafe and some ideas on how to create a security policy for your company.

The next section of the chapter will deal with one of the maintenance tasks you need to perform when using Visual SourceSafe—analyzing and fixing the Visual SourceSafe database. Even though Visual SourceSafe is designed to provide the ultimate in security, efficiency, and reliability, you may still encounter a problem or two—just as you would when using any other database product.

Finally, the last three sections of the chapter deal with actually using Visual SourceSafe with a project. We'll look at usage techniques for Visual C++, Visual Basic, Visual J++, and Visual InterDev. All four products allow you to use Visual SourceSafe to ensure your project is protected from harm. It's important to understand how Visual SourceSafe works in each environment so that team members using different languages on the same project know how to interact with each other.

Administering Visual SourceSafe

Before you can do much with Visual SourceSafe, you need to know how to administer it. You need to add users, and potentially a database or two, before you'll be able to actually use the product the first time. In addition, you'll need to know how to archive and restore projects as time progresses. This section of the chapter covers all three administration-related tasks: users, databases, and projects. In addition, we'll talk about setting the Visual SourceSafe options that determine how security and other features work. The following sections will help you understand how to use the Visual SourceSafe Administrator to perform a wide range of Visual SourceSafe–related tasks. Figure 6-1 shows the main Visual SourceSafe display (this figure shows two users added).

The first time you start Visual SourceSafe Administrator, you'll see a message saying that an administrator password hasn't been assigned. Make sure you assign a password to the administrator immediately by following the procedure in the Changing User Properties section that follows. Once you assign a password, exit Visual SourceSafe Administrator and restart it to test the password. You'll also want to make sure that you're the only one using Visual SourceSafe at the time. Otherwise, someone else could learn the administrator password and compromise the security that Visual SourceSafe can provide.

Users

Visual SourceSafe comes with two users added to the database: guest and administrator as shown in Figure 6-1. If you allow everyone to log on as an administrator, you'll lose the security benefits that Visual SourceSafe can provide.

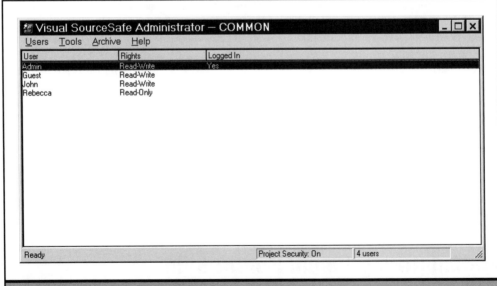

Figure 6-1.   The main Visual SourceSafe Administrator display shows a list of users, their level of overall access, and whether they're logged in

Alternatively, if everyone logs on as a guest, they may not have the rights needed to get any useful work done. In sum, you have to add users to your Visual SourceSafe database before you use it, just as you would for any kind of other secure environment—such as a network operating system.

The following sections will show you how to perform three user-related tasks: adding, deleting, and modifying. As an administrator you'll begin by adding users, but it won't be long before someone leaves the company and you have to delete them from the database or someone loses their password and you have to supply them with a new one. Whatever the reason for change, you can be sure that you'll need to change the user setup on a more than occasional basis.

Adding Users

Adding a new user to the Visual SourceSafe database is relatively easy. Just use the Users | Add User command to display the Add User dialog box shown here:

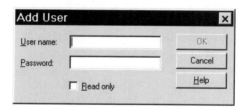

Type the user name (the one that the user will use to log into Visual SourceSafe) into the User name field. Type the password you want them to use in the Password field. Note that the Read only option allows you to restrict the user to only reading what the project contains. This is a useful feature for support personnel like technical writers who need access to the project but don't need to change it in any way. Click OK and the new user will appear in the main Visual SourceSafe window like the one shown in Figure 6-1.

 Using the user's network name for their Visual SourceSafe login allows the user to log in faster. Visual SourceSafe can automatically add the user's login name to the Log In dialog box.

At this point, the user can access Visual SourceSafe. However, if you have project security enabled, the user won't be able to work with any projects until you assign the user some rights to it. We'll cover setting rights in the Changing User Properties section of the chapter.

Deleting Users

You'll need to remove users as people leave the company. Keeping an old user in place is one sure way to create a security breach, and it happens more often than most administrators would like to admit. All you need to do to remove a user from Visual SourceSafe is to highlight their name in the main window list (Figure 6-1) and press DELETE. Alternatively, you could use the Users | Delete User command to remove a user. In either case, you'll see a message box asking if you're sure that you want to delete the user in question. Click Yes to complete the process.

 Deleting users from Visual SourceSafe is a one-way process. You can't recover the user once you delete him or her from the Visual SourceSafe database. If you do delete a user by accident, you'll need to re-create them from scratch. Make sure you assign the new user entry to any projects that they may have had access to in the past if project security is set to On.

Changing User Properties

Adding a user to the database usually isn't the end of the process. Depending on how you have Visual SourceSafe set up, you may need to add the user to one or more projects and set the level of access they have to those projects. However, even if you use the default setup for Visual SourceSafe, there are going to be times that you need to change a user password or even the user's name.

Changing a user's password is one of the easiest things to do, so let's look at that first. All you need to do is highlight the user's name that you want to change in the main Visual SourceSafe Administrator display (Figure 6-1) and select the Users | Change Password command. You'll see a Change Password dialog box like the one shown here:

Change Password	✕
User name: John	OK
New password:	Cancel
Verify:	Help

Type the new password in the New password field, then again in the Verify field. Click OK to make the change permanent. As long as you typed the same password in both the New password and Verify fields, Visual SourceSafe will change the password in the current database.

Although you won't do this very much, you may have to change a user's name or their read access to the Visual SourceSafe database. To change either of these items, highlight the user's name in the main window list (Figure 6-1) and select the Users | Edit User command. You'll see an Edit User dialog box like the one shown here:

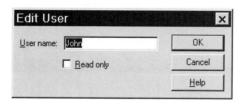

 You cannot change the name or read rights of the Admin user. Visual SourceSafe Administrator will display an error message if you try to do so.

Type a new user name or change the Read only option as needed. Click OK to make the change permanent.

Now we get to the three tasks that require you to set Project Security to On: setting user rights by project, determining the current rights of a user, and copying the rights of one user to another. You can access this option on the Project Security tab of the SourceSafe Options dialog box that we'll discuss in the Setting Visual SourceSafe Options section of the chapter.

The first task is to set the user's options by project. You'll need to select the Tools | Rights by Project option. Visual SourceSafe Administrator will display the dialog box shown here:

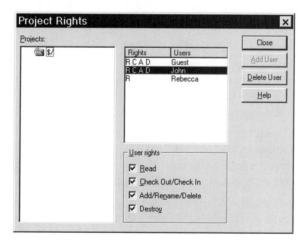

The Projects list in this dialog box shows you the current projects that Visual SourceSafe is managing. The default project is $/. When you add a new project to Visual SourceSafe, its name will appear in the list. Simply highlight the name of the project and click Add User. You'll see an Add Users for <Project Name> dialog box like the one shown here:

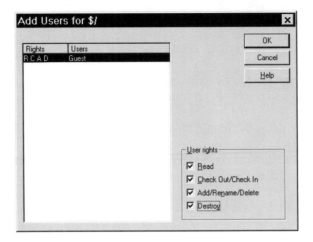

You'll need to select a user from the list provided, then click one or more of the User Rights options. Click OK to add the user to the project. There are four security options provided by Visual SourceSafe. The following list provides an explanation of each security option.

- **Read**   Allows the user to read the project files, but not to modify them in any way. You might assign this right to a guest or someone who needs to look at the source code for a project for documentation purposes. Obviously, anyone who wants to edit the file would need this right as well, but this right alone isn't sufficient to allow someone to edit the file.

- **Check Out/Check In**   Allows the user to check a file out for editing. Everyone else on the team is locked out while the file is checked out. The user must check the file in before someone else can check it out (which is why both rights are assigned together). Adding this right automatically adds the Read right as well.

- **Add/Rename/Delete**   Allows the user to add new files to the project and either delete or rename existing files. Adding this right automatically adds the Check Out/Check In right as well.

- **Destroy**   Allows the user to destroy the project. This is the most powerful of all the rights that Visual SourceSafe provides and should be given with care. In most cases, only a project manager or the Visual SourceSafe administrator will have this right. Adding this right automatically adds the Add/Rename/Delete right as well.

Removing a user from a project is just as easy as adding one. Highlight the user you want to remove in the Project Rights dialog box, then click Delete User. Visual

SourceSafe will ask if you really want to remove the user. Click Yes to complete the process. Use this option with care since there isn't any way to undo a deletion.

Our second project-security-related task is to determine the current rights of a user. You may find that you don't want to manage user rights by project. Selecting the Tools | Rights Assignments for Users command will display an Assignments for <User Name> dialog box like the one shown here:

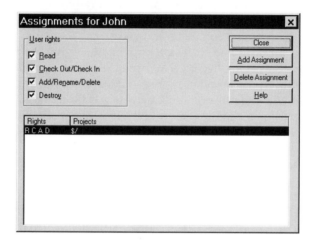

This dialog box will still allow you to change the user rights for a specific project (and the rights options are still the same as before). However, the emphasis this time is on the user, not the project. To add a user to a new project, click Add Assignment. You'll see an Add Assignment for <User Name> dialog box, as shown here:

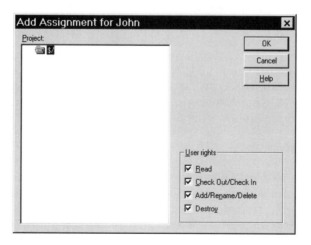

Highlight a project name, choose one or more rights options, then click OK to add the user to a new project. The new project will appear in the list shown in the Assignments for <User Name> dialog box.

Deleting an assignment is equally easy. Highlight the name of the project that you want to remove the user from, then click Delete Assignment. Visual SourceSafe Administrator will ask if you're sure that you want to delete the user's rights to the project. Click Yes to complete the process. (As with everything else, deleting an assignment is a one-way process, so you'll want to be sure that you want to remove the user from the project before you complete the process.)

That brings us to our third and final task, copying the rights of one use to another. As your Visual SourceSafe setup becomes more complex, you may find that adding users to a project one at a time becomes more of a chore than you want to take on. Copying from a user with the same or similar rights greatly reduces the time required to set up a new user. All you need to do is add the new user using the procedure in the Adding Users section of the chapter. Highlight the new user, then select the Tools | Copy User Rights command. You'll see a Copy Rights Assignments to <User Name> dialog box like the one shown here:

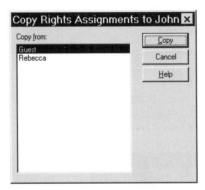

Highlight the user that you want to copy the rights from, then click Copy. Visual SourceSafe Administrator will copy the rights of the user you selected in the Copy Rights Assignments to <User Name> dialog box to the user that you selected in the main Visual SourceSafe window (refer to Figure 6-1).

Databases

There are essentially two tasks when it comes to databases in Visual SourceSafe: creating a database and maintaining it. Creating a new database allows you to keep groups of users or project types separate. You'll also need to create a new database every time you want to use a different server to store project information. This section of the chapter explores database creation, since you'll need to perform this task as part of setting Visual SourceSafe up for use for the first time. (We'll cover database maintenance in the Analyzing and Fixing the Visual SourceSafe Database section of the chapter.)

Each database has its own set of rules and security setup. In other words, each database is a completely separate environment, which offers you another way of enforcing project security. Simply create a new database for each project, for each project type, or group of programmers.

Visual SourceSafe creates a default database on your local hard drive when you install it, which is fine if you plan to use Visual SourceSafe in the stand-alone mode. However, if you plan on using Visual SourceSafe in a team environment, you'll need to create a database in a central location such as a server. The following procedure will help you create a database on a Windows NT Server, simply modify it to fit your particular needs (I'm assuming that you've already started Visual SourceSafe Administrator).

1. Select the Tools | Create Database command. You'll see the Create New VSS Database dialog box shown next. Notice that you must select a location for the database, as well as the kind of database you want to create. In most cases, you'll want to create a Visual SourceSafe 6.0 database if all of the people using the database have Visual Studio 6.0. The reason is simple—the new database format is much more efficient.

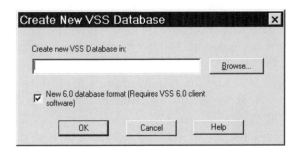

2. Type a path to the database location on the Windows NT Server (as an alternative, you can click the Browse button to search for a new location).

3. Choose the New 6.0 database format option if all the users for this database have Visual Studio 6.0 installed on their workstations. Visual SourceSafe Administrator will display a variety of dialog boxes as it creates the database for you. Be patient, because the new database creation process can take time. Once the creation process is complete, you'll see a Database Creation Complete dialog box like the one shown here:

4. Click OK to clear the Database Creation Complete dialog box. The creation process is complete, but you can't actually use the database yet.

5. Use the Users | Open SourceSafe Database command to display the Open SourceSafe Database dialog box shown here (your dialog box may not contain an entry for the newly created database as shown in the following illustration):

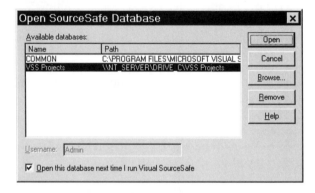

6. If the newly created database appears in the Available databases list, then highlight it; otherwise, use the Browse button to find the database on the Windows NT Server.

7. Click Open. Visual SourceSafe Administrator will open the new database. The new database won't contain any old user names—you'll need to enter everything from scratch.

8. Add users, set any required Visual SourceSafe options, and set any required security.

Projects

Visual SourceSafe Administrator allows you to do two things with the projects you create. You can archive the projects when you finish (this will save all of the required state information for later) or restore them when you need to start working on them again. Since most development systems can only handle so many projects at once, archiving and restoring projects will be one of the more common tasks that an administrator will need to perform. The following sections will help you understand how to perform both tasks.

Archiving a Project

Archiving (preparing for offline storage) a project allows you to store it in such a way that you can restore it later, and as far as your system is concerned, it appears that the project never left the hard drive. Maintaining an archive of completed projects is an important part of the administrator's job because those old projects normally require some kind of update along the way. The following procedure will show you how easy it is to create an archive of a project maintained by Visual SourceSafe (this procedure assumes that you have Visual SourceSafe Administrator open).

1. Select the Archive | Archive Projects command. You'll see the Choose Project to Archive dialog box shown here. This is where you'll choose the project you want to archive.

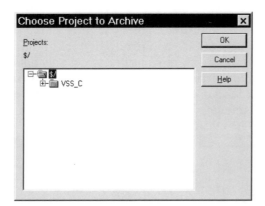

2. Highlight the project you need to archive. The example will use the VSS_C project throughout this procedure, but you can substitute any project name.

3. Click OK. You'll see the Archive Wizard, Step 1 of 3 dialog box shown next. Notice that you can choose to archive more than one project at a time by clicking the <<Add button. You'll see the Choose Project to Archive dialog box again, where you can choose another project to archive. If you need to remove a project from the archive list, highlight the project, then click Remove>> in the Archive Wizard, Step 1 of 3 dialog box.

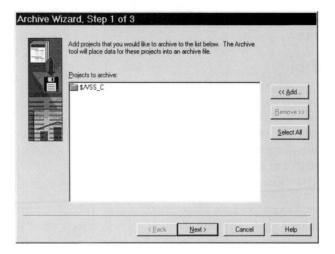

4. Click Next. You'll see the Archive Wizard, Step 2 of 3 dialog box shown here. Visual SourceSafe Administrator gives you three storage options: save the data to a file, save the data to a file and remove it from the database, and delete the data permanently. It's pretty obvious that you'd only delete the data permanently without archiving it if you didn't intend to update the project later. For the purposes of this example, I'll assume that you'll want to archive the project and remove it from the database so that you can restore it later.

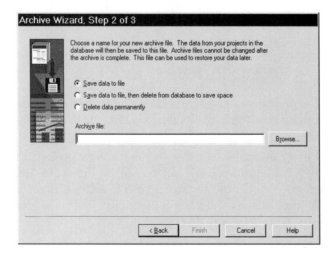

5. Select one of the archive options. The example uses the Save data to file, then delete from database to save space option (space on the server).

6. Type a name in the Archive file field. The example uses **C:\Temp\MyArchive.ssa** as the archive file.

7. Click Next. You'll see the Archive Wizard, Step 3 of 3 dialog box shown here. This is where you'll choose which files get archived. Normally, you'll want to archive all of them to ensure you get a complete copy of the application.

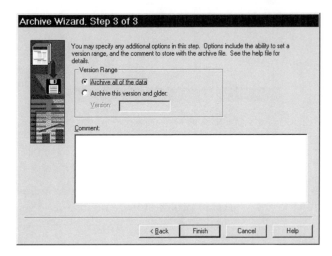

8. Choose the Archive all of the data option (unless you want to save only part of the application data archive).

9. Type a comment in the comment field to identify the contents of the archive later.

10. Click Finish. You'll see an Archive Wizard dialog box, like the one shown next, as Visual SourceSafe Administrator creates an archive of your project. There may be additional dialog boxes displayed during the archive process since Visual SourceSafe Administrator may have to ask your permission to delete certain checkout and other administrative files from the database. Be patient. The archiving process can take a long time, depending on the size of your project.

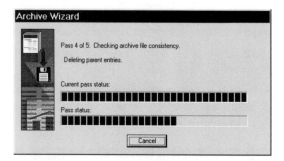

11. At some point, you'll see an Archive/restore successfully completed dialog box like the one shown here:

12. Click OK to complete the process. Now that you have an archive file, you can back it up to tape or some other offline storage media.

Restoring a Project

In most cases, you'll eventually want to work on a project that you archived. That's when you need to use the restore features of Visual SourceSafe Administrator. The following procedure will show you a typical restore process. We'll be using the same example program that I showed you in the previous section (the procedure assumes that you have Visual SourceSafe Administrator open).

1. Use the Archive | Restore Projects command to display the Restore Wizard, Step 1 of 3 dialog box shown here:

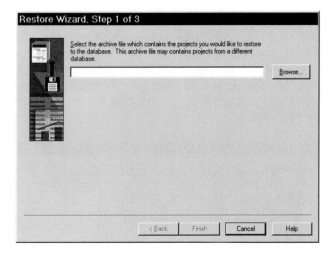

2. Type the name and full path to the archive file that you want to restore (as an alternative, you can use the Browse button to find the file).

3. Click Next. You'll see the Restore Wizard, Step 2 of 3 dialog box shown here. This dialog box allows you to choose which of the projects in the archive that you want to restore. The default action is to restore the entire archive. Notice that you can choose to restore subprojects as well as complete projects. You'd use this option if you had used the archive for backup purposes and only needed to restore part of the project.

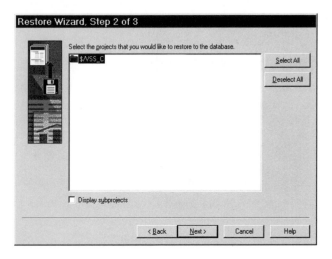

4. Choose one or more projects to restore, then click Next. You'll see the Restore Wizard, Step 3 of 3 dialog box shown here. This dialog box allows you to restore the project to its original directory or to an alternative location. In most cases, you'll retain the current directory when restoring a project that requires additional work. You may want to use an alternative directory if you're restoring a partial project or restoring a complete project for comparison purposes.

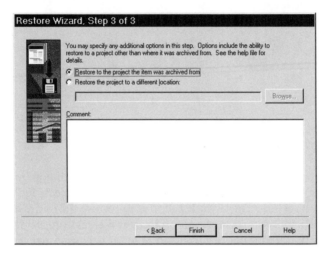

5. Click Finish. You'll see the Restore Wizard dialog box shown here. Restoration may take some time as Visual SourceSafe restores all of your project information.

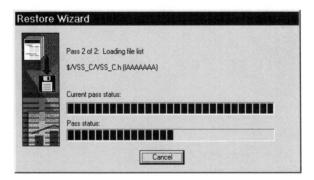

6. At some point, you'll see an Archive/restore successfully completed dialog box like the one shown here:

7. Click OK to complete the process. At this point, you should be able to access the project just as if it had been in the database all the time. You'll then need to perform additional steps, such as assign users to the project and give them rights to it.

Setting Visual SourceSafe Options

You probably won't need to spend a lot of time setting up Visual SourceSafe. In most cases, you'll set it up once after the initial installation, then change the options from time to time as conditions in your company change. Even so, it's important to know what options you have available to you to make Visual SourceSafe easier to use.

Displaying the Visual SourceSafe options is easy. Just use the Tools | Options command within Visual SourceSafe Administrator to open the SourceSafe Options dialog box shown here:

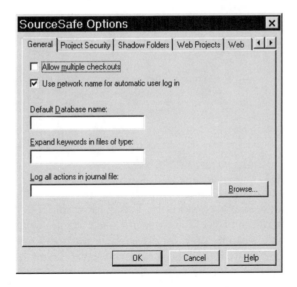

The General tab of the SourceSafe Options dialog box allows you to choose a default database and log events to a journal. There's a special field where you can place the names of files that use keyword expansion. Keyword expansion is a special process that Visual SourceSafe can perform when you check in or add files. For example, if you place the string "$Revision: $" in a file that uses keyword expansion, Visual SourceSafe will replace it with the word Revision followed by the current revision number for the file. There are also two options on the General tab. The first, Allow multiple checkouts, tells Visual SourceSafe that you want to allow more than one person to check out a file at a time. The second option, Use network name for automatic user log in, tells Visual SourceSafe to display the user's network name automatically in the login dialog box when the user logs into Visual SourceSafe.

Using multiple checkouts is a dangerous practice that could lead to corruption of project files. Always use this feature with care. In fact, consider it an option of last choice on large projects where the need to provide multiple access is a necessity.

The next tab is Project Security. We've already talked about the options on this dialog box. The most important option, of course, is Enable project security. This option allows you to set security for each user on a project-by-project basis. Here's what the Project Security tab of the SourceSafe Options dialog box looks like:

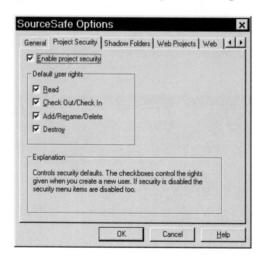

A shadow folder contains the most recently checked in copy of all of the files for your project. All of these files are read-only. The shadow folder is not designed to replace the local copy of the project files, nor is it used to replace the Visual SourceSafe database. Shadow folders can be used for a variety of purposes. The most common reason that you'll use shadow folders is as a repository of source files for team members who only need to read the source data, not modify it in any way. You can also use a shadow folder as a central repository for compiling purposes. The programmer would grab the parts of the application that he or she isn't working on from this repository and combine them with the parts that he or she is working on. Here's what the Shadow Folders tab of the SourceSafe Options dialog box looks like (normally there isn't a project selected—the illustration shows a project so that the other fields on the tab become visible):

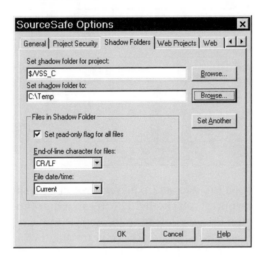

As you can see from the Shadow Folders tab, there are three steps in setting up a shadow folder for your project. First, use the Browse button for the Set shadow folder for project field to set the project name. This will enable the Set shadow folder to field. Second, use the Browse button for the Set shadow folder to field to set a location for the shadow folder. Since this is going to be a shared resource, you'd normally select a location on a network drive. Finally, you'd set the various options for the shadow folder. One of the options that's set by default is to set the read-only attribute for all the shadow folder files. You also have to determine things like the end-of-line character for the files and how the time and date stamps are set for the files.

You can use multiple shadow folders to create a repeater setup on multiple servers so that one server doesn't get bogged down by requests for information. The Set Another button on the Shadow Folders tab of the SourceSafe Options dialog box allows you to provide multiple shadow folders for a single project.

It's fairly certain that you'll work on at least one Web project with Visual Studio. Visual SourceSafe is ready to help you make accessing the project as easy as possible. The Web Projects tab of the SourceSafe Options dialog box (shown next) allows you to set up your project for Web access:

The first thing you need to do to set up a Web project is to specify the project name in the This project represents a Web site field. You can either type the name of the project manually or use the Browse button to locate it within the Visual SourceSafe database. Second, you need to specify a URL for your Web project. Finally, you need to set up one or more optional fields like the Deployment path, which contains either a local or remote location to deploy the files in your project. The Site map filename field contains the name of the file you want Visual SourceSafe to use to create a site map. The default setting for this field is Sitemap.HTM. Some server setups also support a virtual root directory. If your server setup includes a virtual root directory, then enter this value in the Virtual Root field.

There are three default options that you can specify for all Web projects. These settings appear on the Web tab of the SourceSafe Options dialog box. The first setting specifies the proxy used to access Web sites outside of the local network when you use a firewall for outside access. The second setting tells Visual SourceSafe which Web sites are local and therefore don't require proxy access because they're already inside the firewall. Finally, you can specify the name of the file to use for default Web pages. Visual SourceSafe will use the name Default.HTM if you don't specify a value for this field.

The last tab of the SourceSafe Options dialog box is File Types. You'll use it to specify the kinds of files that Visual SourceSafe will recognize for specific types of projects. Here's what the File Types tab looks like:

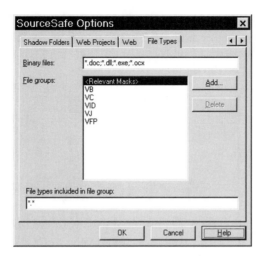

The first field, Binary files, overrides what Visual SourceSafe normally sees as a binary file. The values shown in the illustration represent the default file types that Visual SourceSafe recognizes. Below the Binary files field, you'll see the File groups list and associated File types included in file group field. Selecting one of the entries in the File groups list will show you the files that Visual Studio associates with that type of project in the File types included in file group field. You can change these entries to allow Visual SourceSafe to automatically recognize more or fewer file types automatically.

So, what happens if the file group you want to use doesn't appear in the list? Click the Add button and you'll see an Add File Group dialog box. You can use this dialog box to add new entries to the File groups list. Likewise, highlighting an entry in the File groups list and then clicking delete will remove the file group from consideration when Visual SourceSafe manages a project for you.

Analyzing and Fixing the Visual SourceSafe Database

There are all kinds of maintenance procedures that the average administrator has to perform on a daily basis, so you're probably not too thrilled to hear that you should perform some maintenance on the Visual SourceSafe database as well. Fortunately, the maintenance procedure is almost too simple. All you need to do is choose either the Analyze VSS DB or the Analyze & Fix VSS DB option from the Microsoft Visual Studio 6.0 | Microsoft Visual SourceSafe submenu of the Start menu. If the database is in good shape, you'll see a dialog box like the one shown here:

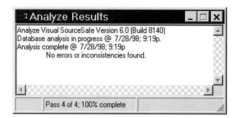

In the unlikely event that there is a problem with your database, the Analyze & Fix VSS DB menu option will fix the problem automatically in most cases. If you suspect that there might be damage to your database, try to analyze the database first without fixing it. In some cases, the maintenance utility will be able to provide suggestions that you can use without trying the fix part of the utility first. In addition, Microsoft support may be able to provide you with some assistance. Just take things slow in repairing your database to minimize potential data loss.

Using Visual SourceSafe with Programming Language Products

It's finally time to take a look at how Visual SourceSafe interacts with the programming language products provided with Visual Studio. Every language is a little different, but there shouldn't be too many surprises. We'll follow the same process in every one of the examples that follow. First, we'll create a very simple program shell (which may not be functional). Then, we'll add that project to the Visual SourceSafe database using the language product's built-in features.

Visual C++

Using Visual SourceSafe with Visual C++ is relatively easy for most project types. Let's begin by creating a simple dialog-based application project. The following procedure will help you create the project.

1. Use the File | New command to display the New dialog box.

2. Choose the Projects tab, then highlight the MFC AppWizard (exe) icon.

3. Type **VSS_C** in the Project Name field, then click OK. Visual C++ will display the MFC AppWizard - Step 1 dialog box.

4. Choose the Dialog-based option, then click Finish. You'll see the New Project Information dialog box shown here:

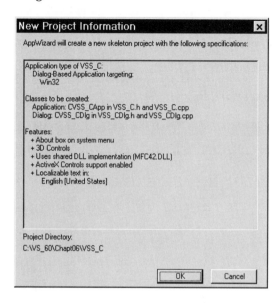

5. Click OK, Visual C++ will create the project for you.

Now it's time to add source control support to the project. Performing this task will place a copy of the files in the Visual SourceSafe database. The programmers working on the project will need to check files out before they can use them, and back in once they're finished. The following procedure shows you how to add source control support.

1. Use the Project | Source Control | Add to Source Control command to display the Visual SourceSafe Login dialog box shown here:

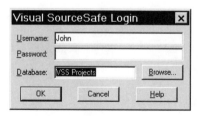

2. Type your name and password in the appropriate fields.

3. Choose an appropriate database for storing the project information. Normally, you'll want to use the Visual SourceSafe database on a server for team projects. The COMMON database found on the local machine drive is fine for individual projects where you want the single-user benefits that Visual SourceSafe can provide.

4. Click OK. Visual C++ will attempt to log you into the Visual SourceSafe database. You'll see the Add to SourceSafe Project dialog box shown here if Visual C++ successfully logs you in:

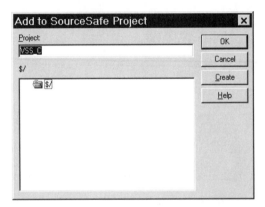

5. Click Create to add your project to the Visual SourceSafe database. You'll see the new project added below the $/ folder in the Add to SourceSafe Project dialog box.

6. Click OK. You'll see the Add to Source Control dialog box shown here. What this dialog box is asking is which files you want to add to the Visual SourceSafe database. In most cases, you'll want to add all of the project files to ensure you have total source control support for the project.

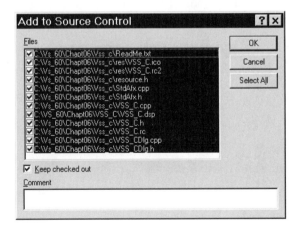

7. Choose one or more files in the Files list to add to source control.

8. Decide whether you want to keep all of the files checked out so that you can work on them immediately. If so, check the Keep checked out option.

9. Type a comment in the Comment field.

10. Click OK. You'll see a SourceSafe Command Status dialog box as Visual C++ adds files to the Visual SourceSafe database. This dialog box will disappear once all of the selected files are added.

Your project is now under source control. The first thing you'll notice is that there are some new options enabled in the Project | Source Control menu. These options will allow you to do things like check files in or out and get a new copy of the source file from the Visual SourceSafe database. You'll also be able to start the Visual SourceSafe Explorer utility that we'll discuss in the Working with Visual SourceSafe Explorer section of the chapter.

Visual Basic

Visual Basic provides one of the best environments around for fast prototyping of projects containing many forms and dialog boxes. However, the ability to create a prototype quickly also means that there is a much higher potential for collisions with other team members. That's why it's so important to have source control for every aspect of your Visual Basic project. This section is going to look at how Visual Basic provides for your source control needs. We'll begin by creating a very simple project shell using the following procedure. Once the project is created, we'll go right into the process for placing it under source control (Visual C++ requires two separate steps).

1. Open Visual Basic. You'll see the New Project dialog box.

2. Highlight the Standard EXE icon, then click Open. Visual Basic will create a simple dialog-based application for you. At this point, it's important to create a local copy of your project—even though you could place the project under source control without doing so, the local copy makes it less likely that you'll end up with an unusable entry in the SourceSafe database.

3. Use the File | Save Project command to display the Save File As dialog box.

4. Click Save twice to save Form1 and Project1 using the default names. You'll see the Source Code Control dialog box shown here. This is where we'll begin to place the project under source control.

5. Click Yes. You'll see a Visual SourceSafe Login dialog box like the one shown here:

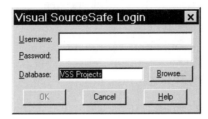

6. Type your name and password.

7. Check the database name to make sure it's correct. If not, either type the name of the database that you want to use or click the Browse button to find it.

8. Click OK. You'll see an Add to SourceSafe Project dialog box like the one shown here:

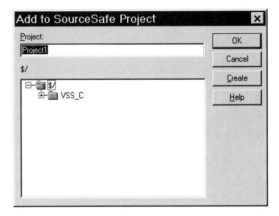

9. Type the name for your project. The example program uses **VSS_C**.

10. Click Create. Visual Basic will create a new Visual SourceSafe database entry for you.

11. Click OK. You'll see the Add Files to SourceSafe dialog box shown next. This is where you'll choose which files get placed in the SourceSafe database. In most cases, you'll want to place all project files under source control to ensure you have a complete project for everyone to look at.

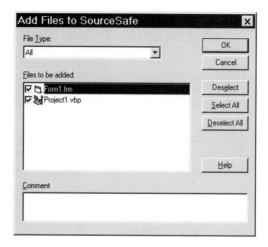

12. Make sure all of the project files are selected (you should see a check in the check box next to each file in the list).

13. Type a comment in the Comment field.

14. Click OK. Visual Basic will display a SourceSafe Results dialog box for a few moments as it adds the files in your project to the SourceSafe database. Once this process is complete, the SourceSafe Results dialog box will disappear and your project will be under source control.

Once you've placed your project under source control, you'll see some new entries in the Tools | SourceSafe menu enabled. For example, you'll be able to check the files out or get the latest version of your source code file. There are some differences between the way Visual C++ and Visual Basic handle source code files under source control. For example, Visual Basic automatically assumes that you want to check all your source files in when you place them under source control, while Visual C++ allows you to keep them checked out. In addition, if you open a file in the Project Explorer without checking the file out first, what you'll see is a read-only copy of the file—Visual Basic won't display any kind of an error message until you try to make a change to the file.

Visual InterDev and Visual J++

Visual J++ and Visual InterDev share the same IDE, so it's not too surprising that their method of handling source control is precisely the same. In fact, you'll notice a lot of similarities between the way these two language products work and what we talked about in the Visual Basic section of the chapter. The following procedure is going to help you create a project shell.

1. Open Visual J++. You'll see the New Project dialog box.

2. Open the Visual J++ Projects\Web Pages folder on the New tab of the New Project dialog box.

3. Highlight the Applet on HTML icon, type the name for your project (the example uses VSS_J), and click Open. Visual J++ will create a new project shell for you.

Now that we have a new project shell, let's place it under source control. The following procedure will show you what you need to do to place either a Visual J++ or Visual InterDev project under source control.

1. Use the Project | Source Control | Add to Source Control… command to display the Visual SourceSafe Login dialog box shown here:

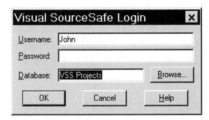

2. Type your name and password.

3. Select an appropriate database. You can either type the database name into the Database field or use the Browse button to find it.

4. Click OK. Visual J++ will establish contact with the Visual SourceSafe database. Once it does, you'll see the Add to SourceSafe Project dialog box shown here:

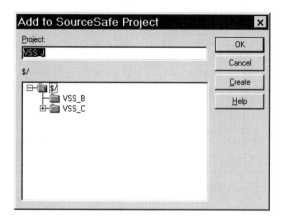

5. Click Create (the Project field should already contain the name of your project). Visual J++ will create a new Visual SourceSafe database entry for you.

6. Click OK. You'll see an Add to Source Control dialog box like the one shown here. Notice that Visual J++ allows you to keep the source code files checked out so that you can continue to work on the project after you place it under source control. Also notice the "Don't show any more Add dialogs" option. You can check this box if you want Visual J++ to take care of the rest of the source control details in the background instead of displaying dialog boxes in the foreground so that you can monitor the process.

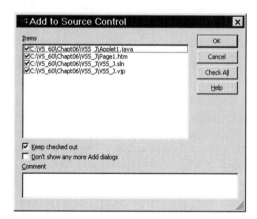

7. Choose whether you want to keep the files checked out so that you can continue working on them.

8. Choose whether you want to see any more dialog boxes. Checking the Don't show any more Add dialogs option will prevent you from monitoring the database update process, but will also allow you to get back to work faster.

9. Make sure all of the files that you want to place under source control are checked. In most cases, you'll want to place all of the files for a project under source control so that you have a complete project available for other people to access. In addition, if you use SourceSafe for backup purposes, placing all of the files under source control ensures that you have a complete copy of the project available should something happen to your local copy.

10. Type a comment in the Comment field.

11. Click OK. If you chose not to view any more dialog boxes, the project is under source control. Otherwise, you'll see a series of SourceSafe Command Status dialog boxes as Visual J++ adds files to the Visual SourceSafe database. These dialog boxes will disappear once all of the selected files are added.

Your project is now under source control. Visual J++ will enable some new commands under the Project | Source Control menu. One of the more interesting menu entries allows you to remove the project from source control—a feature that doesn't appear with some of the other Visual Studio language products. Obviously, you'll see the familiar commands as well. You'll be able to check files out or in and refresh your local copy of a source code file from the copy stored in the SourceSafe database.

Working with Visual SourceSafe Explorer

Visual SourceSafe Explorer works just like Windows Explorer. The difference is that it interacts with a Visual SourceSafe database rather than the contents of your hard drive. With that difference in mind, this section is going to cover some of the unique features of Visual SourceSafe Explorer rather than talk about features that you're already familiar with based on using Windows Explorer. Figure 6-2 shows the Visual SourceSafe Explorer display that you'll see when you first start the project (you may have to log in first).

As you can see, this display looks remarkably similar to the one that you're used to using with Windows Explorer. The left pane provides a list of Visual SourceSafe project folders that you can expand as needed to show all of the subfolders for a particular project. The right pane provides a list of files in each folder. Notice that instead of file statistics, you get project statistics. Figure 6-2 shows that three of the files for the VSS_C

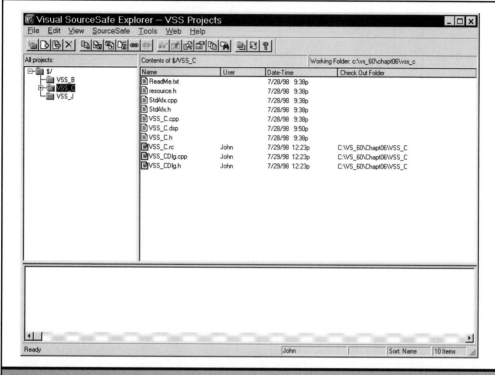

Figure 6-2.   Visual SourceSafe Explorer allows you to explore your project database just as you would explore your local hard drive

project are checked out to John and stored on his local hard drive. In other words, you could look at this display and instantly find out who was working on what part of a project at any given moment.

Just about everything you'll ever need to do with Visual SourceSafe Explorer can be done with the buttons on the toolbar right under the menu. The following list defines the purpose of each button.

- **Create Project**   Allows you to create a new project. The new project is essentially an empty folder that you can add files to later using the Add Files button.

- **Add Files**   Adds new files to the folder highlighted in the left pane. Clicking this button displays an Add File dialog box that contains everything needed to select folders and files on your local hard drive, as shown here:

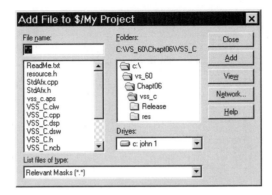

If you want to add an entirely new folder to an existing project, don't select any files in the file list. All you need to do is select the folder you want to add in the directory hierarchy displayed on the right side of the Add File dialog box. Make sure you select the Recursive option in the Add Folder dialog box that appears when you click Add. The Recursive option tells Visual Studio to add the folder and all that it contains to the project.

- **Label Version**   Adds a label to the current folder or file. The label is used for identification purposes when viewing the project history.

- **Delete Files/Project**   Removes a file or project folder. The Destroy Permanently option in the Delete dialog box allows you to remove the file or project folder permanently from the Visual SourceSafe database—this option doesn't affect any local file or folder copies that you may have. It does, however, remove your chances of undeleting the file or folder later.

- **Get Latest Version**   Retrieves a copy of the file or project folder that you can use locally. The default settings retrieve the current copy. However, by overriding the default setting, you can get files from a previous version of the project. In addition, you can choose where to save the files (which allows you to create multiple local copies of a project) and what you want to do with existing local files. Here's what the Get <File or Project Name> dialog box looks like:

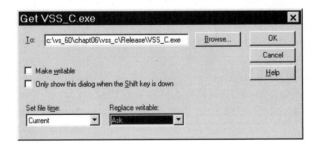

- **Check Out Files/Project**   Allows you to check files out for local use. Other users won't be able to edit the file or project while you have it checked out. They can, however, view the files in a read-only mode.

- **Check In Files/Project**   Allows you to check files in after editing them locally. This option updates the copy of the file in the Visual SourceSafe database with the latest copy contained on the user's local hard drive.

- **Undo Check out**   Returns the state of the selected file to it's pre-checkout state. In essence, this command undoes any changes you've made to the file or project. This command doesn't affect any local copies of the file or project.

- **Share Files**   Places the file or project into share mode. This allows more than one project to use a single file. Any changes to the file by any project using it will be reflected in all other projects. Sharing files encourages code reuse and reduces development time since only one copy of the file needs to be maintained. Most important of all, any bug fixes you make to the file will automatically appear in all projects that use it.

- **Branch Files**   Breaks the share link for a file, creating a new development branch and an independent version of the file for the project in question.

- **View File**   Allows you to see the contents of a file in a read-only mode.

- **Edit File**   Allows you to edit a file. This button also checks the file out so that no one else can modify the file while you're editing it.

- **File/Project Difference**   Compares the contents of two files or projects and displays a dialog box showing any differences. Here's a typical example of a report that you'll see when using this Visual SourceSafe Explorer feature:

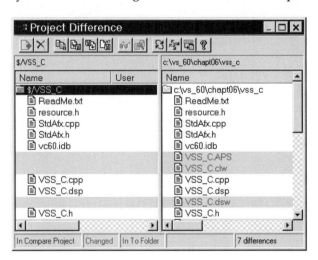

- **Show Properties**   Displays a list of file or project properties. Some of the contents of the Properties dialog box look just like what you'd see in Windows Explorer. There are also Visual SourceSafe-specific entries, including any checkouts, the status of any links, and a list of branches for the file.

- **Show History**   Displays the update history of the file, including any check-ins, changes of label, or other Visual SourceSafe-specific operations.

- **Find in Files**   Allows you to find a file based on its filename and contents. Works just like its Windows Explorer counterpart.

- **Set Working Folder**   Sets the working folder used for storing retrieved copies of files in the Visual SourceSafe database on the local hard drive.

- **Refresh File List**   Retrieves the latest file list from the Visual SourceSafe database.

- **Help**   Displays the Help dialog box.

As you can see, the buttons provide just about every feature you might need when using Visual SourceSafe. Fortunately, like most of Microsoft's newer applications, the toolbar is fully customizable using the Tools | Customize Toolbar... command. You can add commands that don't appear to the toolbar (which are very few) and remove commands that you don't use very often to free up space or make the toolbar less cluttered.

Chapter 7

Working with the Enterprise Features

Visual Studio comes in several editions. However, the edition that we'll concentrate on in the book, for the most part, is the Enterprise Edition, and for good reason. The Enterprise Edition of the product comes with many features that the Professional Edition lacks. Many of these features are team development oriented or help speed development of large projects along. However, there's another difference in the Enterprise Edition: It provides six additional utility programs that you won't find in other versions of the product.

That's what this chapter's all about. We'll look at the extra utilities that the Enterprise Edition adds to the Visual Studio package. In most cases, these utilities are designed to make working with large projects easier. For example, the Application Performance Explorer helps you find bottlenecks in code that might otherwise defy analysis. In other cases, you'll use these tools to manage the large projects that only the enterprise environment can generate. For example, Visual Modeler will help you create better applications through better design.

The goal of this chapter is to provide you with an overview of the various enterprise tools at your disposal. It's amazing to see how using one or two of these tools can greatly reduce project complexity and reduce development time. When you get finished with this chapter, you should have enough information to get started using these products on your next project.

Using Application Performance Explorer

Designing distributed applications takes a lot more in the way of planning than working with a single desktop or with a client/server architecture. Not only do you have concerns about passing data across network boundaries, but now parts of your application will also execute on other machines. The problem with a distributed application is that you can't really determine in advance how such an application will perform, at least not by using the methodologies that most people use right now. The only way to really get statistics on how an application will run in such an environment is to build a test case, then see how it performs. You could then extend the information you get from this test case to the application as a whole. Application Performance Explorer is designed to help you do just that—it allows you to see how a distributed application, or at least a test case of that application, is going to work on your system once you get it developed.

Application Performance Explorer isn't some magic forecasting tool. You need to set it up to mimic the conditions that your application will run under. Once you've set up a set of conditions, the utility runs a series of tests to see how the application will perform given the hardware you've provided for the utility to use. It's important to stress this last point; you need to use Application Performance Explorer on your production system unless your test system is precisely the same because the hardware configuration that you test with is going to affect the test results.

Not only does Application Performance Explorer allow you to test the design decisions you make for the application as a whole, but you can also use it to judge the effect of design decisions on individual components. Component technology is no longer just a nice way to promote code reuse; it's the basis of creating a distributed application. Your application can use DCOM to execute some of the components that it needs on a remote server rather than use local resources.

There are a lot of different ways to view testing. For example, you could look at individual components or you could divide the task into task areas. Application Performance Explorer uses three site-based levels of testing. The following list explains all three levels:

- **Client**   A client can be anything that uses resources or makes requests. Most of the time you'll see a client as a workstation connected to a network. However, clients could be any number of object types, including tasks running on the server itself. A server- or client-based DLL can provide a callback routine that accepts feedback from the server and generates new requests. A real-time process monitoring utility would fall into this category, as would an ISAPI Filter monitoring Web access.

- **Server**   A server is anything that provides resources and processes requests. In most cases, a server will be some process running on a machine dedicated to multiple-user access. However, just like the client, you can define alternative forms of servers, so it's important to understand this very basic definition of a server. For example, you could have a COM server on the client machine that processes requests for shared application data. This data might be something as simple as access requests between your application and an Excel worksheet.

- **Database**   Unlike clients and servers, the definition for a database is very restricted when using Application Performance Explorer. You have a choice between SQL Server and Microsoft Access databases. The utility will exercise the data that these databases contain within the parameters set by your application programs. In other words, simply adding a database won't suddenly provide you realistic figures for what you can expect from your application. You need to provide the Application Performance Explorer with a component designed to exercise the database in the way that you intend the user to use the database within the final application.

Now that you have a better idea of what Application Performance Explorer can do and how it does it, let's take a quick look at the interface. Figure 7-1 shows what Application Performance Explorer will look like when you start it. Notice that the display shows the three site-level testing areas that I just mentioned. You can configure each level separately (we'll discuss the mechanics of doing so in the sections that follow). Above the three site-level buttons is a Profile drop-down list box. This is where you'll find a list of preconfigured test jobs. Application Performance Explorer comes with a collection of preconfigured jobs as part of the package, but you can add new jobs as needed. Finally, notice the blank edit box below the three test buttons. This is where Application Performance Explorer will display the results of any tests that you perform.

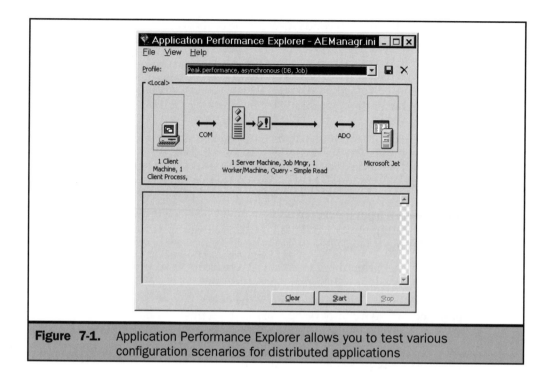

Figure 7-1. Application Performance Explorer allows you to test various configuration scenarios for distributed applications

As you can see, the interface for this utility is relatively simple. However, configuring the utility requires a good understanding of how Application Performance Explorer performs the requested tests and how you expect your application to work. Make sure you spend some time working on the design of your application before you start testing various scenarios. Of course, you won't want to start coding until you know that your application has a good chance of working as anticipated. The following sections will tell you more about how to configure Application Performance Explorer for your specific needs.

Working with Clients

As previously stated, a client is an object that generates requests or uses resources. Of course, this is a very basic client and not very useful for testing purposes. To make the client useful, it must also be able to accept input from the server and process that input in some way to ensure the data received is the data that was expected. That's what client configuration for Application Performance Explorer does. You'll configure the utility to understand how requests will be generated and how those requests will be processed when your application gets the data back from the server. Click on the Client button (the first button shown in Figure 7-1) and you'll see the General tab of the Client Options dialog box shown here:

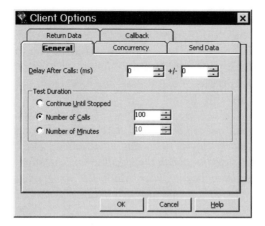

This is where you'll configure the way that Application Performance Explorer calls the server. You can tell it to keep sending requests to the server until stopped, call the server a specific number of times, or conduct the test for a specific time interval. Notice that you can also determine the interval between calls. You could set the interval short to simulate a fully loaded high-stress situation or extend the interval to test for nominal performance levels.

There are other ways to place a load on the application and its components. For example, you can test the application's ability to handle concurrent operations by changing the settings on the Concurrency tab of the Client Options dialog box shown here:

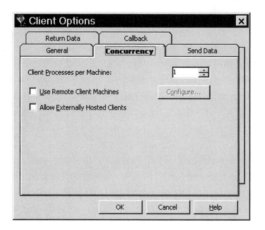

The Client Processes per Machine field contains the number of processes that Application Performance Explorer will place on each client. The default client is the local machine. You can, however, add remote clients by checking the Use Remote Client Machines option. The first time you check this box, you'll see a Configure

Remote Client Machine dialog box. This dialog box contains the names of all the remote client machines that you plan to use for the test. An Add button allows you to add more clients to the list, while a Remove button allows you to remove existing clients. The Configure Remote Client Machine dialog box allows you to create a custom test setup that takes certain types of client machine loads into account, allowing you to design your application around them.

> **Tip** *It's important to create a client setup that matches the setup used by your business as a whole or the target market if you're developing an application for general distribution. A developer machine may not match the machine configuration commonly used by the people who will use the application later. Make sure you create a test machine environment that reflects the actual usage conditions of your application.*

There's one more check box on the Concurrency tab that requires some additional thought on your part. What if you want to see how a test will work when there's more than one test being run at a time? Checking the Allow Externally Hosted Clients check box will allow another copy of Application Performance Explorer running on another machine to perform tests on the current machine. The whole effect of running multiple tests simultaneously is to better model the business environment as it actually works. Few business users run just one application at a time; they run multiple applications. When you create a test setup that checks the anticipated performance of your custom application, you'll initially want to see how the application runs by itself. However, once you make this assessment, you'll also want to verify that the application will run well with other applications.

> **Tip** *Strive for the type of application load that the user will actually encounter when using your application when running multiple tests simultaneously. Using a balanced load of CPU and disk-bound tasks may not reflect reality and will definitely degrade the feedback you receive from Application Performance Explorer. A user survey may help you determine what applications a user actively uses during the day. However, you may also need to resort to monitoring software to ensure you see the actual application load on your network.*

Most applications work with some type of data. As a result, it's important to test data flow from the client to the server in some meaningful way. That's where the Send Data tab of the Client Options dialog box comes into play. You'll use the options on this tab to tell Application Performance Explorer how to send data to the various server components that your application will interact with. Here's what the Send Data tab looks like:

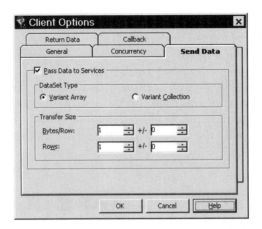

The first thing you'll need to do to pass data to a service is check the Pass Data to Services option. If you're using the asynchronous model, Application Performance Explorer will pass data to both the job manager and a worker. On the other hand, if you use the synchronous model, Application Performance Explorer will pass data to the worker alone.

Note   *In the asynchronous model, calls get made to services, but the client doesn't wait for a response. The client provides a callback function that the service uses to return a response and data from the call. On the other hand, when using the synchronous model, the client does wait for a response from the service after making a call. The response and data are normally read directly in the calling function rather than using a callback function to process the data. Asynchronous calls are normally used for streaming data like binary large objects (BLOBs), while synchronous calls are more appropriate for small data transfers like integers and strings.*

There are two kinds of data that you can send to the service: A variant array and a variant collection. You choose the kind of data using the DataSet Type options. Microsoft recommends using a variant array because it's more efficient. All you send to the server is an array of pointers to the data—which reduces the network traffic that you might otherwise encounter passing entire collections of data. The Variant Collection option is provided more for testing the worst-case data transfer scenario than anything else.

Once you decide on a dataset type, you need to define some parameters for the data itself. The final set of fields on the Send Data tab define the number of bytes per row and the number of rows of data that you'll send. These values should roughly correspond to what you expect to send to the service when using the application for real. Notice that there are also boxes for determining a variation of the data size. In most cases, you'll want to test your application by sending what you think will be the range of data sizes (bytes per row) that your application will produce.

Most applications expect to receive data back from the server when they send a request of some type. The Return Data tab looks much like the Send Data tab that we just discussed. The difference is that you're specifying the parameters for the data that the client will receive rather than what it will send.

Applications rely heavily on callback functions to receive the data that they've requested, to be notified of events, or to handle messages generated by various sources. Part of the client configuration process is to determine how the callback function (if any) will get registered with the server. That's where the Callback tab, shown here, comes into play:

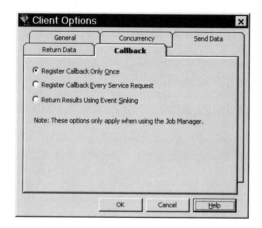

Notice the note that says that this tab only applies to applications that rely on the Job Manager. This implies that you can only set the Callback option for applications that rely on the asynchronous model, which makes sense because the synchronous model relies on the application waiting for return data. There are three different ways to register your callback function. You can register the callback once, which implies that your application maintains a constant connection to the server (something that may not happen with some types of Internet or intranet calls). Application Performance Explorer will also register the callback function with every service call, which is more appropriate for most Internet and intranet applications where the connection gets broken and the service gets unloaded when no longer needed. Finally, you can tell Application Performance Explorer that the service will fire an event, rather than perform a callback, to return the requested data to the application. This is the method used by many ActiveX components.

Working with Servers

Servers can process client requests as well as provide resources of various types. With this in mind, you need to perform two kinds of server configuration tasks when using Application Performance Explorer. The first task is to tell the client where to find the data it needs. The second task is to tell the server how to interact with the client.

Let's begin by looking at the connection process. Use the View | Service Connection Options command to display the Application Service Connection dialog box shown here:

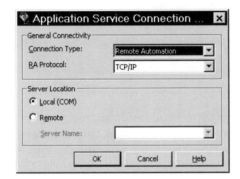

The first thing you need to decide is what kind of connection you want to create between the client and the server. This initial connection defines the method used to launch the server and any associated components. Application Performance Explorer defaults to using remote automation because that type of connection is more commonly available right now. However, you can also choose to use DCOM. If you choose remote automation, then you'll also need to choose a remote automation protocol (TCP/IP, SPX, or named pipes).

If you decide to enable remote automation during testing, make sure you run the Automation Manager utility. This utility passes remote automation requests from the client through the automation proxy to the appropriate Remote Automation Server components.

Once you configure the connection, you'll need to define the server location. Application Performance Explorer defaults to using the local machine. This setting is handy for checking your settings, to make sure that they'll work, or for performing a local test rather something that includes the entire network. If you do choose to use a remote server (which is probably what you'll use for any real testing), then you need to choose the Remote option and type a server name in the Server Name field. Application Performance Explorer will make sure you can actually create a connection before it makes the settings permanent.

Now that you have access to a server, you need to configure it for use with the client. Click the Server button (second button shown in Figure 7-1) and you'll see the DB Task tab of the Application Service Options dialog box, like the one shown here:

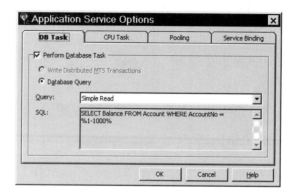

As you can see, this tab allows you to configure the server to interact with a database. Checking the Perform Database Task check box tells the server to make a connection to the database (the connection is defined as part of the database configuration, which we'll talk about in the "Working with Databases" section of the chapter). There are one or two types of connection you can make depending on the capabilities of your server. Application Performance Explorer will allow you to use Microsoft Transaction Server (MTS) transactions if your server supports them. Normally, you'll use a predefined database query by selecting the Database Query option. Just choose the query you want to perform on the test database by selecting it from the drop-down list box.

Tip   *Application Performance Explorer comes configured with a test database and predefined queries that interact with that database. If you want to create queries to interact with your database or expand the queries that you can make on the test database, then you'll need to modify the contents of the APETest database. The Query table of this database contains the queries that you see in the DB Task tab of the Application Service Options dialog box. In addition, you may need to modify the source code for the ACCOUNT.CLS file found in the Ape\Source\Aemtssvc folder of the Application Performance Explorer installation. This is a Visual Basic source code file that contains the queries for MTS transactions.*

Besides database tasks, you can also ask the server to simulate a CPU task. Just select the CPU Task tab shown here and check the Simulate CPU Based Task check box:

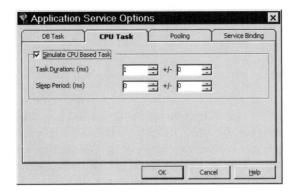

The Task Duration field allows you to choose the length of time that the server will simulate a CPU task. The number in the first field determines the median duration of the task in milliseconds. You can randomize the task times by adding a number to the +/- field. Likewise, you need to specify the task sleep time—in other words, how long the server will wait between CPU task simulations. As with the Task Duration field, the Sleep Period field allows you to set both a median time and the range of randomized times that the server should use. The combination of these two fields determines the relative CPU task load on the server. A high setting for task duration and a low setting for sleep time will simulate a heavy load.

Resource pooling allows your server to work more efficiently. However, the application you create has to be programmed to make use of this feature. In most cases, it makes sense to use resource pooling because you want to get the most out of your server. In other cases, like a low-usage application designed for administrator use, you may not want to expend development dollars adding this feature. The kind of resource pooling also makes a difference. You need to determine whether the server will pool resources locally or use remote worker machines to get the job done. The Pooling tab of the Application Service Options dialog box, shown here, allows you to make all these resource-pooling configuration choices.

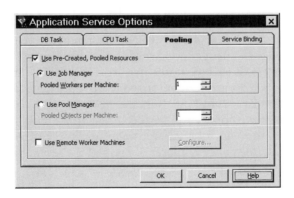

The Pooling tab allows you to set resource pooling in motion by checking the Use Pre-Created, Pooled Resources check box. Notice that Application Performance Explorer allows you to use either the Job Manager or the Pool Manager. If you select the Use Job Manager option, both jobs and workers will be queued. On the other hand, the Pool Manager only queues objects. In other words, these options allow you to optimize the level of local or remote resource pooling used for the test. The number of objects or workers that you pool determines the stress level on server resources, with 1 being the lowest stress level.

You can also use remote worker machines when conducting tests. Click the Use Remote Worker Machines check box and you'll see a Configure Remote Worker Machine dialog box that allows you to add new workers to the list. As with client machines, you'll want to make sure that these remote workers actually reflect your final network setup so that the test results aren't skewed. The Add to Test button allows you to add new workers to the list, while the Remove button allows you to remove them.

The final tab in our Application Service Options dialog box is Service Binding. This tab allows you to change the method used for binding objects used for testing purposes. Here's what the tab looks like:

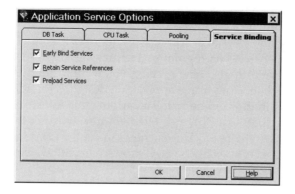

The Early Bind Services check box determines when services get bound during testing. An early bound service will improve application performance, but could limit flexibility because you can't change service properties during run time. Checking the Retain Service References check box means that workers will retain any service options required for test objects. This means that the work will only have to instantiate the service one time. After this first instantiation, the worker will use a reference to the service, which will improve application performance. You'll probably want to uncheck this box if you want to simulate Internet or intranet access. The Preload Services check box tells Application Performance Explorer to preload the server before it begins timing the test. If you'd normally preload your services, then you'll want to check this option to get accurate test results. Otherwise, checking this box will make the application appear more efficient than it really is.

Working with Databases

Many applications require access to a database. However, the method and type of access required depends a great deal on how your application is set up, what environment you intend to use it in, and whether you have any legacy code to support. Application Performance Explorer provides two methods for configuring your database connection: the connection itself, and how the server and client interact with the database.

Let's begin by looking at what you need to do to define a connection. Use the View | Database Connection Options command to display the Database Connection Options dialog box shown here.

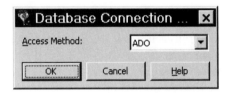

Notice that the only feature you can change in this dialog box is the method used to create the connection. By default, Application Performance Explorer chooses the fastest and newest connection method, ADO (ActiveX Data Objects). The Access Method drop-down list box also provides you with access to the RDO (Remote Data Objects), DAO (Data Access Objects), and ODBC (Open Database Connectivity) API connection methods.

Now that we've determined what connection method to use, it's time to determine what database engine we'll use. Remember that Application Performance Explorer limits you to using either Microsoft Jet or Microsoft SQL Server. However, since the source code for this product is provided in the Ape\Source folder, you could add other database types to the list. Click the Database button (third button shown in Figure 7-1) and you'll see a Database Options dialog box like the one shown here.

You may look at this dialog box and feel that it's lacking a few things, like a place to type the name of the database you want to use for testing. If you choose the Microsoft Jet option, then Application Performance Explorer will look for a database named APETEST.MDB in the Ape folder. The program ships with a default test database that you can modify to meet your needs. It allows you to do everything from simple query changes to complex database structure changes to make the test database look more like the one used by your finished application. However, in some cases the test database won't serve your purposes or provide very realistic test results. In those cases, you'd probably need to modify the Application Performance Explorer source code.

The Microsoft SQL Server option is a little more flexible than the Microsoft Jet option. If you choose this option and click OK you'll see an APE Database Setup Options dialog box like the one shown here:

This is where you choose between using the default test database that Microsoft provides or using one of your own. If you choose to use the default Microsoft database, then Application Performance Explorer will display an APE Database Connect Information dialog box like the one shown here:

All you need to do is enter the name of your server, a user name, and a password and you're ready to test. On the other hand, if you choose to install a new database, then you'll see a Wizard dialog box. The following procedure will show you how to install a new Application Performance Explorer database on your SQL Server.

1. Choose the Install new APE SQL Server database option on the APE Database Setup Options dialog box, then click OK. You'll see the APE Database Setup Wizard dialog box shown here:

2. Click Next. You'll see the System Administrator Login dialog box shown here:

3. Type your server name, the administrator name for SQL Server (not for the server itself), and the SQL Server administrator password.

4. Click Next. You'll see a Destination Directory dialog box like the one shown here:

5. Ensure the default SQL Server data directory supplied in the Server Device Path field is correct.

6. Type a new Device ID value, if necessary (the default value is normally correct).

7. Type a Device Size value if necessary. However, in most cases, you'll want to make the size greater than the default size shown. Otherwise, you may get error messages when the test database runs out of space.

8. Click Next. You'll see the Who's the DBO? dialog box shown next. The database owner (DBO) is the one who actually owns the test database. This is the name you'll type when setting up for the test. If you're planning on eventually making this test database into the permanent application database, make sure you use a DBO that reflects the final owner of the database rather than the test name supplied.

9. Type the name of the DBO in the Log on dbo ID field.

10. Type the DBO password in both the Password for log on and Confirm password fields.

11. Click Finish. Application Performance Explorer will create the new test database on the SQL Server for you. If everything goes well, you'll eventually see a Successful Installation dialog box.

12. Click Exit, then OK at the Database Options dialog box. Application Performance Explorer will be configured to use the new SQL Server database you've set up.

Using Visual Modeler

It's easy to get lost when looking at a large application design. Trying to figure out where various components fit into the big picture can be confusing to say the least. Because of the complexity of today's applications, most enterprise developers use diagrams to create a picture of the custom applications they create. This picture helps other people see what the application will eventually look like from a flow or component perspective. Visual Modeler helps you create pictures of your application using simple tools that speed the design process and allow you to think more about the application you're creating than the tools used to design it.

Visual Modeler goes further than simple diagrams, though. The diagramming process that it uses allows you to separate the design task into functional areas, or services. Microsoft defines three types of services as described in the following list:

■ **User services** Anything to do with the user interface falls into this functional area. A user will interact with the user services to get information from the server and to provide information to the server. Normally, this part of the application contains forms and dialog boxes that the user will interact with. However, this functional area could include multimedia and other forms of user communication as well. The user services also bundle any information required by the server and send it off to the business services functional area.

- **Business services**   This functional area consists of all of the business logic required to make your application run. For example, if the user requests an address from the address database, this set of routines would create the SQL code required to access the data in the database, then format the result to send back to the user. The business services normally appear on the server. However, there isn't any reason that they couldn't appear on another workstation or as part of the application. Microsoft does recommend placing the business services in separate components to make it easier to update your application as business needs change.

- **Data services**   It's important to keep the business logic required to run your business separate from the code required to access the data you need. That's why Microsoft included a special functional area for routines that manipulate data. The data services area has only one purpose—to ensure safe data access. Data isn't useful if you can't access it. On the other hand, data corruption could result in a large business loss or other problems.

Seeing the forest for the trees is another problem. Even if you've used good diagramming techniques to create your application model, you may still run into problems seeing what you want. That's why Visual Modeler provides three kinds of views for you to see your application design. The following list provides an overview of each view.

- **Logical**   This view displays all of the classes in your application and how they relate to one another. It's the lowest level view of your application.

- **Component**   This view shows all of the DLLs, EXEs, OCXs, and other component files that make up your application. You'll use this application to see how all of the parts of your application fit together—it's the only view that provides you with an overview of your application as a whole.

- **Deployment**   This view shows how you'll eventually deploy the application. For example, you'd use it to see what parts of the application will appear on servers and what parts would appear on workstations.

One of the best ways in which Visual Modeler helps you with the application design process is that it can actually generate code for you. All you need to do is use the Tools | Generate Code command to export your design as code that you can use within Visual Basic or Visual C++. Obviously, you need to fully define the application before the code can be generated and you'll likely still need to perform a lot of hand coding, but any help in getting an application up and running is usually appreciated by the developer.

This section of the chapter is going to provide you with a brief overview of Visual Modeler. While we'll definitely touch on the mechanics of using this complex application, you'll need to spend time learning the theory behind computer-aided software engineering (CASE) in general before this product will become really useful.

(Obviously, this advice would apply even if you were creating the application using a white board—an application won't replace the theoretical knowledge required for good engineering practices.) In addition to the theoretical knowledge you'll require, it's also important to work through a few simple projects before you attempt a complex enterprise-level application.

A Tour of the IDE

Visual Modeler is a special version of a CASE program developed by Rational Software for Microsoft. Like the version of InstallShield provided with Visual Studio for Visual C++, this version of Visual Modeler has a more capable twin that you can purchase directly from Rational Software. In addition, even though the interface is very Microsoft-like, it still bears the marks of being created by another company. What this means is that you will notice some differences in using Visual Modeler as compared to the rest of Visual Studio.

Let's take a look at the IDE. Figure 7-2 shows what Visual Modeler will look like when you first start it to work on a new project. (You may need to use the View | Toolbars | Toolbox command to display the Toolbox toolbar shown in the figure.)

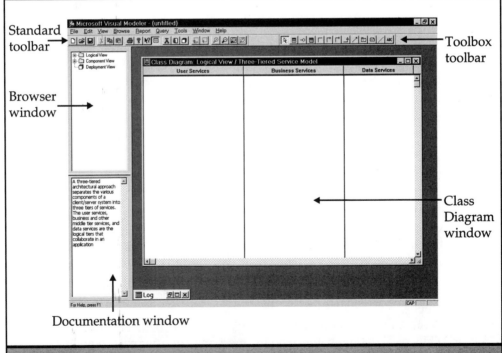

Figure 7-2. Visual Modeler allows you to create diagrams of your application using a set of specialized drawing tools

We'll see that Visual Modeler provides more windows than the ones shown, but these are the basic windows you need to start working on a new project. The Documentation window displays help information about the various objects you select; once you have worked with Visual Modeler, you probably won't need to display it. The Browser window displays a hierarchical view of the components of your project and the various design windows that you can open to work with them. The Class Diagram window allows you to start adding new features to your application.

I won't cover the standard toolbar here because it contains most of the same features that you would find in any application. We'll cover any special features as the chapter progresses. On the other hand, the Toolbox toolbar contains all of the tools you need to start your application. You start with a group of standard tool buttons. The following list provides information about each of the standard tool buttons on the Toolbox toolbar (you can customize the toolbars in this application, just like you can with most 32-bit Windows applications).

Button Name	Button	Description
Pointer		Allows you to choose one of the objects in your diagram.
Class		Use the Class tool to create the beginning of a definition for an object. A class contains the structural and behavioral parameters of the object. This includes the class name, a list of properties, and a list of methods associated with the object. It also includes the return type of the object, if any.
Interface		You can't use this particular tool by itself; it has to be attached to a class or component. The Interface tool allows you to define a bundle of externally accessible methods for the class or component in question.
Class Utility		The Class Utility tool allows you to define a set of extra functions for a class. (In some parts of the Visual Modeler documentation, this tool also appears as Utility.) This kind of component is normally used to define one or more free subprograms, or to define a class that contains only static members or static member functions.

Button Name	Button	Description
Association		This tool allows you to create a semantic relationship between two classes or between a class and an interface. An association creates a bidirectional relationship, which means that data, properties, or other adornments can flow both ways. This is the weakest of all relationship types because there are no limits on what either object in the relationship can do.
Unidirectional Association		Like the Association tool, the Unidirectional Association tool creates a relationship between two objects. However, the unidirectional association is more specific because adornments can only flow in one direction. You would use this where a distinct hierarchical relationship is an advantage. For example, you might create a superclass that defines a class as a whole, then a group of subclasses that a user would actually need to write an application.
Aggregation		The Aggregation tool defines a relationship where a class or class utility supplies resources used by another class. Aggregate objects are either completely composed of other objects or at least logically contain another object.
Generalization		Use this tool to show one object inheriting the features of another object. For example, you'd use this tool to define the relationship between a subclass and one or more superclasses.
Dependency or Instantiates		This tool allows you to define a relationship where one component depends on the methods and properties provided by another component. For example, you might have a clock component that relies on the methods and properties of a timer component. The clock would display the current time, but the timer would actually track the time. The primary component (the one that relies on another component) is always instantiated after the second component to ensure that all of the methods and properties required by the primary component are available.

Button Name	Button	Description
Package		A package is a grouping of some kind of object. You can use the Package tool to create logical groups, physical groups, node groups, and distribution units. In essence, this is an organizational tool that helps you keep like components together.
Note		Use this tool to annotate your drawing. Make sure you include any assumptions that you made during the design process and conditions that must be met during the implementation phase of the project.
Anchor Note to Item		This is a special tool that attaches a note to another item.
Text Box	ABC	This is another form of documentation tool like the Note tool. Unlike the Note tool, this tool is designed to create notes that everyone needs to see on a continual basis. The text produced by this tool is not enclosed in a box and appears as part of the diagram.

Tip

Visual Modeler uses the idea of an adornment to suggest details that you can attach to any of the tools that it provides. For example, an adornment for a class might consist of a method or property. You can create classes, interfaces, associations, and other drawing objects without defining the adornments. This allows you to get an overview of the project started quickly. Once all of the elements are in place, you can begin to add adornments to each of the project elements, defining them in full detail so that every member of your team knows exactly how the various components of the project will go together.

Let's look at the Browser window in a little more detail for a moment. Here's a more detailed look at what you'll see when you create a new project:

> **Tip** *You can right-click on every object in the Browser window to display a context menu containing commands that you can perform with the selected object. This is an important feature for the Browser window since you'll use it to create new application elements like components or classes. When in doubt about what you can do in a particular area of Visual Modeler, always right-click to see what the context menu contains.*

Notice that the Browser windows contains a hierarchical view of our project using the three views that I mentioned at the beginning of this chapter. The Logical view breaks our project down using the three-tiered service model. In addition, you'll find folders for each of the services that contain the various elements provided by that service. The folders are relatively unpopulated now, but will contain more entries as your project gets bigger. A look at the Component view shows the default component that you'll see in every Visual Modeler project: Main. Finally, you'll see a place for the Deployment view. It's empty right now because we haven't created anything to deploy.

Creating Classes Using the Class Wizard

One of the tasks that you'll perform most often with Visual Modeler is creating new classes. You can create a class using the Toolbox toolbar button, but right-clicking in the appropriate place in the Class Diagram window and selecting Class Wizard is much easier in the long run. The following procedure will show you how to use the Class Wizard to create a class specification.

Tip   *Visual Modeler starts without any knowledge of any classes that are provided by the programming language suites supplied with Visual Studio. This is a help if you want to create an application that doesn't rely on the Microsoft Foundation Classes (MFC). On the other hand, if you want to reduce the amount of code you have to write, it might be handy to have those predefined classes loaded into Visual Modeler so that you can include them in your design plans. Simply use the Tools | Visual C++ | Import MFC 4.21 command to import the current set of classes supplied by MFC.*

1. Right-click in the User Services area of the Class Diagram window and choose Class Wizard from the context menu. You'll see the Class Wizard - Name of new class dialog box shown here:

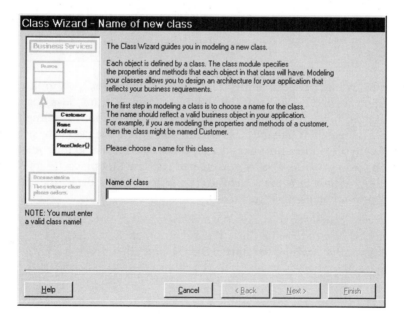

2. Type a name for your new class (the example uses MyClass).

3. Click Next. You'll see a Class Wizard - Documentation of class <Class Name> dialog box like the one shown here for the MyClass class:

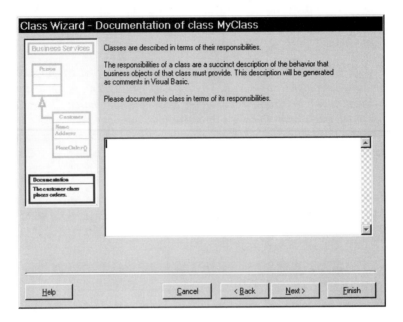

4. Type the overall purpose of this class. The example uses, "A sample class definition created using Visual Modeler." Obviously, your class documentation would need to be more extensive for a real class definition. You might want to include information like the class creator and where the user can contact him or her. Always include a purpose and function for the class so that other people don't have to guess as to why you created it in the first place. Users will actually see these comments when using the class within Visual Basic (they may or may not appear when using Visual C++).

5. Click Next. You'll see the Class Wizard - Service type of class <Class Name> dialog box. Notice that the Class Wizard automatically selected the User Service for us since that's where we started the class creation process.

6. Choose a different Service type option if necessary, and then click Next. You'll see the Class Wizard - Inheritance of class <Class Name> dialog box like one shown here:

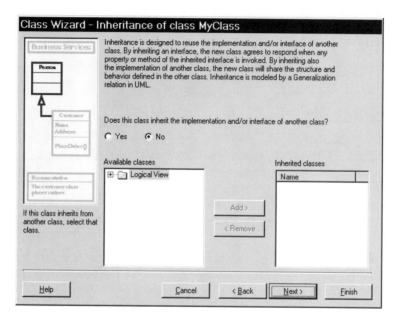

7. Choose the Yes option if you need to inherit from another class. Class Wizard will enable the Available classes list on the left side of the dialog box.

8. Find the class that you need to inherit from in the Available classes list, highlight it, then click Add. The name of the class you chose will appear in the Inherited classes list on the right side of the dialog box. If you need to remove a class, highlight its entry in the Inherited classes list, then click Remove.

9. Click Next. You'll see the Class Wizard - Methods of class <Class Name> dialog box shown here:

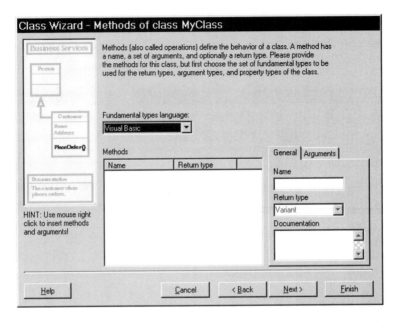

10. Choose the programming language that you want to use to create this class from the Fundamental types language drop-down list box. The default setting is Visual Basic, but you can also choose Visual C++ or Visual J++ (listed as Visual Java in the drop-down list box) as programming languages. The example program uses Visual C++ as its fundamental programming language.

11. Right-click within the Methods list and choose Insert from the context menu if you want to add a method to the class; otherwise, skip to Step 17 (the example will add one method for illustration purposes). This is the technique that Class Wizard uses for adding new methods to the list. You can also right-click on an existing method and choose Delete from the context menu to remove it from the Methods list.

12. Type the name of the method in the Name field. The example program uses a name of MyMethod.

13. Choose a return type from the Return type drop-down list box. The example returns void.

14. Type some documentation for the method in the Documentation field. You'll usually want to include things like the number and type of parameters that the method uses. Always include a purpose for the method and what the user can expect as output. The example uses, "This is an example method." for documentation.

15. Click the Arguments tab and add any arguments needed by the method (the example doesn't require any). Use the same technique to add arguments as you did to add the method.

16. Perform Steps 11 through 15 for all of the methods that your class requires. The example uses only one method, so you can proceed to the next step if you're following the example.

17. Click Next. You'll see the Class Wizard - Properties of class <Class Name> dialog box. As you can see, this dialog box looks much like the one used to add methods to the class. It works about the same way, except that there are few elements to define than with a method. The example uses a single property named MyProperty. It's a char value and has an initial value of "Hello World." The Documentation field contains, "This is an example property." Here's the one property that I added for our example:

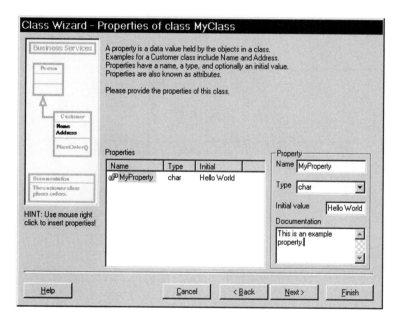

18. Add any properties required for your class. The example uses only the one described in Step 17.

19. Click Next. You'll see the Class Wizard - Summary of class <Class Name> dialog box. This is your last opportunity to make changes (by clicking the Back button) before the class gets added to your design. Here's what the Class Wizard - Summary of class MyClass dialog box looks like:

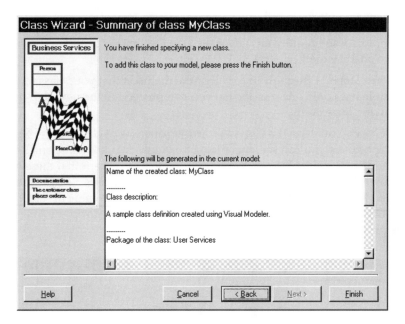

20. Click Finish to complete the process. Visual Modeler will display the Class
Diagram: User Services/Package Overview window shown here:

Working with Specifications

There are a lot of different ways to work with the objects used within Visual Modeler.
However, no matter what you do, you'll eventually need to work with the
specifications for those objects to create a finished product. This section will give you a
whirlwind tour of specifications under Visual Modeler. We'll concentrate on the Class
Specification dialog box, since you can access most of the other important specification
dialog boxes from this one. Right-click on just about any object and you'll see an Open
Specification entry on the context menu. Choosing this option will display a dialog box

similar to this one used for classes (the screen shots in this section of the chapter use the example class created in the previous section using the Class Wizard):

The General tab of the Specification dialog box normally contains the name of the object and a description of its purpose. In the case of a class specification, you'll also find the name of the parent class. Finally, if this is an interface, you'll see the Interface item selected in the Stereotype field.

Methods and properties are part of most classes, so it's important to see how you work with them. (We'll cover only methods in the following discussion, but properties work about the same.) Here's what the Method tab for the Class Specification for MyClass dialog box looks like:

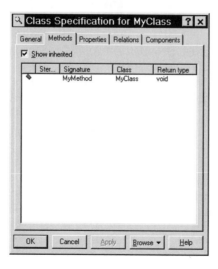

Click on MyMethod and the Documentation window will display the documentation you provided for this method. We discussed documentation in the previous section, so I won't cover that again here. Notice that the dialog box displays the associated class and return type for the method, but no arguments (which is why it's important to include them in your documentation). If you want to see what the arguments for this method are, simply right-click the method and choose Specification from the context menu. Visual Modeler will display a Method Specification dialog box that you can use to view the arguments for your method. Adding a new method consists of right-clicking anywhere within the method list on the Method tab of the Class Specification dialog box and choosing Insert from the context menu. A new method will appear that you can name immediately. You'll need to open the method specification to define the details for it.

Using Visual Studio Analyzer and Visual Studio Analyzer Server

There are a variety of ways to analyze the performance of an application or your system when using that application. We saw one method of doing this using the Application Performance Explorer earlier in the chapter. That utility provided you with the means to stress test the application design before committing it to code.

Visual Studio Analyzer works at the opposite end of the spectrum from Application Performance Explorer. Now that you have a component or application, you need to see if it actually performs as you thought it would during the design phase. It's important to verify that your design works as anticipated.

Visual Studio Analyzer requires you to start the Visual Studio Analyzer Server before you open the IDE. In addition, you must install DCOM95 version 1.2 on Windows 95 machines and Service Pack 4 on the Windows NT 4.x machines before you'll get full use from Visual Studio Analyzer. If you haven't installed the required DCOM support, Visual Studio Analyzer will display an error message when you try to connect to the machine. In some cases, you can still get useful statistics from Visual Studio Analyzer, but it's important to install the required DCOM support as soon as possible. You can find DCOM95 Version 1.2 at: http://www.microsoft.com/com/dcom/dcom1_2/download-f.htm and Service Pack 4 for Windows NT 4.x at: http://www.microsoft.com/ windows/ downloads/default.asp?product=Windows+NT+Server.

There are actually two parts to Visual Studio Analyzer: a server and an application. The server just sits in the background collecting any data you need. In fact, the only evidence that you'll see that this part of the package is running is a little icon in the

Taskbar Tray. Right-click on this icon and you'll see three entries in a context menu that allow you to start or stop the service, or exit from the server altogether.

Visual Analyzer itself relies on the same Visual Studio interface that we've explored for Visual Basic, Visual J++, and Visual InterDev, so using this product should be fairly easy. You already have a good idea of how the interface for this product works from the previous chapters of this book. This section will concentrate on an example of how to use Visual Analyzer to track the communication that takes place when you execute an application. In this case, we'll see what happens when we try tracking Visual Basic.

Before we can go too far, though, we'll need to create a Visual Analyzer project. Start Visual Analyzer and you'll see the familiar New tab of the New Project dialog box that we've seen in the past. Choose the Visual Studio | Visual Studio Analyzer Projects folder. Highlight the Analyzer Wizard icon, type **COMView** in the Name field, then click Open. You'll see the Visual Studio Analyzer Project Wizard - Step 1 of 4 dialog box shown here:

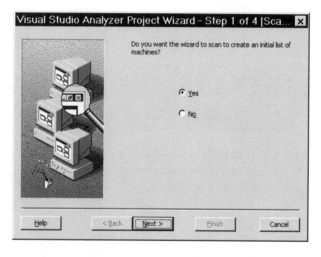

Note   *You don't have to use the wizard if you don't want to. The wizard is provided as a fast way to get your project up and running quickly. However, as we'll see in the remainder of this section, Visual Studio Analyzer projects are fairly simple to set up, so using the wizard isn't absolutely essential.*

At this point, we're ready to create a project. This first step of the wizard will allow you to scan your network for acceptable workstations. If you're using a test setup, this is probably a good idea. On the other hand, if you're working on a large network, the scanning process could take quite a while and tie up network resources as well. The following procedure will take you through the process of creating an example Visual Analyzer project that assumes you're working on a small test setup.

1. Choose Yes at the Visual Studio Analyzer Project Wizard - Step 1 of 4 dialog box and click Next. Visual Studio Analyzer will scan your network for suitable test machines. It'll only pick up machines that are running the Visual Studio Analyzer Server, so if a machine you expected to see in this list doesn't appear, then you may need to check the status of the server. Once the scanning process is complete, you'll see the Visual Studio Analyzer Project Wizard - Step 2 of 4 dialog box shown here:

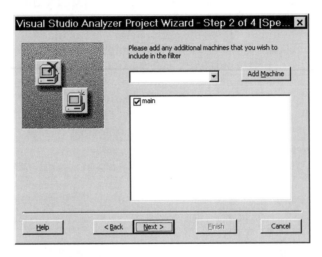

2. Check the boxes next to the machines you want to test. If you don't see a machine you want to test in the list, you can add it by typing its name in the blank field supplied at the top of the dialog box and then clicking Add Machine. However, you'll still want to ensure that the test machine is actually set up to use with Visual Studio Analyzer.

3. Click Next. You'll see the Visual Studio Analyzer Project Wizard - Step 3 of 5 dialog box. We need to set up filters for the information that we want to analyze. The first step in setting up a filter is to choose a source for the information. In this case, we only need to track COM events. However, as you can see from the list, Visual Studio Analyzer can track a wide range of sources.

4. Uncheck all of the source options except COM Event Source so that your Visual Studio Analyzer Project Wizard - Step 3 of 5 dialog box looks like the one shown here:

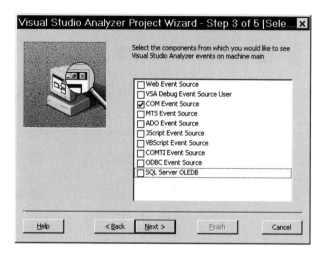

5. Click Next. You'll see the Visual Studio Analyzer Project Wizard - Step 4 of 5 dialog box. It's time to select a set of filters to monitor. This dialog box shows groups of filters. You can refine the selections you make here once the project is created.

6. Uncheck all of the filter groups you don't need. Here's the selection we'll be using for the example:

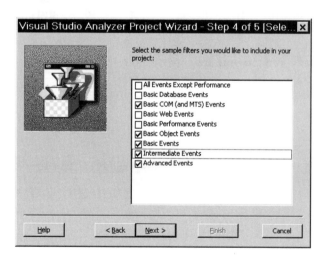

7. Click Next. You'll see the Visual Studio Analyzer Project Wizard - Step 5 of 5 dialog box shown here. This is your last opportunity to modify the project parameters.

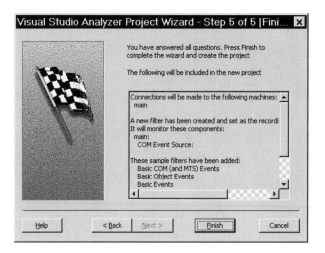

8. Click Finish. Visual Analyzer will create the project for you.

At this point, we have a project that's ready to go, but it really won't do anything. There are a couple of things we need to do to activate it. The first thing you'll need to do is open the log used to display the events. It's under the Event Logs folder in the Project Explorer window. If you open the log, you'll see that it's currently unfiltered, which means it can't receive any information. We'll change that situation by right-clicking the COMView filter (in the Project Explorer window) and choosing Apply Filter to View from the context menu.

You also need to start the recording process using the Set Record Filter option on the COMView filter context menu. It's easy to tell if this option is on—just look for a check mark next to the option on the context menu.

Try starting Visual Basic (without doing anything else to your machine first). Visual Analyzer will record four COM events and place them in the Event List window as shown here:

As you can see, Visual Analyzer provides a wealth of information and the log format makes it possible to record that information over an extended period of time. You can export the log, if you'd like, using the Analyzer | Export Events option. Visual Analyzer will create an Excel-compatible Comma Separated Variable (CSV) format file.

Visual Analyzer isn't limited to plain text display. The New Chart button will create a chart that shows a graphic representation of time versus even occurrence. You can use this display to look for patterns in application execution. Another useful display is the Process Diagram. Clicking on an event in the Event List highlights the process responsible for that event in the Process Diagram. In fact, you can play back the events from beginning to end and use the Process Diagram to see an animated graphic display of the interaction of the various processes in your application.

Part III

Desktop Applications

Chapter 8

A Basic Multilanguage Example

Using any of the programming languages in Visual Studio as a separate product can be a feat of skill that many people can't reproduce with ease. Using all the languages at the same time, at least with any efficiency, may well be beyond even the most expert programmer. Yet, when you look at Visual Studio, it very obviously has the capability to create extremely large, extremely complex applications that rely on multiple languages.

Obviously, the first question you would need to ask is why you would want to use more than one programming language in the first place. After all, you can create a database application using either Visual Basic or Visual C++. In the final analysis, given a relatively flexible programming language, you could create any type of application that you really want to create. The point is not that Visual Basic is able to create an application that Visual C++ can't (or vice versa), but that Visual Basic is more efficient at creating some types of applications than Visual C++. In other words, given two programmers with equal skills, the Visual Basic programmer will finish some applications before the Visual C++ programmer will because Visual Basic is simply more efficient than Visual C++ in some situations.

Saving development time and money is indeed one of the major reasons to use a multilanguage product like Visual Studio. However, for some people, the savings in time and money alone probably wouldn't be enough reason to assemble a team of developers with a variety of language skills to work on a single product. Let's look at the question from another direction. You need to ask yourself just how much employee satisfaction counts toward productivity in the workplace. Here's a scenario that I've actually seen occur at more than one company. An employee knows how to use a single application, a spreadsheet. He or she uses that application for everything, including typing reports and creating simple database applications. Sure, you can do this type of work with a spreadsheet, but it's very frustrating and time-consuming to do so. In most cases, these employees were much more productive once they learned a new product in addition to the spreadsheet. The frustration of trying to use the spreadsheet for a task that it was ill-designed to perform greatly impacted the productivity of the employee.

Okay, enough analysis of why it's important to use more than one language for now. You obviously have some idea of what you'd like to accomplish with a team of programmers who can use the full capabilities of Visual Studio or you wouldn't be reading this book. I just wanted to make the point that there is something to be gained from using a product like Visual Studio when creating complex applications. Using the right tool for the job is always important if you want to get the job done quickly and efficiently.

This chapter is going to concentrate on a very simple multilanguage programming example. What you'll learn is the basic principles for getting a team to work together on a single project where their best skills are used in concert with those of the other programmers. We'll begin by looking at what we need the application to do, go through the various phases of application construction, enhance the application once it works, and, finally, get the application ready for distribution. Some steps could be performed simultaneously, but we'll have to settle for looking at them one at a time.

One of the other things we'll begin to look at in this chapter is what you need to do to make the various languages work together. There are situations when perfectly good code won't work with multiple languages, and we'll look at one of those situations in this chapter. If you really do want to save time and effort using more than one programming language for a project, then it's essential to make sure you design the project properly from the very beginning. Part of that design process is looking for potential interoperability problems.

Scenario

The first step we'll always perform when working on a new project in this book is to talk about what the final application will do. We'll answer the question of what the application has to do to satisfy some basic needs on the part of the user. In addition, the "Scenario" section of the chapter will tell you what prompted the need for the application in the first place and provide you with a few ideas about what you can learn by following the entire course of application development. Performing this analysis will help you see how the various tools provided with Visual Studio work in concert to achieve a particular goal. In addition, you'll learn why certain tools are more efficient than others at performing a particular programming task.

The scenario for this chapter is creating a basic application. All we'll do is create a system clock-monitoring program that relies on a special ActiveX control. The goal of this example is to show you some of the basic steps in using the Visual Studio products together. Since Visual C++ is great at helping you get low-level programming done quickly, we'll use it to create the clock-monitoring control. In this case, we'll create one control that outputs the date or time based on input criteria provided by the application program in which it's used. A programmer could attach the control to a menu or use it to display system time in a dialog-based application. You could even use this type of control to show local server time for a Web-based application. Of course, once we create the control, we'll publish it so that other team members can use it. Even though Visual Studio provides a wealth of enterprise-level tools like Visual SourceSafe, none of the team-level programming is worth anything if everyone isn't willing to share. The act of publishing a control is part of the sharing process.

Note   *Visual C++ is the product of choice when it comes to low-level programming like ActiveX controls. Visual Basic is the product of choice when it comes to high-level programming like application building. Even though you can use Visual Basic for low-level programming and Visual C++ for high-level programming, you'll find that using each product for its specialty area will make programming faster and easier.*

Once you have the controls designed for your application, you can begin to build the application itself. Visual Basic is a higher-level language that allows fast application prototyping and relatively quick programming as long as you don't try to perform too many low-level tasks with it. Since Visual Basic does so many things for you automatically, you'll find that the amount of code required for our application is relatively small when compared to the same type of application in Visual C++. So, while it's true that we could have created the application using Visual C++, Visual Basic will prove to be the more efficient tool for performing the task.

Creating ActiveX Controls with Visual C++

We've already created a very simple ActiveX control in the "Simple ActiveX Control" section of Chapter 4. If you'll remember, this particular example used simple text and numeric properties to make the On/Off button work correctly. A time and date control, however, can't really get by with using simple text properties. What we really need is a property that fully represents the time and date in a way that allows someone using the control to manipulate the value if they want to do so. What this means to you, as a programmer, is that we'll need an OLE property in this example.

Of course, not everyone will want to write the code required to manipulate the time and date, so we'll also include a couple of properties that allow the programmer to obtain a simple text equivalent of the time or date. There are a number of methods that we could use to get the text output, but for this example we'll provide separate time and date text output properties, along with two properties for choosing the output format.

The final consideration is the control's update interval. (After all, time and date aren't constant, so the control will need to update the field values in some way.) If we create a control that updates constantly, then it'll use clock cycles that could be used for other types of processing. Obviously, this is an inefficient use of computing potential if you don't need to update the clock constantly (as in a display of the current system time and date on the application title or status bar). Another way to do things would be to update the time and date fields of the control only on request. In other words, the control wouldn't perform any sort of update once it was initialized until the programmer requested one. While this approach is extremely efficient, it means that the programmer needs to provide additional timing logic in the application. A third approach is to provide an intermittent update. The control could fire an event every time the clock got updated, notifying the application that it was time to change any settings. This approach represents the middle road in control efficiency. It does, however, require additional programming on the part of the control developer. Even so, we'll be using the third approach in this example. We'll provide a property for setting the control update frequency and an event to notify the application using the control about the update.

Defining the Control Shell

Let's begin by creating an MFC ActiveX project using the MFC ActiveX ControlWizard. I've provided you with detailed instructions for doing this in Chapter 4, so I won't provide them again here. I've used ClockIt as the name of my project, but you could use any name that you wanted. Accept the default settings on the first page of the MFC ActiveX ControlWizard. You'll need to change a few settings on the second page. First, we don't need to see the control during run time, so check the Invisible at runtime option. The programmer using the control will need to provide any required display logic. The only purpose of this control is to provide the date and time. Second, we want the programmer to be able to see our control, so you'll need to check the "Available in 'Insert Object' dialog" option. This is an especially important setting if you want programmers who use products like Visual Basic to use your control. Click Finish and you'll see a New Project Information dialog box like the one shown here. Click OK to complete the project shell.

It's time to add some properties to our control. Open the MFC ClassWizard using the View | ClassWizard command. Choose the Automation tab of the dialog box. Table 8-1 provides a list of the properties you'll need to add along with their data type. All of the properties use the Method variable option. If the MFC ClassWizard chooses the Get/Set methods option for you, then choose the Method variable option instead.

Before you move from the Automation tab, we'll need to add a method to the list. Our clock control will need some method for stopping and starting. Click the Add Method button and you'll see an Add Method dialog box. Type **StartIt** in the External name field. This is what outside applications will call the method. Normally, you'll use the same name internally as well, so MFC ClassWizard automatically adds whatever name you choose to the Internal name field as well. You also need to define a return value. In this case, we won't return anything, so you can choose void in the Return type field. Finally, we need to know whether the user wants to turn the clock on or off, so you'll define a bStart parameter in the Parameter list field. Choose BOOL as the

Property Name	Type	Custom/Stock
Clock	DATE	Custom
Enabled	BOOL	Stock
TextDate	CString	Custom
TextDateFormat	short	Custom
TextTime	CString	Custom
TextTimeFormat	short	Custom
UpdateInterval	Short	Custom

Table 8-1. Clock ActiveX Control Property Listing

parameter type. Click OK to make the change permanent and close the Add Method dialog box. At this point, the Automation tab of the MFC ClassWizard should look like the dialog box shown in Figure 8-1.

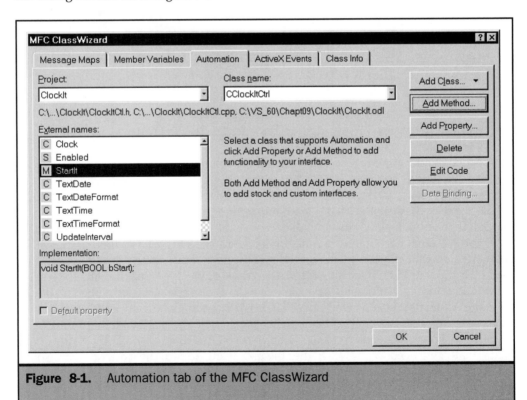

Figure 8-1. Automation tab of the MFC ClassWizard

We'll also need to add an event to the project skeleton, so you'll need to open the MFC ClassWizard to the ActiveX Events tab. For this example, we only need to add one event, Tick. Click the Add Event button to display the Add Event dialog box. The Tick event doesn't require any parameters and the MFC ClassWizard will automatically know that this is a custom event. All you need to do is type **Tick** in the External name field, then click OK. The ActiveX Events tab of the MFC ClassWizard should look like the dialog box in Figure 8-2 when you finish adding the Tick event.

Besides properties and events, our control will need to monitor two Windows messages that appear in the application's message queue when another application or thread either sends or posts a message. Since this is a clock, we'll need to monitor the WM_TIMER message to know when to fire the timer event. In addition, we need to know when the user has enabled or disabled the control. That means we need to monitor the WM_ENABLE message. To add the functions required to monitor the message, open the MFC ClassWizard and choose the Message Maps tab. Choose CClockItCtrl in the Class name field, the MFC ClassWizard should automatically select CClockItCtrl in the Object field as well. Find the WM_ENABLE message in the Messages list, then click Add Function. Do the same thing for the WM_TIMER message. In both cases, you'll see a new function added to the Member functions list.

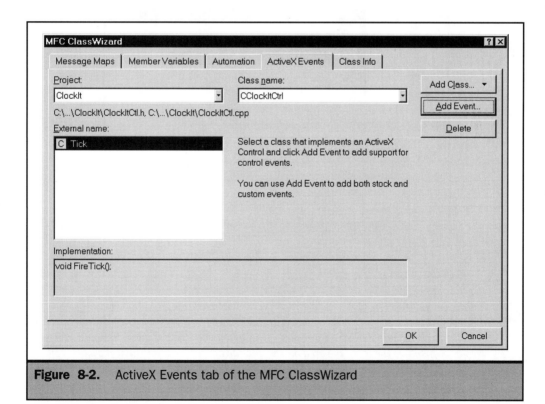

Figure 8-2.   ActiveX Events tab of the MFC ClassWizard

Close the MFC ClassWizard dialog box. At this point, you have a completed control shell, but we can't add code yet; we need to define some resources first.

Defining the Resources

We're going to look at what you need to do to define a variety of resources in this example. The first thing we need to do is design an icon for our control, something that will tell the control user about the purpose of the control immediately. There are three places you have to include this icon:

- IDI_ABOUTDLL (Standard 32 × 32)
- IDI_ABOUTDLL (Small 16 × 16)
- IDB_CLOCKIT

Unfortunately, all three icons (bitmaps) are different sizes, so you'll need to draw the icon three times. Choosing an icon that scales to different sizes well and is easy to draw is important if your drawing skills are like mine (nearly nonexistent). Here's the icon I'm using for this example, although you could use anything that you like.

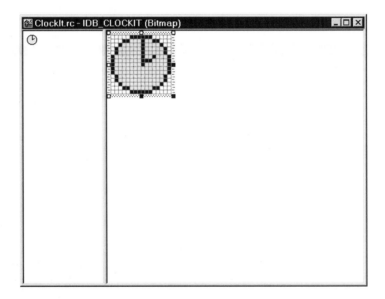

| Tip | *Make sure you use the special background color when drawing the two sizes of IDI_ABOUTDLL for the area outside of the clock. The background color is the green monitor in the Colors toolbar. It appears green when you draw it on-screen, but when Windows displays the icon, the area on the outside of the clock will turn the same color as the background of whatever the clock is displayed on. This gives the application user the impression that the icon is round instead of square.* |

At some point, you'll want to update the information in VS_VERSION_INFO. This resource contains information like the name of the company that created the control, any copyright or trademark information, and version information. You'll want to review these three areas as a minimum. I normally include a comment as well that tells the user a little bit about the control's function.

The About Box (IDD_ABOUTBOX_CLOCKIT) comes next. All you really need for an ActiveX control is the copyright and version information. You may also want to include the name of the company that created the control. Here's what the About Box looks like for this ActiveX control:

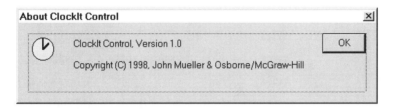

Always use two ampersands (&&) in a row when you want to see a single ampersand in a resource like an About Box. A single ampersand appears as an underline. Normally you'll use a single ampersand to create a shortcut on menus.

OK, all of the easy resources are out of the way. Now it's time to create our Property Page resource (IDD_PROPPAGE_CLOCKIT). The first thing you'll need to do is draw the controls on-screen. Here's the Property page I designed for this ActiveX control (note the use of combo boxes for the two format controls):

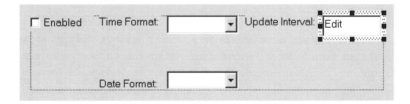

Let's start configuring the controls. We'll want to give them better IDs first. Right-click on the Enabled check box and choose Properties from the context menu. Choose the General tab of the Properties dialog box and type **IDC_ENABLED** in the ID field. Now we'll follow the same process for the other three controls. Give them the following ID values: **IDC_TIMEFORMAT**, **IDC_DATEFORMAT**, and **IDC_UPDATE_INTERVAL**.

Now that all our controls have readable names, let's get them ready for use. You won't need to do anything with either IDC_ENABLED or IDC_UPDATE_INTERVAL right now, but you will need to change IDC_DATEFORMAT and IDC_TIMEFORMAT as shown in Table 8-2.

Control	Tab	Property	Value
IDC_TIMEFORMAT	Styles	Type	Drop List
	Styles	No integral height	Checked
	Styles	Sort	Unchecked
	Data	Enter list box items	hh:mm:ss am hh:mm am hh:mm:ss 24 hh:mm 24
IDC_DATEFORMAT	Styles	Type	Drop List
	Styles	No integral height	Checked
	Styles	Sort	Unchecked
	Data	Enter list box items	dd/mm/yy mm/dd/yy dd/mm/yyyy mm/dd/yyyy dd Month yyyy Month dd, yyyy DOW dd Month yyyy

Table 8-2.   ClockIt Property Page Configuration

Note   *Press* CTRL-ENTER *to add more lines to the Enter list box items field of the Data tab. Each entry you want to see in the drop-down list box must appear on a separate line in this field.*

There is one final task to perform with the Property page. We need to create a connection between the controls on this page and the properties we created earlier. (I described this process in detail in Chapter 4.) Now, CTRL-double-click on each control to display the Add Member Variable dialog box, type in the associated memory variable: **m_textTimeFormat**, **m_textDateFormat**, or **m_updateInterval**. We'll need to create a new member variable for the Enabled field. I've used m_Enabled for the example. Make sure you include a property name in the Optional property name field of the Add Member Variable dialog box. Open the MFC ClassWizard when you finish defining the member variables. Choose the Member Variables tab, then select

CClockItPropPage in the Class name field. Your dialog box should look like the one shown in Figure 8-3.

Our ActiveX control won't need to display itself when the program is executing. It's a background control like the common dialog box control used with Visual Basic. If you were to retain the default image provided by the control, what you'd see when you placed it on an application is a square with an ellipse inside—hardly a good presentation for a production-level control. Though we won't take the time to change the displayed appearance of all the ActiveX controls we create for the book, it's important to at least see one example of how you can do it. With this in mind, you'll need to add another bitmap to the default resources. Right-click the Bitmap folder in ResourceView, then choose Insert Bitmap from the context menu. Right-click on the new bitmap entry, then choose Properties from the context menu to display the Properties dialog box. Change the ID to something more appropriate—the example uses IDB_DISPLAY. Now it's time to draw the bitmap we'll display whenever someone

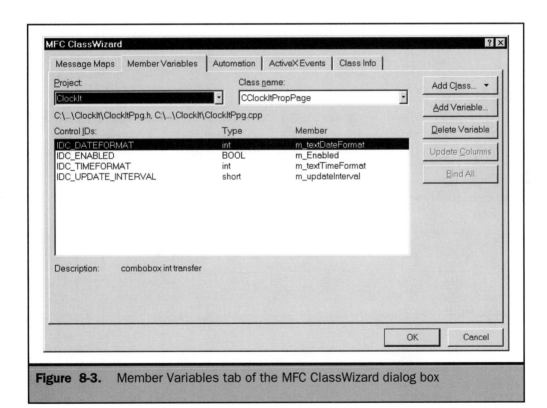

Figure 8-3.   Member Variables tab of the MFC ClassWizard dialog box

places the control on a form. Here's the button look that I drew for the purposes of this example:

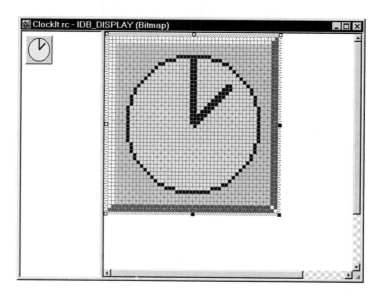

Adding Some Code

Now it's time to add some code. Listing 8-1 shows the code for the ClockItCtrl.CPP file. Almost all of function shells are defined for you in advance. You'll need to add the UpdateTime( ) and IntMonthToString( ) functions to the list of those that will appear in your source file by default. Adding these functions also means changing the ClockItCtrl.H file, a part of which appears in Listing 8-2. The code you need to add appears in bold type. Note the m_nTimerID variable. I'll show you how it comes into play later.

Listing 8-1

```
// ClockItCtl.cpp : Implementation of the CClockItCtrl ActiveX Control class.

#include "stdafx.h"
#include "ClockIt.h"
#include "ClockItCtl.h"
#include "ClockItPpg.h"


#ifdef _DEBUG
#define new DEBUG_NEW
#undef THIS_FILE
static char THIS_FILE[] = __FILE__;
#endif
```

```
IMPLEMENT_DYNCREATE(CClockItCtrl, COleControl)


/////////////////////////////////////////////////////////////////////////
// Message map

BEGIN_MESSAGE_MAP(CClockItCtrl, COleControl)
    //{{AFX_MSG_MAP(CClockItCtrl)
    ON_WM_ENABLE()
    ON_WM_TIMER()
    //}}AFX_MSG_MAP
    ON_OLEVERB(AFX_IDS_VERB_EDIT, OnEdit)
    ON_OLEVERB(AFX_IDS_VERB_PROPERTIES, OnProperties)
END_MESSAGE_MAP()


/////////////////////////////////////////////////////////////////////////
// Dispatch map

BEGIN_DISPATCH_MAP(CClockItCtrl, COleControl)
    //{{AFX_DISPATCH_MAP(CClockItCtrl)
    DISP_PROPERTY_NOTIFY(CClockItCtrl, "Clock", m_clock, OnClockChanged, VT_DATE)
    DISP_PROPERTY_NOTIFY(CClockItCtrl, "TextDateFormat", m_textDateFormat,
OnTextDateFormatChanged, VT_I2)
    DISP_PROPERTY_NOTIFY(CClockItCtrl, "TextTimeFormat", m_textTimeFormat,
OnTextTimeFormatChanged, VT_I2)
    DISP_PROPERTY_NOTIFY(CClockItCtrl, "UpdateInterval", m_updateInterval,
OnUpdateIntervalChanged, VT_I2)
    DISP_PROPERTY_NOTIFY(CClockItCtrl, "TextDate", m_textDate, OnTextDateChanged,
VT_BSTR)
    DISP_PROPERTY_NOTIFY(CClockItCtrl, "TextTime", m_textTime, OnTextTimeChanged,
VT_BSTR)
    DISP_FUNCTION(CClockItCtrl, "StartIt", StartIt, VT_EMPTY, VTS_BOOL)
    DISP_STOCKPROP_ENABLED()
    //}}AFX_DISPATCH_MAP
    DISP_FUNCTION_ID(CClockItCtrl, "AboutBox", DISPID_ABOUTBOX, AboutBox,
VT_EMPTY, VTS_NONE)
END_DISPATCH_MAP()


/////////////////////////////////////////////////////////////////////////
// Event map

BEGIN_EVENT_MAP(CClockItCtrl, COleControl)
    //{{AFX_EVENT_MAP(CClockItCtrl)
    EVENT_CUSTOM("Tick", FireTick, VTS_NONE)
    //}}AFX_EVENT_MAP
END_EVENT_MAP()
```

```
/////////////////////////////////////////////////////////////////////
// Property pages

// TODO: Add more property pages as needed.  Remember to increase the count!
BEGIN_PROPPAGEIDS(CClockItCtrl, 1)
    PROPPAGEID(CClockItPropPage::guid)
END_PROPPAGEIDS(CClockItCtrl)


/////////////////////////////////////////////////////////////////////
// Initialize class factory and guid

IMPLEMENT_OLECREATE_EX(CClockItCtrl, "CLOCKIT.ClockItCtrl.1",
    0xf16a8f06, 0xf0be, 0x11d1, 0xae, 0x3, 0, 0x60, 0x97, 0x5b, 0xf7, 0x84)


/////////////////////////////////////////////////////////////////////
// Type library ID and version

IMPLEMENT_OLETYPELIB(CClockItCtrl, _tlid, _wVerMajor, _wVerMinor)


/////////////////////////////////////////////////////////////////////
// Interface IDs

const IID BASED_CODE IID_DClockIt =
    { 0xf16a8f04, 0xf0be, 0x11d1, { 0xae, 0x3, 0, 0x60, 0x97, 0x5b, 0xf7, 0x84 } };
const IID BASED_CODE IID_DClockItEvents =
    { 0xf16a8f05, 0xf0be, 0x11d1, { 0xae, 0x3, 0, 0x60, 0x97, 0x5b, 0xf7, 0x84 } };


/////////////////////////////////////////////////////////////////////
// Control type information

static const DWORD BASED_CODE _dwClockItOleMisc =
    OLEMISC_INVISIBLEATRUNTIME |
    OLEMISC_ACTIVATEWHENVISIBLE |
    OLEMISC_SETCLIENTSITEFIRST |
    OLEMISC_INSIDEOUT |
    OLEMISC_CANTLINKINSIDE |
    OLEMISC_RECOMPOSEONRESIZE;

IMPLEMENT_OLECTLTYPE(CClockItCtrl, IDS_CLOCKIT, _dwClockItOleMisc)
```

```
/////////////////////////////////////////////////////////////////////////
// CClockItCtrl::CClockItCtrlFactory::UpdateRegistry -
// Adds or removes system registry entries for CClockItCtrl

BOOL CClockItCtrl::CClockItCtrlFactory::UpdateRegistry(BOOL bRegister)
{
    // TODO: Verify that your control follows apartment-model threading rules.
    // Refer to MFC TechNote 64 for more information.
    // If your control does not conform to the apartment-model rules, then
    // you must modify the code below, changing the 6th parameter from
    // afxRegInsertable | afxRegApartmentThreading to afxRegInsertable.

    if (bRegister)
        return AfxOleRegisterControlClass(
            AfxGetInstanceHandle(),
            m_clsid,
            m_lpszProgID,
            IDS_CLOCKIT,
            IDB_CLOCKIT,
            afxRegInsertable | afxRegApartmentThreading,
            _dwClockItOleMisc,
            _tlid,
            _wVerMajor,
            _wVerMinor);
    else
        return AfxOleUnregisterClass(m_clsid, m_lpszProgID);
}


/////////////////////////////////////////////////////////////////////////
// CClockItCtrl::CClockItCtrl - Constructor

CClockItCtrl::CClockItCtrl()
{
    InitializeIIDs(&IID_DClockIt, &IID_DClockItEvents);

    // Set the initial control size.
    SetInitialSize(48, 48);
}


/////////////////////////////////////////////////////////////////////////
// CClockItCtrl::~CClockItCtrl - Destructor

CClockItCtrl::~CClockItCtrl()
{
    // Kill the timer.
```

```
        KillTimer(m_nTimerID);
}


//////////////////////////////////////////////////////////////////////
// CClockItCtrl::OnDraw - Drawing function

void CClockItCtrl::OnDraw(
            CDC* pdc, const CRect& rcBounds, const CRect& rcInvalid)
{
    CPoint    oPoint;         // Starting point for the bitmap.
    CBitmap    oBitmap;       // A variable to hold the bitmap.

    // Define the upper left corner of the drawing area.
    oPoint.x = 0;
    oPoint.y = 0;

    // Load the bitmap.
    oBitmap.LoadBitmap(IDB_DISPLAY);

    // Draw the bitmap.
    pdc->DrawState(oPoint,
        CSize(48, 48),
        oBitmap,
        DST_BITMAP | DSS_NORMAL,
        NULL);
}


//////////////////////////////////////////////////////////////////////
// CClockItCtrl::DoPropExchange - Persistence support

void CClockItCtrl::DoPropExchange(CPropExchange* pPX)
{
    // Default actions on the part of the Class Wizard.
    ExchangeVersion(pPX, MAKELONG(_wVerMinor, _wVerMajor));
    COleControl::DoPropExchange(pPX);

    // Get the updated time for our control.
    UpdateTime();

    // Make all of our properties persistent.
    PX_Short(pPX, "TextDateFormat", m_textDateFormat, 1);
    PX_Short(pPX, "TextTimeFormat", m_textTimeFormat, 0);
    PX_Short(pPX, "UpdateInterval", m_updateInterval, 1);
    PX_String(pPX, "TextDate", m_textDate);
    PX_String(pPX, "TextTime", m_textTime);
```

```
}


///////////////////////////////////////////////////////////////////////////
// CClockItCtrl::OnResetState - Reset control to default state

void CClockItCtrl::OnResetState()
{
    // Resets defaults found in DoPropExchange
    COleControl::OnResetState();

    // Set the clock output fields.
    UpdateTime();
}



///////////////////////////////////////////////////////////////////////////
// CClockItCtrl::AboutBox - Display an "About" box to the user

void CClockItCtrl::AboutBox()
{
    CDialog dlgAbout(IDD_ABOUTBOX_CLOCKIT);
    dlgAbout.DoModal();
}



///////////////////////////////////////////////////////////////////////////
// CClockItCtrl message handlers

void CClockItCtrl::OnClockChanged()
{
    // Don't do anything special,
    // just the default action.
    SetModifiedFlag();
}

void CClockItCtrl::OnTextDateFormatChanged()
{
    // Update the time.
    UpdateTime();

    // Make sure the change shows up.
    SetModifiedFlag();
}

void CClockItCtrl::OnTextTimeFormatChanged()
{
```

```
    // Update the time.
    UpdateTime();

    // Make sure the change shows up.
    SetModifiedFlag();
}

void CClockItCtrl::OnUpdateIntervalChanged()
{
    // Kill the existing timer.
    KillTimer(m_nTimerID);

    // Create a new timer.
    m_nTimerID = SetTimer(1, m_updateInterval * 1000, NULL);

    // Make sure the change shows up.
    SetModifiedFlag();
}

void CClockItCtrl::OnTextDateChanged()
{
    // Don't do anything special,
    // just the default action.
    SetModifiedFlag();
}

void CClockItCtrl::OnTextTimeChanged()
{
    // Don't do anything special,
    // just the default action.
    SetModifiedFlag();
}

void CClockItCtrl::OnEnable(BOOL bEnable)
{
    // Perform the default action.
    COleControl::OnEnable(bEnable);

    if (!bEnable)
    {
        // Kill the existing timer.
        KillTimer(m_nTimerID);
    }
    else
    {
        // Create a new timer.
        m_nTimerID = SetTimer(1, m_updateInterval * 1000, NULL);
```

```
    }
}

void CClockItCtrl::OnTimer(UINT nIDEvent)
{
    // Update the control properties.
    UpdateTime();

    // Tell the world that we've updated the clock.
    FireTick();

    // Perform the default action.
    COleControl::OnTimer(nIDEvent);
}

void CClockItCtrl::UpdateTime()
{
    // Declare a series of variables to hold the time.
    COleDateTime    oDateTime;
    CString         sMonth;
    CString         sDay;
    CString         sYear;
    CString         sHour;
    CString         sMinute;
    CString         sSecond;
    CString         sDOW;

    int             iCurrentHour;       // Hour manipulation.
    LPTSTR          sBuffer = "0000";   // Date/Time buffer.
    CString         sAmPm = " a.m.";    // A.M./P.M. String.

    // Obtain the current time.
    oDateTime = COleDateTime::GetCurrentTime();

    // Get the day of week.
    switch (oDateTime.GetDayOfWeek())
    {
    case 1:
        sDOW = "Sunday";
        break;
    case 2:
        sDOW = "Monday";
        break;
    case 3:
        sDOW = "Tuesday";
        break;
```

```
case 4:
    sDOW = "Wednesday";
    break;
case 5:
    sDOW = "Thursday";
    break;
case 6:
    sDOW = "Friday";
    break;
case 7:
    sDOW = "Saturday";
    break;
}

// See if we need to convert the hour to am/pm format prior to
// converting it to a string.
iCurrentHour = oDateTime.GetHour();
if ((m_textTimeFormat == 0) || (m_textTimeFormat == 1))
    if (iCurrentHour > 12)
    {
        iCurrentHour = iCurrentHour - 12;
        sAmPm = " p.m.";
    }

// Convert the time to text.
itoa(iCurrentHour, sBuffer, 10);
sHour = sBuffer;
itoa(oDateTime.GetMinute(), sBuffer, 10);
sMinute = sBuffer;
if (sMinute.GetLength() == 1)
    sMinute = "0" + sMinute;
itoa(oDateTime.GetSecond(), sBuffer, 10);
sSecond = sBuffer;
if (sSecond.GetLength() == 1)
    sSecond = "0" + sSecond;

// Convert the date to text.
itoa(oDateTime.GetDay(), sBuffer, 10);
sDay = sBuffer;
if (sDay.GetLength() == 1)
    sDay = "0" + sDay;
itoa(oDateTime.GetMonth(), sBuffer, 10);
sMonth = sBuffer;
if ((m_textDateFormat >= 0) && (m_textDateFormat < 3))
    if (sMonth.GetLength() == 1)
        sMonth = "0" + sMonth;
itoa(oDateTime.GetYear(), sBuffer, 10);
```

```
    sYear = sBuffer;

    // Fill the TextDate property with the appropriate value based
    // on format selection.
    switch (m_textDateFormat)
    {
    case 0:
        m_textDate = sDay + "/" + sMonth + "/" + sYear.Right(2);
        break;
    case 1:
        m_textDate = sMonth + "/" + sDay + "/" + sYear.Right(2);
        break;
    case 2:
        m_textDate = sDay + "/" + sMonth + "/" + sYear;
        break;
    case 3:
        m_textDate = sMonth + "/" + sDay + "/" + sYear;
        break;
    case 4:
        m_textDate = sDay + " " + IntMonthToString(sMonth) + " " + sYear;
        break;
    case 5:
        m_textDate = IntMonthToString(sMonth) + " " + sDay + " ," + sYear;
        break;
    case 6:
        m_textDate = sDOW + " " + sDay + " " + IntMonthToString(sMonth) + " " +
sYear;
    }

    // Fill the TextTime property with the appropriate value based
    // on format selection.
    switch (m_textTimeFormat)
    {
    case 0:
        m_textTime = sHour + ":" + sMinute + ":" + sSecond + sAmPm;
        break;
    case 1:
        m_textTime = sHour + ":" + sMinute + sAmPm;
        break;
    case 2:
        m_textTime = sHour + ":" + sMinute + ":" + sSecond;
        break;
    case 3:
        m_textTime = sHour + ":" + sMinute;
        break;
    }
```

```
    // Set the Clock property value.
    m_clock = DATE(oDateTime);

    // Make sure the change takes place.
    SetModifiedFlag();
}

CString CClockItCtrl::IntMonthToString(CString sMonth)
{
    // Find the integer string value of sMonth and return
    // the month it corresponds to as a full text value.
    switch (*LPCTSTR(sMonth))
    {
    case '1':
        return "January";
    case '2':
        return "February";
    case '3':
        return "March";
    case '4':
        return "April";
    case '5':
        return "May";
    case '6':
        return "June";
    case '7':
        return "July";
    case '8':
        return "August";
    case '9':
        return "September";
    case '10':
        return "October";
    case '11':
        return "November";
    case '12':
        return "December";
    }

    // Just in case we get some odd value from the calling
    // function.
    return "Error in Month Value: " + sMonth;
}

void CClockItCtrl::StartIt(BOOL bStart)
{
    if (!bStart)
```

```
    {
        // Kill the existing timer.
        KillTimer(m_nTimerID);
    }
    else
    {
        // Create a new timer.
        m_nTimerID = SetTimer(1, m_updateInterval * 1000, NULL);
    }
}
```

ting 8-2

```
// Dispatch maps
    //{{AFX_DISPATCH(CClockItCtrl)
    DATE m_clock;
    afx_msg void OnClockChanged();
    short m_textDateFormat;
    afx_msg void OnTextDateFormatChanged();
    short m_textTimeFormat;
    afx_msg void OnTextTimeFormatChanged();
    short m_updateInterval;
    afx_msg void OnUpdateIntervalChanged();
    CString m_textDate;
    afx_msg void OnTextDateChanged();
    CString m_textTime;
    afx_msg void OnTextTimeChanged();
    afx_msg void StartIt(BOOL bStart);
    //}}AFX_DISPATCH
    DECLARE_DISPATCH_MAP()

    afx_msg void AboutBox();

    // Add in our time update function.
    void UpdateTime();

    // Add in an integer month to string month converter.
    CString IntMonthToString(CString sMonth);

    // Timer event tracking variable.
    UINT m_nTimerID;
```

Understanding the Control Code

Listing 8-1 probably looks like a lot more code than you'd ever want to type, but it's really not all that difficult to understand once you break it into pieces. Let's take the functions in order, starting at the beginning of the source file.

A control constructor always has the same name as the control, while the destructor adds a tilde (~) in front of the function name.

The first function we'll look at is the constructor, CClockItCtrl( ). The only thing we do here is use the SetInitialSize( ) function to set the initial control size to the size of our bitmap. This call doesn't appear to make any difference when using the control with Visual C++, but it does affect the control's initial size in other language products like Visual Basic. Not setting the control size means that the control will get drawn in the default size, which doesn't match the size of our control bitmap and leaves a white space around the control when you see it on a form.

The destructor, ~CClockItCtrl( ), also contains a single call. In this case, we kill a timer. You'll see where the timer comes into play later. All you need to know for the moment is that it's important to kill any timers you create. The best place to do that for the last time (when you're closing the application) is in the destructor.

OnDraw( ) is totally changed from the default function provided by the MFC ActiveX ControlWizard. The reason is simple. The original OnDraw( ) function places a white rectangle with an ellipse in it on your form. It's a default for controls that aren't derived from a control that normally gets displayed on-screen. You'll want to use something like the code shown here whenever you create an invisible control to make sure that another programmer will be able to identify your control on a form. The steps required to make this work are simple. Just define a CBitmap object to hold the bitmap we created earlier, load the bitmap into our object, then display it using a function like DrawState( ).

The DoPropExchange( ) function is very much like the one described in the "Breaking the Code into Pieces" section of Chapter 4, so we won't talk about it in this chapter. The only difference is that we call the UpdateTime( ) function described later in this section to update the time-related property values prior to the property exchange.

The next major function we come to is OnClockChanged( ). Note that we don't have to do anything to this function since the other functions handle any changes required to this property. I feel that it's important to find what I term "output properties" early in the design process. The Clock, TextTime, and TextDate properties all fall into this category—their only purpose is to provide an output to the application in which the control is used. This means that you won't see any code for the OnTextTimeChanged( ) or OnTextDateChanged( ) functions either.

We do have two formatting properties to think about: TextDateFormat and TextTimeFormat. Their associated functions, OnTextDateFormatChanged( ) and OnTextTimeFormatChanged( ), have a single call to UpdateTime( ). We then set the modified flag using the SetModifiedFlag( ) function to ensure the changed values take effect.

Note *The easiest way to look at Windows timers is as little alarm clocks that you set using SetTimer( ) and turn off using KillTimer( ).*

It's time to look at one of the more complex functions (at least from a conceptual point of view): OnUpdateIntervalChanged( ). Every time we change the UpdateInterval property, we need to make a change in how the control operates. It's not enough to simply make the change to the property value; we need to make a change to the clock functionality of the control itself. The first thing you need to understand is that Windows provides a limited number of timers. You can set a timer just as you would an alarm clock. Every so many milliseconds, Windows will call a function that you've designed to tell it that the alarm has gone off. To set the time, you use the SetTimer( ) function. The SetTimer( ) function requires three inputs: the timer identifier (any nonzero number), the amount of time between alarms in milliseconds, and the address of a timer callback function. If you supply a NULL value, then Windows will use the application's message queue and generate a WM_TIMER message. Windows will return a number that corresponds to the alarm clock that your application is using. When you decide that you no longer need to use the alarm, you call the KillTimer( ) function with the timer number included.

Tip *The easiest way to create a timer callback function for your control is by accessing the WM_TIMER message through the OnTimer( ) function. A standard callback has to be declared outside of your class as a CALLBACK EXPORT function. This means a standard callback has to use a lot of extra code to gain access to the control's methods and properties using the Window handle. The only time that it makes sense to use a callback function is if you need to perform special processing with a number of window messages and want to combine the code required into one function.*

Now let's look at the code in OnUpdateIntervalChanged( ). The first thing we do is turn off any existing alarm using the KillTimer( ) function. Then, we set a new alarm using the SetTimer( ) function. Notice that I save the timer number using the m_nTimerID variable that we created in the header shown in Listing 8-2. Finally, we set the modified flag to ensure our changes have taken hold.

The OnEnable( ) and StartIt( ) functions both work in a similar way to the OnUpdateIntervalChanged( ) function. They both use the KillTimer( ) function to remove alarms and the SetTimer( ) function to create new ones. The example code uses the passed BOOL to determine when it needs to set or kill the timer. Note that this code doesn't include any error trapping for situations where a user may try to set a timer or kill a timer more than once. A production control would need to include this type of error checking since Windows has a limited number of timers available.

The OnTimer( ) function performs three tasks. First, it updates the current time properties for the control. Next, it fires the Tick event. The Tick event will be monitored by the application program. Finally, the OnTimer( ) function allows Windows to perform any default timer processing.

It's time to look at the UpdateTime( ) function. There's a lot of code here because we have to maintain control over three properties and the contents of those properties can vary according to the TextTimeFormat and TextDateFormat properties. In essence, this is the meat and potatoes function of the whole control.

Let's look at the time portion of the UpdateTime( ) function first. We begin by converting the hour value from a 24-hour format (the Windows default) to an A.M./P.M. format, if needed. In addition to converting the number used to represent the time, we need to change the string that holds either A.M. or P.M., depending on the current time. Obviously, we only need to perform the conversion if the user has selected the correct time format and the hour is later than 12 noon. Once we have the hour converted, we can place the hours, minutes, and seconds into strings. I find that CStrings are easier to work with than most string formats, so we need a buffer to grab the string, then place it in the CString used to hold it permanently. Finally, we use a switch statement to choose a particular time format and place the numbers in their desired position.

Working with the TextDate property in UpdateTime( ) is similar to working with the time. We begin by converting the day of the week value to text using a switch statement. The next thing we do is grab all of the date values and place them into CString variables. Finally, we use a switch statement to place the numbers into their desired position and add the day of week, if needed. Notice that there are three date formats that spell out the month name rather than displaying it as a number. That's where the IntMonthToString( ) function comes into place. It takes as input a CString containing the month as a numeric value. A simple switch statement converts the number to a text value. The spelled out month value gets placed into the TextDate property in place of the normal number.

The Clock property is the easiest part of the whole UpdateTime( ) function. All we need to do is take the oDateTime object, used to hold the date and time, and convert it to a DATE format. Notice that the UpdateTime( ) function ends by setting the modified flag. This is an important thing to do if you want to ensure your property changes show up at the control.

Publishing the Control Using Visual Component Manager

You've just created one of the best ActiveX controls available for monitoring the time (or at least we'll say that you have for the purposes of this example). Now you need to place the control in a location where everyone can use it. One of the best ways to do this is to publish your control using the Visual Component Manager. You'll find this tool in a variety of places, but the easiest place to access it if you still have Visual C++ open is through the Tools menu. Once you start the program, you'll see an Internet Explorer window like the one shown in Figure 8-4. (This copy of Visual Component

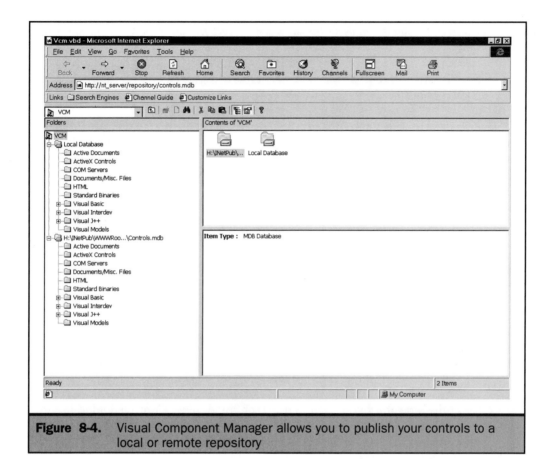

Figure 8-4.   Visual Component Manager allows you to publish your controls to a local or remote repository

Manager has already been set up to use a remote repository on a server drive in addition to the local repository that you'll be able to access by default.)

> **Note**   *The Visual Component Manager provides access to both local and remote repositories of customized programming aids like ActiveX controls.*

As you can see, this is an Explorer style view of the repository. On the left are folders used to store various types of objects, including ActiveX controls. You can also use the repository to store custom project wizards, HTML pages, and various binary files like bitmaps. The whole purpose of this repository is to make it easier to access customized programming aids on either a local or company-wide basis (though you'll likely use it on a company-wide basis more often than not).

> **Note** *This section is not meant as a tutorial for using every feature of the Visual Component Manager. Our only goal at the moment is to publish an ActiveX control so the entire team can use it. You can, however, use the procedures in this section any time you need to publish ActiveX controls and most other types of objects that the repository is designed to handle.*

Now that you have a better idea of what Visual Component Manager can do for you, let's look at ActiveX controls in particular. We need to publish the ClockIt control that we just created so that the other team members have access to it. The following procedure shows what you need to do to publish an ActiveX control (ClockIt in particular) either locally or remotely:

1. Open the Visual Component Manager, if you haven't done so already. You'll see a Main window like the one shown in Figure 8-4.

> **Note** *At this point, you may need to select a different repository than the default. Figure 8-4 shows the local repository and a repository located on a network server. In a team situation, you'll need to set up a remote repository on a server and switch to that repository before publishing your ActiveX control. If you already have a connection to the remote repository, you'll see it listed along with the local repository. To open a remote repository that you haven't accessed before, right-click the VCM folder and choose Repository | Open from the context menu. You'll see a File Open type dialog box that will allow you to find and then access the remote repository.*

2. Select the repository you want to use, then the ActiveX Controls folder within that repository. For the purposes of this example, I'll be using the remote repository located on my H: drive. You can use any repository you like, including the local repository, for this example.

3. Click the Publish a New Component button on the toolbar. You'll see the Visual Component Manager Publish Wizard - Introduction dialog box.

4. Click Next. You'll see the Visual Component Manager Publish Wizard - Title and Properties dialog box shown next. This is where you'll tell Visual Component Manager about the control so that it can enter the details for you into the component repository. Notice that the wizard automatically enters some information for you, such as in the Author field.

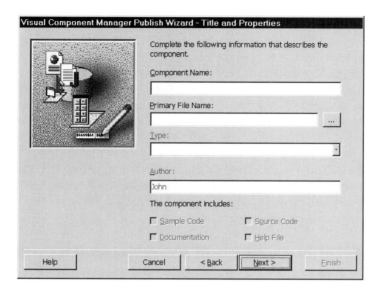

5. Type **ClockIt (Time and Date Display) Control** in the Component Name field.

6. Click the Ellipses button next to the Primary File Name field. Use the Primary File dialog box to find the ClockIt.OCX file. This is the file that contains the control we just created. Click Open in the Primary File dialog box to enter the control name in the Primary File Name field.

7. Choose ActiveX Control in the Type field. Note that the Visual Component Manager won't allow you to type in a new Type field entry—you must use the defined types.

Note *At this point, you could also change the Author field entry, though the default is normally sufficient for publishing your control. The default is based on your login name for Windows, which should be unique on the network. In other words, as long as you maintain unique names for your network login, the name supplied here should be unique (and easily identifiable) as well.*

8. Select one or more The component includes options. These options include sample code that shows how to use the control, source code for the control itself, a help file, and component documentation. For the purposes of this example, check the Source Code option since that's all we have for this control. Later, we could include the sample code that we'll create in the next section of the chapter.

It isn't always a good idea to publish more than just the ActiveX control to the repository since Visual Component Manager always installs whatever you provide to the client machine. Not everyone will require the source code for your control, so placing it on their machine will waste space and make it hard for them to use your control. In some cases, you may even want to make multiple entries. For example, you might have one entry that includes just the control, another that includes both a sample program and a help file along with the control, and yet another that includes everything, even the source code.

9. Click Next. You'll see the Visual Component Manager Publish Wizard - More Properties dialog box shown here. This is where you'll type a control description and provide some keywords to make it easier for people to search for your control on the network.

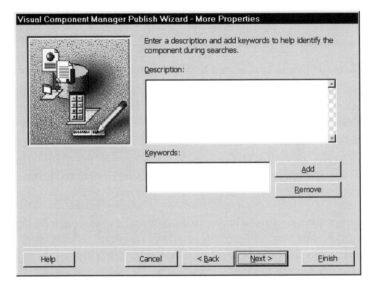

10. Type **This control allows you to monitor the date and time in both DATE and text formats. It includes properties for setting the output format and the timing interval.** in the Description field.

11. Click Add. You'll see the Item Keywords dialog box shown next. In the left pane is a list of keywords that already appear in the repository database (there won't be any the first time you use Visual Component Manager). In the right pane is a list of keywords applied to this component. I've already added one, Time.

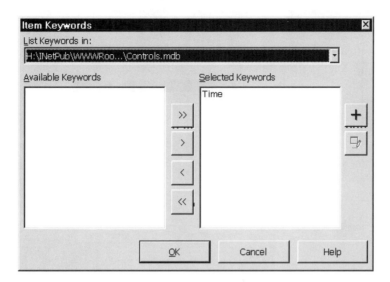

12. Click the + (plus) key. You'll see the Add a Keyword dialog box. Type **Date**, then click OK. You'll see the word added to the right pane of the Item Keywords dialog box. Follow these same steps for **Automatic Update** and **Time**. You could add additional keywords as desired, but this should be sufficient for the example.

13. Click OK to close the Item Keywords dialog box. The list of keywords that you just typed will appear in the Keywords field of the Visual Component Manager Publish Wizard - More Properties dialog box.

14. Click Next. You'll see the Visual Component Manager Publish Wizard - Additional Files dialog box. This is where you'd add any documentation, help, source code, or sample files for the control. We need to add the source code for our example since we selected the Source Code option earlier in the procedure.

15. Add all of the ClockIt project files to the list by clicking Add Files…, then using the File Open style dialog box to locate the files. Your dialog box should look similar to the one shown here:

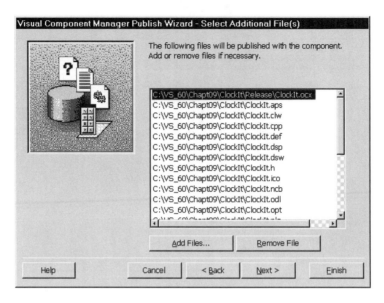

16. Click Next. You'll see the Visual Component Manager Publish Wizard - COM registration dialog box shown here:

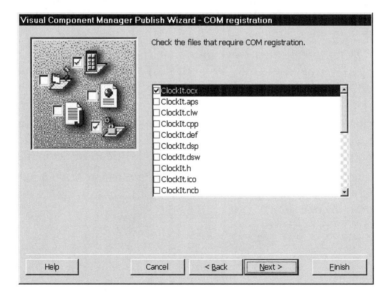

17. Ensure that the ClickIt.OCX entry is checked since this is the only file that requires COM registration.

18. Click Next. You'll see the Visual Component Manager Publish Wizard - Finished dialog box.

19. Click Finished. Visual Component Manager will create the required entries in the repository for you. You'll see a new entry in the repository like the one shown in Figure 8-5 when it gets finished.

Now you have a new control published at a central location for everyone to use. The problem now is how to allow someone else to use your control. Whenever you want to use a resource stored in the Visual Component Manager repository, all you need to do is right-click the control (or other object) and choose Install on this computer... from the context menu. You'll be asked where you want to install the control and perhaps a few other questions, depending on the type of object you want to install. If there are multiple copies of a control in the repository, make sure you choose the one that includes all the features you need. For example, if you need just the control, find a repository entry that includes just the control in the File name field. Otherwise, you'll get all of the files that the component author has chosen to publish for that particular repository entry installed on your machine.

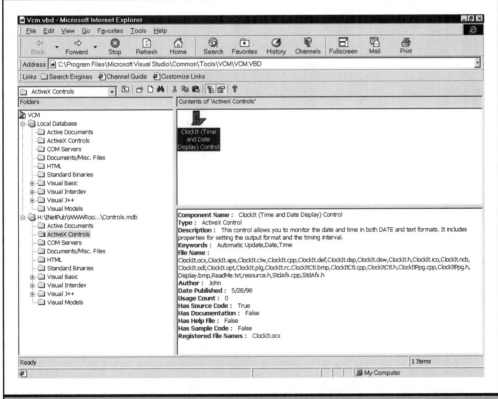

Figure 8-5. Visual Component Manager displays complete information about your control once it's entered in the repository

Using the Control Within Visual Basic

Creating an ActiveX control in Visual C++ to use in Visual Basic for application development occurs more often than you might think in the computer industry. It's a perfect match. Visual Basic provides fast prototyping and easy application development, while the strength of Visual C++ is its access to low-level programming constructs.

In this section, we'll begin by creating an application in Visual Basic that uses the ActiveX control we created in the "Creating ActiveX Controls with Visual C++" section of the chapter. The whole purpose of this example is to exercise the test control. Normally, you'd be using the control as part of an application designed to perform some type of work like accessing a database. We'll look at that kind of application as the book progresses.

One of the reasons for the orientation of this example is that you'll find that creating ActiveX controls for Visual Basic using Visual C++ isn't always as easy as it might first appear. That's where the last part of this section comes into play. Our first attempt at using the ActiveX control in the previous section is going to fail, even though the code is perfectly good and will work just fine if you use it with a Visual C++ application. We'll look at the reason for the failure and what you can do to fix it. Performing this kind of analysis will help you work through other problems related to developing tools in one language for use in another.

Note *Even though we're not including the Visual C++ test program in this chapter, you can download it from the Osborne Web site at: http://www.osborne.com. The project appears in the ClockItTest2 folder. Make sure you use this test program with the original version of the ClockIt control. You'll see that the control works perfectly with the Visual C++ version of the test application, but not at all with the Visual Basic version of the same application.*

Designing the Visual Basic Form

This section of the chapter will help you get our Visual Basic test application set up and ready for use. Since we've already gone through the steps required to create a simple Visual Basic application in Chapter 4, we'll use an abbreviated procedure in this section. The following procedure will take you through the steps required to create the project and design the form:

1. Start Visual Basic. You'll see a New Project dialog box.

2. Double-click the Standard EXE entry. You'll see a new dialog-based Visual Basic application, which includes a blank form.

3. Right-click the toolbox and choose Components… from the context menu. You'll see the Components dialog box shown here:

4. Check the Clock ActiveX Control Module entry, then click OK. You'll see the ClockIt control added to the toolbox. Notice that our control appears as the little clock symbol that we drew as a resource earlier.

5. Add components to the form to allow testing of the ClockIt control. Figure 8-6 shows the layout I used for this example. Notice that the ClockIt control appears as a push button on-screen. Table 8-3 will provide you with a complete list of properties for the controls on our form. Note that a blank in the table means that the property is blank for the control. In addition, I've already renamed the controls to appropriate values in most cases, using the (Name) property.

Adding Some Code to the ClockItTest Application

Just in case you haven't figured it out yet, I've called this application ClockItTest, though you can name it anything you like. It's time to add some code to the form we created previously. As with any Visual Basic application, double-clicking on the form or control will display the Code Editing window with the default function selected for you. All you need to do to change objects is choose one from the Object list box. Likewise, you can choose object-specific procedures by choosing one in the Procedures

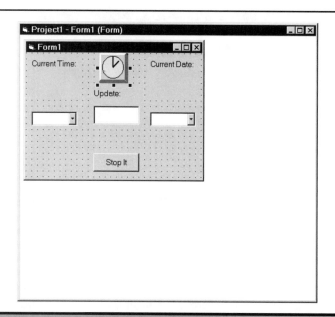

Figure 8-6. The ClockItTest application provides everything needed to fully test the control

Control	Property	Value
Label1	Caption	Current Time:
	Height	252
Label2	Caption	Current Date:
	Height	252
Label3	Caption	Update:
	Height	252
lbTime	Caption	
lbDate	Caption	
tbUpdate	Text	
cmdStart	Caption	Stop It
cbTimeFormat	Text	

Table 8-3. Control Property Settings for the ClockItText Application

Control	Property	Value
	Style	2 - Dropdown List
	Width	1200
	ItemData	hh:mm:ss am hh:mm am hh:mm:ss 24 hh:mm 24
cbDateFormat	Text	
	Style	2 - Dropdown List
	Width	1200
	ItemData	dd/mm/yy mm/dd/yy dd/mm/yyyy mm/dd/yyyy dd Month yyyy Month dd, yyyy DOW dd Month yyyy
Form1	Caption	ClockIt Control Test

Table 8-3.   Control Property Settings for the ClockItText Application (continued)

list box. Listing 8-3 shows the code we'll use for this example. All of the code is shown in the listing. I'll describe the various procedures after you get a look at the code.

Listing 8-3

```
Private Sub cbDateFormat_Click()
    ' Change the date format.
    ClockIt1.TextDateFormat = cbDateFormat.ListIndex

    ' Update the display.
    lbDate.Caption = ClockIt1.TextDate
End Sub

Private Sub cbTimeFormat_Click()
    ' Change the time format.
    ClockIt1.TextTimeFormat = cbTimeFormat.ListIndex

    ' Update the display.
```

```
        lbTime.Caption = ClockIt1.TextTime
End Sub

Private Sub ClockIt1_Tick()
    'Update our time and date displays.
    lbTime.Caption = ClockIt1.TextTime
    lbDate.Caption = ClockIt1.TextDate
End Sub

Private Sub cmdStart_Click()
    ' Stop or start the clock depending on the
    ' current state.  Change the caption on the
    ' command button as well.
    If cmdStart.Caption = "Stop It" Then
        cmdStart.Caption = "Start It"
        ClockIt1.Enabled = False
    Else
        cmdStart.Caption = "Stop It"
        ClockIt1.Enabled = True
    End If
End Sub

Private Sub Form_Load()
    ' Make our format selections match the
    ' ClockIt control settings.
    cbTimeFormat.ListIndex = ClockIt1.TextTimeFormat
    cbDateFormat.ListIndex = ClockIt1.TextDateFormat

    ' Initialize the output displays.
    lbTime.Caption = ClockIt1.TextTime
    lbDate.Caption = ClockIt1.TextDate

    ' Set the update interval.
    tbUpdate = ClockIt1.UpdateInterval

    ' Start the clock.
    ClockIt1.StartIt (True)
End Sub

Private Sub tbUpdate_Change()
    ' Change the update interval.
    ClockIt1.UpdateInterval = tbUpdate.Text
End Sub
```

Running the Example and Finding the Problem

At this point, we should have a working application. If you start the program, you'll see that you can change the date and time format just fine. In addition, the time and date output fields (lbTime and lbDate) will contain the correct time and date as of the time you started the program. In fact, there's only one problem with this whole picture—the clock doesn't appear to update at all. You can change the date or time format, or even the update interval, and the clock will just sit there, motionless.

You may suspect that there is a problem with the ActiveX control's code. However, a search through the code won't yield any problems at all. In fact, if you try using this control to create a Visual C++ dialog-based application that provides precisely the same functionality as our Visual Basic example in Listing 8-3, you'll find that the control works completely correct. The clock updates just as it should and you can change any of the properties as needed. (You'll find a Visual C++ project that does just this—it tests the original control for you—at the Osborne Web site: http://www.osborne.com. The name of the project is ClockItTest2.)

So, what's the problem? It turns out to be a very subtle difference in the way that Visual Basic and Visual C++ instantiate (create an instance) a control. The problem lies in the flags in Listing 8-1. That's the section that looks like this:

```
static const DWORD BASED_CODE _dwClockItOleMisc =
OLEMISC_INVISIBLEATRUNTIME |
    OLEMISC_ACTIVATEWHENVISIBLE |
    OLEMISC_SETCLIENTSITEFIRST |
    OLEMISC_INSIDEOUT |
    OLEMISC_CANTLINKINSIDE |
    OLEMISC_RECOMPOSEONRESIZE;
```

At first look, you won't see any problem with this code at all. However, after you spend many days digging through some obscure documentation somewhere, you'll find out that Visual Basic won't in-place-activate a control that's invisible—unlike Visual C++, which does. Since the control is inactive, MFC doesn't create a window for it. A control without a window can't have a callback function. If you'll remember right, our callback function requires a window handle to do anything with the control. No window means no handle, which ultimately means that the clock display won't update.

OK, so you comment out the OLEMISC_INVISIBLEATRUNTIME flag, recompile the ActiveX control, then run the Visual Basic application again. Voilà, the clock updates just fine and you can do everything with the Visual Basic application that you can with the Visual C++ version. Even the update interval works as anticipated. However, now you have another problem—the control is visible. We wanted the ClockIt control to disappear so the user wouldn't have to see it. Here's the solution to that problem:

```
void CClockItCtrl::StartIt(BOOL bStart)
{
    if (!bStart)
    {
        // Kill the existing timer.
        KillTimer(m_nTimerID);

        // Make sure the control is invisible.
        COleControl::SetControlSize(0, 0);
    }
    else
    {

        // Create a new timer.
        m_nTimerID = SetTimer(1, m_updateInterval * 1000, NULL);

        // Make sure the control is invisible.
        COleControl::SetControlSize(0, 0);
    }
}
```

Notice the two sections in bold. All we need to do is set the control size to 0. Since any application using this control has to call the StartIt( ) method to start the clock, it's unlikely that an application developer will forget to perform this simple task. The control will still disappear from the form, but since it's active, both Visual Basic and Visual C++ application developers will see a clock that automatically updates.

This may seem like a simple problem to avoid, and it is. However, the fix doesn't correct any code or make any major changes in the control itself. All we've done is remove a flag and add two lines of additional display code. A problem like this could take you weeks to find if you didn't have at least some clue of where to look. Consider some of the problems in finding it. For one thing, your debugger is useless, for the most part, because the debugger will tell you that the code is absolutely correct. If you look at the Microsoft documentation, it doesn't tell you directly that using the OLEMISC_INVISIBLEATRUNTIME flag can be harmful to your application's health. Finally, it's very likely that you'll set this flag as part of the development process since you'll want the control to be invisible when someone uses it. The OLEMISC_INVISIBLEATRUNTIME flag is always there when you check the Invisible at runtime option in the MFC ActiveX ControlWizard. As you can see, running into this problem is a very natural part of the development process. It's problems like these, not major problems in your code, that will cost you the most time to repair.

Packaging and Deploying Your Application

The application is done. We've built the control, placed it in the application, and created and tested all the code. However, it's still not in the hands of your users. That's where the matter of packaging comes into play. Even though the application is all ready to go on your machine, you have to get it on the user's machine for it to do any good. The Package and Deployment Wizard will allow you to create several kinds of packages, the most common of which are self-installing EXE files and CAB files that get used on the Internet.

This section is going to show you one example of how to use the Package and Deployment Wizard. The following procedures will show you how to package our ClockItTest application and get it ready for distribution to users needing a fully configurable clock on their machine. There are two main steps: packaging and deployment. We'll cover both procedures in separate sections.

*You must create an EXE file for the ClockItTest application. All you need to do is use the File | Make <Project>.EXE command to create the executable file. When you see the Make Project dialog box, type **ClockItTest** in the File name field. Click OK and Visual Basic will create the executable for you. There are more complex setups that you can perform when creating an EXE file; we'll visit them as the book progresses.*

Packaging

This section shows you how to package an application before you deploy it to a Web site or a location on a network drive. Normally, you'll package the application so that it contains a few highly compressed files. Using this technique makes it easy for you to ensure the user has everything needed to use your application.

1. Start the Package and Deployment Wizard. You'll see a dialog box like the one shown here:

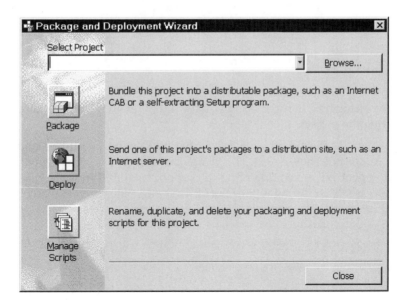

2. Use the Browse button to find the VBP (Visual Basic Project) file for the ClockItTest application. If you didn't rename your project, it'll appear as Project1 in the ClockItTest folder.

3. Click Package. You may get one or more messages once you click the Package button. For example, one of the more common messages is that the project file is newer than the project executable. The Package and Deployment Wizard will ask if you want to recompile the application. In most cases, you'll want to tell the Package and Deployment Wizard to perform the required work. Once the wizard has performed the work required to get a package together, you'll see a Package Type dialog box like the one shown here:

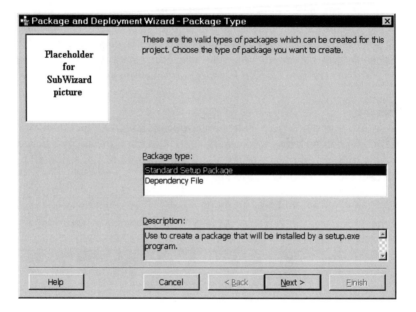

4. Choose the Standard Setup Package option, then click Next. You'll see a Build Folder dialog box. In most cases, you'll want to retain the default directory for building the project.

5. Click Next. At this point, you'll see a Missing Dependency Information dialog box like the one shown next. This dialog box simply says that the Package and Deployment Wizard couldn't find the support required for a package element. In this case, it's referring to the ClockIt.OCX file. Since there are no other files required in this case, you can ignore the problem.

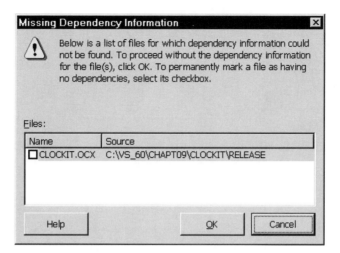

6. Click OK. You'll see a Files dialog box that contains a complete list of the files required to run the application. In most cases, you'll make a careful check of the file list to make sure all of the files associated with your application are included. For this example, all you really need to check is the ClockIt.OCX file. Make sure that the Package and Deployment Wizard has included it in the list of files to package.

Tip *Notice that the Files dialog box includes an Add button. Clicking this button will display an Add File dialog box that will allow you to add files to the list. For example, you may need to add supplementary files for a database application if the Package and Deployment Wizard doesn't find them all.*

7. Click Next. The Package and Deployment Wizard will ask how you want to distribute your application, as shown next. You can choose between a single file or floppy disk distribution. (By the time you read this, Microsoft may have added additional distribution methods, including CD.)

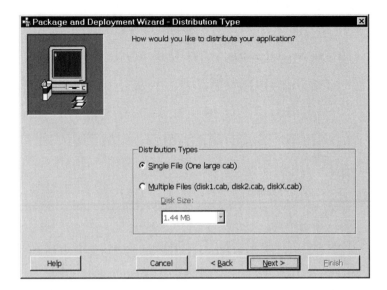

8. Choose Single File, then click Next. You'll see the Installation Title dialog box. This is the title that the Setup program will use throughout the installation process.

9. Type the name of the project, ClockIt Test (or whatever name your project is using), then click Next. You'll see the Icons dialog box shown here. This dialog box is a lot more than it seems at first. The Groups list is a list of Start Menu folders where your application icons will appear. You'll normally give the Groups list the name of your main application program or company. Obviously, you can create subgroups and arrange the application icons in other ways. The Icons list tells what icons will appear in the various group folders. Step 10 is specific to this example, but you can use it as a guideline for modifying your own groups and icons.

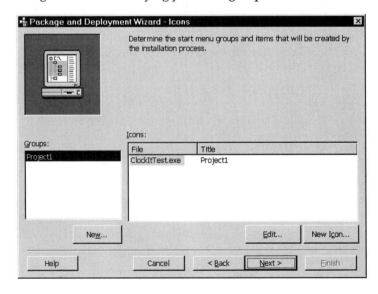

10. Highlight the Project1 entry in the Group list and press Delete. You shouldn't have any groups or icons at this point. Click New... You'll see the Add G&roup dialog box. Type **ClockIt Test**, then click OK. Click New Icon... You'll see the A&dd Icon dialog box. Select ClockItTest.EXE from the File to create an icon for list box. This entry determines which file gets the icon title that you choose. Type **ClockIt Test** in the Icon Title field. This is the entry that will appear in the Start menu for this application. Click OK. Your Icon dialog box should look like the one shown here:

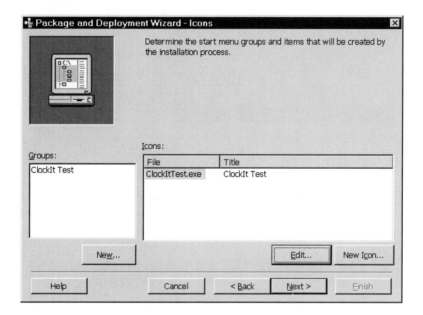

11. Click Next. You'll see the Install Locations dialog box. The Files list provides a complete list of the files that you'll install for the application and their current location on the development machine. The Install location list box tells where Setup will place the file on the user's machine. This dialog box is where you'll determine the location of each file during installation. Normally, you'll want to retain the default settings provided by the wizard.

12. Click Next. You'll see the Shared Files dialog box shown next. As you can see, this dialog box lists all of the files that could be shared by other applications. If you check a box next to a filename, then Setup will install the file as shared. What this means is that when a user uninstalls your application, Setup will spend extra time making sure that no other applications are using the file. The file will only get removed if no other applications are using it.

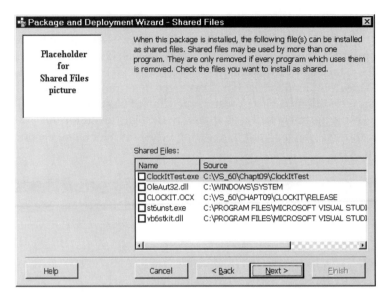

13. Check the ClockIt.OCX entry since our control might be shared by other applications.

14. Click Next. You'll see the Finished dialog box shown here. You still need to enter a name for saving the package. In this case I used ClockIt Install. Make sure that you give the package a meaningful name so that you can find it easy later. Click Save Script so that the options you've selected will get saved to disk.

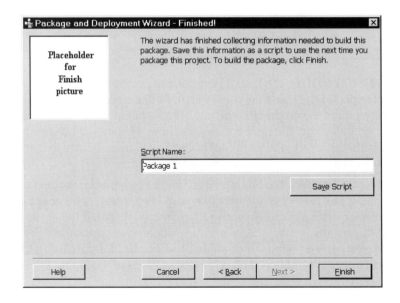

15. Click Finish. The Package and Deployment Wizard will display a dialog box telling you that it's creating the CAB file required for your installation package. You'll see a Packaging Report dialog box like this one when the Package and Deployment Wizard completes its work:

16. Click Close to close the Packaging Report dialog box.

Deploying

This section continues where the previous one left off. Deploying your application means that you're ready for a user to install it on their machine and you want to get it to a central distribution point. Always package your application before you try to deploy it. Using a package makes it easier and faster to download the application from Web sites. It also means that you'll spend less time trying to figure out which files are lost. The following procedure assumes that you've just completed the packaging procedure in the previous section and still have the Packaging and Deployment Wizard open.

1. Click the Deploy button on the main Package and Deployment Wizard dialog box. You'll see the Choose Package dialog box shown next. Normally, you'll choose the (Most Recent) option shown because you'll want to deploy your package as soon as you finish creating it. However, you can also choose from one of the existing packages in the Package to Deploy list box.

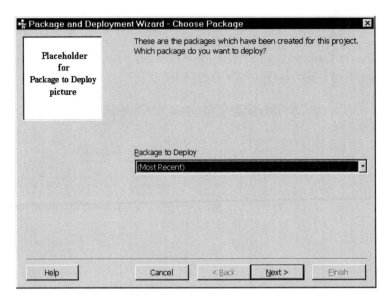

2. Click Next. You'll see the Deployment Type dialog box shown here. This dialog box allows you to choose between Internet (intranet) or network deployment. For the purposes of this example, choose the Folder option in the Deployment type list.

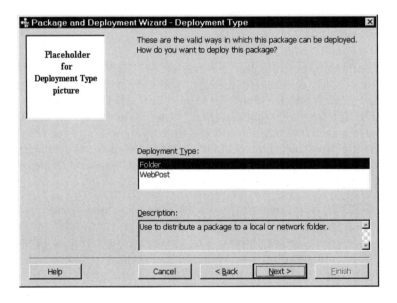

3. Click Next. You'll see a Folder dialog box. This is where you'll decide where to deploy your application. Normally, you'll choose a common network drive that everyone who needs to use the application can access.

4. Choose a directory to use for application deployment. Click Next. You'll see the Finished dialog box shown here:

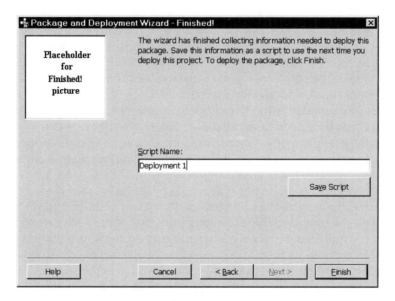

5. Type a name for the deployment script in the Script Name field. For this example, I used ClockIt Network Install for the script name. Click Save Script.

6. Click Finish. You'll see a Deployment Report dialog box that tells which files were copied to the deployment directory.

7. Click Close to close the Deployment Report dialog box.

8. Click Close to close the Package and Deployment Wizard.

At this point, your application is ready for the user to install from a network directory. The process for deploying to the Internet is similar; however, it relies on your ability to post files to the Web server, so make sure you have sufficient rights on the server to do so.

Lessons Learned

By this time, you should have a better idea of what to expect when it comes to working with multilanguage applications. One of the best things you can learn from this example is to expect the unexpected. There are going to be problems getting one language to interface with another and in ways that you can't expect from the outset of the project. It's important to keep your options open as well. We could have built this control using Visual Basic, but it may have taken a bit more effort to do so, and we couldn't be sure the Visual Basic control would work any better than the one created with Visual C++. Since this isn't a time-critical control, the slower speed of the Visual Basic version of the control wouldn't have been a major obstacle.

Publishing common parts of your application programming environment is also an important consideration in team projects. Using Visual Component Manager makes this task relatively easy. However, getting the programmers in your company to actually publish their controls may be another story. It's important that every team member understand that they are working together and that publishing their control is part of the design and development process.

One of the things you may not have noticed is that most of the Visual Basic part of the project could have been developed even before the control became available. For example, the prototyping phase didn't require any input from the ClockIt control at all. Since the control is invisible at run time, you can place it anywhere you like on the form.

Theoretically, you could also begin the coding process without having the ClockIt control available, though development becomes problematic at this point. You really need to have the controls available for testing purposes as the team develops the code. Here's where the publishing process comes into play again. Notice that Visual Component Manager doesn't really care how many copies of the control we upload to the database. You could maintain a complete collection of the beta controls for testing purposes. This would allow you to check for things like control functionality changes. Since the act of installing the control on your machine also registers it, checking variations between beta releases of the control becomes fairly easy.

The final part of the application development process for most people is designing some kind of distribution package. If you plan to distribute the application over the Internet, you may want to use a CAB file. On the other hand, local installation usually requires the use of self-executing EXE files. Whatever method of distribution you decide on, you have to make sure that the package you create is both friendly and easy to use. The package you design to hold your application will affect the user's view of the program as a whole; we all know how important first impressions are.

Chapter 9

A Data Entry Example

Database management applications are one of the most common types of applications you'll find in business today. The reason is simple: Managing data, everything from product inventory to all of the accounting records, is central to making any business run properly. A database management system (DBMS) allows a business to manage data with minimal fuss and a maximum of reliability.

There are a lot of different DBMSs on the market today, all of which have one thing in common—they help you store data. The exact technique used to store the data differs from DBMS to DBMS. In addition, the various DBMSs provide different feature sets and are compatible with one or more database standards currently endorsed by standards groups. We could spend literally chapters discussing the merits of each DBMS, but I'd rather show you how to use Visual Studio to write a database application. Since this book focuses mainly on enterprise-level programming, I've decided to use SQL Server 6.5 for all programming examples. Not only does this DBMS provide industrial-strength database storage features, but a developer version also comes with Visual Studio Enterprise Edition.

Note *Don't get the idea that I'm endorsing SQL Server for all of your database storage needs, nor am I saying that SQL Server is the best product out there. You'll need to spend some time comparing the feature sets provided by the DBMSs available today to see which one meets your needs best. In fact, there's no one best-fit product out there, despite what the vendors would have you believe. DBMSs are a highly customizable and complex application. It's important that you look through the list of DBMSs supported by Visual Studio (the list is impressive to say the least), then find a DBMS that will allow you to perform the kinds of tasks that you need to perform. Cost is certainly a factor in your decision, as are factors like types of data that the DBMS can store. (You'll definitely want BLOB support if you need to store graphics.) Don't forget to take factors like scalability and reliability into account. You'll also want to make sure your DBMS can access all your data, especially if you have data stored on an older system like a mainframe or minicomputer.*

The chapter begins by telling you the scenario for our example application. We'll go over the particulars of this particular application. Once you have an idea of what the application will do, we'll build a database and create a connection to it. Now that we have some method for accessing our data, we'll create a Visual Basic application to view and modify it. This means using the Data View window to see what the database has to offer. Creating a form to view and modify the data comes next, then adding a report so that we can print the database contents.

Creating an application to work with our data isn't the end of the process. We also need to provide help. In this case, we'll look at how you can provide HTML-based help from a central server. Using centralized HTML-based help means that you can update the help files easily and even provide service for users on the road. The final stage of our application development process will be to package our application. In this case, we'll use the InstallShield product that comes with Visual C++, rather than the Visual Basic alternative that we looked at in the previous chapter. One of the benefits of using InstallShield is that you gain flexibility over the distribution media and installation parameters.

Scenario

Have you ever had to deal with a company that lacks a centralized database of customer and employee names and addresses? It can be a very frustrating process. The first thing that happens is that you need to tell everyone individually about how you anticipate working with the company and then provide them with your name, address, and telephone number. Of course, the next thing that happens is that your company decides to move to a new location. Now you need to call each one of those people at the company individually to tell them about the change in address and telephone number. What can happen is that you get mail sent to the wrong address and missed calls.

Your boss decides that he or she has had enough problems with wrong addresses and that the company will use a centralized database of names and addresses. That's what this example is all about—building a database that allows you to store all of that name and address information in a central location. Never again will you send a package to the wrong place or lose contact with someone because you don't have the right telephone number. In addition, you'll probably hope that they install a centralized name and address management system as well.

Obviously, this is a very common example of one type of database that every company can use, and that's one of the reasons I chose it. Any other form of database example (except accounting, which can get to be quite complex) is probably too specialized to meet everyone's needs. During the course of this example, we'll set up a name and address database, then create a Visual Basic application to access it.

The goal of this exercise is to show how programmers and database administrators can work together to create an application. In this case, the programmers and database administrators would likely work together during the design phase. The programmers would need to wait, then, until the database administrators at least had a simple database design in place. Once that was finished, the two groups could work simultaneously to accomplish their particular tasks. In addition to these two application-specific groups, you'd also need writers to create the help file text. They could work in tandem with the programmers to ensure that the help files actually match the final product. Obviously, all three groups would need to work together during the debugging process to ensure that everything works as anticipated.

One potential group that I didn't mention here is the group of Webmasters. We'll look at a database example that relies on the Internet in Chapter 12. However, there isn't anything stopping your company from creating a single database for both Internet and network access of a particular database, especially a name and address database. In fact, the HTML-based help we'll discuss in this chapter works right into that picture. There's another place where the Webmaster comes into play, though. While your writing staff can create the text that goes into those help files, they probably aren't versed in writing HTML code. You'll need the services of a Webmaster (or programmer versed in working with HTML tags) to take the help file text created by the writers and transform it into something that a browser can understand.

Setting Up the Database

Every good database application starts with a database. That might seem like a very obvious statement to make, but some application writers never seem to get the point. They'll start with the user interface or other concerns without taking the capability of the database into account first. Trying to create a database application without a database is a real exercise in frustration. The following procedure assumes that you have the Enterprise Edition of Visual Studio, with SQL Server Developer Edition installed. I'll also assume that you've set up any security required to access both the database server and the SQL Server installation.

> **Note** *Your screen may or may not match the screen shots shown in this section of the chapter. I used a Windows NT Server and the version of SQL Server 6.5 that comes with the Visual Studio package for this example. If you're using a different version of Windows or a different configuration of SQL Server, your screen will most likely look different than mine. In addition, this chapter assumes that you've created a clean test installation of SQL Server on your server. Finally, the test application will always access the database over a network, which is what you'll need to do to check central file access.*

1. Open SQL Enterprise Manager. You'll see a Microsoft SQL Enterprise Manager window like the one shown in Figure 9-1. This is where you'll perform all management functions with SQL Server, including designing databases for use by clients. Notice that the figure shows both the Database Devices and the Database folders open. We'll use these two folders as the example progresses. The first thing we need to do is create a database device.

2. Right-click the Database Devices folder, then choose New Device... from the context menu. You'll see the New Database Device dialog box shown next. A database device is the physical file used to hold the database. The database has everything needed to store your data, including both tables and procedures. We'll look at the contents of our test database later in the procedure.

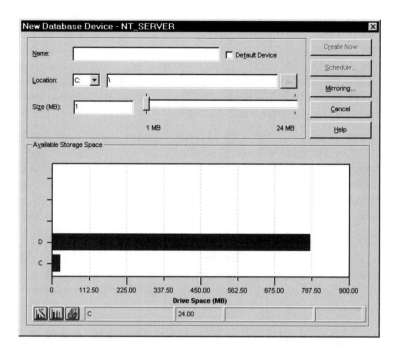

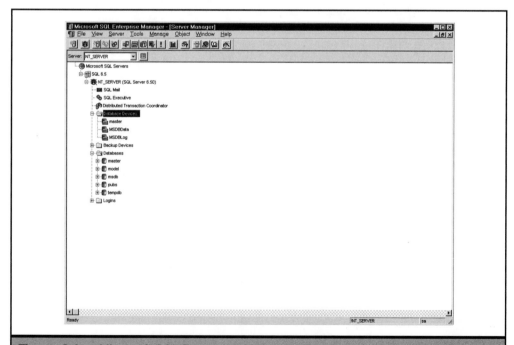

Figure 9-1. Microsoft SQL Enterprise Manager allows you to design and manage databases on your database server

3. Type a database device name in the Name field. I used Sample for the purposes of this example.

4. Type the initial size of the database file in the Size (MB) field. I used 5 for this example since our test data won't be very large. Obviously, a production database will be much larger, and you'll need to provide additional space for growth while keeping the available space on your server in mind.

5. Click Create Now. SQL Server will create the database device that you requested. It'll display a success message once the database device is available for use. (If you don't see a success message, you'll need to stop the procedure now and check your SQL Server installation. Also, make sure that you actually have the space required to hold your database on the server.)

6. Click OK. You should see a new database device named Sample appear in the Database Device folder. Now it's time to add the database itself.

7. Right-click the Databases folder, then select the New Database... option on the context menu. You'll see the New Database dialog box shown here. Notice that it contains a list of all the database devices that SQL Server currently has installed.

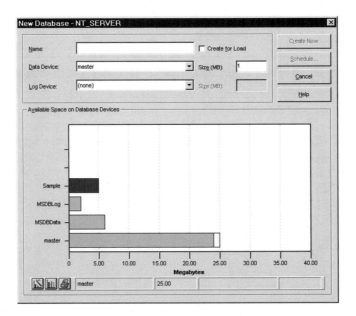

8. Type the name of your database in the Name field. I used Address for the sample application.

9. Choose the Sample database device in the Database Device field.

10. Click Create Now. You'll see the Address database added to the Databases folder.

At this point, we're ready to start designing the database. There are actually three steps in the design process (at least for this simple example). First, we need to create the fields that the user will need to store name and address data. Second, we'll need to assign permissions to access the database. Without these permissions, no one will be able to access the database and enter data into it (except the system administrator, of course). Finally, we'll provide some indexes to order the data for display. Let's begin by adding fields to our database.

The system administrator account (sa) can access every part of SQL Server, including any new databases you create.

The process for adding fields to a table is easy. Open the Address database hierarchy and you'll see two folders, one of which is Objects. Right-click on the Objects folder and choose New Table… from the context menu. You'll see a Manage Tables dialog box like the one shown here:

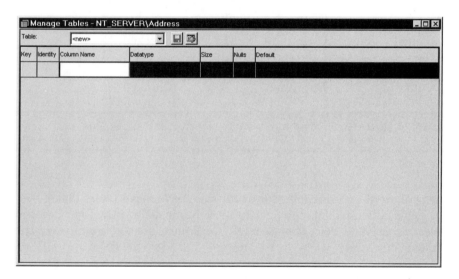

The Manage Tables dialog box is where you'll type in the field names, decide on their data type and size, and assign them a default value (if required). The Nulls column determines if the field requires a value. A checked field allows null entries (no value). Table 9-1 shows the fields that we'll use for this example. All you need to do is type these values into your Manage Tables dialog box to create the table. A blank value in the Default column means that you don't need to type anything in the Default column of the Manage Tables dialog box.

Column Name	Datatype	Size	Nulls	Default
LastName	Char	40	Not checked	
FirstName	Char	40	Not checked	
MiddleInitial	Char	1	Checked	
Title	Char	40	Checked	"Owner"
Company	Char	40	Checked	
Address1	Char	50	Not checked	
Address2	Char	50	Checked	
City	Char	50	Not checked	
State	Char	2	Not checked	"WI"
ZIP	Char	10	Not checked	
Telephone1	Char	13	Checked	
Telephone2	Char	13	Checked	
LastContact	DateTime	N/A	Checked	

Table 9-1. Field Values Used for the Sample Database Application

When you finish entering the information into the Manage Tables dialog box, click the Save Table button. You'll see a Specify Table Name dialog box. Type **Contacts** in the New Table Name field, then click OK. Click the Close box to close the Manage Tables dialog box.

Tip
If you want more control over the initial appearance of your table, click the Additional Features button in the Manage Tables dialog box. You'll be able to set up the primary key, one or more foreign keys, any unique constraints, and a set of rules for checking those unique constraints. There are other ways that you can set things like the primary and foreign keys, but the Additional Features button allows you to set everything from one place.

There are two tasks left to perform before we can start creating a connection to our database. The first task is to set the security for our database. Right-click the Contacts table entry, then choose Permissions… from the context menu. You'll see an Object Permissions dialog box like the one shown here:

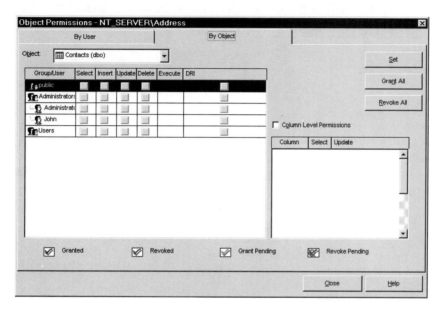

The Object Permissions dialog box allows you to determine who gets what level of access to a particular table. It's important to give each user only the level of access they actually require to prevent damage to your database and its contents. Notice that I've set up three groups for my example table: Public, Administrators, and Users. The public at large only needs to view the contents of the database. We really don't want them to change anything, so they only get the Select permission, which allows them to view the records. Users need to be able to view and modify the records. They also need to add new records and delete old ones, so users as a group get the Select, Insert, Update, and Delete permissions. Finally, the Administrator group requires full access to the table, so they get all of the available permissions. You'll need to be careful handing out this privilege since anyone in the Administrator group will have full access to everything the table has to offer. When you finish setting security for the Contacts table, click Set to make the changes permanent, then Close to close the Object Permissions dialog box.

Our final task is to set up the required indexes for our table. An index allows the user to see the table in sorted order. All you need to do is right-click the Contacts table entry, then choose Indexes... to open the Manage Indexes dialog box shown here:

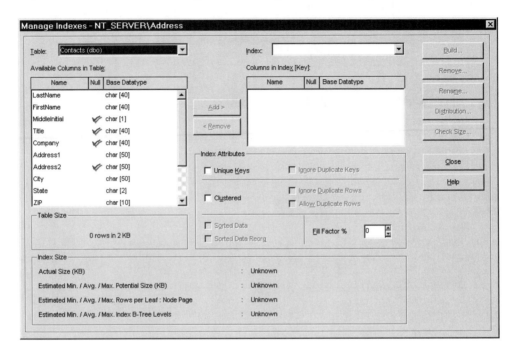

We'll create two indexes for our Contacts table—the number that you actually need to set in a given circumstance depends on how many ways you need to see the data ordered. Type **LastName** in the Index field. Highlight the LastName entry in the Available Columns in Table list, then click Add. Do the same thing for the FirstName entry. Click the Build button. You'll see an Index Build dialog box that asks if you want to build the index now or wait until later. Click Execute Now. SQL Server will pause for a few moments, then take you back to the Manage Indexes dialog box. You've just created the first index.

The second index is built using the same technique. Type **ZIPCode** in the Index field. Choose the ZIP, LastName, and FirstName fields (in that order) from the Available Columns in Table list. Click Build, then Execute Now to create the index. The second index is ready to go. Click Close to close the Manage Indexes dialog box. At this point, we're ready to create a connection to the database.

Creating the Database Connection

There are a number of ways to create connections to a database. We'll actually use two different methods in this chapter, though normally you'll choose only one. This section looks at what you need to do to create an *ODBC* (or *open database connectivity*) connection. You'll normally use ODBC for a network connection to Microsoft products like Access and SQL Server. There are a number of other products that support ODBC as well, but you always need to check with the vendor first. ODBC is also an established technology, which makes it more likely that you'll find a needed driver for an older DBMS. The following procedure will help you create an ODBC connection for the example database.

> **Tip** *Microsoft hopes to make OLE-DB (which stands for "object linking and embedding for databases") the connection method of the future. OLE-DB has several advantages over ODBC, one of which is remote access over the Internet. We'll spend more time talking about OLE-DB as the book progresses, but it's important to note that OLE-DB does provide superior capability in almost every category when compared to ODBC. Obviously, the one place where OLE-DB lags right now is in vendor support, where ODBC has better driver support because it's been available longer. You can get around this hurdle as well since there is a special OLE-DB provider for using ODBC drivers—at least those from companies that fully conform to Microsoft's specification.*

1. Open the ODBC applet in the Control Panel (Windows 95 may have a 32-bit ODBC applet). You'll see the ODBC Data Source Administrator dialog box shown here:

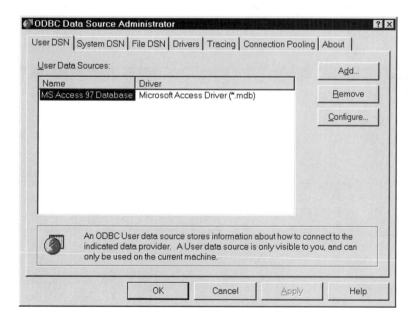

2. Click Add. You'll see the Create New Data Source dialog box shown here. This dialog box lists all of the ODBC drivers installed on your machine. Since we're using a SQL Server database, we'll need to choose the SQL Server driver.

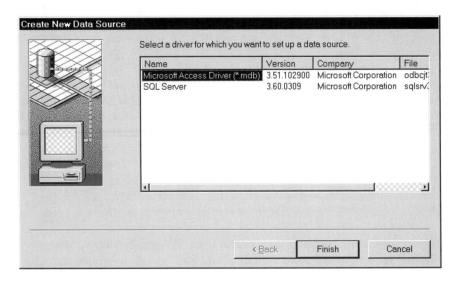

3. Highlight the SQL Server driver entry, then click Finish. You'll see the Create a New Data Source to SQL Server dialog box shown here. This is where we'll begin creating the connection.

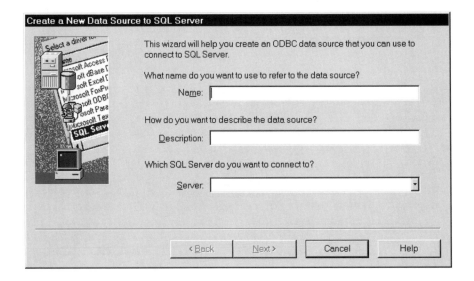

4. Type the name you want to use to refer to the connection in your programs in the Name field. The example program using AddressConnect.

5. Type a description of the connection in the Description field. The example program uses "A sample address database" as a description.

6. Type the name of the server where the database is located. This has to be the actual network name for the computer holding the data. (The actual name for a computer will appear in places like Network Neighborhood.) You can't use something like http://www.mysite.com or an IP address.

7. Click Next. You'll see a dialog box asking what method of authentication to use when accessing SQL Server. In most cases, you'll want to use the default settings.

8. Click Next. You'll see the dialog box shown here. Notice the Change the default database to field. This field must contain the name of the database you intend to use with your Visual Basic application.

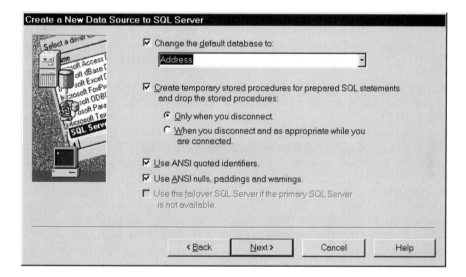

9. Check the Change the default database to option, then select the Address database from the list.

10. Click Next. You'll see some translation options. Normally, these options will only get used when you need to support more than one language.

11. Click Next. You'll see a dialog box asking how to log transactions on your machine. In most cases, you don't need to log the transactions (and wouldn't want to because the logs can quickly use up a large portion of your hard drive). The one time these options come in handy is when you need to troubleshoot the database connection.

12. Click Finish. You'll see the ODBC Microsoft SQL Server Setup dialog box shown here. Notice the Test Data Source button. Always click this button to ensure you have a good connection to the server.

13. Click the Test Data Source button. You should see a dialog box like the one shown here.

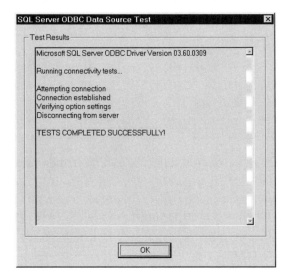

14. Click OK twice to close the two setup dialog boxes. Click OK again to close the ODBC Data Source Administrator dialog box. You've just created an ODBC data source for our sample database.

Using the Data View Window

Visual Basic provides a Data View window that allows you to see and test your database connection before you spend a lot of time writing code. The Data View window makes it possible for you to find potential problems with the connection long before you start debugging the application. What this means to you as a developer is that you have one less major cause of failure to worry about when honing your application's capabilities.

Before we can use the Data View window, we'll have to create a new Visual Basic project. The following procedure will help you create an example shell. Once we have the shell in place, you'll learn how the Data View window can make working with databases a lot easier.

1. Open Visual Basic. You'll see the New Project dialog box.

2. Highlight the Data Project icon, then click Open. Visual Basic will create a new database project for you.

Note that we haven't set up anything for the database yet. That's where the Data View window comes into play. Click the Data View Window icon on the toolbar (or use the View | Data View Window command). You'll see the Data View window shown here:

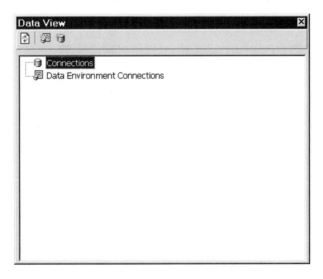

There are two icons in the Data View window at the moment. The first is the Connections icon. You'll use this icon to create a connection to the SQL database. Right below it is a Data Environment Connections icon. This icon represents our connection between the application and the database. Let's begin by creating the SQL connection using the Connections icon.

1. Right-click on the Connections icon, then choose Add Connection... from the context menu. You'll see the Create New Data Link dialog box shown here:

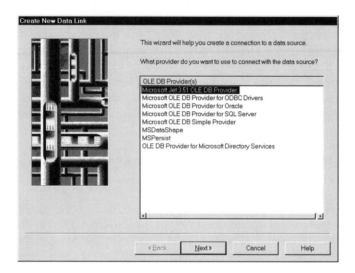

2. Highlight the Microsoft OLE-DB Provider for SQL Server option, then click Next. You'll see the dialog box shown here:

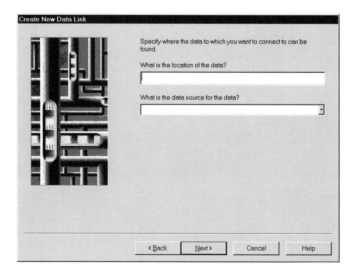

3. Type the location of the data. This entry normally contains the server name. (The example uses a local network, so I used the name of my server in this case.) You can also enter a uniform resource locator (URL). We'll cover how to do that in Chapter 12.

4. Type the name of the data source. In this case, we're using the Address database. Make sure you type the database name, not the name of the table within the database that you want to use. We'll set up the detailed information later.

5. Click Next. You'll see a Password dialog box. Make sure you enter the name and password you need to access the server (if you've used server security) or SQL Server (if you've used database-level security).

6. Type your name and password in the appropriate field.

7. Click Next. You'll see a Test Connection dialog box. It's extremely important that you test the connection before you complete this wizard. Otherwise, you'll need to start creating the connection from scratch.

8. Click Test Connection. If your connection is successful, you'll see a dialog box like the one shown here. Make sure your connection works before your proceed with the example.

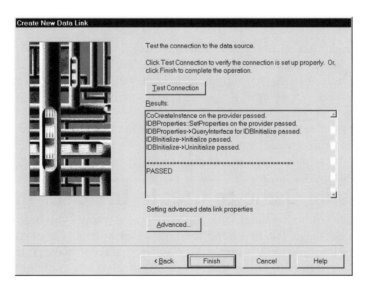

9. Click Finish. You'll see a new connection added to the Data View window. Note that the connection name is set so that you can type one in.

10. Type a connection name. The example program uses AddressConnect.

The connection to the database should be all ready to go. There's one more test you can perform to be absolutely certain that you've connected to the right database and table. Open the database connection, then look at the table. You should see something like this:

You can right-click on any of the objects, including fields, in the Data View window and select properties from the context menu. The resulting dialog box will tell you the particulars about an object. This information comes in handy when you want to learn how to interact with the database and the objects that it contains.

At this point, we're ready to start creating a user interface for our application. Close the Data View window by clicking the Close box.

Using Visual Basic to Create the User Interface

This section helps you understand the various display elements you need when working with a database. The first thing we'll do is look at what you need to create a very simple grid interface to the sample database. Visual Basic makes it simple to create such an interface without too much code. (There isn't any code for the grid interface except what you need to resize the various display elements.)

Grid interfaces are fine when you want to work with a lot of records at once or if you need to get an overview of the content of your database. A Single-Record view allows you to see an entire record at once (or at least as much of the record as will fit on the display). We'll also create a simple single-view record so that you can see what's required when working with individual display elements.

In addition to a grid or single-record interface for adding, deleting, and modifying database records, you need some method to print the records. This section of the chapter will also look at what you need to create a simple report.

Creating a Grid Interface

Let's begin with the easiest part of the application, the grid interface. The Application Wizard automatically created a form for you to use, so open the frmDataEnv form. You'll only need two controls: a DataGrid and an Adodc. Double-click on both controls in the toolbox to place them on the form. Place the DataGrid near the top of the form and the Adodc near the bottom. The exact placement of the controls isn't important right this second because we'll make some changes to the control properties to make things line up. (We'll also add some code to take care of resizing the DataGrid control.) Table 9-2 contains a list of the changes you'll need to make to the two controls. (A blank entry in the Value column means to make that property blank, arrow-bracketed values mean that you need to replace that value with something appropriate to your server setup.)

We need to set one more property for the Adodc1 control, the ConnectionString property. Click on the ellipses next to this property and you'll see the Property Pages dialog box. The following procedure tells you how to create a connection string for the Adodc1 control. (This procedure should look familiar since it's very similar to the one for creating a connection using the Data View window.)

Control	Property	Value
Adodc1	Align	2 - vbAlignBottom
	Caption	
	Password	\<Your Password\>
	RecordSource	Select * From Contacts
	UserName	\<Your Name\>
DataGrid1	Align	1 - vbAlignTop
	AllowAddNew	True
	AllowDelete	True
	DataSource	Adodc1

Table 9-2.   Data Grid Form Control Properties

1. Select the Connection String option, then click Build. You'll see the Create New Data Link dialog box shown here:

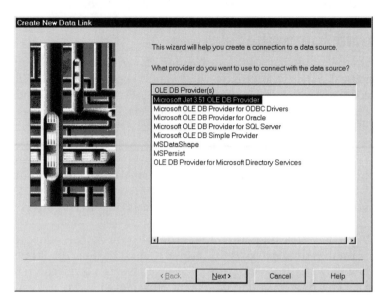

2. Highlight the Microsoft OLE-DB Provider for SQL Server entry since that's the kind of database we're using.

3. Click Next. You'll see a dialog box requesting the location of the data and the data source.

4. Type the name of your server in the first field, and the name of your data source in the second (Address for the purposes of this example).

5. Click Next. You'll see a Password dialog box.

6. Enter your name and password, if necessary.

7. Click Next. You'll see a Test Connection dialog box.

8. Click Test Connection. If your connection passes, then click Finish to complete the process. Otherwise, find where the connection has failed.

9. Click OK to close the Property Pages dialog box.

At this point, you should have a long string of information in the Connection String property. Make sure you don't disturb this property during the rest of the design process. In fact, you may want to save your application at this point. The example application uses a name of SmplData for the folder used to hold the project files. (To keep things simple, I haven't actually changed the name of any of the project files.)

Now we have to perform one more setup step for the DataGrid control. We have to populate the grid with the names of our data fields. Right-click the DataGrid control, then choose Retrieve fields from the context menu. You'll see a dialog box asking if you want to replace the current field definitions with the ones from the Contacts table. Click Yes. Your form should now look similar to the one shown here.

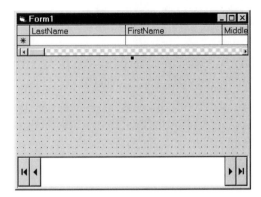

The form is fully functional right now. You could start the application and use it to enter data into the database. However, there's one fit and finish item we need to take care of with a little code. DataGrid1 will automatically resize itself to the width of the form, but it won't change in height. The code in Listing 9-1 makes sure that DataGrid1 resizes as needed.

Listing 9-1

```
Private Sub Form_Resize()
    'Make DataGrid1 height follow the form height.
    DataGrid1.Height = frmDataEnv.ScaleHeight - Adodc1.Height
End Sub
```

Creating a Single-Record Interface

This section shows how to create a single-record interface form. You'll use this kind of form to view one record at a time. The advantage of this kind of form over the data grid is that you can see everything the record contains without scrolling. To create the single-record interface, we'll need another form. The following procedure will help you create a new data form.

1. Right-click the Forms folder in the Project window. Choose the Add | Form option on the context menu. You'll see the Add Form dialog box shown next:

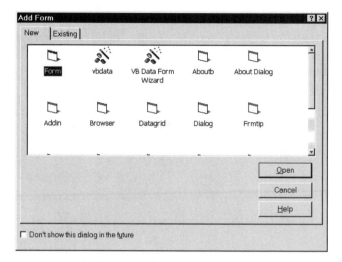

2. Highlight the VB Data Form Wizard icon, then click Open. You'll see the Data Form Wizard - Introduction dialog box shown here. Note that the Profile field allows you to use a previously created profile. We talked about this feature in Chapter 4, so I won't discuss it at length now.

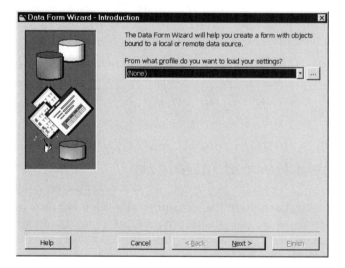

3. Click Next. You'll see a Data Form Wizard - Database Format dialog box. This is where you'll choose the source of the data that you want to use for your form.

4. Choose the Remote (ODBC) option. This form will use the ODBC connection that we created earlier in the chapter. Remember that ODBC is only good for a network setup—you can't use it on the Internet.

5. Click Next. You'll see the Data Form Wizard - Connect Information dialog box shown here. This is where you tell the form how to connect to your database.

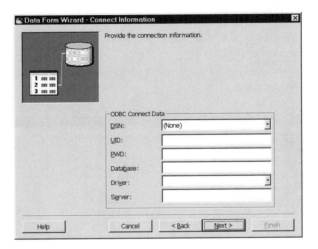

6. Choose AddressConnect in the DSN (data source name) field. This is the connection that we defined earlier in the ODBC applet of the Control Panel.

7. Type your user name in the UID field.

8. Type your password in the PWD (password) field.

9. Type Address, the name of our database, in the Database field.

10. Click Next. You'll see the Data Form Wizard - Form dialog box shown here. This is where you define how the form will look.

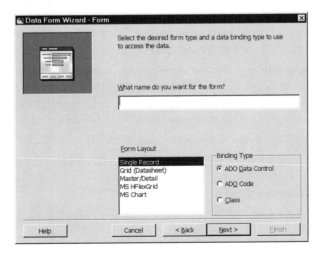

11. Type **frmSingleRecordView** in the What name do you want for the form field.

12. Choose Single Record for the Form Layout and ADO Data Control for the Binding Type. We used the ADO Data Control (Adodc) in the previous section of the chapter as well. Using this control makes it easy to move from record to record without adding a lot of code.

13. Click Next. You'll see the Data Form Wizard - Record Source dialog box shown here. The purpose of this dialog box is to allow you to choose a specific record source, then add specific fields to your form (just in case you don't want all of the fields from a table).

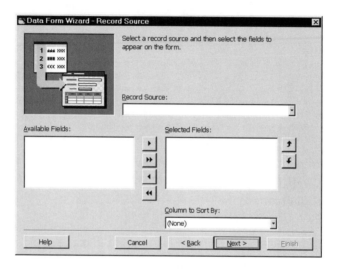

14. Select Contacts in the Record Source field. The Data Form Wizard will fill the Available Fields list with the fields from the Contacts table as soon as you do this. If you don't see this happen, there's a problem with your connection. Make sure you stop defining the form now and check the connection to your server. You'll need to start the form over again after solving your connection problem.

15. Click the right-pointing double arrow to add all the fields in the Available Fields list to the Selected Fields list. Use the up and down arrows to change the order of the First name and Last name fields so they appear as FirstName, MiddleInitial, and LastName in the Selected Fields list.

16. Choose LastName in the Column to Sort By field.

17. Click Next. You'll see the Data Form Wizard - Control Selection dialog box. This is where you define which controls to add to the form. We'll use the default setting of all controls.

18. Click Next. You'll see the Data Form Wizard - Finished dialog box. Note that you can choose to save these settings in a profile.

19. Click Finish to complete the form creation process. You'll see a Data Form Created dialog box.

20. Click OK. You'll see the single-record dialog box shown here:

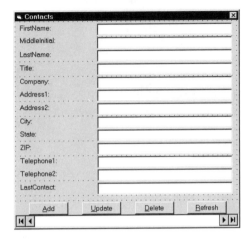

Now we have a single-record view to look at in addition to our Grid view. Unfortunately, if you start the application at this point, you won't be able to see what you've done. One way to get around this problem is to add a menu to our original form. All we need is a single menu entry for selecting the single-record view. Begin by opening the frmDataEnv form that we worked with in the previous section. Right-click the form, then choose Menu Editor from the context menu. Fill out the Menu Editor dialog box as shown here:

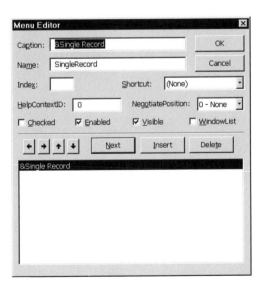

Click OK to close the Menu Editor dialog box. Now, click on the new menu entry on the frmDataEnv form. You'll need to add the code shown in Listing 9-2.

Listing 9-2

```
Private Sub Form_Unload(Cancel As Integer)
    'End the application
    End
End Sub

Private Sub SingleRecord_Click()
    'Update the single-record view.
    frmSingleRecordView.datPrimaryRS.Refresh

    'Show the single-record view.
    frmSingleRecordView.Show

    'Hide the grid view.
    frmDataEnv.Hide
End Sub
```

Since our Grid View dialog box gets hidden when we display the single-record view, it's important to have a menu entry on the frmSingleRecordView form as well. Use the same method that we used for the previous menu to add one for frmSingleRecordView. Use "&Grid View" for the Caption field, and "GridView" for the Name field. Listing 9-3 shows the code you'll need to add to the procedure for the Grid View menu entry.

Listing 9-3

```
Private Sub Form_Unload(Cancel As Integer)
    'Added by Wizard
    Screen.MousePointer = vbDefault

    'End the application
    End
End Sub

Private Sub GridView_Click()
    'Update the grid view.
    frmDataEnv.Adodc1.Refresh

    'Show the grid view.
    frmDataEnv.Show

    'Hide the single record view.
    frmSingleRecordView.Hide
End Sub
```

The code for both forms is essentially the same. The Form_Unload( ) function contains a single new command, End. This tells Visual Basic to end the application. Since you might have both forms open (hiding the form does not close it), you need this command to ensure the application shuts down. Notice that I haven't included any error trapping, something you would normally add to any database application. In this case, you'd probably want to verify that any updates the user had requested actually got made before you end the application.

The Click( ) function (for either GridView or SingleRecord) contains three commands. The first thing we do is refresh the Adodc control (or datPrimaryRS, as the wizard named it). The refresh process tells the control to get the current record information from the database. This is important because the user may have added, modified, or deleted a record during the time that the current view was open. If you don't refresh the Adodc control, then the view you switch to will show the old information. Remember that you need to refresh the Adodc control, not the form that it's on. The second step is to show the form that we're going to so that the user can see it. Finally, we hide the current form.

Note   *Hiding a form is not the same as closing it. A hidden form is still active, you just can't see it.*

Working with Reports

Reports are an extremely personal thing, contrary to common belief. If you look at the forms produced by any two companies, you'll see two completely different sets of forms. In fact, look at the forms produced by two different people in a single company and you're still apt to see a lot of very big differences in style. Even strict guidelines are often circumvented in order to get some preferred form feature in place. With this in mind, I won't insult your sense of style by attempting to tell you how to lay out a report in this section of the chapter. We will, however, look at what you need to create a form. That way, you can get just the layout of data you want from your database when creating your database application.

Our database report will make use of DataEnvironment1. We discussed the data environment earlier as part of the Data View window. Currently, DataEnvironment1 has a connection to a database, but nothing else. We need to add a command to it in order to access the data that the database contains.

Let's begin by opening DataEnvironment1. What you'll see are two folders: one contains connections, the other commands. Right-click the Commands folder, then choose Add Command from the context menu. You'll see a Command Properties dialog box. Configure your Command Properties dialog box so that it matches the one shown here.

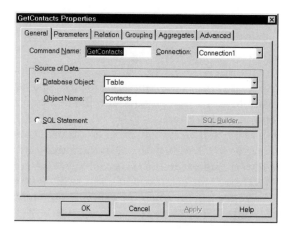

Tip

You can gain additional flexibility by selecting the SQL Statement option in the Command Properties dialog box, then using the SQL Builder to create a command. A SQL statement can retrieve data or perform a variety of other tasks. When used in reports, you could create separate SQL commands to order the data in various ways. On the other hand, using objects is fast and efficient, especially during the initial design stage of a project. Using an object means that you have one less piece of code to worry about as you try to get the application as a whole to work. Always add SQL Statements to your project later in the design process, once you have the main program code debugged.

Click OK to close the Command Properties dialog box. At this point, you should see a GetContacts command added to the Commands folder. Click the plus sign next to the command and you'll see a list of fields that you can drag and drop onto the report we'll create next. Here's what DataEnvironment1 should look like at this point:

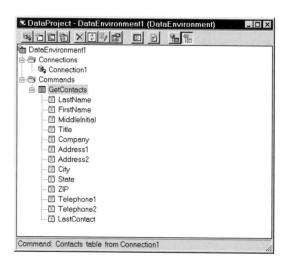

Now that you have a command to execute, you can open DataReport1. Set the DataSource property to DataEnvironment1, then choose GetContacts from the list box in the DataMembers property. These two properties give you access to the fields in the Contacts table of the Address database. Right-click on the Detail section of the report, then choose Retrieve Structure from the context menu. You'll see a dialog box that asks if you want to replace the current report hierarchy. Click Yes. At this point, you're ready to create your report.

There are a number of ways to design a report, but the fastest and easiest method is to drag and drop the fields from the DataEnvironment1 window. In fact, if you drag the GetContacts command from the DataEnvironment1 window to the DataReport1 window, all of the fields from the Contacts table will get added at once. Here's the report format that I designed once I got all of the fields added to DataReport1:

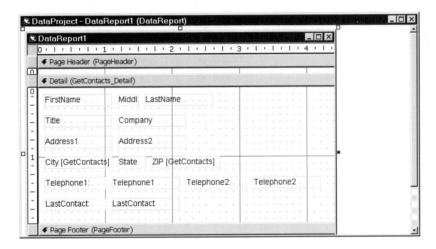

The report is ready to go, but there isn't any way to print it right now. We need to open the frmDataEnv form again. This time we'll add a Print menu option using the same technique we did in the previous section for switching views. Just type **&Print** in the Caption field of the Menu Editor dialog box, and **Print** in the Name field. Listing 9-4 shows the code you'll need to add for this menu command.

sting 9-4

```
Private Sub Print_Click()
    'Print our database.
    DataReport1.Show
End Sub
```

Adding HTML-Based Help Using Visual InterDev

Up to this time in the computer industry, the standard method for adding help to your application was through Windows Help. In many cases, Windows Help is still the best choice for a number of reasons, not the least of which is the higher level of integration you can achieve with it when designing your application. It's difficult to add context-sensitive help to an application when you're using HTML-based help, but with Windows Help it's a snap.

So, if you don't get the same level of integration using the new technology, why bother to use it at all? There are a few benefits in favor of using HTML-based help as well. Have you ever installed a patch to your application, only to discover that the help files didn't keep pace? That's one of the problems that vendors face every day. Support calls increase as a product gets older because the help file on the user's machine gets out of date. Timeliness is the number one reason to use HTML-based help.

Another good reason to use HTML-based help is that you can monitor user help activity, and hone your help files better as a result. Every time someone requests a Help page from your Web site, you can log that event. After a while, you'll get a picture of which pages people use most often and the areas that are most difficult to use in your application.

Windows Help files are also limited in the amount of extra help they can provide. For example, you can place a link to a patch download area on your Web site within HTML-based help. In fact, you can highlight the changing condition of your application on a What's New page. You can't provide these kinds of services with standard Windows Help.

Finally, there's the matter of size over availability. A Windows Help file is always available because it's stored on the user's hard drive. This means that a user can access help no matter where they are, even if there isn't a Web connection available. On the other hand, the Windows Help file does take space on the user's drive, space that might be rather limited when you're talking about a laptop. HTML-based help has the advantage here. It doesn't require any permanent space on the user's machine because it's stored on your server. The user can simply download the parts of the help file required for the current question. The browser automatically frees the space required by the Help page after a certain amount of time.

The first section that follows will show you how to add a browser to your Visual Basic application. You'll use menu commands to set the browser up and get it ready to view a specific page on your Web site. Fortunately, adding this part of help is relatively easy. Visual Basic does most of the work for you automatically.

The second section will show you how to use Visual InterDev to create the required help files. Since we have an automatic connection to our Web server when using this product, you won't even need to publish the help files. This section may not show you every nuance to writing help files, but it will get you started.

The Visual Basic Part of the Picture

Adding HTML-based help to your application means that you have to provide some type of browser to view the Web pages. Fortunately, Visual Basic version 6 makes it easy to add this capability to your application, though you may have to perform some modification to the default browser if you want to restrict user access to the Help pages you provide for your application. All you need to do is add another form, then manipulate that form from one or more menu entries.

Let's begin with the new form. Right-click the Forms folder in the Project window. Choose Add | Form from the context menu. You'll see the same Add Form dialog box that we saw earlier when adding the Single-Record view to our database application. Highlight the Browser icon, then click Open. You'll see a new browser form, as shown here:

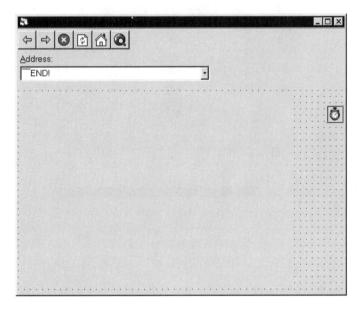

As you can see, this is a full-featured browser that the user could use to access any part of the Internet, not just your Web site or the Help pages associated with the application. If you want to limit the user's ability to access the entire Internet, you'll need to modify this default form by removing things like the Address field. Two of the features you will want to keep in place are the forward and back arrows. These two buttons allow the user to move from one place to another with relative ease and reduce the number of links you need to add to your Help pages. For the purposes of this example, we'll leave the default browser form as is. That way, you can experiment with it later as part of the process of working with your help files.

Adding a browser form isn't enough to make our help display work. We also need an MDI window (*MDI* stands for "multiple document interface") to display the browser form in. To add the MDI form to your application, right-click the Forms folder in the Project window. Select Add | MDI Form from the context menu. You'll see an Add Form dialog box with a MDI Form entry. Highlight the MDI Form entry, then click Open. You really don't need to do much with this form except change the title; its only purpose is to hold the browser form.

Let's add some Help menu entries to the frmDataEnv form. Right-click the form, then choose Menu Editor... from the context menu. We're going to add three menu entries: a main Help menu, and both a Search and a Contents submenu entry. Here's what the Menu Editor dialog box looked like after I added the three menu entries:

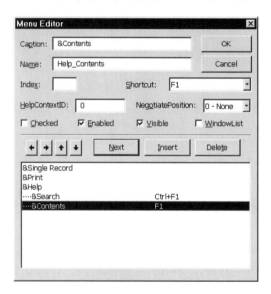

Notice that the Search and Contents submenu entries are indented below the Help menu entry. I've also included speed keys for these two menu entries. Table 9-3 shows the entries you'll want to make in the various Menu Editor dialog box fields.

Menu Entry	Field Name	Value
Help	Caption	&Help
	Name	Help
Search	Caption	&Search
	Name	Help_Search

Table 9-3.   Help Menu Configuration Parameters

Menu Entry	Field Name	Value
	Shortcut	CTRL-F1
Contents	Caption	&Caption
	Name	Help_Contents
	Shortcut	F1

Table 9-3. Help Menu Configuration Parameters (continued)

Now that we have some menu entries to use, let's create some code to access the browser form. Listing 9-5 shows the code you'll need to add for the two menu entries. (The source code does contain server-specific information for my Web server—you'll need to change these server-specific entries to match your server setup.)

sting 9-5

```
Private Sub Help_Contents_Click()
 'Display the help form, then maximize it.
 frmBrowser.Show
 frmBrowser.WindowState = 2

 'Display the URL in the Address field.
 frmBrowser.cboAddress.Clear
 frmBrowser.cboAddress = "http:\\nt_server\Help\Contents.HTM"
 frmBrowser.cboAddress.AddItem "http:\\nt_server\Help\Contents.HTM", 0

 'Go to the required URL
 frmBrowser.brwWebBrowser.Navigate2 ("http:\\nt_server\Help\Contents.HTM")
End Sub

Private Sub Help_Search_Click()
 'Display the help form, then maximize it.
 frmBrowser.Show
 frmBrowser.WindowState = 2
```

```
'Display the URL in the Address field.
frmBrowser.cboAddress.Clear
frmBrowser.cboAddress = "http:\\nt_server\Help\Search.HTM"
frmBrowser.cboAddress.AddItem "http:\\nt_server\Help\Search.HTM", 0

'Go to the required URL
frmBrowser.brwWebBrowser.Navigate2 ("http:\\nt_server\Help\Search.HTM")
End Sub
```

As you can see, the process for displaying the required help Web page is the same in both cases. The first thing we do is display the browser form. You'll want to make sure that it's maximized in the MDI window, so it's important to set the WindowState to 2. Displaying the URL in the Address field of the browser form comes next. You don't need to perform this step if you eliminate the Address field from the browser form. Notice that we need to clear the old address, display the new search address, and then add the address to the list of available addresses in the Address field. That way, the user will be able to select previously displayed search sites. Finally, we navigate to the appropriate Web site using the Navigate2( ) function. Make sure you perform this step last since it's likely that finding the Web site will take at least a few moments. You'll want to have all of the other display elements in place before the navigation takes place so the user has a nice display to look at and the Web browser can display any required error messages.

Creating the Web Pages

The help features of the application are complete, but we don't have anything to display on the Web site. That's where Visual InterDev comes into play. We need to create two Web pages as a minimum: one that provides a list of topics the user can research (Contents), and another that allows the user to perform ad hoc searches of the Help pages (Search).

Let's begin by creating a new project. The following procedure will get you started. (We looked at creating Web projects in Chapter 4, so this section will use an abbreviated procedure designed to get you going quickly.)

1. Open Visual InterDev and you'll see the New Projects dialog box. Make sure the Visual InterDev Projects folder is selected.

2. Highlight the New Web Project icon, then click Open. You'll see the Web Project Wizard - Step 1 of 4 dialog box. The wizard will automatically enter a server name for you if you've created projects before. (See Chapter 4 for instructions on creating a server connection, if needed.)

3. Choose the Master Mode option. We want all changes made to the Web pages to appear automatically on the server. Unlike some projects, where you want to be sure that the page is complete and fully tested before you post it to the Web site, informational Web pages, like those used for help files, can be posted immediately.

4. Click Next. You'll see the Web Project Wizard - Step 2 of 4 dialog box. This is where you'll enter the project parameters.

5. Choose the Create a new Web application option.

6. Type **Help** in the Name field. Make sure you also check the Create search.htm to enable full text searching. (As you can see, Visual InterDev makes it relatively easy to create the search page—all you really need to worry about is creating the Contents page.)

7. Click Next. You'll see the Web Project Wizard - Step 3 of 4 dialog box. This dialog box allows you to apply a layout to your Web pages. In many cases, you'll want to use a custom layout, especially for pages you intend to allow the public to view. However, for our purposes, one of the standard layouts will work just fine.

8. Choose the Bottom 1 layout, then click Next. You'll see the Web Project Wizard - Step 4 of 4 dialog box. This dialog box allows you to apply a theme to your Web page. In some cases, themes are nice because they dress up the page and ensure consistency from one page to the next. However, Help pages normally look and work better plain.

9. Choose <none>, then click Finish. Visual InterDev will create the project for you.

What you have at this point is a project shell and a basic Search page provided by the wizard. In fact, if you try the Search option of the Help menu for our sample application, you'll find that it's functional. Obviously, you'll at least want to look at the Search.HTM file to see if you need to make any modifications to it. At least you have a starting point with this page of your help system.

Now it's time to add a Contents page to our sample help system. Begin the process by right-clicking the <server name>/Help folder in the Project window. (In my case, the <server name> variable gets replaced with nt_server and the setup reflects my particular server setup, so your screen shots may differ slightly from mine.) Choose Add | HTML Page from the context menu. You'll see an Add Item dialog box that contains a list of items that you can add to the current project, including an HTML Page. Highlight the HTML Page icon, type **Contents** in the Name field, then click Open. You'll see a new Contents.HTM window added to the IDE. There are three tabs on this window: Design, Source, and Quick View. As you can see, this new page provides everything we've used to create Web pages in the past. Figure 9-2 shows the simple design I've created for our sample help file.

Figure 9-2. The Contents page will provide an overview of the help available to the user

This page isn't finished by a long shot, but there is enough information there for you to see one way to lay out a help file Contents page. Notice that there is a general informational paragraph at the top. A link to the search page is included as part of this information paragraph. To create a new link, all you need to do is drag the page that you want to reference from the Project window to the Web page that you're designing. The text will contain the URL for the link, which isn't really the best way to tell the user what the link contains. Simply highlight the URL text and type in whatever you want. In this case, it's the word Search. This link offers more than just a simple link. Right-click on the link and choose Properties from the context menu. You'll see a Property Pages dialog box. One of the most important fields in this dialog box is the Popup text field. You can place helpful text in this field that appears as balloon help when the user places the mouse cursor over the link. Here's how I modified the Property Pages dialog box for the Search link in our example:

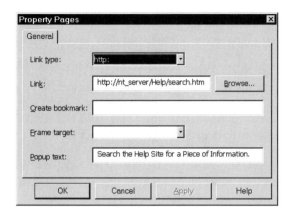

You should strive to make your Contents page approachable and easy to use. This page shows one method that you can use to accomplish this task. Notice that I've used a Table of Contents (as in a book) approach to this particular Web page. At the very top is the title of the whole Web site. Following that are chapter headings, which just happen to be form titles for this example. Below the form titles are major headings. In this case we have three: Controls, Menu Entries, and Data Fields. Finally, we have subject headings for each of the major sections. I've only filled in one for the controls. The Grid Entry View form has only one set of user accessible controls, and they're contained in the Adodc control at the bottom of the form. Each bullet describes one of these controls in brief. If the user needs additional information, they can click the link for that particular control. (To keep the example simple, I've used pseudolinks that point back to the Contents page.)

Our application now has two functional Help menu entries. Obviously, for a production-quality application, you'd add appropriate pages for each of the individual controls and graphics to help the reader see how the project pieces go together.

Packaging Your Application with InstallShield

Visual Studio doesn't require you to use the Visual Basic Package and Deployment Wizard we used in Chapter 8 to get your application ready for distribution. There's also a C++ equivalent called InstallShield. For Visual Basic users, this particular product is going to look extremely complex, perhaps even unwieldy. Fortunately, it's a lot easier to use than it looks once you break the task down into pieces. The advantage of using the Visual Basic Package and Deployment Wizard is simplicity—the Wizard makes most of the decisions for you. On the other hand, InstallShield provides a lot in the way of flexibility. This section is going to show you how you can put that flexibility to use.

There are some additional things you need to do before you can use InstallShield. For example, you should have a complete list of the files needed to run your application. Make sure your file list includes specific installation areas for each file. For example, you'll want to note which files you have to install in the SYSTEM folder. Finally, you should have tested your application and associated files on a clean machine—one that has had only Windows installed. It doesn't pay to start writing an installation program until you're certain you have included all of the files it requires and that the setup works as anticipated on a clean machine.

Note   *This section relies on the version of InstallShield provided with Visual C++ 6.0. Earlier versions of Visual C++ may not have this version of InstallShield, which means you'll probably need to modify the procedures in this section to meet your needs. Even if you are using the same version of InstallShield outlined in the book, you may see slightly different screens or have a few different options, depending on the application you're trying to package. In short, it's not going to be too unusual to see a few variations from what I'm presenting here when you're using InstallShield. You'll need to install the InstallShield product—it's located in the IShield directory on your Visual Studio CD. The procedures in this section assume you've already installed the InstallShield product on your hard drive.*

So far, we've created a simple database application with two views and a print form, then added HTML-based help to it. Now it's time to package this application to send to someone else—well, at least for example purposes. The following procedure is going to show you how to put a typical installation program together. We won't do anything really fancy; the whole idea is to get the application ready to send to someone else. The type of installation we'll cover is one that's very appropriate for the corporate environment. Independent developers or makers of shrink-wrap products would need to modify this procedure somewhat and perform some additional packaging tasks that fall into the fit and finish category.

Note   *We'll cover a generic installation program in this section; you'll need to modify it to meet the needs of your particular application and installation environment.*

1. Start the InstallShield 6 Free Edition program. You'll see a Projects window similar to the one shown in Figure 9-3. Notice that we don't have any project defined yet, but that there is an Installation Wizard entry in the Projects window. This window doesn't look precisely like the one in Visual C++, but as the procedure goes on you'll notice certain similarities that tend to ease the installation program creation process.

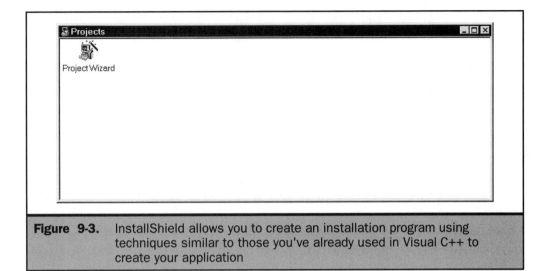

Figure 9-3.   InstallShield allows you to create an installation program using techniques similar to those you've already used in Visual C++ to create your application

2. Double-click on the Project Wizard icon in the Projects window. You'll see a Project Wizard - Welcome dialog box similar to the one shown here:

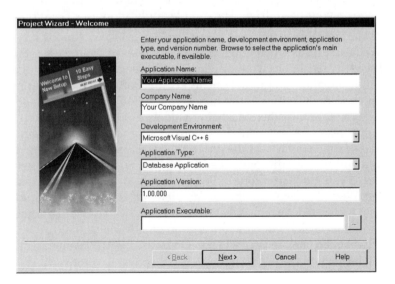

The Professional Edition of InstallShield offers advanced features on the Welcome (and other) page—make sure you read about the enhancements in the help file.

3. Type the name of your application. The example program is "SQL Database Access Example."

4. Type your company name. The example program uses "A Sample Company."

You can't choose anything but Visual C++ 6.0 as the development environment for this example. The Professional Edition of InstallShield includes more development environments, making it easier to use in situations like this one where the application was developed using something other than Visual C++ 6.0. Fortunately, you can still derive a great number of flexibility benefits from using the Free Edition of InstallShield.

5. Choose one of the entries in the Application Type field. The example program uses Database Application.

6. Type the application version number in the Application Version field. Our example program uses 1.0, but you can use any numbering scheme consistent with your company policies.

7. Click the ... button next to the Application Executable field. You'll see a standard Open dialog box that you can use to find the application you want to package on your hard drive. The sample application uses DataProject.EXE.

8. Click Next. You'll see a Project Wizard - Choose Dialogs dialog box like the one shown next. This is when you'll choose the series of dialog boxes that the user will see when installing your application. Since we're using the corporate model for our installation program, I unchecked the Software License Agreement, Setup Type, and Custom Setup dialog boxes. You'd choose some or all of these dialog boxes for the other packaging models. For example, you'd retain the Software License Agreement dialog box as a minimum if you wanted to create a shrink-wrapped version of the program for resale. There are a few things you should notice about this particular dialog box. First, look in the lower-left corner as you move from one dialog box entry to the next. You'll see that the Project Wizard gives you a thumbnail view of the dialog box in question to make it easier to determine whether you actually want it. Highlighting a dialog box and then clicking the Preview button will display a dialog box that looks exactly like the one the user will see. Obviously, you'll be able to modify this dialog box later, but it helps to know what you're starting with.

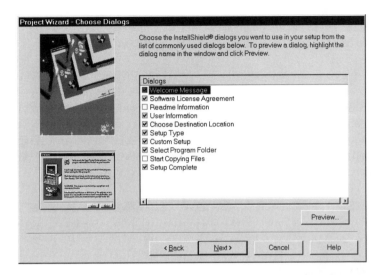

9. Choose which dialog boxes you want to add to the installation program, and then click Next. You'll see a Project Wizard - Choose Target Platforms dialog box like the one shown here. Since we want to be able to install our program on any of the supported programs, we won't have to make any changes. However, there may be situations where you'll want to be a little more selective. Reducing the number of supported platforms accomplishes two things. First, it reduces the size of the installation program you create—a real plus for shareware developers who are short on space to begin with. Second, it reduces the chance that someone will try to use your program under the wrong version of Windows—a real plus for any developer.

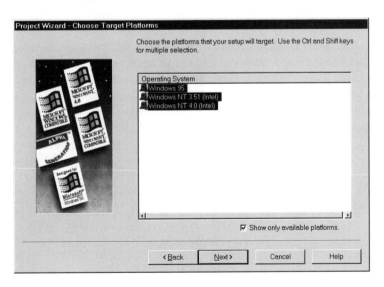

It's educational to uncheck the Show Only Available platforms check box to see all of the choices offered by the Professional Edition of InstallShield.

10. Select one or more platforms as needed (but at least one), and then click Next. You'll see a Project Wizard - Specify Languages dialog box like the one shown here. Since the Free Edition only supports one language, we don't have to make any changes here. Like other selections you've had to make so far, more is not necessarily better. Adding languages will increase the size of the installation program and could add user confusion as well—choose only the languages you need.

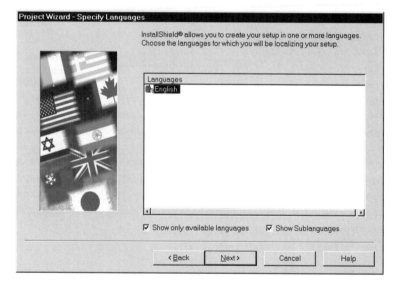

11. Highlight one or more languages (but at least one), and then click Next. You'll see a Project Wizard - Specify Setup Types dialog box like the one shown next. Since we're using the corporate packaging model, I've already chosen the Network setup type. Other packaging models will require you to make other selections, including the most common of all: Custom, Typical, and Compact. It's interesting to note that InstallShield does offer a wealth of other choices, though.

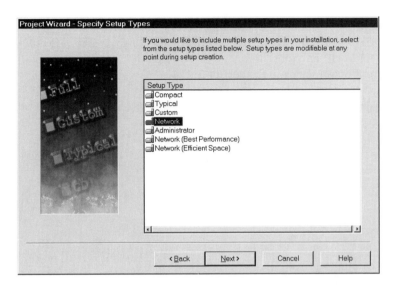

The next step sets up a Help Files component type. You may wonder why an application that uses HTML-based help would require this component since the help files should be available on the central server. This is one of those situations where you may want to include the HTML files on a laptop machine, but not a desktop machine. If the laptop user is away from the company and can't access the central help files through an Internet connection, they can still access the local copy of the HTML-based help files. Obviously, you have to build this capability into the application (we didn't) and provide a multiple installation platform capability. It's important to take all of the needs of the users at your company into account when creating an installation program. Providing local help may not seem like a big deal until a user calls a 1:00 A.M. asking for help.

12. Choose one or more setup types and then click Next. You'll see the Project Wizard - Specify Components dialog box like the one shown next. The Project Wizard doesn't assume anything about the components you want to install. The example program uses Program Files, Shared DLLs, and Help Files. You'll need to choose each of these options one at a time to define the files that go under each component type. A component type is a definition of a major program area. For example, the user may want to include all of the sample files, but none

of the help files. A component type doesn't necessarily define which files you'll
need to perform the task, but simply that the task is a separate entity that the
user could either choose to install or perhaps that needs to be installed in a
different directory from the rest of the files.

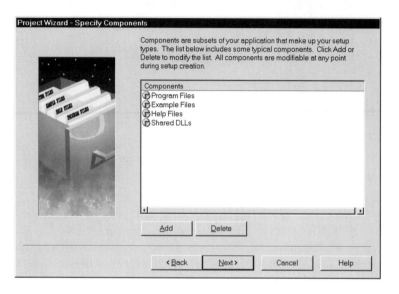

*You can add new component types as needed to your installation program. For example,
you might need to add a Database File component if you've written a database
application. All you have to do is click the Add button, and the Project Wizard will add
the new entry for you. Type the name of the component, and press* ENTER *to complete the
addition process. We'll need a Database File component for this example, even though
the database will already be installed on the central server for everyone to use. The user
requires the ADO drivers required to access the database.*

13. Highlight Example Files and then click Delete. Project Wizard will remove this
    component type from our installation program.

14. Click Add. Type **Database Files** as the component type name. We'll use this
    component type to hold the ADO drivers.

15. Add or delete component types as needed and then click Next. You'll see a
    Project Wizard - Specify File Groups dialog box like the one shown next. Our
    example program uses three standard entries: Program Executable Files, Help
    Files, and Shared DLLs. (We'll need to add another custom file group for
    database files.) Normally, you'll create file groups so that all of the files needed
    for a specific task are copied at one time. File groups can cross component type

boundaries. For example, say the spell checker and the grammar checker both rely on the same set of DLLs but require different rule files. You could define a common file group for the DLLs and two other file groups for the rule files. If the user selected the spell checker but not the grammar checker, InstallShield would copy the spell checker file group and the common DLL file group, but not the grammar checker file group.

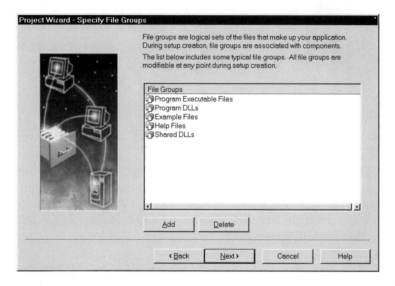

16. Highlight Program DLLs and then click Delete. Highlight Example Files and then click Delete. We've just eliminated the two file groups that we won't need for the example program. Obviously, the selection of file groups will depend on how your application is put together and where you need to copy the files. Remember that all the files in one file group will go to the same directory on the hard drive.

17. Click Add. Type **Database Files** for the file group name. This is the file group where we'll list ADO drivers for our database example. We're using a separate file group because these files have to be stored in a special location. If they were stored in the program or in the Windows System directory, we could have used one of the standard groups. Always make sure you take special storage requirements into account when designing your file groups.

18. Add or delete file groups as needed and then click on Next. You'll see a Project Wizard - Summary dialog box like the one shown next. At this point, you should check the list of options to make sure everything is correct before you ask the Project Wizard to build the installation program for you.

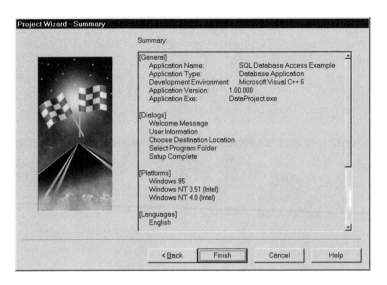

19. Click Finish. InstallShield will create the installation program using the parameters you've just specified. At this point, the InstallShield interface will change as shown in Figure 9-4. Notice that you can now see the C++ code required to create the installation program and that you can modify it just like you would any other project.

Note   *Don't get the idea that InstallShield generates source files that are precisely like the ones used in a general Visual C++ project. There are some ancillary files that you haven't seen in the past, such as the setup rule (SETUP.RUL) file shown in Figure 9-4.*

At this point, you should have a barely usable installation program shell. There's still quite a bit of configuration to do, though, and we'll look at all of it in the sections that follow. The important thing to realize is that you'll write very little code during this process—InstallShield will do most of the work for you as you define the various program elements.

Web Link   *If you've still got questions about how to use InstallShield after reading this section, there are a couple of ways to get more information. This is one of those times when it really pays to look in the product README file, because it contains links to a lot of places you need to know about on the Internet. For example, you'll find a link to the newsgroups site at http://support.installshield.com/newsgroups/default.asp. This site contains links to several InstallShield-specific newsgroups. Just clicking one of the links will create a new folder in your newsreader containing the newsgroup you wanted to look at. There's even a special newsgroup for the Free Edition at installshield.is5.free-edition. You'll also find links for newsgroups covering things like the IDE, scripting, and the use of multimedia. In short, these newsgroups provide you with the contacts you need with other developers interested in finding solutions to packaging their applications successfully.*

Figure 9-4.   Once you've created a project, InstallShield will generate it for you and then display the resulting source code

Setting Up the Components

The first task we'll need to accomplish is setting up the various components. Remember that a component is a selection that appears during the installation. If you've ever used the Custom Install feature of an installation program, then you know what a component is. It's the series of check boxes that allow you to choose whether you want to install a particular program feature like the help files.

Configuring the components for your installation program is fairly easy. Click on the Components tab and you'll see a Components - Program Files dialog box like the one shown next:

Components - Program Files	
Field	Value
Description	
Status Text	
Display Name	
Visible	Yes
Overwrite	ALWAYSOVERWRITE
Destination	<TARGETDIR>
File Need	STANDARD
Include in Build	Yes
Password	
Encryption	No
CD-ROM Folder	
FTP Location	
HTTP Location	
Miscellaneous	
Comment	
Required Components	None Selected
Included File Groups	None Selected

The Components dialog box contains a complete list of all the values for the selected component. Remember that we have three components in this case: Program Files, Help Files, and Shared DLLs. It's important to set up all three before you go to the next section. Double-click on the Description property and you'll see a Properties dialog box containing two fields and a description. The first field shows the current Description property text, while the second field allows you to input a new value for the Description property. The descriptive text at the top of the dialog box tells you more about the Description property.

All of the other properties will show similar dialog boxes. Each Properties dialog box will describe what you're supposed to do with this particular property. It will also allow you to type in a value for the property. In this case, type **All the files required to run the application.** Then click OK. The Description property will now contain the text you just typed.

You don't need to change all of the component properties—what you do need to change depends on the kind of application package you're creating. For example, in our corporate model installation, we don't ever allow the user to choose the components that get installed, so providing a component description is pointless. The user won't ever see it anyway. There are some properties that you should consider changing regardless of the packaging model you're using, and the following list looks at each one.

■ **Status Text**   This is the text that the user will see while the installation program copies the files from the source to the destination. The Progress dialog box will say something like "Copying program files...," which works fine for default components. You may want to define something special for custom components.

■ **Installation** If you've ever been annoyed by the fact that some program came along and copied over the new DLLs you just installed with really old ones that don't work, then you'll know why this property is important. It tells InstallShield whether you want to look at the time and date stamp on the component files before you overwrite them. I always choose NEWERVERSION/NEWERDATE or SAMEORNEWERVERSION/ SAMEORNEWERDATE instead of the default ALWAYSOVERWRITE. In essence, these options tell InstallShield to only overwrite a file if the source has both a newer (or same) date and a newer (or same) version than the one on the user's hard drive.

■ **Destination** The standard destination for all of your application files is the target directory, the one the user chose for the program. However, there are some circumstances where using the target directory won't work like it should or could waste space on the user's machine. For example, most Visual C++ applications require the C runtime files and the MFC files. What if every application you installed added these files to a program directory instead of a centralized place? It wouldn't take very long to fill your hard drive with useless files. In most cases, you'll probably want to copy your Shared DLLs component files to the Windows SYSTEM folder. All you need to do is change this property. (When you open the Property dialog box, you'll see a map of the various locations you can use for copying the file; just choose the one you want.)

■ **Required Components** This is where you'll set up dependencies between components as shown here. What I'm telling InstallShield in this case is that if the user installs the Program Files component, he or she must install the Shared DLLs component as well (which only makes sense since without the Shared DLLs, the program won't run). Here's what the Shared DLLs component looks like when you make it a dependent component:

Pay special attention to the FTP Location and HTTP Location properties if you plan to install your application from an Internet or intranet site. These properties will allow a user to start the installation from a Web site link and then copy the needed files from your Web server. You would normally choose the FTP Location property if the files were under the control of the FTP server.

There's one last item that you absolutely must take care of to configure the components. Look at the Included File Groups property in the Components - Program Files dialog box. Right now we haven't assigned any file groups to the Program Files (or any other) component. Double-click on this property and you'll see a Properties dialog box that contains a complete list of the file groups assigned to a particular component. Remember that I previously talked about an example where you might want to make the spell checker and grammar checker optional components of your installation. They both use the same DLLs but require different rule files. I mentioned setting up three file groups: one with the spelling rule file, another with the grammar rule file, and a third with the common DLLs needed by both. This is the property where you set up that relationship. Click on the Add push button and you'll see an Add File Group dialog box like the one shown here:

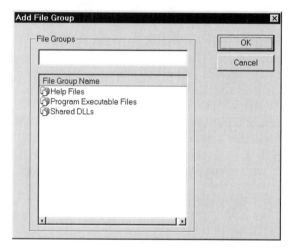

As you can see, the Add File Group dialog box contains the three file groups we defined using the Project Wizard. You'll need to make the following assignments between components and file groups before going on in the chapter. Table 9-4 shows the settings I used for the example program.

Component	Property	Value
Program Files	Description	All the files required to run the application
	Status Text	Copying Program Files...
	Overwrite	SAMEORNEWERVERSION/ SAMEORNEWERDATE
	Required Components	Shared DLLs&&Database Files
	Included File Groups	Program Executable Files
Help Files	Description	Files that show you how to use the program
	Status Text	Copying Help Files...
	Overwrite	SAMEORNEWERDATE
	Included File Groups	Help Files
Shared DLLs	Description	Common files used by the program
	Status Text	Copying Shared DLLs...
	Overwrite	SAMEORNEWERVERSION/ SAMEORNEWERDATE
	Destination	<WINSYSDIR>
	Included File Groups	Shared DLLs
Database Files	Description	Files used to access the SQL database
	Status Text	Copying Database Access Files...
	Overwrite	SAMEORNEWERVERSION/ SAMEORNEWERDATE
	Destination	<svDatabase>
	Included File Groups	Database Files

Table 9-4. Component Settings for the Sngl_Doc Installation Program

If you're looking for that <Database> destination in Table 9-4, you won't find it. You need to create this destination in the Script-defined Folders area. Just highlight Script-defined Folders, then click New Folder. Type **svDatabase** as the new destination name, which is a script variable. Now, open the Setup.RUL file and add the following code (in bold):

```
// your global variables
#define  svDatabase "C:\Program Files\Common Files\System\ado";
```

This is the first place that we've used the flexibility provided by InstallShield to customize our setup program. You'll see further examples of this flexibility as the chapter progresses. For right now, just keep in mind that InstallShield allows you to completely configure the installation paths for your setup program, something you won't find with the Visual Basic Package and Deployment Wizard. (Of course, the latter product isn't designed to provide this flexibility, and you should have also noticed by now that our setup for InstallShield has been much longer than the one for the Visual Basic Package and Deployment Wizard.)

Setting Up File Groups

Creating a set of components doesn't help the installation program very much. You've told the user what components can be copied to the hard drive, but you still haven't told the installation program what those files are. This is the step where you do that. We'll define a set of files for each of the file groups that we defined previously.

The first thing you'll need to do is click on the File Groups tab. What you'll see is a list of the file groups and the File Groups dialog box shown in Figure 9-5. Choosing which file group you want to configure is easy. Just click on its entry in the File Groups window on the left side of the display.

Click on the plus sign (+) next to the Help Files folder in the File Groups window. Click on the Links entry under the Help Files folder and you'll see the File Groups - Help Files\Links dialog box shown in Figure 9-5. This is where you'll define a list of one or more files to include for this file group.

> **Tip**
>
> *If you want to find out what project files to include in your InstallShield package (setup program), you can always use the Visual Basic Package and Deployment Wizard to build a Dependency File package instead of the usual Standard Setup Package. You'll find the Dependency File package option on the Package and Deployment Wizard - Package Type dialog box. We talked about the Visual Basic Package and Deployment Wizard in Chapter 8. Please refer to that chapter for details on how to use this wizard. The file you want to look at once you create the package is the <Application Name>.DEP file. All of the Uses<number>= entries in that file contain the names of files that your project needs to work. Make sure you check individual files for dependencies as well. For example, StdOle2.TLB always uses three additional files: OleAut32.DLL, OlePro32.DLL, and AsycFilt.DLL. Unfortunately, only the executable files are included in the DEP file. You'll also need to include help and other resource files (like databases).*

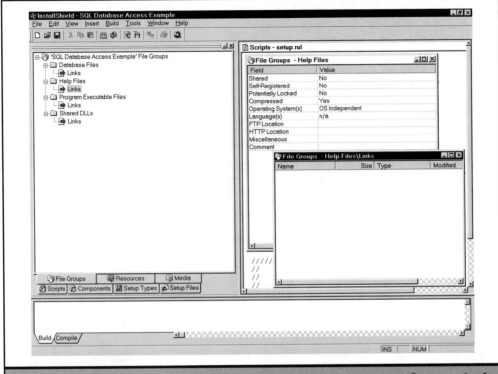

Figure 9-5. The File Groups - Help Files dialog box allows you to configure each of the file groups that we defined previously

Right-click on the File Groups - Help Files\Links dialog box and choose Insert Files from the context menu. You'll see a standard File Open type dialog box. Find the Search.HTM and Contents.HTM files that we created earlier in the chapter. Click OK to add these files to the Help Files file group. Note that we didn't add any graphics or other bells and whistles to our help files; you'd need to include these files in the list as well if you wanted to create a complete list of help files.

The Program Executable Files file group comes next. All we need to add in this case is the DataProject.EXE file. The Database Files group requires the following list of files: MSADOR15.DLL, MSDERUN.DLL, and DAO350.DLL. You'll find these files in the \Program Files\Common Files\System\ado, \Program Files\Common Files\Microsoft Shared\Dao, or \Program Files\Common Files\designer directory. The last file group, Shared DLLs, requires that you add the following list of files: MSVBVM60.DLL, OleAut32.DLL, OlePro32.DLL, AsycFilt.DLL, StdOle2.TLB, ComCat.DLL, MSBIND.DLL, MSStdFmt.DLL, MSDATREP.OCX, MSADODC.OCX,

MSDATGRD.OCX, MSDATLST.OCX, MSDBRPTR.DLL, MSDatSrc.TLB, MSJtEr35.DLL, MSJInt35.DLL, MSVCRT40.DLL, MSCOMCTL.OCX, and SHDOCVW.DLL. You'll find these files in the Windows SYSTEM folder.

Defining Resources

By this time, you should have the components and the file groups set up. What we need to do now is provide some identification information for the users. After all, they'll want to know a little something about the program they're installing. Click on the Resources tab and you'll see the Resources window shown in Figure 9-6. This same window contains two dialog boxes: Resources - String Table and Resources - String Table\English. The resources we want to change are in the Resources - String Table\English dialog box.

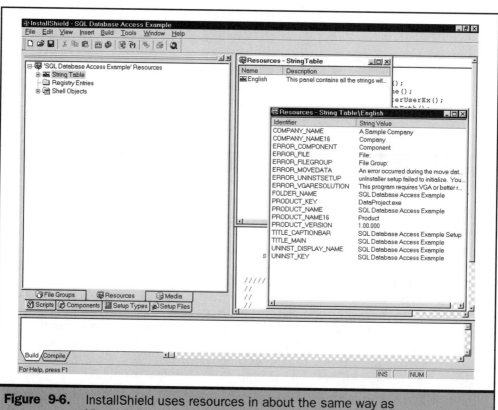

Figure 9-6. InstallShield uses resources in about the same way as Visual C++ does

Most of the changes we'll make in the Resources - String Table\English dialog box won't affect the program at all. We're making them for identification purposes or to help the user in some way. Changing one of the resource values is much the same as changing a property in one of the other dialog boxes. All you need to do is double-click on the Identifier you want to change, and InstallShield will display a dialog box that allows you to make the required change. Table 9-5 shows the changes I made for the example program—obviously, many of the strings will be different for your installation program.

Determining a Media Type

We've come to the very last thing you must do from a configuration perspective—simply tell InstallShield what type of media you want to use for distributing your application. In most cases, you'll use CD as the main distribution method, and you may decide to use floppies as a secondary method if the application is small enough. You'll need to use the Media Build Wizard to add media to your installation program. The following procedure will take you through the steps required to add a floppy media type.

Note   *As we'll see in a few seconds, the Default media type is CD. You won't see anything in the Media window that says Default is CD, but you'll see it when you use the Media Build Wizard to create other distribution types. If your only goal is to distribute your application on CD, then you can begin building the setup program immediately using the Default media type.*

Identifier	Value
COMPANY_NAME	A Sample Company
PRODUCT_KEY	DataProject.EXE
PRODUCT_NAME	SQL Database Access Example
UNINST_DISPLAY_NAME	SQL Database Access Example
UNINST_KEY	SQL Database Access Example

Table 9-5.   String Values for the Sngl_Doc Installation Program

1. Click on the Media Build Wizard entry and you'll see the Media Build Wizard - Media Name dialog box shown here:

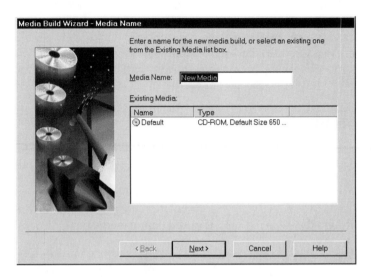

2. Type **3.5 Floppy** and then click Next. You'll see the Media Build Wizard - Disk Type dialog box shown here. Notice that InstallShield supports a wide variety of media types, including 2.88MB and 4.0MB floppies.

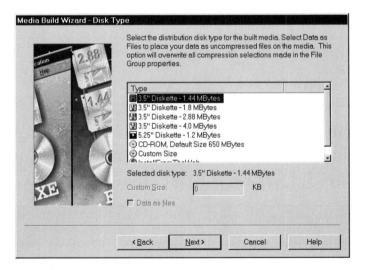

3. Highlight the 3.5" Diskette - 1.44 MBytes option and then click Next. You'll see the Media Build Wizard - Build Type dialog box. A full build will compress all the files for your application, create the required CAB files, and create the

full-fledged installation program. The Quick Build option is designed for testing purposes. It allows you to see if your installation program works as anticipated.

4. Choose the Full Build option and then click Next. You'll see the Media Build Wizard - Tag File dialog box. All this dialog box does is allow you to enter your company name and associated application information.

5. Type all the required information into the dialog box. The example program uses "A Sample Company" for the Company Name field, "SQL Database Access Example" for the Application Name field, "Personnel" for the Product Category field, and "Simple Database Editing and Printing Tool" for the Misc. field.

6. Click Next. You'll see a Media Build Wizard - Platforms dialog box.

7. Click Next. You'll see a Media Build Wizard - Summary dialog box like the one shown here. This is your last chance to verify the settings you've used.

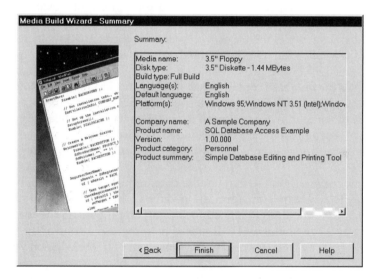

8. Verify your settings, and then click Finish. InstallShield will create the new build that you requested.

Note   *The Free Edition of InstallShield may present an error message at this point, saying that it doesn't have enough memory to create the requested build. Ignore the problem and try setting up the build again. If you still can't get it to work, complete the rest of the chapter using the default build setting. What you'll need to do is right-click on the Default folder and choose Media Build Wizard... from the context menu. Choose the Default option on the first screen of the Media Build Wizard dialog box and then click Next until you get to the final screen, where you got the error before. Click Finish and InstallShield will create the media for you.*

At this point, you'll see a Building Media... dialog box. InstallShield is actually creating your installation program for you. When the process is complete, just click the Finish button and you're finished!

Lessons Learned

Database management programs are one of the strongholds of the computer industry. Almost every programmer you talk to has created at least one of these kinds of programs. Yet, for all of the experience that we've accumulated over the years, database programming is also one of the most difficult and error-prone kind of application that you can create. The problem isn't one of knowing what to do; it's one of sheer scale and complexity. That's why most large database applications are also team projects.

This chapter has shown you that creating a simple database with Visual Basic doesn't have to be hard. In fact, the simple database-programming example contains less code than just about any other example you'll find in this book. However, as the complexity of the data model increases, you will see a corresponding increase in the complexity of the application. Don't assume that because Visual Basic helps you create a connection to the DBMS and provides aids in creating the forms required to access the various tables the database contains that all of the programming is going to be easy. Quite the contrary, you'll still find yourself spending hours trying to untie the knots of data created by other people in an attempt to understand the model that you should be programming to. Fortunately, the tools provided by Visual Basic do make it possible to prototype a database application with lightning speed once you do understand the data model.

Applications, especially those that handle data, require some form of help. There is no one best way to add help to an application, only a best method given your specific company situation. Companies that need to support employees on the road as well as at home have a decision to make. HTML-based help represents one of the very best methods for allowing everyone access to the same font of knowledge on your company server. HTML-based help offers the additional capability of instant upgrades on everyone's machine since a single HTML file on the server contains the required information. It's when access to the server becomes less than optimal that the decision of what kind of help to use becomes harder to make. Standard Windows Help is always available on a user's machine. They don't require any kind of a connection to the company network or the Internet to use it. In addition, Windows Help provides better linkage to the application program. It's very difficult to add any level of context-sensitive help to an application that uses HTML-based help.

Finally, packaging your application doesn't have to revolve around a specific product. Most Visual Basic programmers likely rely on Visual Basic Packaging and Deployment Wizard, which is a great choice in most situations. However, as we've seen in this chapter, you can also use InstallShield when flexibility is of greater concern than ease of setup program creation. It does take more time and effort to create a setup program using InstallShield. However, the resulting program can provide more options and even perform some tricks that the Visual Basic Packaging and Deployment Wizard alternative can't.

Chapter 10

A DHTML Application Example

There are a lot of traditional application types on the market right now. You could find yourself creating a utility program or a database application on any given day. Because of the prominence of the Internet, you may find yourself creating an entirely new application type: the Dynamic Hypertext Markup Language (DHTML) browser. In fact, we've already looked at one use for such an application in Chapter 9 as a means for implementing HTML-based help.

This chapter is going to explore the DHTML application more completely. Our first topic of discussion is what the application will look like. We'll explore things like what you want the user to see and how they'll access those items. Obviously, this means we'll also spend a little time talking about what kind of a user the application will interact with.

The topic of how to create a Web page with Visual InterDev for your DHTML application comes next. We'll look at some of the pluses and minuses of this new browser environment. We'll also look at different ways that you can mix your Web pages with Java applets and how you can create fully functional Internet applications.

Finally, we'll create some sample DHTML applications. One example will use Visual Basic as the programming language; the other will use Visual C++. The use of multiple language examples, in this case, should help you get started with DHTML quickly. This is one situation in which there are definite advantages in using Visual C++ as the language of choice in some situations, while Visual Basic will do a better job in others.

The next section contains the scenario for this chapter. We'll take a more in-depth look at the particulars of this programming task. In particular, we'll look at why you would want to create a DHTML application in the first place. Believe it or not, there are a lot more corporate uses for this new gizmo than you might think.

Are you confused about how DHTML differs from the HTML that you've been using all along for your Web pages? There are lots of good resources on the Internet for finding out more about DHTML. One of the better sites is the Dynamic HTML Index at http://www.all-links.com/dynamic/index.htm. Not only does this site include a lot of very practical information, but there's a chat group available as well. I was even able to find a DHTML bookstore on this Web site. A good place to look for links is the Microsoft site at http://www.microsoft.com/msdn/sdk/inetsdk/help/dhtml/references/dhtmlrefs.htm. This site doesn't provide a lot in the way of information, but the list of links is impressive. Do you want to see some demonstrations of what DHTML can do for you? Then check out the Web site at http://www.wmcentral.com/dhtml/. There's even a DHTML site of the week link that allows you to view DHTML at its best—at least in the opinion of the person running the Web site. There's also a site you can go to if you don't want to write your own DHTML. The SII Dynamic HTML site at http://www.sunriseintl.com/web/dhtml.htm offers to help you create a DHTML-enabled Web site (for a price of course).

Scenario

Your company has finally decided to create an intranet. There are lots of different kinds of information that management wants you to put on the site, such as safety procedures and employee information packages. Several departments want to make files available for download from the site. For example, there are a number of forms that you'll need to make available. In addition to the usual intranet fare, you'll also need to do some special things like make an employee survey form available from the Personnel department. Suffice it to say that information is not one of the problems you face—perhaps information overload is a much greater concern. A good first task, then, is to organize the information you want to present and to condense it into a summary page (with a pointer to the full source material) as needed.

The initial problem, of course, is convincing the employees to use the intranet once it's put together. Anyone who has spent any time at all trying to get much in the way of employee participation, without the threat of instant termination, knows that most employees would rather spend their time around the water cooler than looking at your latest gizmo. So, the first thing you need to do is figure out how to get an employee interested in what you have to offer. After all, the information provided is for their benefit for the most part. (Even if the employees won't benefit directly from the information, getting the information to them will help them perform their job better.)

Once you have the employee's attention, you'll need to prove it to management. It's hard to provide evidence of the economic value of some kinds of software aids, and to quantify in terms so that the management can understand the value of the intranet site that you've set up. Maintaining statistics is one way to ensure that you can provide evidence of your intranet's value to the company once it is set up and running. Obviously, one of the statistics you'll have to maintain is a count of the number of employees visiting your site and the precise pages that the employee visited while there.

Tip	*While this chapter shows you a very obvious way to keep count of how many employees visit a Web page, there are other, more covert methods of doing so. For example, there are programs designed to help you analyze the contents of your Web site log files. The method you choose for keeping track of your Web site statistics is nearly as important as the statistics you choose to monitor. Another consideration is the usability of those statistics later. You may decide that you need to derive another statistic from the information you already have. There are situations when using a direct monitor approach, like the applet we'll look at in this chapter, that just won't provide the additional information you need. That's when indirect monitoring methods like log files come into play. Often, you can use the contents of a log file to derive the statistics you need.*

Now that you have the employees' attention, and have provided them with the information they initially came to find, you might want to direct their attention to another location on the intranet site. That's when banners come into play. You see banners used all the time on the Internet to introduce people to new ideas and new sites. Banners can likewise be used on your intranet site to advertise underused or new pages.

Consider for a second that an employee has filled out a request for a large forms delivery. Wouldn't it be nice if the employee also knew how much space to clear to store the forms and the weight of those forms? That's when local calculations can really help. Instead of burdening the server with a lot of calculations and overflowing the cabling between the server and workstation with a lot of traffic, you can have the Web page perform these calculations locally. Another problem that you'll need to think about, then, is when to perform calculations locally rather than at the local server.

So far, this scenario has focused on the needs of the corporate employee. What if your intranet site will also serve the needs of customers or other interested parties? Banners can just as easily advertise products that your company makes. You'll still want to count which customers visit various areas of your Web site as well. Certainly customers will have need of local math functionality. They'll likely need to know the total of their order or the amount of taxable versus nontaxable items. In other words, don't get the idea that our scenario is only meant to address the needs of a narrow group of people; the things that we're discussing in this chapter with regard to content apply to many other groups as well.

> **Note**   *It's useful to view a Web page from three perspectives: what you want to sell, what you want to get, and how you can prove that you achieved your goals.*

Getting the content together is only one part of the bigger picture. You have to provide a method for the employee to grab that information from the company intranet. Normally, you'd rely on a browser to do the job. After all, the browser is free for the asking (at least, in most cases) and it will display any standard Web page. The ability to display just about any Web page, though, is where problems begin. You may want to restrict the employee's ability to view certain kinds of content. In addition, a standard Web browser can go anywhere on your intranet or the Internet as a whole (at least, unrestricted sites). You may want to limit your employees' interaction with the company intranet or the Internet as a whole to certain sites.

All these problems can be resolved by creating a custom browser. Designing and coding such a browser used to be a major undertaking. Visual Studio makes it easy to write the code for a custom browser using either Visual Basic or Visual C++. This new browser project type can do anything that a full-fledged browser can do because it relies on Internet Explorer for much of its functionality. All you need to do is write code that takes the restrictions you want into account. We'll look at simple custom browsers created with both Visual Basic and Visual C++ in this chapter. What you'll find is that both browsers are equally capable of displaying standard Web pages.

So, what kind of team will you need to pull this kind of project off? There are going to be two main groups. You'll have a group of people who contribute content to the Web site and a second group performing the various programming tasks. Both groups will have to work together during the planning stages or the Web site will lack cohesiveness. In addition, once your programming group has some basic code together, they'll need to test it with a subset of all the content types that the first group has to contribute. Be sure that you have a complete list of planned content types so that you can check them off as you test them. Obviously, this means that both groups need to be working on their part of the Web site simultaneously. Since a Web site can be a complex undertaking, you'll want to set up some type of monitoring. Don't forget that the content providers will continue to work on the site long after the programming effort is complete. You'll need to define some type of maintenance parameters for the site so that it doesn't become a jumbled mess as content gets added.

Let's talk about that first group—the content providers—a little more. In most cases, you'll be dealing with a manager, but it could just as easily be an administrative assistant that helps you out. What this means is that you'll need to provide feedback in a simple, easy-to-understand manner. Planning packages that contain information on how the Web pages will be laid out and what templates the content provider should use will also be a big plus.

The second group, the programmers, will include people who will use Visual InterDev to create the actual Web pages and those who will use Visual J++ to create the required controls. In addition, our example will include either Visual Basic or Visual C++ programmers who will create the custom browser used to view the site. All three programming groups need to work together at the beginning of the project to define what's needed. Once the planning phase is done, the Visual C++/Visual Basic browser programmers can work on their part of the project independently until it's time for the first testing phase. The Visual J++ programmers will need to work with the Visual InterDev programmers a little longer to define what controls will have to appear on the site. Once testing has begun, all three programming groups will continue working together until project completion. Interaction is essential if you want the user to see a cohesive, well-designed Web site.

Defining What You Want the User to See

The process of creating a Web page begins with determining what you want the user to see. What the user sees defines your Web page as a whole. Graphics, text, and sounds all work together to create a specific kind of experience for the user. Since what a user sees is so very important to how your Web page is viewed, it's important to define what effect you want to create at the outset. However, before you can define an effect, you have to consider what materials you have to work with. Let's look at this question from two different perspectives to begin with: individual and corporate (most Web page projects are actually a combination of the two perspectives).

When a small company or an individual begins to create a Web page, what they face is empty page syndrome. The effort of getting those first few words on the page can amount to more than getting the rest of the page put together. It's not that the individual has no idea of what they want to say; rather, they face a problem of how to say it. Getting the words, graphics, and sounds together to produce a desired effect can prove more difficult than you might think at first. Listing potential discussion areas, along with the desired effect and possible solutions for each, makes creating an effective Web page easier for everyone involved. Some factors to consider when you're developing Web content include:

- **Emotional impact**   A Web page almost always produces a certain emotional impact, even if it doesn't produce any emotional response at all. A designer page doesn't necessarily guarantee the kind of response you want. If all the user does is say an unemotional "ho hum" when they see your Web page, then you've probably lost the attention that you were hoping to gain in the first place. Of course, it's equally important to make sure you get the emotional response that you were hoping to achieve. Making the user sad or angry when you were trying to achieve something else will almost certainly result in total rejection of your Web site.

- **Educational value**   When users look at a Web site, they usually want to learn something. For example, a user may want to learn how to request vacation or what the company policy is regarding sick days. Even a data entry screen can teach if it's designed properly. The user may request information from the database, or use the data entry screen to learn how to perform a certain task. Obviously, there are exceptions to this rule, but in most cases you'll want every Web page on your site to teach something.

- **User participation**   Getting a user to participate with the page you designed is very important. A user that participates with the page will get a lot more out of it than a user who sits on the outside looking in. There is a wide variety of tactics that Web page designers use to get the user involved, everything from background music to buttons that the user needs to push to get a certain level of output. The whole purpose of a Web page is to draw the user in. You want to make the users ask questions so that they'll want to know more about whatever it is that you're trying to present.

- **Page focus**   Every page needs to focus on very specific issues. Nothing is more distracting than a page that tries to cover everything. Some Web sites that I've visited actually use a single page for everything. A table of contents at the beginning does make it easier to navigate the page, but most people would rather download several short pages instead of one long one. In fact, try to make each Web page talk about one topic in the list of topics that you need to cover. Use anchors wisely when needed to make navigation on your page easier.

- **Overall statement**   It's equally distracting to view a Web site that has no central theme. You might design a Web site specifically to discuss company policy. If that's the case, don't discuss the latest soap opera gossip in it. Make sure that the Web site makes an overall statement and that it has a central theme and purpose.

■ **Media impact**   Some Web pages actually work best when you dazzle the user with loud graphics and even louder sounds or other multimedia. As a general rule, though, Web sites used for business purposes should use graphics, sounds, and other forms of multimedia sparingly. Light use of several media together can often achieve the same impact as you would by heavily using one.

Corporations usually face the opposite problem of the individual Web page designer. The team putting a corporate Web page together has more than enough ideas—the sample page literally overflows with copious quantities of text. The problem for a corporate team is getting all that information into an understandable format and making it small enough that someone will actually want to view it (which means downloading the page). Obviously, the one effect that you don't want to produce with a Web page, especially one designed for a corporate intranet, is to make the information unwieldy and difficult to use. There are several development issues that a corporate team needs to consider as well.

■ **Consistency**   Every page in a corporate Web site needs to have the same overall layout. If you place the corporate logo in the upper-right corner of the page on the first page, you'll need to do the same thing with all the rest. Consistency affects things like color as well. If the first page uses a blue background with white text, then all the pages should use this color combination. Finally, there should be consistency in the way that things are worded. Using a single editor to perform the final adjustments to the page content should help in this regard.

■ **Fit and finish**   People expect a corporate Web site to look polished. After all, a corporation is supposed to have more in the way of resources than an individual designer would. Everything from the type of text used to the layout of the pages and the quality of the art reflects on the company itself. A well-designed Web page that uses high-quality art gives the user the feeling that the company is solid and well run.

■ **Accessibility**   Nothing is worse than looking at a corporate Web page and not knowing whom to contact for further information. As a minimum, every corporate Web site needs a page containing contact information—a list of phone numbers if nothing else is available. In addition, every page should have a mailto: shortcut. Providing the user with a method to contact the site's Webmaster is essential, even if the Web page is only used on an intranet, out of sight of the rest of the world.

■ **Well defined**   There are a number of ways to pursue this particular design goal. One way to achieve it is to ensure the entire team has a single vision of what information the site will contain and how that information will be presented. Some people actually compare pages on a Web site. If one page says that the corporation places quality above performance, and another page says the opposite (performance is more important than quality), you tend to confuse the public. In addition to defining the information, you need to provide definitions for the content as well. For example, there should be a way to find out the meanings for acronyms and jargon used on the site. You can't assume that a user will know what a technical term means simply because it's used a lot in a particular industry. The user may be a new employee who simply doesn't know what the terms mean.

Note *Single users need to find content to fill a page, while corporate teams need to organize and edit the excess of information they usually have on hand.*

Both of these groups can benefit from a feature that Visual InterDev provides: the ability to outline your Web site just as an author of a book would do. Here's an example of the Project window (the method used to outline the overview of your Web site) for the help file we created in Chapter 8:

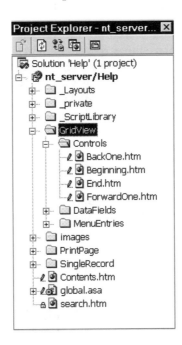

Notice that the Contents and Search pages appear at the very top level. If you'll remember from that example, we divided the program up into three sections, one for each of the major forms in the application. Notice that those form names appear as top-level folders within our outline. The next level of help was to divide each form into functional areas like menus, controls, and data fields. If you'll look at the GridView folder, you'll notice that there are subfolders for each of these functional areas. Finally, the example help file defined each object within a functional area. Look at the outline in the sample Project window again. There's one Web page dedicated to each object. It's easy to see that a user wouldn't have any trouble at all finding a particular piece of information using this layout.

Note *The Project window provides a place where you can organize your Web site as a whole.*

Once you have the overview in place, you can begin to outline individual pages. Tackling either a data overflow or underflow by working with one small piece of the puzzle at a time is a technique that writers have used for centuries to make books both understandable and fit within the constraints established by the publisher. Using an outline on every page is one way to ensure uniformity of content as well. Here's an example of a page outline (and associated content) for one of the buttons on the Grid View form of the example in Chapter 8:

Every control page in the help file could use exactly the same layout. Other types of pages, like those used for menus, could use a similar layout to give the entire help file the same look and feel. The whole purpose of this example page is to show you that breaking a page down into component parts makes it easier to write the page a section at a time. All you really need to do is define the object's properties or the way in which the user will use it. The Beginning Button Web page provides the user with everything needed to use the Beginning button in the example program, including some warnings that everything may not be as it seems. (For example, the beginning record may rely on index order or filtering criteria.)

Note *Always create an outline for each page that's consistent with the Web site as a whole and that fully defines the page content.*

Outlines work to the Web author's benefit in another way as well, especially when working with a team. If you stay at a low level all the time, you could lose sight of the project as a whole. An outline can keep you on track. For example, a team leader could outline the entire Web site plan using Visual InterDev. Individual team members could fill in details at the page level. Finally, a single editor (most likely the team leader) could edit the content before the pages are made public. In sum, the whole idea of outlining your project first is to ensure you take all of the needs of a particular Web site into account before any major components are in place. You'll find it a lot harder to make changes after the fact than to design the site properly in the first place.

Determining Where to Place Access Points

The help file that we created in Chapter 9 was fairly easy to set up because it has only two access points: the contents page and the search page. In most cases, you don't need more than these two access points in a help file unless you want to implement some form of context-sensitive help within the application. (Since Visual Basic isn't set up to do this, adding context-sensitive help for HTML-based help files is difficult to say the least.) Most Web sites aren't so easy to set up. You need to determine in advance what access points the user will have to your Web site. In most cases, there will be more than one access point for the whole Web site, and perhaps even more than one per page.

The placement of access points is more important than you might initially think. The following list provides some ideas of why access points are important.

- **Site flow**   There are times where getting to a specific page without viewing the pages before it is like telling just the punch line of a joke: The joke isn't funny and the page isn't useful. If your Web site provides several layers of information, make sure the user accesses the site from an overview page, then drills down to the detailed information. This ensures that the user gets the maximum benefit from the material you have to provide.

- **Accurate site statistics**   Unless you're planning on monitoring each and every page of your Web site (a nightmare scenario on larger sites), you'll want to control the access points to make sure that every user who views your site gets counted. Otherwise, you may find it difficult to get the help you need from management later to perform upgrades of equipment or make changes to the site setup.

- **Forms and controls**   While multipage forms are rare, they do exist. What would happen if a user accessed a form halfway through and only completed the last half of it? Neither of you would benefit. The user will have wasted time partially completing a form that will need to be resubmitted later and you'll waste time trying to locate the user to inform them of the problem. The same holds true of certain controls. You may find that the content of a control relies on the answers provided on a previous page. If this is the case, you'll want to make sure the user actually fills out the previous page.

■ **Return points**   A lot of sites lack what many people call return points. These links allow the user to get back to an upper level of the same page or other pages (like the home page) without using the Back button on their browser. Providing return points means that the user can navigate your site with ease using just the mouse and your Web page. This is an especially important feature to have if you plan on having the user browse your site with the browser in kiosk (full screen) mode.

As you can see, the placement of access points on your Web site can determine, in part, how a user views the site and whether the site is even usable. Controlling site access is especially important if you plan to include a mix of secure and nonsecure pages. (Even though a user couldn't easily override your security by accessing a secure page from the wrong place, it's less likely that the user will be able to use the page contents without experiencing problems of some kind.) As we'll see in the next section, not only do you need to control how the site is configured, but you need to control things like meta tags as well. Full control over how a user accesses your site ensures that both you and the user will get what you need out of the experience.

Creating the Web Pages Using Visual InterDev

It's time to begin building the Web site part of our project. We won't spend a lot of time looking at the content of the Web site since content will vary from site to site depending on its purpose. What we'll do instead is look at how the Web site goes together. The whole purpose of this example is to provide you with guidelines for constructing a Web site. What you put into the Web site is determined solely by your company's needs.

Note   *The four tasks for creating a Web site are defining the project, creating an overview outline, designing the page outline, and filling the pages with content.*

There are four main tasks that we'll perform when constructing our sample Web site. The first is to define the project. We partially explored this topic in Chapter 9. However, the project in that chapter was a help file. In this case, we'll be building something a lot more complex, which means that we'll spend more time building a foundation.

The second task is to create an outline. We looked at the theory behind creating an outline earlier in this chapter. Now we'll put that theory into practice. I won't tell you exactly what each Web page contains, and certainly the outline we'll look at isn't intended as a guideline for all Web sites; but the ideas that I'll present will be central to most Web sites. In other words, you'll probably use this part of the chapter as a source of ideas for your own Web site.

The third task is to design a Web page. We'll be using a layout and theme in this example, which makes creating the Web page a lot easier. In addition, using layouts and themes ensures a certain level of consistency between Web pages on a single site. Again, the content of this page isn't nearly as important as getting some ideas to use on your own Web pages. We'll also look at some procedural aspects of using layouts and themes. Even if you choose to create a custom layout and theme, you'll find that these procedures will work just fine.

Finally, we'll explore the task of creating page content. We started with an overview outline, then outlined each of the pages. Now it's time to fill in the blanks. This section will show you how to take the outlines we've created and use them to generate completed Web pages. Since the content for our example page is totally arbitrary, what you should be looking at is the procedures that I'll present. (You may even get a few ideas for content on your own Web pages, but that would be a secondary consideration.)

Defining the Project

This section will help you define the Visual InterDev project used as a Web page source for this chapter. Since I've already shown you a generic project example in Chapter 4, I won't go into all the options at your disposal in this chapter. We will, however, look at some of the things you can do to personalize your project in more detail. The following procedure is meant as a guideline for creating a corporate Web site project (obviously, any content you see, along with specific project parameters, are exclusive to this example).

1. Open Visual InterDev. You'll see the New Project dialog box.

2. Ensure the New tab is selected and that you're looking in the Visual InterDev folder. Highlight the New Web Project icon, type a name for your project (the example uses **CorpSite**), then click Open. Visual InterDev will display the Web Project Wizard - Step 1 of 4 dialog box.

3. Choose the server you want to use (we set this list box up in Chapter 4).

4. Choose the Master Mode option, since we want any changes to appear immediately on the test server.

Caution   *Don't use your production server for any of the examples in this book. Always use a test server when learning to create new project types. In addition, you should always have a test server available when creating new projects for company use. You'll want to fully test the project on the test server (where it doesn't matter if the program crashes the machine) before making it available on your production server for general use. In addition, taking a test server offline to work with the project won't cause network traffic headaches like you would get when taking a production server offline.*

5. Click Next. Visual InterDev will attempt to contact your Web server. If the server responds, you'll see the Web Project Wizard - Step 2 of 4 dialog box. Everything in this dialog box should be set up for you. You'll want to check the application name to ensure that it's the same one that you typed in the previous dialog box. In addition, make sure you check the Create search.htm to enable full text searching option.

6. Click Next. You'll see the Web Project Wizard - Step 3 of 4 dialog box. This is when we'll select a layout for the project. You may or may not want to use the canned layouts, depending on personal preferences. However, it never hurts to at least try the capabilities provided with the language product, especially on an example project like the one we're creating.

Tip

The number of layout choices that Visual InterDev offers might overwhelm you when you first look at them. However, it's relatively easy to find what you need. Look carefully through the layout selections and you'll notice that only a few of them include a banner as part of the layout. Since most corporate layouts will require a banner to display the company name and logo, you've already eliminated some of the choices. It's also important to think about your specific needs with regard to fast access. If you're creating a complex Web site, you'll need plenty of buttons to make access easier. For example, every Web page should have a link to the Search page, Corporate Information page, and the Site Map. In some cases, you may want to provide quick links to the sibling pages or to some of the more important first-level pages. We'll see how this process works as the example progresses.

7. Choose the Top, Left, and Bottom 1 option for this example. This particular layout is extremely flexible and gives you maximum automatic links for a complex Web site. I also chose it because this layout gives you a good idea of how the various automatic link types work. Here's what the layout we'll use looks like:

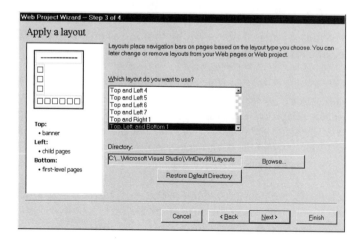

8. Click Next. You'll see the Web Project Wizard - Step 4 of 4 dialog box. This is where you'll decide on a theme for your Web page. Obviously, the art you use for your Web site has a great influence over how the user views your Web site as a whole. You'll want to get some help from a graphic artist if none of the canned themes will work for you.

9. Choose the Construction Zone option for this example. (It doesn't really matter which theme you choose, but your screen shots will differ from mine if you choose a different theme than the one I chose.)

10. Click Finish. Visual InterDev will create both a local and master copy of the project for you.

The project creation process for this example will take a noticeably longer time than the one in Chapter 4 because there are more files and more information in each file to process. Wait patiently and Visual InterDev will eventually complete the project shell for you.

Creating an Overview Outline

There's more than one phase to create an overview outline for your Web site. You have to take a lot of things into account. It's important to ask questions like, "How easy will it be for users to access the various pages on the site?" and "What kind of pages should I include?" Some of these questions are taken care of automatically for you by Visual Studio. For example, creating a site diagram automatically takes care of any navigation problems for you. The following sections show you how to create an overview outline, beginning with the site diagram.

Creating a Site Diagram

At this point, you should have a Web site shell that includes a Search page and not much more. Obviously, you'll need to add a lot more in the way of site structure before you can begin to add any content. Fortunately, there are a few shortcuts you can take to add some of the required pages. Let's begin by looking at one of the requirements for any complex Web site: The Site Map.

The top folder for a project normally contains the server name, followed by a slash, followed by the project name like this: nt_server/CorpSite. Rather than repeat all this information every time that it's needed in the chapter, I'll simply refer to the project as CorpSite. You'll need to add in your server name (which won't be the same as mine in most cases). Likewise, all of the screen shots will reflect the specifics of my Web server. Just substitute your server's name in the place of mine when working with the project files.

1. Right-click the CorpSite folder. Choose the Add | Site Diagram… option from the context menu. You'll see the Add Item dialog box shown here. Notice that the Site Diagram icon is already highlighted for you.

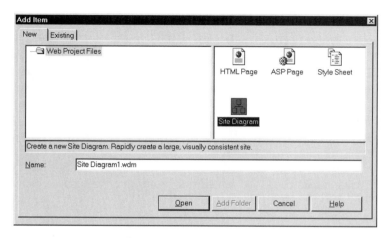

2. Type a name for the Site Diagram in the Name field (or use the default name). The example uses **Site Diagram1**, but you should use any name that you want.

> **Tip**
>
> *Visual InterDev will use names with spaces for many of the default filenames. The spaces will make filenames more readable on your Web server, but could present problems if you use them in the filenames of objects like HTML and graphics files. While you can use names that include spaces with many browsers, some won't accept the spaces (especially older browsers like Netscape 3). If you plan on creating a Web site for Internet use, you'll normally want to use names without spaces in them. In fact, this is probably a good habit to get into anyway since most people won't be used to typing the spaces for URLs.*

3. Click Open. You'll see a Site Diagram like the one shown here:

If you right-click on the Home page and choose Property Pages from the context menu, you'll see a Property Pages dialog box like the one shown in Figure 10-1. Notice that the Title field contains the name of the Web page as it appears in the site map, while the URL contains the filename of the Web page on the server. The page name, in this case, is Default.HTM, but we haven't added a Default.HTM file in the outline. We won't need to add Default.HTM because Visual InterDev adds it for you automatically; however, it's important to know that this page exists and why. The Home page for a Web site is normally named Default.HTM, but you can call it anything you like. Just make sure you reconfigure your Web server as needed for the change in name. Most Web servers also use Default.HTM as the default Home page (the one selected automatically when a user tries to access the site without any filename included). In this case, we'll follow convention and retain Default.HTM Web page as our default Home page for the site.

Arranging Global Pages in the Site Diagram

We already have another Web page to add to the Site Diagram1 page. Just click on Search.HTM in the Project window, then drag it to the Site Diagram1 window. Visual InterDev will automatically create a connection for you from the Home page entry to the Search page if you place Search below the Home page. However, we want Search to be an upper-level page, so place it beside Home as shown here:

Right-click on the Search page object and choose Property Pages from the context menu. You'll see a Property Pages dialog box like the one shown in Figure 10-1. Note that the search page title is in lowercase. Change it to uppercase to match the Home page entry.

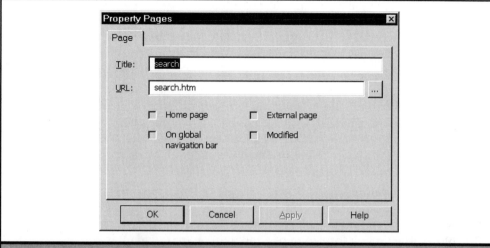

Figure 10-1.   Visual InterDev provides a Property Pages dialog box for changing the Site Diagram object properties

The third default page that every Web site should have is an About page that talks about your company and how to contact you. It's important that users know what your company is about. To create the About page, just right-click on CorpSite and choose Add | HTML Page… from the context menu. Type **About** in the Name field of the Add Item dialog box, then click Open. You'll have a new page added to the Project window. Now you can add this page to the Site Dialog1 page, just as you did Search.HTM. Make sure that you make the About object a top-level entry, just as we did for Search.

Deciding On Which First-Level Pages to Add

There's a wealth of other default page types that you'll find on the Internet. Spend some time looking at the Web sites of other companies to see which page types you might like to add. The following list will give you some additional ideas as well.

- **Human Resources (Personnel)**   This page can list new jobs, requirements for advancement, work hours, vacation policies, and other job-related information. If you have an Internet site, you can use this page to tell people where to send resumes and who to talk with regarding job opportunities.

- **Products**   If you make a product, you have to let people know about it. The Products page normally lists all of your products, provides a brief description, and then provides a link to some marketing information. For most Internet sites, a product is something tangible that the person using your site could purchase outright or lease. The difference between a product and a service is important. For example, a computer would be considered a product because you can hold it, while computer programming would be considered a service because you only see the results of running it.

■ **Services** Intangible offerings like building Web pages or accounting normally appear on a Services page. Like the Products page, you'll include a list of all of the services your company offers, then add links to marketing information that someone could use to make a purchasing decision.

■ **Sales** Once a person decides to buy something from your company (make sure you include employees as potential buyers), they need to know how to do it. The Sales page could be anything from a simple list of telephone numbers that the viewer could call to make a purchase over the phone, to a secure Web page that allows them to make the purchase electronically. Make sure this page contains a link for dealer information if your company relies on outside dealers for sales.

■ **Press Information** In addition to the normal marketing information about your current products and services, you may want to prepare the public for future products and services that are either in development or on the drawing board. The Press Information page allows you to provide this kind of information. However, you don't have to limit this page to just new product and services information. If you receive kudos for something you've done, this is the place to put that information as well. One of the more interesting applications that I've seen for this page is a Success Stories section where outside parties provide testimonials about your products or services.

■ **Partnerships** Sometimes it helps to let other people know who you're affiliated with and how. For example, a customer may be looking for a set of products that work well together. Even if your company doesn't produce all of the products required, the Partnerships page could show the customer that other companies make add-ons that are compatible with your products. In other words, this page could help you compete against larger companies with greater resources.

Tip *Make sure that if you list a company on your Partnership page, that they list your company on their Partnership page as well. Getting a listing on another company's Partnership page is one way to greatly increase your exposure on the Internet.*

■ **Legal Notices and Information** Yes, just like anything else to do with business these days, you should probably include a page with all the normal disclaimers about product suitability. Putting all this information in one place means that you don't have to repeat it and that there's little chance of someone getting the wrong information. Make sure you include trademark and copyright information on this page as well.

■ **Technical Support** Some places call this page the Help Desk now. Whatever you end up calling your Technical Support page, the purpose is simple—to provide help with using a product or service. It doesn't matter whether your Web site supports employees on the road using a custom application or a Fortune 500 client who has just purchased your entire stock of widgets. What's important is that when someone needs help, they can find it with ease on your Web site.

■ **Feedback**   Always provide some method of getting feedback from the people who use your site, services, or products. Some companies use a simple mailto: entry at the bottom of their Web page, which works fine in some cases; but in many cases, you'll need more information than a general email will provide. This page could contain one generic form for everything, or you could provide links for specific kinds of user feedback. Just how complex this area of your Web site gets depends on how much you want to customize the feedback that you get from the user. The Feedback page is also a good place to include surveys and other kinds of input, such as new product suggestions. In fact, an intranet site could use this page in place of the suggestion box used by many companies.

■ **Investor Information**   One of the more unusual kinds of pages that is cropping up on many company sites these days is an Investor Information page. This page is normally associated with stock offerings for the company in question. You could also use it to provide access to the company report and to show how well the company is doing financially.

■ **Clubs/Support Groups**   Making the users feel like they're integral parts of your company is very important if you want them to continue using the Web site after they see it the first time. In other words, you have to give the user a good reason to come back. A Clubs or Support Groups page can make a big difference in the participation level of a Web site. It doesn't matter whether you have an intranet or Internet site (after all, employees are users of the Web site, too). Normally, this page will include meeting information. However, you could also use it to sponsor a chat group.

Obviously, not all of these pages will work for every company, but you'll find that most of them are generic enough that you can add them in some way. For example, even if you're running an intranet site with no outside access, the Personnel page can list new jobs that are available to people within the company.

Modifying the Default Layout

There's one more task we have to perform before we can start to add child pages to our Web site. The current setup will display the child pages for the currently displayed page (those that are under the current page in the site diagram hierarchy) and the first-level pages (those pages under the Home page). We don't have any method for the user to conveniently get back to the Home page. We need to change the layout slightly using the following procedure.

1. Open the _Layouts | tp1 folder in Project Explorer. You should see the LAYOUT.HTM file that is used for all layouts in the site. Changing this file will change all the files that you create after the modification. That's why we're changing the file now, instead of at the beginning of the project when there was no need to add a Home page button.

2. Right-click the LAYOUT.HTM file, then choose Get Working Copy from the context menu. This command gets a copy of the file from the server and locks everyone else out. You must get a working copy of any files you need before attempting to modify them. Visual InterDev assumes that you want working copies of any files you create. A pencil next to a filename entry in Project Explorer means that you have a working copy of that file, while a lock signifies that you don't.

3. Double-click LAYOUT.HTM to open the file. You'll see the layout, but not the theme, for all of the pages we'll create for the Web site.

4. Right-click the bottom PageNavbar control. You'll see the PageNavbar Properties dialog box shown here. (Notice that the diagram shows which pages are selected by highlighting them in red and that the Home page isn't selected.)

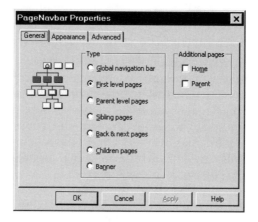

5. Check the Home option in the Additional Pages block. This will add a Home page button to all of the Web pages that we'll create from this point on. Notice that the Home icon in the diagram is now highlighted in red.

6. Click OK to close the PageNavbar Properties dialog box.

7. Save the changes to the LAYOUT.HTM file, then close it.

8. Right-click the LAYOUT.HTM file entry in Project Explorer, then choose Release Working Copy from the context menu. Choosing this option will release the copy of the LAYOUT.HTM file so that other people can use it.

Tip *You can use the techniques shown in this section to modify the default layout in other ways. For example, you could add a company logo to the top of every page or create a special tips and pointers banner to help people get more from the Web site. If you want a particular modification to appear on every page of your Web site, you'll need to add it to the layout before adding the site diagram or any pages. Make sure you modify the Search page as well since it gets created for you by the wizard.*

Adding First-Level and Child Pages

At this point, you're ready to add new child pages to your Web site. Now that you have a better idea of what you can add to your Web site, let's add some of those pages as shown here. (Notice the use of folders to keep various kinds of information separate.)

As you can see, even a simple test site can quickly accumulate pages. The use of folders is important if you want to keep the pages in some semblance of order. Make sure you use enough folders to maintain the site's hierarchical arrangement, so that other programmers know where to find specific files. Notice also that even though there are no spaces in the filenames, they're still very descriptive. Using the right kind of descriptive filename also reduces the time required to update the site diagram.

Once you've created all of the required Web pages, add them to Site Diagram1. This will make it easier for you to see how the site will actually appear to the user. In addition, updating the site diagram will also update the PageNavbar controls that allow the user to move from one area of your Web site to the other. I've used the following layout for my site diagram, though you could use anything you wanted. (In fact, it would probably be a good idea to experiment at this point and see the effect various layouts have on the final appearance of the Web pages.)

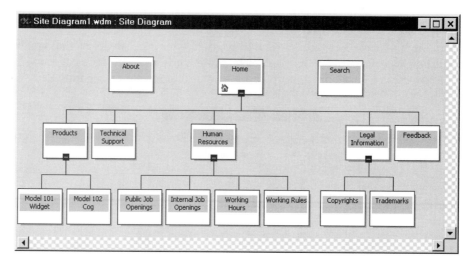

Defining Global Links

At this point, we have a functional Web site, even though none of the pages contain any content. Let's take a look at the Home page. Figure 10-2 shows what the Home page looks like. Notice the set of links that get included on this page automatically as a result of creating Site Diagram1. Normally, you'd have to create and update these links

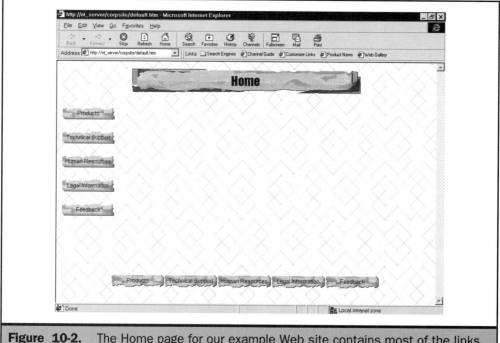

Figure 10-2. The Home page for our example Web site contains most of the links you would expect

manually. In addition, the PageNavbar control at the top creates a page banner based on the title for the current page in the site diagram, which is why it's so important to define meaningful block names. Noticeably absent though are the Search and About page links. In addition, it seems a little redundant to have two sets of buttons that show exactly the same thing. If you click on the Products button, you'll notice that these buttons normally show different entries (child pages on one, first-level pages on the other). We'll correct both of these problems next.

The first thing we need to do is provide a method for accessing the two pages (About and Search) that we can't see at the Home page level. Visual InterDev supports a Global Navigation Bar feature that allows us to access these top-level pages. All you need to do is mark the page so that it gets added. Select the About block in Site Diagram1. Use the Diagram | Add to Global Navigation Bar command to add About to the list. Do the same thing for Search and then save the project.

Now that we have a means for accessing the pages, let's add them to the Home page. Open Default.HTM. Right-click the bottom PageNavbar control, then choose Properties from the context menu. You'll see a PageNavbar Properties dialog box. Choose Global Navigation Bar from the Type group and Home from the Additional Pages group. Click Ok to close the PageNavbar Properties dialog box. Make the same changes to both the About.HTM and Search.HTM files. Save the changes. Figure 10-3 shows the changes you should see to the Home page.

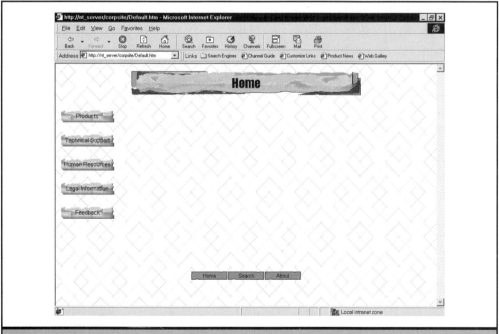

Figure 10-3. The Home page now includes all of the links required to access our entire Web site

Designing a Typical Page

Getting the overview of your Web site completed is only part of the task. Now you have a host of blank Web pages to fill out. However, if you simply attack each page in its entirety, what you'll probably end up with is a gush of ideas that are presented in no particular order. Adding content begins with an outline, just as you would use when writing a report or a book. That's what we'll do in this section—outline a Web page.

Using a top-down approach when designing the Web pages in your site is a good idea because you can create a better flow of ideas. Normally, I start with the Home page since that's the first page that everyone will see. We'll begin this section, then, by opening Default.HTM so that we can add an outline to it.

If you look at the layout we've chosen for this example, you'll notice that there are three main areas where you can add content. Each of these areas is designated by a DesignerControl that tells you to either add your content above or below the control. The first is the heading area at the very top of the page. You could add a company logo or other global information here. The second area, the one that we'll concentrate on, is in the middle of the page. It's where you'd add headings as part of the Web page design process. Finally, there's a footer area at the bottom of the page where you would add a mailto: or copyright information. Some Web sites include the entire company address and telephone number in this area. However, people tend to ignore footers that get too large and complicated.

> **Tip**   *Visual InterDev provides an HTML toolbar that also includes a Paragraph Format list box. You can use the predefined styles in this list box to set things up, such as the heading level for the outline of your Web page. This feature works just like the formatting feature of any word processor, which should make it easy for everyone to get up and running quickly.*

The problem, at this point, is figuring out what kind of headers to add. Just think if you were trying to add content at this point, you'd probably have a very bad case of empty page syndrome by now. If you look at most Web sites, the Home page normally contains links to other areas on the Web site, but Visual InterDev has already taken care of this for us. What we really need is something to spark the viewer's attention and provide them with a reason to look further. Here are some ideas for Home page headings that you might consider:

- **Breaking News**   Even if you have a Press page, you really need to add breaking news to your Home page. The Press page normally contains older news that has already happened or news of events in the future. The Home page is where you should provide the news that's happening today. Of course, you really don't want to provide the user with the whole story on the Home page. Pique their curiosity, then redirect them to the appropriate places in your press section.

- **New or Improved**   This heading goes by a lot of different names, but the purpose is always the same—to tell customers about new products or improvements to released products.

- **Statement of Purpose**   Some companies that have more than one Web site will state the purpose for each of their Web sites. In a few cases, I've even seen this extended to companies with a single Web site who want to make sure you know what you're getting before you spend the time looking. A statement of purpose can be helpful if it's written correctly because it helps the user know what to expect immediately.

- **Big Picture**   Besides links to the rest of the Web site, some companies refuse to do anything else with their Home page. However, that leaves a big hole on the page as well. Some of these companies fill that hole with a big picture, which is fine if the picture provides some meaningful input to the user. Be aware, however, that many users will click the Stop button before they see the big picture—especially if they access your site over a dial-up line.

- **Promotions**   There are a lot of different forms of promotion. Anything you want to give a special nudge to on your Web site is a candidate for promotion. A promotion might be as simple as employee of the week or a sale on your latest product. On the other hand, you might choose to emphasize a little-used resource like the Search page or technical support section.

- **Widgets**   Sometimes a Web site will have something that falls into the widget classification. For example, the counters that many Web sites sport don't provide much in the way of useful input, but they're still fun to see. Banners can usually advertise promotions more effectively than plain text. Other widgets include automated menus and graphics. For the most part, widgets are designed for emphasis and a little fun.

For the purposes of this example, I chose to provide a simple Home page. Here's what the headings for that page look like. (Obviously, you're free to experiment with what works best for your company—this page only represents a simple example of how to perform the task, not what to put on the Web page.)

This outline contains three levels of headings. The first level contains major areas of coverage such as breaking news. The second level covers a particular story, like the company president's good news for the shareholders. Finally, a third level is added if a particular story is too long to cover in one or two paragraphs. Notice that there are three main points in the company president's good news speech, and each point is covered by a separate heading.

Developing Page Content

This is the last thing you need to do with the Web page before releasing it to the general public. All of the steps we've taken so far have led up to the creation of some content that'll help the Web site user in some way. Unfortunately, even with all of the aids that we've built into the Web site creation process, this part of the task will still take the most amount of time. There are a few things, though, that you can do to make it easier. The following list won't help you write content, but it will help you get started.

- **One area at a time**   Some people have a hard time writing content for their Web site because they try to concentrate too hard on the big picture. Smaller is better in some situations. If you've done a good job of designing your Web site, you should be able to concentrate on one small area of text at a time. Obviously, you'll still need to make sure that text fits in with the topic that you're discussing.

- **Graphics that count**   A picture is often worth a thousand words, or a thousand minutes of download time, whichever comes first. If you need a picture to get your idea across without writing a novel the size of *War and Peace* on your Web site, then make sure you use a good one. The picture has to clearly present your point or you'll lose your audience. Make sure that you provide some kind of text description of the picture, especially if you're working on an Internet site. Blind users (or those with other physical handicaps) may not own browsers that allow the user to see the picture. They may need a simple description of the picture instead.

- **Clutter that kills**   Keep a single topic in mind as you write the content for each section of your Web page. Don't ramble about topics that are covered elsewhere. You may find that you have to add another heading or two to provide adequate topic coverage. The idea is to make sure your text is clear and concise. Get what you need to say written in the fewest words possible.

- **Don't leave anything out**   There's an opposite extreme to the verbose Web page that says little or nothing about the topic that's supposedly being discussed—one that says nothing at all. Make sure that you say enough, that your user is clear about what you want to say. Remember that the user won't be able to ask questions very easily, so make sure you answer any potential questions as you write the content for your Web page.

Augmenting the Web Pages with Visual J++

Everything we've done for the example Web site so far has involved static content. The content may be of a more advanced sort than what you might see on most Web sites; but it stays the same during the entire session. Even though the buttons will change given a change in the Web site configuration, the page the user sees at their browser won't change once they receive it.

There's absolutely nothing wrong with static pages. In fact, it's fairly safe to say that almost all of the pages you create for your Web site will be static. There isn't any reason to add any dynamic content in most cases. However, what if you did want to add some kind of content that changed either from session to session or during the session? You'd require some type of applet or control to make the content dynamic (or at least change from session to session).

Note *This section is going to show you just one method of creating dynamic content, through a Java applet that also acts as an ActiveX control. There's a wealth of other methods that you can use to create various kinds of dynamic content. For example, ActiveX controls, whether created with Visual C++ or Visual Basic, are good candidates for creating dynamic content. (Visual C++ is a better choice, in this case, because it can create smaller controls, which decreases download time.) You can also create streaming content with a variety of server packages like the one from Real Audio. The point is that you shouldn't necessarily limit yourself to using Java applets unless they'll do the job for you.*

This section is going to show you how to create a simple counter—in this case, a clock to display on a Web page. It tells the viewer what the current time is on their machine. Normally, you can't provide this kind of feature on a Web page because the display is static. However, having a clock available helps the user keep track of the time they're spending on the Web.

Once we get the clock completed, we'll publish it to the repository, then add it to the sample Web site that we've been working on throughout the chapter. We've already created a simple Java applet in Chapter 4 and published an ActiveX control in Chapter 8, so many of the procedures in this chapter will use an abbreviated format.

Obviously, this isn't the only kind of counter you'll ever need; there are counters that simply keep track of how many times a certain event has happened. For example, you may be interested in tracking how many people have visited your Web site. Another use for counters is user-generated events like key or mouse clicks. Counting the number of system-generated events such as time-out messages is also important.

Clock examples are a good way to see how various kinds of implementations compare. For example, we created a ClockIt ActiveX control in Chapter 8 that performs at least some of the functions of the counter applet in this chapter. You may want to spend some time comparing the two examples to see how the implementations differ and how they are the same. Learning how one language differs from the other is one way to improve overall team efficiency. Often, the choice of language is the determining factor in how long a project takes. Using the wrong language is not only frustrating, but time consuming as well.

There are a lot of extensions you could add to this counter applet besides simply using it as a clock. One potential extension would allow you to time user events, like the time required to answer questions on a test. Another potential use would be an alarm clock. You could signal the user when a given time period is over. You could also keep the counter in the background and have it time system or application events.

 This example relies on the Windows Foundation Classes (WFC). You won't be able to use the applet we create in this example on a non-Windows machine, nor will you be able to modify the source code using anything other than Visual J++ 6.0 (or above). While the Microsoft-supplied WFC will help you create more capable applications, the price you pay for this flexibility is portability. Unfortunately, it's all too easy to use the WFC without really knowing that you have. Some wizard-generated output does rely on the WFC to get the job done. Always be absolutely certain about the level of compatibility you need for an applet (or application) before creating one using the WFC. If an applet won't run on a non-Windows machine, but runs fine on your Windows development platform, check your code for inadvertent use of the WFC.

Creating the ClockDisp Applet

In this section, we'll create a new applet called ClockDisp. The only thing that this applet will do is display the system time, though it can easily be extended to do a lot more. The following procedure will help you get started creating the applet.

1. Open Visual J++. You'll see the New Project dialog box.

2. Choose the Visual J++ Projects | Components folder, then highlight the Control icon as shown here. Choosing this option will create a control that relies on WFC instead of the standard Java package. There are a few other differences between this option and the control we worked with in Chapter 4. For one thing, you don't get a test Web page as a default and the control itself starts out blank. You'll need to define a few additional items that we didn't have to in Chapter 4.

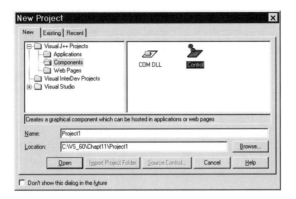

3. Type **ClockDisp** in the Name field, then click Open. Visual J++ will create a new project for you.

4. Right-click Control1.JAVA in Project Explorer, then choose Rename.

5. Type **ClockDisp.JAVA**, then press ENTER.

6. Right-click the project folder, then choose Add | Add Web Page... from the context menu. You'll see an Add Item dialog box.

7. Choose the Web Page folder, then click Open. Visual J++ will create Page1.HTM for you and add it to the project.

8. Open both ClockDisp.JAVA and Page1.HTM.

Note

Renaming your project and control files may seem like a nuisance, but they are necessary steps to ensure you can access your control using a unique name. Otherwise, you may find that you can't find your control when you need to use it in a project because it's stored under some generic name of Microsoft's choosing.

The first time you open ClockDisp.JAVA, you'll see a code-editing window, just like the one we saw in Chapter 4. However, when using WFC, there's another mode—the form view window—for adding controls that looks just like Visual Basic. We need to edit two lines of code to make this change in our control as shown here (the changes are in bold):

```
public class ClockDisp extends UserControl
{
    public ClockDisp()
```

Close ClockDisp.JAVA, then reopen it. What you'll see is a Visual Basic–like graphical editing window. Now we need to add two controls to the form. The first is a label for displaying the time, the second is a timer control for making clock events happen. Your form should look like the one shown in Figure 10-4 when you get finished adding the two controls.

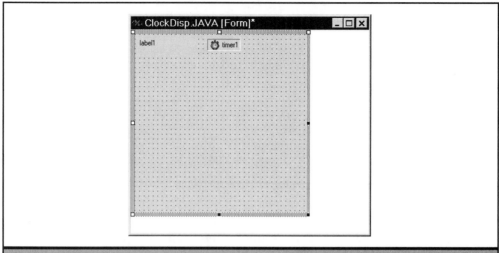

Figure 10-4. Visual J++ can provide an editing screen that looks just like Visual Basic as long as you use WFC

We'll need to set some properties for these two controls (I've renamed the label TimeDisp for ease of code reading). Table 10-1 shows a list of the properties for each control and their new values. If you see a blank for the property, then make that property blank in your project as well.

Control	Property	Value
TimeDisp	borderStyle	Fixed 3d
	text	
Timer1	enabled	True
	interval	1,000

Table 10-1. ClockDisp Form Control Properties

Adding Some Code to ClockDisp

Now that we have a project set up, it's time to add some source code. Double-click Timer1 to open the Code window and create the appropriate function. Listing 10-1 shows all of the source code for this example. Make sure you add all of the required code, including the imports.

Listing 10-1

```
import com.ms.wfc.core.*;
import com.ms.wfc.ui.*;

// Add support for the Calendar object.
import java.util.*;

/**
 * This class is a visual component. The entry point for class execution
 * is the constructor.
 *
 * This class can be used as an ActiveX control. Check the checkbox for this
 * class on the Project Properties COM Classes tab, or remove the // from
 * the next line:
 * @com.register ( clsid=FCE40920-1D5E-11D2-B06E-0060975BF784,
 * typelib=FCE40921-1D5E-11D2-B06E-0060975BF784 )
 */
public class ClockDisp extends UserControl
{
    public ClockDisp()
    {
        // Required for Visual J++ Form Designer support
        initForm();
    }

    private void Timer1_timer(Object source, Event e)
    {
        // Create a Calendar object.
        Calendar oTime = Calendar.getInstance();
```

```
         TimeDisp.setText(oTime.get(oTime.HOUR_OF_DAY) + ":" +
                     oTime.get(oTime.MINUTE) + ":" +
                     oTime.get(oTime.SECOND));
}

public String getLabelForeColor()
{
   Color   oColor = TimeDisp.getForeColor();   // Current foreground color.

   // Return the color as a string.
   return new String(colorToString(oColor));
}

public void setLabelForeColor(String oColor)
{
   // Set the foreground color.
   TimeDisp.setForeColor(stringToColor(oColor));
}

public String getLabelBackColor()
{
   Color   oColor = TimeDisp.getBackColor();   // Current background color.

   // Return the color as a string.
   return new String(colorToString(oColor));
}

public void setLabelBackColor(String oColor)
{
   // Set the background color.
   TimeDisp.setBackColor(stringToColor(oColor));
}

 // Converts a string formatted as "rrggbb" to an awt.Color object
private Color stringToColor(String paramValue)
{
   int red;
   int green;
   int blue;
```

```
    red = (Integer.decode("0x" + paramValue.substring(0,2))).intValue();
    green = (Integer.decode("0x" + paramValue.substring(2,4))).intValue();
    blue = (Integer.decode("0x" + paramValue.substring(4,6))).intValue();

    return new Color(red,green,blue);
}

// Converts a color value to a string formatted as "rrggbb".
private String colorToString(Color paramValue)
{
    String   colorValue;   // String to hold converted values.

    // Obtain the hex value for each color and combine it into a single
    // string.
    if (paramValue.getRed() < 15)
        colorValue = "0" + Integer.toHexString(paramValue.getRed());
    else
        colorValue = Integer.toHexString(paramValue.getRed());

    if (paramValue.getGreen() < 15)
        colorValue = colorValue + "0" + Integer.toHexString(paramValue.getGreen());
    else
        colorValue = colorValue + Integer.toHexString(paramValue.getGreen());

    if (paramValue.getBlue() < 15)
        colorValue = colorValue + "0" + Integer.toHexString(paramValue.getBlue());
    else
        colorValue = colorValue + Integer.toHexString(paramValue.getBlue());

    return colorValue;
}
```

```java
/**
 * NOTE: The following code is required by the Visual J++ form
 * designer.  It can be modified using the form editor.  Do not
 * modify it using the code editor.
 */
Container components = new Container();
Label TimeDisp = new Label();
com.ms.wfc.app.Timer Timer1 = new com.ms.wfc.app.Timer(components);

private void initForm()
{
    this.setBackColor(Color.CONTROL);
    this.setSize(new Point(300, 300));
    this.setText("Control1");

    TimeDisp.setLocation(new Point(8, 8));
    TimeDisp.setSize(new Point(100, 25));
    TimeDisp.setTabIndex(0);
    TimeDisp.setTabStop(false);
    TimeDisp.setText("");
    TimeDisp.setBorderStyle(BorderStyle.FIXED_3D);

    Timer1.setInterval(1000);
    Timer1.setEnabled(true);
    Timer1.addOnTimer(new EventHandler(this.Timer1_timer));
    /* @designTimeOnly Timer1.setLocation(new Point(128, 8)); */

    this.setNewControls(new Control[] {
                TimeDisp});
}
// NOTE: End of form designer support code

public static class ClassInfo extends UserControl.ClassInfo
{
    public static final PropertyInfo labelForeColor =
        new PropertyInfo(ClockDisp.class,
                    "myString",
                    String.class,
                    CategoryAttribute.Appearance);
```

```
public static final PropertyInfo labelBackColor =
    new PropertyInfo(ClockDisp.class,
                "myString",
                String.class,
                CategoryAttribute.Appearance);

public void getProperties(IProperties props)
{
    super.getProperties(props);
    props.add(labelForeColor);
    props.add(labelBackColor);
}
   }
}
```

There are two different tasks that this code will perform. The first is creating the clock, and the second is to provide properties for changing the color of the label used to display the clock on-screen. We'll look at the clock code first, which appears in the Timer1_timer( ) function.

Double-clicking on Timer1 automatically creates the Timer1_timer( ) function for you. A timer event automatically calls this function, just like it would in any other programming language. The timer itself consists of a standard Calendar class object, which is why we have to add the import java.util.*; statement at the beginning of the file. Once we have the current time, all we need to do is update the display. The very next statement retrieves the various time element values and places them within the label that we've set aside for the purpose.

Providing property values for changing the label color is a bit more difficult than filling it with a time value. One of the things you should have noticed is that the wizard automatically creates a blank ClassInfo class for you. This is where you'll start the process of adding new properties to your applet. The first part of the property creation process is to create the properties themselves. That's where the PropertyInfo class comes into play. Notice that we call it twice, once for each of the properties that we want to add (labelForeColor and labelBackColor). There are several forms of the PropertyInfo constructor method. The form used in this example is going to be optimal for most people. It takes four variables: The name of the class that contains the property get and set functions, the name of the property, the property class type, and the attribute that the property will appear under if the user chooses to list the applet properties by category.

Note *At the time of this writing, you can't reliably use any type for a property other than the String class. Even though the Microsoft documentation shows that you can use other classes, the reality is that only the String class will allow you to actually use the property in the environments that normally support Java applets and ActiveX controls. (Theoretically, you should be able to use other property types based on the abilities of other programming languages like Visual C++.) Hopefully, Microsoft will have this problem fixed by the time you read this since most applets are going to require more than string properties to get the job done. Unfortunately, the only clue you get that a property type won't work is that the property won't appear in one of the environments that you use it in, which means that you need to perform extensive testing. The Java code will still update and the container used to hold the applet will still accept it. If you don't see the list of properties you think you should see for an applet in the Properties window, then try changing the property's type to string temporarily for testing purposes.*

The second part of the property creation process is to add the property to the applet's default property list. We'll override the getProperties( ) function to perform this task. Notice that the first thing we have to do is obtain a list of the default properties using the super.getProperties( ) method. Once we have a list of default properties, the add method of the object used to store the property list will allow us to add the two new properties for the applet.

If you tried using the applet at this point, you might see the properties, but you couldn't do anything with them. Every property that you add to your applet also requires a get and set function. In our example, that means adding four functions: getLabelForeColor( ), setLabelForeColor( ), getLabelBackColor( ), and setLabelBackColor( ).

Setting either the labelForeColor or labelBackColor property value is relatively easy. All you need to do is retrieve the current color settings from TimeDisp and convert it to a string for display in the Properties window. Fortunately, the stringToColor( ) method that's supplied as a default part of the Applet on HTML project will work just fine here as well. All I did was copy and paste it from our project in Chapter 4 for the purposes of this example.

Getting the properties is a little more complex. The first thing we need is a function that converts a color to string, since neither Java nor WFC provides this functionality for us. The colorToString( ) method does just that. This function may look like it contains a lot of code, but most of it is repetitive. We need to get three color values—red, green, and blue—using the get method for that color in the paramValue object. Once we have a color value, the toHexString( ) method of the Integer class allows us to convert it to a string. If the hex value of the color is less than 0x10, then we also need to append a 0 to the beginning of the string value so that we'll end up with six numbers in the resulting string.

The getLabelForeColor( ) and getLabelBackColor( ) methods work much like you would expect. We get the required color, then convert it to a string using the colorToString( ) method. All we need to do then is display the color value as a string of three hex values: rrggbb (two digits of red, green, and blue each).

There's one last bit of coding we need to do and it would be easy to miss. You can use a WFC version of a Java applet as an ActiveX control. This means you could use the same applet on a Web page or within a Visual Basic application. The only thing you need to do to implement this functionality is remove a single comment from the lines of code shown here (the code is generated automatically for you by the wizard):

```
* This class can be used as an ActiveX control. Check the checkbox
* for this class on the Project Properties COM Classes tab, or
* remove the // from the next line:
* @com.register ( clsid=FCE40920-1D5E-11D2-B06E-0060975BF784,
* typelib=FCE40921-1D5E-11D2-B06E-0060975BF784 )
```

Publishing the ClockDisp Applet

We've already looked at the topic of publishing a control in Chapter 8. Make sure you spend some time reading through the detailed publishing information in that chapter before you go too much further in the book. We still need to publish our Visual J++ control if we want others to use it—control publication is one of the tenets of team development. The following procedure will help you publish the example control—it assumes that you already have Visual J++ open with the ClockDisp project loaded. (Remember that publishing a component allows other people to install it on their machine—you won't really do anything with the published control unless you need a fresh copy to work with.)

> **Note**   *The procedure for publishing controls is slightly different in each of the Visual Studio language products. This consistency problem can be very confusing, especially for new users of Visual Studio. Make absolutely certain that you understand what Visual Studio is asking for each time you publish a control to ensure the control gets published as intended.*

1. Choose the Tools | Publish Component | Project File(s)… command. You'll see the Visual Component Manager Publish Wizard - Introduction dialog box.

2. Click Next. You'll see a Visual Component Manager Publish Wizard - Select a Repository dialog box like the one shown here. This is where you select the location of the published component. For the purposes of this example, it doesn't matter if you use a local or remote repository, though a remote repository will allow you to access the component from more than one machine.

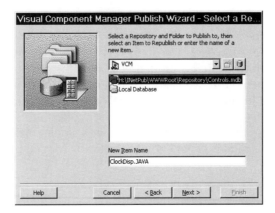

3. Double-click the repository you want to use. You'll see a list of publication locations within that repository.

4. Double-click on the Visual J++ folder, then again on the Applets folder. Placing ClockDisp in the Applets folder will allow other people to find it quickly.

5. Click next. You'll see the Visual Component Manager Publish Wizard - Title and Properties dialog box shown here. Notice that Visual Component Manager automatically fills in most of the essential information for you.

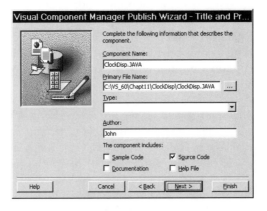

6. Choose Java Source in the Type field, then click Next. You'll see the Visual Component Manager Publish Wizard - More Properties dialog box shown here. This is where you'll type a control description and provide some keywords to make it easier for people to search for your control on the network.

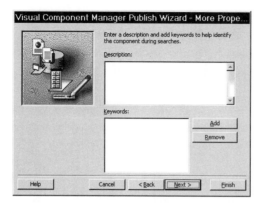

7. Type **This applet allows you to monitor the time in text format. It includes properties for setting the output color.** in the Description field.

8. Click Add. You'll see the Item Keywords dialog box. In the left pane is a list of keywords that already appear in the repository database. Since we've already published at least one component, there should be some keywords in the left pane. In the right pane is a list of keywords applied to this component.

9. Choose the Time and Automatic Update keywords, then click the right arrow if you performed the example in Chapter 8. These keywords will appear in the right pane. Otherwise, click the + (plus) key. You'll see the Add a Keyword dialog box. Type **Time**, then click OK. You'll see the word added to the right pane of the Item Keywords dialog box. Follow this same step for **Automatic Update**. You could add additional keywords as desired, but this should be sufficient for the example.

10. Click OK to close the Item Keywords dialog box. The list of keywords that you just typed will appear in the Keywords field of the Visual Component Manager Publish Wizard - More Properties dialog box.

11. Click Next. You'll see the Visual Component Manager Publish Wizard - Select Additional Files dialog box shown here. This is where you'd add any documentation, help, source code, or sample files for the control. The only file that the user will need in this case is the JAVA file shown.

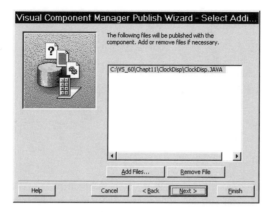

12. Click Finish. Visual Component Manager will create the required entries in the repository for you. You'll see a new entry in the repository.

Adding the ClockDisp Applet to the Sample Web Site

It's finally time to enhance our Web site using the ClockDisp applet. If you were going to use this applet throughout the project, it would be better if you had the design team create it before you create you initial Web page design. That way, you could incorporate the applet into the Layout.HTM file (found in the _Layouts\tp1 folder).

In this case, we're going to place our clock control on a single Web page—Default. HTM (Home page)—so that the users can see the time when they first access the site. The use of the PageNavbar control allows the user to get back to the Home page quickly, so it's not really necessary to add the clock to other pages.

The first thing you'll need to do is open Default.HTM. You'll also need to add the control to your toolbox. Here's where things are different than our previous Visual J++ applet example. In this case, you'll find the ClockDisp applet under the ActiveX Controls tab as ClockDisp.ClockDisp, as shown here:

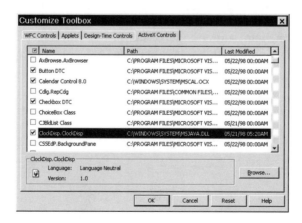

However, don't get the idea that ClockDisp is an independent ActiveX control. It still relies on Java classes. In fact, if you look at the Path column of the Customize Toolbox dialog box, you'll notice that ActiveX functionality is provided through MSJAVA.DLL, not through the applet itself. Using this applet on an intranet site means that you also need to provide the user with a copy of MSJAVA.DLL in addition to ClockDisp.JAVA.

Adding the control to our default Web page is easy. Select the Source tab of the Default.HTM window, place the cursor on the line after the <BODY> tag, then double-click the ClockDisp. Visual InterDev will add a new <OBJECT> tag for you. You'll need to set two properties for the applet, as shown here:

Property	Value
Width	120
Height	39

At this point, the updated Web page is ready to go. (If you were going to deploy this page in a production environment, you'd need to add values to the codebase and class properties.) The user will see a clock as shown in the upper-left corner of Figure 10-5.

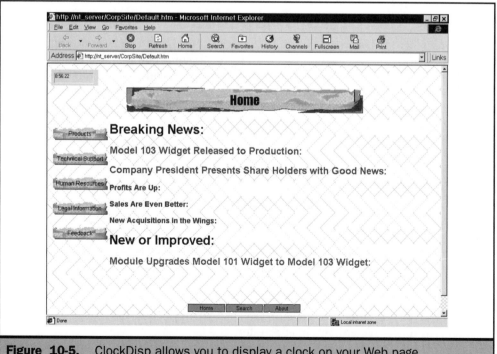

Figure 10-5.   ClockDisp allows you to display a clock on your Web page

Using ClockDisp Within Visual Basic

Remember that I mentioned in the previous section of this chapter that ClockDisp acts like an ActiveX control. The proof is in the fact that you can use ClockDisp within a Visual Basic application. That's right. By creating a WFC Java applet, you gain some extra flexibility in where you can use the applet within Windows. (You still lose the ability to use the applet on other platforms.)

Let's try ClockDisp with Visual Basic. Begin by opening Visual Basic. You'll see a New Project dialog box. Highlight the Standard EXE icon on the New tab and click Open. Visual Basic will create a new dialog-based application for you.

Now we need to add ClockDisp to the toolbox. Right-click the toolbox and choose Components… from the context menu. You'll see a Components dialog box. Look through the list and find ClockDisp (note that it's not called ClockDisp.ClockDisp in Visual Basic). Check the box next to ClockDisp and click OK. You should see the ClockDisp applet (actually an ActiveX control) added to your toolbox.

Double-click the ClockDisp icon in the toolbox to add it to your project form. Notice that the clock automatically starts to run. You'll also be able to change the labelForeColor and labelBackColor properties to change the colors in the label. Once you get done working with the Visual Basic project using ClockDisp, just close it—you won't need to save it for later use.

Creating the DHTML Application

The Web page we've designed is fully functional—you could view it in Internet Explorer and not experience any problems. However, some companies may not want to allow everyone to use a browser—they may want more control over how their employees view the data contained on an intranet or Internet site. That's where Dynamic Hypertext Markup Language (DHTML) applications come into play. This application allows you to see the content provided by an intranet or Internet site in a controlled environment. In most cases, this will allow you to enforce security while making the Web site easier for users to access.

Both Visual C++ and Visual Basic provide the means to access a Web site through a DHTML application. Of the two, Visual C++ provides the greater flexibility and ability to extend the usual definition of browser into nontraditional areas such as a help desk. Visual Basic has the advantage of allowing you to develop the application faster and with fewer lines of code than you'll need with Visual C++.

The next two sections will show you two examples of a DHTML application that you can use to display the sample Web site that we've created. The best reason for showing both languages is so that you can see the relative merits of each. In addition, since both languages produce about the same end result, you may find that you want to use your favorite language to develop the DHTML application to reduce any language learning curve you might encounter.

Using Visual C++

This section is going to show you how to create a very simple DHTML application using Visual C++. The whole purpose of this application is to show you that it's possible to create a fully customizable DHTML application with relative ease. Of course, the actual amount of coding you need to perform will increase as you ask the application to perform more work. (We'll look at a more complex DHTML application in Chapter 14, when we create a help desk setup.) The next two sections help you set up and enhance a Visual C++ DHTML application.

Setting Up the Visual C++ DHTML Application

Visual C++ does most of the hard work for you when it comes to creating a DHTML application. In fact, as the following procedure shows, there really is only one important setting you need to worry about—the base class for the document view. The following procedure will help you set up the Visual C++ version of the DHTML application.

1. Open the New dialog box using the File | New command. You'll see the New dialog box.

2. Highlight the MFC AppWizard (exe) icon on the Project tab. Type a name for your DHTML application (the example uses **Viewer1**).

3. Click OK. You'll see the MFC AppWizard - Step 1 dialog box. We don't need much document support for this application, but we do need to be able to display at least one document at a time.

4. Choose the Single document option, then click Next five times. You should see the MFC AppWizard - Step 6 dialog box. Notice that the Base class field has a drop-down list box where you can select a new base class to use for the document view. A browser relies on the CHtmlView class, not the CView class currently shown.

5. Click Finish. You'll see the New Project Information dialog box shown here:

If you compiled this application right now, you could use it to display Web pages, but you wouldn't see the custom page we developed earlier in the chapter. We need to make a few small changes to the code to provide this minimal functionality. In fact, all we really need to do is change one line in the OnInitialUpdate( ) function, as shown in bold type here:

```
void CViewer1View::OnInitialUpdate()
{
  CHtmlView::OnInitialUpdate();

  // TODO: This code navigates to a popular spot on the web.
  //  change the code to go where you'd like.

Navigate2(_T("http://nt_server/corpsite/Default.HTM"),NULL,NULL);
}
```

Compile and run the application. Figure 10-6 shows a typical example of what you'll see.

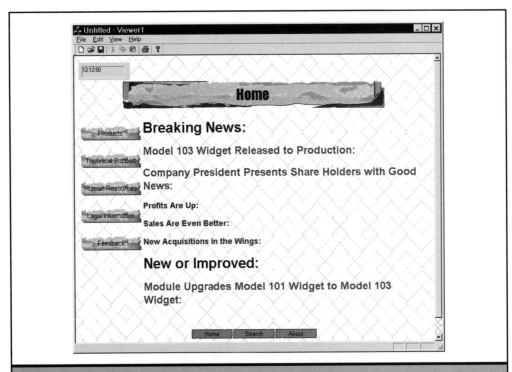

Figure 10-6.   Our custom browser displays the Web site that we created earlier

Enhancing the Visual C++ DHTML Application

Now that we have a basic browser built, let's talk about a few of the things you could do to enhance it. There are a number of ways to add functionality to this application, but one of the most important things you can do is add a method for getting back to the Home page quickly. It's frustrating for the user to have to go through endless Web pages looking for the Home page (especially if you haven't provided an address bar for entering URLs with the application).

Another important addition is an address bar. Our sample application comes without one, but adding one isn't hard. Of course, adding an address bar means that the user can enter any address and you lose a certain amount of application security unless you want to monitor those addresses on a case-by-case basis.

There's one enhancement that our application does need and that you should consider adding for most applications: the ability to move forward and backward through the history list. Even our sample browser maintains a history list. You can use this list to allow the user to go back and forth between the list of sites they have already visited.

Let's look at the process for adding a forward and backward capability to our sample application. The first thing you'll need to do is add two buttons to the IDR_MAINFRAME toolbar as shown here:

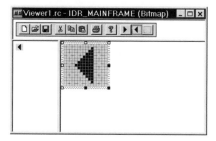

We also need to give our toolbar buttons some names. All you need to do is double-click a button to display its Toolbar Button Properties dialog box. I gave the first button an ID of ID_FORWARD and the second an ID of ID_BACKWARD. If you want, you can also fill the Prompt field with an appropriate prompt like "Go to the next Web site.\nGo Forward" for the forward button and "Go back to last Web site.\nGo Backward" for the backward button.

Now that we have buttons, we need to add functions to support them. CTRL-double-click on the forward button. You'll see the MFC ClassWizard dialog box. Visual C++ assumes that you want to add any new functions to the CMainFrame class, but that won't work in this case. Make sure you select the Viewer1View class in the Class name field. Visual C++ will automatically select the correct Object ID for you. All you need to do is choose Command in the Messages list and click Add Function. Accept the default settings for the function name. Now choose ID_BACKWARD in the Object ID list and Command in the Messages list. Click Add Function and accept the default function name. Click Edit Code and Visual C++ will take you to the new functions in the code. Listing 10-2 shows the code you'll need to add for this example.

Listing 10-2

```
void CViewer1View::OnForward()
{
    GoForward();

}

void CViewer1View::OnBackward()
{
    GoBack();

}
```

Lest you think I'm pulling your leg (especially those of you who have been working with Visual C++ for a long time), this really is all the code you need to make those buttons work. If you want to add menu entries as well, just give them the same ID values as the buttons and you won't need to add any additional code.

Obviously, there are a lot more interesting and harder to add features that you could add to this application. For example, we don't have a Favorites list right now and such a list might be very helpful with a help desk application (as we'll see in Chapter 14). It's important to brainstorm the various elements of your DHTML application and weigh the cost of security versus the features that users need.

Using Visual Basic

Visual Basic provides both more and less than Visual C++ does when it comes to creating a standard browser. For the most part, creating the application is easier, but you do have to get around a couple of assumptions that Microsoft made before you get a functional browser of the sort that we created in the previous section. (In all actuality, the Visual Basic version of the application will probably prove superior for most developers from the very outset.) The following procedure will help you set up a simple DHTML application using Visual Basic.

1. Open Visual Basic. You'll see the New tab of the New Projects dialog box.

2. Highlight the VB Application Wizard icon and click Open. You'll see the Application Wizard - Introduction dialog box.

3. Click Next. You'll see the VB Application Wizard - Interface Type dialog box. This is where you'll choose what type of view that Visual Basic will use.

4. Choose the Single Document Interface (SDI) option. You'll also need to give your project a name. The sample application uses **Viewer2**.

5. Click Next four times. You'll see the Application Wizard - Internet Connectivity dialog box shown here:

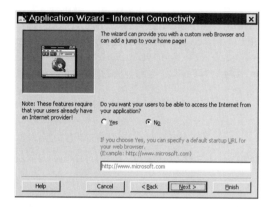

6. Choose the Yes option. We need to add Internet connectivity to this application. It's also important to type the URL for the CorpSite Web site that we created earlier in the chapter in the blank provided. The Application Wizard - Internet Connectivity dialog box will provide an example of how to type the URL.

7. Click Finish. Visual Basic will create the application for you, then display an Application Created dialog box.

8. Click OK to clear the Application Created dialog box.

At this point, the first problem we have should be evident. Visual Basic assumes that you want to display a main form first, then display the browser form. We want to display the browser form from the outset, so we need to make a couple of small changes. First, open Module1. Make sure the (General) object is selected and the Main procedure. You'll need to change the default code as shown in bold in Listing 10-3. The (Declarations) procedure also requires changes as shown in bold in Listing 10-3.

Listing 10-3

```
Public fMainForm As frmBrowser



Sub Main()
    Set fMainForm = New frmBrowser
    fMainForm.Show
End Sub
```

At this point, we no longer need frmMain. Right-click on frmMain in the Project window and choose Remove frmMain.frm from the Context menu. The form will disappear from the Project window (though it should still be on disk if you saved the project after creating it).

Our application still isn't ready to use. Even though we typed a starting address in the VB Application Wizard dialog box, Visual Basic hasn't added it to our application in a way that the application can use. Right-click frmBrowser in the Project window and choose View Code from the context menu. Choose Form from the Object list and Load from the procedure list. You'll need to initialize the StartingAddress variable as shown in bold in Listing 10-4.

Listing 10-4

```
Private Sub Form_Load()
    On Error Resume Next
    Me.Show
    tbToolBar.Refresh
    Form_Resize

    'Add a starting address.
    StartingAddress = "http://nt_server/corpsite/Default.htm"

    cboAddress.Move 50, lblAddress.Top + lblAddress.Height + 15

    If Len(StartingAddress) > 0 Then
        cboAddress.Text = StartingAddress
        cboAddress.AddItem cboAddress.Text
        'try to navigate to the starting address
        timTimer.Enabled = True
        brwWebBrowser.Navigate StartingAddress
    End If
End Sub
```

The program is now functional. Figure 10-7 shows what this browser variation looks like. Notice that Visual Basic automatically includes a Home button, along with both a Forward and Backward button. In fact, you may find that you need to remove some of this functionality for security reasons. For example, a user could use the Address field to navigate to a location on the Internet. In other words, Visual Basic assumes that you want to build a standard full-featured browser, so you'll definitely need to modify it in some situations.

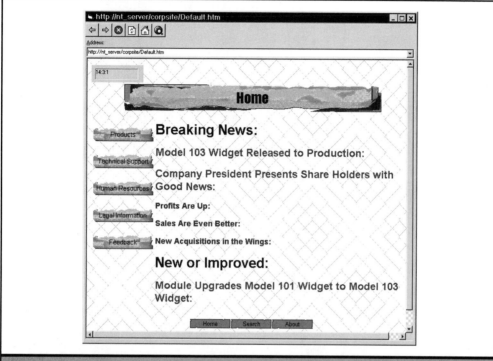

Figure 10-7. The Visual Basic version of a simple browser contains many features that the equivalent Visual C++ application doesn't

Lessons Learned

Developing Web content is becoming increasingly complex as vendors offer new capabilities in existing products and develop new ones. Users are becoming more aware of what the Web can do as well, which means that they expect more than simple text from a Web site in many cases. Finally, business expects a Web site to better service both employee and customer needs. In sum, whatever kind of Web site you plan to develop, you'll find that you need to use the latest technology to do it. The Internet is no longer a community of scientists sharing the latest information about a favorite research project—it has developed into a business tool that includes the local variant—intranets.

Determining what you want the user to see and how you want the user to access your Web site is an important part of the development process—something that you must do before you begin to design anything. You'll also want to think about the aesthetics of your Web site—what colors you want to use and how you plan to incorporate graphics or other multimedia. In addition, you need to plan for dynamic content and decide whether you want to use off-the-shelf components or design them yourself. Finally, you need to determine the application that you'll use to access the Web site. Many companies use browsers because they're inexpensive and require no development time. However, as more companies begin to use Web sites for employee-specific concerns such as a help desk, the need for a custom application designed to access the Internet in a specific way becomes more important.

We even looked at two languages that you can use to develop a DHTML application in this chapter—both languages have specific features that make them better suited to certain situations. Obviously, if your only concern is restricting access to the Internet and providing limited access to the company intranet, then Visual Basic is probably the best tool for the job since it offers the fastest development speed. On the other hand, Visual C++ becomes the best choice once you start needing to provide more flexibility in the application and a wider range of low-level controls (especially when it comes to managing the data stream between the client and server).

That leads us back to the use of custom controls. We looked at a Java applet that you could also use as an ActiveX control in this chapter. The idea of using one control for multiple environments isn't new, but using them in such diverse environments is. If you're used to grabbing for Visual Basic or Visual C++ every time you need to develop an ActiveX control, you may want to consider some of the alternatives. Certainly, Visual J++ offers some of the features of both Visual Basic and Visual C++ when it comes to developing ActiveX controls, but it can't really replace either. Every tool in Visual Studio has a niche where it fits into the whole picture, and it's important to realize that you can optimize team efforts by using the right tool in the right place.

Part IV

Internet Applications

Chapter 11

Enhanced Web Pages with
ActiveX

Web sites are a lot of different things to different people. Consider the most common use for a Web site: Information dissemination. Some people will look for short, concise bits of information that they can use to complete some task. If they find an endless labyrinth of information, even information that's related to the topic at hand, the first thing they're likely to do is press the Stop button on their browser. Other people do want that additional level of information. They may not know what questions to ask and the additional material is welcome because it helps them get the full picture without having to spend too much time thinking about the issues. Still other people want to see information in graphic, rather than text, format whenever possible. Trying to come up with a Web site design that will suit everyone's content format needs can be daunting to say the least.

Adding to the dilemma of what kind of content to present is the new question of how to present it. Component technology makes it possible for a browser to display content in more than just the static format used in ages past by Web sites. Now you can have various types of dynamic content on a Web site as well for the small cost of a little extra download time. Components can also take over tasks that are traditionally performed on the server. For example, order entry forms can really benefit from some type of component technology. You can provide the user with instant feedback about any calculations on the page—an application that traditionally relies on another trip to the server. Providing the user with the ability to get instant feedback from the form encourages "what if" analysis that may not normally take place. Of course, there are several schools of thought on the issue of component technology as well. Most people won't be willing to wait a long time for a component to download if all they need is the text content on the page. On the other hand, some people will wait for the entire page to download because they require the additional interaction provided by the various components on the Web page.

No matter how you look at it, though, there are some applications where you absolutely have to rely on component technology. Say you want to provide company-wide training on how to use some new software. An intranet site may provide the perfect venue for doing so if your company is in several locations. Component technology provides the multimedia and instant feedback capabilities required in such a case. You can create a Web page that looks every bit as good as a stand-alone application running on the user's machine. The Web site is actually better than the stand-alone application, though, because you can upgrade it as needed without worrying about old copies sitting on the user's machine. In addition, an intranet allows everyone in the company to participate as soon as the Web site becomes available. When writing a stand-alone application, you have to worry about how to package the application for distribution.

This chapter will help you understand how to use component technology—most notably an ActiveX control—on your Web site. The first few sections of the chapter will answer the question of what precisely an ActiveX control is. Microsoft has changed the terms it uses for various types of Component Object Model (COM) technology over the last few years, leaving some users of that technology confused. Even if these sections don't precisely reflect Microsoft's viewpoint of ActiveX at the time you read this, you'll at least know what ActiveX means in reference to the rest of the book.

Once we've gotten all of the theory about ActiveX out of the way, we'll use it to create an ActiveX control that you can use in a variety of situations, including a Web page. In this case, we'll create an ATL-based ActiveX control that provides the same functionality as the MFC-based ActiveX control, OCXExmpl, that we created in Chapter 4. One of the benefits of this example is that you'll get to see how two controls with the same functionality compare when created using one technique over the other.

Scenario

Web development efforts at your company have gotten bogged down in a mire of competing standards and old code. You begin to see a pattern of down time, lost documentation, and spaghetti code that demands attention. One of the few alternatives at your disposal is an incremental update of the code on your intranet site. As part of this effort, you decide to create a set of standardized components that everyone will use to reduce coding time and create a consistent look on the Web pages of your intranet site. In addition, these new components will provide a fully documented method of accomplishing specific tasks using a variety of programming languages.

There are three main tasks you want to perform to start the incremental upgrade. First, you'll want to get all of the development groups together. It's important to create a list of required controls and define their functionality before you begin the coding process. The only problem, in most cases, is that a Visual Basic developer will likely have very different requirements for a push button than a Visual J++ developer. Getting the teams together will help you derive a set of specifications that will work for everyone so that your controls are truly universal. In addition, you'll want to prioritize control development. Make sure that the controls that will be used by everyone get developed first so that everyone can become productive faster. Categorize controls by their difficulty in implementation and reliance on other controls as well so that you don't leave one control out of a set required to perform a specific high-priority task.

Second, you'll want part of the development team to begin work on a set of standardized components. The controls developers will start out working on a single control that can be tested later in a variety of environments by other teams. Obviously, you'll focus on the easiest high-priority control first so that you can establish procedures for control creation and testing. Using a simple control as the initial development project will also build team spirit and reduce the time required to show a successful implementation to management.

Third, you'll need to test the control in all of the programming environments currently supported by your company. It's important to test the controls as they are developed so that any potential problems can be uncovered quickly and you can modify any counterproductive trends in control development.

Unlike many of the other projects that we've looked at in the book so far, this one has a long development cycle and a constant maintenance cycle. In other words, you'll want to devote a lot of resources to get started, but then create a special team to keep all of the controls up-to-date as your company expands and grows.

 This chapter tells you how to create custom controls that do something out of the ordinary when compared to off-the-shelf controls. While it's nice to develop your own set of controls so that you know precisely how they'll work in a given circumstance, a single control can require a lot of development time. Always try to find an off-the-shelf component first that will perform the task for you. Then, if there are no commercially created components to do the job, you can resort to custom component creation.

What Is an ActiveX Control?

There's been a lot of confusion about ActiveX controls in the past, and part of the problem stems from Microsoft's continuing redefinition of all terms related to COM. The following sections are designed to help you gain a fuller appreciation of precisely what ActiveX is and how it relates to COM as a whole. We'll define what an ActiveX control is, and more importantly, what it isn't (at least in terms of ActiveX in this book).

 Microsoft has introduced a plethora of new OLE-related technologies like ActiveX and COM+ over the past few years. Trying to keep up with these technologies could prove daunting for even the best programmer. Microsoft's view of technologies like COM+ and DCOM appears at http://www.microsoft.com/com/. If you'd like some help from fellow programmers, check out the microsoft.public.activex newsgroup folder. This folder contains a wealth of newsgroups you can join to get various kinds of COM help, though they do specialize in ActiveX support. A great place to learn about the use of ActiveX on the Internet using current browser technology is the microsoft.public.inetexplorer.ie4.activex_ contrl newsgroup. There are also a lot of component newsgroups spread throughout the Microsoft news server like those in the microsoft.public.inetsdk.programming.components newsgroup folder.

It's easier to divide the discussion of ActiveX into two parts. The first section that follows will help you understand what an ActiveX control is and how it compares to older technology like OCX. The second section will help you understand how ActiveX can help you personally. It helps you understand that ActiveX is a very important part of an overall application development strategy, but that it can't fix every problem that you'll ever encounter.

What Is ActiveX?

Here's the simplest definition of ActiveX you'll ever find. ActiveX is an advanced form of OCX (maybe a simpler form of OLE is a better way to look at it). However, this simple definition doesn't even begin to scratch the surface of what you'll actually find under the hood of an ActiveX control. OLE is the user's view of ActiveX. For the programmer, ActiveX is also a set of enabling technologies for the Internet. It provides a method you didn't have in the past for exchanging information.

> **Note**   *Microsoft is currently working on a new Internet-specific component technology named COM+. ActiveX was never widely adopted on the Internet, though many intranets use it and ActiveX controls will always be used as application components. There were three reasons for the failure of ActiveX on the Internet: component size, security concerns, and lack of non-Microsoft browser compatibility. With this in mind, you should probably consider ActiveX controls as solutions for your company's internal use and not as an enabling technology for the Internet.*

To really appreciate ActiveX as a programmer, you have to look at OLE from the programmer's perspective, and that means looking at OCXs. From the user's perspective, all that an OCX does is exchange data between two applications (or between the operating system and an application). OCXs are a lot more than just data exchange. They include an idea called the *Component Object Model* (COM). COM is a specification that defines a standard binary interface between object modules. This interface defines a function-calling methodology, standard structure-based data-passing techniques, and even a few standard function calls. Using COM means that it doesn't matter which language you use to write an application module such as an OCX; the interface for that module is the same at the binary level.

> **Note**   *At the time of this writing, Microsoft was working on WebView, an integration technology between Internet Explorer and Windows 95's system Explorer. This new technology will make Web sites as easy to access as the drives and other resources listed in Explorer right now. You'll also see plain English names in place of the more familiar URLs that you need to know now. The first place you'll see this technology in action is in Windows 98.*

So, how does COM affect applications you write? The answer is fairly complex because of the number of ways in which COM gets used, not because the technology itself is so overwhelming. When a user places a graphic image object within a container controlled by your application, what do you know about that object? The only thing you really know about it is who created it in the first place. Knowing this information allows you to call on that application for a variety of services, such as displaying the graphic or allowing the user to edit it. In reality, what you're doing is sharing that application's code.

Programmers benefit from using COM as well. When you install an OCX into your programming environment, what have you really accomplished? In most cases, you have a new control that you stick on a form somewhere. You really don't need to know about the control's inner workings. The only important factors are what the control will do for your application and how you interact with it. Again, you're calling a particular module of code installed on your machine using a standard interface—that's what COM is all about.

ActiveX is an extension of this idea. You're still using a standard interface. However, instead of simply calling that code from the local machine environment or over the persistent connection of a LAN/WAN, you'll call it from the Internet. In addition, this new code can take the form of applets or mini-applications.

The one thing you have to understand about ActiveX is that it's only part of COM—it's not the whole picture. ActiveX controls are in-process servers. This means that ActiveX relies on the client application for a container in which to store itself and that it has no application-specific capabilities of its own from a traditional perspective. ActiveX controls are essentially DLLs with very special capabilities that are not designed for stand-alone use. The fact that an ActiveX control is an in-process sever means that it relies on the client's address space for resources like memory and that an errant ActiveX control can crash the entire application. There's a wealth of other types of COM component types, like the ActiveDocument (previously known as ActiveX Document) applications we'll look at in Chapter 13, that are designed for stand-alone use.

What Will ActiveX Do for You?

ActiveX will do for the Internet what OCXs have done for the desktop. However, you'll find ActiveX controls in places that you hadn't really thought about in the past. For example, NetManage, Inc. plans to create a new email client called Z-Mail Pro. This package supports ActiveX technology in a way that allows users to exchange, create, and view HTML documents directly in the message-viewing window. What this means to users is that they now have the ability to create dynamic Web pages, something that you have to really work at today.

Remote connections will also benefit from the use of ActiveX. For example, Proginet Corporation is currently working on ActiveX technology that will bring mainframe data to the desktop. Their Fusion file transfer management system (FTMS) will work with any development language that supports OLE containers, such as Delphi, Visual C++, and PowerBuilder. Essentially, you'll place an ActiveX control on a form, define where to find the data, and then rely on the control to make the connection. No longer will remote access over the Internet require the user to jump through hoops. A special transfer server on the mainframe will complete the package by automating all transfer requests. No longer will an operator have to manually download a needed file to the company's Web site before a client can access it.

Even Microsoft Exchange will benefit from ActiveX. Wang Laboratories, Inc. and other companies are creating new add-ons that mix Exchange and ActiveX together. Wang's product is a client/server imaging add-on. It'll allow users to scan, view, annotate, manipulate, or print graphic images no matter where they are located. This same product will include a hierarchical storage management ActiveX control. The two technologies will work together to make graphics easier to access and use in a large company. They'll also make it easier to find a needed graphic—which should ultimately result in a storage savings to the company.

Microsoft itself has issued a whole slew of ActiveX controls. Some of these controls are free for downloading from their Internet site (http://www.microsoft.com). Examples of these new controls include Animation Player for PowerPoint and Internet Assistant for both Access and Schedule+. The Internet Assistant for Access will create a snapshot of a database table that gets uploaded as a static image. The snapshot automatically updates every time the user accesses the page. The Internet Assistant for Schedule+ will allow you to upload scheduling information to a Web page. Since the data gets updated every time a user accesses the site, you no longer have to worry about compute-at-home employees missing meetings. Finally, the PowerPoint Animation Player will allow you to play a PowerPoint presentation from within any ActiveX-compliant browser.

Tip   *Even if an ActiveX control is available for performing a certain task, the data transfer rate determines whether the ActiveX control will work as anticipated. In other words, don't expect PowerPoint presentations to work well over a 33.6 Kbps connection, even if you have a great ActiveX control to play it with. Make sure that you take the data transfer rate and capabilities of the client machine into account before using an ActiveX control to accomplish a given task.*

Finally, if you think ActiveX won't help with security, think again. A lot of new firewall and certificate strategies are making the rounds these days. One of them is Net2000. It's a set of APIs that will allow developers to tie NetWare core services (including directory, security, and licensing) into their applications. You'll be able to tap this API through ActiveX controls over an intranet. How will this help users and developers alike? It means that with the proper programming constructs, a network administrator will be able to track license usage throughout the entire network, even across Internet connections. This is going to become a much bigger issue as more people begin to compute from home rather than the office.

Deciding When to Use an ActiveX Control

As previously mentioned, ActiveX isn't always the technology of choice. There are times when you may want an out-of-process server solution like ActiveDocument. In other cases, another form of object technology like a Java applet may be the best choice. One of the more important things you can determine before you even begin an ActiveX control project is whether it's even the right choice for you.

The following sections will answer two questions when it comes to ActiveX control usage. First, we'll look at how ActiveX compares to an older technology like OCX. Second, we'll compare ActiveX control development environments: MFC versus ATL.

There are a lot of ways to create an ActiveX control other than using Visual C++. Both Visual Basic and Visual J++ will allow you to create ActiveX controls. In fact, there are times when using one of these languages may be a plus, especially if you don't know how to use Visual C++ and development time is a factor. The main reasons for using Visual C++ to create your ActiveX controls are the size of the final control (Visual C++ produces the smallest controls), speed of execution (Visual C++ also produces the fastest controls), and packaging (the ATL version of ActiveX controls are self-contained). Check out the ClockDisp control in Chapter 9 if you want to see the Visual J++ version of ActiveX.

ActiveX vs. OCX Controls

For the most part, ActiveX and OCX controls are totally interchangeable. You'll see ads for ActiveX controls that have nothing to do with the Internet. Look a little closer, and you'll find that those controls probably appeared in an OCX listing sometime in the not-too-distant past. Of course, you'll have to watch these ads carefully. An ActiveX control isn't the same thing as an OCX—even if they do share the same heritage. Remember that an ActiveX control has to be able to work with the Internet.

The Internet places some special challenges on the programming environment. For one thing, you don't have the luxury of high-speed loading anymore. The size of an OCX becomes a critical issue when used within the Internet environment. Downloading a 60KB OCX may test a user's patience—trying to download a 200KB OCX will probably result in the user stopping the download altogether. ActiveX controls are small versions of OCXs.

ActiveX controls also suffer from various machine-specific requirements. When you install an OCX on your machine, the installation program can check the machine and make allowances as needed. The same can't be said about an ActiveX control. You can't assume anything about the client machine at all. It could be anything from a new Pentium to yesterday's 80386. (If your ActiveX control does have some kind of platform limitation, you'll have to either find some way to work around it or make certain that everyone who uses it knows about the limitation.)

You'll also need to deal with some situations that an OCX programmer would never have to think about. For one thing, what happens if the browser doesn't support ActiveX at all? The current method of dealing with this is that the browser would simply ignore any HTML tags that it doesn't know how to work with. Dealing with a browser that is non-ActiveX-compliant is easy in this case—just leave a message telling the user the browser won't work with the current page, and direct the user to an alternative.

MFC- vs. ATL-Based Controls

One of the ways that Visual C++ shows its robust development environment when compared to other programming languages is the inclusion of two ways to create ActiveX controls: MFC or ATL. Unfortunately, this flexibility can cause some problems that other developers don't have to face. For one thing, how do you determine which type of control to create? Some developers have rendered the question moot by using the same technology for all their controls, but following this route means that you haven't really explored and used Visual C++ to its full potential.

There really isn't any way to say definitively that one method of creating a control is better in a given situation. What you really need to do is define what you expect the control to do, what you're willing to invest to get that functionality, and your level of expertise. Obviously, there are situations where one control creation method is preferred over another, because the two methods do have distinctly different advantages and disadvantages. To give you some idea of what you need to consider when looking at an ATL ActiveX control versus one created using MFC, read through the following list. What you'll find are ideas that you can use to help you make a decision on which route is best for you.

- **Development speed**   Using the MFC ActiveX Control Wizard is the fastest method to create a control. The wizard takes care of most of the interface details so that what you end up with is a skeleton that's ready for some control logic. In fact, it usually takes the developers twice as long to use the ATL method for creating a control. Obviously, your results will vary depending on factors like control complexity and your programming experience.

- **Control size**   If you want to create the smallest possible ActiveX control, then go the ATL route. ATL gives you full control over every aspect of the control and makes it feasible for you to hand-tune every control element without getting bogged down in MFC-specific code. Not only are MFC-based controls larger, but remember that the client may also have to download the MFC libraries before they can use the control, which is a significant amount of code.

- **Learning curve**   ATL controls are much harder to create than MFC controls simply because you have to consider more things like interfaces. In most cases, it pays to create your first couple of controls using the MFC ActiveX Control Wizard so that you can learn the ropes of creating the control logic.

Tip   *If you're used to the Visual C++ version 5.0 ATL support, try the new ATL COM AppWizard in version 6.0. The new ATL COM AppWizard helps you create controls much faster than the manual techniques of the past. However, using the MFC ActiveX Control Wizard is still far faster than using the ATL COM AppWizard to create a control.*

- **Compatibility**   By definition, MFC-based ActiveX controls require the client to have the MFC libraries installed on their machine. However, there are more than a few versions of those libraries floating around and they aren't all compatible. What happens when a user downloads your control and the associated libraries, then can't use an important application because the new libraries are incompatible with their application? Since the MFC libraries are stored in the SYSTEM directory, a client machine can only have one version. That's where the compatibility problems come into play.

■ **Ease of use**   The MFC ActiveX Control Wizard tends to throw everything but the kitchen sink into a control because it assumes nothing about your ability to write control code. What this means is that you end up with a wealth of interfaces you may not need or use. All of this wasted functionality bloats the size of the control and makes it harder to use.

■ **Ease of code modification**   Creating an MFC-based control is very easy the first time around. Since the wizard adds much of the code for your application, development goes quickly. However, what happens when you decide to update that control? Now you have source files that may contain a good deal of code that wasn't written by a staff programmer and that may require additional time to research and understand.

To get a better idea of how MFC and ATL versions of the same control compare, let's compare the OCXExmpl control in Chapter 4 to the OnOffButton control in this chapter. Both controls provide similar functionality and features, including things like the property page and events. First the coding part of the picture. It took nearly three times longer to create the ATL version of the control in this chapter compared to the MFC version in Chapter 4. Not only that, but a quick look at all the code required to create the control in this chapter should tell you something about development time for an ATL-based control. The ATL-based control itself is also slightly larger at 68KB when compared to the MFC-based version at 36KB. However, appearances can be deceiving. Figure 11-1 shows the Dependency Walker views for both controls. Notice that the

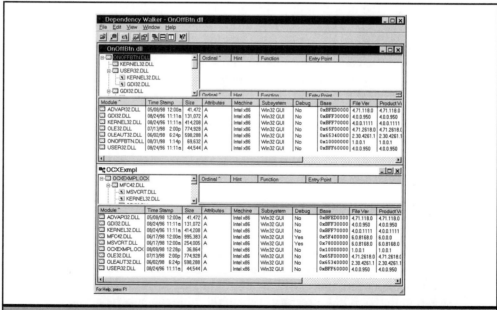

Figure 11-1.   ATL-based ActiveX controls are self-contained; the MFC-based control requires support files

MFC-based control requires two additional support files: MFC42.DLL and MSVCRT.DLL, both of which are quite large. If you can be absolutely certain that the user will have the correct version of both of these support files, then the MFC-based ActiveX control is actually a better way to go from several standpoints. However, it's easy to see why some Internet developers are a little less than thrilled about using anything other than ATL to develop their ActiveX controls.

Understanding the Required Interfaces

All COM components use interfaces. At its core, an interface is nothing more than an array of pointers to the methods provided by your ActiveX control or other COM components. An interface provides a reliable, language-independent method for accessing your control. You'll use interfaces to provide every piece of information about your ActiveX control, even the properties that it supports. Using interfaces allows anyone to use an ActiveX control and ensures that the control itself remains safe from the vagaries of data corruption (if the interface is created correctly and the control adheres to Microsoft specifications).

Interfaces also encompass the idea of standardized access. Microsoft publishes standards that allow everyone who creates an ActiveX control to create something that everyone can use. These standards enforce the idea that the interface will follow a specific set of rules when providing information about the control that it supports. So, at a higher level, an interface is also a standard—an ideology about how things should work.

No matter how you view interfaces, they are a fact of life for anyone who creates ActiveX controls. You must create specific interfaces that do certain things for the control to work properly in all environments. That's what the next three sections are all about. We'll begin by looking at the common interface that every component will require, IUnknown. This particular interface is the starting point for all communication with your control. However, it doesn't take long to figure out that IUnknown is very limited. You need other interfaces to provide a robust control that everyone can use. The next two sections look at common interfaces for ActiveX controls and ActiveDocument applications. You'll learn how interfaces work in real life and, potentially, how you can use them for your own benefit when creating your own controls.

IUnknown, the Generic Interface for Everyone

Working with COM components is all about communication of some type. You want to create some code that is easy to reuse because it can communicate with the client using it and adapt, if necessary. ActiveX control communication consists of a client, a server, and an interpreter named COMPOBJ.DLL between them. Essentially, these three objects are the basis of what we'll discuss throughout the book because they encompass the three objects that most people work with.

That's not all there is to know about the communication, though—an ActiveX control needs to provide a standard interface to make it useful. When an application instantiates a copy of an ActiveX control (the component object), it receives a pointer to a list of functions. That list of functions is housed in what's termed an interface. To make it easier for you to understand what an interface is (at least in the context of an ActiveX control), think of it as a set of semantically related functions implemented as part of a component object. You'll normally see an interface as an array of functions defined in the OLE 2 headers for your programming language.

An interface can perform a variety of tasks. For example, you might add a data operation interface like GetData or SetData. The more complex an ActiveX control, the more interfaces it requires to perform its task.

There's one interface called IUnknown that every ActiveX control must provide. It's the basis of all other interfaces—every other interface inherits from this basic interface. This is the interface that gets passed back to your application when you instantiate a copy of the control as a component object. Within this interface (and every other interface supported by an ActiveX control) are the three function calls listed here:

- **QueryInterface( )**   This function allows the application to determine what interfaces the object supports. If the application queries an interface and the ActiveX control supports it, the application receives an array of pointers to the functions supported by the interface. Otherwise, the application receives a null pointer.

- **AddRef( )**   This function creates a new relationship to a component object interface. Using this function creates another pointer to the array of function pointers supported by the interface. A component object maintains a reference count of the number of relationships that it has established. The component object only gets unloaded from memory when the reference count is 0.

- **Release( )**   This function allows you to destroy the relationship between an application and an ActiveX control. It decreases the reference count by 1. If the component object's reference count is 0, then this function call also requests the destruction of the component object.

The presence of IUnknown means that your application can communicate with any component object it encounters. If your application recognizes the interfaces that the component object supports, it can communicate with that object at a fairly high level. For example, an ActiveX control provides very specific interfaces that your programming environment will know about if it supports them. If your application only recognizes a few of the interfaces, it still might be able to communicate with the component object, but at a much lower level.

There are a lot of interfaces that the OLE 2 specification already supports for specific kinds of component objects. The Microsoft OLE 2 SDK provides a full synopsis of all of these component object types and the interfaces that they're required to support. We'll also cover a few of the ActiveX-specific requirements throughout this book. However, just because Microsoft hasn't defined a particular interface doesn't mean that you can't define it yourself. The specifications we'll talk about throughout this book and those that you'll learn from other sources are the minimum interfaces that you can implement. Nothing says that you can't implement more interfaces, then publish an API that tells how to use them. That's the beauty of using COM—you can extend it as needed to meet specific requirements.

ActiveX Control Required Interfaces

Visual C++ supports a variety of ActiveX control types, everything from a full control to one that's optimized for working with Internet Explorer alone. The interfaces you need to provide for the component to work with a specific environment depends a great deal on the environment itself. With that in mind, we'll look not only at required interfaces in this section, but also at the interfaces required to work in a specific environment. Table 11-1 provides a comparison of various ActiveX control environments and the interfaces they require. Note the special I<Class> entry in the list. This particular interface is different for every component because it contains the elements specific to that component, including both methods and properties.

Interface	Full	Lite	Composite[1]	HTML	Lite Composite[1]	Lite HTML
I<Class>	✓	✓	✓	✓	✓	✓
IDispatch	✓	✓	✓	✓[2]	✓	✓[2]
IPersistStreamInit	✓	✓	✓	✓	✓	✓
IOleControl	✓	✓	✓	✓	✓	✓
IOleObject	✓	✓	✓	✓	✓	✓
IOleInPlaceActivateObject	✓	✓	✓	✓	✓	✓
IViewObjectEX, IViewObject2, IViewObject	✓	✓	✓	✓	✓	✓
IOleInPlaceObject-Windowless	✓	✓	✓	✓	✓	✓
IPersistStorage	✓		✓	✓		

Table 11-1. Interface Support Required for Various ActiveX Control Types

Interface	Full	Lite	Composite[1]	HTML	Lite Composite[1]	Lite HTML
IQuickActivate	✓		✓	✓		
IDataObject	✓		✓	✓		
IProvideClassInfo, IProvideClassInfo2	✓		✓	✓		

Table 11-1.   Interface Support Required for Various ActiveX Control Types (continued)

[1]Based on CComCompositeControl class instead of CComControl class. The CComCompositeControl class allows the control to contain other Windows controls and to host multiple controls in a single control.

[2]Implements two IDispatch interfaces. The first interface interacts with the control itself. The second interface is designed to handle user interface events, methods, and properties. The second interface includes one default method, OnClick( ).

Note   *There are many other interfaces that ActiveX controls have to support to obtain certain levels of functionality. For example, if you want to support events in your ActiveX control, then you'll need to provide an IConnectionPointContainer interface. There are some cases when you'd need to provide interfaces in addition to the one that you want to support. For example, the IConnectionPointContainer interface also requires you to implement the IEnumConnectionPoints, IConnectionPoint, and IEnumConnections interfaces. Another common supplementary interface is ISpecifyPropertyPages, which tells the container application that your control includes at least one property page. The property page itself will need to support the IPropertyPage or IPropertyPage2 interface.*

Now that you have a little better idea of which interfaces are required where, let's talk a little about what those interfaces are for. The following list provides a brief description of each major ActiveX control interface.

- **IDataObject**   This interface defines everything needed to transfer information between two objects, including the data format and the method used to transfer the information. If there's more than one format that the data can appear in, this interface will provide an enumerated list of available formats. This is also the interface that provides information about data rendered for a specific device (making it unsuitable for devices that don't conform to a specific standard).

- **IDispatch**   There are two methods for accessing the methods and properties provided by an ActiveX control. IDispatch provides an indirect method that relies on a type library for implementation purposes. This interface is always used as part of a dual-interface control. A dual interface isn't necessarily a requirement by Microsoft standard. However, most developers implement a dual interface today to allow their control to work with more than just the language that it was developed in. IDispatch is a late bound interface.

■ **IPersistStreamInit**   Making sure that a control's data remains intact between uses is important (otherwise you'd have to reconfigure your applications every time you used them). You'll use this interface to make sure that any stream data required by your control is persistent or saved between sessions. This is a replacement for the older IPersistStream interface. The main difference between the two interfaces is that IPersistStreamInit also includes initialization code in the form of the InitNew( ) method, which initializes a control to a default state.

■ **IOleControl**   Communication is key with ActiveX controls. The overall purpose of this interface is control communication between the client and server. The normal purpose of this interface is to provide keyboard information. For example, a client could ask about the control's keyboard behavior and whether it provides full or partial support for control key combinations.

■ **IOleObject**   This is the most essential of all interfaces for an ActiveX control since it provides both basic control functionality and communication features. Along with this interface, a control must provide support for both IDataObject and IPersistStorage for every embedded object that it supports. IOleObject contains a wide variety of methods designed to enhance control functionality. There's a minimum of 21 interface-specific methods along with the 3 standard methods (QueryInterface( ), AddRef( ), and Release( )) for a total of 24 methods in a standard IOleObject interface. Of the 21 interface specific methods, 6 can be ignored by returning E_NOTIMPL (error not implemented) if you don't require the functionality they provide: SetExtent( ), InitFromData( ), GetClipboardData( ), SetColorScheme( ), SetMoniker( ), and GetMoniker( ). Three of the methods—DoVerb( ), Close( ), and SetHostNames( )—require a full control specific implementation.

■ **IOleInPlaceActivateObject**   Some types of ActiveX controls require a method for communicating with the container frame and documents. Normally, you'll find this interface used when a control needs to support MDI or other complex application environments. This particular interface allows visual editing of the control in certain application types like a programming language IDE.

■ **IViewObjectEx, IViewObject2, and IViewObject**   All three of these interfaces have one thing in common: they allow the ActiveX control a certain measure of autonomy in displaying itself without passing a data object to the container. Not only does this speed up the drawing of the control, but it ensures there's a minimum of drawing problems. The caller can request specific types of drawing features. For example, it can choose between a full or iconic display of the object. The IViewObject2 improves on IViewObject by returning the size of the drawing required to represent the object when using a specific presentation. You would normally use this interface when working with compound document containers. The IViewObjectEx interface includes all of the features of IViewObject2. It improves on IViewObject2 by adding flicker-free drawing for nonrectangular objects, hit testing for nonrectangular objects, and control sizing. You would use this interface to implement irregularly shaped controls.

- **IOleInPlaceObjectWindowless** Use this interface to allow a windowless control to receive window messages and to participate in drag-and-drop operations.

- **IPersistStorage** Storing your data objects from one session to the next is an important part of making the control react the same way each time you use it. This interface provides a structured storage medium where each object has its own storage area within the container's storage medium. You must implement this interface along with IOleObject and IDataObject to make the control work within an embedded environment.

- **IQuickActivate** Performance is often a factor when working with ActiveX controls, especially if the user has already spent time waiting for the control to download from the Internet. This interface allows the control and container to combine load-time or initialization-time handshaking into a single call, greatly improving control performance.

- **IDataObject** This interface works with the control's data. It allows the container and client to exchange information and also provides the means for one object to notify the other of data changes. The data transfer methods supported by this interface allow objects to specify the format of the data or enumerate the available data formats. The client can also specify that data is rendered for a specific device.

- **IProvideClassInfo and IProvideClassInfo2** Use this interface to access a control's coclass entry in its type library. The IProvideClassInfo2 interface is simply a faster version of the IProvideClassInfo interface. It also provides an ancillary method, GetGUID, which returns the object's outgoing IID for its default event set.

ActiveDocument Required Interfaces

There's actually an easy way of looking at the OLE interface functions required to create ActiveDocuments. In fact, we can summarize the functionality of an ActiveDocument using what you've learned so far in the book as a basis for understanding. If you want your application to support this specification, it has to perform the four steps listed here:

- **Implement IPersistStorage** Your application must support this class and associated methods so that it can use OLE compound files as a storage medium.

- **Support OLE document embedding features** This particular feature is implemented in many different ways. The current trend is toward providing the user with two embedding methods through menu functions: Insert Object and Paste Special. The functions used to do this are IPersistFile, IOleObject, and IDataObject.

- **Provide in-place activation support**   There are two interfaces that you need to implement in order to support in-place activation: IOleInPlaceObject and IOleInPlaceActivateObject. To implement these classes, you'll have to gather information about the container using methods provided by the IOleInPlaceSite and IOleInPlaceFrame classes.

- **Add the ActiveDocument extensions**   Most OLE 2 servers perform the first three steps right now. To make them work on the Internet, you have to add the four functions we'll discuss in this section.

Let's talk about the fourth item on this list in greater detail. ActiveDocuments are fairly new in some ways. Since Microsoft kept the specification for them a secret for so long, few compilers out there provide direct support for an ActiveDocument server. What this means to you, as a programmer, is that you'll either have to build the added interfaces yourself (not really too difficult) or upgrade your compiler. What we'll look at in the next four sections are the four added interface calls that you'll have to support in order to create a fully functional ActiveDocument server. (Fortunately, they aren't all required. For example, Microsoft Excel only implements three of them.) The good news is that the ActiveX SDK provides the header and other support files needed to create these interface elements. We'll take a look at those in this section as well.

> **Note**   *Microsoft Visual C++ versions 4.2 and above include direct support for creating most ActiveX object types, including ActiveDocument. If you have an older version of Visual C++, it's definitely time for an upgrade. The newer versions of Visual C++ will literally build all of the elements we'll talk about in this section for you—reducing the time it will take for you to create your new control or application.*

IOleDocument

Whenever an Internet client sees a server that implements the IOleDocument class, it knows that the server can act as an ActiveDocument server. This is the first thing that Internet Explorer and other Internet client applications will look for when they see a document that's associated with your application. Don't confuse standard in-place activation with the kind used by an ActiveDocument server. You can build an application that supports in-place activation alone and it'll work fine on a local machine, but it won't support in-place activation over the Internet.

> **Note**   *In many cases, it doesn't matter if you implement this interface—you can still support OLE 2 without it. A server that's missing this interface will simply be opened in a separate window, even if it normally supports in-place activation with local clients like Word for Windows.*

So, what does this class do besides telling Internet Explorer that your application supports ActiveDocuments? The methods it supports get called every time the client needs to create new server views (CreateView( ) method), enumerate those views

(EnumViews( ) method), or retrieve the MiscStatus bits associated with the ActiveDocument (GetDocMiscStatus( ) method). In essence, this class helps you manage the server as a whole. It provides the low-level functionality required for the client and server to communicate.

A server view isn't the same thing as the view that the user sees when they click on a link to one of your documents—that's managed by the IOleDocumentView function we'll talk about in the next section. What a server view provides is a single instance of the server itself. A client application uses this view for communication purposes. For example, if the client needs to find out what features the server supports, it would use a server view to do so. We'll see how this works when we get into the actual application code.

There are four standard miscellaneous status bits. The first bit, DOCMISC_CANCREATEMULTIPLEVIEWS, tells the client whether the server can create multiple views. In other words, this bit defines whether you can run multiple copies of the application at one time. In most cases, a modern server can do this. About the only exceptions are for CAD or drawing programs where the memory requirements might be too prohibitive. Another class of application that may not support this is a communications program, since most people only have one modem. The second bit, DOCMISC_SUPPORTCOMPLEXRECTANGLES, tells whether the server can support complex view area commands. An example is whether or not the server will allow the client to determine the position of things like scroll bars and sizing boxes. The third bit, DOCMISC_CANOPENEDIT, is used to tell the client whether the server can open a document for editing. Setting this bit prevents the user from editing a document online (something you may want to consider for security reasons, or if you want to create a server for viewing purposes only). The final bit, DOCMISC_NOFILESUPPORT, tells whether the server supports any kind of file manipulation. Setting this bit usually forces the client to display an error message since the user won't even be able to read the selected file.

IOleDocumentView

Like the IOleDocument class, you must implement IOleDocumentView to make ActiveDocument work. This particular interface element is reliant on the IOleDocument class. You need to have a server running before you can open a document. In addition, the client relies on information it gets from the GetDocMiscStatus( ) method of IOleDocument to know how to interact with this class. Each copy of the IOleDocumentView class controls a single instance of an ActiveDocument view. In most cases, this means that the single instance of the IOleDocumentView class controls a single document. However, you could just as easily create one instance of the class for each view of the single document you have opened.

The IOleDocumentView class supports a variety of methods. Table 11-2 lists the most common methods that you'll find. As you can see, the methods allow you to resize the screen or create another copy of the view that you're looking at. Some of the other methods allow you to reset the view's bounding area or determine which document is currently displaying within the view.

Method	Description
SetInPlaceSite( )	Associates a view site object with this view. The client supplies the view site object. In essence, this is the method that will associate a document with the current view.
GetInPlaceSite( )	Returns a pointer to the view site object associated with the view.
GetDocument( )	Returns a pointer to the document associated with the view.
SetRect( )	Defines the bounding area for the view. In other words, this method sets the size of the window that the user will see.
GetRect( )	Returns the coordinates for the view's bounding area.
SetRectComplex( )	Defines a complex bounding area for the view. Not only does this method determine the size of the window the user will see, but things like the placement of scroll bars and other view elements. A view doesn't have to support this feature. You do need to set a miscellaneous status bit if your application doesn't provide the support. (See the IOleDocument class description for more details.)
Show( )	The client can use this method to either show or hide the view.
UIActivate( )	Determines whether the user interface is active or not. Normally, the user interface is only active when the view has the focus. It's normally deactivated at all other times to prevent conflicts with the view that does have focus.
Open( )	Requests that the server open the view in a separate window. You can turn off this feature using a miscellaneous status bit. (See the IOleDocument class description for more details.)
CloseView( )	Shuts the view down.
SaveViewState( )	Writes the current view status information to an IStream.
ApplyViewState( )	Requests that a view return its state to the settings defined in a previously saved IStream.
Clone( )	Creates a copy of the current view. The cloned view will have the same context, but use a different view port (instance of the IOleDocumentView class).

Table 11-2.   Methods Associated with the IOleDocumentView Class

IOleCommandTarget

This is one of the classes you don't have to implement to make ActiveDocument work. However, it's a lot more than a simple convenience item. IOleCommandTarget allows the client and server to talk with each other without resorting to tricks like assigning fixed-menu IDs. Of course, there are limitations to this communication. For one thing, the communication is still limited to a fixed number of commands (which we'll talk about a little further down). There's a two-step procedure required to make this part of the interface work.

The first part of the client-to-server communication is to find out what commands the server supports. The client does this using the Query( ) method. Table 11-3 provides a complete list of the commands that the server can support along with their associated identifiers. The first thing you should notice is that most of the commands are standard menu entries.

Command	Identifier
Edit Clear	OLECMDID_CLEARSELECTION
Edit Copy	OLECMDID_COPY
Edit Cut	OLECMDID_CUT
Edit Paste	OLECMDID_PASTE
Edit Paste Special	OLECMDID_PASTESPECIAL
Edit Redo	OLECMDID_REDO
Edit Select All	OLECMDID_SELECTALL
Edit Undo	OLECMDID_UNDO
File New	OLECMDID_NEW
File Open	OLECMDID_OPEN
File Page Setup	OLECMDID_PAGESETUP
File Print	OLECMDID_PRINT
File Print Preview	OLECMDID_PRINTPREVIEW
File Properties	OLECMDID_PROPERTIES
File Save	OLECMDID_SAVE
File Save As	OLECMDID_SAVEAS
File Save Copy As	OLECMDID_SAVECOPYAS

Table 11-3. Common Commands Supported by IOleCommandTarget

Command	Identifier
Not a standard command. This identifier asks the server if it can perform the following three tasks: return a zoom value, display a zoom dialog box, and set a zoom value. This identifier is normally associated with View menu commands (or their equivalent) if the server supports them.	OLECMDID_ZOOM
Not a standard command. This identifier retrieves the zoom range supported by the server. It's normally associated with the View Zoom command if the server supports it (or an equivalent).	OLECMDID_GETZOOMRANGE
Tools Spelling	OLECMDID_SPELL

Table 11-3.   Common Commands Supported by IOleCommandTarget (continued)

The second phase of the client-to-server communication uses the Exec method. The client passes the server one or more OLECMD structures. Each structure contains a single command, any required input arguments, and a place to put informational flags on return from the call. You won't need to provide any input arguments, so that part of the structure will contain a NULL. The standard options appear in Table 11-4. Table 11-5 describes the flags that you'll see on return from an Exec call.

Flag	Description
OLECMDEXECOPT_PROMPTUSER	Prompts the user for some kind of input prior to executing the command. For example, you'd want to use this option with a File Open command.
OLECMDEXECOPT_DONTPROMPTUSER	Don't ask the user for any kind of input. For example, you might want to use this option when the user asks you to print a document.

Table 11-4.   Standard Exec Method Input Arguments

Flag	Description
OLECMDEXECOPT_DODEFAULT	You're not sure whether to prompt the user or not. In this case, you want the application to perform the default action. In most cases, this means it will prompt the user for input.
OLECMDEXECOPT_SHOWHELP	Don't execute the command at all. Display its help screen instead. You might want to use this command if your ActiveDocument provides an alternative help button.

Table 11-4. Standard Exec Method Input Arguments (continued)

Flag	Description
OLECMDF_SUPPORTED	The view object supports the requested command.
OLECMDF_ENABLED	The command is available and the view object has enabled it.
OLECMDF_LATCHED	This command uses an on-off toggle and it is currently set to on.
OLECMDF_NINCHED	The view object can't determine the state of a command that uses a toggle state. In most cases, this means that the command uses a tristate configuration and that it is in the indeterminate state. For example, a three-state check box will return this value if the user has selected some suboptions for an install program but not others. (The check box appears grayed on-screen.)

Table 11-5. Standard Exec( ) Method Return Values

IPrint

IPrint is another optional class that you can implement. This class allows an object to support programmatic printing. There are three methods supported by IPrint: print (Print), retrieve print-related information (GetPageInfo), and set the initial page number for a print job (SetInitialPageNum). Of the three methods, only the Print method accepts any flags as input. Table 11-6 provides a list of these flags and tells how to use them.

Flag	Description
PRINTFLAG_MAYBOTHERUSER	Tells the server that user interaction is allowed by the client. If this flag isn't set, then any print requests have to run by themselves. In most cases, the client will allow user interaction—the only exception will probably involve batch printing jobs or situations when the print operation proceeds in the background.
PRINTFLAG_PROMPTUSER	Prompts the user for input regarding the print job using the standard print dialog box (like the one supported by Windows). For example, the user can select the number of copies when this option is specified. You must also specify the PRINTFLAG_MAYBOTHERUSER flag to use this option.

Table 11-6.   Flags Supported by the Print( ) Method of IPrint

Flag	Description
PRINTFLAG_USERMAYCHANGEPRINTER	Allows the user to change the printer. There are some situations when you won't want to enable this option—like network setups where the user can't easily access the printer. You must also specify the PRINTFLAG _PROMPTUSER flag to use this option.
PRINTFLAG_RECOMPOSETODEVICE	Tells the print job to recompose itself for the target printer. For example, if the target printer supports a higher resolution than currently specified as part of the print job, then the print job should make use of that higher resolution.
PRINTFLAG_DONTACTUALLYPRINT	Test the print job out, but don't actually create any output. This option allows you to test a user interface feature like prompting without wasting paper in the process.
PRINTFLAG_PRINTTOFILE	Send the printed output to a file instead of a printer.

Table 11-6.   Flags Supported by the Print( ) Method of IPrint (continued)

Designing the Control with Visual C++

ATL-based ActiveX controls don't have to be difficult to put together; however, no matter how you look at it, they do take more time to write. Unlike the MFC-based ActiveX control we created in Chapter 4, an ATL-based ActiveX control provides very little in the way of automatic code entries for you. There's no MFC ClassWizard to create and maintain all of the required entries. The result is that you need to remember to do more things by hand, but at least you'll know why all that code is required. In addition, you'll find that using ATL is a lot more flexible and customizable than MFC, which makes ATL the best solution when you need maximum control over your programming environment.

This section of the chapter is going to help you create an ATL-based ActiveX control. Since this is your first control in the book, it might be interesting to create an OnOff button like the one we created in Chapter 4. That way, you'll be able to compare the two buttons later and draw your own conclusions about where each technology works best.

Defining the Project

Defining the project is the first phase of creating an ATL-based ActiveX control, just as it is for any other project. The following procedure will get you started creating an ATL-based ActiveX control (the procedure assumes that you have Visual C++ 6 ?? started).

1. Use the File | New command to display the New dialog box.

2. Choose the Projects tab of the New dialog box and highlight the ATL COM AppWizard icon.

3. Type **OnOffBtn** in the Project Name field, then click OK. You'll see the ATL COM AppWizard - Step 1 of 1 dialog box shown here. Notice that there are three kinds of projects that you can choose from: Dynamic Link Library (DLL), Executable (EXE), and Service (EXE). An OCX is essentially a renamed DLL file, so that's the option we would choose to create an ActiveX control. There are also three options to choose from. The Allow merging of proxy/stub code option allows you to create a single DLL that contains everything needed for the ActiveX control in a single file, so we would check this option. Normally,

the proxy/stub code appears in a separate DLL. The Support MFC option allows you to use MFC calls in your OCX, but that defeats the purpose of using the ATL options for an ActiveX control in the first place. You should use the MFC ActiveX Control AppWizard (as we did in Chapter 4) to create the control if you want MFC support. Finally, the Support MTS option allows you to use Microsoft Transaction Server with your ActiveX control. This is a very valuable option for server-side controls, but we won't be using it for this example.

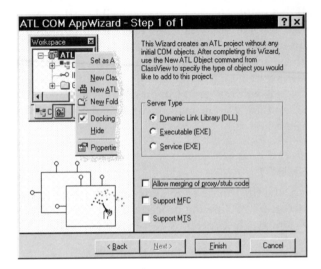

4. Choose a Server Type option. The example uses the Dynamic Link Library (DLL) option.

5. Check any of the support options. The example uses the Allow merging of proxy/stub code option.

6. Click Finish. You'll see the New Project Information dialog box shown here:

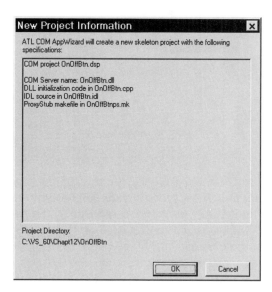

7. Click OK. The ATL COM AppWizard will create the new project for you.

Inserting an ATL Object

At this point, we have a server shell. If you look at the methods provided, you'll find everything needed to create the IUnknown interface, and nothing more. That's one of the benefits of using ATL. You get to decide exactly what your control contains and what functionality it provides. Nothing is done for you.

However, now we have to make our shell into an ActiveX control because that functionality doesn't exist in the current setup. Fortunately, making this shell into an ActiveX control isn't hard. All we really need to do is add the appropriate ATL object and some code to make the control functional. The following procedure will show you how to add one type of ATL object to the code. There are many more options than the one we'll look at here, but at least this example will get you started.

1. Use the Insert | New ATL Object command to display the ATL Object Wizard dialog box shown here. One look at the number of available categories should tell you that ATL is extremely flexible.

2. Choose the Controls category. Notice that this category includes a wealth of ActiveX control types. These types include full (you can use it everywhere), lite (a control with limited functionality), composite (contains more than one full control), and HTML (a special control used on Web pages). There are also combinations of these basic control types, such as lite composite.

3. Highlight an object icon. The example uses Full Control so that we can test it out in a variety of environments and so that we can make some comparisons against an MFC version of the same control (see the "Simple ActiveX Control" section of Chapter 4).

4. Click Next. You'll see the ATL Object Wizard Properties dialog box shown here. This is where we'll define the various properties for our ActiveX control.

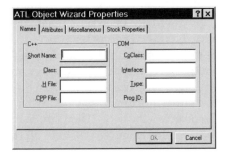

5. Fill out the various pages of the ATL Object Wizard Properties dialog box to meet the needs of your particular control. Table 11-7 shows the settings you'll need to use to create the example ActiveX control. Note that many properties get filled out automatically when you type in one property value on a particular tab. The table won't include these automatic entries and you should assume that the automatic entries are correct unless the table tells you otherwise. While you can change the automatic entries, using them as is tends to make the code easier to read and your control work with less debugging later.

6. Click OK. The ATL Object Wizard will create the required class and interface for you.

Tab	Property	Value
Names	Short Name	OnOffButton
Attributes	Support Connection Points	Checked
Miscellaneous	Add control based on	Button
	Acts like button	Checked
Stock Properties	Supported	Caption
		Enabled
		Font

Table 11-7.   On/Off Button ATL Object Property Values

Initializing Stock Properties

When you create an MFC-based ActiveX control, most or all of the initialization of stock properties is performed for you. In fact, about the only thing you really need to worry about is handling the stock property if you require some type of customized performance. An ATL-based control won't do as much for you at the outset because Microsoft assumes that you're using ATL to gain its small footprint and flexibility. That's why you may need to initialize some stock properties when using ATL. In addition, the ATL form of the control may require some extra handling for events and methods.

One of the stock properties that we added, Font, does require initialization. If you try to compile our example control and display the current property pages, you'll see that the Font page doesn't contain any information. There are fields for entering property values like typeface and point size, but these fields will contain no information at all. Attempting to set the properties on this property page will likely result in an error as well.

Most stock properties are easy to initialize since all you have to do is assign a value to them. Initializing our Font property is a little more difficult. For one thing, you need to make certain that the property doesn't already have a value. Assigning a value to the Font property if it already has a value will mean that the property will get reset every time it's used. Once you determine that the Font property isn't initialized, you get the current default font, then use that font to initialize the Font property. Likewise, you'll need to initialize both the Caption and Enabled properties to standard values.

| Tip | *There are times when it's difficult at best to determine whether to initialize a property. For example, since the ModalResult property will always have some value (0 if nothing else) you can't determine whether to initialize it. Fortunately, some properties have a NULL value when the control is first instantiated, but always have a value otherwise. For example, the Caption property will always be NULL when you first place the control on a form. However, once you initialize it the first time, it's unlikely that the Caption property will continue to be NULL. Using a known NULL property as a method for detection is one way to be certain that your control will react as planned.* |

Besides stock properties, our control will contain three custom properties. We'll actually add these properties in the next section of the chapter, but it's easier to talk about initializing them now. All you normally need to do to initialize a stock property is assign a value to its member variable. Listing 11-1 shows how you would initialize the various properties for this control (added code is in bold type).

Listing 11-1

```
LRESULT OnCreate(UINT /*uMsg*/, WPARAM /*wParam*/, LPARAM
/*lParam*/, BOOL& /*bHandled*/)
{
    CComPtr<IFont> p;          // The ambient (default) font pointer.
    CComPtr<IFont> pFont;      // A copy of the font for local use.

    RECT rc;
    GetWindowRect(&rc);
    rc.right -= rc.left;
    rc.bottom -= rc.top;
    rc.top = rc.left = 0;
    m_ctlButton.Create(m_hWnd, rc);

    // See if the Font property has been initialized.  If not, then
    // get the default font, create a copy of it, then initialize our
    // Font property with it.
    if(!m_pFont)
    if(SUCCEEDED(GetAmbientFont(&p)) && p)
       if(SUCCEEDED(p->Clone(&pFont)) && pFont)
          pFont->QueryInterface(IID_IFontDisp, (void**)&m_pFont);

    // Initialize the Caption, Enabled, ModalResult, and StdButtonType
    // properties if necessary.  Using the Caption property as a basis
    // of detection ensures the properties will only get set during the
    // initial placement of the component.
    if(!m_bstrCaption)
```

```
{
   m_bstrCaption = "Button";
   m_bEnabled = TRUE;
   m_lModalResult = mrNone;
   m_lStdButtonType = 0;

   // Initialize our button caption.
   m_ctlButton.SetWindowText("Button");
}
else
{
   // Allow for conversion of a CComBSTR to LPTSTR.
   USES_CONVERSION;

   // Convert the Caption property to an LPTSTR.
   LPTSTR    lptstrCaption;
   lptstrCaption = OLE2T(m_bstrCaption);

   // Display the caption on our button.
   m_ctlButton.SetWindowText(lptstrCaption);
}

return 0;
}
```

The code in Listing 11-1 has one other initialization feature. Look at the m_ctlButton.SetWindowText( ) calls. There are two of them, one in the initialization part of the **if(!m_bstrCaption)** statement, and the other in the else part of the same statement. The first call allows us to display a default text value in the button when it's first created. The second call maintains the current caption value in the button. Both of these calls are absolutely essential for maintaining button appearance as the user works with it. The second call requires some additional code that the first one doesn't. Notice the USES_CONVERSION macro. This macro tells the compiler that you want to convert an OLE string to a C string. The OLE2T( ) macro performs the actual conversion. Finally, we set the button text using the LPTSTR created by the OLE2T( ) macro.

Adding Properties

Our OCXExmpl control in Chapter 4 contains more than just stock properties. We also included three custom properties: ModalResult, OnOff, and StdButtonType. ModalResult and StdButtonType are both type long, while OnOff is type VARIANT_BOOL. Adding these custom properties to the OnOffButton component is relatively easy. Right-click the

IOnOffButton entry in ClassView and select Add Property from the context menu. You'll see an Add Property to Interface dialog box like the one shown here:

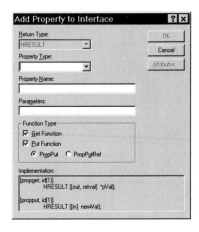

All you need to do is type the property name in the Property Name field and choose a type from the Property Type drop-down list box. (The drop-down list box may not have the VARIANT_BOOL option, but you can type it in without any problem.) Visual C++ will show you what the interface declarations will look like in the Implementation field. Click OK to add the new property to the control. Make sure you perform this process for all three of the custom properties that we need to add for the example. When you get done, you should see [IN] and [OUT] entries for each of the new properties under the IOnOffButton interface entry in ClassView.

Adding the properties won't do much for our control. You'll also need to add member variables to store the current value of the properties. Right-click COnOffButton in ClassView, then choose Add Member Variable from the context menu. You'll see an Add Member Variable dialog box like the one shown here:

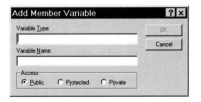

Type the type of your variable in the Variable Type field and the name you want to use in the Variable Name field. The example program uses three variables: m_lModalResult, m_lStdButtonType, and m_bOnOff. The type of the variable normally matches the type of the property that you want to track. One exception is that you'll use a BOOL in place of a VARIANT_BOOL for Boolean properties. In addition, you'll normally want to keep the property variables public.

Once you have the properties and property variables in place, you need to add some code to make them work together. The code is relatively simple. Just send the current value of the property variable when asked by the client. Likewise, you'll need to store any new values for the property as the client sends them to you. Obviously, you can make these functions as complex or as simple as you like. Listing 11-2 shows the minimum code required to make the properties work.

Listing 11-2

```
STDMETHODIMP COnOffButton::get_ModalResult(long *pVal)
{
    // Send the current ModalResult value to the client.
    *pVal = m_lModalResult;

    return S_OK;
}

STDMETHODIMP COnOffButton::put_ModalResult(long newVal)
{
    // Get a new ModalResult value from the client.
    m_lModalResult = newVal;

    return S_OK;
}

STDMETHODIMP COnOffButton::get_StdButtonType(long *pVal)
{
    // Send the current StdButtonType value to the client.
    *pVal = m_lStdButtonType;

    return S_OK;
}

STDMETHODIMP COnOffButton::put_StdButtonType(long newVal)
{
    // Get a new StdButtonType value from the client.
    m_lStdButtonType = newVal;

    return S_OK;
}

STDMETHODIMP COnOffButton::get_OnOff(VARIANT_BOOL *pVal)
{
    // Send the current OnOff value to the client.
```

```
    *pVal = m_bOnOff;

    return S_OK;
}

STDMETHODIMP COnOffButton::put_OnOff(VARIANT_BOOL newVal)
{
    // Get a new OnOff value from the client.
    m_bOnOff = newVal;

    return S_OK;
}
```

Our example in Chapter 4 required some special code to make the custom properties persistent using the PX_Bool( ) and PX_Long( ) functions. Likewise, we need to add some special code to this example to make the properties persistent for this example. Listing 11-3 shows the property map entries we have to add to the OnOffButton.H file (in bold type) to make the properties persistent.

Listing 11-3
```
BEGIN_PROP_MAP(COnOffButton)
    PROP_DATA_ENTRY("_cx", m_sizeExtent.cx, VT_UI4)
    PROP_DATA_ENTRY("_cy", m_sizeExtent.cy, VT_UI4)
    PROP_ENTRY("Caption", DISPID_CAPTION, CLSID_NULL)
    PROP_ENTRY("Enabled", DISPID_ENABLED, CLSID_NULL)
    PROP_ENTRY("Font", DISPID_FONT, CLSID_StockFontPage)

    // Add our properties to the control.
    PROP_ENTRY("ModalResult", 1, CLSID_NULL)
    PROP_ENTRY("StdButtonType", 2, CLSID_NULL)
    PROP_ENTRY("OnOff", 3, CLSID_NULL)
```

The PROP_ENTRY( ) macro takes three arguments: the name of the property, the ID number for the property, and the class ID of any property pages used to change the property value. (If your property doesn't require a property page to make changes, then you can use the special CLSID_NULL value in place of a property page class ID.) The only one of the three arguments that should be a mystery is the property ID number. You get this number from the interface entries in OnOffButton.IDL as shown here for ModalResult:

```
[propget, id(1), helpstring("property ModalResult")]
HRESULT ModalResult([out, retval] long *pVal);
```

Notice the id(1) entry. The number is what you'll use with the PROP_ENTRY( ) macro to identify the property that you want to add to the property map.

Inserting a Property Page

Unlike the MFC-based ActiveX control, the ATL-based ActiveX control doesn't include any property pages. You need to add a property page object to the project. We'll use the same property page that we did in the OCXExmpl project in Chapter 4. However, you'll notice a distinct difference in the technique required to add the property page this time. The following procedure will allow you to add a property page to the OnOffButton example.

1. Use the Insert | New ATL Object… command to display the ATL Object Wizard dialog box.

2. Highlight Controls in the Category list and the Property Page icon in the Objects list.

3. Click Next. You'll see the ATL Object Wizard Properties dialog box. Table 11-8 contains a list of the changes you'll need to make in this dialog box. Remember that some changes will take place automatically and you don't need to change them unless the table contains a specific entry telling you to do so. A blank property value means that you need to remove any text from that field.

4. Click OK. The ALT Object Wizard will create a blank property page for you.

At this point, you have a blank property page that you can use, but it's not linked to the ActiveX control in any way. Try compiling using the control in a Visual Basic or Visual C++ test application and you'll see that you can't access the property page

Tab	Property	Value
Names	Short Name	PropPage1
Strings	Title	On/Off Button Properties
	Doc String	Allows you to set the default button values.
	Helpfile	

Table 11-8. On/Off Button Property Page ATL Object Property Values

through the programming language IDE. To make the property page accessible, you have to add some code to the OnOffButton.H file as shown in bold in Listing 11-4.

Listing 11-4

```
BEGIN_PROP_MAP(COnOffButton)
    PROP_DATA_ENTRY("_cx", m_sizeExtent.cx, VT_UI4)
    PROP_DATA_ENTRY("_cy", m_sizeExtent.cy, VT_UI4)
    PROP_ENTRY("Caption", DISPID_CAPTION, CLSID_NULL)
    PROP_ENTRY("Enabled", DISPID_ENABLED, CLSID_NULL)
    PROP_ENTRY("Font", DISPID_FONT, CLSID_StockFontPage)

    // Add our property page to the control.
    PROP_PAGE(CLSID_PropPage1)
```

The PROP_PAGE( ) macro allows us to access the property page object that we created. Every property page that you create will require a separate entry in the property map for ConOffButton. Where did we get the argument for the PROP_PAGE( ) macro? Look at the top of the PropPage1.H file and you'll see a line of code like this:

```
EXTERN_C const CLSID CLSID_PropPage1;
```

Visual C++ automatically adds an external constant you can use to access the property page as needed. All you need to do is look at the top of the header file to figure out what it is and add it to your PROP_PAGE( ) macro.

Now that you have a property page to work with, you can resize it to the 250 × 110 size used by the property page in Chapter 4. Add the same radio button controls as before and configure them the same way. (See the "Defining the Property Page" section of Chapter 4 for details.)

We'll be dealing with three properties through this property page: Caption, ModalResult, and StdButtonType. Unlike our MFC-based ActiveX control, you have to manipulate these properties locally. This means you'll also need some member variables to hold the property values. We've already added member variables to the project earlier in the chapter, so I won't bore you with details again. The names of our member variables are m_bstrCaption (type CComBSTR), m_lModalResult (type long), and m_lStdButtonType (type long).

Creating a blank property page with some controls on it doesn't make it useful. We also need to add code to connect the buttons on the property page to the actual properties within our control. The first thing we need to do is add some event handlers to our property page. Right-click anywhere on the property page and choose Events from the context menu. You'll see the New Windows Message and Event Handlers dialog box shown here:

This dialog box may seem a little intimidating at first, but it's really easy to use. Simply select the object that you want to work with in the Class or object to handle field. Highlight the message or event that you want to handle in the New Windows messages/events list, then click Add Handler. Visual C++ will add the appropriate handler shell to your application code. We need several handlers in this case. You'll want to add a BN_CLICKED handler for each of the ten buttons on our property page. In addition, you want to add a WM_INITDIALOG handler for the property page class. This last handler will allow us to select the button that matches the current control settings every time the user opens the property page.

Now that we have the event handler headings in place, our property page is finally ready for coding. Listing 11-5 shows the code for making our property page work.

Listing 11-5

```
//////////////////////////////////////////////////////////////////////
// CPropPage1
class ATL_NO_VTABLE CPropPage1 :
    public CComObjectRootEx<CComSingleThreadModel>,
    public CComCoClass<CPropPage1, &CLSID_PropPage1>,
    public IPropertyPageImpl<CPropPage1>,
    public CDialogImpl<CPropPage1>
{
public:
    long m_lStdButtonType;
    long m_lModalResult;
```

```
    CComBSTR m_bstrCaption;
    CPropPage1()
    {
        m_dwTitleID = IDS_TITLEPropPage1;
        m_dwHelpFileID = IDS_HELPFILEPropPage1;
        m_dwDocStringID = IDS_DOCSTRINGPropPage1;
    }

    enum {IDD = IDD_PROPPAGE1};

DECLARE_REGISTRY_RESOURCEID(IDR_PROPPAGE1)

DECLARE_PROTECT_FINAL_CONSTRUCT()

BEGIN_COM_MAP(CPropPage1)
    COM_INTERFACE_ENTRY(IPropertyPage)
END_COM_MAP()

BEGIN_MSG_MAP(CPropPage1)
    CHAIN_MSG_MAP(IPropertyPageImpl<CPropPage1>)
    MESSAGE_HANDLER(WM_INITDIALOG, OnInitDialog)
    COMMAND_HANDLER(IDC_RADIO1, BN_CLICKED, OnClickedRadio1)
    COMMAND_HANDLER(IDC_RADIO10, BN_CLICKED, OnClickedRadio10)
    COMMAND_HANDLER(IDC_RADIO2, BN_CLICKED, OnClickedRadio2)
    COMMAND_HANDLER(IDC_RADIO3, BN_CLICKED, OnClickedRadio3)
    COMMAND_HANDLER(IDC_RADIO4, BN_CLICKED, OnClickedRadio4)
    COMMAND_HANDLER(IDC_RADIO5, BN_CLICKED, OnClickedRadio5)
    COMMAND_HANDLER(IDC_RADIO6, BN_CLICKED, OnClickedRadio6)
    COMMAND_HANDLER(IDC_RADIO7, BN_CLICKED, OnClickedRadio7)
    COMMAND_HANDLER(IDC_RADIO8, BN_CLICKED, OnClickedRadio8)
    COMMAND_HANDLER(IDC_RADIO9, BN_CLICKED, OnClickedRadio9)
END_MSG_MAP()
// Handler prototypes:
//  LRESULT MessageHandler(UINT uMsg, WPARAM wParam, LPARAM lParam, BOOL& bHandled);
//  LRESULT CommandHandler(WORD wNotifyCode, WORD wID, HWND hWndCtl, BOOL& bHandled);
//  LRESULT NotifyHandler(int idCtrl, LPNMHDR pnmh, BOOL& bHandled);

    STDMETHOD(Apply)(void)
    {
        IOnOffButton* pOnOffButton;    // Create a pointer to our control.

        ATLTRACE(_T("CPropPage1::Apply\n"));
```

```
    for (UINT i = 0; i < m_nObjects; i++)
    {
        // Query the interface.
        m_ppUnk[i]->QueryInterface(IID_IOnOffButton,
        (void**)&pOnOffButton);

        // Change the property values.
        pOnOffButton->put_ModalResult(m_lModalResult);
        pOnOffButton->put_Caption(m_bstrCaption);
        pOnOffButton->put_StdButtonType(m_lStdButtonType);

        // Release the interface.
        pOnOffButton->Release();
    }
    m_bDirty = FALSE;
    return S_OK;
}
LRESULT OnInitDialog(UINT uMsg, WPARAM wParam, LPARAM lParam, BOOL& bHandled)
{
    IOnOffButton* pOnOffButton;     // Create a pointer to our control.

    for (UINT i = 0; i < m_nObjects; i++)
    {
        // Query the interface.
        m_ppUnk[i]->QueryInterface(IID_IOnOffButton, (void**)&pOnOffButton);

        // Get the current property values.
        pOnOffButton->get_StdButtonType(&m_lStdButtonType);
        pOnOffButton->get_ModalResult(&m_lModalResult);
        pOnOffButton->get_Caption(&m_bstrCaption);

        // Set the current button so the user can see it.
        switch(m_lStdButtonType)
        {
        case 0:
            CheckRadioButton(IDC_RADIO1, IDC_RADIO10, IDC_RADIO1);
            break;
        case 1:
            CheckRadioButton(IDC_RADIO1, IDC_RADIO10, IDC_RADIO2);
            break;
        case 2:
            CheckRadioButton(IDC_RADIO1, IDC_RADIO10, IDC_RADIO3);
```

```
                break;
            case 3:
                CheckRadioButton(IDC_RADIO1, IDC_RADIO10, IDC_RADIO4);
                break;
            case 4:
                CheckRadioButton(IDC_RADIO1, IDC_RADIO10, IDC_RADIO5);
                break;
            case 5:
                CheckRadioButton(IDC_RADIO1, IDC_RADIO10, IDC_RADIO6);
                break;
            case 6:
                CheckRadioButton(IDC_RADIO1, IDC_RADIO10, IDC_RADIO7);
                break;
            case 7:
                CheckRadioButton(IDC_RADIO1, IDC_RADIO10, IDC_RADIO8);
                break;
            case 8:
                CheckRadioButton(IDC_RADIO1, IDC_RADIO10, IDC_RADIO9);
                break;
            case 9:
                CheckRadioButton(IDC_RADIO1, IDC_RADIO10, IDC_RADIO10);
                break;
        }

        // Release the interface.
        pOnOffButton->Release();
    }
    return 0;
}
LRESULT OnClickedRadio1(WORD wNotifyCode, WORD wID, HWND hWndCtl, BOOL& bHandled)
{
    // Set our properties.
    m_lModalResult = mrNone;
    m_lStdButtonType = mrNone2;
    m_bstrCaption = CComBSTR("Button");

    // Enable the Apply button on the Property Page dialog box.
    IPropertyPageImpl<CPropPage1>::SetDirty(TRUE);

    return 0;
}
```

```
LRESULT OnClickedRadio10(WORD wNotifyCode, WORD wID, HWND hWndCtl, BOOL& bHandled)
{
    // Set our properties.
    m_lModalResult = mrOff;
    m_lStdButtonType = mrOff;
    m_bstrCaption = CComBSTR("Off");

    // Enable the Apply button on the Property Page dialog box.
    IPropertyPageImpl<CPropPage1>::SetDirty(TRUE);

    return 0;

}
    LRESULT OnClickedRadio2(WORD wNotifyCode, WORD wID, HWND hWndCtl, BOOL& bHandled)
{
    // Set our properties.
    m_lModalResult = mrOK;
    m_lStdButtonType = mrOK;
    m_bstrCaption = CComBSTR("OK");

    // Enable the Apply button on the Property Page dialog box.
    IPropertyPageImpl<CPropPage1>::SetDirty(TRUE);

    return 0;
}
LRESULT OnClickedRadio3(WORD wNotifyCode, WORD wID, HWND hWndCtl, BOOL& bHandled)
{
    // Set our properties.
    m_lModalResult = mrCancel;
    m_lStdButtonType = mrCancel;
    m_bstrCaption = CComBSTR("Cancel");

    // Enable the Apply button on the Property Page dialog box.
    IPropertyPageImpl<CPropPage1>::SetDirty(TRUE);

    return 0;
}
    LRESULT OnClickedRadio4(WORD wNotifyCode, WORD wID, HWND hWndCtl, BOOL& bHandled)
{
    // Set our properties.
    m_lModalResult = mrAbort;
```

```
        m_lStdButtonType = mrAbort;
        m_bstrCaption = CComBSTR("Abort");


        // Enable the Apply button on the Property Page dialog box.
        IPropertyPageImpl<CPropPage1>::SetDirty(TRUE);


        return 0;
}
LRESULT OnClickedRadio5(WORD wNotifyCode, WORD wID, HWND hWndCtl, BOOL& bHandled)
{
        // Set our properties.
        m_lModalResult = mrRetry;
        m_lStdButtonType = mrRetry;
        m_bstrCaption = CComBSTR("Retry");


        // Enable the Apply button on the Property Page dialog box.
        IPropertyPageImpl<CPropPage1>::SetDirty(TRUE);


        return 0;
}
LRESULT OnClickedRadio6(WORD wNotifyCode, WORD wID, HWND hWndCtl, BOOL& bHandled)
{
        // Set our properties.
        m_lModalResult = mrIgnore;
        m_lStdButtonType = mrIgnore;
        m_bstrCaption = CComBSTR("Ignore");


        // Enable the Apply button on the Property Page dialog box.
        IPropertyPageImpl<CPropPage1>::SetDirty(TRUE);


        return 0;
}
LRESULT OnClickedRadio7(WORD wNotifyCode, WORD wID, HWND hWndCtl, BOOL& bHandled)
{
        // Set our properties.
        m_lModalResult = mrYes;
        m_lStdButtonType = mrYes;
        m_bstrCaption = CComBSTR("Yes");


        // Enable the Apply button on the Property Page dialog box.
        IPropertyPageImpl<CPropPage1>::SetDirty(TRUE);
```

```
        return 0;
    }
    LRESULT OnClickedRadio8(WORD wNotifyCode, WORD wID, HWND hWndCtl, BOOL& bHandled)
    {
        // Set our properties.
        m_lModalResult = mrNo;
        m_lStdButtonType = mrNo;
        m_bstrCaption = CComBSTR("No");

        // Enable the Apply button on the Property Page dialog box.
        IPropertyPageImpl<CPropPage1>::SetDirty(TRUE);

        return 0;
    }
    LRESULT OnClickedRadio9(WORD wNotifyCode, WORD wID, HWND hWndCtl, BOOL& bHandled)
    {
        // Set our properties.
        m_lModalResult = mrOn;
        m_lStdButtonType = mrOn;
        m_bstrCaption = CComBSTR("On");

        // Enable the Apply button on the Property Page dialog box.
        IPropertyPageImpl<CPropPage1>::SetDirty(TRUE);

        return 0;
    }
};
```

It may look like there's an overwhelming quantity of code here, but most of it is very repetitive. Let's look at the easiest function type first, the OnClickedRadio[Button Number]( ) function. There is one of these functions for each of the radio buttons on our property page. Each button's function does the same thing. First, we set all of our properties, then we call a function to enable the Apply button. When the user clicks the Apply button, the changes we made to the local variables will be sent to the ActiveX control through the STDMETHOD(Apply)(void) call or Apply( ) method.

The Apply( ) method is relatively straightforward as well. The first thing this function does is to create a variable to hold an instance of a pointer to our control. However, this pointer variable is NULL when you first create it. The next thing we do is use the QueryInterface( ) function to fill the variable with an actual pointer to the control. Now that we can see the control, we look at each interface it provides in turn.

The goal is to find the three functions required to place our local memory variable values into the control properties. Once we find the functions (put_ModalResult( ), put_StdButtonType( ), and put_Caption( )), we use them to change the control properties. The last two things we need to do are reset the local dirty property value variable and release our pointer to the control.

The OnInitDialog( ) function works similar to the Apply( ) method. However, in this case the process is reversed because we use the get_ModalResult( ), get_StdButtonType( ), and get_Caption( ) functions to retrieve the current control property values. The switch statement allows us to depress the button that reflects the current StdButtonType property setting. This allows the user to see which setting is selected when he or she first opens the property dialog box.

Adding a Resource

We've used a resource twice now in this section of the chapter in the form of a ModalResult property value. We created default values for this property in the OCXExmplCtrl.H file using the MODALTYPE enumeration. Unfortunately, this technique won't work with our ATL-based control. What we need to use this time is a series of defines placed in a custom header file and added to our program.

Adding the header to our project is easy. Use the File | New command to display the New dialog box. Choose the Files tab and highlight the C/C++ Header File icon. Notice that the dialog box defaults to adding the header file to our current project, but it never hurts to double-check and make sure you'll add the header file to the right location. Type **ModalResult** in the "File name" field. Click OK and you'll see a blank text area you can use to type in our ModalResult values. Listing 11-6 shows the contents of this header file.

Listing 11-6

```
// Create the defines required for the ModalResult
// and StdButtonType properties.
#define    mrNone        -1L;
#define    mrNone2        0L;
#define    mrOK         1L;
#define    mrCancel     2L;
#define    mrAbort       3L;
#define    mrRetry       4L;
#define    mrIgnore     5L;
#define    mrYes         6L;
#define    mrNo         7L;
```

```
#define    mrOn       8L;
#define    mrOff      9L;
```

Once you have the ModalResult.H file created, you'll also need to add it to both the OnOffButton.H and PropPage1.H files. Here's the code you'll use to do it:

```
// Add our custom ModalResult and StdButtonType
// property values.
#include "ModalResult.h"
```

Adding Events

Adding events is a lot different when using ATL than it is using MFC. You have to worry about more things going wrong as you set the events up. However, if you follow the same procedure each time, you'll find that your events will work as expected and that you even get some flexibility in implementation that would be hard to get with MFC.

The first thing we need to do is add some methods to our _IOnOffButtonEvents interface. These methods will have the same name as the events that we eventually want to create. To start, right-click _IOnOffButtonEvents in the ClassView window and choose Add Method from the context menu. You'll see an Add Method to Interface dialog box like the one shown here:

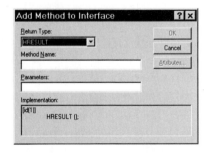

Notice that you can control the result type returned, the method name, and the parameters passed to the method. In most cases, you won't require anything but the method name for an event. However, in this case, we'll have to add some parameters for some of the methods. We'll need seven new methods for our interface: Click( ), KeyDown( ), KeyPress( ), KeyUp( ), MouseDown( ), MouseMove( ), and MouseUp( ). The MouseDown( ), MouseMove( ), and MouseUp( ) methods require four parameters: Button, Shift, X, and Y. The KeyDown( ) and KeyUp( ) methods require two parameters: KeyCode and Shift. Finally, the KeyPress( ) method requires a single parameter: KeyAscii. All of these parameters are of type int. Enter the methods one at a time by opening the Add Method to Interface dialog box, typing the method name in the Method Name field, then click OK.

Once you have all of your methods in place, you need to implement the connection point interface. The way you do this is right-click on the COnOffButton entry in ClassView and choose Implement Connection Point from the Context menu. You'll see the Implement Connection Point dialog box shown here:

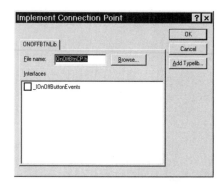

Check the _IOnOffButtonEvents option in the Interfaces field, then click OK. Visual C++ will create the code required to implement the connection points. What you'll see in the new CProxy_IOnOffButtonEvents class is a series of fire methods like Fire_Click( ) for our Click( ) event. These methods allow you to fire an event from within your code. What happens is that the control intercepts Windows messages telling of user interaction events and uses the fire methods to send a message to the connection interface, which in turn uses the requisite event method to send a message to the control container.

Adding the Windows message handlers required to fire events from within your code comes next. Right-click on COnOffButton in ClassView and choose the Add Windows Message Handler option from the context menu. You'll see the New Windows Message and Events Handlers dialog box. We'll need to add methods that will intercept user interactions with the control, like a keypress or mouse click. In sum, we'll need to add handlers for the following windows messages: WM_KEYDOWN, WM_KEYUP, WM_LBUTTONDOWN, WM_LBUTTONUP, and WM_MOUSEMOVE. This set of message handlers won't completely replicate the way the OCXExmpl control works—which demonstrates that you actually have more flexibility using an ATL control.

Tip	*You can use the ActiveX Control Test Container utility to monitor the activity of the control you create as compared to other controls. For example, the default MFC behavior generates a Click event when you release the mouse button and it doesn't matter which mouse button you click. We're still going to generate the Click event when the mouse button is released, but the Click event will only occur when the left button is released. ATL will allow you to do this with relative ease; MFC would require some fairly convoluted programming to perform the same task. Note also that you'll get both a KeyDown and a KeyPress event when ENTER is pressed. The KeyUp event occurs when you release ENTER. Neither the keypress nor the key release generates a Click event. Again, you could modify this behavior if desired using ATL (something that we won't do in this example).*

Keyboard events do require a little special handling. The shift state has to be monitored between the KeyDown and KeyUp events. When the user presses either the SHIFT or CTRL key, you have to set some kind of a variable to track the pressed state. Likewise, you have to monitor when the user releases either the SHIFT or CTRL keys. With this in mind, we need two additional member variables: m_bCtrl and m_bShift. Both are protected BOOL variables. You can create both by right-clicking COnOffButton in ClassView and choosing the Add Member Variable entry on the context menu. The Add Member Variable dialog box will allow you to make the required entries.

Now that you've got message handler shells in place, we can begin to add code to fire our events. Listing 11-7 shows the code you'll need to add to make the message handlers active and fire events as a result of user actions on the control.

Listing 11-7

```
LRESULT OnKeyDown(UINT uMsg, WPARAM wParam, LPARAM lParam, BOOL& bHandled)
{
    int     iKeyCode;    // Key code for key pressed.
    int     iKeyAscii;     // ASCII code once Shift and Ctrl taken into account.
    int     iShift;        // Shift status.

    // Set the shift status variables.
    if(wParam == 16)
        m_bShift = TRUE;
    if(wParam == 17)
        m_bCtrl = TRUE;
```

```
    // Determine the shift status.  Only Ctrl and Shift are sent
    // as part of message handling call.
    iShift = 0;
    if(m_bShift)
        iShift = 1;
    if(m_bCtrl)
        iShift = iShift + 2;

    // Determine the current key code.
    iKeyCode = wParam;

    // Determine the current ASCII code.  Shifted keys always equal
    // the key code. Non-shifted keys above 64 (a) are equal to the
    // key code plus 32.
    if(m_bShift)
        iKeyAscii = wParam;
    else
    {
        if(iKeyCode >= 65)
            iKeyAscii = wParam + 32;
        else
            iKeyAscii = wParam;
    }

    // When determining the current ASCII code, the Ctrl key takes
    // precedence over the Shift key, so we need to place this second
    // check after the first.  Pressing the Ctrl key always produces a
    // control key result for the ASCII value (a is equal to ASCII 1).
    if(m_bCtrl && (iKeyCode >= 65))
        iKeyAscii = iKeyCode - 64;

    // Fire the KeyPress and KeyDown events.  Fire the KeyPress event
    // only if we're not working with a shift key.
    Fire_KeyDown(iKeyCode, iShift);
    if(!(iKeyCode == 16) && !(iKeyCode == 17))
        Fire_KeyPress(iKeyAscii);

    // Allow the normal processing to take place.
    bHandled = FALSE;

    return 0;
}
LRESULT OnKeyUp(UINT uMsg, WPARAM wParam, LPARAM lParam, BOOL& bHandled)
{
    int    iKeyCode;    // Key code for key pressed.
    int    iShift;       // Shift status.
```

```
    // Set the shift status variables.
    if(wParam == 16)
        m_bShift = FALSE;
    if(wParam == 17)
        m_bCtrl = FALSE;

    // Determine the shift status.  Only Ctrl and Shift are sent
    // as part of message handling call.
    iShift = 0;
    if(m_bShift)
        iShift = 1;
    if(m_bCtrl)
        iShift = iShift + 2;

    // Determine the current key code.
    iKeyCode = wParam;

    // Fire the KeyUp event.
    Fire_KeyUp(iKeyCode, iShift);

    // Allow the normal processing to take place.
    bHandled = FALSE;

    return 0;
}
LRESULT OnLButtonDown(UINT uMsg, WPARAM wParam, LPARAM lParam, BOOL& bHandled)
{
    int     iXPos;     // Mouse horizontal position.
    int     iYPos;     // Mouse vertical position.
    int     iShift;    // Shift status.

    // Get the position of the mouse.
    iXPos = LOWORD(lParam);
    iYPos = HIWORD(lParam);

    // Determine the shift status.  Only Ctrl and Shift are sent
    // as part of message handling call.
    iShift = 0;
    if((wParam & MK_SHIFT) == MK_SHIFT)
        iShift = 1;
    if((wParam & MK_CONTROL) == MK_CONTROL)
        iShift = iShift + 2;

    // If the mouse was clicked on our control, then fire both a
    // Click and a Mouse Down event.
    Fire_Click();
    Fire_MouseDown(1, iShift, iXPos, iYPos);
```

```
    // Allow the normal processing to take place.
    bHandled = FALSE;

    return 0;
}
LRESULT OnLButtonUP(UINT uMsg, WPARAM wParam, LPARAM lParam, BOOL& bHandled)
{
    int     iXPos;     // Mouse horizontal position.
    int     iYPos;     // Mouse vertical position.
    int     iShift;    // Shift status.

    // Get the position of the mouse.
    iXPos = LOWORD(lParam);
    iYPos = HIWORD(lParam);

    // Determine the shift status.  Only Ctrl and Shift are sent
    // as part of message handling call.
    iShift = 0;
    if((wParam & MK_SHIFT) == MK_SHIFT)
        iShift = 1;
    if((wParam & MK_CONTROL) == MK_CONTROL)
        iShift = iShift + 2;

    // If the mouse was clicked on our control, then fire a
    // Mouse Up event.
    Fire_MouseUp(1, iShift, iXPos, iYPos);

    // Allow the normal processing to take place.
    bHandled = FALSE;

    return 0;
}
LRESULT OnMouseMove(UINT uMsg, WPARAM wParam, LPARAM lParam, BOOL& bHandled)
{
    int     iXPos;     // Mouse horizontal position.
    int     iYPos;     // Mouse vertical position.
    int     iShift;    // Shift status.

    // Get the position of the mouse.
    iXPos = LOWORD(lParam);
    iYPos = HIWORD(lParam);

    // Determine the shift status.  Only Ctrl and Shift are sent
    // as part of message handling call.
    iShift = 0;
    if((wParam & MK_SHIFT) == MK_SHIFT)
        iShift = 1;
    if((wParam & MK_CONTROL) == MK_CONTROL)
        iShift = iShift + 2;
```

```
    // If the mouse was moved over our control, then fire a
    // Mouse Move event.
    Fire_MouseMove(1, iShift, iXPos, iYPos);

    // Allow the normal processing to take place.
    bHandled = FALSE;

    return 0;
}
```

There are some common elements for all of the methods shown here. First, we don't actually handle the mouse or keyboard events. What we do is monitor the event and fire an event to the client as a result. Because of the way that we handle these events, you have to set the bHandled variable to FALSE so that the normal keyboard or mouse handler will perform its normal function.

The second common element is firing the event. Notice that each method provides some type of event firing call near the end of the method. You must pass the parameters required to fire each event. These parameters appear as part of the event message when you view the control within ActiveX Control Test Container. In addition, you'll find that these parameters are passed to the server for further processing.

Now let's look at the KeyUp( ) and KeyDown( ) methods. The first thing you need to know here is that every key pressed gets passed to the event handler except one, the ALT key. You can't monitor this key because the message handler never sees it. Notice the order in which the various key events are processed. First, we look at the shift status to make sure it's correct, then act on that shift status. Since the user could continue pressing the CTRL or SHIFT keys while pressing several other keys, you need to perform this two-step process. Once the shift status is determined, you can place the key code value into iKeyCode. The KeyUp and KeyDown events report the raw key code value, which is what you get passed in wParam. The KeyPress event reports the true ASCII value of the key, which includes some modification for the SHIFT and CTRL key status. That's where the additional code comes into play in the KeyDown( ) method. We need to modify the key code value so that it reflects the true ASCII value of the key the user pressed. In addition, notice that we only report a KeyPress event when the user has pressed a key—not when the user has pressed either the CTRL or SHIFT keys. This allows the server to perform actions based on what the user has actually typed rather than the raw keystrokes.

The mouse event handlers are a lot easier to understand than the keyboard input handlers. All we need to do, in this case, is process the incoming data and pass it along to the server. The lParam variable contains the X and Y positions of the mouse. Using the HIWORD( ) and LOWORD( ) macros allows us to extract this information with ease. The shift status information is contained in the wParam variable. A simple comparison allows us to determine the current mouse shift status. No other processing is required.

Adding Some Display Code to the OnOffButton Control

At this point, we have a control that's fully functional except for one thing—you don't see any of the changes that occur internally. The final bit of coding for our ATL-based ActiveX control occurs in the OnOffButton.CPP file.

The first thing we'll need to do is add a member variable similar to the one we added to the MFC-based example in Chapter 4. This variable will track the current OnOff button state (whether it's on or off). Add a protected BOOL named m_bSetOn to COnOffButton to take care of this need.

Coding won't be much different than our MFC-based example, in this case. In fact, the code is so similar that you should recognize it right away (though some of the names are changed, the functionality is the same). We'll modify the custom property methods that we created earlier so that they'll also change the appearance of the button and interact with other properties as required. Listing 11-8 shows the updated version of this code.

Listing 11-8

```
STDMETHODIMP COnOffButton::put_StdButtonType(long newVal)
{
    // Get a new StdButtonType value from the client.
    m_lStdButtonType = newVal;

    // Change the ModalResult property and the button
    // text to match the button type.

    switch(m_lStdButtonType)
    {
    case 0:
        m_ctlButton.SetWindowText("Button");
        m_bstrCaption = "Button";
        m_lModalResult = mrNone;
        m_bOnOff = FALSE;
        break;
    case 1:
        m_ctlButton.SetWindowText("OK");
        m_bstrCaption = "OK";
```

```
        m_lModalResult = mrOK;
        m_bOnOff = FALSE;
        break;
    case 2:
        m_ctlButton.SetWindowText("Cancel");
        m_bstrCaption = "Cancel";
        m_lModalResult = mrCancel;
        m_bOnOff = FALSE;
        break;
    case 3:
        m_ctlButton.SetWindowText("Abort");
        m_bstrCaption = "Abort";
        m_lModalResult = mrAbort;
        m_bOnOff = FALSE;
        break;
    case 4:
        m_ctlButton.SetWindowText("Retry");
        m_bstrCaption = "Retry";
        m_lModalResult = mrRetry;
        m_bOnOff = FALSE;
        break;
    case 5:
        m_ctlButton.SetWindowText("Ignore");
        m_bstrCaption = "Ignore";
        m_lModalResult = mrIgnore;
        m_bOnOff = FALSE;
        break;
    case 6:
        m_ctlButton.SetWindowText("Yes");
        m_bstrCaption = "Yes";
        m_lModalResult = mrYes;
        m_bOnOff = FALSE;
        break;
    case 7:
        m_ctlButton.SetWindowText("No");
        m_bstrCaption = "No";
        m_lModalResult = mrNo;
        m_bOnOff = FALSE;
        break;
```

```
    case 8:
        m_ctlButton.SetWindowText("On");
        m_bstrCaption = "On";
        m_lModalResult = mrOn;
        break;
    case 9:
        m_ctlButton.SetWindowText("Off");
        m_bstrCaption = "Off";
        m_lModalResult = mrOff;
        break;
    }

    return S_OK;
}

STDMETHODIMP COnOffButton::get_OnOff(VARIANT_BOOL *pVal)
{
    // Send the current OnOff value to the client.
    *pVal = m_bOnOff;

    return S_OK;
}

STDMETHODIMP COnOffButton::put_OnOff(VARIANT_BOOL newVal)
{
    // Get a new OnOff value from the client.
    m_bOnOff = newVal;

    // Set the StdButtonType property to the appropriate
    // value so that we can change the button status.
    if(m_bOnOff)
    {
        m_lStdButtonType = mrOn;
        m_lModalResult = mrOn;
        m_ctlButton.SetWindowText("On");
        m_bstrCaption = "On";
        m_bSetOn = TRUE;
    }
    else
```

```
    {
        m_lStdButtonType = mrNone2;
        m_lModalResult = mrNone;
        m_ctlButton.SetWindowText("Button");
        m_bstrCaption = "Button";
        m_bSetOn = FALSE;
    }

    return S_OK;
}


STDMETHODIMP COnOffButton::get_OnOff(VARIANT_BOOL *pVal)
{
    // Send the current OnOff value to the client.
    *pVal = m_bOnOff;

    return S_OK;
}


STDMETHODIMP COnOffButton::put_OnOff(VARIANT_BOOL newVal)
{
    // Get a new OnOff value from the client.
    m_bOnOff = newVal;

    // Set the StdButtonType property to the appropriate
    // value so that we can change the button status.
    if(m_bOnOff)
    {
        m_lStdButtonType = mrOn;
        m_lModalResult = mrOn;
        m_ctlButton.SetWindowText("On");
        m_bSetOn = TRUE;
    }
    else
    {
        m_lStdButtonType = mrNone2;
        m_lModalResult = mrNone;
        m_ctlButton.SetWindowText("Button");
        m_bSetOn = FALSE;
    }

    return S_OK;
}
```

As you can see, the code for manipulating the property values based on what type of button the user selects is almost identical to our MFC example in Chapter 4. For this reason, I'll let you read about the inner workings of this code in Chapter 4.

There's one additional change we need to make. The current button doesn't allow us to switch between the on and off states when the user has selected. We'll need to add a little code to the MouseDown handler that we created earlier. Again, this code is almost exactly the same as the code we worked with in Chapter 4. Listing 11-9 shows the required additions in bold.

Listing 11-9

```
LRESULT OnLButtonDown(UINT uMsg, WPARAM wParam, LPARAM lParam, BOOL& bHandled)
{
    int     iXPos;     // Mouse horizontal position.
    int     iYPos;     // Mouse vertical position.
    int     iShift;    // Shift status.

    // Get the position of the mouse.
    iXPos = LOWORD(lParam);
    iYPos = HIWORD(lParam);

    // Determine the shift status.  Only Ctrl and Shift are sent
    // as part of message handling call.
    iShift = 0;
    if((wParam & MK_SHIFT) == MK_SHIFT)
        iShift = 1;
    if((wParam & MK_CONTROL) == MK_CONTROL)
        iShift = iShift + 2;

    // Determine if we need to do anything special with the button.
    if(m_bOnOff)
    {
        if(m_bSetOn)
        {
            m_lStdButtonType = mrOff;
            m_lModalResult = mrOff;
            m_ctlButton.SetWindowText("Off");
            m_bSetOn = FALSE;
        }
        else
        {
            m_lStdButtonType = mrOn;
            m_lModalResult = mrOn;
            m_ctlButton.SetWindowText("On");
            m_bSetOn = TRUE;
        }
    }
```

```
    // If the mouse was clicked on our control, then fire both a
    // Click and a Mouse Down event.
    Fire_Click();
    Fire_MouseDown(1, iShift, iXPos, iYPos);

    // Allow the normal processing to take place.
    bHandled = FALSE;

    return 0;
}
```

Adding a Control to a Web Page Using Visual InterDev

Now that we have a new ActiveX control to try, we should test it. Normally I would suggest starting the test using a Visual Basic or Visual C++ application. In fact, you'll find both a Visual Basic and a Visual C++ test application on the CD that accompanies this book that does test the control in an application environment. However, our main goal in this chapter wasn't creating components for application use; we needed them for use on an intranet site to clean up all of those old application files. With that in mind, we'll test our OnOffButton control on an intranet site in this chapter.

We'll actually follow a four-step process for creating the test Web site in this section of the chapter. The first step will be to create the project itself. However, instead of adding a theme and layout during the design process as normal, we'll add them later. There are times when you may want to add these items later or perhaps need to change the design decision you made at the beginning of the project.

Now that we have a Web site ready to go for testing, it's time to add the test ActiveX control. That's where the second step comes into play. We'll add the ActiveX control that we designed earlier in the chapter to our test Web page, add a few testing controls, and then see how it performs.

The third step will be to add a theme and layout to our project. Adding these items at the outset of a project really is the best way to go, but it's important to know how to change your setup later in the project as well. Few of us can say that we always get everything right the first time around.

The fourth step will be to perform the same test as we did the first time on the ActiveX control. However, this time we'll be able to check for potential interaction problems with the theme and layout we've chosen.

Starting the Project Design

The first thing we'll need to do to test our **OnOffButton** control is to create a test Web page product. The following procedure will get you started; it assumes that you've already started Visual InterDev.

1. Select the Visual InterDev Projects folder on the New tab of the New Projects dialog box.

2. Highlight the New Web Project icon, type OnOffBtnVI in the Name field, then click Open. Visual InterDev will display the Web Project Wizard - Step 1 of 4 dialog box. We have explored this dialog box several times in the book so far, so I won't provide detailed information about its contents again. You should have a Web server connection set up and ready to go (see Chapter 4 if you don't).

3. Click Next to accept the default setup. Visual InterDev will contact the Web server and establish a connection with it.

4. Click Finish. Visual InterDev will create the application shell for you.

Note that we didn't apply a theme or layout during the design process. What we created was a very simple Web project that doesn't include any bells and whistles. Obviously, this is the best setup for testing an ActiveX control for the first time since you won't have to worry about any interaction problems. Normally, you'll create a test page at this point, add your ActiveX control and a few support controls, then proceed with testing.

Adding the ActiveX Control to the Project

In this section, we'll create a simple Web page for testing our OnOffButton control. The first thing you'll need to do is right-click on the <Server Name>/OnOffBtnVI folder, then choose Add | HTML Page… from the context menu. You'll see the Add Item dialog box. Highlight the HTML Page icon if necessary, type **Test.HTM** in the Name field, then click Open. Visual InterDev will add the test Web page to the project.

 If you want to debug the page anytime during the design process, right-click the Test.HTM entry in Project Explorer and choose Set as Start Page from the context menu. Otherwise, Visual InterDev will complain there's no start page when you click Start on the toolbar.

The next thing we need to do is add the OnOffButton control to our toolbox. Begin by clicking the ActiveX Controls tab. Right-click the toolbox and choose Customize Toolbox… from the context menu. You'll see the Customize Toolbox dialog box. Click on the ActiveX Controls tab and find the OnOffButton Class entry. Check the box next to the entry, as shown here:

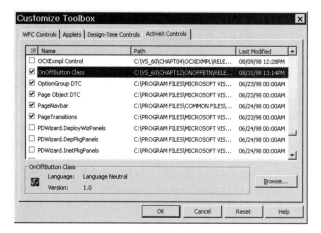

Click OK and Visual InterDev will add the control to your toolbox. Double-click the button in the toolbox and Visual InterDev will add it to the test Web page. Table 11-9 contains a list of property values you'll need to change for our test control in this example. A blank value in the table represents a blank property value.

At this point, there's an important consideration to discuss when it comes to ActiveX controls. You've been working with the control on your local machine, so there isn't any problem with accessing it. On the other hand, the user who will access your Web site won't have the control installed on their machine. They'll need to get a copy of the control from somewhere. That's why you need to include the Codebase entry. It tells Internet Explorer where to download a copy of your control. Of course, the copy needed by the user won't magically appear on your server, you have to get it there somehow. What I normally do is use Windows Explorer to find the control on my local hard drive, highlight it, then use the Copy button to copy it to the clipboard. I then go to the copy of Visual InterDev that I have open with my project loaded, choose the folder that I want to use to store my control, then press CTRL-V to paste the control

Property	Value
Height	25
Width	75
(ID)	PbTest
Codebase	http://<Your Server Name>/OnOffBtnVI/OnOffBtn.DLL

Table 11-9.   Test OnOffButton Settings

there. What will happen is that the control you're using will appear as both part of the project and on your Web server at the same time. Use the location where you store the control on your server as the source for the Codebase property. The example assumes that the OnOffButton control is stored in your main project folder.

We'll also need a test script to check out the results of using the control. Listing 11-10 shows the script we'll use in this case (which should look similar to the test scripts we used in Chapter 4).

Listing 11-10

```
<SCRIPT LANGUAGE="VBScript">
<!--

sub pbTest_Click()

'Determine which button is active, then display the appropriate
'message box for the user.
Select Case pbTest.ModalResult
    Case -1
        MsgBox "Modal Result Value -1 or " + pbTest.Caption
    Case 1
        MsgBox "Modal Result Value 1 or " + pbTest.Caption
    Case 2
        MsgBox "Modal Result Value 2 or " + pbTest.Caption
    Case 3
        MsgBox "Modal Result Value 3 or " + pbTest.Caption
    Case 4
        MsgBox "Modal Result Value 4 or " + pbTest.Caption
    Case 5
        MsgBox "Modal Result Value 5 or " + pbTest.Caption
    Case 6
        MsgBox "Modal Result Value 6 or " + pbTest.Caption
    Case 7
        MsgBox "Modal Result Value 7 or " + pbTest.Caption
    Case 8
        MsgBox "Modal Result Value 8 or " + pbTest.Caption
    Case 9
        MsgBox "Modal Result Value 9 or " + pbTest.Caption
End Select


end sub

-->
</SCRIPT>
```

As you can see, this script gets called whenever the user presses the pbTest button and generates a Click event. All that the script does is look at the current value of the ModalResult property, then display a message box based on the value it finds. Overall, the code's very simple, but will work fine for testing the functionality of our ActiveX control.

Using Themes and Layouts on Web Pages

Testing your ActiveX control on a blank page is just fine for starters, but it really doesn't provide a real-world situation. In the real world, the control would be expected to work on a page that included graphics and other bells and whistles. This example is going to add some complexity to the environment by adding a theme and layout to our test Web page. There are two places we need to add this information.

First, we'll want to add a theme and layout to the project as a whole. All you need to do is right-click on the <Server Name>/OnOffBtnVI folder in Project Explorer and choose Apply Theme and Layout from the context menu. What you'll see is the Apply Theme and Layout dialog box shown here:

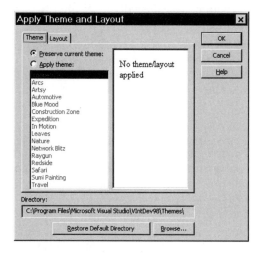

Start by choosing the Apply theme (on the Theme tab) and Apply layout and theme (on the Layout tab) options. Now, all we need to do is choose a theme on the Theme tab and a layout on the Layout tab. For the purpose of this example, I chose Leaves for the theme and Top and Left 1 for the layout. Click OK to complete the process. Visual InterDev will add a series of files to your project and then apply the theme to the project as a whole. At this point, you'll see a message telling you that Test.HTM has been modified outside of the project and asking if you want to reload it. Choose Yes and you'll see the new theme and layout applied to the test page. We're now ready for another testing session with the OnOffButton control. (Any content on your Web page should automatically appear in the new body area of the layout for that page.)

Testing the ActiveX Control with Themes and Layouts in Place

Themes won't normally present much of a problem for your ActiveX control. After all, what you're really doing with a theme is adding some graphics and a few stylistic changes to the Web page. Unfortunately, there are times when you'll run into a problem that only becomes visible when you do add a theme to your Web page. One example of this situation is an ActiveX control that uses a lot of memory or other resources. Loading the theme and the ActiveX control could overwhelm the test system and cause memory or other resource-related problems. That said, you won't run into this situation very often.

Layouts are another story. Because a layout depends on a lot of interaction with the server and the client, and since it relies on FrontPage extensions, you may find that your perfectly functioning ActiveX control no longer works as anticipated. It's important to test all of the features on your Web page when working with a new ActiveX control. For example, go one at a time to all of the links that automatically get attached to the page (like global or child pages). You'll want to be sure that the ActiveX control works after each change. It's especially important to check pages where there's a lot of script activity, like the Search page.

Once you've gotten your ActiveX control tested with the theme and layout you want to use with your Web site, you might start adding other controls to the page just to see how the control is affected by interactions with other controls. Create some complex test scripts that'll allow you to test all of the control features. In addition, you'll also want to make sure you check both client-side and server-side scripting capability.

So, what happens if you find a problem? Some problems will be pretty obvious. For example, if the ActiveX control is supposed to make a caption change when you modify a particular property and doesn't, you at least have a good idea of what functions to check. On the other hand, some problems can be difficult (if not impossible) to find. For example, you may have a problem that only appears when you use a certain layout. What you'll need to do is isolate what makes that layout or other environmental condition unique. If there are several factors, then try testing one factor at a time. Normally the process of fully defining the exact characteristics of a problem will help you figure out exactly where to look in your ActiveX control's code. Finally, remember that you have tools at your disposal for diagnosing ActiveX control related problems. Both the ActiveX Control Test Container and OLE View utilities can help you isolate particular kinds of problems. Just make sure you take the time to examine the control thoroughly before attempting to find the problem within the code.

Lessons Learned

This chapter covered a lot of ground in the area of ActiveX control creation. Not only did you learn about all of the interfaces required to create the control, but you also learned about the advantages and disadvantages inherent with each creation technique. With all of the component technologies around today, this chapter should have shown you that choosing the right technology for your particular situation is no small undertaking. However, you should have at least gotten a few answers to guide you in the decision-making process as well.

One of the most important lessons that this chapter taught is that ATL and MFC are not mutually exclusive. Some people prefer one technique over the other for personal reasons, but both techniques are equally important in different ways. The simplest way to look at the ATL versus MFC question is that you need to use ATL if portability, small control size, and control performance are your main goals. However, remember that these good ATL features are more than offset by longer development time and code complexities. You really need to know COM to make ATL work properly.

Another important lesson to learn from this chapter is the importance of the various utility programs that Microsoft provides. The ActiveX Control Test Container, OLE View, and Depends applications were all essential in getting the information required to complete the control you see in this chapter. More than that, these utilities provided essential information about the utility of the control and how it performs against its MFC-based counterpart in Chapter 4. Many programmers forget that they have a wealth of test utility programs just waiting to help them complete a programming task. Even if Visual Studio lacks the comprehensive all-in-one feel that some developers were hoping for, using the utilities at hand is essential to getting the kind of results that you want.

Testing your ActiveX control in a variety of environments is important because each environment will react differently to it. In this chapter, we didn't actually test the control with anything other than Visual InterDev (though I did on the side, and the test code is available to you on the CD). However, we did test the control on both a blank Web page and one that had a theme and layout added. Even the addition of a theme or layout to your Web page could change how the ActiveX control works. It's important to realize that you need to perform incremental testing so that the true source of any problems is easier to detect.

Chapter 12

Remote Data Access over the Internet

Remote data access used to be a nice feature to have for the few salespeople in a company that spent most of their time on the road. A few static updates of the data each week would allow them to keep up on current company prices or availability for specific products. In many cases, sales from those road trips were still recorded on paper and added to the company database after the salesperson returned from their trip.

As more and more people in a company have begun to rely on remote data access, the need to provide accurate and timely information has increased. No longer is it enough to provide a static display of data in the company database—the information must be accurate as of the time of the request. In addition, many people now update those databases remotely instead of waiting to return to the company.

It doesn't take long to figure out that creating the kind of database access required by today's employee is going to be a nightmare waiting to happen unless you have the appropriate tools to make the job easier. Visual InterDev provides just the kind of tools you're looking for in the form of Design-Time Controls. Even though there are other solutions available to you in Visual InterDev, like the ADODB ActiveX controls, you'll find that the Design-Time Controls option works the best and provides the fastest results.

This chapter is going to help you understand two things. First, we'll look at what kinds of situations require remote data access. In other words, we'll answer the question of when that old static display is no longer adequate, and when it's time to add the ability to both display and change the contents of your company database remotely.

The second section will show you how to create two different kinds of remote access Web pages using Visual InterDev. We'll discuss both a Grid view and a Record view display that you can use to meet a user's database needs in various situations. Obviously, a Grid view display on a Web page will work in about the same situations that a Grid view will work on the desktop. Likewise, you'll likely find that a Record view is the best one for adding new records or viewing all of the details about a single existing record. Not much will change about the theory behind which display to use, just the media for displaying that data will be different. Of course, the tools required to create the display will be different as well.

Protecting your data investment is an important part of any database setup. The third section of this chapter will show you how to enhance the security of your database by using an Internet Server Application Programming Interface (ISAPI) Filter to monitor the data stream. In this case, we'll secure the entire Web site using the Basic Authentication technique. However, the methods you learn in this third section will enable you to create other kinds of security ISAPI Filters that can both stop hackers from entering your Web site in the first place and monitor their activities should the hacker get through your defenses.

Scenario

It's come to your attention that more and more employees are going on the road to garner sales for your company at a time of high competition. The problem is that the salespeople can never quite rely on the information they get from the company Web site because the data changes daily and the Web site is only updated twice a week. In addition, the static data can't adjust for new contact information that is brought to the main office by other salespeople.

Management is concerned that giving the salespeople access to data on the road will also expose potentially sensitive data to hackers as well, so security is a major concern on this project. There are two ways that you'll take care of security concerns in this case. The first method is to create an ISAPI Filter to actually secure the data, making it harder for someone to break into your Web site.

Another method of security for the data comes at the database end of the project. Since this database doesn't handle actual invoice data, there isn't any reason to allow the salespersons to update it remotely. All they really need is the latest contact information, which means you need the ability to read the database dynamically each time a request is made. By opening the database for read-only access, you'll help prevent a hacker from modifying the data they find on your Web site, even if they manage to bypass the ISAPI Filter protecting it.

The database portion of this project won't require a very large team. In fact, you could make it a team of three. The first person is the Visual InterDev developer who will create the Web pages required to display the database information. You'll also need the services of a salesperson to test the output of the database in a real-world situation. Finally, this project will require the services of the database administrator to ensure that the data displayed on-screen matches the data in the database. Obviously, it will be up to both the Visual InterDev developer and the database administrator to ensure that behind-the-scenes issues like security are handled properly.

The ISAPI Filter will require a team of Visual C++ programmers. The ISAPI Filter can be created anytime during the database development process and tested using existing Web resources. Obviously, all of the security measures will need to be tested once the database project is completely finished and in place. This final testing process will require the efforts of the network administrator, the Visual C++ programming team, and users who are versed on using the new database product.

Determining When Remote Access Is Required

There are people who will tell you that every new Web site requires complete and dynamic access to all of the data that your company has to offer so that employees on the road can remain in contact. To a certain extent, they're right. Giving people access to your company's data in the most efficient way possible is always a good idea.

Making sure that the data they see isn't out of date is one way to ensure your business runs smoothly. However, even if you do decide to get rid of all those static Web pages hanging around on your Web site, you still have to answer two major questions, "How much access should we provide?" and, "How often should we update the content?"

These two questions are at the crux of many company discussions today. Providing a constantly updated source of information to employees is obviously optimal to ensuring they have the best possible source of data for making decisions. However, constant updates come at the price of both network bandwidth and increased server load. In addition, if full updates of every bit of information in your database take too long to download, you can be certain an employee will spend less time looking at that information than they should.

Deciding how often data changes is one of the things you need to consider. A pricing index for a hot commodity may change daily or even more often. In this case, a dynamic connection to the database like the one shown in this chapter is probably the best way to go if you want to be sure the employee has the very best information for decision making. On the other hand, if that data only changes on a weekly or monthly basis, you may want to stick with those static Web pages. Batch updates of slowly changing Web pages is still a smart choice when data changes slowly. You'll want to reserve these more exotic methods for data that employees know changes quickly.

Another question is how much access to provide. Giving everyone read/write access to a database is one sure way to invite a hacker to change the information for you. You should reserve full database access for those situations where it's a necessity. For example, if you decide to give employees access to an invoicing database on the road, then you would probably need to provide the ability to both read and write the data. You could reduce your risk in this situation by maintaining a separate Web database for updates. A database administrator could review these updates prior to making them part of the main database.

There are situations, like the one in this chapter, when read access is all that is required. In this chapter, a contact database that may change often but requires little update from employees on the road is a perfect example of a situation where you can provide the employee what they need with only a modicum of security risk. Other read-only examples include inventory control or company policy statements. An employee on the road may need to know that you have a certain number of parts in stock before making a sale, but they don't need to actually change the quantity in the inventory database because that will be taken care of by the people fulfilling the order.

One situation that some people don't consider is the write-only database. The employee sees a form on-screen, fills it out, and then sends the completed form back to the company. If there isn't a need to review these records until the employee arrives back at the office, allowing write-only access isn't a concern. Examples of a write-only database might include a suggestion or a customer survey form.

Designing an Access Page Using Visual InterDev

Visual InterDev provides a variety of tools for creating database applications. You could conceivably create remote access database applications using these tools that would rival their counterparts on the desktop. This section will show you one of the easier methods of creating a read-only database application that users could use on the road to view the company's current contact list. Simple modifications of this project would allow you to fulfill a number of read/write scenarios as well. The following sections will show you how to create, define, and, finally, test a database application created with Visual InterDev.

Creating a Project Shell

The first step in our project is creating a project shell. In this case, we'll use a minimum of gizmos like themes and layouts to ensure you can see how the database elements actually work when looking through the code. The following procedure will get you started with the project shell.

1. Start Visual InterDev, if you haven't done so already. You'll see the New Project dialog box.

2. Type **ViewAddr** in the Name field.

3. Click Open. You'll see the Web Project Wizard - Step 1 of 4 dialog box.

4. Choose a server (see Chapter 4 if you need additional information about setting a server up).

5. Select Master mode, then click Next. Visual InterDev will contact the Web server and set up a new project. You'll see the Web Project Wizard - Step 2 of 4 dialog box.

6. Uncheck the "Create search.htm to enable full text searching" option since we won't need this feature for this project.

7. Click Finish. Visual InterDev will create a new project for you.

Defining a Connection

Databases, whether on a Web site or the desktop, require a connection. Visual InterDev makes creating the connection to a database a little easier than many Microsoft products do by keeping all of the connection elements strictly within the IDE. There are actually two types of ODBC database connection that you can create for Windows: file-based and registry-based. We created a registry-based connection in Chapter 9. This kind of connection has the advantage of residing in the registry—making it unlikely that the user will lose the connection by performing some unexpected action with the client machine. The file-based connection that we'll create in this chapter has the advantage of allowing an administrator to transport the connection from machine to machine using a simple file transfer. Obviously, this is the way to go for a Web application since the client machine may require an ODBC connection update before it can access the database on the Web site. The following procedure shows you how to create a file-based connection.

1. Right-click Global.ASA, then choose Add Data Connection... from the context menu. Visual InterDev will add a data environment to your project, then display the Select Data Source dialog box shown here:

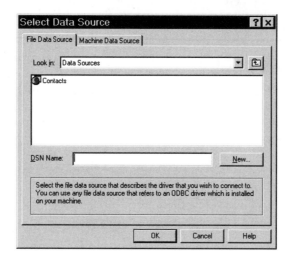

2. Click New. You'll see the Create New Data Source dialog box shown here:

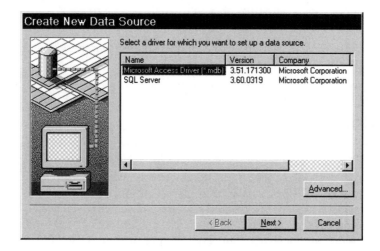

3. Select the SQL Server option, then click Next. You'll see a dialog box like the one shown here asking what name to use for the data source:

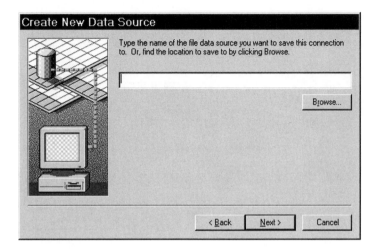

4. Type a name for the data source. The example uses Addresses.

5. Click Next. You'll see a final summary dialog box like the one shown here:

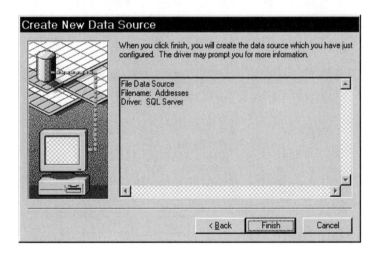

6. Click Finish. Visual InterDev will create a blank data source for you. You'll see the Create a New Data Source to SQL Server dialog box shown here.

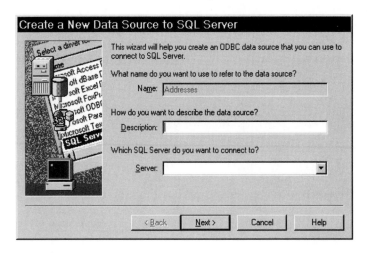

7. Type a description for the data source. The example uses "The client contact information database for our company."

8. Select a server in the Server field. You may need to type the server name if this is a new connection.

9. Click Next. You'll see an authentication dialog box like the one shown here:

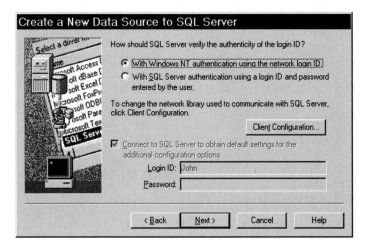

10. Choose the "SQL Server authentication" option, then type **sa** in the Login ID field.

11. Click Next. You'll see a database connection information dialog box like the one shown here:

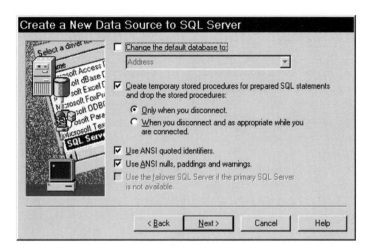

12. Check the "Change the default database to" option, then select Address from the drop-down list box.

13. Click Next twice. Click Finish. You'll see an ODBC Microsoft SQL Server Setup dialog box like the one shown here:

14. Click Test Data Source. You should see a SQL Server ODBC Data Source Test dialog box with a successful completion message like the one shown here:

15. Click OK twice to close the Data Source dialog boxes. You should see an Addresses entry in the Select Data Source dialog box.

16. Highlight the Addresses entry, then click OK. Visual InterDev will display a SQL Server Login dialog box like the one shown here:

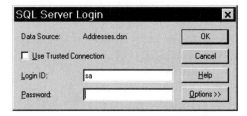

17. Type a password, if necessary (we didn't set the example database up to require security for this user name), then click OK. Visual InterDev will establish a connection with SQL Server and open the connection to the database. You'll see a Data View window open when this occurs. Visual InterDev will also create a

connection for you and display a <Connection Name> Properties dialog box like the one shown here.

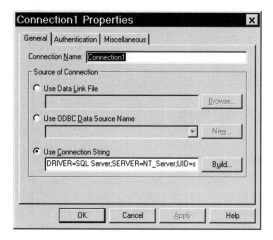

18. Click OK. Visual InterDev will create the connection for you.

19. Right-click Connection1 in Project Explorer and choose Add Data Command... from the context menu. You'll see the <Command Name> Properties dialog box shown here:

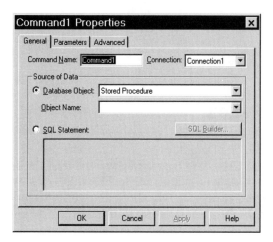

20. Choose Table in the Database Object field and dbo.Contacts in the Object Name field.

21. Click OK. Visual InterDev will execute the command and add the fields of the Contacts database to the Project Explorer Window beneath the Command1 entry as shown here:

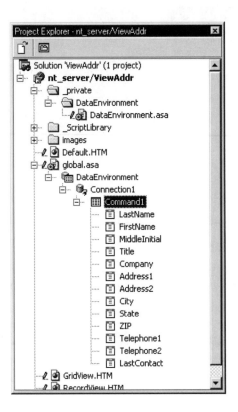

Adding the Web Pages

This example uses three Web pages to display the data contained in the Contacts table of the Address database. The Default page will allow the user to select between one of two database views. The GridView page will show the user the database contents using a grid format. In other words, the user will be able to see more than one record at a time. Finally, the RecordView page will allow the user to see one complete record at a time. This is the optimal solution for record editing or for viewing larger records that don't display completely in the Grid view. The following procedure will help you add the three Web pages required for this project:

1. Right-click the <Server Name>/ViewAddr folder, and choose the Add | HTML Page... option from the context menu. You'll see the Add Item dialog box.

2. Type **Default.HTM** in the Name field, then click Open. You'll see a new Web page added to your project.

3. Repeat Steps 1 and 2, but name the new Web page GridView.

4. Repeat Steps 1 and 2, but name the new Web page RecordView.

5. Right-click Default.HTM and choose Set as Start Page from the context menu.

Designing the Grid View

Now that we have the three Web pages we'll use for this project in place, it's time to start defining the contents for each one. The following procedure will help you define the contents of the GridView.HTM file:

1. Select GridView.HTM using the Window menu.

2. Select the Design-Time Controls tab of the toolbox and add a Recordset control to the GridView display. Visual InterDev will automatically fill the data fields in for you. We need to modify these fields for use with the Internet connection we set up.

3. Choose DE Commands in the Database Object field and Command1 in the Object Name field.

4. Press ENTER, then add a Grid control to the GridView display. We'll need to configure this control to display the information contained in the Contacts table of the Address database.

5. Right-click Grid1, then choose Properties from the context menu. Select the Data tab. You'll see a Grid Properties dialog box like the one shown here.

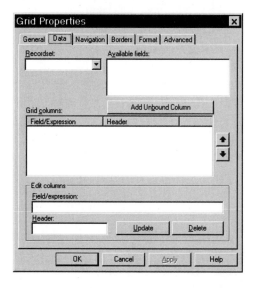

6. Choose Recordset1 in the Recordset field. You'll see a list of "Contacts table" field names displayed in the Available fields list box.

7. Check all of the fields in the "Available fields" list box, then click OK. Your GridView.HTM display should look like the one shown in Figure 12-1.

Designing the Single Record View

The second data display Web page is the RecordView.HTM file. Unlike the GridView.HTM page, you'll need to add a control for moving from record to record, and separate controls for each field in the database to this view. The following procedure will show you how:

1. Select RecordView.HTM using the Window menu.

2. Select the Design-Time Controls tab of the toolbox and add a Recordset control to the GridView display. Visual InterDev will automatically fill the data fields in for you. We need to modify these fields for use with the Internet connection we set up.

3. Choose DE Commands in the Database Object field and Command1 in the Object Name field.

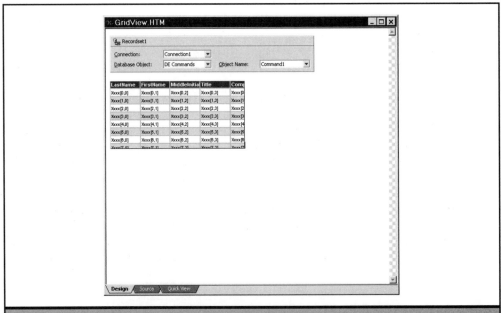

Figure 12-1. The GridView.HTM display will allow the user to see all of the database fields in a grid format

4. Press ENTER, then add a RecordsetNavbar. This is the control we'll use to move from record to record in the Single Record view. You can use a RecordsetNavbar anytime a control lacks the ability to move from record to record. Fortunately, the Grid control used in the previous section includes a navigational aid.

5. Right-click RecordsetNavbar1 and choose Properties from the context menu. You'll see a RecordsetNavbar1 Properties dialog box like the one shown here:

6. Choose Recordset1 in the Recordset field, then click OK. The RecordsetNavbar is now set to move the record pointer as needed to display new records.

7. Add the 13 labels and descriptive text to create the form shown in Figure 12-2. Use the Label control on the Design-Time Controls tab of the toolbox for this task. You'll need to right-click each control in turn and choose the Properties option on the context menu to display the General tab of the <Label Name> Properties dialog box. Set the Recordset field to Recordset1 and the Field/ Expression field to the name of the "Contacts table" field that you want to display. You can set the format of the Label control on the Format tab of the <Label Name> Properties dialog box. The example uses a Font field value of Times New Roman and a Size field value of 3. In addition, the name and first telephone number fields are displayed in bold type.

Designing the Default Web Page

The Default.HTM file will require the least amount of design time for this example. All we really need is a little descriptive text and links to our other two pages. Just type to create the descriptive text. Creating a link is easy as well. All you need to do is drag the name of the file you want to link to from the Project Explorer window to the Default.HTM window. Carefully highlight the underlined text and type in something more descriptive for the line. Figure 12-3 shows the page I created for this example.

Figure 12-2. The RecordView.HTM will allow a user to see all of the fields for a single record

Testing the Results

At this point, our Visual InterDev database access example is ready to go. The first thing you'll see, of course, is the Default.HTM page shown in Figure 12-3. It won't look much different than what you see there, so I won't talk about it again. The only purpose for the default Web page, in this case, is to act as a link between the two database pages.

> **Note** *Displaying database pages in Internet Explorer (or other browsers) can take quite a bit of time. Your browser may actually appear frozen. The "E" in the upper-right corner of the browser will stop rotating and you'll see a done message in the status bar. Don't worry, give the browser a little time to display the information. After a while you'll see the various design-time controls appear on-screen. Once the screen has fully drawn itself, you'll be able to use the project as normal. The display will draw itself much faster if you start the browser outside of Visual InterDev, so that's the best route to go unless you're actually troubleshooting a bug in the Web page code.*

Let's look at the GridView.HTM page. Click the GridView link on the default Web page and you'll see something like Figure 12-4. Notice that the Grid control automatically performs some data formatting for you, which makes the display more attractive. In fact, the Grid control allows you to use the equivalent of a theme to choose a predefined appearance for the data you want to present.

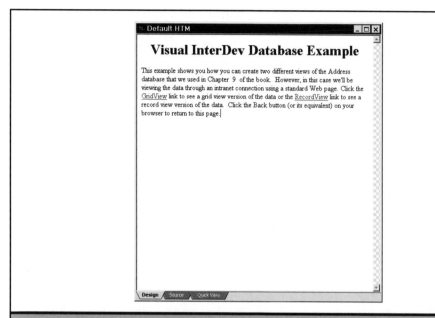

Figure 12-3.   The Default Web Page provides simple links to the other two pages in our example

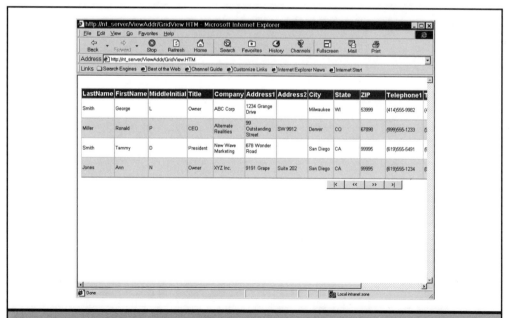

Figure 12-4.   The GridView display provides many default formatting features that allow you to create an attractive display with a minimum of work

The RecordView.HTM display is next. Click the Back button on your browser, then choose the RecordView link on the default Web page. You'll see something like the display shown in Figure 12-5. Unlike the GridView display that we saw in Figure 12-4, this one will require additional formatting. However, it does provide a single-record display, which allows you to see all of the data for a single record in one view.

Using Visual C++ to Create a Security Filter

Our database example works just fine at this point; the user can access the Web site and garner any contact information required prior to their next meeting. However, there's one thing lacking in this picture—security. There are a lot of different ways in which you can add security to any Web application. This section is going to look at one particular method—an ISAPI Filter designed to enforce security on your Web site. The following sections will help you build the ISAPI Filter, install it, and then test it using our sample database Web site.

Note   *There are a lot of different types of ISAPI Filters. While this section provides you with just a taste of what you can do, Chapter 17 provides a description of the various forms of ISAPI Filters at your disposal. Make sure you also read about ISAPI in general in Chapter 16. Both chapters together show you why ISAPI is such a power, yet underutilized feature of IIS installations today.*

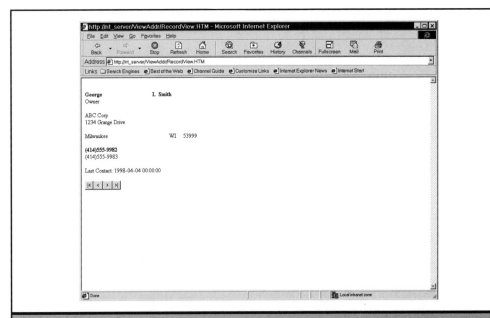

Figure 12-5.   Use a display like RecordView to allow the user to see all of the data for a single record at once

Creating the ISAPI Filter Shell

As with any Visual C++ project, the first thing you need to do is create a program shell that helps define the ISAPI Filter as a whole. In this case, we'll actually start out using the ISAPI Extension Wizard since Visual C++ uses the same wizard for creating ISAPI Filters. The following procedure will get you started.

1. Start Visual C++ if you haven't done so already.

2. Use the File | New command to display the New dialog box. Select the ISAPI Extension Wizard. (Even though we're creating a filter, you'll still need to use the ISAPI Extension Wizard to do it.)

3. Type the name of the ISA filter you want to create. I used DBProtect for the example ISA, but you could use any name that you want. Your New dialog box should look like the one shown here:

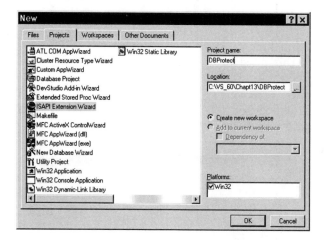

4. Click OK. You'll see the ISAPI Extension Wizard - Step 1 of 1 dialog box. This is where you'll select the various characteristics for your ISA. There are three main areas to the dialog box. You can choose to create a filter by checking the first check box and an extension by checking the second check box. The third area defines how you'll link MFC into your application.

5. Check the filter option, and uncheck the extension option. (Notice that adding the filter also adds another step to the process.) You'll want to provide a short, concise statement of what your ISA does in the Filter Description field. The description appears as a string that you can use within the DLL as needed. This description won't show up in the Properties dialog box when someone opens it for your ISA, so you'll want to add some additional text to the version information for your DLL as well.

6. Type **Protect the Address database from snooping** in the Filter Description field. Here's what your dialog box should look like at this point.

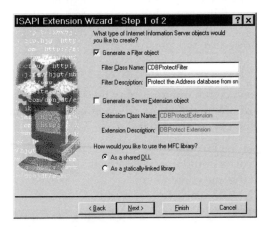

7. Click Next. You'll see the ISAPI Extension Wizard - Step 2 of 2 dialog box shown here. This is the page you'll use to select the events and type of monitoring your filter will provide. There are three areas to consider. See the sidebar entitled "Choosing Filter Options" in Chapter 17 to get more details about these options. For right now, all you really need to consider are the requirements for an ISAPI Filter used to monitor security.

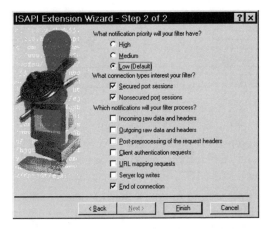

8. Choose the High option for the notification priority. Security is a major concern, so we want to make sure that the ISAPI Filter will get to look at the data stream almost immediately. Unfortunately, selecting this option can slow server performance, so you only want to use it when absolutely required. The default setting of Low is normally appropriate for a filter that performs work like mapping URLs.

9. Check the "Client authentication requests" check box, and uncheck the "End of connection" check box. We want to activate our filter when the user requests specific kinds of access to the server since we're creating a simple filter to keep the Address database safe.

10. Click Finish. You'll see a New Project Information dialog box like the one shown here. Make sure you double-check all the settings for your filter because the New Project Information page provides a detailed breakdown of the events that it'll get to see.

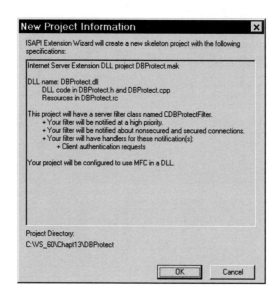

11. Click OK. The ISAPI Extension Wizard will create the required program shell for you.

Adding Some Code

It's time to make our ISAPI Filter functional. The code that we'll use is relatively simple, in this case, because the security filter will perform the minimal work required to start the authentication process. Listing 12-1 shows the code you'll need to add to the OnAuthentication( ) method. We'll talk about how this method works once you get a chance to view the code.

Listing 12-1

```
DWORD CDBProtectFilter::OnAuthentication(CHttpFilterContext* pCtxt,
    PHTTP_FILTER_AUTHENT pAuthent)
{
    CString    oBuffer;         // Buffer for client output.
    DWORD      dwSize;          // Size of the buffer.
    LPVOID     pvInOut;         // Client input or output.
```

```
// See if we're getting an anonymous request.
if (strlen(pAuthent->pszUser) == 0)
{

    // Get the user's name.
    dwSize = 100;
    pvInOut = " ";
    pCtxt->GetServerVariable("REMOTE_USER", pvInOut, &dwSize);
    dwSize = strlen(LPTSTR(pvInOut));

    if (strncmp(LPTSTR(pvInOut), " ", 1) == 0)
    {

        // Set an error condition.
        pCtxt->ServerSupportFunction(SF_REQ_SEND_RESPONSE_HEADER,

            "401 Access Denied",
            NULL,
            NULL);
    }
    else
    {

        // Indicate the user has supplied a password.
        pCtxt->ServerSupportFunction(SF_REQ_SEND_RESPONSE_HEADER,
            NULL,
            NULL,
            NULL);

        // Store the user's name.
        strncpy(pAuthent->pszUser, LPTSTR(pvInOut), dwSize);

        // Get and store the user's password.
        dwSize = 100;
        pvInOut = " ";
        pCtxt->GetServerVariable("AUTH_PASS", pvInOut, &dwSize);
        dwSize = strlen(LPTSTR(pvInOut));
        strncpy(pAuthent->pszPassword, LPTSTR(pvInOut), dwSize);
```

```
        }
    }

    // return the appropriate status code
    return SF_STATUS_REQ_NEXT_NOTIFICATION;
}
```

This code may look a little complicated at first, but it's relatively simple once you understand how the filter does its job. One of the things we need to do is pass information from the filter directly to the server, which in turn passes it onto the client. It takes three passes to complete the trip through this filter, as listed here:

1. Determine if the user is trying to access the server anonymously by using the GetServerVariable( ) function to retrieve the user name. (A blank return value for the user name indicates that the user is trying to access the server anonymously.) If so, tell the server to send a 401 error message to the client using the ServerSupportFunction( ) function. This displays the browser's Password dialog box where the user can enter a password and name.

2. Once the user enters a password and name, retrieve it from the input stream using the GetServerVariable( ) function. Pass the name and password along to Windows NT security for verification.

3. Tell the server that the filter has successfully completed its mission using the SF_STATUS_REQ_NEXT_NOTIFICATION return value.

Since you have three loops to work with, there are always a few surprises when working with a security filter. For example, any decryption will happen during the second pass through the filter, between the time you retrieve the user name and password using the GetServerVariable( ) function and the time you copy this information to the pAuthent structure using the strncpy( ) function. Some things happen during the third loop. For example, you may decide that you need to interact with the user directly. This usually happens during the third pass through the filter.

Notice that I provided a return value of SF_STATUS_REQ_NEXT_NOTIFICATION. That's the server's signal that you want it to handle the details of validating the user and displaying a Web page. If you want to perform all of the validation yourself, you'll also need to display the requested information. There isn't any middle ground when it comes to this step.

IIS normally gives you three chances to enter the password correctly before it displays an error message. You could circumvent this behavior in two ways. First, you could perform your own authentication between the second and third passes of the security filter. This way, you could give the user additional chances to provide the correct password and pass the correct user name and password to the server the first time around. The second method is to use the SF_STATUS_REQ_ERROR return value to stop any attempt to access the Web server after the first failed attempt. This will display a server error message and could possibly convince less knowledgeable users that the server is down, reducing further attempts at access.

Installing the Security ISAPI Filter

Once you compile this filter, you'll need to install it using the technique shown in the "Installing the ISAPI Filter" section of Chapter 17. Obviously, you'll use the DBProtect.DLL file in this chapter instead of the ViewMap ISAPI Filter discussed in that chapter. The ISAPI Filters tab of the Default Web Site Properties dialog box should look like the one shown here when you finish.

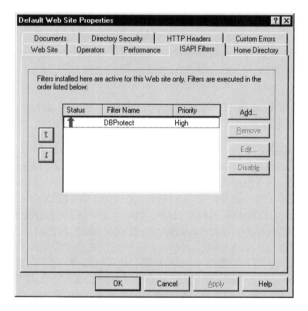

Our example still isn't ready to run. You'll need to set the Web site up for restricted access. The following procedure will help you set up the restricted access required for this example (write down the default settings so that you can return your security settings to their prior state).

1. Right-click the Default Web Site entry, then choose Properties from the context menu. You'll see the Default Web Site Properties dialog box.

2. Choose the Directory Security tab. You'll see a display like the one shown here:

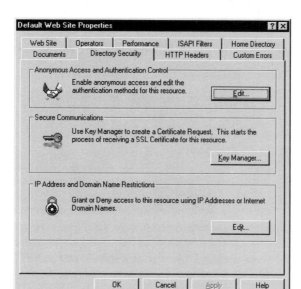

3. Click Edit in the Anonymous Access and Authentication Control group. You'll see the Authentication Methods dialog box. This is where you choose the methods that Windows NT will use to try to authenticate a user. Our simple ISAPI Filter is designed to work with the Basic Authentication method.

4. Check the Basic Authentication option and uncheck everything else. IIS may display a message box when you click the Basic Authentication option; click OK to clear it. Your dialog box should look like the one shown here:

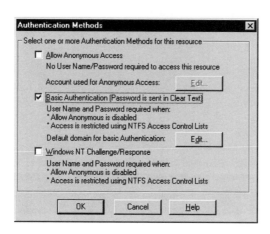

5. Click OK twice to make the setting permanent. IIS may display an Inheritance Overrides dialog box when you click OK to close the Default Web Site Properties dialog box. Click OK to clear it.

We're finally ready to run the example. When you try to access the database now, you'll see a Password dialog box like the one shown here:

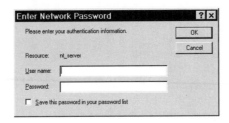

Try entering a nonexistent user name or password. IIS will require you to try three times before it gives up asking for a name and password. After the third time, you'll see a server-generated error message like the one shown in Figure 12-6.

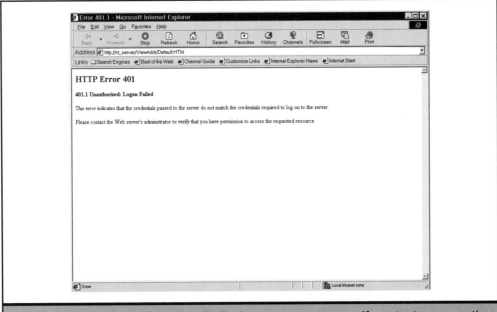

Figure 12-6.   Internet Explorer will display an error message if you try to access the Web site without providing an authorized name and password

You may need to close Internet Explorer to display the Password dialog box again, so that you can test the results of a correct name and password. Entering a valid name and password will give you access to the Web site.

Lessons Learned

Visual InterDev allows you to create database applications that include all of the functionality of their desktop counterparts. However, the environment in which these pages operate poses certain security risks that you probably wouldn't encounter at the desktop. For example, a hacker can easily access your Web site and may even be able to gain access to the database using just a simple browser. With this in mind, security becomes a much more important issue when creating a Visual InterDev application than it is normally.

There are many ways to create a database application using Visual InterDev. For example, you can use the ADODB ActiveX controls. However, the easiest way to get an application up and running using Visual InterDev is by using the Design-Time Controls that come with the product. You'll find that the Design-Time Control method offers you more Visual InterDev–specific configuration options and that you can actually create simple database applications with little or no coding. Obviously, using ActiveX controls would have an advantage if you wanted to use custom controls that you had previously created for desktop application in your company, or if you were looking for the greatest amount of consistency with the look presented by desktop applications used in your company.

Both IIS and Visual InterDev offer methods for securing your application that require little effort beyond some configuration. However, none of these standard security methods offer you a method for providing customized security. ISAPI Filters can provide a completely custom solution or they can be designed to provide a combination of custom and standard security, as you saw in this chapter. While developing an ISAPI Filter to provide a fully customized and secure solution may seem like a lot of work, consider the benefits to your company and the problems that a breach of security could cause. A custom security feature can offer just that little bit of additional security that will keep hackers at bay or at least increase the time it takes for them to break into your system.

Chapter 13

Designing an ActiveDocument
Application

W e've talked about all kinds of new technologies in the book so far—including ActiveX and COM+, which promise to make the Internet into a business tool for everyone. There are a lot of different ways in which ActiveX is being used (and COM+ will be used in the future). For example, Microsoft released a new ActiveX API called ActiveX Accessibility. This API is designed to add to the Internet what the Accessibility applet added to Windows 95/98. Things like Sticky Keys (a method for creating control-key combinations by pressing one key at a time instead of all the keys simultaneously) will appear not only on your Windows 95/98 and Windows NT 4.0 desktops, but also within your ActiveX-compatible Internet browser.

If you haven't had a chance to work with the accessibility features provided with Windows 95/98 and Windows NT yet, take the time to try them. There are times when I'll use some of the features while programming. For example, the MouseKeys feature comes in handy for precise placement of the mouse on-screen (which in turn makes it easier to precisely place components on a form). Even if you don't find any of the accessibility features useful for your own needs, knowing about these features will help you create better applications that a larger group of people can use with ease.

There are other ActiveX-based technologies in the works as well (by Microsoft and other companies)—too many to talk about here. One of the more important ActiveX technologies is ActiveMovie. In fact, the MSNBC Internet site is already using ActiveMovie to show you clips from the NBC news network. Essentially, ActiveMovie allows you to view film clips on the Internet, and play AVI and other kinds of movie files.

Web Link

There's more information available about the technologies just described. You can find out about ActiveX Accessibility at: http://www.microsoft.com/enable/dev/msdn4.htm. Usage instructions and a technological description of the ActiveMovie control appear at: http://www.microsoft.com/msdn/sdk/inetsdk/help/complib/activemovie/activemovie.htm.

The most important ActiveX technology, though, isn't a new and exciting one—it relates to that old and mundane problem of sharing documents on the Internet. This has always been a problem because the interface is static—just consider the number of tags you'd need and the complexity of the program required to create any kind of a dynamic interface. Sure, you can export a word-processed document into HTML and come up with a realistic representation of the data, but that data won't change and it will be difficult for the user to edit it. The same holds true for spreadsheet data. Showing the data isn't too hard as long as you're willing to sacrifice up-to-the-minute information. ActiveX provides an answer in this case. It allows you to create a dynamic document—one that you can edit and see the changes in real time.

So, where did this technology mysteriously come from? It's not new at all: Microsoft has simply modified the technology found in Microsoft Office. The original name for ActiveX Document is *OLE Document Objects*. (Most people, including

Microsoft, have now shortened *ActiveX Document* to simply *ActiveDocument*—the term we'll use throughout the book since it's clearer and more explicit.) It's part of the Microsoft Office Binder technology and was never meant to become a public specification. Originally, you had to sign up for the Office-compatible program before you could even get a specification for OLE Document Objects. It was only after the appearance of Windows 95/98 that this specification became something that anyone could get. However, it only makes sense that Microsoft would make this specification public since it's the next logical step in the evolution of OLE.

ActiveDocument is what this chapter's all about. We're going to examine what will be the most important use of ActiveX besides database applications. You'll learn just how easy it is to create ActiveDocuments for browser use. We'll also examine what you need to do to create custom document setups of your own.

> **Note**
>
> *You can find out more about the interfaces used to create ActiveDocument by reading the "ActiveDocument Required Interfaces" section of Chapter 11. While you don't absolutely have to know this information to create an ActiveDocument application using the techniques in this chapter, knowing the information will help you create more complex applications later. A good knowledge of the interfaces required for ActiveDocument will also help you create ActiveDocument-enabled ActiveX controls or COM servers.*

Future Direction for Microsoft Office 2000

Microsoft plans further integration of Microsoft Office with the Internet when it releases Office 2000. This updated version of Microsoft Office will offer direct support for creating Web pages and publishing the results on the Internet or an intranet. In addition, people will be able to view the document using a browser if they don't have Microsoft Office installed on their machine, or using Microsoft Office when it's installed. While the new version of Microsoft Office will definitely make it easier for people to create enterprise-level content for their Web site with ease, there are still situations where you'll definitely want to provide ActiveDocument support. For example, creating an ActiveDocument application will allow you to enforce security and document editing protocols without resorting to a lot of complex macros. ActiveDocument will remain a viable technology for quite some time to come—the latest upgrade to Microsoft Office will simply provide the tools required to fully support user needs from within an ActiveDocument application. You can find out more about the future of Microsoft Office and how changes Microsoft makes to it will affect ActiveDocument at: http://www.microsoft.com/presspass/press/1998/aug98/ofbetapr.htm and http://www.microsoft.com/msoffice/2000/default.asp.

We'll examine four main ActiveDocument topics in this chapter. First, we'll look at using the Web Publishing Wizard. If you don't know how ActiveDocument works from the user perspective, you'll want to pay close attention to this section. After all, how can you be expected to write an application for something you don't understand?

Second, we'll create a simple program that implements the interfaces required for ActiveDocument. There are two versions of this application: one written in Visual C++, and the other in Visual Basic. Not only will this second section tell you how to create the application, we'll look at some simple ways to test it as well without creating a full-fledged Web page.

Next, we'll discuss things you need to consider when installing ActiveDocument-enabled applications. Simply placing the application on the user's machine may not guarantee that everything works as anticipated. Complex application setups like ActiveDocument require some additional planning on your part.

Finally, we'll create a full-fledged Web presentation of our ActiveDocument applications using Visual InterDev. This presentation will allow you to see the power of ActiveDocument and how it can fit into your intranet or Internet site needs.

Scenario

The scenario for this chapter is pretty basic. Your boss needs to provide a method for people in various company locations around the globe to work on documents together without incurring the cost of travel. ActiveDocument is a perfect solution to the problem since each person can work on the document from his or her office and store it in a central location on a server of your choosing. You can even provide multiple security levels by using the various security features provided by both Windows NT Server and Microsoft Office itself.

There are actually three groups of people who need to work together on this application, though at first glance you might only expect two. The first group is the programmers who will create the ActiveDocument application. This group will need to work closely with the other two groups to ensure the ActiveDocument application performs as anticipated. The application developers may need to provide special security or formatting features that a standard browser or Microsoft Office setup may not provide.

The second group is the Web site developers. They'll need to create three levels of Web site support, two of which can be worked on in tandem. The more important part of the Web site development task is to create a presentation of the application links. These links will allow the ActiveDocument application to open specific documents based on the user's needs. A second task is to create help pages for new users. The typical user isn't going to have any idea of how an ActiveDocument application is supposed to work. As a minimum, you'll need to provide plenty of help pages so that the user can get specific help as needed. A good addition to the help page support is some type of tutorial. You could present the tutorial as a series of Web pages that the user could interact with. Obviously, this task can be performed in tandem with the first task of creating the Web site links. Finally, the Web site developers will have to create some type of search mechanism for finding the right document. Remember that the user will no longer have access to any of the search features provided by Microsoft Office. Unfortunately, you may find it difficult to use the standard search page provided by Visual InterDev since the standard search page relies on being able to read the content of the files. Using any form of encryption on the documents would also mean coming up with an alternative search technique. You'll want to wait to perform this task until there's sufficient test data to make a good test of the search capability of the Web site.

The third group is the sampling of the users who will need to collaborate on documents together using the ActiveDocument application. Make sure you have at least two users per site so that you can reduce the chance of one site not working properly when you deploy the application. This group will need to start to create test data immediately so that the other two groups have something to test with. Better still, they could create actual documents so that the applications can be tested in a real-world situation. (Make sure that these are documents your company can afford to lose or have compromised since security and application errors could create data compromise or integrity problems.)

This chapter concentrates on word processing documents since that is the kind of document that your users will need to collaborate on most often. However, the principles described here will work on a wide variety of other application types as well. For example, there's little difference from an ActiveDocument implementation perspective between sharing word processing documents and sharing spreadsheets. Obviously, the application and Web site specifics will need to be tailored to your company's needs.

What Is an ActiveDocument?

Up to this point, we haven't looked very much at the kinds of documents users would be familiar with in regard to the Internet. For example, while a user is going to be very familiar with the Word document they just modified on their local hard drive, the really neat ActiveX control they used on the Internet is going to be totally unfamiliar. We've also looked at the scripting language used to display specific page elements in a way that only a programmer would love (a user probably isn't all that interested in the latest techniques for creating JavaScript). Of course, this begs a question that nearly everyone will ask—what's in the Internet for the user besides a bit of information, a few forms, and your dazzling ActiveX controls? ActiveDocuments provide part of the answer. They're a means for just about anyone to create content and display it on a Web page.

However, ActiveDocuments are more than merely a way to share information—you can actually use them to get real work done. Think about this scenario: Your company has its own intranet that employees can contact as needed from anywhere in the world. They use it to get their email and perform a variety of other tasks. As previously mentioned, that same intranet can be used for another purpose—collaboration between the various experts in your company. In the past, such collaboration would have required one or more parties to travel to a central location to work together. Besides the cost of doing this, there are other negatives to consider like the effects of jet lag on your workgroup and the need for local resources that will now be unavailable to the parties that traveled from a remote location. In sum, using ActiveDocument allows your company to maximize workgroup potential without inconveniencing the employee or incurring the cost of travel.

Note   *Netscape Navigator and earlier versions of Internet Explorer let you view nonstandard documents through the use of helpers. The browser would start a full copy of the application and then pass it the contents of the file on the Web site. The problem with this approach is that you use more memory to start another application and you don't have a live connection to the Internet server. Changes made to the file wouldn't be reflected in the server copy. Even though Microsoft still uses the term "helpers" with regard to Internet Explorer 3.0 and above, the view from the user's standpoint is completely different.*

ActiveDocuments can be easy to implement within a Web page. Simply place a link to the document in an HTML document using the standard HTML tags. When users click on the document link, they'll see an editable copy of the document in their browser with the appropriate changes to their browser menu and toolbar. Figure 13-1 shows a Word for Windows document displayed in an Internet Explorer browser window. Notice that all of the browser features are still intact—the only thing that's changed is the way the document gets displayed. This particular OLE technique isn't new—it's called *in-place editing*. We have, in fact, still used Word to edit a local downloaded copy of the document (it appears in your browser's temporary directory). Most OLE 2 servers can now provide this capability to an OLE 2 client. Try it out in Word for Windows or CorelDRAW! sometime. The menu and toolbar will change to match that of the client anytime you click on an OLE object. The big difference is that this is happening in a browser through an Internet connection.

Note   *If you test this sample on a LAN-based Internet server, you may get a dialog box asking whether you want to open or save the file. In most cases, you'll definitely get it when testing the connection over a live Internet connection (depending on how you set up security for your browser). Simply open the file to see it as shown in Figure 13-1.*

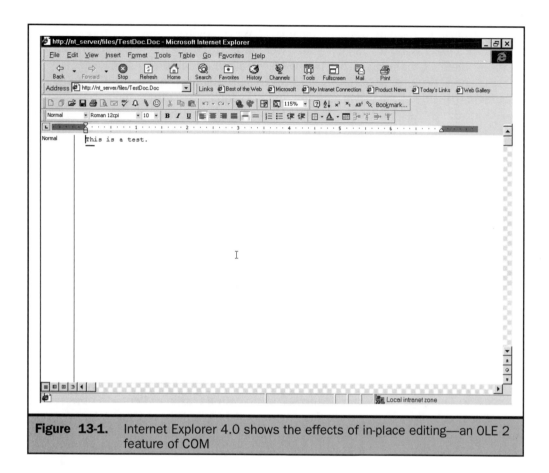

Figure 13-1.   Internet Explorer 4.0 shows the effects of in-place editing—an OLE 2
feature of COM

You'll notice another difference as well. If you were to make a change to this
document and then click the Back button on the Internet Explorer browser toolbar,
you'd see the following dialog box asking if you want to change the file:

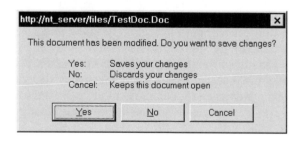

If you click on Yes, you'll see a typical File Save dialog box. The unfortunate part of this setup is that saving the file using this technique will place it on your local hard drive—something that won't work in our scenario, but possibly could in other circumstances. (Future versions of Microsoft Office will allow you to publish your documents directly to the server without an intervening step. Office 2000 promises to streamline the entire process of saving documents to an intranet or Internet site.) There are other ways of saving the file. You could use the File | Save As File... command. You could also use the File | Send To | Web Publishing Wizard command to actually send it back to the Web server—that would be our choice in this situation. (Some combinations of Internet Explorer and Windows won't provide a File | Send To | Web Publishing Wizard command, which means that you'll need to save the file locally and use the Web Publishing Wizard to send it to the Web server as a separate step.) We'll look at the steps needed for using the Web Publishing Wizard in the "Using the Web Publishing Wizard" section of this chapter.

Tip	*There are some situations when none of the techniques for posting changes in this section will help very much. For example, you may want to post the document on the Web server, but you may want each post to arrive individually. In that case, you could always tell the user to use the File	Send To	Mail Recipient command. Obviously, this would mean coordinating all of the documents you receive; but this method will work when others won't.*

ActiveDocument also presents some changes in the way a programmer has to think about OLE. There are three levels of object participation within a client. An object can simply appear in the viewing area, it can take over the window, or it can take over the entire application frame. Let's look at how these three levels differ.

Originally, you could create an object and place it in a container. When OLE 1 came out, the container would simply display an icon showing the presence of the object and nothing more. To edit an object, you double-clicked on its icon within the container. Windows would bring up a full-fledged copy of the document in a separate window. This is what's meant when someone says an object simply appears in the viewing area.

OLE 2 changed the way clients and servers interacted. With it, you could actually see the contents of the object. For example, if you placed a spreadsheet object within a word processing document, you could see its contents without double-clicking on the object. This is the window level of participation. The client and server share a window; the client displays its data, then relies on the server to display any information within an object. OLE 2 also provides in-place activation. In most cases, double-clicking on the object starts an out-of-process server that actually takes over the entire client frame. The server takes over the menus and toolbars normally reserved for client use. From a user perspective, the application was the same; the tools just changed to meet their needs for editing an object.

ActiveDocument moves this technology from desktop to the Internet through the use of a browser. Now your browser tools will automatically change to meet the needs of the user, and they no longer need to open a separate program to edit a document. An out-of-process server will take care of changing the browser menus and toolbars to match the ones normally used by the application. In fact, future versions of Windows will go still farther. We may eventually see total integration of every application with every other application. The user will no longer need to worry about which tool to use to edit the document; they'll simply open it and the operating system will automatically set their display up as needed to edit the document. In a way, this is the direction that Microsoft Office 2000 is already heading with its more complete integration with the Internet.

Windows 95/98 and Windows NT 4.0 both use the Explorer interface. If you right-click on just about any document that's associated with a registered application, you'll see a menu with a variety of choices. This list of choices reflects the combined ability of all applications and the operating system to work with the document. The most common choices are to open or print the document. In some cases, you'll also see an option to use the Quick View utility to see what the document contains.

The interface will probably change in the near future. Double-clicking on a document will perform an in-place activation. The server will actually take over the Explorer menus and toolbars. No longer will the user leave Explorer to open another application window. In addition, Internet sites will appear within Explorer as hard drives, combining the functionality of a browser with what we have today.

Are all of these changes welcomed by the programmer community? Not by a long shot. A few people are already claiming that this technology is only tightening Microsoft's grip on the computing world. Of course, that would only happen if you couldn't install another server in the place of Internet Explorer—which is something that definitely won't happen. ActiveDocument is going to be an extremely important technology as computing matures. That's why this chapter is so important—its purpose is to get you up to speed on this emerging technology so that you can use it to meet your current computing needs.

Tip

The current HTTP 1.0 specification doesn't allow the user to publish a document to the WWW server. The newer 1.1 specification remedies this oversight. If you want to allow users to publish documents back to the server from a Web page, then providing a server that uses the 1.1 specification is the way to go. Not only will you save time and effort by not having to write mundane scripts or jump through other hoops, you'll also reduce support calls by making things easier for the user. (All current versions of both Netscape and Microsoft products support this 1.1 specification—check your documentation if you own an older version of either vendor's product.)

Creating the Connection

Now that we've seen the result of using an ActiveDocument and discussed why this technology is important, let's take a look at the HTML code required to implement it. Listing 13-1 shows the code used to create this example (it's short and to the point). I didn't add any bells or whistles so that you could see the absolute minimum required to create an ActiveDocument link. As you can see, the code uses a simple link and nothing more. All of the "magic" behind this application is located in Internet Explorer. This is the same link tag that you've used to create links to other documents—nothing has changed. The simplicity of ActiveDocument from the Web developer's perspective is one of the things that makes it such an enticing technology.

Listing 13-1

```
<HTML>
<HEAD>
<TITLE>ActiveX Document</TITLE>
</HEAD>
<BODY>
<Center>
<H2>ActiveX Document Test Page</H2>
<EM>Requires Microsoft Word or WordPad</EM><P>
</Center>
<A HREF="http://nt_server/files/TestDoc.Doc">Test Document</A>
</BODY>
</HTML>
```

OK, so you've got a document displayed in your browser that you can edit. That really isn't such a big deal, is it? Sure it is. Since the document remains in the browser, you save memory. There's only one application running, and although you do have to pay the cost of some additional processing overhead and memory to view and process the document, it's a lot less than running two applications. For example, the in-place activation features are the result of using an out-of-process server. An *out-of-process server* is essentially a fancy form of DLL that provides the right kinds of interfaces to communicate with the client application. The point is that the DLL will take less memory than a full-fledged application if for no other reason than that it doesn't have to worry about displaying anything (that's the job of the client). We take a look at some of the requirements for this DLL in the "ActiveDocument Required Interfaces" section of Chapter 11.

There are two other ways to create an ActiveDocument connection that we won't spend much time looking at here. The first method is to use the Microsoft Web Control. The Microsoft Web Browser Control allows you to browse the Internet looking for any kind of document—including those that you don't normally associate with the Internet, like Word for Windows documents. The second method is to use an <OBJECT> tag to embed the out-of-process server for the application right into your Web page. There are several advanced <OBJECT> tag attributes that will help you in this regard. One of them allows you to pass the name of the file you want the user to see, just as you would do when using a link tag. The advanced attributes for the <OBJECT> tag are currently in a state of flux—that's why we won't look at them here.

Using the Web Publishing Wizard

You don't have to settle for the old methods of keeping documents up to date. It only takes a little bit of effort to use the Web Publishing Wizard to keep a document current on the Web server. These changes to the document won't solely appear on your local machine, as they would with older browser technology. They'll actually appear on the Internet server. By providing a written procedure for using the Web Publishing Wizard (and possibly setting up the connection information in advance), you've allowed an employee to make a change to what's essentially an HTML page from a remote location.

You'll need a copy of the Web Publishing Wizard to work with this section of the chapter. Visual Studio normally installs this utility automatically for you, but you may want to check on the Start menu for the appropriate icon. You should also see the Web Publishing Wizard on the Explorer Send To menu (right-click on a file and then look at the context menu entries). You'll also see the Web Publishing Wizard entry in your Word File | Send To menu when you open a document in a browser, but not when you open Word normally. You can download the latest version of the Web Publishing Wizard at http://www.microsoft.com/windows/software/webpost/default.htm. Windows 98 users will find that the Web Publishing Wizard appears in the Internet folder on the Windows Setup tab of the Add/Remove Programs Properties dialog box. The Web Publishing Wizard gets installed as part of various Internet programming tools offered by Microsoft, so you'll want to see if the Web Publishing Wizard is available before you install it.

So how do you start the process? The following procedure will get you going the first time around. You can make this an easy four-step process after this first attempt—we'll look at that part of the procedure once we go through this first phase. We'll start with a document like the one shown in Figure 13-1 and assume that you've already edited it. Now you want to save the change to your Internet site.

1. Use the File | Save As File command to display a File Save dialog box. You'll need to save the file locally before you can send it to the Web server. Perhaps Microsoft will change this part of the procedure later, but for now you'll have to take the time to make a local copy. Give the file the same name as the Web site page. In the case of our sample Internet site, the name of the file is TESTDOC.DOC (as shown in the Internet Explorer title bar in Figure 13-1).

2. Use the File | Send To | Web Publishing Wizard command within Word or Windows Explorer to display the Web Publishing Wizard dialog box shown

here (make sure you highlight the file or folder first if you send it using Windows Explorer):

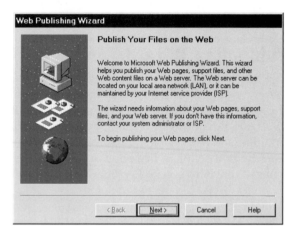

3. Click Next. You'll see the next page, as follows, if you're using an older version of Web Publishing Wizard or if you started Web Publishing Wizard from the Start menu. Web Publishing Wizard automatically places a filename in the File or Folder Name field in some cases. You won't want to use this filename right now. (If you're using a newer version of the product and you did select a file before starting the Web Publishing Wizard, you'll see a dialog box that asks which Web server connection to use; skip to Step 5 in this case.)

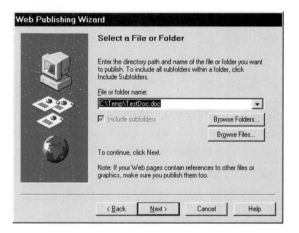

4. Click the Browse Files... button to display a Browse dialog box (it looks like a standard File Open dialog box). Locate the local copy of the document you just saved, then click on Open. Now you'll see the name of the Web document in the File or Folder Name field. Click Next.

5. If you've defined a Web server connection in the past, you'll see a single drop-down list box that contains names of the connections. You can select one of those connections or define a new one by clicking the New button. We'll assume that you need a new connection for the purposes of this example. (If you really don't need a new connection, select an existing one and skip to Step 14.) Whether you click the New button or you've never defined a server connection in the past, you'll see the next page as illustrated here (the illustration shows the latest version of Web Publishing Wizard, which includes one field and one command button; older versions have two fields). This page is where you begin to define the connection between the client machine and the Internet server. Fortunately, you only have to do it once.

Note   *Older versions of Web Publishing Wizard provided two fields on this dialog box. The first contained the connection name, the second the type of connection to create. You can access this second field on newer versions of Web Publishing Wizard by clicking the Advanced button shown on the dialog box.*

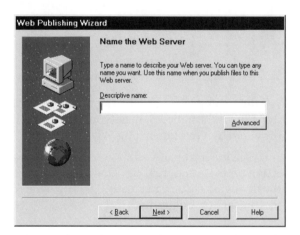

Tip   *A network administrator could perform this task once on each machine to reduce support calls from users. Unfortunately (at least as of this writing), there doesn't appear to be any way of doing this automatically like making a registry change or copying a file to the target machine.*

6. Type the name you want to use for your Internet connection. In most cases, leaving My Web Site is just fine if you only need one entry. Select an Internet service provider from the second list box. (Users of the latest version of Web Publishing Wizard will need to click the Advanced button.) If you're creating a connection for a LAN intranet site, then select Other Internet Provider when using an older version of Web Publishing Wizard or Automatically Select Service Provider when using a new version of Web Publishing Wizard.

7. Click Next. You'll see the next page, as follows. Notice that you'll need to define a connection to the Internet server. Simply type in the URL for your site. Users of the newer version of Web Publishing Wizard will also need to provide a local directory that corresponds to the remote Web site. This is where Web Publishing Wizard will look for files to publish to the Web server. Use the default directory in most cases. If you're using an older version of Web Publishing Wizard, skip to Step 9.

8. Click Next. Web Publishing Wizard will ask you for the URL that you want to use for publishing the information. Unless you're using an unusual setup, the default URL provided by Web Publishing Wizard will work fine.

9. Click Next. You'll see the next page, as shown here. This page allows you to select a connection type: LAN or dial-up. Don't be fooled by the description provided by the dialog box. You can create a dial-up connection for an intranet just as easily as you can for an Internet.

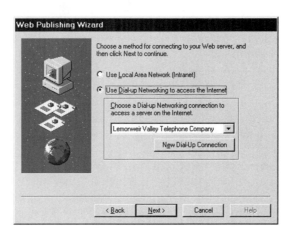

10. Choose between a LAN connection (no modem connection) or a dial-up connection. If you pick a dial-up connection, you'll also need to select one of the dial-up connections in the list box. Clicking the New Dial-Up Connection button allows you to create a new connection definition.

11. Click Next. The Web Publishing Wizard displays the next page, which simply states that it needs to verify the information you provided. Click Next to begin the verification process. If you're trying to create a LAN connection, you'll almost certainly get the error message shown next when using an older version of Web Publishing Wizard. Don't worry about it—the next few steps will show you how to fix the problem. If the Web Publishing Wizard successfully found your site, you can proceed to Step 15.

12. Click OK to clear the error message dialog box. You'll see the first page of an extended connection configuration, as follows. This is where you'll select a file transfer method. If you're working with an Internet site through a dial-up connection, you can choose between an FTP or HTTP file transfer. The HTTP method is only available to Web sites using HTTP version 1.1 or above. If you're working with a LAN, the FTP and Windows file transfer options are available. At this point, the various connections require a bit more definition. The procedure will continue by showing you the Windows file transfer option, since it's the one you'll need most often.

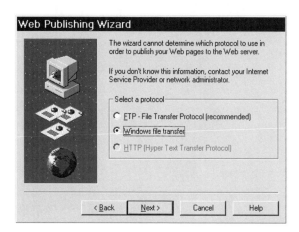

When configuring a LAN connection, use the Windows file transfer method whenever possible, since it's faster. The FTP connection requires an added file transfer layer that really isn't needed in the LAN environment. However, on a WAN, the FTP method could provide an added layer of security.

13. Click Next. You'll see the next page as shown in Figure 13-2. This is where the connection problem will become obvious. Web Publishing Wizard almost never gets the UNC (uniform naming convention) destination for your file right. The reason is pretty simple: the name is obscured by the server in most cases. You'll need to provide a fully qualified UNC to your storage directory like the one shown in Figure 13-2. Make absolutely certain that you provide a UNC name, not a standard DOS drive and directory location. The reason for using a UNC is that it allows you to use the same entry technique no matter what file system the server is using.

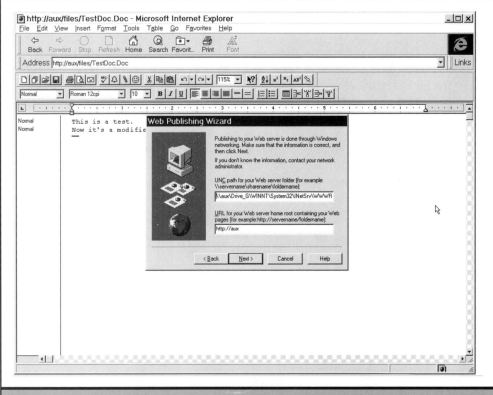

Figure 13-2. This page shows the source of almost every problem you'll have configuring Web Publishing Wizard

14. Click Next. The Web Publishing Wizard displays the next page, which simply states that it needs to verify the information you provided. Click Next to begin the verification process. This time you should see a success message.

15. Click Finish. This will allow you to complete the file transfer process. You'll see a file transfer dialog box while Web Publishing Wizard copies the file for you. Once it's finished, you'll see the success dialog box shown here. You've just modified this document—anyone visiting the Web site will see the changes automatically.

Once you finish these setup steps the first time, the user can complete the process in four easy steps. All you need to do is save the document to a local drive, use the File | Send To | Web Publishing Wizard command to start the Wizard, select the file, select a connection, and then click Finish to complete the process, which are Steps 1 through 4, and 15 if you want to look at it from a procedural view.

Creating the ActiveDocument Application

Now that you have some idea of how ActiveDocument works from the user perspective, let's look at it from the programmer perspective. In the previous section we looked at what you can do with an ActiveDocument application such as Word for Windows or Excel. That's fine if you're a power user who needs to get a little added performance or a Webmaster who wants to optimize a Web site; but you're a programmer who needs to create an application with these capabilities.

This section of the chapter is going to look at two different methods for creating an ActiveDocument application. The first example will use Visual C++ as the programming language, while the second uses Visual Basic. Before we proceed with the examples, though, let's talk a little about the choice of programming language.

There are times when you need to choose a language based on what it can do for you, not necessarily how easy it is to develop the application. Visual C++ offers better optimization than Visual Basic, which results in smaller executable sizes. In addition, you'll find that Visual C++ provides better low-level access to the interfaces required to create an ActiveDocument application. Visual C++ is normally a better choice when you need to develop a small ActiveDocument application that the user may need to download before using.

Visual Basic has a lot to offer when it comes to ActiveDocument as well. For one thing, you'll find that you can develop a complex application a lot faster. (As we'll see later in the chapter, the Visual Basic version of an ActiveDocument application requires a lot more work up front when compared to the Visual C++ version, but the fast prototyping the Visual Basic offers tends to offset this initial investment in time when working with complex applications.) Unlike most Visual Basic applications, you'll find that there are a lot of details to take care of when first creating an ActiveDocument application. However, these details become mundane after a while, and the complex portions of the application are definitely easier to create in Visual Basic than in Visual C++. The combination of features that Visual Basic provides makes it a good choice for larger, more complex ActiveDocument applications.

So, what language would you choose if your application is somewhere between these two extremes? That depends a great deal on the language that your programmers are used to using and the development schedule for the project. Visual C++ is always going to be the slower choice of the two languages simply because it requires a lot more coding on the part of the application developer for most application-related tasks. On the other hand, don't trade away the flexibility that Visual C++ provides when you need it; trying to do anything out of the ordinary with Visual Basic can become messy, and you may actually require more code in the long run to get the job done. In other words, weigh your language choices carefully when working with ActiveDocument because there isn't any answer that is always right. The only right answer is the one that's right for you.

Note   *The ActiveDocument application examples in this chapter use Microsoft Visual C++ 6.0 or Visual Basic 6.0. You can also use Visual C++ versions 4.2 and above or Visual Basic 5.0 with a few small procedural changes (the code itself should work just fine). You must have one of these versions of Visual C++ or Visual Basic to follow the examples in this chapter from start to finish (the 6.0 version is preferred). There are ways of at least using the examples with Visual C++ 4.1, but you may need to work with them a little first. For example, you'll need to add references to the various new classes supported by default by Visual C++ versions 4.2 and above. In addition, creating the examples won't be as automatic as when using the newer products. Theoretically, it's possible to create these examples with Visual C++ 4.0 as well, but the amount of work required will certainly make getting an updated version of the compiler seem like a good idea.*

Using Visual C++

As previously mentioned, Visual C++ provides a great deal of flexibility when creating an ActiveDocument application. However, that flexibility comes at a cost. You need to know more about the interfaces that an ActiveDocument application requires and have a better understanding of COM in general. We studied the special interfaces used by an ActiveDocument application in the "ActiveDocument Required Interfaces" section of Chapter 11, so I won't cover them again here.

Trying to add all four of the required interfaces that we looked at in Chapter 11 manually might prove troublesome to even the most accomplished programmer. In addition, there really isn't any need to go through the trouble now that Microsoft has released their new version of C++ (versions 4.2 and above work, but you'll find that version 5.0 works with fewer glitches than version 4.2, and version 6.0 is completely seamless). What we'll look at in this section is the methods you'll need to work with all types of ActiveDocument applications written in Visual C++.

The first section shows a quick method for creating an ActiveDocument-enabled application. We'll skip some of the details that you'd find in just about any application and concentrate on the ActiveX-specific portions of the project instead.

The next section will show you a very fast method for testing your application once you have it built. The reason for such a simple test is that you want to eliminate any outside factors during the initial test. Later, you'll want to test the application using the production Web page that you'll use on your Web site. We'll perform this level of testing near the end of the chapter.

The final section will show you how to upgrade an existing application written in a previous version of Visual C++. Even though you're currently working with Visual C++ 6.0, you may not have the luxury of rewriting all of your code in the environment that it provides. In some cases, you'll need to update an existing application to reduce development time and get the application running sooner. This section will help you get the job done faster and easier using a simple five-step approach.

Creating the ActiveDocument Application

The first thing you need to do is create a new project workspace. We saw how to do that in Chapter 4. You'll want to select the MFC AppWizard and give your application a name—the sample application uses ActivDoc. Click on OK to start the process, and you'll see the first page of the MFC AppWizard. To make life a little simpler, check the Single Document option on the first page of the wizard. Click Next twice to get past the first and second pages of the wizard. What you'll see next is the third page.

The third page is where you'll do most of the ActiveDocument configuration for the application. You can provide five different levels of OLE support with your application. The last three levels also allow you to add ActiveDocument support. The Mini-Server option won't allow you to run the application alone—you'd have to run it from Word for Windows, Internet Explorer 3.0, or some other container. This level of support is fine if you want to create a file browser or a simple server of some type. The next option is Full-Server, which allows the application to execute by itself. You can use this kind of application to support objects, but not to display them. Paint programs are usually good examples of an application that acts as a server, but not necessarily as a container. The final level, Both Container and Server, is the one that we'll select for this application. It allows you to provide full OLE 2 capabilities in your application, including embedding objects. You'll also want to check the Active document server option, as shown in the following illustration. Make sure you also check the

Automation and ActiveX Controls options. Here's what your dialog box should look like at this point:

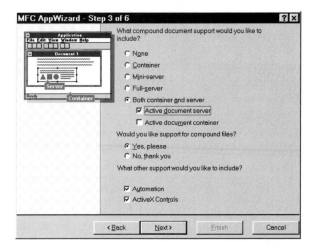

<table>
<tr><td>Note</td><td>The Active document container option is new to Visual C++ 6.0. It allows you to build applications that can contain other ActiveDocuments. For example, you could use this capability to display an Internet Explorer document within your application without actually providing HTML capabilities.</td></tr>
</table>

Click Next to see the fourth page of the MFC AppWizard. Most of the settings on this page are just fine. You may want to set the Recent File List setting higher since most people really like this feature (it sure beats hunting around on the hard drive). A setting of 9 or 10 works fine in most cases (the example program uses a setting of 10).

This page also contains an Advanced... button—which most programmers might whiz right by if they didn't look hard enough. Unfortunately, this button really shouldn't be labeled Advanced... (or perhaps Microsoft should consider reworking the Application Wizard a bit to make one of the required settings more obvious). Click on the Advanced... button and you'll see a dialog box similar to the one in Figure 13-3.

The Document Template Strings page of the Advanced Options dialog box allows you to set the file extension for your application. It also performs some important behind-the-scenes work for you automatically. The example program uses a file extension of AXD. All you need to do is type the extension in the first field (which starts out blank). You may want to change some additional strings—for example, the Main frame caption field. The example uses "ActiveX Document Editor." You may want to make the entry in the Filter name field a little more descriptive as well. It starts out as "ActivD Files (*.axd)," but changing it to "ActiveX Document Files (*.axd)" is a lot more readable. Some people really don't care too much about the long File Type Name field (which defaults to ActivD Document), but changing it to "ActiveX Document" will certainly help later as you search through the registry. In addition, this is the string used to display your new document within the Windows context menu (more on this

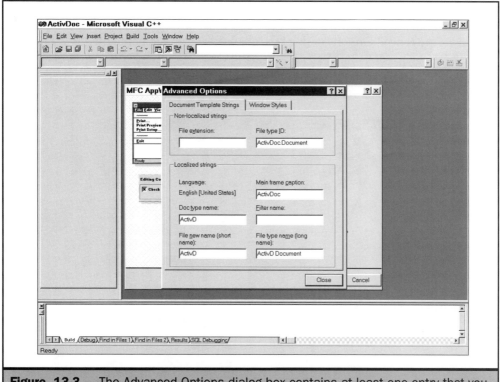

Figure 13-3. The Advanced Options dialog box contains at least one entry that you really need to change before creating an application

in a few paragraphs). Once you make all of these changes, your Advanced Options dialog box should look like the one here:

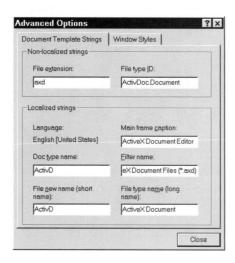

At this point, we've made all the selections required to create a simple ActiveDocument server, but we'll want to make one additional change. Click on Close to close the Advanced Options dialog box. Click Next twice to get to the MFC AppWizard - Step 6 of 6 dialog box. Choose the CActivDocView entry in the classes list, and then select CRichEditView in the Base class field. Your dialog box should look like the one shown here:

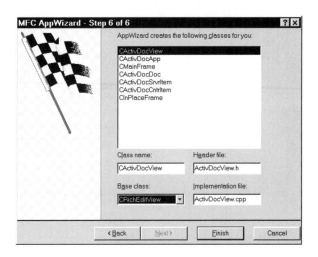

The whole purpose of this last step is to allow you to use the sample application as a simple editor should you wish to do so. You could have implemented the standard CView class if you had wanted to—it wouldn't affect the ability of the program to act as an ActiveDocument server. Now click on Finish to complete the project shell. You'll see a New Project Information dialog box like the one shown here:

Take a few seconds to look through the list of features to ensure that the ActiveX support is complete. (After working with a few projects, you'll find that you can detect any problems very quickly by looking at this dialog box.) Click on OK to generate the project shell.

Testing the Default Application

Right now, our sample application can't do much, but there are a few things it can do right out of the wizard. Compile and run the application once the MFC AppWizard finishes creating it. Running the application is important because the application makes some registry entries the first time you do so. The first change you'll notice is that the Windows context menu now contains an entry for your application file type, as shown in the following illustration. Notice that this is the same name that we typed in the File type name field of the Advanced Options dialog box shown in Figure 13-3 (Figure 13-3 shows the dialog box before we made any changes to its contents).

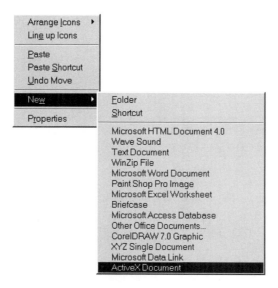

You'll see another change as well. Figure 13-4 shows the ActiveDocument application within the OLE/COM Object Viewer utility (we worked with this utility in Chapter 11 while discussing the interfaces used by various types of ActiveX controls). As you can see, it's listed with the other Document Objects, such as Word for Windows. You should immediately notice that none of the four interfaces we talked about in Chapter 11 are listed here, as they would be for Word for Windows or other Binder programs. We'll see later in this section that checking your interfaces before saying that a program is ready for testing can save you a lot of time and effort later.

The ActivDoc program can also create a basic container file. All you need to do is use the Insert | Object command to add an existing object to the current document. You can save the file to disk. Try creating one now so that you can test the application

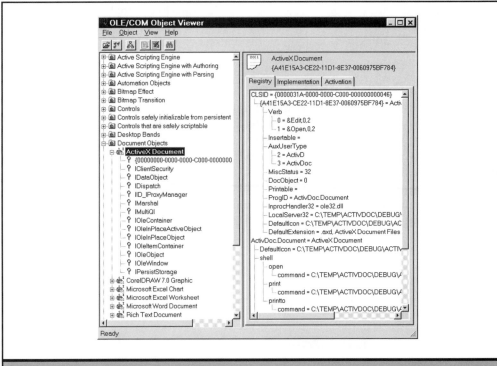

Figure 13-4. The ActivDoc application appears within the OLE/COM Object Viewer utility as a Document Object

frame with Internet Explorer. Make sure you insert an object and then save the file, or you won't see anything when opening the document. This example uses the ColorBlk.BMP file shown in other parts of the book (Chapter 8, for example) as the object—the file itself is saved as TESTDOC.AXD. Once you create the test document, you'll need to create an HTML page to test it. Listing 13-2 shows the code we'll use in this case.

Listing 13-2

```
<HTML>
<HEAD>
<TITLE>New Page</TITLE>
</HEAD>
<BODY>

<!-Display a heading.->
<CENTER><H2>ActiveX Document Test</H2></CENTER>
```

```
<!-Create a link to the test document.->
Click <A HREF="TestDoc.AXD">Here</A> to test the AXD file.

</BODY>
</HTML>
```

Now that we have a test bed, let's see how the application works. Open the test Web page in Internet Explorer and then click on the test link. What you should see is a copy of our test application within Internet Explorer, as shown in Figure 13-5, just as you saw when working with Word for Windows. Notice that the sample application has taken over the menus and toolbar of the browser, just as a Word for Windows document would. In addition, you can insert new objects and perform other tasks using the menu, just as if the application were working on a local document. You can also use the Web Publishing Wizard to save changes (see the "Using the Web Publishing Wizard" section earlier in this chapter for details on this utility).

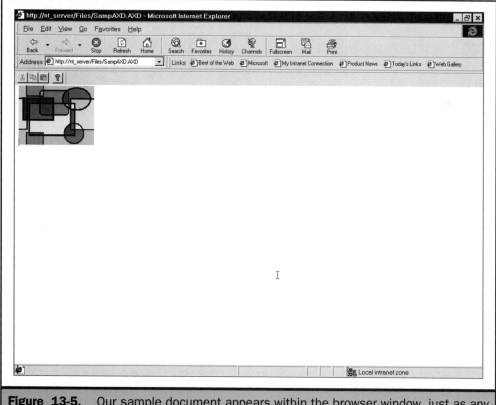

Figure 13-5.   Our sample document appears within the browser window, just as any ActiveDocument would

If everything works properly, you'll see a dialog box asking if you want to either save or open the file (assuming, of course, that you haven't turned the dialog box off during a previous session). Make sure you tell the browser to open the file so that you can actually view it.

Converting an Existing Application

Don't worry if you have a perfectly good application lying around that just doesn't happen to support ActiveDocument. You can convert it to provide this level of support with a minimum of effort—well, at least a lot less effort than writing the program from scratch. In this section we're going to look at a five-step process that you can use to convert just about any existing OLE server to a rudimentary ActiveDocument server. However, it's important to remember that you'll only provide rudimentary support. Some applications will work just fine with this; others won't. Spend some time reading the "ActiveDocument Required Interfaces" section of Chapter 11 again to get the theory down before you start adding support items. Once you do get the additional support items worked out, make sure you test them using an actual Internet setup rather than a local drive. This ensures that you test the complete interface and that the application won't try to do an end around by using standard OLE interfaces rather than the ActiveDocument interfaces that you really want to test.

STEP 1: IMPLEMENT THE CLASSES The first and most obvious step is to implement the classes required to create an ActiveDocument server. If you look at the example we just created in the previous section and any other pre-C++ 4.2 application, you'll notice some very basic differences in the way the classes are declared. That's because Microsoft has subclassed the original MFC classes and added some functionality to them. Table 13-1 shows which classes have changed and how. The first column shows the class declarations used in a pre-C++ 4.2 application. The second column shows the new declarations. The third column tells you which file is affected. The fourth column

Original Class Declaration	New C++ 4.2 and above Declaration	ActivDoc Example Program File	Alternate MFC Class Declaration
class CInPlaceFrame : public COleIPFrameWnd	class CInPlaceFrame : public COleDocIPFrameWnd	IPFrame.H	class CInPlaceFrame : public CDocObjectIPFrameWnd

Table 13-1.   ActiveDocument Class Declarations

Original Class Declaration	New C++ 4.2 and above Declaration	ActivDoc Example Program File	Alternate MFC Class Declaration
class CActivDocDoc : public COleServerDoc	class CActivDocDoc : public COleServerDoc	ActivDocDoc.H	class CActivDocDoc : public DocObjectServerDoc
class CActivDocSrvr: public COleServerItem	class CActivDocSrvr: public CDocObjectServer	SrvrItem.H	class CActivDocSrvr: public CDocObjectServerItem

Table 13-1. ActiveDocument Class Declarations (continued)

shows an alternate class declaration that you may find implemented in older MFC class files—they're based on the Microsoft Office Binder declarations.

Once you replace these declarations in your header files, you'll also need to replace them in the associated CPP files. Using the search and replace capability of Microsoft Developer will make this easier. You won't have to worry too much about missing any of the places where the new class names are used—the compiler will point out any discrepancies automatically once you make the header file changes. Therefore, it's important to make the header file changes first and double-check them before you move on. (Notice that if you're trying to implement an ActiveDocument server using the ActiveX SDK and an older set of MFC files, you'll need to change three header files, whereas moving to Visual C++ 4.2 or above requires a change of only two header files.)

STEP 2: ADD A SIMPLE DECLARATION   The second step is to add a simple declaration to the STDAFX.H file for your application:

```
#include <afxdocob.h>
```

This header file contains all of the declarations needed by your application to get document object support. In fact, a quick look at this file can be quite educational, as it shows exactly how the four ActiveDocument interface elements get implemented.

STEP 3: CHANGE A REGISTRY ENTRY The third step is to change the way you make one of the registry entries. The application you're creating is no longer just an in-place server, so you'll need to change the registry entry in your CWinApp.CPP file (in the case of the example program, it's the ActivDoc.CPP file) from OAT_INPLACE_SERVER to OAT_DOC_OBJECT_SERVER. The actual line of code looks like this:

```
m_server.UpdateRegistry(OAT_DOC_OBJECT_SERVER);
```

STEP 4: CHANGE THE PARSE MAPS The fourth step is to change some of the parse maps, since you'll need to tell your application where to send the print commands and other OLE-related information. You'll need to change two files. The first is the application document header file—ActivDocDoc.H in the case of our sample program. You'll need to add the following highlighted line:

```
// Generated message map functions
protected:
    //{{AFX_MSG(CActivDocDoc)
        // NOTE - the ClassWizard will add and remove member functions here.
        //     DO NOT EDIT what you see in these blocks of generated code !
    //}}AFX_MSG
    DECLARE_MESSAGE_MAP()
    DECLARE_OLECMD_MAP()
};
```

If the message map includes a DECLARE_MESSAGE_MAP( ) message map function, make sure the DECLARE_OLECMD_MAP( ) line appears after it. The second file is the application-document CPP file. At the very beginning of the file, you'll find at least one mapping area for messages. You'll need to add another mapping area, as shown here:

```
BEGIN_OLECMD_MAP(CActivDocDoc, COleServerDoc)
    ON_OLECMD_PAGESETUP()
    ON_OLECMD_PRINT()
END_OLECMD_MAP()
```

As you can see, these additions allow the application to print by routing the print functions through their handler functions using the ID_FILE_PAGE_SETUP and ID_FILE_PRINT standard identifiers. All you need to do to complete the picture is add command maps for the actual handler functions, like this:

```
ON_COMMAND (ID_FILE_PRINT, OnFilePrint)
```

STEP 5: ADD A NEW FUNCTION The fifth (and last) step is to add a new function to your application document header and CPP files. If you were modifying our previous example, you would work with the ActivDocDoc.H and ActivDocDoc.CPP files. Here's the change you'll need to make to the application document header (the function is in bold type):

```
class CActivDocDoc : public COleServerDoc
{
protected: // create from serialization only
    CActivDocDoc();
    DECLARE_DYNCREATE(CActivDocDoc)

// Attributes
public:
    CActivDocSrvrItem* GetEmbeddedItem()
        { return (CActivDocSrvrItem*)COleServerDoc::GetEmbeddedItem(); }

    // Added to implement ActiveX Document Interface.
    CDocObjectServer* GetDocObjectServer(LPOLEDOCUMENTSITE pSite);

// Operations
```

The change to the document CPP file is just as easy. Here's what the new function looks like:

```
// Added for ActiveX Document interface.
CDocObjectServer* CActivDocDoc::GetDocObjectServer(LPOLEDOCUMENTSITE pSite)
{
    return new CDocObjectServer(this, pSite);
}
```

Once you've completed these modifications, you'll need to compile and test the updated application. In most cases, you'll want to test it locally first to make sure you haven't broken anything with the changes. After you're satisfied that the changes haven't affected local performance, try to open a document from the browser. You should see the document open within the browser instead of within a separate window (just as the example program does in Figure 13-5). Make sure the application provides the same level of functionality (sans the File | Save command) as it would when used locally.

Using Visual Basic

Developing an ActiveDocument application in Visual Basic can be difficult the first few times you try to do it. Unlike Visual C++, Visual Basic actually provides two special projects just for the purpose of creating ActiveDocument applications. However, neither of these project types creates a stand-alone application. You must run the application within a container application like Microsoft Word or Internet Explorer. As an alternative, you can build your own container application to launch the Visual Basic ActiveDocument application.

The first project type allows you to create an ActiveDocument DLL. This is an in-process server—it executes in the same memory and thread of execution as the container application. The DLL version is used when you want to create an ActiveDocument application that operates at maximum efficiency and with the least possibility of corruption. The EXE version of the ActiveDocument application is susceptible to data and variable corruption when two or more container applications access it. Two of the greatest advantages of the DLL version of the ActiveDocument application are that it requires less memory to host and is smaller in size so that it's easier to download from the Internet. One of the downsides of using the DLL option is flexibility. For example, you'll find that there are some environments where you can't use modeless dialog boxes with the DLL version of the Visual Basic ActiveDocument application because of limitations in the container environment.

The second project type creates a standard EXE file that you can use either in stand-alone mode or within another application. This is an out-of-process server—it executes in its own memory and thread of execution. One of the advantages of the EXE version of the ActiveDocument application is that it won't normally crash the container application because it executes separately from the container. The EXE version also allows you to host other ActiveDocument applications. In most cases, you'll find that the EXE version of the ActiveDocument application is more flexible and offers more features to the end user. Of course, you pay for this flexibility with reduced efficiency—all calls to the EXE form of the ActiveDocument application have to be marshaled across process boundaries.

There are also some differences between the Visual Basic version of an ActiveDocument application and the one we created with Visual C++. For one thing, the Visual Basic version of the application is designed to use a host application. You can't run it as a separate application. In most cases, you'll run an ActiveDocument application created with Visual Basic using a host application like Internet Explorer or Microsoft Word. This doesn't mean you can't create a stand-alone ActiveDocument application with Visual Basic, just that you'll need to perform a lot more programming to get the results that you're looking for.

Converting Visual Basic Applications to ActiveDocument

If you want to create an ActiveDocument application using Visual Basic, the simplest way to do so is to use one of the predefined projects. The VB Application Wizard isn't set up to allow you to easily create an ActiveDocument application. You can, however, change a standard Visual Basic application to an ActiveDocument application by right-clicking the project folder, then choosing Project Properties from the context menu. Change the Project Type property on the General tab of the Project Properties dialog box to either ActiveX EXE or ActiveX DLL. If you choose ActiveX EXE and want your application to run in stand-alone mode, you'll also need to choose the Stand-alone option on the Component tab of the Project Properties dialog box. Click OK to make the project change permanent. At this point, your project will no longer run because it's not set up to run as an ActiveDocument application. You'll also need to add some additional support to the application like a User Document object. The User Document object is where execution begins when you start your application. The VB ActiveX Document Wizard will allow you to convert an existing form into a User Document object, but you'll still spend some time making the form work properly in the new environment. In sum, you'll need to rework at least part of your standard application to work as an ActiveDocument application.

Designing the VB ActiveDocument Application

This section of the chapter is going to look at the steps for creating an EXE version of an ActiveDocument application created with Visual Basic. Since the requirements for creating the less flexible, but smaller, DLL version is about the same as the EXE version, we'll concentrate on the EXE version in this chapter. The following procedure will help you get the project started, I'll assume that you've already started Visual Basic.

1. Highlight the ActiveX Document Exe icon on the New tab of the New Project dialog box, then click Open. Visual Basic will create an application shell for you consisting of the project file and a User Document object.

2. Right-click Project1 in Project Explorer and choose Properties from the context menu. You'll see the Project Properties dialog box. This dialog box allows you to configure the project before we add any new objects to it. For example, you'll use this dialog box to change the project name and the compilation options. This is also where you'll set debugging options and insert any version-specific information that your project may need like company name or product version.

3. Type a suitable project name in the Project Name field. The sample application uses VBActiveDocument as a project name. Here's what your Project Properties dialog box should look like:

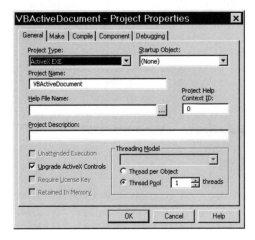

4. Click OK to change the project name. Now we need to begin configuring the User Document object.

5. Double-click UserDocument1 in the Project Explorer. You'll see a blank form open.

6. Change the UserDocument1 (Name) property to some suitable name. The example program uses frmMain to make it easier to find all of the forms in a list, even if they're User Document objects. Now we need to add some controls to our form to make it functional. The first thing we'll need to do is add some components to the toolbox.

7. Right-click the toolbox and choose Components… from the context menu. You'll see the Components dialog box shown here:

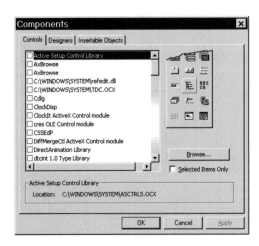

8. Check the Microsoft Common Dialog Control 6.0, Microsoft Rich Textbox Control 6.0, and Microsoft Windows Common Controls 6.0 options on the Controls tab. Click OK to add the controls to your toolbox. These controls will allow you to create a simple rich text format (RTF) text editor that can store information like fonts and graphics as well as text.

9. Save your project using the File | Save Project command. The example project uses VBActiveDoc.VBP as the project filename and frmMain.DOB for the User Document object filename. It's important to remember the names of both the main project and the main form files since you'll need to know both to create a Web page later on. A Web page won't use the EXE file directly; it'll use the VBD file created as a result of compiling the User Document object. It's important to remember this nuance of working with Visual Basic ActiveDocument projects.

10. Add four controls to frmMain, as follows: Toolbar, RichTextBox, CommonDialog, and ImageList. Table 13-2 contains a complete description of the control names and how you need to configure them. Properties that include a Property Page value can be accessed by clicking the (Custom) property in the Properties window. Change the component name using the (Name) property. Finally, any blank values in the table signify blank property values. Here's what frmMain will look like once you add the controls.

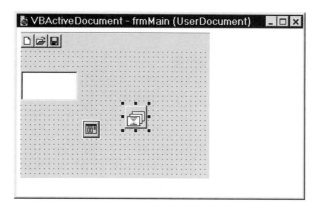

Component	Property Page/Property	Value
imlToolbarIcons	Images (Index 1)/Key	New
	Image	Blank page picture
	Images (Index 2)/Key	Open
	Image	Open manila folder picture

Table 13-2. frmMain Component Property Values

Component	Property Page/Property	Value
	Images (Index 3)/Key	Save
	Image	Floppy picture
tbToolbar	General/ImageList	imlToolbarIcons
	Buttons (Index 1)/Description	Create a new file
	Buttons (Index 1)/Key	New
	Buttons (Index 1)/ToolTip Text	New File
	Buttons (Index 1)/Image	New
	Buttons (Index 2)/Description	Open an existing file
	Buttons (Index 2)/Key	Open
	Buttons (Index 2)/ToolTip Text	Open File
	Buttons (Index 2)/Image	Open
	Buttons (Index 3)/Description	Save file to disk
	Buttons (Index 3)/Key	Save
	Buttons (Index 3)/ToolTip Text	Save File
	Buttons (Index 3)/Image	Save
ctrlTextEdit	Left	0
	MultiLine	True
	ScrollBars	2 - rtfVertical
	Text	
dlgCommonDialog	N/A	N/A

Table 13-2. frmMain Component Property Values (continued)

Adding Some Bells and Whistles

At this point, our project is marginally ready to go. However, there are a few additional features you'll want to add to this experimental project just to see how they work. Add an About dialog box by right-clicking on VBActiveDocument in the Project window and choosing Add | Form from the context menu. You'll see an Add Form dialog box like the one shown here:

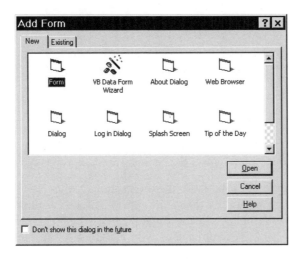

Highlight the About Dialog icon, then click Open. Visual Basic will add an About dialog box form to your project. We won't do anything to this About dialog box other than display it using a menu.

Our ActiveDocument application can also support a menu. Right-click on frmMain and choose Menu Editor… from the context menu. You'll see a Menu Editor dialog box. We need to add the following entries to a File main menu entry: New, Open, Save, and Exit. In addition, we'll need a Help menu with a single submenu, About. The Caption property will always contain the name of the menu as the user will see it when using the application (an ampersand is used to signify the underlined character of the menu entry). The Name property is the value you'll use to access the menu within the application code. You'll normally want to start the menu name with the "mnu" three-letter abbreviation to keep all the menu entries together. I also include all of the names in the menu hierarchy in the menu name. For example, the About entry name would be mnuHelp_About. Using this procedure allows you to keep the menu hierarchy in mind as you write your code. It's also important to provide shortcut keys for keyboard users. You can add them using the Shortcut property.

Here's what the Menu Editor dialog box should look like once you finish adding your menu entries:

There's one other item of interest in the illustration. Notice the NegotiatePosition property. There's every possibility that your application will contain some of the same menu entries as the container application that hosts it. The NegotiatePosition property allows you to tell the container application where to place your menu in case of a conflict. We'll see how this works later. For now, set the NegotiatePosition property for the File menu entry to 2 - Middle and 3 - Right for the Help menu. You don't need to set this property for the submenu entries.

Adding Some Code

Now that we have all of the application components in place, it's time to add some code to make the application work. Listing 13-3 shows the source code for this example. Some of this code should look familiar from Chapter 4, since we used it there for the single document application example. (We won't discuss code that appears in both examples in this chapter, but the code is provided for the sake of completeness and because some object names are different between the two examples.) Note that this example requires more code to do less work than our Visual C++ example in the previous section. That's one of the problems with using Visual Basic for an ActiveDocument application. However, you'll find that there's a point when Visual Basic provides a significant advantage over Visual C++ because of its superior prototyping properties and ability to work with objects using a simple IDE.

Listing 13-3

```
Option Explicit

'Global string used to contain the
'document filename.
```

```
Dim sFile As String

Private Sub mnuFile_Exit_Click()
    'End the program.
    End
End Sub

Private Sub mnuHelp_About_Click()
    'Show the About dialog box.
    frmAbout.Show vbModal
End Sub

Private Sub tbToolbar_ButtonClick(ByVal Button As MSComctlLib.Button)
    'If there is an error, continue processing.
    On Error Resume Next

    'Determine which button was pressed, then call
    'the required menu routine.
    Select Case Button.Key
        Case "New"
            mnuFile_New_Click
        Case "Open"
            mnuFile_Open_Click
        Case "Save"
            mnuFile_Save_Click
    End Select
End Sub

Private Sub UserDocument_Resize()
    'Make sure the text editing control fits on the form.
    ctrlTextEdit.Move 0, tbToolbar.Height, ScaleWidth, ScaleHeight
End Sub
Private Sub mnuFile_Save_Click()
    Dim sFullText As String

    'Display the file open dialog if necessary.
    If sFile = "" Then
        With dlgCommonDialog
        .DialogTitle = "Save As"
        .CancelError = False
        .Filter = "UVW Files (*.UVW)|*.UVW"
        .ShowOpen
        If Len(.FileName) = 0 Then
            Exit Sub
        Else
            sFile = .FileName
        End If
        End With
```

```
        End If

        'Save the file.
        ctrlTextEdit.SaveFile sFile

        'Tell the user that the file is saved.
        MsgBox "The file is saved."
End Sub

Private Sub mnuFile_Open_Click()
        'Dim sContent, sFullText As String

        'Display the Open dialog box so that the user can choose a
        'file to display.  Filter options include *.UVW for the
        'application specific file, all files, and text files.
        With dlgCommonDialog
            .DialogTitle = "Open"
            .CancelError = False
            .Filter = "UVW Files (*.UVW)|*.UVW|All Files (*.*)|*.*|Text Files
(*.txt)|*.txt"
            .ShowOpen
            If Len(.FileName) = 0 Then
                Exit Sub
            End If
            sFile = .FileName
        End With

        'Load the file for viewing.
        ctrlTextEdit.LoadFile sFile

End Sub

Private Sub mnuFile_New_Click()
        'Clear the current document.
        ctrlTextEdit.Text = ""

        'Clear the filename.
        sFile = ""
End Sub
```

This may look like a lot of code, but it isn't even close to what you'd have if we had duplicated our Visual C++ example completely. The code provided in Listing 13-3 only shows what you need to provide very simple application functionality. Fortunately, nothing should be too much of a surprise in this example.

Notice the mnuAbout_Help( ) function. When you want to access a dialog box within your ActiveDocument application, you use the same calling procedure as you would for a normal Visual Basic application. There is one caveat. Some environments won't support modeless dialog boxes when using the DLL form of your ActiveDocument application. Since you may want to use the source you create for one application in several other applications, it's best to go with a modal dialog box whenever possible.

Tip *What happens if you want to call another User Document object? Things quickly get complicated because you have to use one procedure to call that object within Internet Explorer and a completely different procedure to call it from Microsoft Word. For that reason, you'll normally want to avoid using more than the main User Document object in your ActiveDocument applications. It's normally best to use dialog boxes whenever possible.*

The mnuFile_Save_Click( ) function is different in this chapter than it was for Chapter 4. The first difference you should see is that this example will display a File Save As dialog box if you don't have a file currently open. This allows you to create new files as well as save existing ones. However, the big difference in the code is the way that the file gets saved. In Chapter 4 we had to go through a whole routine of opening the file for use and saving it one line at a time. This chapter uses a much shorter method:

```
ctrlTextEdit.SaveFile sFile
```

Likewise, you'll find that the mnuFile_Open_Click( ) function has changed its method of loading the file. Instead of processing the file one line at a time, we simply load it into the RichTextBox control and allow it to do the work. This method of loading and saving the contents of ctrlTextEdit allows us to save things besides text with ease. In the simple testing section that follows, you'll see that we can save graphics as well as text without any problems at all.

A Quick VB ActiveDocument Application Test

It's time to test our application. The first thing you'll need to do is compile it using the File | Make Project1.exe command. This process will create two application files instead of the normal one: VBActiveDoc.EXE and frmMain.VBD. These two files work in tandem to provide the ActiveDocument application functionality. However, it's the VBD file that you'll need to reference in your test code, not the EXE file. Listing 13-4 shows the simple HTML code that we'll use to test this example. It looks much like the test code that we used for the Visual C++ example earlier in the chapter.

isting 13-4

```
<HTML>
<HEAD>
<TITLE>New Page</TITLE>
</HEAD>
```

```
<BODY>

<!-Display a heading.->
<CENTER><H2>VB ActiveX Document Test</H2></CENTER>

<!-Create a link to the test document.->
Click <A HREF="../VBActivDoc/frmMain.VBD">Here</A> to test the VB Active
Document file.

</BODY>
</HTML>
```

Once you have the code typed, you can display the initial Web page using Internet Explorer. This page will contain a link that you can use to display the Visual Basic ActiveDocument application. You can cut and paste text or graphics using the normal shortcut keys (CTRL-V for paste, CTRL-C for copy, and CTRL-X for cut). Obviously, you can also type text into the application as needed. Figure 13-6 shows our sample application in action.

There's something that you should notice about the menus in Figure 13-6. Notice the two File menus. The first menu is the one that is normally provided with Internet

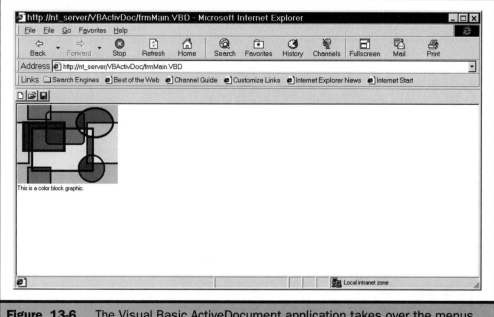

Figure 13-6. The Visual Basic ActiveDocument application takes over the menus and toolbars of Internet Explorer when you activate it

Explorer, while the second is the one that comes with our VB ActiveDocument application. That's how Internet Explorer chose to handle the menu conflict in this case. Now look at the Help menu. Instead of providing two main menus with the same name in this case, the menu entries for our sample application appear on a special submenu of the Internet Explorer Help menu. This is a second method that some applications will use to handle menu conflicts.

Defining Application Installation Requirements

One of the things that will most determine which programming language product you use to create an ActiveDocument application is where you plan to install the application and what you have installed there right now. While Visual C++ provides the better environment for small applications and flexible development, it also requires extra storage in the form of support files. In the case of the example in this chapter, you'd have to send three support files: MFC42.DLL (972KB), MSVCRT.DLL (248KB) and ADVAPI32.DLL (40.5KB). The total upload size for the Visual C++ version of our application is 1,300.5KB.

Visual Basic also requires support files. In this case, however, the size of those files is much greater. You'll need to send MSVBVB60.DLL (1,372KB) and ADVAPI32.DLL (40.5KB). In addition, you need to send application files: Project1.EXE (40KB) and frmMain.VBD (1.5KB). The total size of the upload this time is a whopping 1,454KB.

It may appear at first that Visual Basic is the poorer of the two choices from an upload size perspective. However, there are two things that you need to consider in this case. First, not everyone is going to need to download the application through a dial-up connection to the Internet. If you plan to distribute your application on a CD, then the size of the application may not be such a hindrance. In addition, your client may already have other Visual Basic 6.0 applications installed on his or her machine. If that's the case, then you'd only need to send the small application-specific files instead of both application and support files.

Once you've decided on which application type to use (and we've discussed a lot of trade-offs throughout the chapter that aren't discussed here), you'll need to decide how to package the application. If you're distributing the application over the Internet and are certain that the target machine will have the required support files, you may be able to allow the user to download the file directly or use a CAB file. You can create a CAB file using either the Visual Basic Package and Deployment Wizard or the Visual C++ CabArc utility. If you're going to offer the CAB for public distribution, you'll also need to sign your CAB file so that the person downloading it knows who created it.

You'll find that the Visual Basic Package and Deployment Wizard is the more automatic of the two CAB packaging solutions. (As an alternative, you can also use the DIANTZ utility that ships with older versions of the ActiveX SDK and appears in the FP98 directory on the Visual Studio CD as a replacement for CabArc.) The CabArc utility requires that you also create an INF file containing the requirements for application installation like target directory and the names of the files to include within the CAB file. Table 13-3 contains a complete listing of the items that you might include within this INF file. Listing 13-5 provides an example INF file that you can use to create an INF file for any type of ActiveX component, including an ActiveDocument application.

Entry	Description
Signature=	You must include a signature for the INF file so that Windows 95 and Windows NT know how to handle it. Various versions of the INF file format require different handling.
AdvancedINF=	The version number of the INF file format. The current version is 2.0 (as of this writing). However, older versions of the INF file should work just fine because the operating system will be able to detect its format.
[Add.Code]	
<Filename1>=<Section-Name1> <Filename2>=<Section-Name2> <Filename n>=<Section-Name n>	The [Add.Code] section provides a complete list of all the files that you want to install. This won't include all of the files in the INF file since you won't want to install the INF file as a minimum. The <Section-Name> part of the entry tells Internet Component Download service where to find the installation instructions for a particular file. (See the next section.)

Table 13-3.   INF File Format for Internet Component Download Service

Entry	Description
[Section-Name1]	
Key1=Value1 Key2=Value2 Key n=Value n	Each file-specific section contains one or more keys, just like the keys you've used before with INI files. The following entries explain the key values that Internet Component Download will understand.
File=[<URL> | ThisCAB]	This key tells whether you can download the file from a specific location on the Internet or from this cabinet. Using this key allows you to define locations for files needed by the ActiveX control but not included in the CAB file. Normally, these additional support files are located on the Internet server.
File Version=<a>,<b>,<c>,<d>	This key specifies the minimum acceptable version number for a file. If you don't specify a value, Internet Component Download assumes any version is fine. Each letter designates a level of revision. So if your control's version is 1.0, you'd use Version=1,0,0,0.
File-[Mac | Win32]-[x86 | PPC | Mips | Alpha]=[<URL> | IGNORE]	This key allows you to differentiate required support for various platforms. First you define an operating system, then the CPU type. The <URL> parameter allows you to specify a location for the file. The IGNORE argument tells Internet Component Download that the file isn't needed on the specified platform.

Table 13-3.   INF File Format for Internet Component Download Service (continued)

Entry	Description
[Section-Name1] CLSID=[<Class ID>]	This key allows you to define a class identification for the file. You won't actually create the CLSID—Visual C++ does this step for you automatically, based on a complex equation developed by Microsoft. There are two places to get this value: your C++ source code and the Windows registry. To find it in the Windows registry, just open the registry editor and use the Edit | Find command to find the name of your OCX under the HKEY_CLASSES_ROOT | CLSID key. The registry form of the CLSID for the example in Chapter 2 is {D8D77E03-712A-11CF-8C70-00006E3127B7}. The C++ source location is in the control file. For example, the Chapter 2 source code file to look in is OCXEXMPLCTL.CPP. You'll find the identifier in this call: ///////////////////////////// Initialize class factory and guid IMPLEMENT_OLECREATE_EX (COCXEXMPLCtrl, "OCXEXMPL.OCXEXMPLCtrl.1", 0xd8d77e03, 0x712a, 0x11cf, 0x8c, 0x70, 0, 0, 0x6e, 0x31, 0x27, 0xb7) ///////////////////////////// The CLSID value for an ActiveX control never changes (unless you change something very basic like the name—code changes have no effect), so you only need to find this value once.

Table 13-3.   INF File Format for Internet Component Download Service (continued)

Entry	Description
[Section-Name1] DestDir=[10 | 11]	This key defines where you want to place the file. A value of 10 places it in the main Windows folder. A value of 11 places it in the SYSTEM folder. If you don't specify a value, Internet Component Download will place it in the browser cache directory. Placing a component in the browser cache directory usually won't cause any problems unless the user clears the contents of the cache. If this happens, the control will be downloaded again the next time the user needs it, since Windows won't be able to find it in the location specified in the registry. (For this same reason, you won't want the user to move the control once it's installed.)
RegisterServer=[yes | no]	A yes or no value that determines whether the component is automatically registered on the target machine using RegSvr32. In most cases, you'll set this value to yes for items that you have to register so that the application can see them immediately and the files will be available to your ActiveX control or application. The only time you might set this value to no is if the components must be registered in a certain order and you need to do that manually within your application or control.

Table 13-3. INF File Format for Internet Component Download Service (continued)

Listing 13-5

```
;INF File for ActivDoc.EXE
[version] ; version signature (same for both NT and Win95) do not remove
signature="$CHICAGO$"
AdvancedINF=2.0

[Add.Code]
ACTIVDOC.EXE=ACTIVDOC.EXE
```

```
MFC42.DLL=MFC42.DLL
MSVCRT.DLL=MSVCRT.DLL
ADVAPI32.DLL=ADVAPI32.DLL

[ACTIVDOC.EXE]
File=thiscab
Clsid=[0000031A-0000-0000-C000-000000000046]
FileVersion=1,0,0,0

[MFC42.DLL]
File=http://NT_Server/files/MFC42.DLL
FileVersion=6,0,8168,0

[MSVCRT.DLL]
File=http://NT_Server/files/MSVCRT.DLL
FileVersion=6,0,8168,0

[ADVAPI32.DLL]
File=http://NT_Server/files/ADVAPI32.DLL
FileVersion=4,71,118,0
```

There's something important to note about the code in Listing 13-5. Notice that the three support files lack the "thiscab" designation given to ActivDoc.EXE. Unlike the Visual Basic Package and Deployment Wizard, using CabArc allows you to create a conditional INF file. What you're telling the setup routine is that only the ActivDoc.EXE must be placed on the user's machine and that file is located within the CAB. If the user's machine already has a support file of the right version on their machine, they won't need to download it from your intranet or Internet site. However, if they do need the file, then you provide an URL where the setup routine can go to find the file, download it, and install it on the user's machine. Obviously, this method of creating a CAB file has the potential for saving the user a great deal of download time. After all, it takes just seconds to download a 40KB file as compared to the 1,300.5KB file required for a full Visual C++ installation.

Obviously, if you plan to distribute the application using CDs or floppy disks, then you'll need to build the required Setup program. We've already talked about this particular process several times throughout the book, so I won't talk about it again here.

Creating an ActiveDocument Web Page Using Visual InterDev

It's finally time to add our project to a Web page for testing. Normally the Web page would have been under development by another workgroup so that any content or other needs could be taken care of while the ActiveDocument application is written.

The following procedure will help you set up the application (it assumes you already have Visual InterDev started).

1. Highlight the New Web Project icon on the New tab of the New Project dialog box (you'll find this icon in the Visual InterDev Projects folder).

2. Type a project name in the Name field. The example application uses TestActivDoc as a project name.

3. Click Open. You'll see the Web Project Wizard - Step 1 of 4 dialog box. We already talked about the various settings on this dialog box in Chapter 4, so I won't cover them again here. You should already have a connection to your Web server from previous examples, and we'll want to work in Master mode. Make sure you check the Connect using Secure Sockets Layer option if required for your server setup. In most cases, this option isn't required for a local test server setup.

4. Click Next. Visual InterDev will contact your Web server to create a centralized version of the new project. Once contact is established, you'll see the Web Project Wizard - Step 2 of 4 dialog box. At this point, you could add a layout and theme. We won't in this case since we've already talked about themes and layouts with the CorpSite application in Chapter 10.

5. Click Finish. Visual InterDev will create the new project for you.

Now that we've got a basic application shell put together, it's time to figure out how we plan to use it. There are several ways that you can add an ActiveDocument application to your Web site. However, the two most common ways would be to add the application itself or to add a listing of files for the application (or you could add both).

Adding the application as a link would allow the user to create new files without leaving the browser environment. The browser would simply display the application and allow the user to add content to a blank page. You could use the application link option alone if you wanted to give the user the option of creating new files without having the ability to edit existing ones. For example, you might use this for a company survey or a one-way data entry program of some type.

The file links option would allow the user to edit existing files with ease. They could also create new files provided your application allows that activity, but they would need to open an existing file first to start the ActiveDocument application. In other words, you would use the file links option alone only if you wanted to keep the user from creating new files. Normally, you would combine this option with a link to the ActiveDocument application so that the user could both create new files and edit existing ones.

Let's look at the process for creating a link to the ActiveDocument application. We'll want to create the link on every page of the new Web site, so that means creating a custom layout for our example. The following procedure is going to help you create a custom layout. You can use a modified version of this procedure to create layouts of your own if none of the Microsoft-supplied defaults will work in your situation and you don't want to modify an existing layout.

1. Right-click the <Server Name>/TestActivDoc folder and choose New Folder from the context menu. You'll see a New Folder dialog box. Every layout begins with a _Layouts folder. Since our project lacks this folder, we'll need to create it.

2. Type **_Layouts** in the Folder name field and click OK. Visual InterDev will create the new folder for you.

3. Create a second folder below _Layouts named Custom. This is where we'll store the three files required to create a custom layout: Custom.INF, Preview.HTM, and Layout.HTM. Custom.INF contains the information required to display the layout. Preview.HTM contains a preview of the layout as the user will see it in a browser. Layout.HTM contains the information required to create the custom Web pages within the Visual InterDev IDE.

4. Right-click the Custom folder and choose Add | HTML Page from the context menu. You'll see an Add Item dialog box. Highlight the HTML Page icon and type **Preview.HTM**. Click OK. Perform this same step for Layout.HTM. At this point, we have two of the three essential files for our custom layout. Now we need to create the Custom.INF file.

5. Create a text file using Notepad or some other text editor. There are normally four lines of text in Custom.INF. The first says that this is an information file and not a file for doing something like installing a device driver. The second line provides a title for the custom layout. The third line tells what version of the custom layout file is being viewed. Finally, the fourth line tells what HTML file contains a preview of the layout so that the programmer can view it. Add the following code to the text file:

```
[info]
title=ActiveDocument Link
version=01.00
Description=preview.htm
```

6. Save the text file to a local directory using the name **Custom.INF**.

7. Use Windows Explorer to copy and paste the file into the Custom folder of our project. We need to add one more file to the layout, the ActiveDoc.EXE file. Adding this file will allow us to create a link to it with relative ease and ensures that everyone who uses the layout will also have access to the ActiveDocument application.

8. Copy and paste a copy of ActivDoc.EXE into the Custom folder for our project. At this point your layout should look like the one shown here. Now we need to define the preview and layout pages for our custom layout.

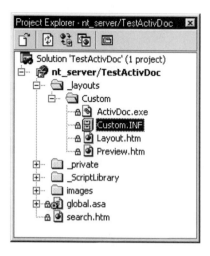

9. Open Preview.HTM and type **A custom layout containing an ActiveDocument application link.**

10. Open Layout.HTM. You must add four controls to Layout.HTM: LayoutHdrStrt, LayoutHdrEnd, LayoutFtrStrt, and LayoutFtrEnd. You may need to add these four Design-Time Controls to the toolbox before you can add them to the HTML page. Drag a copy of ActiveDoc.EXE on the HTML page right between the LayoutHdrStrt and LayoutHdrEnd controls. You'll see a new link added to the layout as shown here:

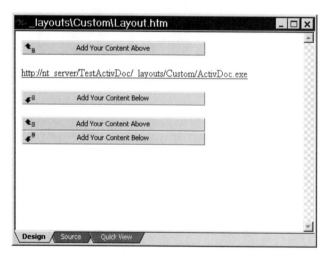

11. Save both the Preview.HTM and Layout.HTM files. We're ready to start using this custom layout.

Any layout you create won't get added to the application automatically. You apply the layout to your application just as you would any of the Microsoft-supplied default layouts.

12. Right-click the <Server Name>/TestActiveDoc folder and choose Apply Theme and Layout from the context menu. You'll see the Apply Theme and Layout dialog box.

13. Click the Layout tab and choose the Apply layout and theme option.

14. Highlight the ActiveDocument Link layout option. Your dialog box should look like the one shown here:

15. Click OK, Visual InterDev will apply our custom layout to the project.

Every HTML page you add to the project from this point on will have a link to our ActiveDocument application on it. This will allow the user to access the application quickly to create new content as needed. If you want to try your new layout, right-click on the <Server Name>/TestActiveDoc folder, then choose Add | HTML Page... from the context menu. You'll see the Add Item dialog box. Highlight the HTML Page icon, then click Open. Visual InterDev will create a new HTML page for you.

Lessons Learned

Developing ActiveDocument applications will become part of the normal flow of application development for most developers in the near future. As companies move at least part of their business to the Internet, it becomes essential to provide applications that will work both on and off the Internet with equal ease. After all, businesses will not want to incur the training costs for showing employees how to use to different applications to perform the same task. Collaboration and other extended forms of workgroup participation will also force companies to create solutions that allow people to communicate even if they aren't in the same room. The bottom line is that you'll very likely develop an ActiveDocument application sometime in the near future—once companies begin to see the need and desirability of using this new technology.

We looked at two different methods for creating ActiveDocument applications in this chapter. There are definitely more ways that you can pursue this technology, but the two methods presented here are probably the most common routes. It's important to remember that unlike many other development areas, Visual C++ and Visual Basic offer very different levels of support when it comes to ActiveDocument. You'll definitely want to spend some time figuring out which development language is best suited to the needs of your company. In this one case, you won't want to make the assumption that Visual Basic and Visual C++ are interchangeable from a results perspective.

The method used to deploy your ActiveDocument application is also a major consideration when it comes to deciding on a programming language. Visual C++ and Visual Basic offer different features in this area as well. In addition, the methods used to deploy the application will determine the cost of doing so. For example, it's probably more cost effective to deploy small applications where you're relatively sure the user will have all of the required support files already installed on their machine from a Web site.

Finally, incorporating your ActiveDocument application into the Web site will take some preplanning. In this chapter, we looked at a very simple method of adding this functionality. A production Web site will likely need something with a more polished look, and you'll definitely need to add online support in the way of HTML-based help files. Supporting your ActiveDocument application once you build it is definitely an important part of the application development process.

Chapter 14

Setting Up a Help Desk Application

What's the total cost of ownership (TCO) for a typical workstation in your company? It's a question that many IT managers ask themselves on a daily basis. PC hardware prices may be taking a nosedive while providing ever higher performance characteristics, but the TCO for that PC is on a never-ending spiral upward. The TCO is a big problem, as witnessed by all of the software on the market designed to reduce it. TCO includes all costs for the PC—hardware, software, maintenance, personnel to operate it, and the cost of training.

Reducing the cost of providing help to end users is one of the big TCO questions that companies are trying to answer today. It doesn't take a rocket scientist to figure out that providing help desk support is one of the more expensive support elements for any company. Just take a look at the proliferation of frequently asked question (FAQ) sheets on just about every Web site on the Internet. In addition, some companies, like Microsoft, are producing huge quantities for white papers that a user can search for using a standard Web-based search engine without disturbing valuable support personnel. In sum, companies are doing whatever it takes to make the user more self sufficient when it comes to getting help for their application needs.

Just about any company can benefit from an automated help desk. There are questions that get asked in every company with such frequency that paying someone to answer them borders on the ridiculous. Not only does this apply to computer software and hardware, but you can also apply it to other things as well, such as personnel management and payroll. Employees in your company should be able to turn to some automated method of getting help for just about every mundane question that exists.

There are benefits to using this approach other than simple cost savings. Consider the number of times that an employee has reacted a certain way because they got bad, misleading, or incomplete information. A help desk application that's fully maintained ensures that everyone gets the same information, in the same way, and that it's always correct (note the emphasis on maintained—Web sites can become inaccurate when the information they contain gets too old).

An automated help desk remedies other problems as well. Consider the problem of outdated paper information. Some employees in your company may still have a copy of the employee handbook from 20 years ago. Do you really want that employee telling new people how the company works based on that old manual? An electronic form of help can be updated and everyone will see the update at the same time. No longer will you need to worry about old materials lurking in the background.

This chapter isn't going to pursue the entire spectrum of potential uses for help desk applications. In fact, we'll concentrate on the first kind of help desk application that most companies will create: An application assistance database. We'll look at what you can do to make your software easier to use for everyone and still reduce the overall TCO for your software application.

We'll begin by creating a special help desk control using Visual C++. This ActiveX control will allow the user to access the help desk without having to think much about where they're going or how they're getting the information they need. The only thing the user will need to worry about is what question they want to ask.

Once we have a control to access the help desk, we'll create some sample Web pages using Visual InterDev that will help you create your own help desk application. This version of the help desk will contain simple text and controls. We'll want to test the content portion of the help desk thoroughly before enhancing it in any way.

Making your help desk friendly and easy to use is essential if you really want someone to use it. Our help desk application will be complete once we add some bells and whistles to it using Visual J++. These additions won't be superfluous—they'll add to the overall appeal of the help desk application.

Finally, we'll make the help desk application a reality to the end user by adding support for it to a Visual Basic application. This section of the chapter will show you how you can implement your help desk in a way that makes its use entirely transparent to the end user. They won't know whether the information they need resides on the local hard drive or on a network drive somewhere.

Scenario

As with many companies, your company is interested in reducing the cost of maintaining the hardware and software needed to run the business. Currently, management is more interested in getting the cost of software under control because training and support costs have skyrocketed. As a result, your team is working on a help desk application to support the software that your company uses. You'll start with the custom software and work your way into the off-the-shelf products like Microsoft Office. Later, when the software portion of the help desk is complete and tested, you'll need to expand the site again to support the hardware end of the computers that your company uses. In other words, you won't just work on this project one time—you'll need to work on it in stages over a long period of time in such a way that each portion of the project is compartmentalized.

There are four phases to the initial part of this project. One development person will create the flexible ActiveX control that will allow the user to access the help desk without knowing much about it. As a result, the ActiveX control will need to offer configuration features that allow it to access whatever resource is needed, whether that resource is in a database, an HTML page, or even a Windows help file. The second thing the ActiveX control will need is the ability to work in a variety of environments. This means that the control will have to be thoroughly tested. Since the ActiveX control development doesn't hinder any of the other team members, and since this control is very generic in nature, you can send the ActiveX control programmer to work on the control until it's complete. Obviously, you'll need to check in with the programmer from time to time to ensure that all of the design criteria are being met and that none of the predefined interface elements have changed.

The second development phase is the creation of Web pages that will work with your custom application. There are actually three groups that will have to work together on this part of the project. The first group will create the Web pages using Visual InterDev. The second group will obtain all of the required content and put it into a format that will work with the help desk application (more on this later). The third group will be a combination of users and experts. You need the users to find out which areas of the application will require the most emphasis. The experts will provide input on how they would solve a particular problem or answer a particular question. All of this input is essential if you want your help desk application to work smoothly the first time around. Obviously, this development team and the ActiveX control programmer will start first; the other two development teams for phases 3 and 4 will have to wait until this part of the project is complete and tested.

The third development phase consists of enhancing the help desk application using Visual J++. While this group is doing all of the programming on the enhancements, the Visual InterDev developers will have to make themselves available for answering design questions. In addition, you may find that parts of the Web page design have to be redone to take certain enhancement requirements into account. In other words, don't disband all of your Visual InterDev team immediately after they finish the Web site and test it.

The fourth development phase is implementation. You'll need to add the new Help ActiveX control to your application and then test to make sure it works as anticipated. This is the one phase where everyone will need to work together. The development team may find that the Help pages they created have broken links or that the Visual J++ enhancements don't work as anticipated. The ActiveX control itself may not provide enough functionality or may be too generic for the job. It's important to ensure that the help desk application is fully tested or you may find yourself cleaning up a huge mess from users who got the wrong information.

Designing a Help Desk ActiveX Control with Visual C++

Our ActiveX control needs to be fairly flexible, easy to use, and, since it's required for later phases of our project, easy to develop. Since the ActiveX control will reside within a Visual Basic application, size isn't quite as important as it would be for an Internet-based component. In addition, we don't need to worry about the number of support files as long as they're kept to a minimum. Finally, since this is a company application and not one that we plan to distribute to the public at large, we have full control over the user's desktop and all that it contains, which means that compatibility problems should be minimal. With all of these facts in mind, this section will show you how to create an MFC-based ActiveX control. We'll follow the same basic steps that we have in the past for creating the control.

Creating the ActiveX Control Shell

As with most of the Visual C++ projects in this book, the first step is to create a program shell. The following procedure will help you get started creating the ActiveX control.

1. Use the File | New command to display the New dialog box. Highlight the MFC ActiveX ControlWizard icon, type the project name (HelpCtrl) in the "Project name" field, then click OK. You'll see the MFC ActiveX ControlWizard Step 1 of 2 dialog box.

2. Click Next. You'll see the MFC ActiveX ControlWizard Step 2 of 2 dialog box. This is where we'll define the control's characteristics. Our control will probably work best as a simple push button, so choose the BUTTON class as the class that you want to subclass for this control. Our control may also need to be used from within applications like Word (remember the criteria in the "Scenario" section of the chapter). This means we'll need to check the "Available in 'Insert Object' dialog" option.

3. Click Finish. You'll see the New Project Information dialog box shown here:

4. Click OK. Visual C++ will create the ActiveX control shell for you.

Adding Some Properties, Methods, and Events

At this point, we have a basic push button like the one we created in Chapter 4. However, since our push button will need to meet a variety of needs, you'll see that there are some differences as well. Let's begin by adding some properties to the control so that it can fulfill its mission of providing simplified help access. Open the MFC ClassWizard dialog box using the View | ClassWizard command. Select the

Automation tab, then add the custom and stock properties shown in Table 14-1. All custom properties will use a Get/Set methods implementation to ensure maximum compatibility for future projects (choose the Get/Set methods option in the Add Property dialog box). Visual C++ automatically provides all needed information for stock properties once you choose a property name in the Add Property dialog box.

We'll see how all of these properties come into play as the chapter progresses. For right now, all you really need to know is that they'll all enhance the flexibility of the final button in one way or another.

Our HelpCtrl button also requires some methods. You add them just as you would a property, by clicking the Add Method button on the Automation tab of the MFC ClassWizard dialog box. The first method you'll add is the stock DoClick( ). All you need to do is select it from the "External name" field found in the Add Method dialog box, then click OK.

We'll also need a custom method called DoHelp( ). Simply type **DoHelp** in the "External name" field and choose BOOL in the "Return type" field. This method also requires the user to pass a parameter, so you'll need to click on the Name column in the "Parameter list" field. Type **lpszHelpURL**, then press TAB. Choose LPCTSTR in the Type column. Click OK to add the custom method. Make sure you close, then reopen the MFC ClassWizard dialog box after adding the properties and before you add the events.

It's time to talk about button events. You'll find the events listed on the ActiveX Events tab of the MFC ClassWizard dialog box. There are two stock events you need to add: Click and DblClick. We won't need any custom events for this control. Once you add the two stock events, click OK to close the MFC ClassWizard dialog box.

Property Name	Implementation	Type
BackColor	Stock	
Caption	Stock	
CursorType	Get/Set methods	long
Enabled	Stock	
Font	Stock	
ForeColor	Stock	
HelpURL	Get/Set methods	BSTR
IconPosition	Get/Set methods	long
IconType	Get/Set methods	long

Table 14-1.   HelpCtrl Stock and Custom Property Values

Adding Member Variables

All of the properties we added in the previous section will require some sort of member variable support so that we can manipulate them as needed. To add a member variable, right-click on CHelpCtrlCtrl in ClassView, then choose Add Member Variable from the context menu. You'll see an Add Member Variable dialog box like the one shown here:

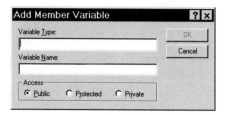

Type the variable name and type, choose an Access option, and then click OK to add the member variable to your application. The class you choose to add the member variable to is important. Make certain you choose CHelpCtrlCtrl so that we can use the variables within the control itself. Table 14-2 shows the member variables you'll need to add to this application. All of the member variables are protected, so the client can't access them. This feature provides data encapsulation, making it impossible for outside influences to affect the ActiveX control.

Tip *The main difference between member variable access and get/set access to properties is that the member variable access method is easier to implement and allows direct access to the member variables. This method is the best option for properties that won't affect the user interface in any way. The get/set method allows you to control access to the member variable. Controlling access means that client input errors are less likely. In addition, the ability to fully check access to your control's properties means that you can change user interface elements as needed. The get/set method is more cumbersome to implement, but provides several distinct features that enhance overall control flexibility as we'll see later in the chapter. Remember that you choose between member variable and get/set access on the Add Property dialog box accessed from the Automation tab of the MFC ClassWizard dialog box.*

Member Variable Name	Type
m_cursorType	long
m_helpURL	CString
m_iconPosition	long
m_iconType	long

Table 14-2. HelpCtrl Member Variables

Obviously, just adding some member variables won't make the properties persistent or store their values in a way that we can use them throughout the control. In Chapter 4 you saw that you needed to add code to the DoPropExchange() method to make the properties persistent so that the values would be saved from session to session. In this instance, since we're using get/set functions to manipulate the properties, we'll also have to add some glue code to make the properties interact with our ActiveX control. The "Adding Some Code" section of the chapter will describe the code you need to add to provide minimal property functions. However, at this point, we have all of the member variables we need to actually implement the functionality that the control will require.

Incorporating Graphics

Previous ActiveX controls in this book have lacked much in the way of graphics. This example will show you how to incorporate graphics into your ActiveX controls in several important ways. First, we'll see how to change the appearance of the ActiveX control within the IDE of the programming language using it. Second, we'll see how you can add a graphic to the button in this example. The same technique will work with other types of controls—all you need to have is a canvas for drawing. The third graphic will change the appearance of the cursor when it appears over the button. Normally, you wouldn't add this feature to a button, but it's a good feature to add when you want the user to know precisely when to click the button. Theoretically, this means that even a button provides a good place to add cursors.

Before we can add any graphics support to this example, we'll have to create the required icon, bitmap, and cursor resources. The first resource, the bitmap used for IDE display purposes, has already been added for you by the wizard. All we need to do is modify it to better meet the purpose of the control in question. Open the IDB_HELPCTRL resource that appears in the Bitmap folder in Resource view and you'll see the standard OCX bitmap. While this 16 × 16 pixel bitmap is functional, it hardly expresses the purpose of our control. Redrawing this bitmap and recompiling the ActiveX control will instantly change the appearance of the control whenever you add it to the IDE of a programming language like Visual Basic. This bitmap can be any of a number of sizes, but the maximum size you should use is 32 × 32 pixels. Here's my rendition of the Help Button control for this example—your control need not use precisely the same representation:

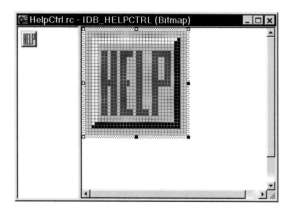

Note *The example uses a 32 × 32 pixel bitmap, the maximum size allowed. The way you draw this bitmap won't affect the functionality of the control, but will change its appearance within an IDE like the one used for Visual Basic. Notice that the sample bitmap provides two rows of light gray pixels around the entire bitmap. These two pixels get highlighted within Visual Basic when you place the mouse over the control in the toolbox, so leaving them blank is usually a good idea.*

While we're at it, we really need an icon similar to the bitmap we just drew for the About dialog box. Fortunately, this resource also exists as IDI_ABOUTDLL. There are actually two icons contained in this resource; the first is 16 × 16 pixels, the second is 32 × 32 pixels. The first icon is used for small icon displays like the ones provided with Windows Explorer. The second icon is used for larger icon displays and within the About dialog box. You need to create renditions of our Help button for both icon sizes to make the ActiveX control work as anticipated in all environments. One final consideration is that unlike the IDB_HELPCTRL resource, this one won't require any kind of an edge because it won't appear in the toolbox. This allows you to create a slightly larger and better-looking icon. Here's the icon I created for the example, though your icon doesn't necessarily have to look this way for the ActiveX control to work properly:

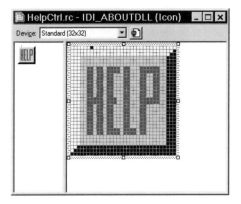

Now it's time to create the special icon that will be displayed on the button itself. Any control will have access to the variety of Windows default icons. In fact, this chapter will show you how to use them. But wouldn't it be nice to be able to display a special icon just for the Help control? That's what this next icon is used for. We'll create a 32 × 32 icon that the user will be able to select from the property page or the IconType property. To add the icon, right-click the Icon folder in ResourceView and choose Insert Icon from the context menu. Visual C++ will create a blank icon for you. We'll want to rename the icon to IDI_HELP by right-clicking the IDI_ICON1 entry in the Icon folder and choosing Properties from the context menu. Simply change the entry in the ID field. Here's what our special Help icon will look like (to get maximum functionality from this example, you need to add the icon, but don't necessarily have to use the same drawing that I did):

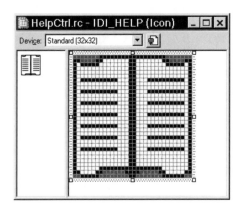

Tip   *Notice that there are two special color selections contained in monitors on your Colors toolbar. The green monitor produces a background color that's invisible. In other words, whatever appears below the icon will show through. The red monitor produces a background that's the same as the Windows desktop color. Using these two special colors judiciously will allow you to create a variety of useful effects found in many applications. The IDI_HELP icon uses the green monitor color as a background so that the button will show through when we use it.*

The final resource we'll need to add is a cursor. The special cursor will allow the user to see instantly that they are working with help rather than the application itself. There's a myriad of these special cursors used in Windows already, so you should be familiar with them. Adding a cursor is similar to adding an icon. Right-click the HelpCtrl resources folder and choose Insert from the context menu. You'll see an Insert Resource dialog box. Choose the Cursor option and click New. Visual C++ will create a blank cursor for you. Right-click IDC_CURSOR1 in the Cursor folder and choose Properties. You'll see a Properties dialog box. Type **IDC_HELP_CURSOR** in the ID field, then close the Properties dialog box. Notice that Visual C++ created a 32 × 32 monochrome cursor for us, which really won't work in this case because we want the user to see the cursor instantly. The following procedure will show you how to insert a new cursor and remove the one we can't use.

1. Click the New Device Image button and you'll see a New Cursor Image dialog box like the one shown here:

2. Click Custom. You'll see a Custom Image dialog box like the one shown next. This is where you'll set the size and number of colors for the new cursor. Remember that even small resources can really boost the size of your application and the memory it requires, so staying small and reducing the number of colors is the way to go. The example will use a 32 × 32 pixel cursor with 16 colors.

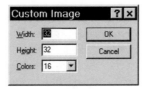

3. Click OK. You'll see the new cursor added to the New Cursor Image dialog box. If you want to add more cursors, you can click the Custom button again. However, the example only requires one cursor.

4. Click OK to add the new cursor image. If you look at the Device drop-down list box, you'll see that there are now two cursors—we really only need one, so the monochrome cursor that we started with must be deleted.

5. Choose the Monochrome (32 × 32) entry in the Device drop-down list box.

6. Use the Image | Delete Device Image command to remove the unwanted image. We can now draw the help cursor.

The Hotspot button allows you to select a new hot spot for your cursor. The hot spot determines what part of the cursor is used for selection purposes and ultimately what coordinates are sent to the Click( ) method of the client application.

At this point, you should have a 32 × 32 pixel cursor that's capable of using 16 colors. Here's the cursor I created for our application:

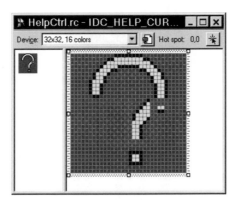

Designing the Property Pages

We've got properties, resources to manage, and a lot of other Help control features in place. Now we need a way to access all of these objects. That's where the property page comes into play for this example. We'll actually need a few properties pages for this example, and of two different types: stock and custom.

There are two stock property pages we'll use in this example, and they're the two that you'll see used most often for ActiveX controls. The first property page, Fonts, will allow the user to change the Font property. Likewise, both the BackColor and ForeColor properties will use the Colors standard property page. Most stock property pages automatically link to the stock properties they control; you may need to do some manipulation in a few cases to get these property pages to work with custom properties. The code for using both the Fonts and Colors property pages appears in the "Adding Some Code" section.

There are also two custom property pages. The first will allow us to control the icon displayed on the button face and where it gets positioned. This property works with the IconType and IconPosition properties. You'll need to resize the standard dialog box used for the property page to 250 × 110 pixels. Table 14-3 contains a complete list of the control names (value in the ID field of the Properties dialog box), properties, and values used for this dialog box. Here's what our first custom property page looks like.

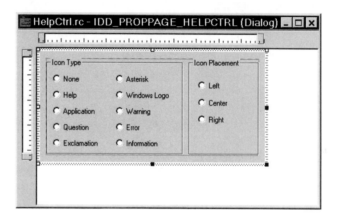

Control ID	Property	Value
IDC_ICON_NONE	Caption	None
	Group	Checked
	Tab stop	Checked
IDC_ICON_HELP	Caption	Help
	Tab stop	Checked

Table 14-3.   IconType and IconPosition Property Page Control Settings

Control ID	Property	Value
IDC_ICON_APPLICATION	Caption	Application
	Tab stop	Checked
IDC_ICON_QUESTION	Caption	Question
	Tab stop	Checked
IDC_ICON_EXCLAMATION	Caption	Exclamation
	Tab stop	Checked
IDC_ICON_ASTERISK	Caption	Asterisk
	Tab stop	Checked
IDC_ICON_WINDOWS_LOGO	Caption	Windows Logo
	Tab stop	Checked
IDC_ICON_WARNING	Caption	Warning
	Tab stop	Checked
IDC_ICON_ERROR	Caption	Error
	Tab stop	Checked
IDC_ICON_INFORMATION	Caption	Information
	Tab stop	Checked
IDC_LEFT	Caption	Left
	Group	Checked
	Tab stop	Checked
IDC_CENTER	Caption	Center
	Tab stop	Checked
IDC_RIGHT	Caption	Right
	Tab stop	Checked

Table 14-3.   IconType and IconPosition Property Page Control Settings (continued)

Notice that we have two groups of radio buttons on this page: one for IconType and a second for IconPosition. You'll see how these two groups work together in the "Adding Some Code" section. However, before we can actually work with the property page, we need to link it to our existing properties. The way you do that is by creating member variables. CTRL-double-click on the None radio button. You'll see an Add Member Variable dialog box like the one shown here:.

For this first member variable, we'll use m_iconType as the member variable name. That's the same name as the member variable used for the property, which avoids confusion later when you're trying to figure out the purpose of each member variable in your code. Since we need the value that the member variable provides transferred to our property, we'll keep the Category field set to Value (the other option is Control, which would allow you to work with the control itself). Notice the "Optional property name" field. This is where the magic happens with our property page. You need to type the name of the property that you want to associate this member variable with. In this case, you'd type **IconType** in this field. (If you're working with a stock property, the name will appear in the drop-down list box, so you can simply select it.) Now we need to do the same thing for the Left radio button. However, in this case, we'll use m_iconPosition as the member variable name and IconPosition in the "Optional property name" field.

There's one additional fit and finish item we need to take care of. If you display the Properties dialog box for the property page, you'll notice that there's no way to change the title used for the property page when it gets displayed in an IDE like Visual Basic. It's possible to change the title, you just have to know where. Look in the String Table resource and you'll see a list of entries like the ones shown here:

ID	Value	Caption
IDS_HELPCTRL	1	HelpCtrl Control
IDS_HELPCTRL_PPG	2	HelpCtrl Property Page
IDS_HELPCTRL_PPG_CAPTI	200	General

Notice that there's an entry named IDS_HELPCTRL_PPG_CAPTION. This is the string that determines the caption used for the property page when it gets displayed in an IDE. Double-click on this entry and you'll see a String Properties dialog box. Change the Caption field value from General to Icons. Close the String Properties dialog box and the name of the property page will be changed.

Let's get to work on the second property. Adding the property page is easy. Just right-click on the Dialog folder in ResourceView and choose Insert from the context menu. (Choosing the Insert Dialog option will give you the wrong kind of dialog box to use as a property page.) You'll see an Insert Resource dialog box. Choose the Dialog | IDD_OLE_PROPPAGE_LARGE option, then click New. Visual C++ will add a new dialog box that you can rename by right-clicking the new entry in ResourceView and choosing Properties from the context menu. Type IDD_PROPPAGE_HELPCTRL2 in the ID field, then close the Properties dialog box. Table 14-4 contains a complete list of the controls used on this property page and their properties. Here's what the property page will look like:

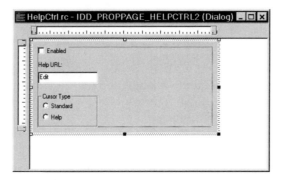

Control ID	Property	Value
IDC_CURSOR_STANDARD	Caption	Standard
	Group	Checked
	Tab stop	Checked
IDC_CURSOR_HELP	Caption	Help
	Tab stop	Checked
IDC_ENABLED	Caption	Enabled

Table 14-4. Miscellaneous Property Page Control Settings

You'll also need to create an Edit Box control with an ID of IDC_HELPURL that will be used for the HelpURL property. There are no special settings for this control other than the ID.

Simply adding a property page to our ActiveX control doesn't make it usable. We have to create a class to hold the property page, which other classes will then use to access the property page. The following procedure will help you create the class required to use the property page in our control.

1. CTRL-double-click the property page (don't do this on any of the controls). You'll see an Adding a Class dialog box like the one shown here:

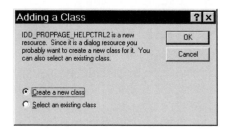

2. Choose the "Create a new class" option since we need a new class to hold the property page.

3. Click OK. You'll see the New Class dialog box shown here:

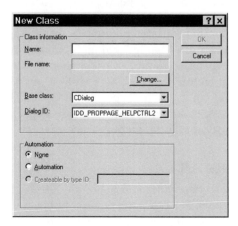

4. Type **CHelpCtrlPpg2** in the Name field. Notice that Visual C++ adds several other entries for you automatically. Normally, you'll accept these automatic settings. Since this is a property page, we'll need to make one additional change.

5. Choose COlePropertyPage in the "Base class" field. This will change our dialog from a standard CDialog class object to a property page we can use with the ActiveX control.

6. Click OK. Visual C++ will add the new class for you.

Visual C++ doesn't provide some of the features for this new property page that you got in the original one. For one thing, if you compile the code at this point and try to use the control in an application, you'll find that this property page lacks a name. You'll need to do two things to add a name for the property page. First, add an entry to the string table similar to the one for the first property page. In this case, we'll give the string table entry an ID of IDS_HELPCTRL_PPG2_CAPTION and a caption of Miscellaneous. After you add the string table entry, you can modify the property page constructor in the HelpCtrlPpg2.CPP file as shown in Listing 14-1 in bold type.

Listing 14-1

```
CHelpCtrlPpg2::CHelpCtrlPpg2() :
    COlePropertyPage(IDD, IDS_HELPCTRL_PPG2_CAPTION)
{
    //{{AFX_DATA_INIT(CHelpCtrlPpg2)
    // NOTE: ClassWizard will add member initialization here
    //    DO NOT EDIT what you see in these blocks of generated code !
//}}AFX_DATA_INIT
}
```

As with our other custom property page, we'll have to associate this one with the properties that it's designed to represent. Simply CTRL-double-click on each control in turn to display the Add Member Variable dialog box. The IDC_ENABLED check box has a Member variable name of m_enabled and an Optional property name of Enabled. The IDC_HELPURL edit box has a Member variable name of m_helpURL and an Optional property name of HelpURL. The IDC_CURSOR_STANDARD radio button has a Member variable name of m_cursorType and an Optional property name of CursorType. We'll look at the code required to make these property page settings operational in the "Adding Some Code" section of the chapter.

Handling Control Events

There are going to be times where you need to handle some of the control's processing needs when it comes to events. For example, what happens when the user clicks the button? If you perform the default processing, the button will appear to go in and out. It'll also fire the click event so that the client can perform any required processing based on user input.

Normally, the default processing would be enough. However, our Help control provides some special features not handled by the default click routine. One of the things we need to do is repaint the icon the application developer has chosen for the button since that's not part of the normal button behavior. With this in mind, we need to add an OnClick( ) method to our Help control, which we'll fill in later.

Adding the OnClick( ) method is easy. Just open the MFC ClassWizard dialog box using the View | ClassWizard command. Choose the Message Maps tab, then the "CHelpCtrlCtl Class name" option. Select the OnClick entry in the Messages list and then click Add Function. What you've done is add a handler for the OnClick event that will allow you to refresh the icon (if any) displayed on the button face.

An event that's a little more difficult to figure out is displaying our special cursor when the mouse pointer is over the Help button. In this case, we need to handle the WM_MOUSEMOVE message because there is no predefined message handler for this even when using a standard control. You add the WM_MOUSEMOVE message handler just as we did the OnClick message. However, in this case, we'll create an OnMouseMove( ) method.

Adding Some Code

It's finally time to make our Help control functional by adding the code that will make it work. All of the code for this example (other than the code covered in previous sections) appears in the HelpCtrlCtl.CPP file. Listing 14-2 contains all of the code for this file since most of the file will change as the result of additions needed to make the control work. We'll discuss the code in the paragraphs that follow the listing.

isting 14-2

```
// HelpCtrlCtl.cpp : Implementation of the CHelpCtrlCtrl ActiveX
// Control class.

#include "stdafx.h"
#include "HelpCtrl.h"
#include "HelpCtrlCtl.h"
#include "HelpCtrlPpg.h"

// Add our second custom property page.
#include "HelpCtrlPpg2.h"

// Add Unicode character conversion support.
#include "AFXPriv.h"

#ifdef _DEBUG
#define new DEBUG_NEW
#undef THIS_FILE
static char THIS_FILE[] = __FILE__;
#endif
```

```
IMPLEMENT_DYNCREATE(CHelpCtrlCtrl, COleControl)


/////////////////////////////////////////////////////////////
// Message map

BEGIN_MESSAGE_MAP(CHelpCtrlCtrl, COleControl)
  //{{AFX_MSG_MAP(CHelpCtrlCtrl)
  ON_WM_MOUSEMOVE()
  //}}AFX_MSG_MAP
  ON_MESSAGE(OCM_COMMAND, OnOcmCommand)
  ON_OLEVERB(AFX_IDS_VERB_EDIT, OnEdit)
  ON_OLEVERB(AFX_IDS_VERB_PROPERTIES, OnProperties)
END_MESSAGE_MAP()


/////////////////////////////////////////////////////////////
// Dispatch map

BEGIN_DISPATCH_MAP(CHelpCtrlCtrl, COleControl)
  //{{AFX_DISPATCH_MAP(CHelpCtrlCtrl)
  DISP_PROPERTY_EX(CHelpCtrlCtrl, "IconType", GetIconType, SetIconType, VT_I4)
  DISP_PROPERTY_EX(CHelpCtrlCtrl, "IconPosition", GetIconPosition, SetIconPosition, VT_I4)
  DISP_PROPERTY_EX(CHelpCtrlCtrl, "HelpURL", GetHelpURL, SetHelpURL, VT_BSTR)
  DISP_PROPERTY_EX(CHelpCtrlCtrl, "CursorType", GetCursorType, SetCursorType, VT_I4)
  DISP_FUNCTION(CHelpCtrlCtrl, "DoHelp", DoHelp, VT_BOOL, VTS_BSTR)
  DISP_STOCKFUNC_DOCLICK()
  DISP_STOCKPROP_BACKCOLOR()
  DISP_STOCKPROP_CAPTION()
  DISP_STOCKPROP_ENABLED()
  DISP_STOCKPROP_FONT()
  DISP_STOCKPROP_FORECOLOR()
  //}}AFX_DISPATCH_MAP
```

```
   DISP_FUNCTION_ID(CHelpCtrlCtrl, "AboutBox", DISPID_ABOUTBOX, AboutBox,
   VT_EMPTY, VTS_NONE)
END_DISPATCH_MAP()


//////////////////////////////////////////////////////////////////////////
// Event map

BEGIN_EVENT_MAP(CHelpCtrlCtrl, COleControl)
  //{{AFX_EVENT_MAP(CHelpCtrlCtrl)
  EVENT_STOCK_CLICK()
  EVENT_STOCK_DBLCLICK()
  //}}AFX_EVENT_MAP
END_EVENT_MAP()


//////////////////////////////////////////////////////////////////////////
// Property pages

// TODO: Add more property pages as needed.  Remember to increase the count!
begin_proppageids(CHelpCtrlCtrl, 4)
  PROPPAGEID(CHelpCtrlPropPage::guid)
  PROPPAGEID(CHelpCtrlPpg2::guid)
  PROPPAGEID(CLSID_CFontPropPage)
  PROPPAGEID(CLSID_CColorPropPage)
END_PROPPAGEIDS(CHelpCtrlCtrl)


//////////////////////////////////////////////////////////////////////////
// Initialize class factory and guid

IMPLEMENT_OLECREATE_EX(CHelpCtrlCtrl, "HELPCTRL.HelpCtrlCtrl.1",
   0x45391a06, 0x49a4, 0x11d2, 0xb0, 0x6e, 0, 0x60, 0x97, 0x5b, 0xf7, 0x84)


//////////////////////////////////////////////////////////////////////////
```

```
// Type library ID and version

IMPLEMENT_OLETYPELIB(CHelpCtrlCtrl, _tlid, _wVerMajor, _wVerMinor)


/////////////////////////////////////////////////////////////////////////
// Interface IDs

const IID BASED_CODE IID_DHelpCtrl =
    { 0x45391a04, 0x49a4, 0x11d2, { 0xb0, 0x6e, 0, 0x60, 0x97, 0x5b, 0xf7, 0x84 } };
const IID BASED_CODE IID_DHelpCtrlEvents =
    { 0x45391a05, 0x49a4, 0x11d2, { 0xb0, 0x6e, 0, 0x60, 0x97, 0x5b, 0xf7, 0x84 } };


/////////////////////////////////////////////////////////////////////////
/
// Control type information

static const DWORD BASED_CODE _dwHelpCtrlOleMisc =
  OLEMISC_ACTIVATEWHENVISIBLE |
  OLEMISC_SETCLIENTSITEFIRST |
  OLEMISC_INSIDEOUT |
  OLEMISC_CANTLINKINSIDE |
  OLEMISC_RECOMPOSEONRESIZE;

IMPLEMENT_OLECTLTYPE(CHelpCtrlCtrl, IDS_HELPCTRL, _dwHelpCtrlOleMisc)


/////////////////////////////////////////////////////////////////////////
// CHelpCtrlCtrl::CHelpCtrlCtrlFactory::UpdateRegistry -
// Adds or removes system registry entries for CHelpCtrlCtrl

BOOL CHelpCtrlCtrl::CHelpCtrlCtrlFactory::UpdateRegistry(BOOL bRegister)
{
  // TODO: Verify that your control follows apartment-model threading rules.
```

```
// Refer to MFC TechNote 64 for more information.
// If your control does not conform to the apartment-model rules, then
// you must modify the code below, changing the 6th parameter from
// afxRegInsertable | afxRegApartmentThreading to afxRegInsertable.

   if (bRegister)
       return AfxOleRegisterControlClass(
           AfxGetInstanceHandle(),
           m_clsid,
           m_lpszProgID,
           IDS_HELPCTRL,
           IDB_HELPCTRL,
           afxRegInsertable | afxRegApartmentThreading,
           _dwHelpCtrlOleMisc,
           _tlid,
           _wVerMajor,
           _wVerMinor);
   else
       return AfxOleUnregisterClass(m_clsid, m_lpszProgID);
}


/////////////////////////////////////////////////////////////////////////
// CHelpCtrlCtrl::CHelpCtrlCtrl - Constructor

CHelpCtrlCtrl::CHelpCtrlCtrl()
{
    InitializeIIDs(&IID_DHelpCtrl, &IID_DHelpCtrlEvents);

    // TODO: Initialize your control's instance data here.
}


/////////////////////////////////////////////////////////////////////////
// CHelpCtrlCtrl::~CHelpCtrlCtrl - Destructor

CHelpCtrlCtrl::~CHelpCtrlCtrl()
{
```

```
   // TODO: Cleanup your control's instance data here.
}


///////////////////////////////////////////////////////////////////////////
// CHelpCtrlCtrl::OnDraw - Drawing function

void CHelpCtrlCtrl::OnDraw(
          CDC* pdc, const CRect& rcBounds, const CRect& rcInvalid)
{
   HICON     hIcon;          // Handle of the icon we'll display.
   int       iWidth;         // Control Width
   int       iHeight;        // Control Height
   COLORREF  crBack;          // Background Color
   COLORREF  crFore;          // Foreground Color

   // Get the control width and height.
   COleControl::GetControlSize(&iWidth, &iHeight);

   // Calculate the right position of the icon by adjusting for
   // the icon size.
   iWidth -= 32;

   // Set the background color.
   crBack = RGB(255, 0, 0);
   SetBkColor(pdc->m_hDC, crBack);
   crFore = RGB(0, 255, 0);
   SetTextColor(pdc->m_hDC, crFore);

   // Perform default paint behavior.
   DoSuperclassPaint(pdc, rcBounds);

   // Load the requested bitmap.
   switch (m_iconType)
   {
   case 1:
      hIcon = LoadIcon(AfxGetInstanceHandle(), MAKEINTRESOURCE(IDI_HELP));
      break;
   case 2:
```

```
        hIcon = LoadIcon(NULL, IDI_APPLICATION);
    break;
case 3:
    hIcon = LoadIcon(NULL, IDI_QUESTION);
    break;
case 4:
    hIcon = LoadIcon(NULL, IDI_EXCLAMATION);
    break;
case 5:
    hIcon = LoadIcon(NULL, IDI_ASTERISK);
    break;
case 6:
    hIcon = LoadIcon(NULL, IDI_WINLOGO);
    break;
case 7:
    hIcon = LoadIcon(NULL, IDI_WARNING);
    break;
case 8:
    hIcon = LoadIcon(NULL, IDI_ERROR);
    break;
case 9:
    hIcon = LoadIcon(NULL, IDI_INFORMATION);
}

// Display the icon on screen.  Offset the icon 4 pixels
// when displayed to the right or left.
switch (m_iconPosition)
{
case 0:
    DrawIcon(pdc->m_hDC, 4, 4, hIcon);
    break;
case 1:
    DrawIcon(pdc->m_hDC, iWidth / 2, 4, hIcon);
    break;
case 2:
    DrawIcon(pdc->m_hDC, iWidth - 4, 4, hIcon);
    break;
}
}
```

```
//////////////////////////////////////////////////////////////////////////
// CHelpCtrlCtrl::DoPropExchange - Persistence support

void CHelpCtrlCtrl::DoPropExchange(CPropExchange* pPX)
{
    ExchangeVersion(pPX, MAKELONG(_wVerMinor, _wVerMajor));
    COleControl::DoPropExchange(pPX);

  // Make all of our properties persistent.
  PX_Long(pPX, "IconType", m_iconType, 0);
  PX_Long(pPX, "IconPosition", m_iconPosition, 0);
  PX_Long(pPX, "CursorType", m_cursorType, 0);
  PX_String(pPX, "HelpURL", m_helpURL, "http://www.microsoft.com");
}


//////////////////////////////////////////////////////////////////////////
// CHelpCtrlCtrl::OnResetState - Reset control to default state

void CHelpCtrlCtrl::OnResetState()
{
    COleControl::OnResetState();  // Resets defaults found in DoPropExchange

    // Set the initial caption.
    COleControl::SetText("Button");
}



//////////////////////////////////////////////////////////////////////////
// CHelpCtrlCtrl::AboutBox - Display an "About" box to the user

void CHelpCtrlCtrl::AboutBox()
{
    CDialog dlgAbout(IDD_ABOUTBOX_HELPCTRL);
    dlgAbout.DoModal();
}
```

```
/////////////////////////////////////////////////////////////////////////
// CHelpCtrlCtrl::PreCreateWindow - Modify parameters for CreateWindowEx

BOOL CHelpCtrlCtrl::PreCreateWindow(CREATESTRUCT& cs)
{
    cs.lpszClass = _T("BUTTON");
    return COleControl::PreCreateWindow(cs);
}


/////////////////////////////////////////////////////////////////////////
// CHelpCtrlCtrl::IsSubclassedControl - This is a subclassed control

BOOL CHelpCtrlCtrl::IsSubclassedControl()
{
    return TRUE;
}


/////////////////////////////////////////////////////////////////////////
// CHelpCtrlCtrl::OnOcmCommand - Handle command messages

LRESULT CHelpCtrlCtrl::OnOcmCommand(WPARAM wParam, LPARAM lParam)
{
#ifdef _WIN32
    WORD wNotifyCode = HIWORD(wParam);
#else
    WORD wNotifyCode = HIWORD(lParam);
#endif

    // TODO: Switch on wNotifyCode here.

    return 0;
}
```

```
/////////////////////////////////////////////////////////////////////////
// CHelpCtrlCtrl message handlers

long CHelpCtrlCtrl::GetIconType()
{
    // Return the value of our internal icon type
    return m_iconType;
}

void CHelpCtrlCtrl::SetIconType(long nNewValue)
{
    // Set our internal value to the one passed by the client.
    m_iconType = nNewValue;

    // Force a repaint of the control.
    COleControl::Refresh();

    SetModifiedFlag();
}

long CHelpCtrlCtrl::GetIconPosition()
{
    // Return the value of our internal icon position.
    return m_iconPosition;
}

void CHelpCtrlCtrl::SetIconPosition(long nNewValue)
{
    // Set our internal value to the one passed by the client.
    m_iconPosition = nNewValue;

    // Force a repaint of the control.
    COleControl::Refresh();

    SetModifiedFlag();
}

BSTR CHelpCtrlCtrl::GetHelpURL()
{
    // Return the value of our internal help URL.
    return m_helpURL.AllocSysString();
```

```
}

void CHelpCtrlCtrl::SetHelpURL(LPCTSTR lpszNewValue)
{
    // Set our internal value to the one passed by the client.
    m_helpURL = lpszNewValue;

    SetModifiedFlag();
}

long CHelpCtrlCtrl::GetCursorType()
{
    // Return the value of our internal cursor type.
    return m_cursorType;
}

void CHelpCtrlCtrl::SetCursorType(long nNewValue)
{
    // Set our internal value to the one passed by the client.
    m_cursorType = nNewValue;

    SetModifiedFlag();
}

BOOL CHelpCtrlCtrl::DoHelp(LPCTSTR lpszHelpURL)
{
    LPCWSTR    lpsURL = NULL;

    // Add a macro that tells Visual C++ we need to convert
    // lpszHelpURL to a Unicode string.
    USES_CONVERSION;

    // Convert the standard string to a Unicode string.
    lpsURL = A2CW(lpszHelpURL);

    // Go right to the appropriate help page.
    HlinkSimpleNavigateToString(lpsURL,
        NULL, NULL, NULL, 0, NULL, NULL, 0);

    return TRUE;
}
```

```
void CHelpCtrlCtrl::OnClick(USHORT iButton)
{
    // Refresh the icon if any.
    COleControl::Refresh();

    // Perform the normal action.
    COleControl::OnClick(iButton);

    // Display the help dialog box.
    DoHelp(m_helpURL);
}

void CHelpCtrlCtrl::OnMouseMove(UINT nFlags, CPoint point)
{
    HCURSOR     hCursor;     // Handle of the cursor we'll use.

    // See if we need to display the special mouse pointer.
    if(m_cursorType > 0)
    {
        // Load the cursor then display it.
        hCursor = LoadCursor(AfxGetInstanceHandle(),
MAKEINTRESOURCE(IDC_HELP_CURSOR));
        SetCursor(hCursor);
    }

    COleControl::OnMouseMove(nFlags, point);
}
```

This control requires a lot of code, but none of it is hard to understand if you take it one piece at a time. The first thing to notice is that you need to add two #include directives to the beginning of the code. The first #include will allow access to the second custom code page. The second #include provides the means to convert standard C character strings into their Unicode equivalent.

Note *Normally, the AFXPriv.h include file would appear in the StdAfx.h file. However, in this case, we aren't using the character conversion macros that the AFXPriv.h include file contains on an application-wide basis. Since we're adding this include manually, placing the #include directive in the file where the include gets used helps in the documentation process.*

The next place you need to look for code additions is in the BEGIN_ PROPPAGEIDS( ) macro. Notice that this macro takes two arguments. It's the second argument that we're interested in because it controls how many property pages the user will see. Make absolutely certain that this argument (4 in this case) reflects the actual number of property pages that you want the user to see. There are situations when your control will compile perfectly; yet because this number is incorrect, you'll fail to see all of the property pages you defined. Rather than spend hours looking for a bug in your property page code, always check this number first.

Each property page also requires a PROPPAGEID( ) macro entry. There are two types used in our ActiveX control. The first type is for custom property pages. You can recognize this property page call by the class name and the use of the guid (in lowercase) method. The second type is used for stock property pages. Each property page will have a special name in this case. The example shows how to use the two most common stock property pages: CLSID_CFontPropPage and CLSID_CColorPropPage.

Drawing our control using the OnDraw( ) method comes next. There are two preliminary steps before we actually draw anything. First, we get the height and width of the control so that we can draw the various elements in the right place. Second, we change the foreground and background color settings so that the control will be present in the right colors should it be in the right mode to do so. Notice that there are several distinct drawing phases for this control. The first drawing phase is to call the superclass to draw the button. Next, we load an icon if the user has selected one. The example control can use either standard Windows icons or custom icons loaded as part of the control. A third alternative would be to allow the user to select an icon from the hard drive—you'd need to add some logic for checking the icon type so that you could load it properly. Finally, a case statement determines where to place the icon on the button, then draws it. Notice that the code assumes that the user will want a 4-pixel border between the icon and the edge of the button. You could potentially add this offset as another property so that the user would gain full control over the appearance of the control and the placement of the icon on it.

As with every other ActiveX control in this book, the DoPropExchange( ) method allows the control to persist its data. The PX_* functions allow you to store the current user property settings as well as set an initial value for each property. However, remember that the DoPropExchange( ) method is solely concerned with custom properties. You'll need to set the initial values of any stock properties using the OnResetState( ) method, which appears next in the list of methods for this control. The only stock property that we really need to set in this case is the button caption. You could also set the button size if desired, but most IDEs provide a default control size, so setting the control size isn't absolutely essential.

The next thing you'll need to change in the skeleton code that we created earlier is the Get/Set methods for the various properties. We've talked about this topic in Chapter 11 with regard to ATL-based ActiveX controls. This example shows you some typical Get/Set implementations when working with an MFC-based ActiveX control. (Remember that our example in Chapter 4 used the member variable technique in place of the Get/Set technique illustrated in this chapter.) Most of the Get/Set methods for this example simply change the values of the member variables that we created earlier. In other words, the Get/Set method provides the means for a client to access the protected variables used to hold state information for the ActiveX control in a safe way.

There are a few things you need to notice about the Set methods used in this control. Look at the SetIconType( ) and SetIconPosition( ) methods. Both of these methods call COleControl::Refresh( ). If you don't refresh the control when making changes to its appearance, then the changes you make won't appear to take effect even though the change has occurred internally. Whenever you write an ActiveX control that changes its appearance in some way, make sure that you add calls to the COleControl::Refresh( ) method as needed.

Now we come to the DoHelp( ) method. This is a custom method that we added early in the design process. The whole purpose of this method is to allow the control to display an HTML-based Help screen for the user. You can either pass the Web page URL directly to the control using the DoHelp( ) method directly, or set the URL in the HelpURL property, then display it when the user clicks the control. Notice that the first thing we need to do is convert the standard C string to a Unicode string. The reason is simple: calling Internet Explorer using the HlinkSimpleNavigateToString( ) function won't work with a standard string. What you'll see is a navigation error (that's right, Internet Explorer won't even have the decency to tell you that you passed what amounts to an unreadable string). There are two conversion steps. First, use the USES_CONVERSION( ) macro to tell Visual C++ that you plan on converting strings from one format to another. Second, use the A2CW( ) macro to convert the standard C string to a Unicode string. The HlinkSimpleNavigateToString( ) function itself is pretty interesting. All you have to supply is a URL in the first parameter. You can further define the part of the page you want to see by including an anchor in the second parameter and a frame name in the third.

The OnClick( ) method allows us to react to a user click. The method contains a mere three steps: refresh the control's appearance, perform the normal click action, then call the DoHelp( ) method to process the default help URL. That's all there is to it.

This example shows one way to add a custom cursor to a control. When the user selects a custom cursor, the OnMouseMove( ) method loads the cursor, then displays it. Since this method only gets called when the mouse cursor is over the Help control, the custom mouse cursor will only appear while the mouse is over the control. This makes it easy for the user to see that clicking this button will perform a special task—in this case, displaying a Help screen. Notice that the OnMouseMove( ) method does call the COleControl::OnMouseMove( ) method to perform default mouse processing.

Creating the Help Desk Web Pages with Visual InterDev

We've already looked at application help in several chapters of the book. In Chapter 5, we looked at the traditional form of help found in the HLP file. In Chapter 9, we looked at a similar form of application help that uses an HTML base. This chapter will look at application, or more properly software, help in a different light. What we'll do in this section is take a help desk approach that assumes the user is no longer just looking for assistance in using the application, but that the application has failed in some way and the user requires some form of problem resolution. (However, since we've already spent some time looking at help file creation, we won't spend a lot of time fleshing these Help pages out—the overall principles are the same, only the skeleton used to organize the information is different.)

Creating the Project Shell

Before we can create a hierarchical question structure or design Web pages, we need to create the project shell that contains the essential resources for this project. The following procedure will help you start the new Visual InterDev application that we'll use for this chapter:

1. Start Visual InterDev, if you haven't already done so. You should see a New Project dialog box.

2. Choose the Visual InterDev Projects folder, then highlight the New Web Project icon.

3. Type **HelpDesk** in the Name field, then click Open. Visual InterDev will display the Web Project Wizard - Step 1 of 4 dialog box. You should already have many of the default setups in place from working with other projects in this book. If not, read through the simple project setup found in Chapter 4.

4. Choose a server and the "Master mode" option. Click Next. Visual InterDev will contact the server and set up a new Web project. You'll see the Web Project Wizard - Step 2 of 4 dialog box.

5. Click Next to accept the default project name of HelpDesk and create the default Search page. You'll see the Web Project Wizard - Step 3 of 4 dialog box. Theoretically, you could get by without a Search page for this project since the user will follow a procedure to find a desired Help page, but its inclusion won't hurt either. Depending on the way you set up your help desk application, including a Search page may be more of a hindrance than a help. You may not want the user to skip valuable diagnostic steps to arrive at a faulty conclusion that may appear to fix the problem. Make sure you uncheck the "Create search.htm to enable full text searching" option if you don't want to include a Search page for this project type.

6. Choose the Top and Bottom 3 layout for this project. We're going to change this layout a bit so that the buttons will appear on the left side of the screen and point to the child pages (the pages with the next step of the solution) instead of the global pages. This will allow us to create pages that automatically get updated with any new answers as your help desk grows. Since you don't know for sure how the user will access the Web page, providing a Previous and Next

button is a good idea. The Bottom 1 layout doesn't provide much else in the way of navigation aids, which is actually a plus for this application. A help desk should be designed in such a way that the user is guided from one page to the next in a logical sequence.

7. Click Next. You'll see the Web Project Wizard - Step 4 of 4 dialog box. Adding a theme isn't absolutely necessary for a help desk; however, you do want to make the help desk as approachable as possible. People react better when they see a friendly interface that looks easy to use. Applying a theme won't add to the functionality of the help desk, but it may allow the user to interact with it better.

8. Choose a theme (the example will use Raygun since it provides a very easy to read interface).

9. Click Finish. Visual InterDev will create a Web site shell.

Modifying the Layout

Let's begin this project by modifying our layout so that it'll work in the way we need it to work. Open the _Layouts\tb3\LAYOUT.HTM file (you'll need to obtain a local copy in most cases). You'll see the layout that we chose in Step 6 of the procedure. What we need to do is change the properties of the second PageNavbar control (the one that is set up for viewing the global pages at this moment). Right-click the PageNavbar control, then choose Properties from the context menu. What you'll see is a PageNavbar Properties dialog box. On the General tab, choose the "Children pages" option, and uncheck the Parent check box. Your PageNavbar Properties dialog box should look like the one shown here.

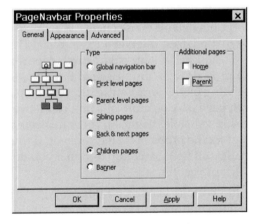

We also need to change the position that the buttons will appear in. Choose the Appearance tab and select the Vertical option. Make sure you choose the Buttons option as well if you want your displays to look like the ones in this example. Here's what the Appearance tab should look like:

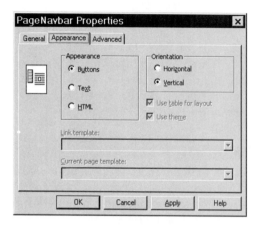

Click OK. We've just modified the layout in a way that makes it perfect for a help desk Web site. What the user will always see is a set of buttons pointing to the next step in the problem solution procedure and a way to get to the previous or next page. This is all you really need if you provide a logical troubleshooting procedure for your help desk Web site.

Creating a Site Diagram

The center of a help desk application is the site diagram. You won't create a very effective or efficient help desk unless you use one. Here's the problem: Without a map of where the user needs to go from one step to another, both you and the user will get lost. A help desk application provides a logical procedure for finding problems with applications, hardware, or some other job-related task. The site diagram helps you map the sequence of events required to reach a particular help solution. This sequence of events (or procedure) can be created in a number of ways, but most generally it's a hierarchical structure that allows the reader to go step by step through a troubleshooting procedure based on technical support input as well as the input of subject matter experts.

Remember that there may be several ways to reach the same solution when troubleshooting a hardware or software problem. Keep the number of Web pages on your site to a minimum by reusing pages whenever possible. Simply place a second (or third) copy of the page where needed in the site diagram. Even though the page has been used more than once, the user will be able to access it as needed.

Use the Add I Site Diagram command to display the Add Item dialog box. Visual InterDev will automatically select the Site Diagram icon for you. Type **HelpProcedure** in the Name field, then click Open. Visual InterDev will create a new site diagram for you. In addition to the site diagram, you'll see a Default.HTM file added once you save the project. Right-click on this file and choose "Set as Start Page" from the context menu to set this as the start page for the help desk Web site.

Organizing the Information

The software that I've chosen to illustrate is a simple utility for displaying user network information, but it could just as easily be something more complex. The important principle to learn in this chapter is how to set up a help desk for an application. We'll actually create this simple application in the "Adding the Help Desk Control to a Visual Basic Application" section of the chapter.

It's time to add a little structure to our example help desk. It's normally better to use a task-based directory structure instead of a hierarchy when working with a help desk. The reason is simple: A single Web page can appear in more than one place in the question hierarchy, so there isn't any good way to create a hierarchical directory structure. So, what task folders do we need to set up for this help desk? For this application, there are going to be two main areas of concern: network and operator errors. What we need to do then is create two folders by right-clicking the <Server Name>/HelpDesk folder and choosing New Folder from the context menu. Name the first folder Network and the second Operator. These two folders will hold all of the content pages for our help desk. (If this were a production Web site, you'd add folders that reflected the kinds of tasks that users normally perform with your application— make sure the folders are general enough to make it easy to find a particular content page later.)

Once you've added the required storage folders, it's time to add some empty Web pages; one for each major question that you intend to answer. Remember that you right-click the folder that you want to add a blank Web page to, then choose the Add I HTML Page... option on the context menu. When you see the Add Item dialog box, simply type the name of the new Web page in the Name field and click OK. The goal here is to use some descriptive name that only uses one word (or several words without spaces). Here's the list of blank Web pages we'll use for this example (look at the Network and Operator folders):

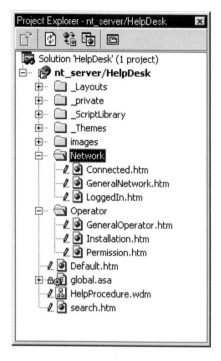

Now that you have some pages to use, let's organize them on the site diagram. Remember that we need to organize the pages in such a way that the user's questions will be answered. It's not necessary to organize the pages in a hierarchical format. I've used the actual page names in the following illustration (except for the default Home entry supplied by Visual InterDev) so that you can see how the pages will go together in this case.

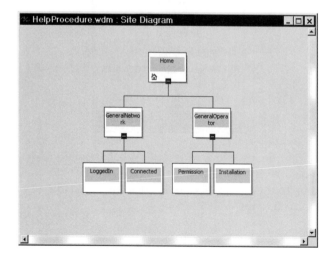

Using ASP to Make Links

At this point, you may be thinking that there is a bit of a gap in our site diagram. What if the user fails to log in? Wouldn't that contingency fit under the GeneralOperator page just as much as it does under the GeneralNetwork page? That's where Active Server Pages (ASPs) come into play. While an ASP is normally used for scripting purposes, you could also use it for something as simple as a page redirection. This is the easiest way to accomplish the task of creating multiple links to the same Web page.

Let's look at the process for adding ASP support to your help desk. Right-click the Operator folder and choose the Add | Active Server Page... entry. You'll see the Add Item dialog box (the ASP Page icon should be highlighted). Type **LoggedIn** in the Name field, then click OK. Visual InterDev will add the LoggedIn.ASP to your Operator folder. You'll also see the ASP displayed on-screen with the Source tab selected. That's because Visual InterDev assumes that you'll want to add some code to the ASP immediately.

Select the Script Outline window. You'll notice that there are two entries in the Client Objects folder: document and window as shown here:

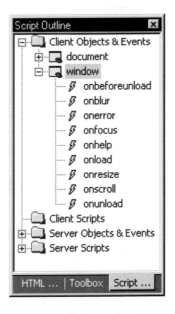

We really don't want the user to see the ASP. What we want to do is make it appear that the user has gone directly to the LoggedIn.HTM page. To do that, you need to add an OnLoad( ) function to the ASP. Just double-click the OnLoad entry in the window folder to add the function to the ASP.

The code required to change the page displayed when the user selects this option is fairly simple. Here's what your window_onload( ) function should look like:

```
function window_onload() {
    // Change the target page to the LoggedIn page.
    window.location.href = "../Network/LoggedIn.HTM"
}
```

Notice that the only thing we need to do is change the window location to the desired page, which is the actual LoggedIn.HTM file. The ASP page only serves as a means for redirecting the user in this case. Here's the new site diagram with the additional LoggedIn entry added:

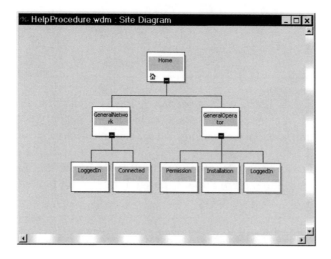

Adding Some Content

We aren't going to add any actual content to our sample—we've already explored most of the content principles needed for a Web site earlier in the book. There are, however, a few special concerns for help desks that you need to consider. The first is how we're using the site diagram in this case. The site diagram we're creating is actually used as answers to a user's question. What you need to do is phrase the site diagrams entries in such a way that the user will actually perceive the buttons as answers. For example, let's look at the entries for the Home page on the site diagram. Right now, it looks like a

Web site. However, if you change the entries as shown here, they look more like answers to a question:

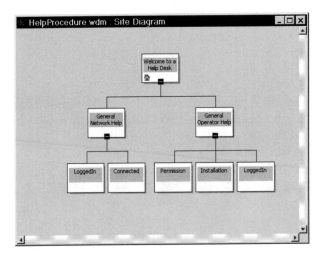

Note *You can change the site diagram entries by right-clicking the icon, then choosing Property Pages from the context menu. Change the Title field to change the icon name and its appearance on the various PageNavbar control buttons.*

Next, you need to add some text to the Default.HTM file so that the user knows what question you're asking. Here's how I changed the default page for this example (obviously, this is a very simplistic approach for the sake of clarity):

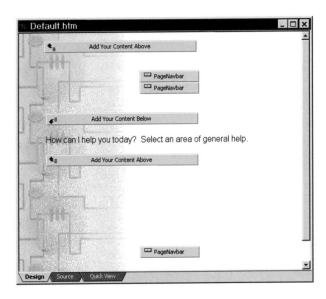

This brings up the second concern you need to address when creating these Web pages. I placed the buttons at the top, which may seem awkward at first (and it does take some time to get used to). However, once the user becomes familiar with the help desk, you'll find that they actually get less frustrated if you put the buttons at the top. An expert user will be able to get from one place to another in the help desk in a relatively short time, further reducing help desk costs by reducing user down time. Here's what our sample help desk looks like in action.

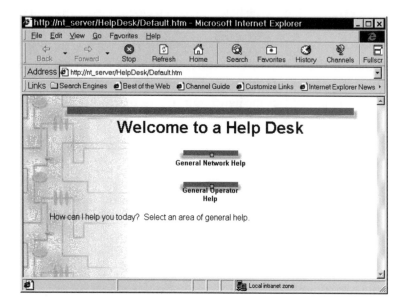

Adding Bells and Whistles Using Visual J++

The help desk that we've created will be very functional, but it won't be complete in at least one respect. This help desk assumes that the answer the user needs will be found somewhere in the Web pages that we've added to the help desk. In many cases, that will be the case. But what happens if it isn't? We need a way to page a support technician when the help desk fails to provide the help that it's supposed to.

Creating the Applet Shell

The Page button will allow a user to access the support technician in a number of ways, including using the standard email message when the current problem isn't a high priority. The following procedure will help you get started creating the Page applet that we'll add to our help desk application later.

1. Start Visual J++ if you haven't done so already. You should see the New Project dialog box.

2. Choose the Visual J++ Projects | Web Pages folder, then highlight the Applet on HTML icon.

3. Type **PageHelp** in the Name field, then click Open. Visual J++ will create a project skeleton for you. We'll need to rename the applet at this point so that we can access it using a more convenient name than Applet1.

4. Right-click on the Applet1.JAVA entry, then choose Rename from the context menu.

5. Type **PageHelp.JAVA** as the new applet name, then press ENTER.

6. Open both the Page1.HTM and PageHelp.JAVA files.

Adding Some Code

Our Java applet is going to be relatively simple. It'll provide a heading telling the user that they can gain additional help. There will also be some buttons for paging help in various ways (including using email). Listing 14-3 provides the code that we'll use to make this applet work.

Listing 14-3

```java
import java.awt.*;
import java.applet.*;
import java.awt.event.*;

/**
 * This class reads PARAM tags from its HTML host page and sets
 * the color properties of the applet. Program execution
 * begins with the init() method.
 */
public class PageHelp extends Applet
{
    /**
     * The entry point for the applet.
     */
    public void init()
    {
        initForm();

        usePageParams();
```

```
}

private  final String backgroundParam = "background";
private  final String foregroundParam = "foreground";

/**
 * Reads parameters from the applet's HTML host and sets applet
 * properties.
 */
private void usePageParams()
{
  final String defaultBackground = "C0C0C0";
  final String defaultForeground = "000000";
  String backgroundValue;
  String foregroundValue;

  /**
   * Read the <PARAM NAME="background" VALUE="rrggbb">,
   * and <PARAM NAME="foreground" VALUE="rrggbb"> tags from
   * the applet's HTML host.
   */
  backgroundValue = getParameter(backgroundParam);
  foregroundValue = getParameter(foregroundParam);

  if ((backgroundValue == null) ||
    (foregroundValue == null))
  {
    /**
     * There was something wrong with the HTML host tags.
     * Generate default values.
     */
    backgroundValue = defaultBackground;
    foregroundValue = defaultForeground;
  }

  /**
   * Set the applet's background and foreground colors.
   */
  lblHeading.setBackground(stringToColor(backgroundValue));
  lblHeading.setForeground(stringToColor(foregroundValue));
  this.setBackground(stringToColor(backgroundValue));
```

```java
    this.setForeground(stringToColor(foregroundValue));

    // Enable our application to listen for events.
    cmdMail.addActionListener(OnMail);
    cmdPhone.addActionListener(OnPhone);
    cmdChat.addActionListener(OnChat);
}

/**
 * Converts a string formatted as "rrggbb" to an awt.Color object
 */
private Color stringToColor(String paramValue)
{
    int red;
    int green;
    int blue;

    red = (Integer.decode("0x" + paramValue.substring(0,2))).intValue();
    green = (Integer.decode("0x" + paramValue.substring(2,4))).intValue();
    blue = (Integer.decode("0x" + paramValue.substring(4,6))).intValue();

    return new Color(red,green,blue);
}

/**
 * External interface used by design tools to show properties of an applet.
 */
public String[][] getParameterInfo()
{
    String[][] info =
    {
        { backgroundParam, "String", "Background color, format \"rrggbb\"" },
        { foregroundParam, "String", "Foreground color, format \"rrggbb\"" },
    };
    return info;
}
```

```
Label     lblHeading = new Label("How You Can Get Help", Label.CENTER);
Label     lblMail = new Label("Low Priority: Use email to contact the administrator.");
Label     lblPhone = new Label("Middle Priority: Contact the administrator by phone.");
Label     lblChat = new Label("High Priority: Get immediate service using network chat.");
Button    cmdMail = new Button("Mail");
Button    cmdPhone = new Button("Phone");
Button    cmdChat = new Button("Chat");
GridBagConstraints  gbc = new GridBagConstraints();
GridBagLayout     gbLayout = new GridBagLayout();

/**
 * Intializes values for the applet and its components
 */
void initForm()
{
  // Set the default colors.
  this.setBackground(Color.lightGray);
  this.setForeground(Color.black);

  // Create a layout for holding the controls.
  this.setLayout(gbLayout);

  // Add the heading.
  gbc.fill = GridBagConstraints.CENTER;
  gbc.weighty = 1.0;
  gbc.gridwidth = GridBagConstraints.REMAINDER;
  gbLayout.setConstraints(lblHeading, gbc);
  this.add(lblHeading);

  // Add the mail button and label.
  gbc.fill = GridBagConstraints.WEST;
  gbc.weightx = 1.0;
  gbc.gridwidth = GridBagConstraints.RELATIVE;
  gbLayout.setConstraints(cmdMail, gbc);
  this.add(cmdMail);
  gbc.fill = GridBagConstraints.CENTER;
  gbc.weightx = 0.0;
```

```
      gbc.gridwidth = GridBagConstrain
      gbLayout.setConstraints(lblMail, gbc);
      this.add(lblMail);

      // Add the phone button and label.
      gbc.fill = GridBagConstraints.WEST;
      gbc.weightx = 1.0;
      gbc.gridwidth = GridBagConstraints.RELATIVE;
      gbLayout.setConstraints(cmdPhone, gbc);
      this.add(cmdPhone);
      gbc.fill = GridBagConstraints.CENTER;
      gbc.weightx = 0.0;
      gbc.gridwidth = GridBagConstraints.REMAINDER;
      gbLayout.setConstraints(lblPhone, gbc);
      this.add(lblPhone);

      // Add the chat button and label.
      gbc.fill = GridBagConstraints.WEST;
      gbc.weightx = 1.0;
      gbc.weighty = 0.0;
      gbc.gridwidth = GridBagConstraints.RELATIVE;
      gbLayout.setConstraints(cmdChat, gbc);
      this.add(cmdChat);
      gbc.fill = GridBagConstraints.CENTER;
      gbc.weightx = 0.0;
      gbc.gridwidth = GridBagConstraints.REMAINDER;
      gbLayout.setConstraints(lblChat, gbc);
      this.add(lblChat);
   }

   // Create a new action listener for the three buttons.
   MailListener  OnMail = new MailListener();
   PhoneListener  OnPhone = new PhoneListener();
   ChatListener  OnChat = new ChatListener();

   // These are the listener classes for the three buttons.  They
   // control how the buttons react when pressed.
   public class MailListener implements ActionListener
   {
      // Create a frame and dialog box for displaying a message to the user.
```

```
    // The dialog box includes a message and an OK button.

    Frame   oFrame = new Frame("Connect Message");
    Dialog  msgBox = new Dialog(oFrame, "Mail Message", false);
    Label   Label1 = new Label("Contact the administrator at:
Admin@my.company.com");
    Button  Button1 = new Button("OK");
    OKButton  OnOK = new OKButton();

    // Impelement the dialog box through the listener for the Phone button
    // on the applet.
    public void actionPerformed(ActionEvent event)
    {
      // Define the dialog box layout.
      msgBox.setLayout(new GridLayout(2, 1));

      // Add the contact message.
      msgBox.add(Label1);

      // Modify and add the OK button.
      Button1.addActionListener(OnOK);
      msgBox.add(Button1);

      // Define the dialog box size, then display it.
      msgBox.setSize(300, 200);
      msgBox.show();
    }

    // Since the mail message dialog box also contains a button, we have to
    // add a listener for it.  The only purpose of this listener is to close
    // the dialog box once the user is finished looking at it.
    public class OKButton implements ActionListener
    {
      public void actionPerformed(ActionEvent event)
      {
        oFrame.dispose();
      }
    }
}
```

```java
public class PhoneListener implements ActionListener
{
  // Create a frame and dialog box for displaying a message to the
  // the user. The dialog box includes a message and an OK button.

  Frame   oFrame = new Frame("Connect Message");
  Dialog  msgBox = new Dialog(oFrame, "Phone Message", false);
  Label   Label1 = new Label("You can contact the administrator at: 555-1212");
  Button  Button1 = new Button("OK");
  OKButton  OnOK = new OKButton();

  // Implement the dialog box through the listener for the Phone
  // button on the applet.
  public void actionPerformed(ActionEvent event)
  {
    // Define the dialog box layout.
    msgBox.setLayout(new GridLayout(2, 1));

    // Add the contact message.
    msgBox.add(Label1);

    // Modify and add the OK button.
    Button1.addActionListener(OnOK);
    msgBox.add(Button1);

    // Define the dialog box size, then display it.
    msgBox.setSize(300, 200);
    msgBox.show();
  }

  // Since the phone message dialog box also contains a button,
  // we have to add a listener for it.  The only purpose of this
  // listener is to close the dialog box once the user is finished
  // looking at it.
  public class OKButton implements ActionListener
  {
    public void actionPerformed(ActionEvent event)
```

```
        {
    oFrame.dispose();
        }
     }
}


public class ChatListener implements ActionListener
{
   // Create a frame and dialog box for displaying a message to the user.
   // The dialog box includes a message and an OK button.

   Frame  oFrame = new Frame("Connect Message");
   Dialog  msgBox = new Dialog(oFrame, "Chat Message", false);
   Label  Label1 = new Label("The Chat line isn't available.");
   Button  Button1 = new Button("OK");
   OKButton  OnOK = new OKButton();

   // Implement the dialog box through the listener for the Phone button on
   // the applet.
   public void actionPerformed(ActionEvent event)
   {
     // Define the dialog box layout.
     msgBox.setLayout(new GridLayout(2, 1));

     // Add the contact message.
     msgBox.add(Label1);

     // Modify and add the OK button.
     Button1.addActionListener(OnOK);
     msgBox.add(Button1);

     // Define the dialog box size, then display it.
     msgBox.setSize(300, 200);
     msgBox.show();
   }

   // Since the chat message dialog box also contains a button, we have to
   // add a listener for it.  The only purpose of this listener is to close
```

```
// the dialog box once the user is finished looking at it.
   public class OKButton implements ActionListener
   {
     public void actionPerformed(ActionEvent event)
     {
       oFrame.dispose();
     }
   }
 }
}
```

Note *Remember to change the applet class and name in Page1.HTM. Visual J++ assumes that you'll retain the name Applet1. Since we've changed the name of both the class and the applet to PageHelp, you'll need to change the entries in the test page as well.*

The code in Listing 14-3 may seem a bit overwhelming at first, but it's fairly easy to understand once you take it apart. The first thing we need to do is import the java.awt.event class. This class will allow us to add listeners for the various push buttons used in this example. In fact, you'll find the java.awt.event class indispensable for any project that requires event handling (which includes anything but the simplest applet).

Most of the code for handling applet arguments is the same as we looked at in Chapter 4, though greatly simplified, so I won't go through it here again. However, it's important to note that once we've handled all of the arguments, there are three special calls for adding handlers to the push buttons we'll talk about in a few moments. The three instances of the event handler classes are OnMail, OnPhone, and OnChat. We'll talk about this code later in the example.

The next thing you'll want to look at is all of the variable declarations for this applet. The applet includes a heading, three buttons, and three labels that explain button functionality. A lot of the code shown here is repetitive, but you need it in order to display the various applet elements in some semblance of order.

Notice that we have to define the layout as a variable instead of simply using it like we did the GridLayout in Chapter 4 (and later in this example). The reason is simple: The GridBagLayout allows you to perform a lot of manipulation in the way the applet gets displayed on various Web pages. The way the user sizes the applet will affect its appearance, and therefore care must be taken in laying the applet out so that none of the components actually disappear.

The GridBagLayout class uses a helper class named GridBagConstraints. The GridBagConstraints contains the parameters for placing various controls within the layout. To get a better idea of how this works, look at the code that follows. All that code is required to obtain a fairly stable layout of components on an applet. However, you'll find that once you get an applet laid out this way, there are very few sizing problems that you have to deal with. Most of the GridBagLayout elements that you have to worry about include the width of each control, how a single control gets displayed with reference to other controls, and the method used to fill in rows of controls.

Once you have the applet components defined and laid out, it's time to take care of any listener objects. The example applet uses three different listener objects for each of the buttons it displays. We could have used a single class to hold all of the code required for the various buttons, but the listener implementation would have gotten difficult to read if the controls varied much from each other. With this in mind, the example uses three different listener classes for each of the push buttons.

Each button on the example applet displays a dialog box containing a contact message. You could easily extend the functionality of these buttons to do things like display a blank email message dialog that contains the address required to reach the administrator or an application like NetMeeting that the user could use to contact the administrator directly. Since each button for the example does about the same thing, I'll describe the inner workings of only one button.

The first thing we need to do in the button listener is define all of the components required to create the dialog box. Notice that a dialog box consists of both a frame and a dialog object. You must have both elements or the dialog box won't display when the user clicks the buttons. There are only two other components required for the dialog box: a label containing the contact information and the push button used to close the dialog box once the user is finished.

Defining the dialog box comes next. The first thing we do is configure each component and add it to the dialog box. Notice that we have to add a listener for the OK button. Leaving this feature out would mean that the user couldn't close the dialog box later. Also, notice that there are two steps in displaying the dialog box. First we have to size the dialog box. If you don't, the user will see a title bar and that's it. Second, you use the show( ) method to display the dialog box on-screen.

The OK button listener is very simple. All we need to do is use the frame's dispose( ) method to get rid of the frame. The frame's dispose( ) method will also get rid of the dialog box and all the components that it contains. This means you don't have to do anything else to get rid of the dialog box on-screen and make sure that the applet doesn't continue to use memory after you get rid of it.

Using the Applet on the Help Desk

There are a variety of ways that we could use the PageHelp applet now that we've put it together. However, before we can do anything at all, the applet has to be deployed. Use the Project | Deploy Solution command to deploy the applet locally. If you want to deploy the applet on a Web site, then you'll need to define a deployment target using the Project | New Deployment Target... command. Once you have a target defined, you can use the Project | Deploy command to deploy the applet.

If you plan to use an applet on a lot of projects, then place it in a general folder on the Web site. I use a folder named Applets on my Web server for general controls. On the other hand, if you are creating a special applet for a single project, then deploy the applet to the load directory and add it as an item to the single Web project. The applet will still end up on the Web server, but it will appear within the individual project directory.

Our example applet will probably be used on this project alone. So, the first thing you'd need to do is deploy it to the local machine. Once you deploy the applet, open the HelpDesk Visual InterDev project. Add a new folder named Applets directly below the <Server Name>/HelpDesk folder. Once you accomplish that task, add the applet by right-clicking the Applets folder and choosing Add | Add Item from the context menu. What you'll see is the Add Item dialog box. Choose the Existing tab, Java Class (*.Class) from the "Files of type" field, and the directory you used for creating the Java applet in the "Look in" field. Your Add Item dialog box should look similar to the one shown here:

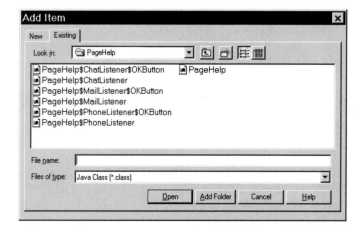

Notice that the Add Item dialog box has an Add Folder button. Click the Add Folder button to add all of the files required for the PageHelp project to the HelpDesk project. The reason you want to do this is so the entire custom project files stay together. (There are a number of other ways to handle this situation, but this particular method works well for small projects where the number of files will remain relatively small.) At this point, you should have all of the files required to add the PageHelp

applet to your HelpDesk project. The Project Explorer window should look similar to
the one shown here with the PageHelp applet files included:

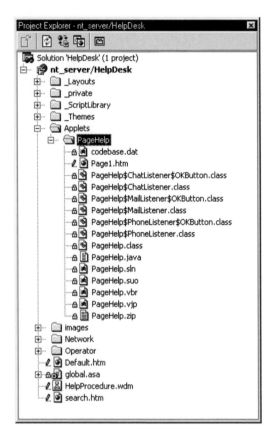

We have access to the PageHelp applet at this point. For the purposes of this
example, I'll assume that you only want to add the applet to the Default.HTM file.
Make sure you open Default.HTM and select the Source tab if necessary. All we need
to do is add some code to add the applet to the Default.HTM file as shown in bold type
in Listing 14-4.

Listing 14-4

```
<!--METADATA TYPE="DesignerControl" endspan-->

<p>How can I help you today?  Select an
          area of general help.</p>
<p>

<!-- Add the PageHelp applet -->
<APPLET
```

```
code=PageHelp.class
codebase="http://nt_server/HelpDesk/Applets/PageHelp"
height=200
name=PageHelp
width=320
id=Applet1>
<PARAM NAME="foreground" VALUE="000000">
<PARAM NAME="background" VALUE="FFD000">
</APPLET>

</p>
<!--METADATA TYPE="DesignerControl" startspan
```

This is the standard code that you'll use to add an applet manually (the best way to do things, in this example). All you need to use is the <APPLET> tag, which includes the applet class, a codebase, the height and width, an applet name within the class, and an ID. The codebase value is essential since leaving it out may make the page nonfunctional. The user needs a codebase to download the required applet files from your Web site. Notice that we also have to include the two parameters for this applet: foreground and background. The colors chosen allow the applet to partially blend in with the theme background. Figure 14-1 shows what our new default Web page looks like in action.

Figure 14-1. The PageHelp applet allows the user to get help for a problem in one of three ways

Adding the Help Desk Control to a Visual Basic Application

We finally have a working help desk solution, so all we need to do is apply it to an application. The Visual Basic application we'll create in this section is purposely short because the help desk was the focal point of this chapter. You'd never develop a help desk application for something as simple as the Visual Basic application shown here. However, this application does provide enough functionality for you to see the help desk at work.

 Error trapping is always difficult to perform and even more difficult to record and log properly. You can download a really helpful ActiveX control named ErrorHandler at: http://www.download.com/PC/Result/TitleDetail/0,4,0-38656-g,1000.html?dd.ax.pc. 0825.004. This ActiveX control makes it very easy for you to trap errors in Visual Basic, then report them to the user in some meaningful way. In addition, the control will place a log entry in the Windows NT event log for you. You can also use this ActiveX control to log other types of events such as task failure, task success, or warnings in the Windows NT event log by raising an exception, then allowing the control to handle it.

Creating the Program Shell

The first thing we'll need to do is create a program shell for our application. The following procedure will get you started:

1. Start Visual Basic if you haven't done so already. You should see the New Project dialog box.

2. Select the New tab, then highlight the Standard EXE icon. Click Open. Visual Basic will create a program shell for you. What you'll see is a simple dialog-box-type application like the one we created in Chapter 4.

Adding Help Desk Support

This project will contain a single control, the HelpCtrl ActiveX control that we created earlier in the chapter. The following procedure will show you how to add the HelpCtrl to your project:

1. Right-click the toolbox and choose Components… from the context menu. You'll see the Components dialog box.

2. Select the Controls tab and check the HelpCtrl ActiveX Control module entry shown here:

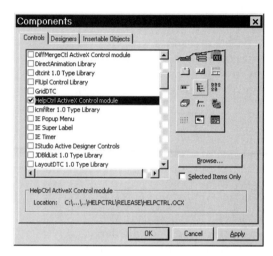

3. Click OK. Visual Basic will add the HelpCtrl to your toolbox as shown here (note that our custom icon is being used).

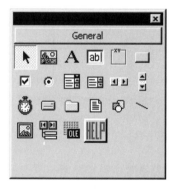

4. Double-click the HelpCtrl to add it to the dialog box. Table 14-5 contains a list of the property values you need to change.

Property	Value
Caption	Help Desk
CursorType	1

Table 14-5. HelpCtrl Property Values

Property	Value
HelpURL	http://<Server Name>/HelpDesk/Default.HTM
IconPosition	2
IconType	1
Width	2000

Table 14-5. HelpCtrl Property Values (continued)

Seeing the Help Desk Support in Action

Make sure you save your project, then start it. What you'll see is a simple dialog-based Visual Basic application with the HelpCtrl displayed in the middle as shown here:

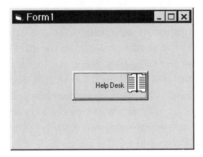

Move the cursor over the top of the HelpCtrl and you'll see it change to the custom cursor that we created. Click the Help Desk button and you'll see a copy of Internet Explorer start. Assuming the URL you provided for the HelpURL property is correct, you'll see the Help Desk Web site appear with the PageHelp applet that we created activated, as shown in Figure 14-1.

Try clicking one of the buttons and you'll see an appropriate help dialog box appear. As previously mentioned, you could easily extend the Java applet to do much more than display a help dialog box. You could also have it display an email form for mailing a message to the administrator or start a copy of NetMeeting so that the administrator could help you directly. The applet could even dial the phone for you and tell you when there is a connection to the administration center.

Lessons Learned

TCO is becoming a bigger issue as more companies realize the PC is eating up valuable resources at an astronomical rate. Creating a help desk is one way to get the knowledge support personnel have accumulated to the user at a much lower cost. While you could use a number of methods for encapsulating this information and making it easy to use, a Web site is one of the most flexible ways to make the information available.

Help desk Web page access can also take a number of forms. However, the button that we've looked at here is one of the easier ways to make the information available from within an application. In addition, the button method allows you to program around a number of potential problems, like changes in the Web site location, and to accommodate users on the road.

The HelpCtrl ActiveX control in this chapter used some new techniques that we haven't used in previous chapters. For one thing, we looked at how you can dress up your controls through the use of various graphics including icons and cursors. Storing the graphics you want to use as part of the control is probably the easiest way to go and ensures that the graphic will be available when needed. Unfortunately, using this technique also means that you'll be limited to the graphics available at the time of control creation. If flexibility is a prime consideration, you'll also want to add the capability to load a graphic resource from disk to your ActiveX control.

There are also different methods for handling ActiveX properties. The MFC-based example in Chapter 4 showed the member variable method of handling properties. The main advantage of using member variables is ease of implementation. Look at the member variable code in Chapter 4 and you'll see that it doesn't take much in the way of support. The Get/Set method used in this chapter has advantages as well. For one thing, you have better control over how the property gets presented to the client. You also have better control over the encapsulation of your control and the ability to better monitor the property values provided by the user.

This chapter also looked at property page handling techniques. Sometimes an ActiveX control requires more than one property page, and this example probably reflects the best way to handle properties for production controls. All essential properties should appear on a property page so that you can be sure the control user has complete access to the properties needed to use the control completely. In addition, it's important to remember that there are both stock and custom property pages. A good rule of thumb for determining which type of property page to use is to look at the property value—colors and fonts are always easier to handle using the stock property pages provided by Visual C++.

Even though this book hasn't mentioned different types of character strings before, it's an important topic in a world that's increasingly using Unicode strings for multiple language support. The code section of the HelpCtrl example shows how you can convert a standard C string to its Unicode equivalent. Knowing how to make this conversion is important when working with products like Internet Explorer that rely on Unicode rather than standard C strings.

Once you get past the goal of creating some method for accessing the help desk, you have to design the help desk itself. Visual InterDev provides the site diagram mechanism for organizing information. It turns out that using a site diagram greatly simplifies the process of creating the help desk hierarchical question structure. All you need to do is decide which questions the user asks most often, and then provide answers for those questions in an easily accessible hierarchical format. The site diagram makes setting this structure up easy.

Creating a site diagram with multiple entry points for some pages wouldn't be possible without the ASP. Using a simple ASP script allows the user to get from one task directory to another without even seeing the change. To the user, the movement from one page to another is seamless—only the programmer knows that the user has moved to a different directory on the server. That's the way things should be. The user really doesn't need to know where the information is stored; it's enough that they can access it when needed.

There are a lot of ways to work with Java applets. One of the better ways to work with them when dealing with small projects is to simply add the applet to your Visual InterDev project. That way, all of the code required for the applet is stored with the Web page files. A larger project will likely require the establishment of an Applets folder on your Web server to ensure they are equally accessible to everyone who needs to use it. In this case, make sure you use Visual SourceSafe to manage the code and only deploy the class files required to actually implement the applet on your Web page.

Part V

Server Applications

Chapter 15

Creating a Basic Java Application

Most Java implementations won't allow you to create stand-alone executables that you can execute from within Windows. Since Visual J++ provides support for the Windows Foundation Classes (WFC), it only makes sense that you should be able to create some level of stand-alone application with it in addition to applets and ActiveX controls. We've already looked at several applet implementations in the book and one ActiveX control. This chapter will help you understand how to use Visual J++ to create a stand-alone application as well.

The first part of this chapter will define the application types that you can create using the special features provided by WFC and Visual J++. The goal is to see where the various application types appear within the grand scheme of Java functionality. Being able to move some of your WFC code from the realm of the ActiveX control to a stand-alone application has certain advantages. Obviously, there are certain situations where you would definitely want to use a Windows version of the Java application rather than the console version, and vice versa. We'll answer that question in this section as well.

We'll get to work on the kind of IIS application we'll look at in this chapter next—the Java Windows application. Visual J++ provides this unique capability by providing access to WFC. Of course, this feature also means that you can't depend on using Java applications on anything but an IIS server and that there may be situations when you'll run into problems interacting with a particular browser. In other words, don't count on the application we produce in this chapter to provide anything in the way of portability—we're working with the WFC extension to the Java language.

Now that we have an application to work with, it's time to create some way to access it. The next section of the chapter will look at ways of building Web pages that access your Visual J++ applications. The general principles you learn here will work with both console and Windows applications, but will concentrate on the Windows version of the WFC application.

Scenario

It's becoming apparent that there are times where your company needs to send field representatives new versions of utility programs while on the road. Unfortunately, your current utilities rely on a lot of runtime files and make downloads lengthy, if they succeed at all. One of the best solutions that you've found to date for your problem has been to create the utility applications using Visual J++. Utilities created using the product may not provide every bell and whistle available, but they're very small and don't require any runtime files.

In addition to the need for new utilities, you'll need some way to distribute them. A second team will create a user-friendly Web page that the field representatives can use to determine if they need the new utility at all. The new Web page will also make it possible for the field representative to download the utility and keep it on their machine, or download it for a single-use application.

There are three phases to this project, two of which can occur simultaneously. The first phase is to create the Visual J++ application. The second phase is to create the Web page. These two phases can be carried on separately using either an old version of the utility or a dummy application for testing. The third phase is to test the application in action. Your two teams will need to work together to ensure the application will work as desired using the slowest connection that the representatives are likely to encounter.

What Is a Java Application?

The first question that you may have had in opening this chapter is "What is a Java application?" The short answer is that outside Visual J++ there isn't any such entity; standard Java doesn't support any type of stand-alone application development. The Windows Foundation Classes (WFC) support provided by Visual J++ allows you to create stand-alone applications as well as ActiveX controls and applets.

We've already spent some time in the book looking at how to create both applets and ActiveX controls with Visual J++, so now it's time to see how you can use it to create applications as well. There are actually two types of applications that you can create with Visual J++: console and Windows. The console application looks much like the console applications you create using products like Visual C++. All you really get is what appears to be a DOS command window. The application shell looks a lot like the one provided for a standard C application. The Windows application is limited to the use of forms. In other words, if you had planned on creating a word processor that uses Java as its basis, you might have a hard time doing it (not that anything is impossible for the determined programmer, but some things are best left to other languages).

The next two sections are going to introduce you to the Visual J++ application. The first thing we'll do is look at what writing applications using WFC is all about. Next, we'll take a little closer look at the two types of WFC applications that you can create using Visual J++ and when you would use one over the other.

It's especially important to realize that any application you write using Visual J++ will rely on WFC, not the standard Java classes. This means that you won't be able to run these applications on non-Windows machines. In addition, the client has to have the WFC classes available on their machine and use the Microsoft version of the Java Virtual Machine. In other words, be prepared to encounter a few compatibility problems to gain the features provided by a Visual J++ application.

An Overview of WFC Applications

There isn't any way that we'll be able to look at every aspect of WFC in one section of a chapter; that would take a book or two. However, what this section will do for you is give you some simple guidelines for making the transition to WFC a little easier as well as a tad more understandable.

Let's begin with the basics. Every WFC-based ActiveX control or application you create will rely on either two or four WFC-specific classes to begin with. The following list tells you about these classes and what they do for you.

- **com.ms.wfc.app.* (application only)**   This class contains all of the application-specific features you'll use within the Windows environment. The main subclasses that you'll use are contained in the Application and Window subclasses. These two classes tell you about the application environment. Also included in this class are subclasses that allow you to manage threads, work with the registry, manipulate the clipboard, and work with the Windows operating system as a whole. One of the handier subclasses for display purposes is SystemInformation, which can help you determine things like the computer name.

- **com.ms.wfc.core.* (ActiveX control and application)**   You won't work much with this class directly. It contains the subclasses required to create other classes that you will use. For example, the Component subclass is used to create all of the WFC components that we'll use to create the application in this section. This particular class also includes a wealth of interfaces that are used to help your Visual J++ application work within the COM environment. It's helpful at times to look at the base class and interface descriptions contained in this class to see how derived classes obtain some of their functionality and provide a consistent interface.

- **com.ms.wfc.ui.* (ActiveX control and application)**   There are few classes that you'll use more than this one. It contains all of the subclasses required to create the interface elements of an application. Not only does this include things like buttons, but brushes and other graphics construction classes as well. Unfortunately, this particular class is also a moving target. Many of the descriptions were still under construction at the time of this writing.

- **com.ms.wfc.io.* (application only)**   Every kind of external access, whether files or a printer, relies on this class. You'll find subclasses that work with streams of various sorts and even helper subclasses that allow you to create complex variables like strings with less code.

Using just these four classes, you could build most simple applications or ActiveX controls. However, there's a limit to the functionality they provide, so it's helpful to look at the other WFC classes that Microsoft provides. For example, the com.ms.wfc.html class allows you to add DHTML capability to both ActiveX controls and applications. Another important WFC-specific class is com.ms.wfc.data.ui, which allows you to work with data bound controls. (The base class for this class is com.ms.wfc.data, which contains few subclasses that you could use directly.) A data bound control will allow you to access and display the contents of a database with a lot less coding than traditional coding methods allow.

You'd miss out on a lot of great functionality if you stuck with just the WFC classes listed in the WFC and Java reference. There are other Visual J++ classes listed in the Platform SDK that allow you to do things that normally require fully developed programming languages like Visual C++. Most of these extra packages are in the com.ms class. For example, com.ms.security allows you to perform a variety of security checks with your Visual J++ application or ActiveX control. The com.ms.dll.callback class will allow you to add a callback to your Visual J++ application, something that's normally not possible.

The bottom line is that WFC applications have at their disposal the wealth of functionality that any Windows application can provide. The problem, of course, is how much compatibility you're willing to give up to get these features. As you incorporate more Windows functionality into your application, the possibility of using it on non-Windows platforms diminishes, making it less likely that you'll get the one feature that many purists feel that Java is best able to offer—something that will work everywhere.

When Should You Use a WFC Application?

There are some overriding questions you need to answer before you even consider using Visual J++ as an application programming language. The most important of those questions is compatibility. Java was never designed to create stand-alone applications, though you could certainly use it to do so in applet form. Microsoft has greatly extended the idea of using an applet to create an application, but at the cost of compatibility. Ultimately, this means that you're at Microsoft's mercy when it comes to support for your application. Whether Microsoft will choose to continue adding their own vision to Java or not remains to be seen. However, it's important to consider whether the Visual J++ application that you create today will be viable tomorrow given the unstable nature of the language additions Microsoft has made.

Another consideration is extensibility. Even with WFC support, a Visual J++ application isn't designed to provide large-scale application support. The forms that Java supports when creating a Windows application look more like the forms used for a dialog-based Visual Basic application than anything else. Even the process for creating the application is similar. This limitation would tend to make Visual J++ applications suitable for small development needs or, perhaps, utilities. The console format is even more limited since you have to program everything from scratch. Normally, you'll relegate these applications to background automation tasks requiring little or no user interaction. In other words, if you need a robust application with lots of features, consider some other language.

One of the other problems that you may run into is with WFC itself. Anyone who has had to deal with the vagaries of different MFC versions will understand the potential problems. Since there's no standards committed to manage WFC, you may end up with the same problems as you have now with MFC. A user may be in the position of not being able to use your application because they have a different version of the Java Virtual Machine (JVM) installed on their machine. WFC is in its infancy right now, which means that changes will definitely occur. Just how Microsoft handles these changes will definitely affect the viability of your application in the future.

Visual J++ does bring a lot of features to the desktop. The most important of these features is the size of the application you get. You can create extremely small applications that perform just as well as their much larger Visual Basic counterparts. In addition, a Visual J++ application doesn't depend on runtime files like Visual C++ and Visual Basic do—all you need to have installed is the Microsoft version of the JVM.

Code reuse is another feature that you need to take into account. If most of your development efforts currently center around the Internet and you already have a large code base of Java code for the applets you've created, it only makes sense to reuse that code for small application development. Just like any Java development effort, you can import your own custom classes, making it possible to reuse objects for a variety of tasks. The bottom line is that any time you can reuse code (either directly or in objects), you reduce both development and debugging time for the project.

In short, you should consider using Visual J++ as an application platform when you need to create relatively small applications that you can distribute through a medium like the Internet or a company intranet. Visual J++ is most useful for companies that can control the environment used by their employees for computing. In addition, like many Microsoft technologies, the Visual J++ application is best used with other Microsoft products like Internet Explorer. You most definitely won't be able to use a Visual J++ application on a non-Microsoft platform like UNIX—at least not at the moment.

The console version of the Visual J++ application is best used for background processing—like an advanced batch file. Unfortunately, the console version doesn't provide much in the way of a user interface, which means that you'd end up spending a lot of time creating one if user interaction is required. The console version does have the advantage of providing a very clean coding environment, and providing a very minimalistic application as a result.

The Windows version of the application is best used for utility programs or applications that can benefit from a forms interface (dialog boxes) since that's all Visual J++ provides. It's extremely important not to use this kind of development product for large-scale applications, though small database projects can work out because Microsoft provides the required hooks. Of course, you won't want to use Visual J++ to develop an application that does much in the way of data manipulation since it's very early in the language development process and Microsoft has a lot of bugs to work out. A database viewer or perhaps a client address application are about the limits of the database products you should tackle with this product right now.

Creating an IIS Application Using Visual J++

Visual J++ provides a lot of features that allow you to create small utility-type programs in a flash, especially if you use the Application Wizard. This section is going to show you how to create an application that makes maximum use of the built-in wizard features—a simple text editor. While this text editor won't help you write another version of *War and Peace*, it will allow you to take simple notes. You'll also find that the application is small enough to download from a Web site, making local storage on a notebook computer unnecessary unless a connection to the Internet won't be available.

Creating the Program Shell

There are three ways to create a program shell using Visual J++, and the method that you use depends on the kind of application you want to create. The first two methods are to create a very simple and basic program shell. The Windows Application and Console Application icons in the New Project dialog box that we'll see later in this section provide the most basic shell you can create. The third method, Application Wizard, is the one we'll use here. The advantage of using this method is that you can configure many program elements before you write the first line of code. The disadvantage is that you have to deal with any assumptions that Microsoft may have made about the application you want to create. The following procedure will help you get started creating an application shell using the Application Wizard:

1. Start Visual J++ if you haven't done so already. You'll see the New Project dialog box.

2. Select the New tab, then the Visual J++ Projects | Applications folder. You'll see three project icons, as shown here:

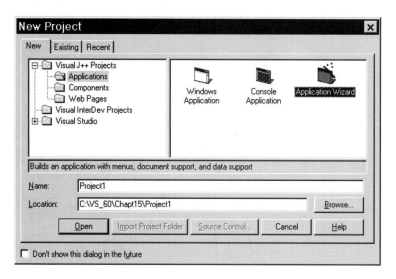

3. Highlight the Application Wizard icon.

4. Type **VJUtil** (or some other project name) in the Name field.

5. Click Open. You'll see the Welcome to the Visual J++ Application Wizard dialog box shown here. Notice that you can choose an existing application profile if you've created this type of project in the past. Since this is a new project, we'll leave the profile set at (None).

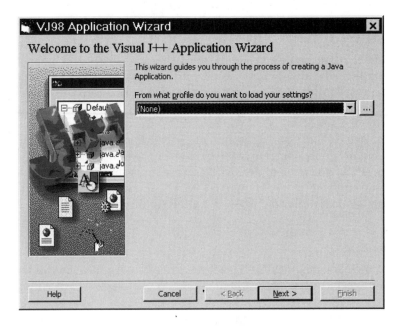

6. Click Next. You'll see the "Choose type of Application" dialog box shown here. Notice that Visual J++ allows you to create form-based applications that rely on databases, as well as the standard utility form-based application. If you choose the "Form Based Application with Data" option, then you'll see the Data Form Wizard next. Once you create the data form based on the contents of a database, you'll proceed with the rest of the VJ98 Application Wizard steps. Visual J++ is not designed to create complex database applications—it's better used as a means for retrieving information from relatively simple database files.

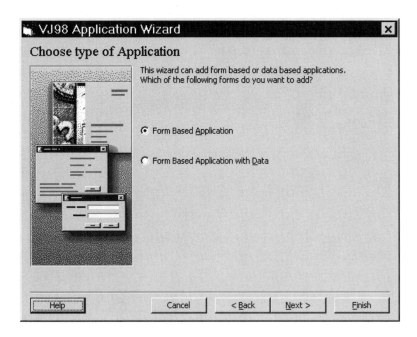

You can always add a form to your Visual J++ application later. Just right-click the project or other folder that will be used to hold the form, then choose Add | Add Form from the context menu. Highlight the Data Form Wizard icon in the Add Item dialog box, type a name for your form in the Name field, and click Open. Follow the wizard dialogs to add a form to your Visual J++ application.

7. Choose Form Based Application, then click Next. You'll see the "Add features to your application" dialog box shown here. Notice that this dialog box contains a list of standard forms you can add to the application. By default, all of the features are checked, so you'll need to uncheck the features you don't need. The Menu, Toolbar, and Status Bar features are normally found on most applications that support data manipulation in some way. The Edit feature will turn your application shell into a simple notepad-type text editor. Since we're going to create a simple text editor, we'll leave all of the features checked.

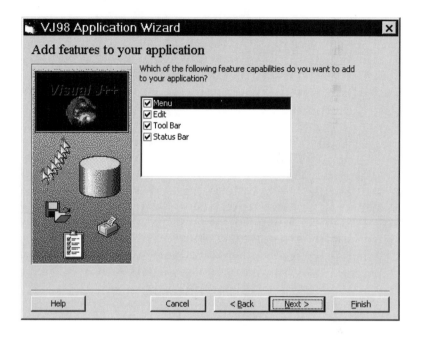

8. Click Next. You'll see the "Choose the kind of comments you want" dialog box shown here. Normally, you'll want to select all three levels of comments while working on the first few Visual J++ applications. The reason is simple: The comments help you get around programming hurdles much faster. However, once you become proficient at using the Application Wizard and creating a default application, you'll find that the "Sample Functionality comments" become less meaningful since you'll have a good idea of what purpose the default code serves. The TODO comments remind you of things you need to do to the default code, and the JavaDoc comments help you document your code faster by automatically adding comments to all classes and their members.

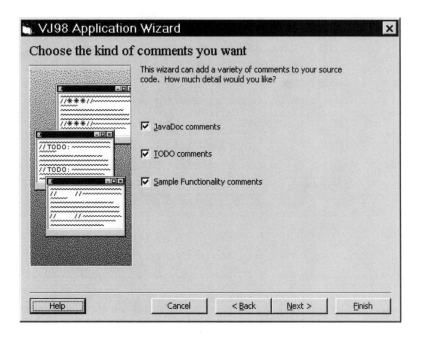

9. Click Next. You'll see the "Choose the program packaging options" dialog box shown here. Notice that you can create a Class, EXE, or CAB file. In addition, you can automatically deploy the application to another location. The Class file format is what Java normally uses for application distribution. You'd use this format if you wanted to create an application for display on a Web page alone. The EXE file format allows you to start the application from the command line, making it the perfect solution for stand-alone applications. Even if you choose this format, you can still create a link to the EXE file and use it from within a Web page. The CAB file format provides a way to hasten the download process for larger applications. The files within the CAB file are in the Class format.

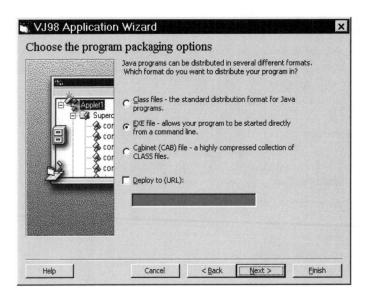

10. Choose the EXE file format, then click Next. You'll see the Application Wizard Summary dialog box shown here. Notice that you can save the current project profile to disk, which will make duplicating a set of project criteria easier.

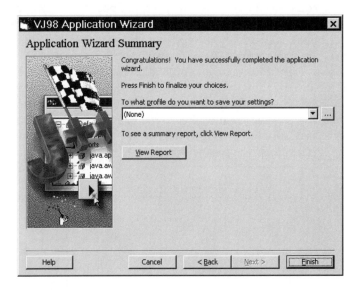

11. Click View Report. You'll see the Summary Report dialog box shown here. This is your last opportunity to check the application settings before creating the project shell. It's always a good idea to check the settings to make certain your project contains all of the features you'll need.

12. Click Close to close the Summary Report dialog box.

13. Click Finish. Visual J++ will create a program shell for you. You'll see a project setup similar to the one shown in Figure 15-1.

This project could be compiled immediately and used as a simple text editor. Just use the Build | Build command to create the EXE file. (The Build | Configuration menu contains the two build options for Visual J++: Debug and Release.) In fact, you may want to try it out, just to see what Visual J++ is capable of creating on its own. You'll find that the EXE file is extremely small at only 20.5K for the release version of the program. What you'll see is a very small text editor like the one shown here:

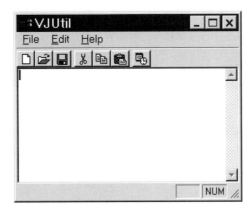

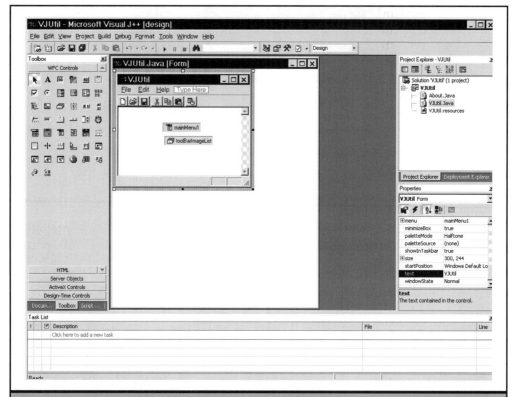

Figure 15-1. Visual J++ can create a fully functional text editor with little effort on the part of the developer

Enhancing the Resources

The sample application will work fine as a basic text editor, but it lacks some important features that just about anyone using it will need. For one thing, there aren't any print features provided with the program. Even the simplest editing need is likely to involve printing an occasional document, so adding the ability to print to our application is essential. Even if you don't provide the ability to preview the document or select something other than the default printer, the application will need to send documents to the default printer.

Another potential problem is the Date/Time button. Normally, you wouldn't concern yourself with this feature because very few users will actually need it. However, since the button is provided by default, you need to make it fully functional. The current button places the date and time in the Edit window, but doesn't allow you to modify their format. It would be nice if the application allowed you to choose from several date/time formats that included just the date alone or the time alone.

The third problem is the font used to display the information on-screen. The application chooses the default font, which may or may not be large enough for the viewer to see. While this isn't an essential feature, it would still be nice to allow the viewer to choose a font that is easily read even while using a notebook computer in full daylight.

All of these problems are easily solved with a combination of resources and code. This section of the chapter will show you how to modify the current application resources so that the user will be able to interact with the application better. The next section will detail the code required to make these resources usable.

Modifying the Menu

The first resource we'll have to modify to correct the three problems with this program is the menu. Anyone who has worked with Visual Basic will have a pretty good idea of how to perform this particular modification. The main menu and all submenus contain a Type Here entry. Simply type some text in the menu to create the new menu entry. You can change the menu entry properties by highlighting the menu entry and changing the settings in the Properties window. Table 15-1 shows the new menu entries you'll need to add, any associated menu settings, and where to add them. An Add To Menu column entry of <Main> means to place the menu entry on the main menu rather than an existing submenu. Make sure the Help menu appears last on the main menu. You can move a menu entry around by highlighting it, then dragging the menu entry to its new location.

Visual J++ doesn't use the same menu naming convention as used by other Microsoft products. This means that you'd need to change the name property for existing as well as new menu entries. One of the better menu naming conventions is to name the menu entry in a hierarchical manner. For example, the File | Open menu entry would use a name property value of FileOpen. Using this convention allows you to have more than one submenu entry with the same name. Unfortunately, because of the way the wizard generates the default code, you'd also need to rework the code to make this naming convention change. Only the new entries in Table 15-1 use the conventional naming scheme to reduce the amount of code rework required by the reader.

You can add a separator to a menu by typing a - (dash) at the Type Here entry instead of typing the normal text. Type an & (ampersand) in front of any menu characters you want to underline for speedier access by the user.

Working with Components

One of our new menu entries will allow the user to select a display font. This font selection won't just affect a little of the text—all of the text will be affected for the Edit control. In addition, we need to make a change to the font used for printing purposes, so that what the user sees on-screen will also appear at the printer.

Menu Name	Add To Menu	Property	Value
FilePrint	File	name	&Print
		shortcut	Ctrl-P
FormatDate	\<Menu\>	name	Format &Date
FormatDateDefault	Format Date	name	&Default
		checked	true
		default	true
FormatDateMMDDYY	Format Date	name	&MM/DD/YY
FormatDateMonthDDYYYY	Format Date	name	Month &DD, YYYY
FormatDate24HourTime	Format Date	name	&24 Hour Time
FormatDateAMPMTime	Format Date	name	&AM/PM Time
Font	\<Menu\>	name	F&ont

Table 15-1. VJUtil New Menu Entry Settings

Tip *If you want to allow the user to change just part of the text to a different font and allow those changes to appear within the saved file, you must use the RichEdit control found on the WFC tab of the toolbox. The Edit control that the wizard provides as a default allows you to work with plain text; none of the changes you make to the font will appear in the saved file. In other words, the Font menu in our example is only used to change the display temporarily.*

The first thing you need to do is add a FontDialog control to the application. You'll find this component on the WFC tab of the toolbox. You can place the FontDialog control anywhere on the Edit control. We'll also need to change one of the properties for this component. Set the fontDevice property to Both, so both the printer and the screen will reflect a change in font setting.

Since we're adding print capability to this application, it would be nice to access the printer from the toolbar. There's a two-step process to adding an icon to the toolbar. The first thing we need to do is add the appropriate icon to the toolBarImageList control. One of the easier ways to do this is to get the picture you want to use and store it as a bitmap in the project directory. Using a 16 × 16 pixel icon-sized bitmap assures that the user will see what you intended them to see. Select the toolBarImageList control, then double-click the images property in the Properties window. You'll see an Image[] Editor dialog box. Click Add and you'll see an Open dialog box. Select your image file and click Open. Visual J++ will add the image to the image list. Your Image[] Editor dialog box should have seven images in it like the one shown here:

Now that we have an image to use, we can add it to the toolbar. Select the toolBar control, then double-click the buttons property in the Property window. You'll see a ToolBarButton[] Editor dialog box. Click Add and you'll see a new toolbar button added to the list as shown here:

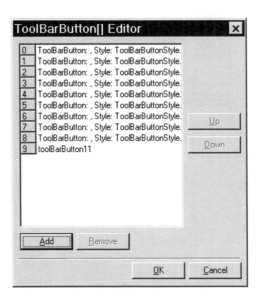

You'll need to configure this button using the standard Properties window, so close the ToolBarButton[] Editor dialog box by clicking OK. Notice that the button's property

Property	Value
imageIndex	7
name	printToolBarButton
text	
toolTipText	Print

Table 15-2. printToolBarButton Properties

has a plus sign next to it. This opens and closes the hierarchical structure for the various buttons' properties and works just the same as it would in Windows Explorer. Table 15-2 contains a list of the properties you'll need to change. Here's what the expanded form of the buttons property for our new button looks like with the properties changed:

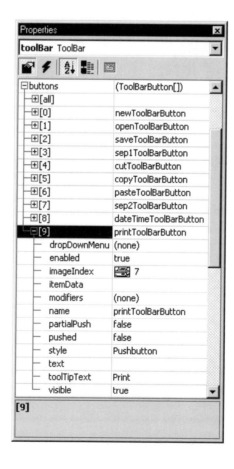

Adding Some Code

At this point, the example application is fully configured—all of the resources are ready to go. It's time to add some code to the application. Simply double-click on the Font menu entry and you'll see the Code window. Listing 15-1 contains the source code for the first half of the application—the part you need to change. Visual J++ can add all new functions for you if you want to go back to the Form window each time and double-click on the associated menu entry. I'll describe all of the code additions once you've had a chance to look at the code.

Listing 15-1

```java
//VJUtil.java
import com.ms.wfc.app.*;
import com.ms.wfc.core.*;
import com.ms.wfc.ui.*;
import com.ms.wfc.io.*;

// Add printer support
import com.ms.awt.*;
import java.awt.Toolkit;
import java.awt.Graphics;

/**
 * @author: Application Wizard
 * @version: 1.0
 * This class can take a variable number of parameters on the command
 * line. Program execution begins with the main() method. The class
 * constructor is not invoked unless an object of type 'VJUtil'
 * created in the main() method.
 */

public class VJUtil extends Form
{
  private String m_sFileName = new String("");
  private boolean m_bIsDirty = false;

  private void editText_textChanged(Object sender, Event e)
  {
    m_bIsDirty = true;
  }

  public void doNew(Object sender, Event e)
  {
    // New
```

```
    if (canCloseCurrent(sender,  e))
    {
      editText.setText("");
      m_sFileName = "";
      m_bIsDirty = false;
    }
}

private void saveAsMenu_click(Object sender, Event e)
{
  // Save As
  doSaveAs(sender, e);
}

private void saveMenu_click(Object sender, Event e)
{
  // Save
  doSave(sender, e);
}

private void doOpen(Object sender, Event e)
{
  // Open
  if (! canCloseCurrent(sender,  e))
    return;

  OpenFileDialog fOpenDlg = new OpenFileDialog ();
      fOpenDlg.setFilter("Text files (*.txt)|*.txt|All files (*.*)|*.*");
  fOpenDlg.setCheckFileExists(true);
  fOpenDlg.setCheckPathExists(true);
  fOpenDlg.setReadOnlyChecked(true);
  fOpenDlg.setFileName ("*.txt");
  if (fOpenDlg.showDialog() == DialogResult.OK )
  {
    try
    {
      File fInputFile = File.open(fOpenDlg.getFileName());
      long nLength = fInputFile.getLength();
      editText.setText (fInputFile.readStringCharsAnsi((int)nLength));
```

```java
        fInputFile.close ();
        m_sFileName = fOpenDlg.getFileName ();
           }
      catch (Exception excpt)
      {
      MessageBox.show (excpt.getMessage(), "VJUtil", MessageBox.ICONERROR |
                   MessageBox.OK);
           }
   }
}

public void wordWrapMenu_click(Object sender, Event e)
{
  // WordWrap
  boolean bWordWrap;
  bWordWrap = ! editText.getWordWrap ();
  editText.setWordWrap (bWordWrap);
  wordWrapMenu.setChecked(bWordWrap);
  if (bWordWrap)
    editText.setScrollBars(ScrollBars.VERTICAL);
  else
    editText.setScrollBars(ScrollBars.BOTH);
}

public void doDateTime(Object sender, Event e)
{
  Time   currentTime = new Time();  // Date/Time variable.
  String  sValue = new String();     // String value of Month.

  // Determine which format to use, then display the time.
  if (FormatDateDefault.getChecked())
  {
    editText.setSelectedText  (currentTime.toString());
  }
  else if (FormatDateMMDDYY.getChecked())
  {
      editText.setSelectedText(Integer.toString(currentTime.getMonth()) + "/" +
         Integer.toString(currentTime.getDay()) + "/" +
         Integer.toString(currentTime.getYear()).substring(2, 4));
```

```
    }
    else if (FormatDateMonthDDYYYY.getChecked())
    {
      // Convert the month value to text.
      switch (currentTime.getMonth())
      {
      case 1:
        sValue = "January ";
        break;
      case 2:
        sValue = "February ";
        break;
      case 3:
        sValue = "March ";
        break;
      case 4:
        sValue = "April ";
        break;
      case 5:
        sValue = "May ";
        break;
      case 6:
        sValue = "June ";
        break;
      case 7:
        sValue = "July ";
        break;
      case 8:
        sValue = "August ";
        break;
      case 9:
        sValue = "September ";
        break;
      case 10:
        sValue = "October ";
        break;
      case 11:
        sValue = "November ";
        break;
```

```java
        case 12:
          sValue = "December ";
          break;
        }

        // Display the date.
        editText.setSelectedText(sValue + Integer.toString(currentTime.getDay())
                  + ", " + Integer.toString(currentTime.getYear()));
      }
      else if (FormatDate24HourTime.getChecked())
      {
      editText.setSelectedText(Integer.toString(currentTime.getHour()) + ":" +
                Integer.toString(currentTime.getMinute()) + ":" +
                Integer.toString(currentTime.getSecond()));
      }
      else if (FormatDateAMPMTime.getChecked())
      {
        if (currentTime.getHour() > 12)
          editText.setSelectedText(Integer.toString(currentTime.getHour() - 12) +
":" +
                Integer.toString(currentTime.getMinute()) + ":" +
                Integer.toString(currentTime.getSecond()) + " p.m.");
        else
          editText.setSelectedText(Integer.toString(currentTime.getHour()) + ":" +
                    Integer.toString(currentTime.getMinute()) + ":" +
                    Integer.toString(currentTime.getSecond()) + " a.m.");
      }
    }

  public void doPaste(Object sender, Event e)
  {
    // Paste
    try
    {
      DataObject myDObj = new DataObject (Clipboard.getDataObject ());
      editText.setSelectedText ((String) myDObj.getData (String.class));
    }
```

```
    catch (Exception ecx)
    {
    }
}

public void doCopy(Object sender, Event e)
{
  // Copy
  Clipboard.setDataObject (editText.getSelectedText ());
}

public void doCut(Object sender, Event e)
{
  // Cut
  Clipboard.setDataObject (editText.getSelectedText ());
  editText.setSelectedText ("");
}

public void exitMenu_click(Object sender, Event e)
{
  // Exit
  if (canCloseCurrent(sender,  e))
    Application.exit();
}

private void aboutMenu_click(Object sender, Event e)
{
  About myAbout = new About();
  myAbout.showDialog ();
}

private void toolBar_buttonClick(Object source,
                            ToolBarButtonClickEvent e)
{
  if (e.button == newToolBarButton) {
    // New
    doNew(source,e);
  }
```

```java
    else if (e.button == openToolBarButton) {
      // Open
      doOpen(source,e);
    }
    else if (e.button == saveToolBarButton) {
      // Save
      doSave(source,e);
    }
    else if (e.button == cutToolBarButton) {
      // Cut
      doCut(source,e);
    }
    else if (e.button == copyToolBarButton) {
      // Copy
      doCopy(source,e);
    }
    else if (e.button == pasteToolBarButton) {
      // Paste
      doPaste(source,e);
    }
    else if (e.button == dateTimeToolBarButton) {
      // Date/Time
      doDateTime(source,e);
    }
    else  {
      // print the document.
      FilePrint_click(source, e);
    }
}

  public VJUtil()
  {
      super();

    //Required for Visual J++ Form Designer support
    initForm();

    //TODO: Add any constructor code after initForm call
```

```java
    wordWrapMenu.setChecked(editText.getWordWrap ());
    Application.addOnIdle(new EventHandler(this.VJUtil_Idle));
}


/**
 * VJUtil overrides dispose so it can clean up the
 * component list.
 */
public void dispose()
{
    super.dispose();
    components.dispose();
}

private void VJUtil_Idle(Object sender, Event e)
{
    // Set the statusBarStates
    StatusBarPanel sbPanel[] = statusBar.getPanels ();
    if ((GetKeyState(VK_CAPITAL) & 1) == 1)
        sbPanel[1].setText ("CAP");
    else
        sbPanel[1].setText ("");
    if ((GetKeyState(VK_NUMLOCK) & 1) == 1)
        sbPanel[2].setText ("NUM");
    else
        sbPanel[2].setText ("");
}

private void VJUtil_closing(Object source, CancelEvent e)
{
    // Check to see if there are changes to save
    if (canCloseCurrent(source,  e))
        Application.exit();
    else
        e.cancel = true;
}

private boolean canCloseCurrent(Object sender, Event e)
{
    boolean bRc = false;
    if (! m_bIsDirty)
```

```
      return true;

   int iRc;
   String sText = new String ();
   sText = "The text in the ";
   if (m_sFileName.length() == 0)
     sText = sText + "Untitled ";
   else
     sText = sText + m_sFileName;
   sText = sText + "file has changed. \n\n Do you want to save the changes?";
   iRc = MessageBox.show (sText, "VJUtil", MessageBox.DEFBUTTON1
|MessageBox.ICONEXCLAMATION | MessageBox.YESNOCANCEL);
   switch (iRc){
   case DialogResult.YES:
     bRc = doSave(sender, e);
     break;
   case DialogResult.NO:
     bRc = true;
     break;
   case DialogResult.CANCEL:
     bRc = false;
     break;
   }
   return bRc;
  }


  private boolean doSaveAs(Object sender, Event e)
  {
    boolean bRc = false;
    SaveFileDialog fSaveDlg = new SaveFileDialog ();
    fSaveDlg.setFileName (m_sFileName);
    fSaveDlg.setFilter("Text files (*.txt)|*.txt|All files (*.*)|*.*");
    fSaveDlg.setCheckPathExists(true);
    fSaveDlg.setOverwritePrompt(true);
    if (fSaveDlg.showDialog() == DialogResult.OK )
    {
      File fOutFile = File.create(fSaveDlg.getFileName());
      fOutFile.writeStringCharsAnsi (editText.getText ());
      fOutFile.close ();
      m_sFileName = fSaveDlg.getFileName();
      m_bIsDirty = false;
      bRc = true;
```

```
  }
  return bRc;
}

private boolean doSave(Object sender, Event e)
{
  boolean bRc = false;

  if (m_sFileName.length() == 0)
    bRc = doSaveAs(sender,  e);
  else
  {
    File fOutFile = File.create(m_sFileName);
    fOutFile.writeStringCharsAnsi (editText.getText ());
    fOutFile.close ();
    m_bIsDirty = false;
    bRc = true;
  }
  return bRc;
}


private void Font_click(Object source, Event e)
{
  // Display the font dialog so the user can make a
  // selection.
  fontDialog1.showDialog();

  // Set the Edit component font property to the value
  // selected by the user.
  editText.setFont(fontDialog1.getFont());
}

private void FilePrint_click(Object source, Event e)
{
  // Create a print job.
  Toolkit    tools = Toolkit.getDefaultToolkit();
  WPrintJob  wpj = (WPrintJob)tools.getPrintJob(null, "Print", null);

  Graphics  oDraw = wpj.getGraphics();    // Drawing area for text.
  int       iStyle = java.awt.Font.PLAIN;  // Font style.
  int       iCounter = 0;                 // Printing loop counter.
```

```java
String    sText[] = editText.getLines();  // Array of print strings.

// Get the current edit control print style.
if(editText.getFont().getBold())
  iStyle = iStyle + java.awt.Font.BOLD;
if(editText.getFont().getItalic())
  iStyle = iStyle + java.awt.Font.ITALIC;

// Use the current font in all draw operations.
oDraw.setFont(new java.awt.Font(editText.getFont().getName(),
              iStyle,
              (int)editText.getFont().getSize()));

// Print the first 20 lines of text.
for (iCounter = 0; iCounter < 20; iCounter++)
{
  // Make sure we handle array bound errors.
  try
  {
    //Draw the text one line at a time.
    oDraw.drawString(sText[iCounter], 20, 20 * (iCounter + 1));
  }
  catch (ArrayIndexOutOfBoundsException exception)
  {
  }
}

  // Dispose of the draw object so that the text gets flushed to the
// printer.
  oDraw.dispose();

  // End the print job.
  wpj.end();
}

private void FormatDateDefault_click(Object source, Event e)
{
  // Check the default entry and uncheck the others.
  FormatDateDefault.setChecked(true);
  FormatDateMMDDYY.setChecked(false);
  FormatDateMonthDDYYYY.setChecked(false);
  FormatDate24HourTime.setChecked(false);
```

```
      FormatDateAMPMTime.setChecked(false);
   }

   private void FormatDateMMDDYY_click(Object source, Event e)
   {
      // Check the MM/DD/YY entry and uncheck the others.
      FormatDateDefault.setChecked(false);
      FormatDateMMDDYY.setChecked(true);
      FormatDateMonthDDYYYY.setChecked(false);
      FormatDate24HourTime.setChecked(false);
      FormatDateAMPMTime.setChecked(false);
   }

   private void FormatDateMonthDDYYYY_click(Object source, Event e)
   {
      // Check the Month DD, YYYY entry and uncheck the others.
      FormatDateDefault.setChecked(false);
      FormatDateMMDDYY.setChecked(false);
      FormatDateMonthDDYYYY.setChecked(true);
      FormatDate24HourTime.setChecked(false);
      FormatDateAMPMTime.setChecked(false);
   }

   private void FormatDate24HourTime_click(Object source, Event e)
   {
      // Check the 24 Hour Time entry and uncheck the others.
      FormatDateDefault.setChecked(false);
      FormatDateMMDDYY.setChecked(false);
      FormatDateMonthDDYYYY.setChecked(false);
      FormatDate24HourTime.setChecked(true);
      FormatDateAMPMTime.setChecked(false);
   }

   private void FormatDateAMPMTime_click(Object source, Event e)
   {
      // Check the AM/PM Time entry and uncheck the others.
      FormatDateDefault.setChecked(false);
      FormatDateMMDDYY.setChecked(false);
      FormatDateMonthDDYYYY.setChecked(false);
```

```
FormatDate24HourTime.setChecked(false);
FormatDateAMPMTime.setChecked(true);
}
```

The first thing you should notice is that the application uses the standard compliment of WFC classes. However, this application will begin showing you that most applications and many ActiveX controls will require a lot more support than WFC provides. In this case, we need to add two standard Java classes (java.awt.Toolkit and java.awt.Graphics) and one specialty Microsoft class (com.ms.awt.*) to enable printer support. Notice that I was very careful not to add all of the standard Java awt classes—doing so would have added ambiguity to the application and made it harder for the compiler to do its job. We'll see how these three classes come into play later in the discussion. For now, all you need to know is that the wizard will generate a generic application that relies solely on the WFC classes for you, which means you'll likely need to add some classes to gain full functionality of everything that Java has to offer.

One of our objectives for this application was to add better date and time support. The menu resource we added (and associated code) won't do the job by itself; we also need to modify the doDateTime( ) method. Notice that about the only thing that's the same as the original function is the currentTime variable, which contains the current system date and time. The function begins by checking the checked status of each Date Format menu entry. If the entry is checked, then the doDateTime( ) method displays the date and/or time in that format. The easiest way to display the date and time is to simply format currentTime as a string using the toString( ) function. All of the other conversions require you to work with individual date or time elements like the month or hour. Notice that in one case we convert the month to a string directly (for the FormatDateMMDDYY menu entry) and in the other we use a switch( ) statement to convert it to a text description of the month (the FormatDateMonthDDYYYY menu entry). The most important thing to remember about the time conversion is that time is always presented as a 24-hour time and not in an A.M./P.M. format.

Adding a button to the toolbar means adding some code to the toolBar_buttonClick( ) method to make it functional. In this case, we only have to add a simple reference to the FilePrint_click( ) method. Make sure you pass the appropriate Object and ToolBarButtonClickEvent variables to any routines that you call so that they can process the event properly.

The Font_click( ) method is the first custom method that we'll talk about. This method gets called when the user clicks the Font menu entry. All that we need to do is display the standard Font dialog box, then retrieve the values for the font selections that the user made and apply them to the editText control. This is actually one of the easier changes to implement for the application.

Printing is a real problem with Visual J++ for a number of reasons. The FilePrint_click( ) method shows you the simplest method for getting the information from the editText control to the printer. As you can see, the first thing we need to do is create a print job. Essentially, the print job is a method for packaging a canvas containing print information and sending it to the printer through standard Windows mechanisms. The print job also takes care of things like displaying the Print dialog box so the user can choose a destination for the print job. There are other variables associated with the print job, the most important of which is a Graphics class variable. This variable is the canvas we'll use for drawing the information. One of the first things we'll do is get the current font information and apply it to oDraw. You should apply the font information before you try drawing on oDraw. Once the font is applied, the method uses a simple for loop to process the lines of text we've gotten from the editText control. Notice that the sText array contains one entry of each hard return found in editText. Unfortunately, there isn't any way to determine just how many elements the sText string array contains. That's why it's necessary to add exception handling to the loop. That way, if the counter goes beyond the end of the sText string array, the program won't issue an error message. The final two steps are to dispose of the Graphics variable oDraw and end the print job. Note that the oDraw.dispose( ) method also flushes the information contained on the Graphics variable canvas to the print job and ultimately the printer.

Note *There are situations where you may have trouble printing from a Visual J++ application due to driver problems, even if your code is perfect. Normally, the problem manifests itself as an inability to print at all instead of less than perfect print results. One of the better MSDN articles to read on the subject is entitled "FIX: Printing Fails with java.lang.NullPointerException." The bottom line is if you have trouble getting your print routine to work, it may not be your code. Check to make sure you have the latest print drivers and the latest copy of the JVM installed on your machine. Doing so will ensure you run into a minimum of problems.*

The final set of custom methods all deal with the Format Date menu. Each item on the menu requires a separate method for controlling its checked state. When the user selects an item, the code checks it and unchecks all of the other menu items. This checked state information was used earlier in the doDateTime( ) method to determine what format to use when the user clicks the Date/Time button or chooses the entry from the Edit menu.

Once you have all of the code put together, you can compile and run the application for the first time. Here's what your application should look like now that you've added all of the required bells and whistles:

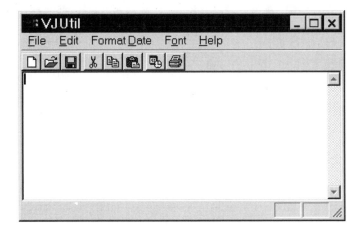

Performing an Initial Test

When testing an application, it's always best to start with the smallest, least complex testing environment and work your way up. The same thing holds true with the Visual J++ application in this chapter. It's important to test the application in a stand-alone mode to ensure you've taken care of any major problems before linking it to a Web page for dissemination across your company.

Unlike some application types though, there are a few special things you need to do with the VJUtil application. For one thing, you need to make sure that it's small enough to download from the company intranet without causing the user a lot of grief. Our application turned out to be a svelte 25.5KB in size—small enough to download in a short time even if the user has an older 28.8Kbps modem.

Appearance and positioning are two other concerns. Remember that this application will be used on a wider variety of machines than normal, including both laptop and notebook computers that may have a smaller than normal display. You'll need to ensure that the visual elements of the application work even when the user is sitting on a plane working with a laptop on the flight home.

Obviously, your testing should include the usual elements. You'll want to make sure that the application works as anticipated. Compatibility testing is extremely important since Visual J++ provides extra challenges in this area. Make sure that the user will have access to a printer that actually works with the application.

Building an IIS Application Access Page with Visual InterDev

At this point, you have a small, lightweight text editor that someone could download from just about anywhere. If we had added some special formatting features or even support for RTF files, the user could use this little text editor for something as complex as writing reports. Word processors like Word for Windows support RTF files, making it possible to import the file with little or no loss of formatting.

What we need is some method for distributing the application. That's where this section of the chapter comes into play. We need a user-friendly method of distributing the original application and any updates that may occur. Building a simple Web page to do the job will make it easy for users to get the text editor when they need it.

Besides providing a link to the word processor so that the user can download it, there are some other features that this Web page requires. The first is a set of operating instructions. It's not too hard to figure out that the users won't have a manual with them. Even though this is a very simple program, you'll still need to include a few instructions for the newer user.

Another Web site consideration is version information. You should provide a set of instructions for finding out what version of the program the user currently has and what version is currently available so that the user knows when they need to download the latest version. In addition, this Web page should probably outline what the differences in versions are and how important the download is. It may be that the user won't be in a position to download a simple upgrade that won't affect the overall functionality of the application. Helping the user know when they absolutely have to download a new version will keep the frustration level to a minimum.

The following sections will help you create a very simple Web site for distributing the example application. The whole purpose of this Web site is to make downloading the example application as easy as possible, then provide the basic support required by the user in a hurry to get things done.

Creating the Web Site Shell

Now that you've got a basic idea of what we'll be doing, let's create a simple Web page shell. The following procedure will get you started (it assumes that you've worked through the example in Chapter 4 and require a minimum of assistance).

1. Start Visual InterDev if you haven't done so already. You'll see the New Project dialog box.

2. Select Visual InterDev Projects folder and highlight the New Web Project icon.

3. Type **TextEdit** in the Name field and click Open. You'll see the Web Project Wizard - Step 1 of 4 dialog box. This dialog box should have the name of your Web server already added to it from previous projects.

4. Select the "Master mode" option and then click Next. Visual InterDev will contact your Web server and set up a new project on it. You'll see the Web Project Wizard - Step 2 of 4 dialog box once this process is complete. This is one time where you might need to attach a Web project to an existing page—most likely your main Web site. We won't be going this route, but it's important to know that you'd make the decision whether to attach to an existing Web project here.

5. Click Next. You'll see the Web Project Wizard - Step 3 of 4 dialog box. We need a simple theme, in this case, that allows the users to find the information they need quickly. There isn't going to be a complex structure for this application, so the ability to get to sibling pages quickly should be enough. Obviously, you'll need to choose a layout based on the complexity of your application.

6. Choose the Left 1 option (for the simple layout required by the example) and then click Next. You'll see the Web Project Wizard - Step 4 of 4 dialog box. The theme you use should match the master page you're attaching to if you're going that route. Stand-alone projects should use a very simple theme to leave the display uncluttered and make the information easy to find. In addition, a high-contrast theme will help laptop users find information quickly, even if their display is partly obscured by less than optimal light conditions.

7. Choose the Sumi Painting theme. It provides relatively high contrast, coupled with a lack of fussy graphics.

8. Click Finish. Visual InterDev will create a new project for you.

Adding the Example Application and Content

Our simple Web page doesn't need a lot in the way of content. Remember that we really need to have two features: a user guide so that even a novice can use the application and version information that allows the user to determine when an update is required. Adding content is as simple as adding the two required sibling Web pages, then designing a site diagram to make them accessible. Since we've performed this task several times in the book already, we won't go through the actual steps here. However, you'll find the completed version of the project on the CD that accompanies the book. You'll definitely want to create one blank Web page to follow along with this section.

Adding the application right to the Visual InterDev project file will make distribution just that much easier. You'll know that the current release version is available to the user because it appears right with the Visual InterDev project. Since our Visual J++ application consists of a single file (you can check this with the Depends utility), adding the application to the Web project is easy. Right-click the <Server Name>/TextEdit folder, then choose Add | Add Item from the context menu. You'll see the Add Item dialog box. Click the Existing tab, change the "Files of type" field to Executable Files, then search for the VJUtil program on your hard drive. Once you find it, highlight it, then click Open. Visual J++ will add the application right to your project. We also need to add the resource file to our project, just in case a user hasn't downloaded the VJUtil text editor before. Find the VJUtil.RESOURCES (may be shown with an RES extension in Windows Explorer) file and add it to your Web project using the same procedure as we used for the VJUtil program.

Don't assume that every Visual J++ application will consist of a single file. Always use the Depends utility to ensure that there really is only one file needed. In addition, the Depends file only shows executable files that an application depends on—a Visual J++ application also relies on a relatively small resource file. If the user is downloading the application for the first time rather than performing a simple upgrade, then they will need both the application and the resource file. Normally, you should perform the first install of the product at your company so that users on the road are required to perform a minimum of work to upgrade their machines.

Now we can add the file to the Web page. Figure 15-2 shows an example Web page that I created for this example. Notice that there are two discrete sections on this page. The first section tells the user when they need an upgrade, while the second tells the user how to download and install the program (which is very trivial in this case). Notice that the second section includes instructions for both new and existing users, but that the existing user's needs come first since it's unlikely that many people will be performing a new installation.

Lessons Learned

Visual J++ represents a major leap in Java technology. It allows you to do something that you couldn't do in the past—create a stand-alone application that allows you to reuse code that you created in the past. However, it's important to remember that this new capability comes at a heavy price in both compatibility and flexibility. You'll also be reliant on Microsoft to provide a smooth upgrade path between versions of Visual J++ to ensure your investment in coding time today is worth something tomorrow.

Two of the biggest advantages of using Visual J++ to write applications are the relatively small size of the resulting application and the fact that Visual J++ applications don't rely on runtime files as a general rule. (You can add support for external DLLs to gain access to a needed function, but the programmer adds this requirement—it's not a hidden secret like some runtime support requirements have been in the past.) Visual J++ applications are perfect for distribution through the Internet because of this feature.

The fact that Visual J++ is still in its infancy is reflected by some of the fit and finish issues that you'll run across. The most important of these problems is the need to have current files for both drivers and the VJM. Even files that are one version too old may not contain an important feature that allows you to print on a specific printer, or worse yet, break an application that would normally work fine on any other machine.

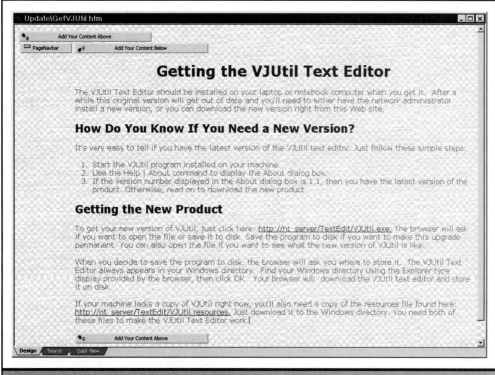

Figure 15-2. The VJUtil download Web page contains both upgrade criteria and download instructions

Visual InterDev is an important partner in making your utility program a success. You need a simple Web page to distribute the application once you've completed it. Since Visual InterDev comes as part of the Visual Studio package, you'll find that it's probably the handiest tool available for creating these simple Web pages fast.

Chapter 16

Getting Feedback with
ISAPI Extensions

The term "application" has been bantered about for many years to represent a wealth of different executable file formats. There has been an ebb and flow of names and definitions that supposedly make the picture clearer but only end up clouding the issue further. Take the browser helper application for example. It's designed to help the browser perform a task such as displaying content on a Web page, but there is nothing in the definition that says that the helper application must also provide stand-alone functionality, which is something that some purists deem necessary to call an executable file an application.

Applications have recently taken on yet another meaning when scripts are combined with an interpreter. It seems that every version of Windows has some new scripting host designed to run everything from simple batch type files to complex applications like those found in some ASP implementations. However, if you look back at the very first BASIC applications for DOS, you'll find that they were well rooted in interpreter technology—the executable version of these files is a relatively recent innovation.

These two paragraphs describe where Internet Information Server (IIS) is today. There is a wide variety of file types that many people consider applications, but which range well outside of the usual definition of an executable file. Everything from scripts to standard executables to DLLs that just look like stand-alone executables float around on most servers today, and you can create them all with Visual Studio.

Rather than engulf you in the flames of yet another dispute, I'll define some very basic IIS application types in this chapter—the ones that we'll actually work with as the book progresses. This list of applications doesn't in any way serve as the definitive list of applications that IIS can host. In fact, as previously mentioned, some of these applications are actually DLLs in disguise. This book will simply refer to them as applications because Microsoft originally called them that. I won't get into the mystical properties that define the purist form of application—I'm simply using these definitions as a convention.

Of course, none of this would be an issue if there weren't other factors that came into play, like the historical methods of working with a Web server. Most of them are along the traditional static HTML route, which requires the use of scripts of various types. For example, you can use a Common Gateway Interface (CGI) script to query a database through a C/C++ program. The script would then format an HTML page containing the results of the query and upload it to the client. We aren't going to cover any of these more traditional routes in this chapter since there are entire books available on the topic. However, it's important to mention that the traditional methods exist because they do work and you may find you need one when the newer methods we'll talk about in this chapter just don't fit the bill. For example, you may already have an existing infrastructure and trying to reprogram everything using new technology may not be cost effective.

On the other hand, using new technology like the Internet Server Application Programming Interface (ISAPI) can give you better flexibility and could greatly enhance your ability to provide content on the Internet. That's what we'll talk about in the first section of this chapter—the theory behind the new technology that you can use to provide great content on your Web site. We'll also look at a specific way to provide that increased flexibility to the users of your Web site. What we'll look at in this chapter is ISAPI as a management tool. More important, we'll look at some of the enabling technologies that go with ISAPI, like ISAPI server applications (ISAs). When you complete this chapter, you'll have a good overview of how this technology will work in a real-world situation. You'll also have a good idea of when you'll need to use those older technologies instead. I'll be sure to tell you about any problem areas you'll need to watch as you implement these new technologies on your own server. Knowing these pitfalls may help you decide whether to go the new-technology route or stick with what you've used in the past.

Web Link   *There's a fast way to learn the bare essentials of some types of IIS access techniques, including ODBC. Dynamic Systems International provides a series of lessons you can download about IIS from http://www.dsi.org/dsi/iis.htm. These lessons include an overview of just about everything you'll need to make some of the older technology access methods work. You may also want to visit the Microsoft IIS FAQ site (sponsored by Stephen Genusa) at http://www.genusa.com/iis/, which includes topics like CGI. In addition, the KLV site at http://www.Adiscon.com/IIS contains links for various Visual C++ programming considerations when using older technology. The same site includes links to places where you can find out the latest information on Internet specification efforts and security concerns like user authentication.*

Once we get past the theory of how ISAPI works and what it can do for you, we'll put some of that theory into practice by creating an ISAPI Extension. (Make sure you also look at Chapter 17 where we'll create an ISAPI Filter.) This ISAPI Extension is designed to make it easy for you to create custom Web pages. These Web pages will be used to help create a report, but you could use them for any of a number of purposes. Our first step in creating the report, then, is to define some report requirements—we need to know what we want out of the report for a given situation before we can create the code to create the report.

Designing the ISAPI Extension comes next. We'll create a fairly basic reporting extension in this chapter, but you could easily add to it to meet your own needs. The whole purpose of this ISAPI Extension is to give you some idea of what's possible. This section of the chapter will also show you how to create simple test scenarios for the new ISAPI Extension. The reason is simple, you have to know that the ISAPI Extension actually works before you can create the rest of the application—including a user-friendly front end that will greatly complicate the application as a whole for you, but make things a lot easier for the user.

We'll use the Address database created in Chapter 9 in this chapter. The ISAPI Extension will access the database and use it as a source of information. You could potentially change the code in this chapter to simply display information from a text file, but using the SQL Server database will allow you to learn more about how ISAPI Extensions work.

The ability to create custom content is enhanced when the user gains access to some of the customization controls in a way that makes it easy to configure that content. One way to allow the user to customize a report is to create a custom Web page for the purpose. Normally, you would use scripts to screen the input from potential user errors before passing it on to the server for processing. The input page, the one that requests the report information, has to be user friendly. That's why we'll use a product like Visual InterDev to create the standard Web page. It allows you to create a user-friendly front end in a modicum of time. Obviously, this input page will be different than the ones we've created in the past since it'll interact with the server through the ISAPI Extension we created in the previous section.

Scenario

Your company has decided that it needs some way of generating report information for everyone at the company, but that not everyone should get all of the information that the report has to offer. In addition, the company needs to know that each employee will get the information that will be most useful for the task at hand. In other words, the employee needs to have some input on precisely what information the report contains so that they won't have to wade through a mire of unneeded information to retrieve the few gems required for a report.

There are actually three tasks to perform in this case, but five groups are required to perform them. The first task is to create the report criteria. This is a document that should spell out the kind of information that a user will receive given a specific set of input criteria and the user's security classification. In other words, a user shouldn't be allowed to receive sensitive information by mistake—they should only be allowed to choose from the information actually available to them.

The first task requires the participation of a relatively large group of people because it affects most of the other tasks involved in this scenario. You'll need to have the C++ programmers involved because they need to create the ISAPI Extension that determines what the user will get as output. Network administrators need to be involved since they are the ones most concerned about security and the implementation of both the Web page and the ISAPI Extension. A group of test users should be included so that the ISAPI Extension will provide the number of report groups required to make the output truly usable. Obviously, this task has to be performed before you can do anything else.

The second task is to create the ISAPI Extension. Once the report criteria are defined, the Visual C++ programmers will have a better idea of what they need to produce. The network administrator group will need to maintain close contact during the development process to ensure the resulting ISAPI Extension doesn't break any security rules. The administrators and Visual C++ programmers will also have to work together to ensure that the ISAPI Extension is feasible from the perspective of both processing power and memory. A report generator can consume huge quantities of both of these resources. During the ISAPI Extension testing phase, the administrator and Visual C++ programmer group needs to be joined by a group of representative users so that the test ISAPI Extension can be checked for both quality of output and technical features like memory usage.

The third task could be started at any time. The Visual InterDev developers can create a Web page that will eventually access the ISAPI Extension. Since the design process can't really end until the ISAPI Extension is ready to use, you may want to wait until the testing cycle is complete. Once all of the pieces are together for creating the input Web page, the Visual InterDev developers can create it, then test it using the users group.

Note	*You can create an ISAPI Filter or ISAPI Extension using Visual Basic 6.0. However, the development machine must have Peer Web Service version 3.0 or above, or Internet Information Server installed to start the project. Visual C++ has no such requirement. The positive part of this arrangement is that you can test a Visual Basic ISAPI Extension with extreme ease just by clicking the Run button. Visual C++ programmers have to compile the control, load it on the server, create a test page, and finally access the ISAPI Extension through Internet Explorer. Obviously, the Visual C++ debug cycle is far longer and more complex than the same cycle for Visual Basic.*

Working with ISAPI

Internet Server API (ISAPI) can be a very complex topic because there is more than one flavor of ISAPI that you can work with. The major division is between ISAPI Filters and ISAPI Extensions. There are many ways to use an ISAPI Extension, which in part determines how you create it in the first place. The ISAPI Extension categories affect the way a programmer and administrator view the whole topic of ISAPI. Likewise, ISAPI Filters are varied to the point that you need to change the creation process to produce a specific kind of ISAPI Filter for a specific task. For example, you use different ISAPI Extension Wizard settings for a security filter than you do for one that redirects URLs. (It's interesting to note that the ISAPI Extension Wizard is used to create both ISAPI Filters and ISAPI Extensions—we'll see later in the chapter and in Chapter 17 that this process is relatively easy and that there isn't any reason to complicate it by providing more than one wizard.)

Don't think that Microsoft has cornered the market when it comes to good newsgroups that deal with ISAPI-related issues. There are quite a few non-Microsoft newsgroups that you'll want to pay close attention to. One of the more interesting non-Microsoft IIS sites is comp.lang.java. I was amazed to find message threads about everything from ASP to ActiveX on this site. Another good non-Microsoft site for IIS-specific help is comp.infosystems.www.servers.ms-windows. I found a great ISAPI thread on this newsgroup at the time of this writing. Needless to say, there are other comp.infosystems.www newsgroups you'll want to check out as well. It's hard to find out what the bugs are in some software, but you won't find it very difficult to do with IIS if you look at comp.os.ms-windows.nt.software.compatibility.

The following paragraphs are going to provide you with the information you'll need to at least understand what the various flavors of ISAPI are all about and how you can use them to your benefit. We'll look at five major issues that you'll need to deal with when working with ISAPI. Perhaps the most important issue is what ISAPI is in the first place. We need to answer the question, "How does ISAPI differ from the myriad of other technologies that are in place today?"

The next question is where ISAPI fits into the general scheme of things. Microsoft has a grand scheme of where all of these pieces of technology will eventually fit. The only problem is that the map often gets lost because people focus on the very smallest part of one technology. This section will help give you a bit more perspective on where Microsoft seems to be headed.

Theoretical discussions are fine for the classroom, but where does ISAPI fit in the real world? That's the topic of the next section. You could replace many of the functions that ISAPI performs with older technologies like CGI, so it's important to know why ISAPI is the best choice. We'll look at why ISAPI is such a compelling technology for administrators with real-world needs and real-world constraints.

Choosing between an ISAPI Filter and an ISAPI Extension should be relatively easy, but some people have trouble doing it. The next topic tells you how to make the right choice and even provides a few clues as to where these two ISAPI technologies overlap. Fortunately, there are fairly simple ways to determine which technology is ultimately correct.

Our final section will deal with the thorny issue of working with the five ISAPI classes supported by MFC. These classes help you create all of the various flavors of ISAPI we've talked about in the previous sections of the chapter. It's important to realize that you need to use specific classes in certain ways to achieve a desired result. This section will help you gain a perspective of where each class fits into the overall ISAPI picture.

What Is ISAPI?

So what is ISAPI? For the purposes of this book, ISAPI is a set of MFC extensions that allow you to work directly with IIS. These classes offer low-level support and access to

IIS-specific features. We'll work with a relatively new kind of project to implement ISAPI in this chapter, the ISAPI Extension Wizard. (The ISAPI Extension Wizard has been available for several iterations of Visual C++ now, but Microsoft continues to refine and improve its operation.) There are also five ISAPI-specific classes that we'll look at: CHttpServer, CHttpServerContext, CHttpFilter, CHttpFilterContext, and CHtmlStream. You'll use these classes to create ISA.

ISAs are called by a whole variety of other names, like ISAPI server extension DLLs in the Microsoft documentation. We'll use ISA throughout the text when referring to an application just to keep things simple.

By necessity, ISAs rely on ISAPI. You'll use ISAPI classes to create ISAPI Extensions and ISAPI Filters for IIS. However, you're not limited to ISAPI classes; there are also WinInet classes for controlling Internet communication and all of the standard MFC classes to provide things such as an interface.

ISAPI comes in two basic flavors: filters and extensions. A filter allows you to keep something out or in by monitoring events on your server. For example, you could create an ISAPI Filter that keeps people out of your Web site unless they enter the right password. Another type of filter could prevent files larger than a certain size from getting uploaded to the FTP server on your Web site. ISAPI Extensions are more like applications, batch processes, or background processes. For example, you could create an extension that allows the user to interact with a database without resorting to using scripts. The same extension could create Web pages dynamically based on the user input and the contents of the database on your server.

There are a lot of newsgroups you can visit to get help with your IIS, ASP, or ISAPI problem. In fact, there are too many to list them all in this chapter, so you'll want to spend a little additional time looking around. For the best Microsoft-specific support for IIS, take a look at microsoft.public.inetserver.iis. There are other newsgroups in the microsoft.public.inetserver area that you'll want to take a look at, too, but this one usually has the most messages. You'll find Microsoft-specific ASP help at microsoft.public.inetserver.iis.activeserverpages. If you're using Front Page as one of your Web page maintenance tools, you'll want to take a look at microsoft.public.frontpage.client for ISAPI-specific help. Finally, if you're searching for that hidden ASP newsgroup, take a look at microsoft.public.activex.programming .scripting.vbscript.

An Overview of ISAPI

Before you can understand ISAPI, you have to understand where it fits into the Microsoft scheme of things. There are actually five levels of Internet support provided with Visual Studio, three of which can reside on the server. The other two levels of support are client-specific—you'll never see them on the server. There are only two Visual Studio products that you can use to implement these levels of Internet support: Visual Basic and Visual C++. You'll find that Visual Basic offers the same features here as it does with any other application: fast development speed and reduced learning curve, because many implementation requirements are hidden from the programmer. On the other hand, Visual C++ provides great low-level access to all of the features that IIS can provide, but exacts a relatively high cost in learning time. The following list defines each level of support and tells where you'll find it:

- **ISAPI (server)** This is the level of support we're talking about in this chapter. You need it to provide an extension or filter for the server itself. In other words, the client won't directly interact with this level of support; it'll merely see the results of the interaction. ISAPI Filters and ISAPI Extensions get loaded on the server as part of your IIS configuration, as we'll see later—both of these levels of support rely on DLLs instead of stand-alone applications.

- **WinInet (server or client)** We don't cover this level of support in the book directly, but we do cover it indirectly. This set of classes allows you to use a specific method of data transfer between the client and the server. There are three levels of protocol support: HTTP, FTP, and Gopher. Essentially, you'd use these classes to create a session (CInternetSession), which is one connection to the server, and then specify a connection type (CFtpConnection, CHttpConnection, or CGopherConnection). After establishing a connection, the user can do things like look for a file (CFtpFileFind or CGopherFileFind). Normally, you don't have to interact with these classes directly because Visual Studio takes care of everything for you, as we saw in Chapter 11 when creating an URL moniker application.

- **Asynchronous URL monikers (server or client)** We looked at this particular area of Visual C++ Internet support in Chapter 11. The important aspect for you to remember is that an asynchronous URL moniker allows you to perform tasks on the Internet without waiting. You simply tell the target application what you want and then go on doing whatever else you wanted to do. The whole idea is that the Internet doesn't provide an instantaneous response in most situations, and even if it does, a long download could render the user's machine useless for hours at a time without the use of asynchronous URL monikers.

- **ActiveX documents (client)** Displaying a document in your browser and allowing the user to edit it is what this level of support is all about. We visited it in Chapter 13.

- **ActiveX controls (client)** Creating the basic elements of a Web page used to involve lots of scripting, and even then you got a static image. Using ActiveX controls on a Web site means that old technology and static displays no longer hold you back—your Web page can change to meet a specific situation. We took a look at this technology in Chapter 11.

There are a lot of places you can visit on the Internet to find out more about IIS, ISAPI, and other Internet server–related technologies like Active Server Pages (ASP). The main Web site to visit for IIS information is http://www.microsoft.com/ntserver/Basics/ WebServices/default.asp. This Microsoft-supported Web site contains links to just about everything you'll need to use IIS itself and even a few of the more common links for enabling technologies like ISAPI. If you value non-Microsoft assistance, take a look at the ASP Developer's Site at http://www.genusa.com/asp/. This Web site contains a lot of valuable information about using Active Server Pages on your Internet server. This same site has non-Microsoft links to both IIS and ISAPI sites.

Using ISAPI in the Real World

There a few things you need to know about ISAPI when it comes to a real-world production environment. For example, your ISA will be a DLL that loads on the server, just like any other DLL. This DLL will share the same address space as the HTTP server does, and you can unload it later if you need the memory it's consuming for something else. (Newer versions of IIS will allow you to create separate address spaces for applications, but using a shared space is still the default setting.) In addition, an ISA has a high level of intimacy with the server, which means that you have more complete access to everything the server has to offer. On the other hand, server access is still controlled, which means you'll gain access to server elements only when there isn't a security prohibition against the access. So what do these features buy you? The following list tells you about the advantages of using ISAs over other techniques like CGI.

- **Automatic load and unload** Unless you tell IIS not to unload the ISAPI Extension, it will unload automatically when no longer needed. However, it doesn't load and unload like the C application used for a CGI script will. The ISAPI Extension loads the first time it's needed, then unloads when memory is needed to perform other tasks. In other words, the ISAPI Extension is available when needed for subsequent calls by the client—only the first call requires the server to load the ISAPI Extension.

You can force IIS to unload the ISAPI Extension after each client call, just as it would do for any other application. There is only one good reason for using this feature— debugging of the ISAPI Extension. You don't want the ISAPI Extension to remain in memory when you're trying to debug it or you won't know if the changes you've made are actually taking effect and what that effect is.

- **Lower memory costs** Since your ISA loads as a DLL on the server and uses the same memory space as the HTTP server, you won't have to waste the memory normally associated with CGI overhead. All you'll really need to load is the logic required to perform the task you're asking the ISA to do.

- **Speed**   Loading a DLL or C application the first time will take essentially the same amount of time, though the DLL will be slightly faster due to its smaller size. However, once you've loaded the DLL the first time, it'll stay in memory until you unload it, which means that you don't have to pay that loading cost more than one time if you don't want to. A CGI script will load the C application every time you call it. That's not the best news, though. Since the ISA DLL shares the same memory space as your HTTP server, you won't have to pay a time penalty for interprocess calls or any of the overhead normally associated with using a C application in a separate address space.

- **Code sharing**   All the server needs to do is load your DLL one time. Any application that requests the services of that DLL has access to it. Obviously, code sharing is one of the factors that leads to the lower memory costs and speed improvements over CGI mentioned in the first two points. However, code sharing results in some not-so-obvious benefits as well. For example, code sharing reduces administration time for your server, since the administrator only needs to replace one copy of any given DLL to affect every application that uses it. The C applications typically used by CGI have a lot of redundant code in them. Change a single routine and you'll need to change every C application that uses the routine on your server, which means greatly increased administrator time and the need for additional application tracking by the programmer.

- **Reliability**   C applications used by CGI scripts load and execute on the server without having much access to the server itself. As a result, it's harder to create a C application that can monitor server events and recover from errors. What usually happens is that the server will terminate an errant CGI script and the client will end up with nothing. ISAs have full access to the server, which means that they can recover from errors more easily. As a result, the client very seldom (if ever) ends up having to make a request the second time.

- **Filtering capability**   You can't provide an event-driven equivalent to an ISA using CGI and a C application. The reason's simple: a C application gets called, does its work, and then unloads. There isn't any way that it can monitor server events over the long term.

- **Multiple tasks in one DLL**   Every task that you want CGI to perform requires a separate executable for each task you perform. As a result, you incur the overhead of calling each routine. ISAs, on the other hand, can contain multiple commands, each of which is a member of the CHttpServer class.

Getting these seven capabilities doesn't mean that you have to pay a big price in either learning curve or excess coding. ISAs are just as easy to use as the CGI equivalent. Here's what the two lines of code would look like in an application:

```
<!-This is a call to a CGI routine with one parameter.->
http://aux/controls/sample.exe?Param

<!-This is a call to an ISA routine with one parameter.->
http://aux/controls/sample.dll?Param
```

As you can see, working with ISAPI doesn't have to be difficult. We called our ISA control using about the same code as we would a CGI routine. In fact, the only difference from a coding perspective is that our ISA control uses a DLL extension, while the CGI routine uses an EXE extension. Theoretically, you could switch your server to ISAs, make a few search-and-replace changes to your Web pages, and no one would notice the difference from an interface perspective. Of course, everyone would notice the higher efficiency of your Web site due to the advantages of using ISAPI.

The last advantage that I mentioned for using ISAs was the fact that you can perform more than one task with a single ISA. We'll see later how you implement this behavior. For right now, all you really need to know is that the calling syntax still doesn't differ much from standard CGI calls you may have used in the past. Here's an ISA routine call that specifies that you want to use the DisplayStr( ) function:

```
<!-Call the DisplayStr function in an ISA routine with one parameter.->
http://aux/controls/sample.dll?DisplayStr?Param
```

As you can see, we called something other than the default task using a second question mark (?) in the calling string. The first parameter now tells which function you want to call within SAMPLE.DLL, and the second parameter contains a list of parameters. This method of calling functions is known as a parse map, which you'll learn how to create in the section later on creating an ISAPI Extension.

ISAs do share some qualities that you'll find in CGI. For one thing, your application executes on the server, not the client. This makes updating your application easy—all you need to do is replace one DLL file on the server. (You do need to stop the service to update the DLL with older versions of IIS, but this is a small price to pay for the convenience of one machine update.) Obviously, this is a lot easier than trying to replace an application on every client machine that accesses your Web site. It's also one of the reasons that companies are taking a serious look at intranets to host things like a help desk and custom database applications—updating one server is a lot easier than updating a lot of clients.

Tip   *IIS Version 4 adds some new capabilities that make working with ISAs easier. For one thing, you can tell the server to unload the ISA after each call. This means that you can try the ISA to see if it works and replace it with a new copy if necessary, all without stopping the service. The disadvantage of this new capability is that you'll see a slight performance hit because the server will need to reload the ISA every time it gets called by a client.*

Choosing Between an ISAPI Filter and an ISAPI Extension

You don't have to spend a lot of time deciding whether to create an ISAPI Filter or an ISAPI Extension (or even both). The differences between the two types of ISA are pretty easy to figure out. Once you do so, choosing the one you need becomes fairly simple.

> **Tip**
> *There are also choices to make about which programming language to use. Visual Basic allows you to create ISAPI Extensions with extreme ease, but doesn't allow you to create ISAPI Filters without a lot of hand programming. If you want to create a small ISAPI Extension on a very short time schedule, then Visual Basic is the tool of choice. On the other hand, if you want to create any kind of ISAPI Filter or complex ISAPI Extensions, then you'll find that Visual C++ offers the best environment. Make sure you choose the right tool to get the job done in the time required.*

A filter will always react to events on the server itself. A user attempting to log into your Web site will generate an event that an ISAPI Filter can monitor. You'll normally use it to modify the data flow between the client and server. For example, if your application saw an SF_NOTIFY_AUTHENTICATION event take place, it could display a dialog for the user to enter a name and password. If these were correct, the user would gain access to the Web site.

Extensions are used in the same situations as their CGI counterparts. For example, if you wanted to create an order entry system, you would likely use an extension. The extension would receive data from a form that the user filled out, process the information, add it to the database, and, finally, send some type of receipt back to the user. This is the same process that you would follow when using a CGI script; the only difference is that now you're using a DLL instead. Unlike a filter, an extension doesn't monitor events on the server—it acts in every way like an application would.

There are some situations where the choice of filter or extension doesn't really matter very much. For example, consider a simple Web counter. Every time someone accesses your Web site, you update the counter to show what number visitor that person is. You could call an ISAPI Extension from the Web page to update this counter if so desired, or have a filter monitor the SF_NOTIFY_LOG event on the server and send the information automatically. The choice is a matter of personal taste.

You'll run into situations where you need to use both an extension and a filter. For example, you might want to display one Web page for an authorized Netscape user, another for an unauthorized Netscape user, and two others for authorized and unauthorized Internet Explorer users. This situation requires some scripting within the HTML form to detect the browser type, a little bit of work on the part of a filter to detect whether the user is authorized or not, and a little work on the part of an extension to generate the proper page. Using this combination of client scripting and ISAPI Extensions to your server represents one way to fully extend your Web site and make it convenient for everyone to use.

Working with the Five ISAPI Classes

Previously, I mentioned that you would be working with five ISAPI-specific MFC classes in this chapter. This doesn't mean that you won't continue to work with the classes you're familiar with, but these classes do provide special capabilities you'll need to design an ISAPI Filter or ISAPI Extension. The following list is meant as an overview of the classes that you'll work with in the sections that follow. Obviously, you'll get a much better view of these classes when we begin to work with the example code.

> **Tip**
>
> *Visual Basic hides many low-level details from the programmer. In fact, a Visual Basic version of an ISAPI Extension or ISAPI Filter relies exclusively on MSVBVM60.DLL for support. While you won't have to know about these MFC classes to get your ISA up and running when using Visual Basic, the principles you'll use are the same. These actions are still taking place in the background. Visual Basic merely makes them inconsequential to the programmer. The positive side of this is that you'll create an ISA with less code and with fewer low-level programming needs to worry about. The negative side is that you'll have less control over the data stream between the client and server, and hence, less flexibility in designing the ISA.*

- **CHttpServer**   This is the main class that you'll need to use to create either a filter or an extension. The CHttpServer class defines an object that works as a server extension DLL or an ISA. The main purpose of the CHttpServer object is to handle the messages generated by the server and the client. As a result, you'll only find one CHttpServer object in any ISA DLL.

- **CHttpServerContext**   The CHttpServer class actually creates this object. It's a single instance of a single request from the client. In other words, you'll see one CHttpServerContext object for every active client request. The object gets destroyed when the client request has been fulfilled.

- **CHttpFilter**   ISAPI Filters require the use of a special CHttpFilter object to monitor server events. This object will look for all of the SF messages that the server generates as the client interacts with it. For example, the client will generate an SF_NOTIFY_LOG message every time a user tries to access the Web site.

- **CHttpFilterContext**   The CHttpFilter object will create one CHttpFilterContext object for each active server event. The CHttpFilterContext class represents a single event generated by a single client during a specific session.

- **CHtmlStream**   You'll use this class to manage data between the client and the server. The CHttpServer class will create an object of this type whenever it needs to transmit information between the client and the server. In most cases, there is only one of these objects per DLL. However, the CHttpServer object can create as many CHtmlStream objects as it needs to transfer data safely. A typical CHtmlStream object contains data and all the tags required to create the content for an HTML page. For example, if you performed a search of a database, the resulting CHtmlStream object would contain not only the data but also the HTML tags required to actually create the Web page used to display the data.

Defining the Reporting Requirements

Any good database application designer will tell you that figuring out what you want as an output is crucial in determining what you need as input. It doesn't really matter what you're using for a source of information (though databases are by far the most common source). You need to know what the end user needs before you can create a method of providing it. The following sections will help you understand the design criteria for Internet or intranet reports in general and our example report in specific.

General Considerations

Every report you ever create will have some general requirements. Some of them are pretty easy to understand. For example, you'll always need to provide some key to understanding complex graphical information. However, there are some concepts that are even more basic than this—you have to provide some method for getting the data from its raw form to a report format that a user can understand. There are three stages of data manipulation for any report, though most reports require more:

- **Input**   You must create some method of inputting the data that provides consistent output results. Database management systems (DBMSs) normally provide rules that determine whether a bit of input is correctly formatted and provides enough in the way of data. (Unfortunately, there is still no reliable way to ensure that most of the data content is actually correct.) Forms help the user format the data input and help files allow the user to find out what information is required when they're unsure. In addition, most input forms provide hints and helps. For example, a blank that requires a state name as input may provide a drop-down list box that contains a list of all of the states or regions that your company normally deals with. Whatever your means of input, the bottom line is that it doesn't pay to input even one piece of data until you can be sure the output will be consistent.

- **Storage**   There are a number of ways to store the information, but some methods are better than others when it comes to retrieving the data for output. For example, you could easily store tips of the day in a text file on disk and be sure that the user would still be able to retrieve the information in a reasonable amount of time. Try storing your company's one million customer contact list in a text file and you may be in for a very long wait. DBMSs have been searching for the fastest, smallest, most reliable, and most convenient means of data storage for years—they haven't found it yet. The best thing to remember here is that data storage is never a one-size-fits-all proposition—there is only the solution that makes the best sense for your particular needs.

- **Formatting**   The format used to input and store the data is very seldom the same format used to retrieve it. In fact, it's more than likely that the users of your report generator will want to see the data in several different formats, depending on their needs at the time. For example, if your report shows the current sales for the quarter, some people may only need an overview by region, others a detailed report by salesperson, and still others a detailed report by product. In other words, formatting is critical if you want to present the information to the user in a useful way.

All reports will have these three items in common. It doesn't matter what environment you create the report for, the size of the report, or the complexity of the information it contains. You always have to provide a method for inputting the data, storing it for later use, then formatting it for output.

Web-Site-Specific Considerations

Web-site-based reports also have some additional requirements that all reports of this type will have. As with the general requirements I just described, the vast majority of your Web-based reports will have additional requirements. We'll look at how you would implement these needs in the coding section of this chapter. Consider this list of report items an overview of what you need just to get started:

- **HTML limitations**   When you create a report for the desktop, it can contain a wealth of features that you can't even consider in a Web environment. For example, you'll find it difficult to create wide reports because the user may be limited to the amount of data that a laptop computer screen can hold. Try creating too many columns and the user may give up trying to read the report out of frustration. In short, you need to choose the format of your report to keep the limitations of HTML in mind. Hopefully, the DHTML specification will provide more in the way of formatting options so that the amount of work required to create a readable and aesthetically pleasing report is diminished.

- **Intranet vs. Internet**   Your company most likely controls the browsers and equipment used to view Web pages through the company intranet. This means you'll be sure of the capability of the hardware and software that the user will have on hand for viewing reports. If you want to use Front Page extensions to spruce a report up, you can do so without fear. On the other hand, there is a very wide variety of both hardware and software available on the Internet. This means you'll need to write a report in a format that will work with the lowest common denominator. In short, reports that you create for the Internet will require more work to complete simply because you have to check for a greater number of potential problems.

- **Channel requirements**   A user may not have a T1 connection to the Internet; they may rely on a dial-up connection from another country. A report you create for display on the Internet or an intranet will need to provide the information the user needs in the smallest possible form. The appearance of the data is important, but even more important is the requirement to actually get the data to the user.

■ **Web page benefits** There are times where the Web page will provide some benefits that you may not be used to using on a paper report. For one thing, you have easy-to-use linking at your disposal. This means that you could use a single report to provide both overview and detail information if you format it correctly. The user can decide on the level of detail based on how many links they follow. However, don't confuse this detail advantage with an organizational need. It's still important to provide some means of getting the data organized in the way the user wants to view it.

Example Report Criteria

Our example report has two specialty criteria that we must consider. The first is that the employee only gets the amount of information requested. There are two ways to meet this requirement. First, we can provide an overview page with links to detail pages that the employee can view. Second, we can provide a menu of options so that the user can select the report sections they want to view. That way the overview won't contain any more sections than what the user requested in the first place.

The second criteria is that the user be able to choose a report format—the method used to organize the information. In this case, we'll have to limit the users' choices to make the ISAPI Extension useful and still resource friendly. Yes, it's possible to provide a report generator that can output the information in any format, but at the expense of both memory and processor cycles. In addition, the user would end up designing the report, which is something we need to avoid over an intranet connection. The amount of bandwidth required to actually process all of the formatting instructions in real time would likely prove prohibitive.

Creating an ISAPI Extension with Visual C++

It's time to create the ISAPI Extension we'll use to create a report. The example program will accept input from the user or Java applet, then create a report based on the input criteria. For the most part, you'll be able to use everything in the following sections for any kind of ISAPI Extension, except for the example-specific code.

Note *The code in this section was developed using Visual C++ version 6.0 exclusively and hasn't been tested extensively on older platforms (the code should work fine with Visual C++ 5.0). While the code may work without modification with Visual C++ 4.2, you'll probably need to make allowances in the procedures I've provided. The code itself will require change to work with versions of Visual C++ older than version 4.2.*

Our example ISAPI Extension will work with the SQL Server database we created in Chapter 9. Make sure you create this database before proceeding with this example. The example will allow you to create two different report organization types: name and ZIP code. In addition, you'll be able to create either an overview or a Detail view of the data. Finally, you'll be able to select a singe name from the database for display purposes.

Creating the ISAPI Shell

The first step in creating our ISAPI Extension is to create a shell that we can add some code to later. The following procedure will take you through all the steps required to create the sample ISAPI Extension. You can use the same procedure to start any ISAPI Extension that you need to create. I'm assuming that you already have Visual C++ running and that you're using the 6.0 version of the product.

One of the best places to look for ideas for your own ISAPI extension or filter is freeware produced by other programmers. The alt.comp.freeware newsgroup lists quite a few of these offerings. For example, at the time of this writing, AAIT Incorporated introduced a new freeware product named CGI Expert. It supports the CGI, win-CGI, ISAPI, and NSAPI interfaces simultaneously. Obviously, you'll want to use freeware products, like any other product, with care. However, they do provide excellent ideas on how to create your own custom extensions when needed (or a solution so you don't have to do any programming at all).

1. Use the File | New command to display the New dialog box shown here. Notice that I've already selected the ISAPI Extension Wizard.

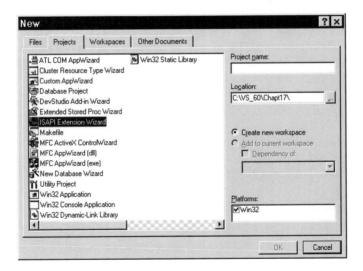

2. Type the name of the ISA you want to create in the "Project name" field. I used ReportIt for the example ISA, but you could use any name that you want.

3. Click OK. You'll see the ISAPI Extension Wizard - Step 1 of 1 dialog box shown here. This is where you'll select the various characteristics for your ISA. Notice that there are three main areas to the dialog box. You can choose to create a filter by checking the first check box and an extension by checking the second check box. Both of these areas allow you to assign a class name and description. The third area defines how you'll link MFC into your application.

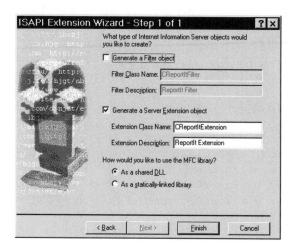

4. Check the "Generate a Server Extension object" option, and uncheck the "Generate a Filter object" option.

Tip   *You'll want to provide a short, concise statement of what your ISA does in the Extension Description field. The description appears as a string that you can use within the DLL as needed. The wizard-generated code will also give this description to the server when the server initializes the ISAPI Extension. This description won't show up in the Properties dialog box when someone opens it for your ISA, so you'll want to add some additional text to the version information for your DLL as well.*

Type **Create a specialized report for the client** in the Extension Description field. Notice that there are no specialized class settings and very few wizard customizations for ISAPI Extensions. You'll start with a very primitive ISAPI Extension shell that actually works if you compile it—though a default shell doesn't provide much in the way of content.

5. Click Finish. You'll see a New Project Information dialog box like the one shown here (as with most projects, this is your last opportunity to view any project settings before the wizard creates the shell).

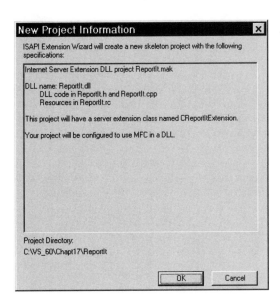

6. Click OK. The ISAPI Extension Wizard will create the required program shell for you.

As you can see, the process for creating an ISAPI Extension shell is very simple and straightforward. We'll see in Chapter 17 that the options for a filter are a bit harder to figure out at first, but that they actually help you create a specific kind of filter with greater ease.

Adding Some Code

At this point, we need to do three things to the skeleton that the ISAPI Extension Wizard has created for us to make the extension functional. These three steps are the same for every ISAPI Extension that you'll ever create. In other words, these steps reflect the minimum work required to create any ISAPI Extension. The following sections will provide a detailed view of how to create the example ISAPI Extension, but more importantly, clue you in on how you would create an ISAPI Extension in general.

Step 1—Create a Parse Map

The first task in designing any ISAPI Extension is to create a parse map for the new functions we want to add. Theoretically, you could use the Default( ) method for your extension code, but I prefer to use this method to display the various settings required to use the ISAPI Extension. In addition, since most of the ISAPI Extensions you create will contain more than one display method, you'll need to add one or more functions to it anyway. You'll find the parse map near the beginning of the ReportIt.CPP file. Listing 16-1 shows the code you'll need to add to the parse map so that we'll be able to access the new function from the HTML page.

Listing 16-1

```
/////////////////////////////////////////////////////////////////////////
// command-parsing map

BEGIN_PARSE_MAP(CReportItExtension, CHttpServer)
    // Create one parse map for each report organization.
    // Organize the report by contact name.
    ON_PARSE_COMMAND(Name, CReportItExtension, ITS_I2 ITS_PSTR)
    ON_PARSE_COMMAND_PARAMS("integer=0 string=''")

    // Organize the report by ZIP code.
    ON_PARSE_COMMAND(ZIPCode, CReportItExtension, ITS_I2 ITS_PSTR)
    ON_PARSE_COMMAND_PARAMS("integer=0 string=''")

    // Display the extension usage instructions.
    ON_PARSE_COMMAND(Default, CReportItExtension, ITS_EMPTY)

    // Set the ISAPI Extension to automatically display the Default()
    // method if no other method is passed on the command line.
    DEFAULT_PARSE_COMMAND(Default, CReportItExtension)
END_PARSE_MAP(CReportItExtension)
```

Even though you only had to add four lines of code to make this example work, we're actually concerned with all six lines of code. The ON_PARSE_COMMAND( ) macro allows you to define a new function. Notice that we supply a function name, the class in which the function is supplied, and the type of parameters the function will use. (In this case, we'll have one integer and one string parameter for our special functions.) The ON_PARSE_COMMAND( ) macro requires a parameter entry, even if you don't need any parameters to make the function work. Notice that the Default( ) function uses a value of ITS_EMPTY since it doesn't need any parameters, but that our new functions, Name and ZIPCode, have a parameter of ITS_I2 for the integer parameter and ITS_PSTR for the string pointer.

That brings us to the ON_PARSE_COMMAND_PARAMS( ) macro on the next line. You have to tell Visual C++ how to deal with the parameters for your function. For example, if we had wanted to force the user to supply a string value for our function, we would simply have "string" in the ON_PARSE_COMMAND_PARAMS( ) macro. Since we don't absolutely have to have the user supply either the integer or string to use our function, I've supplied default values of 0 and '' (a blank string). Be aware that the query will fail if you require a parameter and the user doesn't supply it.

Finally, you need to tell Visual C++ which function to use as a default using the DEFAULT_PARSE_COMMAND( ) macro. Since the Default( ) method is just fine in this case, I didn't change the default setting. As previously mentioned, it's a good idea to get into the habit of providing the usage instructions for your ISAPI Extension in the Default( ) method.

Step 2—Adding Function Declarations

The second thing you'll need to do to the code is add the function declaration entries to the ReportIt.H file. Unless you modify the class specification to include your new functions, Visual C++ won't know anything about it and the DLL won't compile. Fortunately, all we need is the single-line entries shown in bold in Listing 16-2. I've included the surrounding code so that you know where to place the new entries.

isting 16-2

```
{
public:
    CDispStrExtension();
    ~CDispStrExtension();

// Overrides
    // ClassWizard generated virtual function overrides
        // NOTE - the ClassWizard will add and remove member functions here.
        //    DO NOT EDIT what you see in these blocks of generated code !
    //{{AFX_VIRTUAL(CDispStrExtension)
    public:
    virtual BOOL GetExtensionVersion(HSE_VERSION_INFO* pVer);
    //}}AFX_VIRTUAL

    // TODO: Add handlers for your commands here.
    // For example:

    void Default(CHttpServerContext* pCtxt);
    void Name(CHttpServerContext* pCtxt, int iType, LPTSTR lpszName);
    void ZIPCode(CHttpServerContext* pCtxt, int iType, LPTSTR lpszZIPCode);

    DECLARE_PARSE_MAP()

    //{{AFX_MSG(CDispStrExtension)
    //}}AFX_MSG
};
```

As you can see, adding the function call declaration is a pretty simple matter. At this point, though, you may be wondering where the CHttpServerContext* pCtxt part of the declaration came in. We certainly didn't declare it previously in any of the parse map macros. It turns out that the pCtxt parameter gets passed to your function by default. Remember from our previous discussion that the CHttpServer class automatically creates a CHttpServerContext object for every user request. This is where the parameter comes from. What you're getting is a pointer to the CHttpServerContext object associated with the user's call to your function. It's also the way that you keep multiple calls to your function separate—each call has a completely different object associated with it.

Step 3—Write the Functions

There is one last thing that we need to do to make this DLL function: add the function code to the ReportIt.CPP file. I added the function code right after the existing Default( ) function code. This function code isn't complete—we'll add some additional functionality in the following sections. However, this code does represent output you might create for a simple ISAPI Extension. The example also adds two other features: database access and the ability to use a custom <TITLE> tag for the HTML code. Listing 16-3 shows the two functions that I created for this example, along with the modified Default( ) method.

Listing 16-3

```
void CReportItExtension::Default(CHttpServerContext* pCtxt)
{
    // Start creating the Web page.
    StartContent(pCtxt);

    // Display the standard title.
    WriteTitle(pCtxt);

    // Display a helpful message.
    *pCtxt << _T("\r\n\r\n<CENTER><H1>");
    *pCtxt << _T("Welcome to the ReportIt ISAPI Extension");
    *pCtxt << _T("</CENTER></H1>\r\n\r\n");
    *pCtxt << _T("This ISAPI Extension allows you to display a report ");
    *pCtxt << _T("containing the information from the Address database ");
    *pCtxt << _T("we worked with in Chapter 9.<P>\r\n");
    *pCtxt << _T("Using this ISAPI Extension is easy.  All you need to ");
    *pCtxt << _T("do is call it with the name of one of the standard ");
    *pCtxt << _T("reports: Name or ZIPCode.  You can also supply two ");
    *pCtxt << _T("optional arguments:\r\n\r\n");
    *pCtxt << _T("<UL>\r\n\t<LI><STRONG>Type: </STRONG> 0 for overview and ");
    *pCtxt << _T("1 for detailed.\r\n\t");
    *pCtxt << _T("<LI><STRONG> Search Criteria: </STRONG> A name or ZIP ");
    *pCtxt << _T("Code that you want to search for.\r\n</UL>\r\n\r\n");

    EndContent(pCtxt);
}

// Display the report by name.
void CReportItExtension::Name(CHttpServerContext* pCtxt, int iType, LPTSTR lpszName)
{
    // Create a couple of local variables.
    CString   cDate;        // String representation of date.
    CString   cTime;        // String representation of time.
    CTime     oCurDate;     // Current date and time.
```

```
// Get the current date and store it in a string.
oCurDate = CTime::GetCurrentTime();
cDate = oCurDate.Format("%A, %d %B %Y");
cTime = oCurDate.Format("%I:%M %p");

// Start creating the Web page.
StartContent(pCtxt);

// Display the standard title.
WriteTitle(pCtxt);

// Display the time and date.
*pCtxt << _T("\r\n\r\nDate: ");
*pCtxt << _T(cDate);
*pCtxt << _T("<BR>\r\n");
*pCtxt << _T("Time: ");
*pCtxt << _T(cTime);
*pCtxt << _T("<P>\r\n");

// Display a report heading.
switch (iType)
{
case 0:
    *pCtxt << _T("\r\n<H1><CENTER>");
    *pCtxt << _T("Customer Contact by Name (Overview)");
    *pCtxt << _T("</CENTER></H1>\r\n");
    break;
case 1:
    *pCtxt << _T("\r\n<H1><CENTER>");
    *pCtxt << _T("Customer Contact by Name (Detailed)");
    *pCtxt << _T("</CENTER></H1>\r\n");
    break;
}

// Create a table and display the table headings.
*pCtxt << _T("\r\n<TABLE BORDER=3>");
*pCtxt << _T("\r\n\t<TR>");

// Display the correct headings for the type of
// report requested by the user.
switch (iType)
{
case 0:
    *pCtxt << _T("\r\n\t\t<TH>Name</TH>");
    *pCtxt << _T("\r\n\t\t<TH>Title</TH>");
    *pCtxt << _T("\r\n\t\t<TH>Company</TH>");
```

```
            *pCtxt << _T("\r\n\t\t<TH>Telephone</TH>");
            break;
        case 1:
            *pCtxt << _T("\r\n\t\t<TH>Name</TH>");
            *pCtxt << _T("\r\n\t\t<TH>Title</TH>");
            *pCtxt << _T("\r\n\t\t<TH>Company</TH>");
            *pCtxt << _T("\r\n\t\t<TH>Address</TH>");
            *pCtxt << _T("\r\n\t\t<TH>City</TH>");
            *pCtxt << _T("\r\n\t\t<TH>State</TH>");
            *pCtxt << _T("\r\n\t\t<TH>ZIP</TH>");
            *pCtxt << _T("\r\n\t\t<TH>Telephone 1</TH>");
            *pCtxt << _T("\r\n\t\t<TH>Telephone 2</TH>");
            *pCtxt << _T("\r\n\t\t<TH>Last Contact</TH>");
            break;
    }

    *pCtxt << _T("\r\n\t</TR>");

    // End the table.
    *pCtxt << _T("\r\n</TABLE>\r\n");

    // End the Web page.
    EndContent(pCtxt);
}


// Display the report by ZIP code.
void CReportItExtension::ZIPCode(CHttpServerContext* pCtxt, int iType, LPTSTR lpszZIPCode)
{
    // Create a couple of local variables.
    CString    cDate;        // String representation of date.
    CString    cTime;        // String representation of time.
    CTime      oCurDate;     // Current date and time.

    // Get the current date and store it in a string.
    oCurDate = CTime::GetCurrentTime();
    cDate = oCurDate.Format("%A, %d %B %Y");
    cTime = oCurDate.Format("%I:%M %p");

    // Start creating the Web page.
    StartContent(pCtxt);

    // Display the standard title.
    WriteTitle(pCtxt);

    // Display the time and date.
    *pCtxt << _T("\r\n\r\nDate: ");
```

```
*pCtxt << _T(cDate);
*pCtxt << _T("<BR>\r\n");
*pCtxt << _T("Time: ");
*pCtxt << _T(cTime);
*pCtxt << _T("<P>\r\n");

// Display a report heading.
switch (iType)
{
case 0:
    *pCtxt << _T("\r\n<H1><CENTER>");
    *pCtxt << _T("Customer Contact by ZIP Code (Overview)");
    *pCtxt << _T("</CENTER></H1>\r\n");
    break;
case 1:
    *pCtxt << _T("\r\n<H1><CENTER>");
    *pCtxt << _T("Customer Contact by ZIP Code (Detailed)");
    *pCtxt << _T("</CENTER></H1>\r\n");
    break;
}

// Create a table and display the table headings.
*pCtxt << _T("\r\n<TABLE BORDER=3>");
*pCtxt << _T("\r\n\t<TR>");

// Display the correct headings for the type of
// report requested by the user.
switch (iType)
{
case 0:
    *pCtxt << _T("\r\n\t\t<TH>Name</TH>");
    *pCtxt << _T("\r\n\t\t<TH>Title</TH>");
    *pCtxt << _T("\r\n\t\t<TH>Company</TH>");
    *pCtxt << _T("\r\n\t\t<TH>Telephone</TH>");
    break;
case 1:
    *pCtxt << _T("\r\n\t\t<TH>Name</TH>");
    *pCtxt << _T("\r\n\t\t<TH>Title</TH>");
    *pCtxt << _T("\r\n\t\t<TH>Company</TH>");
    *pCtxt << _T("\r\n\t\t<TH>Address</TH>");
    *pCtxt << _T("\r\n\t\t<TH>City</TH>");
    *pCtxt << _T("\r\n\t\t<TH>State</TH>");
    *pCtxt << _T("\r\n\t\t<TH>Telephone 1</TH>");
    *pCtxt << _T("\r\n\t\t<TH>Telephone 2</TH>");
    *pCtxt << _T("\r\n\t\t<TH>Last Contact</TH>");
    break;
}
```

```
*pCtxt << _T("\r\n\t</TR>");

// End the table.
*pCtxt << _T("\r\n</TABLE>\r\n");

// End the Web page.
EndContent(pCtxt);
}
```

This looks like a lot of code, but it really isn't. You'll find that many ISAPI Extensions use a lot of display-oriented code that tends to make the code look cumbersome. Let's look at the modifications to the Default( ) method first. The function itself is pretty easy to figure out. The first thing we do is tell Visual C++ to start a Web page. That's like adding the <HTML> and <HEAD> tags to a document. The second thing we do is output a title—just as if we were typing the <TITLE> tag into a document. The only way to override the default title is to override the WriteTitle( ) function—something that you can do if you'd like. Now that we've got a heading, it's time to create some body content. We have to use the stream operator to send the information. Notice that I freely use all of the HTML tags that you could use on any Web page in this example. Anything you can do with a standard HTML document, you can do with your ISAPI Extension. We'll see in just a few moments how all these tags work together to produce a Web page. You'll also want to notice that we send the string we got from the Web page back to the new Web page—you don't even have to convert the values to text to make them work. The final function call we use, EndContent( ), tells Visual C++ that we're done sending information. It's like adding the </HTML> to the end of the document. Just about any ISAPI Extension method will use these functions to create the Web page. Figure 16-1 shows what the Default Web page would look like at this point.

Note   *At this point you could compile the ISAPI Extension we've created and test it out—all you'll see is the report headings, not the actual report. Once you successfully compile it, move the DLL to your Web server. There are several logical places to put the DLL, but the two most common would be a Scripts directory or a special Controls directory. I normally keep all my controls in one place in a Controls directory to make them easy to locate, but the actual location you use isn't all that important. The only criteria are that the user be able to access the directory containing the DLL through your Web site and that you've marked the directory as executable using the Internet service manager provided with your Web server.*

One of the things you should have noticed in the source for Listing 16-3 is that we use a lot of C escape codes in the output for the Web page. This may seem a bit counterintuitive at first, and you don't actually have to include them, but using the escape codes will make your Web source easier to read. Figure 16-2 shows the output

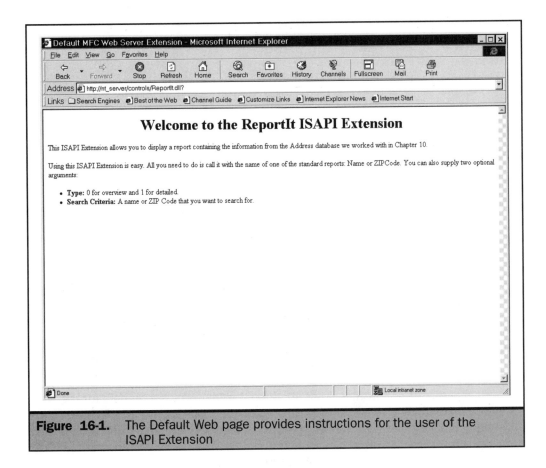

Figure 16-1. The Default Web page provides instructions for the user of the ISAPI Extension

from the Default( ) method. Notice that this code is clear, making it less difficult to debug than if you had to try to read all of the output in one big heap.

Now it's time to discuss the two report methods: Name( ) and ZIPCode( ). Both of these methods are about the same at the moment, so I'll discuss the special features for both at one time. The first thing we do in this case is create some variables for grabbing the system time from the server. It's important to note that this code is for the server and not for the client. If we had wanted to use the client's time, then we'd have to insert a script into the heading of the Web page output. Providing the user with the server's time and date makes it easier for the user to determine exactly what the data is based on, especially when they're overseas and unaware of local time at the company.

Getting and formatting the time comes next. Using the GetCurrentTime( ) method makes it easy to fill the CTime object. The Format( ) method makes quick work of formatting the date and time for display.

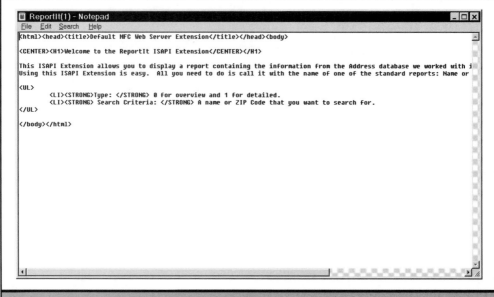

Figure 16-2. Using C escape codes in your ISAPI Extension makes the Web page source easier to read

At this point, we go through about the same display process as we did for the Default( ) method. However, it's important to note that user input will affect the kind of heading that gets displayed along with the number of columns in the table. An overview report contains simple information that the user is likely to need, while the detail report contains everything that the database has to offer. Figure 16-3 shows some typical output from the Name( ) method. In this case, you're looking at the detail report, but the other reports are similar in appearance. (We'll create a test Web page later in the chapter that will enable you to see these various outputs for yourself.)

Using Custom Titles

Take another look at Figures 16-1 and 16-3. You should notice that the title bar contents for both figures are the same—which is the default text that Visual C++ provides if you decide not to create your own Web page title. Look at the code in Figure 16-2 and you'll see that the <TITLE> tag is on one line with the rest of the header tags as well, which could make debugging of this area messy. Obviously, providing a distinct title for each Web page and a clean appearance for the Web source code are only two reasons for creating a custom <TITLE> tag, but they're very good ones.

Consider for a second, though, what would happen if you wanted to include some additional information like meta tags or scripts in the header. You would need some means for creating this content, but it's apparent you can't place this information in the

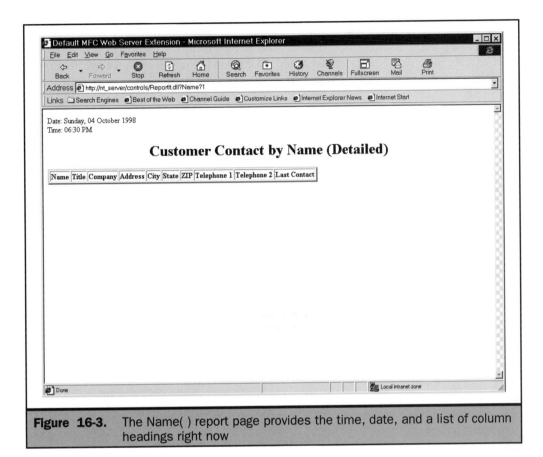

Figure 16-3. The Name( ) report page provides the time, date, and a list of column headings right now

output methods for the Web page—all of that content goes to the body area of the Web page. The answer is simple—you need to override the WriteTitle( ) method so that it produces the kind of result you want.

Unfortunately, overriding WriteTitle( ) isn't as straightforward as you might think. What you actually need to do is create a new method for your ISAPI Extension named GetTitle( ). The method can't take any inputs and must output an LPTSTR. Here's what the declaration will look like in the ReportIt.H header file (place it right after the ZIPCode( ) method declaration):

```
// Function for displaying a custom title.
LPCTSTR GetTitle( ) const;
```

If you want to create a unique <TITLE> tag for each of your output methods, then you'll also have to create a member variable and set it within each of the output methods so that GetTitle( ) will know which <TITLE> tag to output. I've chosen an int for the example application because then I can use a simple switch() to select one of the <TITLE> tag outputs in the GetTitle( ) method. Here's the declaration for the member variable—place it right after the GetTitle( ) declaration in ReportIt.H:

```
// Member variable that determines <TITLE> tag output.
 int iTitle;
```

Now that we have a method declaration and a member variable to track which <TITLE> tag to output, let's add some code to make this work. Listing 16-4 shows the GetTitle( ) method code you'll need to add to your ISAPI Extension for this example. Make sure you also add some code to set the iTitle value in each of the output methods: Default( ), Name( ), and ZIPCode( ).

Listing 16-4

```
LPCTSTR CReportItExtension::GetTitle() const
{
    // Choose one of the defined <TITLE> tags.
    switch (iTitle)
    {
    case 1:
        return "\r\nReportIt Default Page\r\n";
        break;
    case 2:
        return "\r\nReportIt Display by Name\r\n";
        break;
    case 3:
        return "\r\nReportIt Display by ZIP Code\r\n";
        break;
    }

    // return a default value.
    return "\r\nMake sure to set iTitle to an appropriate value.\r\n";
}
```

As you can see, the code in Listing 16-4 is fairly simple. We just return the appropriate <TITLE> tag value from GetTitle( ). There isn't anything special you can do beyond that—the text you return has to contain all of the tags and text that you want to appear in the header area. However, this is still an extremely powerful capability. Here's the Default page with its new title bar.

Defining the Database Connection

It's time to add the database connection to our ISAPI Extension. All that this connection will do is allow us to grab information from the Address database, then display the appropriate information in the right order on the report. The first thing we need to do is add the connection itself, which means adding an entry to the server's ODBC applet using the procedure found in the "Creating the Database Connection" section of Chapter 9. Make sure you add the connection to the System DSN tab of the ODBC Data Source Administrator dialog box or the connection may not work over an Internet connection.

> **Note**
> *You may have to alter the procedure in Chapter 9 slightly depending on how you have your server set up. The example code may require you to use SQL Server authentication in place of Windows NT authentication because the browser will log on to the Web server using an anonymous user ID. You can get around this problem by adding security to the ISAPI Extension—something we won't do in this example. Make sure that if you use SQL Server authentication, that you choose a Login ID value that is always valid like "sa."*

Once you add the connection, you need to start adding code to the ISAPI Extension. The first thing you need is database support. You add this to the StdAfx.H file as shown here:

```
// Add database support.
#include <afxdb.h>
```

Updating the Name( ) and ZIPCode( ) methods comes next. Listing 16-5 shows the changes you'll need to make in bold type. Most of this code should look familiar since we've talked about it in the past. The reason for dividing it into two additions in this case is to reduce the complexity of the programming problem and to allow for two testing stages—a very important consideration for an ISAPI Extension like this.

isting 16-5

```
// Display the report by name.
void CReportItExtension::Name(CHttpServerContext* pCtxt, int iType, LPTSTR lpszName)
{
    // Create a couple of local variables.
```

```
CString     cDate;          // String representation of date.
CString     cTime;          // String representation of time.
CTime       oCurDate;       // Current date and time.

// Create some variables for database access.
CDatabase           oDB;            // Database object.
CRecordset          oRS;            // Recordset object.
CCriticalSection    oCritical;      // Database operation critical section.
CString             oOpenStr;       // Database opening string.
CString             oSearch;        // Special search value.
CString             oField;         // Used to hold field values.
CString             oName;          // Used to hold name value.

// Set the GetTitle() value.
iTitle = 2;

// Get the current date and store it in a string.
oCurDate = CTime::GetCurrentTime();
cDate = oCurDate.Format("%A, %d %B %Y");
cTime = oCurDate.Format("%I:%M %p");

// Start creating the Web page.
StartContent(pCtxt);

// Display the standard title.
WriteTitle(pCtxt);

// Lock the critical section so that other users can't attempt to
// open the database.
oCritical.Lock();

try
{
    // Open the database.
    oDB.OpenEx(_T("DSN=AddressConnect"),
        CDatabase::openReadOnly | CDatabase::noOdbcDialog);

    // Assign the database to our recordset
    //(allows use of the database connection).
    oRS.m_pDatabase = &oDB;

    // Construct the standard query.
    oOpenStr = _T("SELECT LastName, FirstName, MiddleInitial, Title, ");
    oOpenStr = oOpenStr + _T("Company, Address1, Address2, City, State, ");
    oOpenStr = oOpenStr + _T("ZIP, Telephone1, Telephone2, LastContact ");
    oOpenStr = oOpenStr + _T("FROM dbo.Contacts");
```

```
    // See if there is a special search condition.
    oSearch = lpszName;
    if(!(oSearch == " "))
    {
        oOpenStr = oOpenStr + " WHERE LastName='" + _T(oSearch) + "'";
    }

    // Add remainder of query.
    oOpenStr = oOpenStr +  " ORDER BY LastName, FirstName";

    // Open the recordset.
    oRS.Open(CRecordset::snapshot,
        oOpenStr,
        CRecordset::none);
}
catch (CDBException* e)
{
    *pCtxt << _T("\n<H2><CENTER>Database Opening Error</H2></CENTER>\n\n");
    *pCtxt << _T(e->m_strError);
    *pCtxt << _T("\n<P>\n");
    *pCtxt << _T(e->m_strStateNativeOrigin);

    // Unlock the critical section.
    oCritical.Unlock();

    // End the document.
    EndContent(pCtxt);

    // Exit the ISAPI Extension
    return;
}

// Unlock the critical section now that we're done with the database.
oCritical.Unlock();

// Display the time and date.
*pCtxt << _T("\r\n\r\nDate: ");
*pCtxt << _T(cDate);
*pCtxt << _T("<BR>\r\n");
*pCtxt << _T("Time: ");
*pCtxt << _T(cTime);
*pCtxt << _T("<P>\r\n");

// Display a report heading.
switch (iType)
{
case 0:
```

```
        *pCtxt << _T("\r\n<H1><CENTER>");
        *pCtxt << _T("Customer Contact by Name (Overview)");
        *pCtxt << _T("</CENTER></H1>\r\n");
        break;
    case 1:
        *pCtxt << _T("\r\n<H1><CENTER>");
        *pCtxt << _T("Customer Contact by Name (Detailed)");
        *pCtxt << _T("</CENTER></H1>\r\n");
        break;
    }


    // Create a table and display the table headings.
    *pCtxt << _T("\r\n<TABLE BORDER=3>");
    *pCtxt << _T("\r\n\t<TR>");

    // Display the correct headings for the type of
    // report requested by the user.
    switch (iType)
    {
    case 0:
        *pCtxt << _T("\r\n\t\t<TH>Name</TH>");
        *pCtxt << _T("\r\n\t\t<TH>Title</TH>");
        *pCtxt << _T("\r\n\t\t<TH>Company</TH>");
        *pCtxt << _T("\r\n\t\t<TH>Telephone</TH>");
        break;
    case 1:
        *pCtxt << _T("\r\n\t\t<TH>Name</TH>");
        *pCtxt << _T("\r\n\t\t<TH>Title</TH>");
        *pCtxt << _T("\r\n\t\t<TH>Company</TH>");
        *pCtxt << _T("\r\n\t\t<TH>Address</TH>");
        *pCtxt << _T("\r\n\t\t<TH>City</TH>");
        *pCtxt << _T("\r\n\t\t<TH>State</TH>");
        *pCtxt << _T("\r\n\t\t<TH>ZIP</TH>");
        *pCtxt << _T("\r\n\t\t<TH>Telephone 1</TH>");
        *pCtxt << _T("\r\n\t\t<TH>Telephone 2</TH>");
        *pCtxt << _T("\r\n\t\t<TH>Last Contact</TH>");
        break;
    }


    *pCtxt << _T("\r\n\t</TR>");

    // Output the contents of the database.
    try
    {
        while (!oRS.IsEOF())
        {
            // Start a row.
            *pCtxt << _T("\r\n\t<TR>\n");
```

```
// Display the Name field.
*pCtxt << _T("\r\n\t\t<TD>");
oRS.GetFieldValue("LastName", oField);
oName = oField;
oRS.GetFieldValue("FirstName", oField);
oName = oField + " " + oName;
oRS.GetFieldValue("MiddleInitial", oField);
oName = oName.Left(oName.Find(' ') + 1) +
    _T(oField) +
    oName.Right(oName.GetLength() - oName.Find(' '));
*pCtxt << _T(oName);
*pCtxt << _T("</TD>");

// Display the Title field.
*pCtxt << _T("\r\n\t\t<TD>");
oRS.GetFieldValue("Title", oField);
*pCtxt << _T(oField);
*pCtxt << _T("</TD>");

// Display the Company field.
*pCtxt << _T("\r\n\t\t<TD>");
oRS.GetFieldValue("Company", oField);
*pCtxt << _T(oField);
*pCtxt << _T("</TD>");

// Process the special detail fields.
if (iType == 1)
{

    // Display the Address field.
    *pCtxt << _T("\r\n\t\t<TD>");
    oRS.GetFieldValue("Address1", oField);
    *pCtxt << _T(oField);
    *pCtxt << _T(", ");
    oRS.GetFieldValue("Address2", oField);
    *pCtxt << _T(oField);
    *pCtxt << _T("</TD>");

    // Display the City field.
    *pCtxt << _T("\r\n\t\t<TD>");
    oRS.GetFieldValue("City", oField);
    *pCtxt << _T(oField);
    *pCtxt << _T("</TD>");

    // Display the State field.
    *pCtxt << _T("\r\n\t\t<TD>");
    oRS.GetFieldValue("State", oField);
```

```
        *pCtxt << _T(oField);
        *pCtxt << _T("</TD>");

        // Display the ZIP field.
        *pCtxt << _T("\r\n\t\t<TD>");
        oRS.GetFieldValue("ZIP", oField);
        *pCtxt << _T(oField);
        *pCtxt << _T("</TD>");
    }

    // Display the Telephone field.
    *pCtxt << _T("\r\n\t\t<TD>");
    oRS.GetFieldValue("Telephone1", oField);
    *pCtxt << _T(oField);
    *pCtxt << _T("</TD>");

    // Perform some more detail processing.
    if (iType == 1)
    {

        // Display the second Telephone field.
        *pCtxt << _T("\r\n\t\t<TD>");
        oRS.GetFieldValue("Telephone2", oField);
        *pCtxt << _T(oField);
        *pCtxt << _T("</TD>");

        // Display the Last Contact field.
        *pCtxt << _T("\r\n\t\t<TD>");
        oRS.GetFieldValue("LastContact", oField);
        *pCtxt << _T(oField.Left(10));
        *pCtxt << _T("</TD>");
    }

    // Move to the next record.
    oRS.MoveNext();
    }
}
catch (CDBException* e)
{
    *pCtxt << _T("\n<H2><CENTER>Database Data Output Error</H2></CENTER>\n\n");
    *pCtxt << _T(e->m_strError);
    *pCtxt << _T("\n<P>\n");
    *pCtxt << _T(e->m_strStateNativeOrigin);
}

// End the table.
*pCtxt << _T("\r\n</TABLE>\r\n");
```

```
    // Declare a critical section before closing the database and recordset.
    oCritical.Lock();

    try
{

        // Close the recordset.
        if (oRS.IsOpen())
            oRS.Close();

        // Close the database.
        if (oDB.IsOpen())
            oDB.Close();
    }
    catch (CDBException* e)
    {
        *pCtxt << _T("\n<H2><CENTER>Database Closing Error</H2></CENTER>\n\n");
        *pCtxt << _T(e->m_strError);
        *pCtxt << _T("\n<P>\n");
        *pCtxt << _T(e->m_strStateNativeOrigin);
    }

    // Unlock the critical section.
    oCritical.Unlock();

    // End the Web page.
    EndContent(pCtxt);
}

// Display the report by ZIP code.
void CReportItExtension::ZIPCode(CHttpServerContext* pCtxt, int iType, LPTSTR
                        lpszZIPCode)
{
    // Create a couple of local variables.
    CString    cDate;        // String representation of date.
    CString    cTime;        // String representation of time.
    CTime    oCurDate;    // Current date and time.

    // Create some variables for database access.
    CDatabase        oDB;        // Database object.
    CRecordset        oRS;        // Recordset object.
    CCriticalSection    oCritical;    // Database operation critical section.
    CString            oOpenStr;    // Database opening string.
    CString            oSearch;    // Special search value.
```

```
CString                 oField;        // Used to hold field values.
CString                 oName;         // Used to hold name value.

// Create some variables for database display.
CString    oZIPCode;    // Current ZIP Code heading.
CString    oDisplay;    // The rest of the data to display.

// Set the GetTitle() value.
iTitle = 3;

// Get the current date and store it in a string.
oCurDate = CTime::GetCurrentTime();
cDate = oCurDate.Format("%A, %d %B %Y");
cTime = oCurDate.Format("%I:%M %p");

// Start creating the Web page.
StartContent(pCtxt);

// Display the standard title.
WriteTitle(pCtxt);

// Lock the critical section so that other users can't attempt to
// open the database.
oCritical.Lock();

try
{
    // Open the database.
    oDB.OpenEx(_T("DSN=AddressConnect"),
        CDatabase::openReadOnly | CDatabase::noOdbcDialog);

    // Assign the database to our recordset
    //(allows use of the database connection).
    oRS.m_pDatabase = &oDB;

    // Construct the standard query.
    oOpenStr = _T("SELECT LastName, FirstName, MiddleInitial, Title, ");
    oOpenStr = oOpenStr + _T("Company, Address1, Address2, City, State, ");
    oOpenStr = oOpenStr + _T("ZIP, Telephone1, Telephone2, LastContact ");
    oOpenStr = oOpenStr + _T("FROM dbo.Contacts");

    // See if there is a special search condition.
    oSearch = lpszZIPCode;
    if(!(oSearch == " "))
    {
        oOpenStr = oOpenStr + " WHERE ZIP='" + _T(oSearch) + "'";
    }
```

```
        // Add remainder of query.
        oOpenStr = oOpenStr +  " ORDER BY ZIP, LastName";

        // Open the recordset.
        oRS.Open(CRecordset::snapshot,
            oOpenStr,
            CRecordset::none);
    }
    catch (CDBException* e)
    {
        *pCtxt << _T("\n<H2><CENTER>Database Opening Error</H2></CENTER>\n\n");
        *pCtxt << _T(e->m_strError);
        *pCtxt << _T("\n<P>\n");
        *pCtxt << _T(e->m_strStateNativeOrigin);

        // Unlock the critical section.
        oCritical.Unlock();

        // End the document.
        EndContent(pCtxt);

        // Exit the ISAPI Extension
        return;
    }

    // Unlock the critical section now that we're done with the database.
    oCritical.Unlock();

    // Display the time and date.
    *pCtxt << _T("\r\n\r\nDate: ");
    *pCtxt << _T(cDate);
    *pCtxt << _T("<BR>\r\n");
    *pCtxt << _T("Time: ");
    *pCtxt << _T(cTime);
    *pCtxt << _T("<P>\r\n");

    // Display a report heading.
    switch (iType)
    {
    case 0:
        *pCtxt << _T("\r\n<H1><CENTER>");
        *pCtxt << _T("Customer Contact by ZIP Code (Overview)");
        *pCtxt << _T("</CENTER></H1>\r\n");
        break;
    case 1:
        *pCtxt << _T("\r\n<H1><CENTER>");
        *pCtxt << _T("Customer Contact by ZIP Code (Detailed)");
```

```
        *pCtxt << _T("</CENTER></H1>\r\n");
        break;
    }

    // Create a table and display the table headings.
    *pCtxt << _T("\r\n<TABLE BORDER=3 WIDTH=100%>");
    *pCtxt << _T("\r\n\t<TR>");

    // Display the correct headings for the type of
    // report requested by the user.
    switch (iType)
    {
    case 0:
        *pCtxt << _T("\r\n\t\t<TH>Name</TH>");
        *pCtxt << _T("\r\n\t\t<TH>Title</TH>");
        *pCtxt << _T("\r\n\t\t<TH>Company</TH>");
        *pCtxt << _T("\r\n\t\t<TH>Telephone</TH>");
        break;
    case 1:
        *pCtxt << _T("\r\n\t\t<TH>Name</TH>");
        *pCtxt << _T("\r\n\t\t<TH>Title</TH>");
        *pCtxt << _T("\r\n\t\t<TH>Company</TH>");
        *pCtxt << _T("\r\n\t\t<TH>Address</TH>");
        *pCtxt << _T("\r\n\t\t<TH>City</TH>");
        *pCtxt << _T("\r\n\t\t<TH>State</TH>");
        *pCtxt << _T("\r\n\t\t<TH>Telephone 1</TH>");
        *pCtxt << _T("\r\n\t\t<TH>Telephone 2</TH>");
        *pCtxt << _T("\r\n\t\t<TH>Last Contact</TH>");
        break;
    }

    *pCtxt << _T("\r\n\t</TR>");

    // Output the contents of the database.
    try
    {
        while (!oRS.IsEOF())
        {
        // Start a row.
        oDisplay = _T("\r\n\t<TR>\n");

        // Display the Name field.
        oDisplay = oDisplay + _T("\r\n\t\t<TD>");
        oRS.GetFieldValue("LastName", oField);
        oName = oField;
        oRS.GetFieldValue("FirstName", oField);
        oName = oField + " " + oName;
```

```
oRS.GetFieldValue("MiddleInitial", oField);
oName = oName.Left(oName.Find(' ') + 1) +
    _T(oField) +
    oName.Right(oName.GetLength() - oName.Find(' '));
oDisplay = oDisplay + _T(oName);
oDisplay = oDisplay + _T("</TD>");

// Display the Title field.
oDisplay = oDisplay + _T("\r\n\t\t<TD>");
oRS.GetFieldValue("Title", oField);
oDisplay = oDisplay + _T(oField);
oDisplay = oDisplay + _T("</TD>");

// Display the Company field.
oDisplay = oDisplay + _T("\r\n\t\t<TD>");
oRS.GetFieldValue("Company", oField);
oDisplay = oDisplay + _T(oField);
oDisplay = oDisplay + _T("</TD>");

// Process the special detail fields.
if (iType == 1)
{

    // Display the Address field.
    oDisplay = oDisplay + _T("\r\n\t\t<TD>");
    oRS.GetFieldValue("Address1", oField);
    oDisplay = oDisplay + _T(oField);
    oDisplay = oDisplay + _T(", ");
    oRS.GetFieldValue("Address2", oField);
    oDisplay = oDisplay + _T(oField);
    oDisplay = oDisplay + _T("</TD>");

    // Display the City field.
    oDisplay = oDisplay + _T("\r\n\t\t<TD>");
    oRS.GetFieldValue("City", oField);
    oDisplay = oDisplay + _T(oField);
    oDisplay = oDisplay + _T("</TD>");

    // Display the State field.
    oDisplay = oDisplay + _T("\r\n\t\t<TD>");
    oRS.GetFieldValue("State", oField);
    oDisplay = oDisplay + _T(oField);
    oDisplay = oDisplay + _T("</TD>");
}

// Display the ZIP field.
oRS.GetFieldValue("ZIP", oField);
if(!(oField == oZIPCode))
```

```
        {
                // Display a caption.
                if(iType == 0)
                    *pCtxt << _T("\r\n<TR><TH COLSPAN=4>ZIP Code: ");
                else
                    *pCtxt << _T("\r\n<TR><TH COLSPAN=9>ZIP Code: ");
                *pCtxt << _T(oField);
                *pCtxt << _T("</TH>");

                // Set the header value for the next loop.
                oZIPCode = oField;
        }

        // Display the Telephone field.
        oDisplay = oDisplay + _T("\r\n\t\t<TD>");
        oRS.GetFieldValue("Telephone1", oField);
        oDisplay = oDisplay + _T(oField);
        oDisplay = oDisplay + _T("</TD>");

        // Perform some more detail processing.
        if (iType == 1)
        {

                // Display the second Telephone field.
                oDisplay = oDisplay + _T("\r\n\t\t<TD>");
                oRS.GetFieldValue("Telephone2", oField);
                oDisplay = oDisplay + _T(oField);
                oDisplay = oDisplay + _T("</TD>");

                // Display the Last Contact field.
                oDisplay = oDisplay + _T("\r\n\t\t<TD>");
                oRS.GetFieldValue("LastContact", oField);
                oDisplay = oDisplay + _T(oField.Left(10));
                oDisplay = oDisplay + _T("</TD>");
        }


        // Display the data.
        *pCtxt << _T(oDisplay);

        // Move to the next record.
        oRS.MoveNext();
    }
}
catch (CDBException* e)
{
    *pCtxt << _T("\n<H2><CENTER>Database Data Output Error</H2></CENTER>\n\n");
```

```
        *pCtxt << _T(e->m_strError);
        *pCtxt << _T("\n<P>\n");
        *pCtxt << _T(e->m_strStateNativeOrigin);
    }


    // End the table.
    *pCtxt << _T("\r\n</TABLE>\r\n");

    // Declare a critical section before closing the database and recordset.
    oCritical.Lock();

    try
    {

        // Close the recordset.
        if (oRS.IsOpen())
            oRS.Close();

        // Close the database.
        if (oDB.IsOpen())
            oDB.Close();
    }
    catch (CDBException* e)
    {
        *pCtxt << _T("\n<H2><CENTER>Database Closing Error</H2></CENTER>\n\n");
        *pCtxt << _T(e->m_strError);
        *pCtxt << _T("\n<P>\n");
        *pCtxt << _T(e->m_strStateNativeOrigin);
    }

    // Unlock the critical section.
    oCritical.Unlock();

    // End the Web page.
    EndContent(pCtxt);
}
```

All that we've added to this code is the database-specific components not included in the previous section. Notice that you can effectively divide the code additions into three areas: open the database, display any data that it contains, then close the database. Every one of these functional areas is further divided into two sections: the code you want to execute, and the code required to catch any exceptions.

Unlike just about any other type of programming, you can't rely on Visual C++ to provide the user with any type of message at all when it comes to output from an ISAPI Extension. In other words, the user may not see anything at all if an error occurs. You absolutely must provide error trapping of some kind with a database application—even if that error trapping consists of displaying an error message for the user to read on their browser display. In fact, that's what the error trapping code for our example consists of; it displays an error message that will help the user make sense of an unexpected database occurrence.

The act of opening and closing the database also requires some special handling. Neither of these actions is inherently thread safe unless you take certain precautions. In this case, I chose to handle potential problems by declaring a critical section. Only one person at a time will be able to open or close the database. However, once the user obtains a snapshot of the contents of the database, they can use it to their heart's content. That's why there is no critical section declared for the data display sections of the code.

Opening the database is a two-step process. First, we open the database itself using the DSN created with the ODBC Data Source Administrator. When working with a database through a Web connection of any type, you must specify the CDatabase::noOdbcDialog option, which tells SQL Server not to display a Login dialog box. The reason is simple: SQL Server has no idea of how to send such a dialog box over the Internet connection. If you want the user to log in, then you must set up security through some other means—normally, a secure connection between the client and server. The DSN will need to be set up for using Windows NT security, since this is how the user will be identified. It's always easier to check your database application using a nonsecure connection first, then adding security later.

The second step of the opening process is to find a specific table and query it. This requires building a query string that contains the names of the fields you want to see (and in what order you want to see them), the name of the table, any search criteria, and finally, any indexing criteria. That's what all of the oOpenStr manipulation is about in the code—we're building a query string for the user based on input from the Web page. Notice that the search criteria (WHERE clause) is only added if the user actually provided search input on the Web page. Once this step is complete, you have a recordset containing all of the records that matched the criteria you specified.

There are two completely different styles of displaying the data in this case. The Name( ) method displays the contents of the database directly to the browser, while the ZIPCode( ) method builds a complex string, then uses it to display the data. Neither method is better than the other, though the first method does produce faster on-screen results and the second method preserves network bandwidth.

Closing the database is also a two-step process. First, you need to close the recordset, then close the database. It's absolutely essential to close the recordset first to ensure that any changes the user made get sent back to the database and that you don't lose any memory on the server.

A Simple ISAPI Extension Test

Now that you have a new ISAPI extension loaded on your Web server, it's time to test it out. Remember that our ISA only does one task: it displays the contents of the

Address database. However, you can ask the ISAPI Extension to perform that task in one of four ways and then further limit the display by requesting a specific last name or ZIP code. Listing 16-6 shows the HTML code you'll need to create a test Web page for our ISA. I used a name of ReportItTest.HTM for the resulting file.

isting 16-6

```
<HTML>
<HEAD>
<TITLE>ISAPI Extension Example</TITLE>
</HEAD>
<!-Create a form to display our pushbuttons.->
<FORM NAME="MyForm">
<!-Display a heading.->
<H3><CENTER>Display a Report ISAPI Extension</CENTER></H3>

<!-Display an edit box.->
Type a name or ZIP code search value (if desired):
<INPUT TYPE=TEXTBOX NAME="StringValue" SIZE=40><P>

<!-Display a couple of buttons.->
<CENTER>

<!-Perform the default action.->
<INPUT LANGUAGE="JavaScript"
    TYPE=BUTTON
    VALUE="Default"
    ONCLICK="window.location.href = 'controls/ReportIt.dll?'"><P>

<!-Display the Name Overview report->
<INPUT LANGUAGE="JavaScript"
    TYPE=BUTTON
    VALUE="Display Name Overview"
    ONCLICK="window.location.href = 'controls/ReportIt.dll?Name?0&'
    + MyForm.StringValue.value">

<!-Display the Name Detailed report->
<INPUT LANGUAGE="JavaScript"
    TYPE=BUTTON
    VALUE="Display Name Detail"
    ONCLICK="window.location.href = 'controls/ReportIt.dll?Name?1&'
    + MyForm.StringValue.value"><P>

<!-Display the ZIP Code Overview report.->
<INPUT LANGUAGE="JavaScript"
    TYPE=BUTTON
    VALUE="Display ZIP Code Overview"
    ONCLICK="window.location.href = 'controls/ReportIt.dll?ZIPCode?0&'
    + MyForm.StringValue.value">
```

```
<!-Display the ZIP Code Detailed report.->
<INPUT LANGUAGE="JavaScript"
    TYPE=BUTTON
    VALUE="Display ZIP Code Detail"
    ONCLICK="window.location.href = 'controls/ReportIt.dll?ZIPCode?1&'
    + MyForm.StringValue.value">

</CENTER>
</FORM>
</HTML>
```

While Internet Explorer is perfectly happy displaying <INPUT> tags that appear in the body of an HTML document (between the <BODY> and </BODY> tags), Netscape Navigator won't even recognize them. To make a form usable with all browsers, you must place the <INPUT> tags within a form (between a <FORM> and </FORM> tag pair).

The sample code isn't that complex. It consists of a heading, a text box, and five push buttons. The text box will contain the search value that the user wants to display. Notice that we don't include a submit action for our form, but use standard push buttons and JavaScript to initiate an action. This arrangement seems to work better than a submit when using an ISA that contains more than one function, as ours does.

There are a couple of things you should note about the JavaScript provided for the ONCLICK event of each push button. Notice that with the Default push button we only call the ReportIt.DLL itself—we don't specify a particular function. On the other hand, the other push buttons include both a function name and a string parameter as part of the ReportIt.DLL call. The two arguments for our functions are separated by an & (ampersand), just as they would be when using an ASP script or any other technology that accepts input from a Web page. We'll see how this works shortly.

Tip   *HTML doesn't send any text after a space in a text box to the server. For example, if you type **Hello World** in the text box, the server will only receive "Hello." You must place plus signs (+) between words to send them to the server. For example, if you send Hello+World to the server, it'll see "Hello World" (the Web server log will still show the + sign, which indicates the + sign is replaced with a space after it arrives at the server). This means adding some text manipulation code not shown in the example program to replace the spaces in the text box with plus signs before sending the string to the server.*

Open the test Web page and you'll see something like the page shown in Figure 16-4. As previously mentioned, this is a test page, so I didn't add too much formatting code, in order to keep things simple.

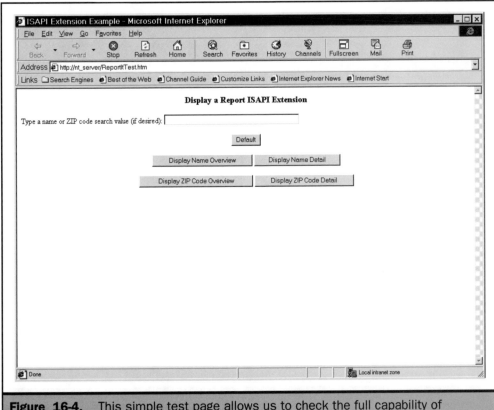

Figure 16-4.   This simple test page allows us to check the full capability of ReportIt.DLL

Note   *Make absolutely certain that the directory you use to store ReportIt.DLL on the server is marked for execute privileges from within the Internet services manager for your Web server. Otherwise, you'll see any number of errors from the browser as it attempts to execute the file—most of which won't tell you that it can't execute the file (the most common error is that the service isn't supported). Marking the directory for execute privileges within the operating system isn't sufficient to allow a visitor to your Web site to use the ISA you've created. In most cases, you can avoid any problems by ensuring the ISA DLL appears in the script directory for your Web server (assuming it has one).*

Let's test the ReportIt.DLL. Begin by clicking the Default button. What you should see is a default string like the one shown in Figure 16-1 that tells what task the ISAPI Extension performs. It's important to include this kind of functionality if anyone else

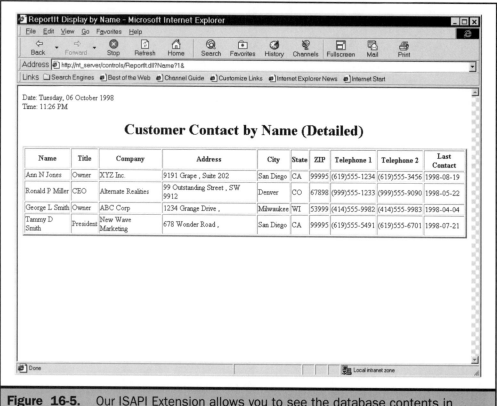

Figure 16-5.   Our ISAPI Extension allows you to see the database contents in name order

will be using your ISAPI Extension. Click the Back button (or the equivalent on your browser) to get back to the ReportItTest.HTM page. Now click the Display Name Detail button and you'll see something like the screen shown in Figure 16-5.

In this case we called ReportIt.DLL with the Name function. In addition, we told it to show the data in format 1, which is detailed. Since we didn't provide a search value, the browser displayed all of the names in the database. Click the Back button on your browser again, then click the Display ZIP Code Detail button. You'll see something like the screen shown in Figure 16-6.

Notice that this time the data is separated into ZIP code areas. If you look at the source code for this Web page, you'll see how all of those display statements in the ISAPI Extension code in Listing 16-6 worked together to produce this display. It's essential to know how to work with HTML tags in addition to C++ when creating an ISAPI Extension. You're literally responsible for generating both the ISAPI Extension code and the Web page code that the ISAPI Extension will display.

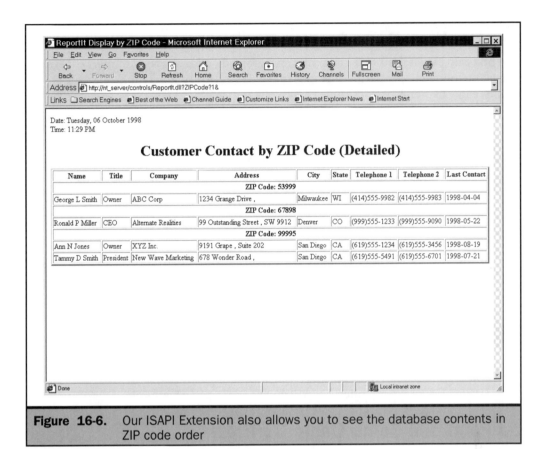

Figure 16-6. Our ISAPI Extension also allows you to see the database contents in ZIP code order

---

Tip

Visual Basic ISAPI Extension programmers have a much easier route to follow when it comes to creating the Web page design. They can rely on the output of Visual InterDev or even FrontPage to create the Web page. This means that a Web page design specialist could work on the Web page while the Visual Basic programmer works on the ISAPI Extension design.

Designing a Feedback Form Using Visual InterDev

We now have an ISAPI Extension that's capable of displaying the contents of our Address database on a Web page. The user can even perform a simple query on the Contacts table to acquire a subset of the information. However, the ISAPI Extension uses some fairly esoteric calling arguments and most users will be unable or unwilling to use it directly. That means we need a Web page to access the ISAPI Extension in a user-friendly manner.

Create the Web Page Project Shell

The first thing we'll need to do is create a program shell for our Visual InterDev Web page. The following procedure assumes that you've already worked through the example in Chapter 4.

1. Start Visual InterDev, if you haven't done so already. You'll see the New Project dialog box.
2. Choose the Visual InterDev Project folder on the New tab.
3. Highlight the New Web Project icon, then type **Addresses** in the Name field.
4. Click Open. You'll see the Web Project Wizard - Step 1 of 4 dialog box.
5. Select a Web server, if necessary, and choose the "Master mode" option.
6. Click Next. Visual InterDev will contact the Web server and create a project directory on it. You'll see the Web Project Wizard - Step 2 of 4 dialog box.
7. Since we don't need full text search on this Web site (we'll use the database to search), uncheck the "Create search.htm to enable full text searching" option.

> **Tip** *You could add a layout and theme at this point, but since you can add these features later on as well, it's usually a good idea to start with a plain Web site for testing purposes.*

8. Click Finish. Visual InterDev will create a new project for you.

Add a Form and Some Basic Controls

The current Web project doesn't have any forms, and we don't need many. At most, you'll need one form that allows the user to query the database and a second that provides help information. Depending on the complexity of the database application, you may need more help or data input forms. However, these are the only two types of pages that you'll need to add to the project.

For this project, all we'll add is the data entry form since we've covered help topics in several other chapters. Right-click the <Server Name>/Addresses folder and choose Add | HTML Page... from the context menu. You'll see the Add Item dialog box. Type **Default.HTM** in the Name field, then click Open. Visual InterDev will add the requested Web page to your project.

Right-click on the Default.HTM Web page entry in Project Explorer. Choose Set as Start Page from the context menu. The project is now ready to run from within Visual InterDev during the debugging process.

Let's begin with some simple controls on the Default.HTM page. Here's what the Web page looks like:

Table 16-1 contains a complete list of the controls and any properties you need to set (two radio buttons in the same group will have the same name).

Control ID	Property	Value
rbName	name	Order
	checked	True
rbZIP	name	Order
rbSimple	name	Detail
	checked	True
rbDetailed	name	Detail
txtSearch	name	txtSearch
cmdSearch	name	cmdSearch
	value	Search

Table 16-1.   Address Database Search Form Control Settings

Creating the Access Script

Now that we have a form with some buttons on it, we need a script to access the ISAPI Extension that we created in the previous section. Click the Source tab of the Default.HTM window, then choose the Script Outline window. Open the cmdSearch folder. You'll see a series of events like the ones shown here:

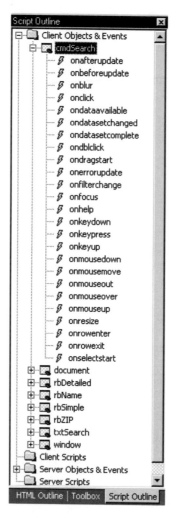

Double-click the onClick event to create a new handler. Listing 16-7 shows the code you'll need to make this Web page function as intended.

Listing 16-7

```
function cmdSearch_onclick() {
    // Determine the report type.
    if (rbName.checked == true)
        sReportName = 'Name';
    else
        sReportName = 'ZIPCode';

    // Determine the report detail.
    if (rbSimple.checked == true)
        sDetail = '0';
    else
        sDetail = '1';

    // Display the report.
    window.location.href = '../controls/ReportIt.dll?' +
                           sReportName + '?' +
                           sDetail + '&' +
                           txtSearch.value;
}
```

The function for selecting the right report is extremely simple in this case. Normally, you'd add some code to ensure the user entered the right kind of search criteria once you had tested this simple form of the function. As you can see, all that we really need to do is choose a report type, a level of detail, then execute the ISAPI Extension required to display the requested information.

Lessons Learned

This chapter has shown you just a bare glimmer of the true power of ISAPI Extensions, though the example is representative of the kinds of tasks you'll probably perform using one. It's important to realize that ISAPI Extensions have full access to the server and everything that it can do. Not only that, but in many ways an ISAPI Extension is much more efficient than any other means of accessing the server simply because you don't have to load and unload it all the time. Make sure you take these factors into consideration when deciding on which technology to use to create your next database access Web page.

Obviously, one of the down sides of using ISAPI Extensions is complexity. Just looking at the code for this relatively simple example tells you what you have to consider when it comes to planning a full-sized project. ISAPI Extension development is time consuming, and you'll definitely run into problems if you don't plan ahead for potential development delays. In sum, ISAPI is a great technology, but it's in its infancy and you need to consider that before devoting a large part of your development dollars to implementing a solution using this relatively new and untested technology.

Error trapping is not an option when it comes to an ISAPI Extension. The user won't have any way of knowing that an error even occurred if you don't at least trap it. Handling the error should consist of two tasks in most cases. First, you need to provide a human-readable error message to the user. This message should include diagnostic information the administrator and programmer can use to fix the problem. Second, error handling should attempt to fix as many problems as possible automatically. However, there is one caveat here as well. Our example ISAPI Extension didn't perform this task because any of the errors it would have trapped and handled would have been indicators of some severe problem with the database or its connection. Make sure you don't end up making problems with the error handling you provide.

Thread safety is also a must for ISAPI Extensions. There is no way to know when more than one user will attempt to use the same portion of the ISAPI Extension at the same time, resulting in possible damage to the data in your database. Make sure you use critical sections whenever necessary to ensure that data transactions are handled in a thread-safe manner. In fact, even though using too many critical sections will slow your code down, it's better to be safe than sorry. Use a critical section to protect your data whenever you have any doubt at all about the thread safety of the system.

Testing also requires special handling with an ISAPI Extension. Consider for a second the lack of real debugging tools. You must find ways to reduce overall testing environment complexity so that you can test in an environment that provides the least outside interference. In this case, we used a simple Web page containing only simple HTML controls and a little JavaScript to test the ISAPI Extension. Obviously, not every ISAPI Extension will be so easy to test using simple methods—you may actually need to break the testing process into fairly small, simple pieces. Make sure you do whatever it takes to test the ISAPI Extension as fully as possible, though, before using it in a production environment.

Chapter 17

**Making Your Own
Administration Tools**

P eople have been making their own tools for as long as people have been around. No matter how good your tool supplier is, or how effective those tools are, there are times when you have a special need that requires you to build your own tool. In fact, the making of custom tools has often led to the creation of whole new industries. While there are fewer opportunities for building your own unique tools in the world of computers, the need to do so still exists.

Microsoft provides several ways for you to create your own administrative tools. For example, the snap-in technology provided by Microsoft Management Console (MMC) provides an opportunity for a third-party supplier to provide custom tools to the market as a whole. In addition, Microsoft provides opportunities for Visual C++ developers to create custom snap-ins for single-company use.

There are other ways to customize your work environment, especially when it comes to working with Internet Information Server (IIS). One of the opportunities for Web customization that many people are likely to overlook is not found on the desktop—it's found within IIS. The ISAPI Filter not only allows you to create specialty extensions to your Web server that affect the user, you can also use them to change the way that you work with your own data.

> **Note**   *Make sure you look at the various theory sections at the beginning of Chapter 16 before proceeding with this chapter. It's important to know how ISAPI works as a whole before you begin looking at the specific example in this chapter.*

The first section of this chapter will provide a little theory on how to use the various filter types and what they can do for you. It's important to figure out precisely what kind of filter you need to use to perform a certain task prior to creating the ISAPI Filter project. That's what this section will help you determine—exactly what kind of ISAPI Filter you need to get the job done. Obviously, there is some level of overlap between the filter types, so it's also important to know when you might have multiple choices. This section will also make you aware of those multiple-choice situations.

The next section of this chapter is going to look at one way you can use an ISAPI Filter to create a tool. In this case, we'll create a simple ISAPI Filter that displays the data input from the client when requesting a certain Web page. You can use this type of information when diagnosing errors with Web pages that include scripts or make requests through an ISAPI Extension. For example, you could use this ISAPI Filter to diagnose errors with the Web pages used to access the ISAPI Extension in the previous chapter.

Once the ISAPI Filter is complete, we'll take a look at a typical Web page setup that could use this kind of tool. We'll design a simple Web site using Visual InterDev that will show how the various features of this ISAPI Filter could help you diagnose communication problems between client and server. Since the Internet does experience these kinds of problems on a regular basis, you'll find that this ISAPI Filter provides a valuable diagnostic aid.

Scenario

Your company has decided to fully embrace Microsoft's ISAPI technology for all new projects. As part of the process of making ISAPI easy for the programmers in your company to learn, you've been tasked with creating some tools to diagnose ISAPI problems not currently detected or supported by existing diagnostic aids. In other words, you need to create some custom tools to meet a particular need.

Obviously, the first thing you'll need to do is find out if there are some areas that programmers need help with right away. For example, client-to-server communication is one problem that many programmers experience since this particular area, while well documented, doesn't exactly appear in the local trade journals as a topic of discussion. Of course, this means you'll have to research how client headers work and what they mean to the server.

> **Tip**
>
> *When working as a tool developer, it's always a good idea to provide some means of getting input from the people that you're creating the tools for. In some cases, this means creating a formal request procedure so that you can document the need for the time and resources required for the tool. However, one overlooked problem is feedback from users once the tool is complete. It's unlikely that a tool will be precisely what everyone needs the first time around. One method you could use to get the input required to improve a tool is to distribute surveys. This would allow the people using your tool to express an opinion using formatting input. In addition, a well-worded survey can help users think about areas of tool use that they may not normally think about, which improves the type of input you receive.*

The first task is to create the ISAPI Filter that will insert itself in the data stream and show the user what kind of input the client is sending to the server. This will help the user create better scripts or correct input problems from a script. It'll also help users diagnose potential problems with ISAPI Extensions by either showing that the extension isn't receiving the input it requires or by showing that the extension is receiving good input and simply not processing it correctly.

The next task is to create a special test Web page. This Web page is important for two reasons. First, it shows the person using your ISAPI Filter what kind of output they should expect from the ISAPI Filter. Second, it allows the user to determine that the ISAPI Filter is installed correctly and working as anticipated. In other words, when they test their Web page using the ISAPI Filter tool, the user can be sure that any erroneous output is the result of their Web page code and not other network problems.

Defining Tool Requirements

Visual C++ makes the decision of choosing an ISAPI Filter type relatively easy, in most cases, since ISAPI Filters rely on message streams flowing between the client and server to activate and perform a task. In other words, part of the process for determining which kind of ISAPI Filter to use is choosing the right method for monitoring data flow. Each kind of ISAPI Filter monitors messages at a different point in the process.

So, what kind of messages can you monitor with an ISAPI Filter? There are seven types that you can choose to monitor as part of the skeleton building process with the ISAPI Extension Wizard. Obviously, you could create hooks to any number of Windows messages should you desire to do so. However, Table 17-1 shows the seven message types that you can choose by default.

Visual C++ Message Type	Code Method Equivalent	Description
Incoming raw data and headers	OnReadRawData	This filter message type allows you the greatest access to direct client input. You get a chance to see the client input before the server processes it. Of course, this means you'll have to dig through a lot of extraneous information before you find what you want, but you can also be sure that the server hasn't removed anything. This message filter uses the PHTTP_FILTER_RAW _DATA data structure to pass data to your application.
Outgoing raw data and headers	OnSendRawData	This filter message type allows you to see the final output of the server before the client sees it. You can modify the data as needed after the server has done everything normally done to the data stream. Again, you'll go through a lot of extraneous information using this type of filter, but then you can also be sure that the client will see exactly what you want it to see. This message filter uses the PHTTP_FILTER_RAW _DATA data structure to pass data to your application.

Table 17-1. ISAPI Filter Message Types

Visual C++ Message Type	Code Method Equivalent	Description
Post-preprocessing of the request headers	OnPreprocHeaders	Use this filter message type if you want the server to perform some preprocessing of the incoming data before your filter sees it. In most cases, you'll get to see everything of value that the server will see, without dealing with a lot of low-level information first. The advantage to this particular message filter type is that you don't have to perform a lot of data massaging to get a desired effect. Obviously, you'll have to be certain that the server won't change the data in some way before you see it. This message filter uses the PHTTP_FILTER _PREPROC_HEADERS data structure to pass data to your application.
Client authentication requests	OnAuthentication	Your client will get called as part of the user authentication process if you hook this message. Doing so allows you to create customized authentication routines. Obviously, you can still call on the standard processing method to complete the task once you complete any custom processing. This message filter uses the PHTTP_FILTER _AUTHENT data structure to pass data to your application.
URL mapping requests	OnUrlMap	Hiding data locations on your server is one reason to hook this message. For example, you may not want a user to know about a virtual directory located on your server, so you redirect the message stream there after the server passes it to you. This process is called mapping a logical address to a physical location on the server. This message filter uses the PHTTP_FILTER _URL_MAP data structure to pass data to your application.

Table 17-1.   ISAPI Filter Message Types (continued)

Visual C++ Message Type	Code Method Equivalent	Description
Server log writes	OnLog	There is any number of reasons to write information to the logs on your server. You may want to provide enhanced message information, hide entries for secret locations on your Web server, or just monitor the logs for specific kinds of entries and raise a flag for the administrator or Webmaster. This message filter uses the PHTTP_FILTER _LOG data structure to pass data to your application.
End of connection	OnEndOfNet-Session	This filter message type allows you to detect the time when the client disconnects from the server. In essence, it's too late to really do anything for the client except send a goodbye message. However, you can use this hook to perform postprocessing of a session. For example, a user may have uploaded data that needs to be verified and placed in a database. Looking for the end of the connection would be a good time to perform this kind processing. That way, your database would always contain up-to-date information. There aren't any data structures associated with this message filter.

Table 17-1. ISAPI Filter Message Types (continued)

As you can see, there's a message-monitoring point to accomplish just about any task. In addition, most message types provide a custom structure that'll make it easy for you to grab certain types of information from the message stream. The following sections describe the most commonly used message types in more detail.

Post-Preprocessing of the Request Headers

There are two messages that allow you to process the incoming and outgoing raw data and headers. However, in most cases, you actually get too much information when looking at raw data, and it's always in a difficult to parse format. Working with the preprocessed request headers, on the other hand, is relatively easy and provides you with just about everything you would need to know about the client request. Before you can really use a request header though, you have to have some idea of what it means.

The various standards committees on the Internet have provided a wealth of request types that a client can make. In addition, you'll find that various browsers have special requests that they support. It doesn't take too long to figure out that you could literally spend all your time monitoring requests from various users to find just one piece of information that you actually need. Fortunately, there's a way to make things a bit easier if all you plan to do is maintain statistics or provide some type of header enhancement. The following list describes the three standard pieces of information that you'll always get from a client:

- **Method**   A method usually defines what the client wants to do. The most common methods that you'll see for a client accessing a Web page are get and post. You'll also find that this standard part of the request header is the most flexible from the client's perspective since there are more than a few standard methods that servers need to respond to.

- **URL**   Every request has to provide a URL of some kind; otherwise, the server can't provide any information in return.

- **Version**   There are several versions of HTTP out now, so it's important to know what version the browser is using. The server normally needs to avoid using special responses with browsers that support older versions of HTTP.

A request header can contain a lot of other information; it just depends on what kind of service the client is requesting. The least complex request headers are for Web services, which is what we'll examine in this chapter. News server and mail server requests become quite a bit more complex as the request header needs to include things like from and date request headers. Here's a list of the standard request headers (though many more exist and there are lots of different options you can use to modify the results produced with the ones in this list).

- **From**   The user's name (normally used with mail requests or for logging purposes). There's no guarantee that the name is actually accurate, so you couldn't use it for security or authentication purposes.

- **Accept**   Provides a list of content types that the client can accept from the server. Each content type is separated by a comma. Parameters for a given content type are separated by a semicolon. Typical content types include audio/mpeg for MPEG audio files and image/jpeg for JPEG images. You may also see wildcard combinations like *.* for all files or audio/* for all audio file formats. Every browser must accept the text/plain and text/html content types as a minimum.

- **Accept-Encoding**   This is similar to the Accept request header, but it defines content encoding types. A typical encoding type would be x-zip for files using the ZIP compression method.

- **Accept-Language**   This is similar to the Accept request header, but it defines the preferred language. Language examples include en for generic English, de for generic German, and en_UK for British English.

- **User-Agent**   The browser will identify itself in this request header. You'll normally see the product name, followed by a slash, followed by the version number.

- **Referrer**   In some cases, you'll see this request header that identifies the Web site that referred the user to your site. It comes in handy for determining whether an advertising banner or link on another site is having much of an effect on your site. This request header can also be used to help find bad links or to perform back tracing to see how a user searches for your site.

- **Authorization**   You'll find security information in this request header. There isn't any specific format since every security scheme uses a different method of presenting itself. Some authentication methods are as simple as a user name and password passed in clear text. Check the documentation for your particular authentication agent for details on what you'll find in this particular request header.

Web Link   *Learn about basic authentication at http://www.w3.org/History/1993/WWW/ AccessAuthorization/. This site provides a complete overview along with links to other pertinent information about basic authentication. Pretty Good Privacy (PGP) maintains a site at http://pilot.msu.edu/user/heinric6/pgp.htm. Not only will you find out about this authentication method, but you can also get details on two books that describe PGP. Kerberos, a newer authentication method, is explained at http://www.cisco.com/warp/public/106/. Another good place to look for Kerberos information is http://www.con.wesleyan.edu/~triemer/network/kerberos/ kerberos_tcp.html. This site includes both white paper and newsgroup links.*

- **Charge-To (or ChargeTo)**   Some sites charge for the information they provide. This request header tells whom to charge for services. The first word of this request header always contains the specification of the namespace providing the charging authority. The exact format of the rest of the header is determined by the charging authority.

- **If-Modified-Since** A browser or proxy server will use this request header if it simply wants to see if the data on a site has changed since a given date. If the data hasn't changed, then the server sends a 304 (not modified) reply in place of the 200 (OK) reply. The server won't download any data to the browser if the data hasn't changed since the specified date.

- **Pragma** For all intents and purposes, this request field is more like a macro than anything else. It simply tells the server to perform a specific task. The only Pragma entry that's defined right now is no-cache. It tells a proxy server to download a new copy of a page from the Web server even though the local content hasn't expired yet. Other Pragma values are possible, but both server and client would need to be designed to understand them.

Every request header consists of one word (multiple words can be linked into a single word using hyphens or underscores) followed by a colon. For example, the from request header that I mentioned earlier looks like this: From: <User Name>. The single word followed by a colon is a standard method of identifying a new request header, which means that you'll want to avoid using this syntax for standard text in any response headers that you create or request headers that you modify. You'll use this syntax when asking to look at a specific request header (there are special keywords for the three standard headers that I mentioned earlier).

Client Authentication Requests

There are lots of ways to verify that a user is supposed to access a particular Web site. For example, you could use some form of digital certification. However, the most common way of verifying access rights is still the client authentication request. The client normally issues this request when the server sends a 401 Access Denied error message in response to a URL mapping request.

As a result, the first thing that a filter would need to do is get some input from the user, which usually consists of a user name and a password. Once a filter has determined that the user has provided some input, it can simply pass control to the server for verification. Of course, this isn't always what you want. You may want to perform some additional processing within the filter that the server doesn't normally do. The filter may also have to provide some additional functionality in the form of decryption or perhaps even specialized error message handling. The following list gives you some ideas on the additional features that a security filter can provide:

- **Decryption** You can always choose to encrypt the password and user name at the client end. This means decrypting it at the server end as well. An ISAPI filter is perfect for this purpose.

- **Authentication** Windows NT doesn't force you to use the built-in authentication. You can always choose to authenticate users yourself and give them an appropriate level of security. For that matter, you could perform an authentication, then assign the user to a group and let Windows NT take care of the details. There are a number of different authentication scenarios.

■ **Custom error handling** You may not like the way that Windows NT handles errors. An ISAPI filter can provide at least limited error handling. Of course, the precise level of error handling you provide is determined by the client as well as the server, which means you'll want to have control over which browser the user uses for access.

■ **Specialized access handling** There are situations when you may not want everyone to have 24-hour access to your Web site. Neither IIS nor Windows NT currently provides any method for shutting down your Web server to the average user while keeping it open for everyone else. An ISAPI Filter can provide access based on the current time (or any other criteria for that matter). You may even restrict access to certain sites based on server load.

URL Mapping Requests

One of the main elements of any client request is the URL that the client wants to retrieve from the server and display for the user. URLs are designed to give the client and server a common ground for identifying a specific resource that is owned by the server and desired by the client. URL mapping is a process where you can redirect a user's request to a more specific, better-controlled, or even hidden area of your Web server. The user can enter the URL they want to look at, and an ISAPI Filter can send them to the most appropriate place to look at the requested information, even if it isn't the originally requested URL. In other words, URL mapping provides the means for giving the user exactly what they want by using a generic input method available to all browser types on an equal basis. The following list gives you some ideas of when URL mapping is especially important:

■ **Hidden information** You may want to keep hackers guessing about where you actually store information on your Web server. Virtual directories provide one method of redirecting traffic, but you can use an ISAPI Filter for this purpose as well. The advantage to using an ISAPI Filter is that you can make changes to your mapping configuration with ease, something that would take a lot of time when using virtual directories.

■ **Browser differences** Every day seems to bring yet another browser compatibility problem to light. The latest problem is how various browsers use Java. You can take several routes to fix these browser compatibility problems, one of which is to maintain two separate sets of pages: one for Netscape and another for Microsoft. An ISAPI Filter can detect which browser is knocking at your door and redirect it as needed.

■ **Company-specific agenda** Imagine for a second that you're a user who wants to access the company's Web site with the least amount of effort. Now, imagine you're a manager who wants to use various Web pages for different purposes based on the day of the week. An ISAPI Filter could read the system clock and redirect a user's request to the right Web page; all they would need to do is type in the same URL every day to get to the right Web page on your server. You could make it as simple as typing **http://www.mycompany.com/today**. For that matter, you could simply make this the user's home page and they would see the specific Web page for a given day.

- **Dynamic reconfiguration**   There may be times when your Web server gets overwhelmed with requests. Wouldn't it be nice if you could detect this condition, then ask another server to help out? ISAPI Filters can do just this. They can help you detect conditions that would normally take your server offline and redirect those requests to another server with a lighter load.

- **Custom pages**   What if someone is trying to access your Web site and they either don't have the correct software installed or don't belong there in the first place? You can actually create a Web page within your ISAPI Filter and send it to the client. For example, if someone with an old version of Microsoft Internet Explorer visits your Web site, you could tell them where to download the latest version. It doesn't matter what URL they type in; your ISAPI Filter could detect the condition and react to it.

- **Web site statistics**   You've probably seen more site counters than you care to remember on the Internet. However, most of these counters have the same problem: they can actually miscount the number of people visiting a site. In addition, you really don't know if the person has visited a particular area of your Web site using this method. In some cases, URL mapping may not involve moving a user from one location to another. You may simply want to monitor their movement between various areas of your site and then record those movements for later use. This is especially important when you want to create a virtual directory setup when the normal logging methods may not work. In other words, the logging methods we looked at in Chapter 12 would produce the wrong results because the user isn't actually going to the directory they first requested.

These are just a few of the potential uses for URL mapping on a Web site. You'll find that URL mapping is one of the more useful things that you can use an ISAPI Filter for. The short take on all this is that you can use URL mapping as a traffic cop on your Web server, it helps redirect traffic as needed to keep things moving.

Server Log Writes

Monitoring user activity is an essential part of maintaining any Web site. For one thing, you want to make sure that hackers haven't discovered a way to get into your Web site, and from there potentially into your network. There are other uses for monitoring as well. For example, you may simply want to know how popular a particular Web page is or if a new Web page has attracted the kind of attention that you originally intended it to.

There are actually two steps in the monitoring process. First, you have to collect a superset of data required for any purpose. In other words, you need to collect the sum total of all the data required to fulfill the needs of any reports you create later. Second, you have to organize that data in an easy-to-use format and output it as a report. This second step may be very important from a user perspective, but you won't be able to do it without making sure you get the data required for the report first.

Let's look at the first step in the monitor process, why you want to collect the information. There are lots of reasons to track server access. The following list provides a few ideas. This is a generic list, which means that you'll probably find reasons that are specific to your situation. What you want to do during this process is come up with a goal for your data collection.

- **Raw data monitoring** There are times when the server will actually hide a potential problem from you. You can create an ISAPI Filter that actually monitors the raw input stream, then extract what you want or save everything that the client sends. Of course, saving everything would produce some pretty big files. The idea here is that you can monitor the stream and then pick what you want to log.

- **Message alerts** Some sites actually monitor incoming data for specific key words. The standard logs created for you by IIS contain log entries for every visitor. What if you don't need to know about every visitor? What if your main goal is to check the input from a few key visitors? An ISAPI Filter can help you perform this kind of monitoring. It allows you to choose specific messages based on keyword searches or other criteria of your choosing.

- **Reporting by location** It's important to know how a new idea is working out. You may want to know how many people are visiting a test location on your Web site and how long they stay to look at it. The default logs provided by IIS will allow you to determine this information, but you'd have to wade through all of the logs for every part of your Web site. You may want to provide a special log just for the test sites, which would make it a lot easier to find out where people are going and what they're doing.

- **URL remapping** Depending on how you have your site set up, you may want to know how many people visit your site and need a URL remapped to another location. This kind of information could tell you things like how many people are finding old site locations vs. new ones.

- **Statistical information** We'll see later that there are all kinds of ways to get statistical information for your Web site by logging various events. For example, you might look at the raw data to see where someone is visiting from or what ISP they use. You might even record specific server events like the number of times that someone requests secure access during the day. The actual number of uses is unlimited.

■ **Custom reports** Some people just don't like the logs created by IIS. If you're using a small- to medium-sized Web site, there isn't any reason to invest in an expensive reporting program just so that you can see your logs in plain English (or whatever other language you're using). An ISAPI Filter can easily replace the standard IIS logs with something that's easy to understand and in the format you want. You can also use this technique to provide extended reports. For example, you may want to know more information about the client than just the user name and location. Creating a custom report is one way to ensure the extra information you want appears in one place. Obviously, the amount of information that you want to include is only limited by your imagination and what the server and client are able to provide.

Microsoft does provide some standard logging options, and you may choose to simply modify one of these existing formats rather than come up with your own. In other words, your ISAPI Filter would simply modify the log entries that would normally get made by IIS anyway. This method has the advantage of allowing you to modify the logs to your needs, but not have to come up with a unique log format of your own. In addition, there are two log file formats. You can log information to standard text files and then view and edit the information in any word processor; or you can log information to SQL/ODBC data files and use the resources of your database management programs to work with log information. Here are the common log file formats.

■ Microsoft IIS Log File Format

■ NCSA Common Log File Format

■ ODBC Logging

■ W3C Extended Log File Format

Whatever log format you use, there are some basic pieces of information you can expect to find in most of them. Table 17-2 shows what kind of information you'll normally find in one of the common log file formats. Note that this is a superset of the information you'll find—not all log formats support every data field shown in the table.

Creating an ISAPI Filter Using Visual C++

The previous section told how you could use an ISAPI Extension to your advantage when constructing a Web site. What we'll do in this section is look at the process for building your own ISAPI Filter. The following sections will take you through the process of creating, developing, and eventually testing the ISAPI Filter. Obviously, the simple test program we create in this section will only verify that the ISAPI Filter is installed on the server correctly and performing its function at least partially. We'll develop a more complete test program in the Visual InterDev section that follows.

Field Name	Meaning	Data Type	Field Size
ClientHost	Client's IP address	Character	50
Username	Client's user name, if a user account logon is initiated	Character	50
LogDate	Date of access	Character	12
LogTime	Time of access	Character	15
Service	Service accessed: W3SVC=Web service MSFTPSVC=FTP service GopherSVC= Gopher service	Character	20
Machine	Name of server that was accessed	Character	20
Serverip	IP address of server (useful if a server has multiple IP addresses)	Character	50
Processingtime	Processing time, in milliseconds	Integer	N/A
Bytesrecvd	Bytes received from user	Integer	N/A
Bytessent	Bytes sent to user	Integer	N/A
Servicestatus	Service status code: 200: Indicate the success of an operation. 300: Indicate the data has been moved. 400: Client errors like incorrect syntax. 500: Server errors like no support for a requested function.	Integer	N/A
Win32status	Windows NT status code (0 means no error)	Integer	N/A
Operation	Name of the operation (type of command)	Character	200
Target	Target of the operation (what the client requested)	Character	200
Parameters	Operation parameters	Character	200

Table 17-2.   Field Characteristics for Common IIS Log File Formats

Creating an ISAPI Filter Shell

Interestingly enough, the process for starting the ISAPI Filter is just about the same as the one for creating an extension. In fact, you'll even use the same wizard to get the job done, though the steps you'll use will be slightly different. The following steps will help you create a program shell:

1. Start Visual C++ if you haven't done so already.

2. Use the File | New command to display the New dialog box. Select the ISAPI Extension Wizard. (Even though we're creating a filter, you'll still need to use the ISAPI Extension Wizard to do it.)

3. Type the name of the ISA filter you want to create. I used ViewMap for the example ISA, but you could use any name that you want.

4. Click OK. You'll see the ISAPI Extension Wizard - Step 1 of 1 dialog box. This is where you'll select the various characteristics for your ISA. There are three main areas to the dialog box. You can choose to create a filter by checking the first check box and an extension by checking the second check box. The third area defines how you'll link MFC into your application.

5. Check the filter option, and uncheck the extension option. (Notice that adding the filter also adds another step to the process.) You'll want to provide a short, concise statement of what your ISA does in the Filter Description field. The description appears as a string that you can use within the DLL as needed. This description won't show up in the Properties dialog box when someone opens it for your ISA, so you'll want to add some additional text to the version information for your DLL as well.

6. Type **View the URL mapping requests from the client** in the Filter Description field. Here's what your dialog box should look like at this point.

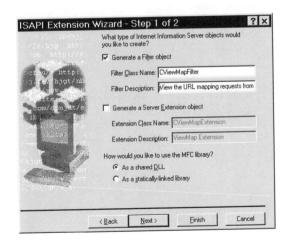

7. Click Next. You'll see the ISAPI Extension Wizard - Step 2 of 2 dialog box shown here. This is the page you'll use to select the events and type of monitoring your filter will provide. There are three areas to consider. See the sidebar entitled "Choosing Filter Options" to get more details about these options. Make sure you also read the beginning of this chapter for a full description of the various message-monitoring options.

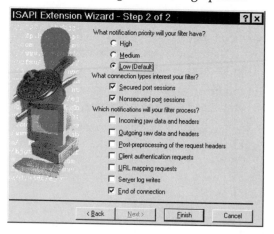

8. Check the "URL mapping requests" check box, and uncheck the "End of connection" check box. We want to activate our filter when the user requests specific kinds of access to the server since we're creating a simple filter to keep some log entries classified.

9. Click Finish. You'll see a New Project Information dialog box like the one shown here. Make sure you double check all the settings for your filter because the New Project Information page provides a detailed breakdown of the events that it'll get to see.

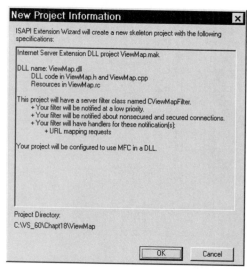

10. Click OK. The ISAPI Extension Wizard will create the required program shell for you.

Adding Some Code

The coding portion of this example is short and to the point. Filters can quickly get out of hand in the complexity department, and debugging them is fairly difficult. In most cases, you'll want to make your filter programs as short as possible. Modularization is a big help as well when it comes time to troubleshoot a faulty filter. Listing 17-1 shows the code you'll need to add to the OnUrlMap( ) function to make it work.

isting 17-1

```
DWORD CViewMapFilter::OnUrlMap(CHttpFilterContext* pCtxt,
    PHTTP_FILTER_URL_MAP pMapInfo)
{
    CString    oBuffer;     // Buffer for client output.
    DWORD      dwSize;      // Size of the buffer.
    LPVOID     pvOutput;    // Client output.

    // Send a response header so that the browser will display our data.
    pCtxt->ServerSupportFunction(SF_REQ_SEND_RESPONSE_HEADER, NULL, NULL, NULL);

    // Create the usual header.
    oBuffer = "\r\n<HTML>";
    oBuffer = oBuffer + "\r\n<HEAD>";
    oBuffer = oBuffer + "\r\n<TITLE>URL Mapping Test Page</TITLE>";
    oBuffer = oBuffer + "\r\n</HEAD>";
    oBuffer = oBuffer + "\r\n<BODY>";
    dwSize = oBuffer.GetLength();
    pvOutput = LPTSTR(LPCTSTR(oBuffer));
    pCtxt->WriteClient(pvOutput, &dwSize, 0);

    // Display a page heading.
    oBuffer = "\r\n<CENTER><H2>URL Mapping Example</H2></CENTER>";
    dwSize = oBuffer.GetLength();
    pvOutput = LPTSTR(LPCTSTR(oBuffer));
    pCtxt->WriteClient(pvOutput, &dwSize, 0);

    // Display the requested URL.
    oBuffer = "\r\nRequested URL: ";
    dwSize = oBuffer.GetLength();
    pvOutput = LPTSTR(LPCTSTR(oBuffer));
    pCtxt->WriteClient(pvOutput, &dwSize, 0);
    oBuffer = LPTSTR(pMapInfo->pszURL);
    dwSize = oBuffer.GetLength();
    pvOutput = LPTSTR(LPCTSTR(oBuffer));
```

```
    pCtxt->WriteClient(pvOutput, &dwSize, 0);

    // Display the default redirection.
    oBuffer = "<P>\r\nDefault Redirection: ";
    dwSize = oBuffer.GetLength();
    pvOutput = LPTSTR(LPCTSTR(oBuffer));
    pCtxt->WriteClient(pvOutput, &dwSize, 0);
    oBuffer = LPTSTR(pMapInfo->pszPhysicalPath);
    dwSize = oBuffer.GetLength();
    pvOutput = LPTSTR(LPCTSTR(oBuffer));
    pCtxt->WriteClient(pvOutput, &dwSize, 0);

    // Display the contents of the response header.
    oBuffer = "<P>\r\nResponse Header Contents:<BR>";
    dwSize = oBuffer.GetLength();
    pvOutput = LPTSTR(LPCTSTR(oBuffer));
    pCtxt->WriteClient(pvOutput, &dwSize, 0);
    pCtxt->ServerSupportFunction(SF_REQ_SEND_RESPONSE_HEADER, NULL, NULL, NULL);

    // Create the usual footer.
    oBuffer = "\r\n</BODY>\r\n</HTML>";
    dwSize = oBuffer.GetLength();
    pvOutput = LPTSTR(LPCTSTR(oBuffer));
    pCtxt->WriteClient(pvOutput, &dwSize, 0);

    // return the appropriate status code
    return SF_STATUS_REQ_FINISHED_KEEP_CONN;
}
```

The first thing you should know is that this test page only reports the contents of the PHTTP_FILTER_URL_MAP data structure. We won't actually do anything with the information. Normally, you would change one or more data members to redirect the user to another Web page based on some criteria like browser type or security restrictions.

Unlike an ISAPI Extension, you won't find a lot of built-in Visual C++ help for creating your Web page with an ISAPI Filter. That's because an ISAPI Filter normally doesn't interact with the user except in the way we're using it—to display an informational message. The first thing we need to do is send a response header to the browser using the ServerSupportFunction( ) function call. You'll use the SF_REQ_SEND_RESPONSE_HEADER service request to automatically create the header. This header tells the browser that it can display the rest of the data and the status of the Web page. I'll show you what this looks like when we view the actual output from the program.

You can also use the AddResponseHeaders( ) function to send a response header to the client. However, in most cases, you'll want to use the ServerSupportFunction( ) call by itself because it requires less work to use.

Once the browser is ready to display the data we want to show, we can create some output, then send it to the client. You'll do this using the WriteClient( ) member function of the CHttpFilterContext class. Notice that I use the WriteClient( ) function to build a standard Web page, just like the one you're used to building on a Web site. You'll need to make absolutely certain to include all of the required tags because an ISAPI Filter assumes nothing about the output, which means the client will see exactly what you provide. It's easier to build the display strings using a CString, then converting the CString to an LPTSTR as shown in the source code (there are actually a number of ways to perform the conversion process, and this is just one of them).

Let's talk a second about the CHttpFilterContext class variable pCtxt that gets passed to the OnUrlMap( ) function. There is one session created between the client and the server, but there is one thread created for each request. The way that your ISAPI Filter keeps track of the current thread is through the pCtxt variable. Each thread (request) uses a unique variable, which makes it more difficult to corrupt the output between threads.

Tip *The example code shows how to create a minimal response header. There are optional parameters that allow you to customize the kind of header you send. The second parameter (first NULL in the example code) allows you to send a status string. In most cases, you'll use this only if there's an error; a value of NULL sends a value of 200 or OK. The third parameter allows you to send additional header data. For example, this parameter could tell the browser what kind of raw data to expect as part of the Web page.*

We'll use a four-step process to output most of the information to the client: create an output string, determine its length, place the string in a LPVOID variable, and then output the data using the WriteClient( ) function. In this case, we'll display the requested URL and the default redirection, which is usually a location on the server's hard drive.

Displaying the response header may not seem like such an important thing to do at first, but you can use this display to check various result values. For example, the standard result value for a new Web page is 200, which means OK. You could display the response header so that you can see the error level, the current time at the server, or any number of other items. We covered at least some of the response header values earlier in the chapter, so I won't talk about them again here.

The last thing we do is display a standard footer. All that the footer will normally contain is the ending </BODY> and </HTML> tags. You must include these tags or the Web page won't get displayed. The Web page must be complete in every way or the client won't display it, even though the client will receive the data. In addition, some strange things can happen when a client receives only part of a page. The best that you can hope for is a time-out, but there have been cases where I've seen a machine freeze after getting an incomplete Web page. Because of the way that this particular error occurs, it's extremely hard to troubleshoot.

This example uses the SF_STATUS_REQ_FINISHED_KEEP_CONN return value in place of the default SF_STATUS_REQ_NEXT_NOTIFICATION return value (which tells the server that you've finished processing the information and want to pass it on to the next filter in line). The SF_STATUS_REQ_FINISHED_KEEP_CONN return value tells the server that you don't want it to do anything else, that you've already handled the client's request. Make sure you use this value or SF_STATUS_REQ_FINISHED by itself whenever you create a Web page within the filter. Otherwise, the Web server will create the default page and send it to the client as well. The result is that your test Web page will get overwritten before you get to see it, in most cases.

Installing the ISAPI Filter

At this point, you can compile the new ISAPI filter. However, even after you move it to the Controls or Scripts directory on your server, you'll still have to perform one other task. Unlike an extension, an ISA filter gets loaded when you start or update the service. This means installing the ISAPI Filter before you use it the first time.

Note	*Users of older versions of IIS don't have any console-specific method for adding ISAPI filters. Unfortunately, this means that you'll have to stop the target service, make a registry entry, and then start up the service again. The filter will get loaded as part of the starting process. The WWW service stores its filter entries in the following registry value: HKEY_LOCAL_MACHINE\SYSTEM\CurrentControlSet\ Services\W3SVC\Parameters\Filter DLLs. You'll probably find one or more values in this location already. All you need to do is add a comma and then type the location of your new ISA filter. Make absolutely certain you perform this step before going on to the next section, or the filter won't load. In fact, this is the setting you'll want to check first if you have trouble getting the filter to work.*

Users of IIS version 4.0 and above will really appreciate the fact that they no longer have to edit the registry manually to load an ISAPI filter. The following procedure will help you get the ViewMap ISAPI Filter installed (this procedure assumes that you're using a full IIS installation on a Windows NT Server):

1. Open the Microsoft Management Console. You'll see a display similar to the one shown here (your display will look different depending on which IIS options you have installed and other system configuration features).

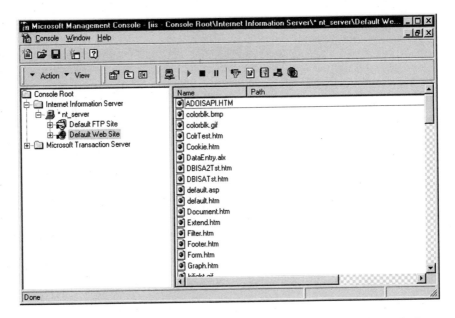

2. Right-click the Web site that you want to add the filter to (normally Default Web Site), and choose Properties from the context menu. You'll see the <Web Site> Properties dialog box.

3. Select the ISAPI Filters tab and you'll see a dialog box like the one shown here:

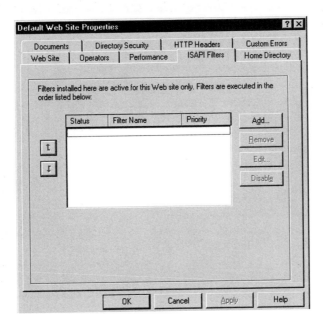

4. Click Add. You'll see a Filter Properties dialog box like the one shown here:

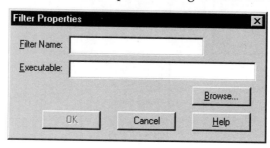

5. Type the human-readable name in the Filter Name field. The example uses URL Mapping Viewer for the File Name field.

6. Use the Browse button to find the ViewMap.DLL file (or whatever ISAPI filter you want to add to the Web site). Once you select the file, its name will appear in the Executable field.

7. Click OK to close the Filter Properties dialog box.

8. Click OK to close the <Web Site> Properties dialog box. IIS will automatically load the filter for you.

9. Open the <Web Site> Properties dialog box again, then choose the ISAPI Filters tab. If your ISAPI Filter loaded successfully, you'll see a display similar to the one shown here:

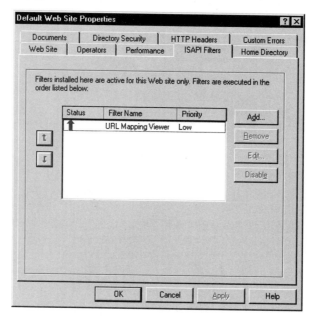

10. Click OK to close the <Web Site> Properties dialog box.

A Simple ISAPI Filter Test

Since our ISAPI Filter will intercept all traffic for the Web server, there isn't any reason to create a complex test for it. You'll know if the ISAPI Filter is working or not if the test Web page shows up when you try to access the Web site. Figure 17-1 shows the test Web page that appeared when I tried to access my Web server.

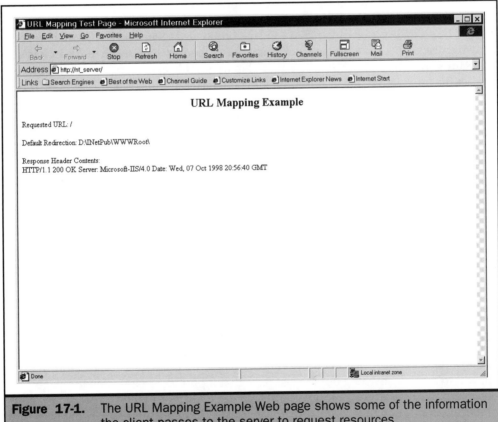

Figure 17-1.   The URL Mapping Example Web page shows some of the information the client passes to the server to request resources

Choosing Filter Options

The second page (Step 2 of 2) of the ISAPI Extension Wizard dialog is very important as far as filter designers are concerned, because it contains the options you'll need to set the filter's monitoring options. There are three sections of options on this page. The first section determines the filter's priority. Low, the default, works just fine in most cases. You'll want to use this level for any kind of filter that performs a general background task. A security filter may require that you set the filter's priority to medium. After all, you don't want the filter to react after the event—a reaction during the event would be much better. Finally, the High priority setting should be reserved for emergency-level filters. For example, you might want to send a message out to everyone that the server is going down due to a power failure.

The second section of the ISAPI Extension Wizard - Step 2 of 2 dialog contains two entries. Check the first entry if you want to monitor events when a user has a secure connection. For example, if you plan to provide extra services to a registered user that an anonymous user doesn't get, you may want to check this option. The second option, Nonsecured Port Sessions, allows you to monitor events when a user doesn't have a secure connection to the server. That's the way most users will access your site if you have a general Web site on the Internet.

The third section contains a list of notifications (events) that your filter will track. Every time the specified event happens, your filter will get called. However, there are two things that will affect when it gets called. If you set the priority of your filter to Low, then any high- or medium-priority-level filters will get to react to the event first. In addition, your filter has to be set to monitor the event with the user's current security level. In other words, your filter won't get called at all if you set it to monitor nonsecured activity and the user is in secured mode.

Creating an ISAPI Filter Test Page Using Visual InterDev

We now have a fully functional ISAPI Filter running on our Web server that won't allow it to display anything but the test page that it provides. While this test page doesn't contain the largest amount of information in the world, it does provide some practical information that could easily be expanded to provide a more in-depth look at how the Web server functions. That's where our Visual InterDev project comes into play. In this section, we'll answer the question of what kind of requests that a Web server normally gets when a user opens a Visual InterDev project. More importantly, this example should provide a better workout for the ISAPI Filter than the short example in the previous section. The following sections will help you create a very simple test application.

Creating the Program Shell

This section will help you create a simple Web project shell. The following procedure will get you started:

1. Start Visual InterDev if you haven't done so already. You'll see the New Project dialog box.

2. Choose the Visual InterDev Project folder on the New tab.

3. Highlight the New Web Project icon, then type **ViewMapTest** in the Name field.

4. Click Open. You'll see the Web Project Wizard - Step 1 of 4 dialog box.

5. Select a Web server, if necessary, and choose the "Master mode" option.

6. Click Next. Visual InterDev will contact the Web server and create a project directory on it. At some point during the contact process, you'll see an error message saying that Visual InterDev can't contact the Web server. This is because the ISAPI Filter is preventing the wizard from making normal contact. You can get rid of the error message by opening the <Web Site> Properties dialog box in MMC on the Web server, selecting the ISAPI Filters tab, highlighting the ViewMap ISAPI Filter, and clicking Remove. Click OK to close the <Web Site> Properties dialog box and remove the ISAPI Filter from IIS. At this point, you can try to make contact with the Web server again. You should see the Web Project Wizard - Step 2 of 4 dialog box.

Tip *The whole reason for this little exercise was to point out that you need to know what effect an ISAPI Filter will have before you leave it installed on the Web server. If this had been a little less obvious, it could have taken hours to figure out what the problem with Visual InterDev was. ISAPI Filters affect every aspect of your Web server, which means that you want to keep your Web server fairly clean during testing to ensure you're seeing an actual error and not the repercussions of using a particular ISAPI Filter.*

7. Click Next. You'll see the Web Project Wizard - Step 3 of 4 dialog box.

8. Choose any layout (the example uses Top and Bottom 2), then click Next. You'll see the Web Project Wizard - Step 3 of 4 dialog box.

9. Choose any theme (the example uses Leaves), then click Finish. Visual InterDev will create a project shell for you.

Creating and Testing a Default Test Page

It's not unlikely that you'll develop a Web project that makes use of both Visual InterDev and the capabilities provided by an ISAPI Filter. However, you may find it more difficult to actually perform this task than you might think. Remember that Visual InterDev requires constant contact with the Web server while working with a Web project. Here's one of the reasons that you need to have additional diagnostic aids when working with ISAPI Filters. If you want to create a project that is looking for a particular result from the ISAPI Filter, then you may find your efforts hindered by the default behavior of products like Visual InterDev. The only way to get around these potential problem areas is to create custom tools that allow you to run and test the ISAPI Filter, while still allowing Visual InterDev to work as usual.

Let's add a test page to the project. Right-click the <Server Name>/ViewMapTest folder, then choose Add | HTML Page... from the context menu. Visual InterDev will display the Add Item dialog box. Type **Default.HTM** in the Name field, then click Open. You'll see a new Web page added to your project. Right-click Default.HTM and choose Set as Start Page from the context menu.

It's time for another experiment regarding ISAPI Filter use and Visual InterDev. Close all files and release all working copies by right-clicking the file and choosing Release Working Copy from the context menu. (You can determine the difference between a file that has a working copy and one that's released by looking for the little lock symbol next to the file—a locked file has no working copy associated with it.) Save your project. Reload the ViewMap ISAPI Filter using the same procedure we used earlier in the chapter. Try running the Visual InterDev project we just created and you'll see the URL Mapping Example Web page shown in Figure 17-1.

Close Internet Explorer to stop the debugging process. Try to get a working copy of the Default.HTM file by right-clicking the file and choosing Get Working Copy from the context menu. You'll see an error message that seems to indicate there was a catastrophic failure of the Web server—obviously this isn't true. This whole exercise demonstrates that you can test a project using an ISAPI Filter from within Visual InterDev—you just can't work with the Web project files during the test process. In sum, you'll probably need to set up separate test and development times for larger projects that require you to use a variety of technologies like ISAPI.

Caution   *Make absolutely certain that you unload the ViewMap ISAPI Filter once you complete this example. It's especially important that you clean the machine up before going back to other sections in the book or the examples will likely fail for the same reasons they did in this section of the chapter.*

Lessons Learned

ISAPI Filters normally sit in the background, performing whatever task we ask them to do. Normally, ISAPI Filters do as their name suggests—filter input from the client before it reaches the server, or filter the server's output before it reaches the client.

It's important to keep the message-based orientation of ISAPI Filters in mind. Not only do you need to have a good understanding of how data flows from one area of the server to the next, but which message interacts with the data flow at that point. Selecting the wrong message for an ISAPI filter may mean hours of rework when you figure out that the filter doesn't have access to the information you require.

Like device drivers, ISAPI Filters are installed on the server and remain resident. They're also installed in a chain, meaning data flows from one ISAPI Filter to the next. The return value you provide for an ISAPI Filter determines whether the next filter in line will get called. You can tell IIS that your ISAPI Filter handled the situation and that no other filters need to get called. The default setup calls all filters in sequence, then creates a page based on the resources that the user requested.

One of the most unique ways to use an ISAPI Filter is as a diagnostic aid. Since the ISAPI Filter has access to the data stream, you can use it to display whatever is happening to the data at that point in the server. Doing so makes it possible for you to monitor data flow and evaluate exactly where data corruption, if any, occurs.

Working with ISAPI Filters can do more than simply make debugging of a Web project difficult. It can also create a situation in which you're also fighting with the very tools that you need for development purposes. This chapter pointed out just a few of these projects. The best thing to do with your development platform is to keep things as simple as possible. Don't load any ISAPI Filters that you don't actually need for development purposes. Obviously, this same caveat applies to anything that might interfere with the normal operation of your server. A clean development environment reduces the risk that you'll chase phantom bugs around your Web server in a failed attempt to create your next project.

On the CD

Visual Studio 6 : The Complete Reference comes complete with a CD-ROM containing all of the source code for every example in the book. This means that you can spend more time learning about the code and less time typing it into your favorite programming language. The CD also contains a few ancillary programs that aren't contained in the book, but I mention all of these extra programs in the book text so you know about them. The following paragraphss will tell you about the CD and how you can use it.

The code is arranged on the CD by chapter. All you need to do is find the chapter you want to use and open it up in Windows Explorer. You'll find one or more subfolders within the chapter folders containing the example code. Each example folder contains one example from the book and uses a single programming language.

There are two ways you can use the code. You can either copy it directly to your hard drive, or you can open the source code directly from the CD. Beware that the CD is read-only and that the programming language IDE will complain if you attempt to make any changes to the example code. The compiled version of each example is also on the CD if you want to see how the example works without compiling it yourself.

If you do copy the contents of the CD to your hard drive, make sure you mark the files as writable. Just right-click the file within Windows Explorer and choose Properties from the context menu. You'll see a <File Name> Properties dialog box containing a list of attributes for the file. Uncheck the Read-only attribute and you'll be able to write to the file as needed. Note that you can select more than one file in Windows Explorer at a time. Selecting all of the files for a project would allow you to set the Read-only attribute with one visit to the <File Name> Properties dialog box.

Make sure you recompile any projects you change to ensure the changes flow through all of the support files. In Visual C++ this means using the Build | Rebuild All command. Otherwise, you won't know whether an error you're seeing is the result of a code compatibility problem with your machine setup or some unforeseen bug in the code itself. If you do find a bug in the code, please be sure to contact me at: JMueller@mwt.net. I'll be more than happy to work with you when you spot a potential problem in the code associated with this book. Your input could help me provide better information to other readers as well.

Index

T